A William Ernest Hocking Reader,
with Commentary

The Vanderbilt Library of American Philosophy offers interpretive perspectives on the historical roots of American philosophy and on present innovative developments in American thought, including studies of values, naturalism, social philosophy, cultural criticism, and applied ethics.

Series Editors
Herman J. Saatkamp, Jr., General Editor (Indiana University Purdue University Indianapolis)
Cornelis de Waal, Associate Editor (Indiana University Purdue University Indianapolis)

Editorial Advisory Board
Kwame Anthony Appiah (Harvard)
Larry Hickman (Southern Illinois University)
John Lachs (Vanderbilt)
John J. McDermott (Texas A&M)
Joel Porte (Cornell)
Hilary Putnam (Harvard)
Ruth Anna Putnam (Wellesley)
Beth J. Singer (Brooklyn College)
John J. Stuhr (Vanderbilt University)

A William Ernest Hocking Reader

WITH COMMENTARY

John Lachs
D. Micah Hester

EDITORS

Vanderbilt University Press

NASHVILLE

Copyright © 2004 Vanderbilt University Press
All rights reserved
First Edition 2004

This book is printed on acid-free paper.

Library of Congress Cataloging-in-Publication Data

Hocking, William Ernest, 1873–1966.
  A William Ernest Hocking reader : with commentary / editors, John Lachs, D. Micah Hester.—1st ed.
    p. cm. — (The Vanderbilt library of American philosophy)
Includes bibliographical references and index.
    ISBN 0-8265-1369-7 (hardcover : alk. paper)
    ISBN 0-8265-1370-0 (pbk. : alk. paper)
    1. Philosophy. 2. Hocking, William Ernest, 1873-1966.
    I. Lachs, John. II. Hester, D. Micah. III. Title. IV. Series.
B945.H641L33 2004
191—dc21
                           2003003842

Contents

Acknowledgments   ix

Abbreviations   x

Editors' Introduction   xi

Hocking in His Own Words

1. "What Does Philosophy Say?" from *Philosophical Review*   3
2. "Preface to the 1912 Edition" from *The Meaning of God in Human Experience* (MGHE)   20
3. "Fact, Field and Destiny: Inductive Elements of Metaphysics" from *Review of Metaphysics*   29
4. "The Self and Nature" from *The Self: Its Body and Freedom*   47
5. "Passage Beyond Modernity: The Possible Universality of Solitude" from *The Coming World Civilization*   62
6. "The Human Will" from *Man and the State* (MATS)   74
7. A. "The Knowledge of Other Minds Than Our Own" from MGHE   83

   B. "Such Knowledge As We Could Desire" from MGHE   91

   C. "That Knowledge We Have" from MGHE   98
8. A. "Are Group Minds Real?" from MATS   106

   B. "Will Circuits" from MATS   119
9. "Institutions and Change" from *Human Nature and Its Remaking* (HNR)   128

10. "The Dialectic of Liberalism" from
    The Lasting Elements of Individualism   136

11. "The Future of Liberalism" from *Journal of Philosophy*   151

12. "Astronomy, Physics and World-Meaning"
    from *Science and the Idea of God*   166

13. "Faith and World Order" from
    The Church and the New World Mind   182

14. "*Vox Dei*" from HNR   192

15. "The Unifying of History" from MGHE   196

16. "The Last Fact" from HNR   201

17. "*Confessio Fidei*" from *Types of Philosophy* (first edition)   208

Hocking as Seen Today

18. W. E. Hocking's "Transfigured Naturalism"   217
    John Howie

19. Passion for Meaning: W. E. Hocking's
    Religious-Philosophical Views   231
    Bruce Wilshire

20. Hocking's Critique of Modernity:
    Countering Solipsism and Cultivating Solitude
    Vincent Colapietro   245

21. Solipsism Surmounted:
    W. E. Hocking's Philosophy of Community   280
    LeRoy S. Rouner

22. Institutions and the Making of Persons:
    W. E. Hocking's Social Personalism   290
    Tom Buford

23. W. E. Hocking and the Liberal Spirit   305
    Douglas R. Anderson

24. The Defects of Liberalism:
    Lasting Elements of W. E. Hocking's Philosophy   318
    John Stuhr

25. W. E. Hocking's Insights
    About the Individual and the State   335
    John E. Smith

26. W. E. Hocking on Marx,
    Russian Marxism, and the Soviet Union   349
    George L. Kline

27. Metaphysics and World Philosophy:
    W. E. Hocking on Chinese Philosophy   367
    Robert Cummings Neville

Selected Bibliography of William Ernest Hocking   383

Index of Selected Names   387

Index of Selected Subjects   389

Acknowledgments

This manuscript was made possible, in part, through generous contributions from the Cabot-Hocking Trust. Also, the scholarly essays in the second part of the book are derived from a lecture series sponsored by the Society of Philosophers in America in conjunction with the Cabot-Hocking Trust. Each scholar presented his thoughts on Hocking to groups of philosophers and other interested participants at an institution of higher education other than his own. This series took place between February 1996 and April 1997. The presentations were as follows:

- Bruce Wilshire (Rutgers University) presented at Seattle University in February 1996.
- Leroy Rouner (Boston University) presented at Southern Illinois University at Carbondale in March 1996.
- George Kline (Bryn Mawr College, Emeritus) presented at Fordham University in April 1996.
- John E. Smith (Yale University, Emeritus) presented at The Penn State University in September 1996.
- Thomas Buford (Furman University) presented at Bryn Mawr College in October 1996.
- Robert Neville (Boston University) presented at Drew University in November 1996.
- Vincent Colapietro (then at Fordham University, now at Penn State University) presented at Boston University in December 1996.
- John Stuhr (then at Penn State University, now at Vanderbilt University) presented at Vanderbilt University in March 1997.
- Douglas Anderson (Penn State University) presented at the University of Oregon in March 1997.
- John Howie (Southern Illinois University at Carbondale, Emeritus) presented at Furman University in April 1997.

The presenting scholars and the editors of this volume wish to thank the sponsoring groups as well as the hosting institutions for their support and encouragement. Also, the editors are in debt to David Hodge for his work on scanning in the Hocking selections, making them editable in a computer-based format.

While several of Hocking's works are in the public domain, many are not. Thus, the editors would like to thank the Hocking family and the respective publishers who gave permission to reprint the following works:

"Astronomy, Physics, and World-meaning" from *Science and the Idea of God* (85–115) by William Ernest Hocking. Copyright © 1944 by the University of North CarolinaPress. Copyright © renewed 1972 by Richard Hocking. Used by permission of the publisher.

"The Dialectic of Liberalism" from *The Lasting Elements of Individualism* (64–102) by William Ernest Hocking. Copyright © 1937, renewed 1965 by the Yale University Press.

"Fact, Field and Destiny," originally published in the *Review of Metaphysics*, vol. 11, 525–549 (copyright © 1958), by William Ernest Hocking.

"The Future of Liberalism," originally published in the *Journal of Philosophy*, vol. 32, 230–247 (copyright © 1935), by William Ernest Hocking.

ABBREVIATIONS FOR HOCKING'S WORKS

CWC	*The Coming World Civilization* (1956)	
FP	*Freedom of the Press* (1947)	
HNR	*Human Nature and Its Remaking* (1918)	
LEI	*The Lasting Elements of Individualism* (1937)	
LRWF	*Living Religions and a World Faith* (1940)	
MATS	*Man and the State* (1926)	
MGHE	*The Meaning of God in Human Experience* (1912)	
MIHE	*The Meaning of Immortality in Human Experience* (1957)	
PTP	*Preface to Philosophy: Textbook* (1946)	
RTM	*Re-Thinking Missions* (1932)	
SBF	*The Self: Its Body and Freedom* (1928)	
SIG	*Science and the Idea of God* (1944)	
SMN	*Strength of Men and Nations* (1959)	
SWP	*The Spirit of World Politics* (1932)	
TP	*Types of Philosophy* (3rd ed., 1959)	
WMCMM	*What Man Can Make of Man* (1942)	

See "Selected Bibliography..." for complete citations. Also, other writings by Hocking cited in chapters 18–27 but not listed here are listed in the "Works Cited" section at the end of each commentary.

Editors' Introduction

Striking things happen in the history of thought. The giants of an age can disappear; when they do, previously unknown figures take their place. It would be comfortable to believe that all of this is to the good and that it is always the cream that rises to the top. But neither Hegelian assurances that nothing positive is lost in the process nor Darwinian celebrations of the survivors seem appropriate: the losses are palpable, and the survivors themselves may soon be submerged.

There is no doubt that excellent philosophers occasionally disappear from the scene. Some of them never resurface. The cost of this to systematic reflection is immense; we lose the guidance of outstanding minds and end up repeating their mistakes. The fruit of decades of investigation goes to waste, and we pursue our projects in ignorance of relevant achievements and useful new ideas.

William Ernest Hocking is one of the important and interesting philosophers who disappeared almost without a trace. His disappearance has been so complete that it is difficult for students and even seasoned scholars of the early twenty-first century to believe that Hocking was a giant in the first half of the twentieth. Few philosophers of his day could match his reputation and his influence. His breadth as a thinker was second only to that of the great American pragmatist, John Dewey. Hocking occupied the arguably most prestigious philosophy chair in the United States as Alford professor of Natural Religion and Moral Philosophy at Harvard (1920–1943)—a post previously held by Josiah Royce—after distinguished service at Yale (1908–1914). Hocking was an international figure, admired in Europe and Asia, and he addressed audiences in countries as diverse as Russia and China. His influence extended beyond the discipline of philosophy to theology, education, law, and political science. His work touched on issues both academic and practical, showing careful reflection and significant depth. Nevertheless, by the time of his retirement, Hocking was a philosopher out of favor, and after his death the visibility of his work rapidly declined.

William Ernest Hocking was born in Cleveland, Ohio, in 1873. His father was a homeopathic physician who, soon after Ernest's birth, moved the family to Joliet, Illinois. Hocking grew up with strong religious convictions, regularly attending the revivals held by the local Methodist church. At the age of thirteen, Hocking came upon Herbert Spencer's work, which shook his faith and captivated his attention, focusing his thoughts on evolutionary philosophy. After working for a few years as a surveyor for the railroad, Hocking saved enough money to attend Iowa State

University as an engineering student. While there, he was introduced to William James's seminal *The Principles of Psychology*, which broke the spell of Spencer and gave Hocking the desire to attend Harvard in order to study with James.

Again taking time to earn the necessary finances for school, Hocking finally entered Harvard in 1899 and, once again, pursued engineering. But he also took a class with Josiah Royce, which so enthralled him that he left engineering to devote himself to philosophy, earning the BA in 1901. In 1902–1903 Hocking continued his philosophical studies in Germany, working with such eminent philosophers as Edmund Husserl, whose phenomenology exerted a powerful influence on Hocking's thought. He returned to Harvard in 1903 and received his doctorate in 1904. After brief stints teaching at a preparatory school and at the University of California, Berkeley, Hocking joined the Yale philosophy department in 1908. Four years later, he published his first—and some think most important—book, *The Meaning of God in Human Experience*. In 1914, Hocking was hired by Harvard president Lawrence Lowell to help fill vacancies left by the departures of G. H. Palmer and George Santayana. A few years later Royce died, and by 1920 Hocking, recognized for his exceptional scholarship and teaching, was given the Alford professorship in Natural Religion, Moral Philosophy, and Civil Polity, the department's only endowed chair at the time. He held the professorship until his retirement in 1943.

During his years at Harvard, Hocking wrote a number of celebrated books, though none came to match the influence of his first. His primary interest was in surmounting "the problem of modernity," which he took to be the Cartesian view of mind, denying us a genuine experience of others. In the preface to the fiftieth anniversary edition of *The Meaning of God in Human Experience*, Hocking wrote:

> Modernity completely failed to resolve the dilemma of "solipsism"; and with its inability to find an experience of other selves would follow its deeper inability to find an experience of God. I had for some time been of the belief that these barriers could be surmounted and that they would fall together. In my own experience they did; this book is to that extent autobiographical. (MGHE, xii)

Recognized nationally and internationally, Hocking received many honors, including the presidency of the American Philosophical Association in 1927 and the prestigious Gifford lectureship on Natural Religion in 1938–1939.

After retirement in 1943, Hocking moved to a farm in New Hampshire and continued to write and lecture in philosophy and politics until his death in 1966.

William Ernest Hocking published twenty books and over 250 articles. At Harvard, he enjoyed the company of such distinguished colleagues as Ralph Barton Perry, Alfred North Whitehead, and C. I. Lewis, and was a major influence in the department when Nelson Goodman and W. V. O. Quine were in residence as doctoral students. He engaged such giant twentieth-century philosophical figures as John Dewey and Bertrand Russell in lively debate. Nevertheless, today most of his books are out of print,* and his work is rarely read and almost never mentioned. What happened? Such questions do not admit of simple, definitive answers. Decline of interest in Hocking's work is due to a number of factors, all of them contingent and perhaps accidental. One is growing distrust throughout the twentieth century of philosophical system building. Another is the current dominance of naturalism, leading to the virtually summary rejection of idealistic speculations. Hocking's philosophical approach went out of style in the last fifty years.

More broadly, the continuing professionalization of philosophy relegated the field to disciplinary isolation, with few contacts to other departments or interest in anything beyond the walls of academic institutions. As a man greatly concerned with practical affairs and the relation of philosophy to the entire enterprise of knowledge, Hocking was caught between a past that celebrated the engaged philosopher and the growing commitment to narrowly academic pursuits. The rise of Anglo-American analytic philosophy in the 1950s and 1960s also contributed to pushing such "older" or "insufficiently rigorous" philosophies as Hocking's to the background and, in some cases, off the philosophical map altogether.

William Ernest Hocking is by no means the only significant philosopher to have been forgotten. Dewey was rediscovered only in the last twenty years; Santayana and Royce have yet to come into their own. Growing excitement about James is offset by Whitehead sliding out of sight; the recovery of every thinker seems to entail the loss of another. Hocking's obscurity is particularly lamentable: the breadth of his vision, his depth on a vast range of issues, his concern for a "passage beyond modernity," his discussions of a "coming world civilization," his devotion to private lived experience and to social relationships demand respect and justify attentive study.

Hocking's system can be characterized as a dialectical idealism, in some respects similar to Hegel's, which develops the deep connections between individuals, communities and the world in which they live. The idealism encompasses pragmatic, empirical, personalist, and phenomenological elements, and presents a unified account of "world historical order." Hocking's starting point is human experience, albeit not of the truncated sort acknowledged by empiricists. He believes that experience rightly understood places us in contact with our fellows and with deeper, religious realities. He views human beings in historical and cultural context and yet manages not to lose sight of the essential unity of the human race. Hocking presents a philosophical system that incorporates the positive elements of nearly all previous thought without becoming an eclectic amalgam of prior opinions. His comprehensive vision shows us our place in nature and offers a strikingly complete account of the realm of values.

His expansive yet unified philosophy addresses not only academic thinkers. It

---

*A new printing of the 1924 edition of *The Meaning of God in Human Experience* was published in the summer of 2003 by Kessinger Publishing.

acknowledges the ambitions of those striving for justice and recognition, treats the claims of cultures different from his own with deep respect, and articulates the hope that human conflicts may be peacefully resolved. In a world fractured by differences large and small, Hocking's philosophy stresses the continuities and unifying connections among us. Hocking's exquisite attention to "the other" and his unwavering commitment to moral decency make his philosophy particularly relevant today. It may well turn out that this philosophy, beckoning to us from the past, will acquire new life and be adopted by many as the thought to guide their future.

The development of this volume is a mark of the conviction of the editors, the contemporary contributors, and all others who have played a role in bringing it to the public that we would do well to examine Hocking's thought for the valuable insights it offers. The idea of resuscitating Hocking's philosophy was first conceived by SOPHIA (Society of Philosophers in America), an organization devoted to turning the attention of philosophers to issues of everyday significance. In 1996 and 1997, ten outstanding philosophers offered a lecture each at ten universities on divergent aspects of Hocking's thought. These lectures constitute the critical/appreciative portion of this volume. Several of the authors knew Hocking personally; others have come to appreciate him only through his published work. None of the essays is naively eulogistic about Hocking's philosophy. They offer both criticism and appreciation as they develop sound appraisals of what is alive, relevant, and of value in what Hocking left us.

The unavailability of Hocking's books and current ignorance of his ideas would have made the publication of essays on his work pointless. It quickly became obvious to the editors that revitalizing Hocking's philosophy required providing a selection from his writings adequate to form a well-rounded picture of their breadth and depth. That is exactly what we have endeavored to do in this volume. We have tried to bring Hocking back to life by offering a representative selection of his best work. Those familiar with his writings may of course find that not all their favorite essays are included here; unfortunate as this may be, exclusion is a necessary part of selection. In looking through Hocking's corpus, one finds such an embarrassment of riches that there is simply no way to include everything one could reasonably want. We hope the day will come when more of Hocking's books will be back in print; for now, we must satisfy ourselves with a judicious pick from his many gems to reawaken an interest in his ideas.

The combination of original texts with critical and appreciative commentary makes this book an ideal addition to courses in American philosophy and provides a more than adequate introduction to Hocking's thought. Anyone wishing to explore his richly nuanced idealism has at hand here all that is needed for an initial yet substantial assessment of its nature and lasting value. The Hocking selections include elements of nine books and three important journal articles. They cover the general framework and many of the details of Hocking's system. Such essays as "What Does Philosophy Say?" (chap. 1) and "Confessio Fidei" (chap. 16) frame all of Hocking's work by setting forth his view of the scope of philosophy and the outlines of his idealism. Chapters 2–5 lay bare some of the features of Hocking's method and the structure of his metaphysics. Chapters from *The Meaning of God in Human Experience* and *Man and the State* (chaps. 6–8) bring out Hocking's attempt to "surmount solipsism" by arguing for the dialectically constitutive relationship between selves and groups.

Additional selections (chaps. 9–11) focus attention on Hocking's social and political philosophy, showing how his analysis of selves and groups relates to the politics of liberalism and the future of the liberal state. Hocking's philosophy of science is covered in chapter 12, in an extract from *Science and the Idea of God*, in which he argues that the deep meaning expressed in Nature and in human life makes any ultimate distinction between the subjective and the objective inappropriate. This naturally leads, in chapters 13–16, to the central ideas of Hocking's philosophy of religion. Discussions of a purposive and orderly world, of religious faith and of God bring the construction of the edifice of his thought to a fitting completion.

The ten essays that form the second part of this volume respond to the elements of Hocking's thought covered in the selections. They analyze, situate, critique, and defend portions of Hocking's philosophy by reference to recent philosophical developments. These essays are living proof of the continuing power of Hocking's philosophy to engage, to stimulate, and in some cases even to convince some of the best scholars of a new generation. We hope that this collection of Hocking's writings and contemporary responses to his thought will serve as an instrument of returning his philosophy to public attention. It is offered to the public with the conviction that we must no longer permit constructive and valuable contributions to the history of human thought to disappear from sight.

Hocking in His Own Words

For all the chapters in this section, Hocking's original footnotes have been converted to endnotes; otherwise, alterations from the original are encompassed by brackets. Furthermore, Hocking's original section numbering has been deleted throughout. His original spelling and punctuation have been preserved.

CHAPTER I

What Does Philosophy Say?

It belongs to our common lot as students of philosophy to meet not once but many times the question, put in all good faith, What does philosophy say about this or that? And we have all had to make the same disconcerting reply:

"Philosophy—does not speak; and no one can speak for it. It has no corporate voice, because it has no corporate judgment. You may ask what mathematics has to say, or even physics; but not what philosophy says. Philosophers are individuals in their work as scientists are not. You cannot expect an orthodoxy among thinkers who become philosophers because they cannot fall in with current orthodoxies. Their thinking is carried on, in part, in the region of strict logic; but in part in the region of belief, where tests of rightness lack sharp finality. I can tell you what I say, or what various camps of philosophy might say: I cannot tell you what philosophy says."

If I may judge from my own experience, we never heartily enjoy making this reply. But many of us have come to believe that it lies in the nature of the case, and find ourselves even more distressed when proposals are made to bring our minds into some program of agreement. We are not insincere in our search for objective truth. We reject outright the complacent view that philosophy is a sort of personal artistry in the making of world-pictures, or a forefated expression of temperament. We believe that those who differ from us are wrong,—otherwise we would not quite believe our beliefs. But we also believe—and with the uncomfortable sense of inconsistency which attends all so-called toleration—in the vital function of differing.

Thus, no philosopher while refuting his antagonist appears wholly desirous of silencing him. It is as if each were aware that his private measures must somewhere fail to hold all of the necessary truth. Each must cherish his opponent, not for the sake of the opposition, but to testify for himself, if perchance the imagined hearer might perform subconsciously that miracle of union which as yet neither disputant can vocally achieve.

Our mode of inducting new members into the philosophic fraternity is not calculated to diminish our differences. We groom our candidate to produce some 'original thesis,' one which marks him out from all his predecessors and from all his brethren. And as he defends his case, we have often found ourselves in the strange position of applauding, not only while we disagree, but to some extent because we

---

President's Address, Eastern Division of American Philosophical Association, University of Chicago, December 27–30, 1927. From *Philosophical Review* 37 (March, 1928): 133–153.

disagree. I exaggerate, but I exaggerate a truth, when I say that our modes of training have in general fostered the will to differ, which in most young thinkers is in no great need of encouragement.

The instinct we thus follow is certainly not unsound. For so long as final solutions are undiscovered, it is in the rankling of discontent and novelty that they must be born. Further, we philosophers, looked at biologically, are agents of mental variation. We have to break up cakes of mental custom, and aid transition by inventing new hypotheses and proposing new values. As agents of variance and growth, we must differ from one another. We cannot endure orthodoxies in philosophy,—at least, not yet.

I would like to set at the head of this discussion my firm belief in the everlasting importance of differing. The question, however, persists, What does philosophy say? And I doubt whether all our disavowals can drive it into retirement—or ought to.

As for the general public, whose naive expectations hold an annoyingly direct and pragmatic standard up to every profession—this general public not only demands from time to time what philosophy has to say, but promptly supplies itself with answers! What some philosopher says it forthwith takes for what philosophy says. Naturally, those philosophers who have gained the widest popular hearing convey this impression in the highest degree, whether they wish to or not. And so far as our involuntary representative misrepresents philosophy the damage is the greater because the likelihood of disillusionment is less. The public will not go far to correct its first impression.

For my part, I look upon the new-born popularity of philosophical reading and study in this country with great satisfaction. We have been an unphilosophical people: we are now at the turn of the tide. We are pragmatically hungry for philosophy: every great social interest—industry, art, politics, education, religion, war-making, the drama—begins to realize today that the thing it has long wanted, and did not know it wanted, is philosophy. Psychology has been tried—and will help; America is groping its way beyond psychology. With the pragmatic hunger goes another and deeper personal hunger. This is for us a great moment, also a responsible and a dangerous moment.

So far, it seems to me, we have been fortunate in those who are representing philosophy to the widening public. The books which have been most largely read have been books of outstanding merit, and they have been taken for their merit, not for their weaknesses. If they have failed in some point, as in accuracy, they have been in other respects nobly honest pieces of work: they have recorded and conveyed an honest and vivid if partial appreciation. Philosophy cannot be truly represented by dull work; for philosophy is intrinsically the most engaging of all activities of the mind. If for example the effort of learned histories of philosophy to be proportionate in treatment and uniformly just leads to their being uniformly dull (as it certainly need not do) the result is nothing less than a betrayal of the great fire that burns at the heart of philosophy. So far as our utterances have failed of the dramatic and irresistible appeal of philosophy to the aspiring reason of men, we must pray for the recovery of the one thing needful.

But with all the great service of the popular philosopher, we view his success, we must view it, with profound uneasiness. For we know that his voice will be taken as the voice of philosophy; and *we know that it is not!* But is this uneasiness due wholly to the stupidity of a public which persists in demanding, What does philosophy say?, like that ancient public which required a sign when no sign should be given? Or is it due in part to a sense of our own inadequacy in meeting a reasonable expectation?

Our students come to us with the same confident faith that philosophy has something to say to them. We promptly disillusion them; we see to it that they shall not fall into the speedy satisfaction of the public. But they are not grateful. They ill conceal their dissatisfaction—indeed they commonly do not conceal it—when they find philosophy a nest of divergent judgments.

This is particularly true if they approach philosophy through its history; for both the conscience and the art of the lecturer require him to develop the issues and to picture in relief the idiosyncrasies of the great thinkers. My own experience as a student leads me to sympathize keenly with the resulting troubled state. I suppose that I am one of the few now living who began life with a devoted discipleship to Herbert Spencer, and who is willing to acknowledge it! I came to Harvard because a chance reading of William James's Psychology broke the spell of Spencer's view. I came hoping to find the truth at Harvard. Needless to say, I did not find the finished product. I found Royce and James, Palmer and Santayana, Münsterberg and Dickinson Miller, engaged in high debate, and rejoicing in the presence of their colleagues as thinkers with whom they might happily differ. My first feeling in that tolerant and lively atmosphere was one of loss and bewilderment. This first feeling was very far from being my last one; but we have to remember the vast majority of our students who do not get beyond the first impression. Knowing the baffled and semi-resentful mood of the student who comes seeking truth, and who is given instead a high discipline in the contemporary methods of seeking truth, I cannot attribute it wholly to the mental idleness of flabby souls who wish results without labor.

The things which we commonly say to ourselves in this situation, true as they are, do not cover the case.

We say that truth cannot live in a final and self-assured proposition; that it must continually fight for its life, unless it is to become (as Mill put it) just one prejudice the more. We say that philosophizing has its chief worth apart from final results; that our most important service is not to convey doctrine but to raise the level of reflection. A competent thinker brings those around him to his own level of competence, whether they agree or disagree. We cannot and dare not give men truth ready made: our first and highest gift is to enable them to think.

These considerations are valid; but if we believed them sufficient we would apply them more radically than we do. The teachers of Zen Buddhism in China in the ninth and tenth centuries could give us lessons in the art of throwing men upon their own mental resources, if that is our real object.

It was the mission of these ancient teachers to denounce the complexities into which Buddhism had fallen, and to bring men back to simplicity, self-dependency and inward depth. The Hindu psychology of *Vijnanevadi*, with its eight faculties and 540 states, had become insupportable and incredible. So they said,[1] "Here in my place there is no truth to tell you. My duty is to lighten your burdens, to free you from your bondage, to cure the sick and to beat the ghosts out of men.... You yourself are not different from the Buddha; do not seek anywhere outside yourself." Since this conviction must be gained by each for himself, the master must not make the matter easy, must not explain. Hence the novice was taught with silence, with ridicule, with blows. And driven from one master, he would take to the great road in search of another, carrying his stick, wearing his straw sandals, begging food and lodging, mingling with all conditions of mankind. Then some day, a chance happening, a casual remark, a song, a bit of nature, and the abrupt illumination took place. It is said that one such novice thereupon returned to his original master, cast himself at his feet, and poured out his acknowledgment saying, "I owe everything to my teacher, because he never told me anything, never explained anything." We shall never deserve such praise!

These thinkers made thorough earnest of the principle of self-help in philosophy, even though they had a truth which they believed final, to convey. If we refrain from such radical measures, is it not in part because we realize that the principle is incomplete? The question I raise is whether, without falling into any of the vices of orthodoxy, we cannot do what the instinct of our students seems to require of us, and present philosophy as having something to say both objective and sayable.

If I seem to be proposing the resuscitation of an ancient and long-buried hope, that of finding a basis of unity in philosophy; it is, I trust, with a reasonable difference. I take due warning from the unhappy fortunes of past efforts in this direction. But I also find frequent helpful instruction even among the ancients.

I find old Simplicius an instructive person, and anything but the idle eclectic he is sometimes reputed to be. With the overt differences of Plato and Aristotle before him, an eclectic would take something from one and something from the other, and patch up a compromise philosophy. Not so Simplicius. Like his predecessors, Syrianus and Proclus, he proceeds on an assumption which we must grant is far more difficult, namely, that Plato and Aristotle were *both entirely right!* For did not both seek the truth? And did not Plato find it? And was not Aristotle far too great an intellect to disagree with the truth? So Simplicius spent gigantic labor and no little originality in the service of that true philosophy which, as he believed, must explain the apparent differences of all other true philosophies.

I find Fichte instructive also, but in a very different way. Simplicius was pacifistic in his methods; but not Fichte. If we were to classify philosophers by the four temperaments, Bacon and Berkeley would surely belong to the sanguine group, Locke to the bilious, Fichte to the sanguine-choleric. Fichte was never more sanguine and seldom more choleric than when he wrote his *Sonnerklarer Bericht* as "Ein Versuch die Leser zum Verstehen zu zwingen." At the outset of this piece he expresses the conviction "that there is only one single philosophy, just as there is only one single mathematics; and that as soon as this only possible philosophy is found and acknowledged, no new ones will arise, but all previous philosophies will signify only attempts and preparatory sketches." It would perhaps not be too hard to guess which philosophy Fichte thought the definitive philosophy would most resemble: but it remained for him an ideal entity, a pure 'ought,' which in its own way and time was to incorporate itself through our unceasing efforts.

Hegel, too, I find instructive; but not so much so for our present direction as a recent commentator of his work, Mr. Stace. Mr. Stace sees in the Hegelian philosophy a kernel of more enduring worth than that philosophy itself; and taking his clue from an *obiter dictum* of William Wallace, he calls it "the universal philosophy which has passed on from age to age, here narrowed and there widened, but still essentially the same. It is conscious of its continuity and proud of its identity with the teachings of Plato and Aristotle"—a phrase which would surely please the shade of Simplicius. But, Mr. Stace, not content with generalities, presents us with the actual substance of this universal philosophy in a series of fairly simple propositions, as these: that all existence is appearance and not reality; that the real is the universal; that the world flows from the universal, not as effect from its cause in time, but as a conclusion from its premise; that the universal is not a thing existing before the world, but is the indwelling reason of the world.

In such episodes as these, none of us, probably, finds any proposition which he can adopt as it stands. There is something melancholy about it all, this immense waste of gifted energy and hope; few episodes in modern philosophy seem to me more pathetic than Fichte's impetuous onslaught on the citadel of finality, and the tragic failure of his last great effort to be *sonnenklar*. From the standpoint of worldly wisdom, there is also, in every serious effort to bring unity to pass in this pluralistic world of untamable wills and thoughts, something subtly diverting.

But even if all past efforts had been pure failures—which I do not grant,—I should be less impressed by the repeated failure than by the immortal persistence of the effort. The problem of the unity of philosophy is thereby qualified—in the words of Miss Calkins' happy title—as one of the persistent problems of philosophy.

And in these episodes, I find intimations of a usable method. Simplicius was doubtless mistaken in aiming to discover a sort of common multiple of the systems he severally accepted, for there can be no common multiple of contradictory judgments. Mr. Stace is equally mistaken in trying to formulate a sort of historical common divisor. Fichte was in error in his apocalyptic vision of the nearness of the great day. But I doubt whether any of them were mistaken in their common belief that a universal philosophy is, in some sense, already in the works. Perhaps the main difficulty has been that these thinkers have begun by trying too hard for something relatively simple and near at hand.

My suggestion is that there are certain views about the universe which are assumed or postulated in the nature of the philosophic enterprise itself, so that every philosopher by his activity, if not by his doctrines, acknowledges them.

It is a large part of the business of philosophy to bring to light the presuppositions of other activities. Philosophy might therefore be expected to be especially keen in the scent for its own presuppositions. But partly because it has been haunted by the ideal of a presuppositionless beginning, and partly because it has been busied with determining the presuppositions of the sciences, its enquiries into its own presuppositions have been (so far as my limited knowledge goes) desultory and incomplete.

And in one respect, at least, we are peculiarly ready at the present moment for renewing the enquiry. For there is a widespread disposition to question whether a presuppositionless beginning of philosophy is possible. Hegel and the pragmatic movement are in complete accord in denying such possibility. Let me recall the words of Charles Peirce:

"We cannot begin with complete doubt. We must begin with all the prejudices we actually have when we enter upon the study of philosophy. . . . Let us not pretend to doubt in philosophy what we do not doubt in our hearts." And Professor Sheldon, in a notable paper recently published in the *Journal of Philosophy* puts the case with even greater vigor:

"Let no one think that the philosopher is, or ever can be, purely empirical or unbiased. He is, on the contrary, deep down in his mind, a dogmatist. He must always look for something which he believes at the bottom of his heart he will eventually find. . . . If he did not have a persisting faith in this matter he would lack sufficient motive for continuing his arduous task."

The words 'prejudice' and 'dogma' are here employed, of course, for their challenging effect. Neither writer intends to urge us to build our philosophic structure on an uncriticised foundation. Each would agree that prejudices and dogmas taken as we find them are individual, variable, obstructive,—the richest field of wild game for the philosophic hunter.

I trust, then, that I am not too far from the intention of these writers if I propose that a part of what they were aiming at is a set of necessary presuppositions, such as all criticism would tend to reinstate. To find such presuppositions would be to clarify our dogmas and prejudices, to recognize the element of necessity in them, and so to win common consent. More than this, it would do justice to the inescapable ideal of a presuppositionless beginning. For to know what our presuppositions are is to know *how far we are* from the presuppositionless beginning, and thus to have such a beginning in mind, and really to depart from it.

Let us agree, for the sake of the argument, upon a tentative statement of what the philosophic enterprise is. Philosophy, as I understand it, is first of all the examination of beliefs,—beliefs being the opinions we live by, as distinct from the opinions we merely entertain. This pluralistic effort to criticise our several major beliefs drives us to some comprehensive belief about the world we live in, so that philosophy becomes the *general interpretation of experience*. The *description* of experience is a part of our business, and to the end of true description, a precise logical scrutiny of the categories; but description is not enough unless description also explains. For after all, it is the necessity of understanding which drives us to philosophy; and whatever interprets the world to men will be to them 'philosophy,' whether we acknowledge it as such or not.

With this understanding, I submit that every one of us as philosopher requires at least these three presuppositions:

First, that things have a meaning;
Second, that we human beings are competent to grasp that meaning, or some of it;
Third, that it is worth while to do so, and ought to be attempted.

Although I am putting these propositions forward as assumptions every philosopher is bound to make, I am aware that they are in need of defence, as well as of further definition. This circumstance will not, in a company of philosophers, at once disqualify them for their proposed rôle as presuppositions. For we are only too often reminded, in the course of our work, of the versatile capacity of the human mind, including our own, to think and act athwart its own foundations.

Thus, in ordinary conversation, we make a number of important presuppositions which the contents of the conversation may belie. For while conversing can only proceed under the tacit profession of good will in the give-and-take, and of equality of the conversers in sharing the meaning of the terms used, it may convey hostilities of all shades or assertions of unmitigated inequality. It may then be useful to bring the implied professions to light, as M. Briand recently did in reminding the belligerent representatives of Poland and Lithuania of their necessary affection for each other! The chief utility of investigating presuppositions depends on the fact that we may not, at once, recognize them as such.

I may, therefore, with a good logical conscience proceed to defend our 'necessary agreements' against potential disagreement; and this may be the best way of exhibiting what they mean.[2]

Our first assumption is that *things have a meaning:* that is to say, there is nothing meaningless in the world (taking things one by one) and (taking them collectively) the world as a whole is not meaningless.

The most obvious difficulty in the way of this postulate is that we are bound in all good conscience to be empirical toward our world; and to be empirical is to accept things as they are, with a 'natural piety' which does not insist on explanation. We have come to believe that there are certain ultimate matters of fact which every philosophy must simply accept as *there*, such as space, or the actual configuration of events, or the amounts and numbers of things, or the existence of anything at all. If some of them should yield up a meaning to us, it would be just another matter of fact that they did so. We have domesticated the word 'datum,' and are growing fond of it. In this respect, our own philosophic age has more natural piety than any preceding age in history.

Still, it seems clear that from the radically empirical standpoint, the postulate that everything has a meaning has the same type of justification as the postulate that everything has a cause. We have the same illusion (if it is an illusion) in both cases,—that of having now and then a direct experience of meaning as of causation. And in each case, if we allow Hume to analyze our experience for us, the supposed object mysteriously eludes us. I seem to see the axe split the wood: but no, I only see the axe fall and the wood then spring apart. Likewise, I seem to see the intention of the wood-cutter: he is preparing his wood-pile for winter. But no, I only perceive the events, and their meaning is a subjective act of interpretation. Personally, I do not accept Hume's analysis; but even at that, if experience does not *give* causes nor meanings, neither can it *reject* them.

Our inability to see a meaning in any case would not afford justification for supposing that no meaning is there. This we could do only if we are prepared to *prove* some aspect of the world to be necessarily meaningless. But in that case, though there is no overt self-contradiction,[3] we should have brought the inexplicable or irrational fact within the world of our meanings, so that it has ceased to be a mere and meaningless matter of fact. If we conceive that an ideal park plan will include some places of natural wildness, they do not cease to be wild; but they are brought within the scope of the rational artifice.

Our present obdurately empirical bent is a sign of good health. It is a normal mental appetite for stuff to be interpreted, together, no doubt, with much justified impatience with former interpretations. It may well be that our accumulation of the raw material of experience will always outrun our interpretative powers, and keep us duly humble and naturally pious. But the empirical attitude in the sense of pure acceptance must be regarded as preliminary, not eventual, unless the impulse of philosophy is to be withered at its root.

So far, we have been speaking of the meanings of things taken piecemeal. But after all, that is not our main concern. Our interpretations have the ambition to deal with the whole situation; and the meaning of the whole filters through to confer significance upon the parts. The most formidable difficulty we have to face is the doubt whether the whole of things can have any meaning.

This difficulty is of a logical order. Meaning is a relative term: it can apply only to what is partial. The whole, then, as a sort of Absolute, must be without meaning. Whatever is true of the whole must bear alike on all the parts, and can make no difference to any of them: it must bear alike on high and low, matter and mind, good and evil. Conversely, we cannot describe the whole in terms of one side of any antithesis, when both sides are found in experience. The whole cannot be good, for experience contains both good and evil. It cannot be mental, for experience contains both mental and non-mental. It cannot have specific meaning, because all meanings come in contrasting pairs.

This type of consideration is familiar under a hundred forms. It applies to the ultimate logical analysis of experience as well as to its totality. It gives the realist like Mr. Holt his neutral entities, just as it gives the logical mystic his indescribable unity or substance. It unites the pragmatist and the pluralist in the corollary that since the whole, if there is a whole, can make no difference, it can make no difference to treat it as if it does not exist, and give our interest and loyalty to meanings which, because of what they are opposed to, as good against evil, have definable work to do in a real time order. We are dealing, in fact, with a sort of metaphysical frontier, in the sense that many explorative thinkers are halted at this line. *Neutralism*, if I may coin the title, is the prevalent belief regarding ultimate reality. All the gods worth worshipping are finite.

Experience lends a certain support to this logic. For even in such small editions of wholeness as we find in a single human career, there is as we pass from the part to the whole an *evanescence of meaning*. The sense of a day's work can be told. But who can tell the entire tendency or significance of his life? The definable meanings are partial; and when we enquire what on the whole they lead to, they vanish, like dream-bridges without abutments, into unspecified termini, or else merge into the ancient and meaningless round which Goethe celebrates:

Warum treibt sich das Volk so und schreit? Es will sich ernähren,
Kinder zeugen und die nähren, so gut es vermag.
Merke dir, Reisender, das, und thue zu Hause desgleichen!
Weiter bringt es kein Mensch, stell' er sich, wie er auch will.[4]

The whole of life is less convincingly meaningful than the parts, and the same is true, only more strikingly, of more inclusive wholes, state, humanity, world.

My belief is that this is a point in which our intuitions must give instruction to our logic. We know, as Tolstoi knew, that unless the whole of a life has meaning, the meanings of the parts are illusory; and the same is true of every totality. We know, then, that *this logical frontier of neutralism must be passed*. And my belief is that we have in hand the means to pass it. We cannot do it by an Hegelian attack, or pseudo-attack, on the principle of contradiction; for to attack that principle is to commit philosophical suicide. But I believe that Hegel was not wholly on the wrong track, and that there is no more important logical task for the present than to find what is valid in his peculiar logical bent.

If I may sketch my own mode of expressing the case, it is that, beside the concepts which have a single boundary, there are also concepts which have, or may have, a *double or multiple boundary.*

Take the concept of 'the mutual.' The mutual is opposed to the non-mutual or exclusive. Thus common property is among the mutual things, private property among the non-mutuals. But since, when A has nothing in common with B, B also has nothing in common with A, all pure exclusions are mutual. Thus the private properties of A and B are *mutually non-mutual.* I need not dwell on the immense social importance of this situation. It means that Plato was radically mistaken, not in desiring that friends should have as much as possible in common, but in failing to see that they may have more in common by having less in common, as when the exclusions of private properties and families allow sharable personal developments not otherwise possible. Thus the concept of the mutual gains a new and wider boundary; and it does so without abandoning the old one, because the original contrast between the mutual and the non-mutual must be kept intact.

This kind of concept is thoroughly familiar; but it is relegated by most reputable logicians to a sort of logical *demi-monde.* I wish to defend its respectability. There is nothing smeary or irresponsible about its behavior. It cannot be accused of "turning into its own opposite" or of having overflowed its banks; there is no twilight zone about it, and no irrational flux. It is a matter of clear saltation.

Now the existence of such concepts as these enables us to see how the whole of things can be significant. For granted that all terms which express meaning come in contrasting pairs, so that each applies primarily to only a part of the world, it yet remains to be asked whether one of the pair may have a double boundary, and *apply also to the whole.* From my own point of view, the concept of *self* has seemed the most perfect example of this class of concepts: for while the self has always a not-self over against it, it is always *taking that not-self in,*—its life may be said to consist in a process of consuming its limits. It has seemed to me to offer the best instance of a concept which could apply at once to the whole and to a part. But perhaps it is not private selfhood which best describes the whole: perhaps it is the mutual, in the form of the social or the 'we'; while private selfhood, as the most completely non-mutual aspect of existence, is included within it. Professor Dewey's address of this afternoon strongly inclines me toward that view. But these are controversial matters. I am not here arguing for the application of any special one of these concepts to the whole of things. I am simply pointing out that if we can find such a concept, neutralism, with its logical objection to our postulate, falls to the ground.

And if the logical difficulties fall, the difficulties raised by experience will not stand. Although the world is well-stocked with the apparently waste,—the uncounted sand grains, the bad lands, the deserts, the empty spaces, the unused interiors and other-sides of things, the unnoticed and innumerable heavenly bodies, the many-too-many insects and perhaps also to our dull eyes the many-too-many of mankind,—our judgment is never tenacious in holding to the verdict, 'meaningless.' For we have seen too many things, in the course of history, swing out of that category into relation with our tangible concerns, too many deserts have become gardens and waste rocks precious ores.

Then, too, in a world in which everything is momentarily affecting everything else, nothing is functionless. The myriads of organisms in the early stages of evolution are not left behind by the highest, but are organized into its life-cycle. Humanity cannot be itself without animal, vegetable, micro-organism: thus the highest, by itself, is not so high as a union of the highest with the not-highest. The 'highest' in biology turns out to be a concept with a double boundary. It begins to appear to our slow political vision that the 'highest races' so far from rendering the less high superfluous, are not so high as a possible just union of the 'highest' with the 'backward.' The failure of aristocracy is in supposing that there is a class of 'the best,' a class with a single boundary which clearly excludes the not-best. And perhaps if there is a Highest Being, its boundary also will extend to include lower ranges of the scale. This is the clear sense of Augustine's remark:

"With a sounder judgment I apprehended that the things above were better than the things below, but all together better than the things above by themselves."

When the relatively meaningless is thus in many ways caught up into the circuits of meaning, we recognize that if logic allows our postulate, life will not deny it.

Our second proposition, as philosophers, is that the *meaning of things can be known by us;* or, to put it in the negative form, that a true understanding of things as they are is not beyond our grasp.

Modern philosophy has gone through a curious reversal on this point. It began with a vehement rebuke to our native presumption in thinking to read God's intention or nature's intention in the arrangements of the world. If it is dangerous to impute motives to our neighbors, how much more so to impute motives to nature, and how much deeper folly to treat such fancies as knowledge. It required a philosophic revolution to cure this folly; but the campaign against the appeal to 'final causes' was one of the most successful of philosophic movements. An humble and Job-like agnosticism about values was well-established long before the corresponding agnosticism in ontology.

Now, in various quarters, we find a complete resumption of confidence; but on the ground that there are no objective and non-evident meanings in things to be sought for. Value is simply the projection of our human interests upon the frame of events. It is the external counterpart of wish, instinct, desire or imagination; and were these to vanish, this aspect of meaning would vanish also. A value, according to Professor Perry, is "any object of any interest." The world of values, according to Mr. Bertrand Russell, is our contribution to the world: it is the realm of our freedom, for here we rule as kings. Our philosophies, according to Mr. Santayana, are works of art; they belong to the domain of that "rhetorical and emotional rendering of existence, which when deepened and purified becomes poetry and music. If meanings are thus determined by our own natures, or products of our own devising, the question of our competence to know them cannot arise.

I am convinced that we must decisively reject this easy route to self-confidence, which is, in substance, the route of subjective idealism. As a revolt from the impossible and long-lasting repression of our value-judgments, these doctrines are refreshing. Their validity is in their unqualified assertion that if we are to philosophize at all, *we must judge and must believe in our power of judgment*. But their way to security and freedom is not less destructive of the life of philosophy than the way of repression. They purchase confidence at the cost of robbing meaning of its metaphysical roots, and making it a painted aspect of the surface of experience.

When we postulate that things have meanings, we are putting the meanings on the same plane of objectivity with the things. The logical issue can be placed on this point. If our interpretations of the world are really emotional renderings, the question of their truth or falsity becomes impertinent. They may be clever, interesting, elevating, or beautiful, but not true or false. But we intend them to be subject to the test of truth. If some one tells us that our philosophy is classic or romantic or profoundly imaginative, we may think these worthy graces; but if that is all, we know we have failed. Ruskin, who might excusably have been concerned with the aesthetic quality of his thought, felt himself outraged by the persistence of this type of appreciation. I have lost his words; they are something as follows: "We tell men their social order is wrong, their souls are in danger, and they reply,— 'It is very beautiful.'" We should have the same reason for indignation. We intend our philosophies to convince and move men to action because they are reliable reports of the nature of the world. It is their business to be beautiful; and would that they could all be as beautiful as the works of Plato or Dante or Santayana. But their primary virtue is their truth, their primary vice, their falsity; and no one can withdraw his philosophy from this test without convicting himself of essential triviality.

There is some analogy between philosophy and biography in this respect. A good biography must be something better than faithful to fact: it must be a work of art and imagination. It must be so, in part, because without imagination it cannot be true. It is dealing with a living and therefore meaningful theme: it must present the facts of that life in the light of that person's own vision of the world. If it falls into bare chronicle, or if it substitutes the writer's vision for that of the subject, it is so far false biography. Philosophy must also be imaginative in order to be true; and philosophical imagination may also be false, because it has something objective to be true to. And if an interpretation may be false, it follows that the meaning alleged is neither on the surface of things, nor at the sole control of the interpreter. It is the objective world which is passing judgment upon it.

In some sense, then, the structure of the world is in itself significant: there is, in some sense, *an objective reason* in the make-up of things.

I would like to illustrate the relation between imagination and truth in philosophy by reference to the fortunes of our interpretations of space in the nineteenth century.

Kant sharpened the sense of the world to the peculiarities of space: its differences from the objects of sense and from general ideas, its unbanishableness, its infinitude and all-at-onceness, its complete knowableness. Two lines of elaboration proceed from Kant. That of the mathematicians, with which we have become well acquainted in recent years, who with great imaginative power have set the space of Kant and Newton in the midst of a class of spaces as but one form of multiple possibilities, accurately definable and curiously conjoined with the measurements of time. Then that of the metaphysical poets, which has been largely forgotten.

What the poet Fichte saw in space was, as we might expect, a moral attribute; though few objects could be more unpromising than space as a field for moral quality. Fichte however felt in space its *Gediegenheit*,—its genuineness, its candor, its transparent honesty. For space is the absence of all concealment, it shows all it is to a single glance. Fichte further celebrates its stability, its repose, its self-containedness. Things may be agitated in space; but beneath their wildest commotion space stands eternally unmoved. Then Fichte speculates whether this imperturbable placidity may not be the inner repose of the self, made external. Perhaps, as we view space, the will perceives its own calm ground, in the form of an object.

We think of space as a field within which we see objects. But the poet Schelling observed that we also see the eyes of other organisms, and the relation between those eyes and the things they are seeing. Space permits us not only to see things, but also to see the seeing of things. As he put it, space is "the form in which the outer sense becomes its own object.' We are reminded of another word of Fichte's, perhaps his boldest imaginative flight,—space is *"the eternal eye, in itself and for itself,"*—it is vision's own self, everywhere at once!

Again, Schelling observes of space that it can be regarded as a sort of extreme thinning out of things. Consider a simple patch of color, and reduce its intensity gradually to zero by spreading it over a larger and larger room. Then when it fills all space its intensity is zero; it becomes indistinguishable from space itself. Space is thus in Schelling's words "the negation of all intensity." And hereupon Schelling also speculates that space may be just an exhibition to ourselves of the intensity of selfhood dissolved *(aufgelöst)* into the infinite; the precise counterpart of that selfhood's intrinsic concentration at a point!

Hegel we might expect to find playing with antitheses. He declares of space that it is the unity of inclusion and exclusion, of togetherness and apartness, of absolute freedom, since it limits no movement, and absolute imprisonment, since with whatever movement no body can leave its space, and finally of the sensible and the insensible; for space is "eine unsinnliche Sinnlichkeit und eine sinnliche Unsinnlichkeit"!

These are surely not descriptions which mathematics can employ. They are not even the dialectical deductions they were supposed to be. They are flights of philosophical imagination, a sort of poetry, with an aim at conveying in figures and symbols what it could not convey literally. If they had been presented as poetry, instead of in the pretentious guise of a deduction of the categories, we should have been better able to place them and to profit by them. For myself I confess that when I want to realize what space is, I find the mathematical imagination indispensable; but I find the poetical imagination incomparably more intimate with the object and farther reaching.

Now the point of this reference to metaphysical poetry is simply that, like all great art, it undertakes to reveal objective significance, and not simply to exhibit the author's versatile fancy. The meanings, then, which we try to find in our philosophies are the meanings which are *there*. And with this understanding, all of the reasons which led our predecessors to doubt our capacity to judge the meaning of the world resume their force.

But the same conviction, pressed farther, carries with it the cure of that doubt. For *we also* are things in the world: and like other things there, we and our doings have a meaning. Now we are a special variety of thing, namely, philosophers, enquirers after meanings. But to suppose that the world has produced meaning-seekers incompetent to assess meanings is to suppose a typically meaningless situation, such as our first postulate forbids us to assume. Hence we cannot believe that our valuations are irrelevant to, or essentially divergent from, the objective meanings of things: our estimations of the world must be potentially competent estimations.

(Note that our postulate contains no invitation to that anthropomorphism, which we have every historic reason to dread. For the human mind is not limited to knowing 'human' values,—such a notion is a phase of that subjectivism we have been denying. As the mind knows what is first of all other than itself, so our values are first of all what we discover, not what we invent; and we do not limit them by our finding. The present danger is not that we shall be too man-centered in our judgments: it is that we shall fail to do justice to the essential transparency and infinite reach of thought.)

Our second postulate, then, warrants us in taking courage anew from that great word of Aristotle, "Let us live, therefore, as if the immortal quality were our share,"—the immortal quality of valid judgment.

Our third postulate expresses one of these objective meanings of the world, and supplies a first principle of action. It is that it is *worth while to know* the meanings of things; or perhaps we might say that they *ought* to be known by us, in the sense that it is a sort of cosmic pity if they are not known!

In a world of pure fact, there is nothing objectively wrong. In a world of meanings, there are situations which we can say are wrong in themselves; among them this situation, that a meaning and its possible appreciator do not come together. It is the destiny of meaning to be understood; and if its being is not fulfilled in this way, there is just so much tragedy and loss. The fact that the meaning is there, in the object, thus creates a certain imperative, 'Know the meaning of things.' This, I think, is the original of all imperatives: *'Be objective:* open your mind to the objective reason of the world.' Philosophy is the first response of the moral will to the world's summons, that we commit to it our ultimate fortunes, and therein realize a part of the elusive meaning of our own lives.

If interpreting were a subjective enterprise of adorning with meaning a neutral world, it would still be important, but it would lack the imperative quality. And there are various concrete ways in which both we and the world would be the losers.

First, we should limit the possible values of the world to the measure of our desires. We suppose that desire is first and value afterward; whereas desire expands to the measure of the values it finds. Were music not presented to us, we should never know from the state of our untutored desires that *that* glory was one of the possibilities of the world. We have no reason to assume that there is any limit to the objective value of the world. On the surface, we find it moderately good and moderately bad: but moderation has no metaphysical standing. The mystic—the metaphysical mystic—reports that he has perceived a worth in being which outpasses our prudent imaginations; and if among the many mystics there is one true observer, we dare not attempt to measure the meaning of things from the psychological end, condemning ourselves forever to a universe of compromised and middling worth.

Then again we should limit our own fertility and freedom. Creative imagination has its conditions: it grows by what it feeds upon; it springs out of contemplation, and varies with hope. The capacity to invent begins in the capacity to observe,—a law which the biography of genius strikingly confirms. There is no mental parthenogenesis. Subjectivism ascribes to our minds a fertility which is not unconditionally our own; for if at any time we are gravid with meaning, it is the universe which has made us so.

And finally, we limit our own effective realism. For if the world is objectively meaningful, then it is in the most apparently meaningless and forbidding places that the greatest opportunities for the disclosure of new meanings exist: here most of all the world asks to be understood. If the values are our own, these places are in prudence to be avoided. But the philosopher knows by instinct that he is bound to open his mind unreservedly, and even by preference, to experience in its bleakest, cruelest and most refractory characters. The meaning of the meaningless is often that it be overcome or abolished; but in any case it is to be faced and understood. The philosopher must be realistic as only one who believes in objective meaning can be. For it is in the realism of the critically hopeful, not in the critical realism of the hopeless, that the world's hope lies.

It might have been possible, had our interest in this hour of mutual counsel been more technical, to present these theses in the guise of a Critique of Pure Philosophy, in answer to a pseudo-Kantian question, How is philosophy possible? You will not hold it against me that I have refrained from using this form. But in substance I believe that this is what we have been asking.

Our answer has been the reverse of Kantian. Philosophy is possible, we have said, not because the subject throws the categories of meaning over an indifferent manifold of datal stuff; but because the meanings are first of all actually there; because they are such as our reasons are destined to reproduce; and because the incentive to find them is the call of reality itself. And we add, that as knowledge is one of the objective values of the world, the philosopher's joy in the apprehension of meaning is at the same time a realization of the cosmic nisus toward being known.

My fear is that I have burdened you with too much argument rather than too little. And if so, I beg to atone for it by resorting to a form of philosophy sanctioned by the highest of names, the form of myth.

Nature was once thought to be a Sphinx, guarding a deep-wrought riddle; and we men were hypothesis-makers, hazarding guesses at the peril of our lives.

It is commonly held to-day that the Sphinx has nothing to guard. Her pretentious mystery (to adopt the language of Mr. Santayana) is but "a thin deception practised upon me by nature. The great Sphinx in posing her riddle, and looking so threatening and mysterious is secretly hoping that I may laugh. She is not a riddle but a fact.... Why take her residual silence for a challenge or a menace? She does not know how to speak more plainly. Her secret is as great a secret to herself as to me."[5] Then we philosophers who try to fathom her meaning are victimized like those who try to dive deep in shallow waters. The figure is untrue, and we must change the myth: for the only answer to an imperfect myth is a truer one.

According to the old Welsh legend, Merlin, the magician and prophet, after spending some years as counsellor at the court of King Arthur, suddenly and mysteriously disappeared. It was supposed that he fell prey to the sorceress Nimu, who having coaxed his secret from him, used it to throw him into a trance and imprisoned him alive in a great rock.

Many years later, a wanderer lost in the mountains fell exhausted to the ground, and was startled to hear a voice coming as it seemed from the depths of the earth, and speaking in an ancient and uncouth form. He understood that the voice purported to be the voice of Merlin, and that a spell was being told which, if spoken from above, would break the prison and set Merlin free.

But he could distinguish only a few of the syllables. And though they stamped themselves upon his memory; and he set them into a ballad, which he sang up and down the mountain roads; and he fancied sometimes that while he sang there was a trembling and cracking within the hills and a great, distant shout which only he could hear; there was no deliverance. Now every seventh year a traveler is lured to that spot and another fragment of the spell is recovered and another song is made. But Merlin cannot be released until the travellers meet and join their fragments into the complete saying.

We philosophers, the travelers of the myth, are taking part in an age-long labor of release. The meanings we find are actual possibilities buried in the heart of the world. Our different reports are, in part, our own creations, wrought by imagination and added to the wealth of racial poetry. But they are, first of all, our debt to the infinite imprisoned meaning of the world. Our differences cannot be regarded as mere personal accidents; for it is because of these differences that the whole spell may be recovered. If we learn how our thoughts belong together, Merlin may yet walk the earth again.

NOTES

1. I owe this account to Professor Hu Shih.
2. I have used the word 'meaning' and am making an incidental assumption that we can so far control its context as to understand it in the same sense. Perhaps the less I discuss this point the more intelligible my remarks will be. Let me make just this note, that the word 'meaning' has established itself in philosophical discussion because it conveniently covers both reason and value. This is not an ambiguity: it is an extreme generality, almost too extreme to be manageable. Its difficulty coincides with its utility.
3. As Charles Peirce seems to hold, *Chance, Love, and Logic*, p. 3, §4.
4. *Epigramme*, 1790, 10.
5. *The Realm of Essence*, p. xix.

CHAPTER 2

Preface to the 1912 Edition of *The Meaning of God in Human Experience*

The services of thought to religion have been subject to a justified distrust. Of uncertain worth, especially of uncertain recoil, are the labors of reason in behalf of any of our weightier human interests. By right instinct has religion from the beginning looked elsewhere for the brunt of support and defense—say to revelation, to faith, to feeling. A bad defense is a betrayal; and what human philosophy of religion can be better than a bad defense?

Present-day philosophy seems notably inclined to take this view of itself. Is it not Bradley, elder metaphysician to our time, who jots down that metaphysics is the finding of bad reasons for what we believe on instinct? Reason is not incapable of recognizing and confessing its own limits: it may even take pride in expounding them, an attitude which since Hume and Kant has become more or less fashionable. Our current science of religion may now assume without too much discussion that the grounds of religion are super-rational, or sub-rational: and we find philosophy undertaking to define what these other-than-rational grounds are—grounds moral perhaps, or psychological, or social, or historical; grounds pragmatic, or even mystic. Various and variously combined as are these several philosophic trends, they agree in accepting the judgment that religion lies close to the primitive moving-forces of life: deeper, then, than reason or any work of reason.

But a vague territory still is this Beyond-reason or Deeper-than-reason. Once singly-named Faith, now it has many names—instinct, the subconscious, the co-conscious, feeling, will, value-judgment, social sense, intuition, mystic reason, perhaps *l'élan vital*—as its border is touched in various scientific excursions. Some unclearness has come with the abundance of our learning, some confusion of categories, no doubt; we can hardly yet say that we know better than our forefathers what religion is, though perhaps we know better what it is not. The one impression which does distinctly emerge from the multitude of contemporary suggestions is a negative one: a general disaffection from the religion of reason, and from its philosophical framework, absolute idealism.

Some doubt the fundamental proposition of this idealism, namely, that all reality is of the same stuff that ideas are made of, that "whatever is is rational." Some

---

From MGHE, xv–xxx.

doubt its doctrine that everything is known to one absolute Knower, whose being is thought, or Idea. And some there are who do not doubt these propositions; who will not deny logical force, even finality, to idealistic arguments—if one must argue: but who add the comment that whatever is vital in religion is missed in all logic-work, is necessarily and forever missed, thought and religion being once for all incommensurate. They do not find the Absolute of idealism identical with the God of religion: they cannot worship the Absolute. And they do not find that religion consists in our human knowledge of this absolute Knower: *Denken*, they think, *ist nicht Gottesdienst*.

In this general dissatisfaction with idealism, and in our unclear efforts to win elsewhere a positive groundwork for religion, I find the sufficient warrant for such a study as this book undertakes. It enquires what, in terms of experience, its God means and has meant to mankind (for surely religion rises out of experience and pays back into it again): and it proposes, by aid of the labors of all co-workers, critics and criticised alike, to find the foundations of this religion, whether within reason or beyond.

This purpose is not over-bold; though no serious treatment of religion dare be over-modest. It is not over-bold, first, because it is a human necessity. We must reach some working clarity in these matters, every individual soul of us: the problem is there; we shall work it through well or ill, get our solution honorably or by default. Is there not in all positive living a similar necessity for what we may call presumption? The world too is there, with work to be done, votes to be cast, a new generation to be trained and harnessed, and other like requirements—all equally impossible. All such undertakings might well be postponed by any man under the true plea of unfitness: nevertheless all this is to be done, and all will get itself done in some fashion, creditable or discreditable. It is, in fact, an old ruse of nature's, this of clothing the necessary in the guise of the impossible, making a dignified way of escape for him who prefers to escape from complete living, calling for something like presumption on the part of him who will not escape. Let us rather say, calling for performance simply, categorical performance. Nature creates the requirement: let nature supply ways and means.

Our purpose is not over-bold, secondly, because, after all, the truth about religion cannot be in itself obscure or intricate. Subtle religion is false religion. Our difficulties are indeed made by our laboring philosophies themselves. The quaint words of Berkeley still hold good: "*We have first raised a dust and then complain we cannot see.*" The truth about religion is to be had; but not by surpassing others in more mighty floundering and dust-raising: this truth is traditionally for "him that hath eyes to see and ears to hear" in a certain quietude of mind.

Only—be it at once said—the dust-raising in the present case is a much more important process than the words of Berkeley imply. In the new philosophies is new truth, and much of it—no mere new misunderstanding. Whatever murkiness there is marks, I believe, a genuine deepening of spiritual consciousness in our Western world: a new appreciation of faith, a new love of life and its variety, a new ability to be both bond and free—speculatively, spiritually, free, while not less scientifically bond, historically bond, even traditionally bond. It is a symptom of any such valid deepening of thought that men know less clearly what they want than what they do not want. The older philosophy has failed to satisfy; the newer philosophies have not yet succeeded in satisfying: the work of proposing and rejecting must continue until conscience at its profounder level can again rest.

It is just because of this veritable growth that cleverness and erudition poured out in abundance do nowadays visibly pall and fail of their usual effect: for cleverness and erudition operate within the already acquired conceptions of mankind—they stand ineffective before what is new-born. For this reason, in part, the weighty scholarship of Germany loses some little ground in these fields. If we know the kind of thing that a given type of scholarship has to offer, then even great virtuosity, though it be prolific of the Very True, must sweat to provoke an interest, still more to arouse our faith. The thing now required is a simple thing, a common word, a slight increment of ultimate sincerity somewhere that can reunite our roots with mother earth. We are as well off above ground as we can be until we are better off below ground. What boots it though a man can produce out of his inner consciousness a veritable banyan forest if there is, in all, no growth *downward?* There is, I say, a quiet and canny maturity of conscience abroad which knows surely what it does not want, a new-born thing in the world, the source of our new philosophies,—in particular of our pragmatisms, our realisms, our mysticisms,—the doom of the old, the doom also of the new that fail to arrive at reality: the lash at the back of the thinker, and the hope in his soul.

Meanwhile, the general deepening of consciousness, and of conscience, is a deepening of religion itself. The formulae that were once potent here too begin to fail: ideas and phrases, gritty a generation ago, a decade ago, are already worn smooth and lend no more friction to any human work. A new calling has sprung up: that of creed-making, or of creed phrase-making; and many of our wise men take part in it. These too have their new Reality to face, merciless as a child. If the spirit of the age is but feebly responsive to new phrase or old, hasten not to judge that the spirit of the age is becoming irreligious: may not the opposite theory as well explain its indifference to *us* (though with less salve for our vanity)? Potentially, at least, men are becoming more religious. This development of religion is still a latent fact, mightier than any yet-visible shape or movement, discernible at times only as a cloud dim and vast, strained and full of repressed lightning. The release of these forces is no small human object.

In what respect, then, is idealism inadequate to these new demands? And what is the truth which the critics of idealism have to offer? It may be well to state at once (especially for the satisfaction of fellow-students in these fields) the substance of our belief on these points, outlining in rough summary the position in which the work of this book results.

The weakness in the armor of classical idealism has been made apparent, I believe, by pragmatism—or rather, by the pragmatic principle of judgment. *Idealism does not do the work of religious truth; ergo, it is not the truth of religion.* This judgment may be accepted without further commitment to the philosophy that pronounces it (for is it not also Hegel's principle that the true idea is known by its work in this concrete world?)

Idealism fails to work, I believe, chiefly because it is unfinished. Unfinishedness is not in itself a blemish; is professed even as a special excellence by that remarkable antisystemist, Henri Bergson.[1] But there are tolerable and intolerable kinds of unfinishedness. A thing is properly unfinished when *it* is finishable; when it has an identity that finishing will not change. Let an artist sketch a face with all conceivable haste and roughness: the unfinishedness of the thing is wholly justified if only it is a thing; if only it has a character and a significance which all later finishing does but develop without displacement or substitution. Our philosophies must meet the same test. Idealism can entertain much of what pragmatism, realism, and the rest have brought forward, and still remain idealism; whether it can entertain all, is doubtful. It is not incapable of admitting into its world-picture variety, change, growth, personality, freedom, also objectivity of a sort. The question is, of what sort?—whether the variety is a real variety, the risk a real risk, the objectivity a real objectivity, individuality and freedom real—or only shows of reality, infected by that illusoriness and approximateness which idealism tends to impose upon realistic experience generally. Can idealism entertain the Real, and still remain idealism? What pragmatism has specifically required of idealism in religion is more genuinely real opportunity, real freedom, real individual creativity. What realism desires is more valid objectivity, substantiality in the world beyond self. It is the latter want, I venture to say, which chiefly limits the effectiveness of idealism in religion: to satisfy the pragmatic test, idealism must become more realistic: for idealism in religion does not give sufficient credence to the authoritative Object, shows, so far, no adequate comprehension of the attitude of *worship*.

Idealism is unfinished, then, not having found its way to worship: it has not found its way to the particular and the historical in religion; to the authoritative and the wholly super-personal. The salvation it offers men seems still to be, in effect, a salvation from the particular in the general, the *ideal*: even though it names the *concrete* as its goal, it has not yet been able in this matter of religion to accomplish union with the concrete. It might seem that the idealist more than any other should appreciate the function of the positive and authoritative in religion; should know (as Hegel knew) that only the concrete can breed the concrete; should know (as Royce knows) that only the individual can breed the individual; should know, then, that only the historic can bear fruit in history, so that when the pragmatic test comes, a religion which is but a religion-in-general, a religion universal but not particular, a religion of idea, not organically rooted in passion, fact, and institutional life, must fail.

Idealism means, in name and in truth, the freedom in this universe of the thinker, the unlimited right of Idea in a world where nothing that is is ultimately irrational. But it is the exercise of freedom which alone discovers the rightful place of authority. Only he who has tried (or tried to imagine) a pure adventure knows that there is *no such thing as a pure adventure;* for when you have cancelled path, peak, sky, star, all distinguishable points in space, the adventure itself is abolished. The idealist who by right and intention is the pure adventurer in the regions of the spirit has not yet experimented his freedom if he remains unappreciative of authority, in religion as in knowledge. It is he who in the end must be called upon to expound the worth and use of church, dogma, creed, priest, mediator, the whole apparatus of God-worship which religious evolution has produced, and God-worship itself.

If idealism declines this responsibility, as being beyond its province, beyond *reason* in fact, belonging to the practical, or psychological, or anthropological, or historical aspect of the matter only, it does thereby acknowledge the foundations of religion to be beyond reason; implies that to comprehend the truth of religion, idealism must at last *abandon itself.*

The pragmatic test has meant much in our time as a principle of criticism, in awakening the philosophic conscience to the simple need of fruitfulness and moral effect as a voucher of truth. It is this critical pragmatism which first and widely appeals to the intellectual conscience at large. *Negative pragmatism*, I shall call it: whose principle is, *"That which does not work is not true."* The corresponding positive principle, "Whatever works is true," I regard as neither valid nor useful. But invaluable as a guide do I find this negative test: if a theory has no consequences, or bad ones; if it makes no difference to men, or else undesirable differences; if it lowers the capacity of men to meet the stress of existence, or diminishes the worth to them of what existence they have; such a theory is somehow false, and we have no peace until it is remedied. I will even go farther, and say that a theory is false if it is not interesting: a proposition that falls on the mind so dully as to excite no enthusiasm has not attained the level of truth; though the words be accurate the import has leaked away from them, and the meaning is not conveyed. Any such criterion of truth is based upon a conviction or thesis otherwise founded, that the real world is infinitely charged with interest and value, whereby any commonplaceness on our part is evidence of a lack of grasp. Upon this basis (not apart from it), a negative pragmatism must be an effective instrument of knowledge.

This instrument is nowhere so significant as in the field of religious knowledge. What difference is made to you (and necessarily made to you) by your equipment of religious ideas and beliefs? If they are powerless, they are false. Whatever doctrine tends to draw the fangs of reality, and to leave men unstung, content, complacent, and at ease,—that doctrine is a treachery and a deceit. Note well that it is not pleasantness but force that sets the mark for truth: we have to require of our faith not what is agreeable to the indolent spirit but what is at once a spur and a promise. What do you think of hell? The doctrine of hell made religion at one time a matter of first-rate importance: getting your soul saved made a difference in your empirical destiny. If your idealism wipes out your fear of hell, and with it all sense of infinite risk in the conduct of life, your idealism has played you false. Truth must be transformed; but the transformation of truth must be marked by a *conservation of power*; herewith we have a more definite expression for the positive basis of our negative pragmatism. No religion, then, is a true religion which is not able to make men tingle, yes, even to their physical nerve tips, with the sense of an infinite hazard, a wrath to come, a heavenly city to be gained or lost in the process of time and by the use of our freedom. The flesh and blood of historical contingencies cannot be sapped up in the timeless issues of a certain type of idealism without loss of power, hence loss of truth.

What, again, do you think of God? The God of orthodoxy is thought of as being so far like man as to have loves, interests, and powers which make themselves temporally felt: this God does things in the world which, if we like, we may call miracles or, if we like better, deeds of Providence. Upon this *differential* work of God, as contrasted with his total work, was based much of the urgency of former religious observance, prayer, and piety. Pragmatism rightly enquires what becomes of this differential work when God becomes the All-One of idealism; and what, if the historical will of God and the acts of Providence disappear from our creed, is to replace the immediacy and pervasiveness of the religious interest which those theories encouraged, and which in themselves (though not in all bearings) were good. In such wise, the pragmatic principle tends to confront idealism, as it has never before been confronted, with the substantial values of orthodoxy; compelling idealism to complete itself by the standard of these values (I do not say, of these propositions), even if at the cost of its philosophic identity.

This is the type of service which pragmatism can well render. As a positive builder it has little to recommend it. Founding truth ultimately on our human value is but another attempt, more radical than that of idealism, at the "pure adventure": it is an idealism become more subjective, freedom less bound by authority. It is the function of the pragmatic test (as of pain and discomfort generally) to point out something wrong; the work of discovering what is right must be done by other means. Knowledge may be obliged to wait long in a notch well known to be tentative and unsatisfactory because the satisfactory thing cannot be found *as truth requires*. I do not say that *action* must wait. Decision has its hour; and if knowledge is absent, the will-to-believe must come into play: but the will-to-believe is precisely a principle for action, not for knowledge. It has no place in the age-long work of speculation. The adoption of an hypothesis as a working-theory or postulate does not conceal from the adopter its true nature; does not obliterate for him the difference between postulate and knowledge.

But is there, then, no inaccessible truth? no permanent gap in knowledge (such as religious truth might hold), to be filled up *by choice?* There is no inaccessible truth. If any object has possible bearing on human interests, such as to make it matter of choice, it has a bearing on human fact also—there is some cognitive way to it. Truth is indeed variously accessible: there are regions of the world unsounded, long to be unsoundable, ample playground for imagination; but in truth-getting these very regions are to be approached (and are approached) with a more delicate chivalry just because of their comparative helplessness—with more care, not less, to restrain the impulses of subjectivity.

But, at last, is there no *unfinished truth?* No reality yet unmade, or in the making; no chance to co-operate with God in the work of creation, in determining what truth shall be? Have we not here the real meaning of positive pragmatism, and its true significance in religion? The world is infinitely unfinished; here lies the opportunity of freedom, the only excuse, indeed, for *time-existence* at all. But of the world, too, we can define a tolerable and an intolerable unfinishedness: the world must have an *identity* which the work of finishing does not destroy or from moment to moment displace. Unlimited co-operation with God in world-making we have; not, however, in ultimate *God-making.* The religious object offers that *identity* without which creative freedom itself would lack, for us, all meaning. Does it seem that super-nature is the plastic part of reality, nature relatively unplastic?—toward nature must we be relatively empirical, passive; toward super-nature relatively self-assertive, creative? I venture to point out that our creativity in any field follows faithfully the character of our passivity in that same field, varies with it not inversely but directly. Here, where our subservience to objective fact is most massive, here in the world of sense and nature, our practical creations are most massive also. And there, in the world of the religious objects, where myth-making, and world-picturing, even God-character-building, are most exuberant,—there the firm steadfastness of objective reality is at its summit also. An ultimate empiricism, a deference to what is given, not makable, just in these regions of the supersensible and the supernatural, is an attitude wholly necessary to human dignity, and to true religion. Far less than absolute idealism is positive pragmatism (radically taken) capable of worship.

If we are right in this, it may appear that pragmatism, taken in a constructive sense, is a self-refuting theory. The only kind of truth which in the end can comply with the pragmatic requirement that power shall be conserved is a non-pragmatic truth, a truth which has an absolute aspect; which proposition we shall try to make good in the course of this treatise. Pragmatism is a philosophy which cannot be finished without destroying its identity.

Whatever may be the deficiencies of idealism, pragmatism, if we are right, cannot supply them. How may it be with mysticism? Mysticism may have its absolute:

but mysticism finds its metaphysics in experience; and mysticism is no stranger to worship. I believe, in fact, that the requirements both of reason and of beyond-reason may be met in what mysticism, rightly understood, may contribute to idealism. Not every mysticism will do. It is not the "speculative mysticism" of the text-books that we want; it is mysticism as a practice of union with God, together with the theory of that practice. Mysticism may introduce idealism to the religious *deed*, ultimately thereby to the particular and authoritative in religion.

There are mysticisms in which none of us believe. There is the mysticism of mantic and theurgy—mysticism of supernatural exploit, seeking short-cut to personal goods. There is another mysticism equally remote from our affections: world-avoiding, illusion-casting, zero-worshipping mysticism; living (in self-contradiction) upon the fruits of a rejected life. This mysticism has given the name its current color: making it necessary, perhaps, to ask that we be understood and agreed together in rejecting it. From the standpoint of just this sound disparagement of these types of mysticism, I have become persuaded that there is another, even a necessary mysticism. A mysticism as important as dangerous; whose historical aberrations are but tokens of its power. It is this mysticism which lends to life that value which is beyond reach of fact, and that creativity which is beyond the docility of reason; which neither denies nor is denied by the results of idealism or the practical works of life, but supplements both, and constitutes the essential standpoint of religion.

The mystic finds the absolute in immediate experience. Whatever is mediated is for him not yet the real which he seeks. This means to some that the mystic rejects all mediators: the implication is mistaken. To say that a mediator is not the finality is not to say that a mediator is nothing. The self-knowing mystic, so far from rejecting mediators, makes all things mediators in their own measure. To all particulars he denies the name God,—to endow them with the title of mediator between himself and God. Thus it is that the mystic, representing the truth of religious practice, may teach idealism the way to worship, and give it connection with particular and historic religion.

I have thus sketched, in highly crude and unmodified manner, the general philosophic attitude of this book. The philosophies of the present time, when they attain their own free conclusion, complete themselves in the same point. Pure thought, and pure voluntarism, share the fate of the "pure adventure": they must find rest in something other, limiting their freedom, yet required by it. It is the finished pragmatist who best knows the need of the absolute. It is the finished mystic who best knows the need of active life and its mediation. It is the finished idealist who best knows the need of the realistic elements of experience; the mystical and authoritative elements of faith. I know not what name to give to this point of convergence, nor does name much matter: it is realism, it is mysticism, it is idealism also, its identity, I believe, not broken. For in so far as idealism announces the liberty of thought, the spirituality of the world, idealism is but another name for philosophy—all philosophy is idealism. It is only the radical idealist who is able to give full credit to the realistic, the naturalistic, even the materialistic aspects of the world he lives in.

So much it has seemed right to say, by way of general philosophic orientation and confession. But in the work of the book itself no interest is taken in the criticism of thought-systems for their own sakes; our interest there is in the substance and worth of religion, to be found by whatever instruments of thought may be at hand.

[...]

NOTE

1. L'évolution créatrice, p. 209.

CHAPTER 3

Fact, Field and Destiny:
Inductive Elements of Metaphysics

At the outset, let me congratulate the members of the Metaphysical Society on being metaphysicians with conscious intent. For it is the metaphysician who most completely fulfills the ideal of Living Dangerously. It is he who most fully renounces the security of current certitudes in the search for authentic certitude. It is he who chooses—let me say—to *live out of doors* in complete exposure to what we call Fact. And not alone to the facts that happen this way he seeks the vicarious experience of all mankind, he invites their findings and their sufferings: in this sense he must be *the absolute* empiricist. But his task does not stop there.

Most simply stated, the business of Metaphysics is to understand the world, that is to say, the given world which, as given, is one stupendous Fact. This is something more than describing the world. Description, accurate and adequate, is the business of science: understanding the world is making sense of it—a quite different matter. That there is such a task implies that the world does not wear its sense on its sleeve: it presents much that seems nonsense, much that seems anti-sense or what some of our French comrades call absurdity. It is precisely this refusal to make sense that is embodied in the concept of Fact.

Fact is what is there without apology: it is there because it is there. That may be to someone a reason for climbing Mount Annapurna; but it is not the factual mountain that issues the invitation. The demand that Fact make sense is simply an irrelevance: Fact stands as a rebuke to those who call it brutal, unjust, irrational—it stands imperturbable to these epithets, for it admits no obligation to be other than it is. The unwritten constitution of the universe is that living and conscious beings take what they find—to start with; they become empiricists in order to stay alive. Precisely for this reason the metaphysician is bound to steep himself—also from the first—in the inexorable taciturnity of Fact: for conscience's sake, he dare not make his task accidentally easy—he must, I say, live out of doors.

This means, among other things, that metaphysics and science are inseparable, science being a world-wide pressure for the extension of factual awareness. But science is in one respect a prejudiced witness: it is a search for *order* among facts; and

---

From *Review of Metaphysics* 11 (June, 1958): 525–549. Read as the Presidential Address at the ninth meeting of the Metaphysical Society of America. Points marked [...] indicate where Hocking omitted portions of a larger text when he made the address.

order is a wraith of sense, tending to parade as the reality of sense—which it is not. The "starry heavens" have often misled thinking men on just this point. Like every other object of science they have two characters, order and configuration. Of these two, configuration—the actual pattern of things—is pure datum—undeducible, unmitigated Fact. And for human destiny, configuration is as fateful as the astrophysical order: the frequent appearance of *novae* (of which Fritz Zwicky, formerly at Palomar with the 48" Schmidt reflector, has reported dozens) reminds us that stellar explosions are among the possibilities of our galaxy; and one of these could conceivably some day spare us humans all the trouble of more technical explorations of space. We continue our more or less peaceful meditations on the universe as much by grace of the factual pattern as by grace of the laws of nature .
[...]
The formidable scope of science, as well as its refractory residue, may add to the sense of dismay: for nothing that the sciences find in the Facts is alien to our metaphysical exposure.
[...]
As Whitehead's cosmology has developed in close touch with the advances of physics, not only must his categoreal scheme be intricate, but his intellectual conscience must lead him to reject simplicity as a false ideal. I have often heard him comment on the delusion of the hope for ultimate simplicity. But there is one relieving consideration:

The widest inductions of the human mind are not those of the sciences: the widest inductions are also the earliest, and show a certain stability and simplicity. While "things" multiply, the word 'thing' remains useful; while changes and events swarm, the term 'event' retains its value. The word 'Fact' which has the wide generality of including both 'thing' and 'event' holds its own, both for untechnical and technical uses. The major categories are, in truth, compact inductions; and with the formal inductions of the sciences we must align the informal inductions of common speech. The work of metaphysics necessarily debouches in this most comprehensive inductive area, where it rejoins the vocabulary of the common man to whom, after all, its message is addressed.
[...]
The categories I shall be dealing with today, beginning in the rough world, belong to both. "Fact" is one of these.

I. Fact as a Category

I call attention first to Fact because Fact embodies the most literal challenge to the meaning of the world.

Fact incorporates the demand that we first of all "accept the universe." It is the "given" aspect of experience—a gift we cannot help having. We are no doubt active in the process of receiving Fact—for one thing, we actively focus our receptors—but this active attention is in the service of docility. The word 'Factum' suggests an original maker, the word 'Datum' an active offerer of gift; but the English word 'Fact' can dispense with these anterior agents: it suggests an independent entity standing pat toward our encounter—offering itself, if at all, only to our awareness. The self-giving of the particular Fact is a piece of the self-standing of the world.

Fact is the core of the empiricism of perception. It is now generally agreed that experience rests, not on sense-data which are abstractions of analysis, but on Fact. "It is indeed," says C. I. Lewis, "the thick experience of the world of things, not the thin given of (introspective) immediacy, which constitutes the datum for philosophical reflection. We do not see patches of color, but trees and houses."[1] What is given is something of which we may and do make judgment, saying what it is that exists or happens: the concept, the judgment, enter into the experienced context.

Let us note that we are empirical to both—to the universal and to the particular, the essence and the existence, the form and the matter. Kant's attempt to separate the two, making the form subjective and *a priori* while the stuff-to-be-formed, his *Mannigfalligkeit*, is objectively given, is a failure. First, because there is no such thing, even for thought, as matter without form—if the matter is objective, so is the form; second, because there is no form without matter—if the form is subjective, so is all that goes with it in concrete experience. From this concrete union, we may extract the conceptual ingredients. To do this empirically is Husserl's contribution: this is his *Wesensschau*, essence-perceiving. It is also what Hegel had done before him, in broad principle, in singling out of the tangled aspect of historical happening the bidden drive, as essence, *Was wirklich ist, dast ist vernunstig*. But it is with what remains after reason is extracted that we have to do, as well: we have to live with *the particular embodiment* of reason. And if that embodiment is devoid of reason, then an idealism that builds on reason alone confesses failure at the crucial point: the destiny of particular beings is a particular destiny. The term Fact, not closed to reason, keeps us in mind of the non-rational ingredient of experience.

Fact as obvious and as problematic

As the point-blank aspect of the world, Fact might well appear devoid of internal problem; it has however certain contrarieties in structure that require metaphysical notice.

First, in relation to necessity. It has been, at least since Hume, the hallmark of Fact that there is no necessity that it should be what it is rather than otherwise. It may be imagined otherwise in innumerable ways without contradiction: the given universe is to all appearances an arbitrary cast among an infinitude of equally possible universes, in infinitude of an order staggering the imagination of a Cantor: to put it otherwise, its prior probability is zero. At the same time, if anything is to exist, it is absolutely necessary that there be a factual world. Fact exhibits the necessity of the unnecessary—the contingent.

[...]

Fact as prized and disparaged

As with physical status, so with value-judgment: Fact exhibits an internal apposition.

[...]

The pure factuality of the individual lot is ground for complaint: a life is an infinite possibility chained to an arbitrary situation. Each person finds himself in an unchosen world, among unchosen people, in unchosen circumstances. A rude biological fitness of human organism to environment, and vice versa, can be inferred from genetics; but for the unique individual, whose value-horizon is universal, why are we not all in the frame of mind of the young O'Neill, as one "who could never belong and was never really wanted," or of Berdyaev who seems to have been born disenchanted with the existing universe? Fact is simply incommensurable with the outreach of the human value-sense: most persons find in themselves a craving for what they are not and have not—the primitive for the civilized, the civilized for the primitive. After the first World War, my Plattsburg squad-mate Norman Hall flees—not from the enemy's prison-camp, but from the whole artefact of polite living, finding Tahiti more to his taste, with a transitory flavor of Iceland, yet never fully domesticated on earth. In John Bakeless' log-book of "The Eyes of Discovery" one becomes aware how much of human history is the tale—not of the conflict of civilizations but of the flight from settled and stifling civilizations toward a "liberty" which to them, the emigrants, actually means less freedom-to-act than a chance for satisfying the craving for a "home." How can the accidental ever be a home for the living spirit?

Yet the person—is not he himself an accident?—if he rebels against actual accident it is in the name of his own factual individuality, and not of his universality alone: it is this same accidental "Whoever you are" that in Walt Whitman's terms "through angers, ambitions, losses, ennui ... picks its way." And for this same accidentality, partial or total law itself makes sober provision. Is not factual possession at least something, if not "nine points" in the law of property? Will not factual usage, unopposed, in time create right of way? Does not *fait accompli*, no matter how accomplished, tend to pose as confirmed right? Right to real estate is proved by particulars—by the "deed," the deed by the signature with factual seals and stamps, and whatever other factual ritual of decision-reached may be by factual usage accepted. Factual custom by degrees finds its way into positive law. And after all, the birth of a child confronts the world with a new legal status—the fact of life carries the right of life, which as a rule the world respects until the factual death of that individual. And in the course of a life, when Fact crosses biography at an angle, memory lights with special care on the irrational detail: and when biographies merge into history, the "accidental"—like a winter-camp at Valley Forge—often begins to glow with almost sacred warmth. How this reversal of value-judgment occurs, how far it can go, metaphysics will be concerned to enquire.

Summary and Transition

For the moment, we simply point out these duplicities in the conception of Fact.

Fact is certainly a non-deducible element of *what is*. There is no ontological principle that can make this particular universe appear necessary, except in the sense that some particular must exist if any thing exists. Fact is also non-deducible from what is desirable or what ought to be, whether for a total good, or for the good of finite conscious beings. To any such being, it is in the end the arbitrary that happens—this is the theme of the heroic and desperate Existentialism. Schopenhauer's proposal of a total repudiation of life remains a rational possibility. Marcel's strange remark that the contemplation of suicide stands at the threshold of mature philosophizing has here its justification.

If there is a creator-God, he must have been faced—or be eternally faced—with the necessity of an arbitrary choice: among the miracles of creation there would appear this supreme miracle, *that he could decide*, among an infinitude of non-rational possibilities. It is probably on this consideration that for Whitehead God *does not create or decide:* He is, in his primordial nature, himself an "accident" of the principle of creativity—a view that would seem for the existent world, to make Accident—or, with Charles Peirce, Chance—the supreme category.

Yet, from what we have seen of the valuing of the surd-ingredient of Fact, it is equally certain that the non-deducibility of Fact does not of itself condemn the actual world as meaningless. It makes the postulate of the metaphysician, that the empirical world can make sense, extremely hazardous: it constitutes the perennial attraction toward an idealism of the pure universal, whether of the Platonic or of the Advaita-Vedantic type. But if it is the actual world that we propose to understand, we must begin by taking Fact seriously. As a first step in this direction, we may note that Fact is not a category that can stand alone.

It belongs to the concept of Fact that a fact is identifiable—and this trait implies finitude, boundary, and presumably plurality. And if Fact implies facts, there must also be relations among facts, distinguishable from the facts themselves. In giving attention to what is *between facts*, we come upon the notion of a Field.

II. Field as a Category

Inasmuch as facts are given in plural, the relations among them are given with the facts, and are sometimes regarded as facts of a second order. It is usual to consider Relation as itself a category. With Bradley, it becomes the turning point of a metaphysic. Russell indicates that specific relatedness, such as up-and-down, right-and-left, is inseparable from sense-data. Whitehead speaks of "togetherness" in general, and of "nexus" in particular, as an element of "immediate actual experience" (P. R., p. 30). I point out that these relationships—and relations generally—assume a background; and that the background deserves to be brought forward for metaphysical study.

I shall refer to this background as Field. Having no specific sense-properties of its own, it is (in a sense) indistinguishable from Nothing, and has often been referred to as "The Void." But unlike a Nothing, it has properties such as continuity and measurability. In recent times—I mean since the advent of quantum theory—Field has become newly significant because of new aspects of discontinuity in nature. Now discontinuity implies *Interval*; and Interval requires quantitative estimations. The important thing about clock-ticks is not simply that they are discontinuous, but that the interval is exactly measured.

This example suggests that in the sense I now propose for the term Field, Time is a field and likewise Space—as the field-metaphor suggests. For our purposes it is important to empty the field-notion of specific contents. In recent physics, especially since the work of Clerk Maxwell, it has become usual to speak of gravitational fields, of electro-magnetic fields, etc. These terms imply not the empty expanse of space-time, but the permeation of that expanse by electric potentials or energy-gradients. I take the liberty of abstracting from this occupation-by-energy-functions, in order to concentrate on the background-continuum for its own sake. I do not regard this liberty as unwarranted, inasmuch as the term Field is not originally technical but a term of common speech, to which I propose now to return it, but with an ideal emptiness!

In this, its generalized, common sense, the Field has still certain properties which distinguish it from the Void—which has given metaphysicians so much trouble, from Nagarjuna and Democritus to Descartes and Einstein. When the Ether was disposed of as an intangible "medium" occupying all space, little was left of Newtonian space but an "undifferentiated continuum" (to borrow a term from Professor Northrop), as a playground for geometry. But field-emptiness still has its nature, regarding which let us set up a thesis or two:

A Field has an all-or-none totality

Boundaries exist within a field. The field itself can have no boundary; for any attempted boundary would reveal field-region beyond the boundary. If you have any space, you have all space; if any time, all time.

A Field is internally related to its contents

Taking the phrase "internal relation" in its acquired sense, as meaning a relation whose presence or absence makes a difference to the being of the relata, it is obvious that the destruction of a time-field—if we can conceive such a thing—would put an end to all events in time. But the inverse is less evident: could we not destroy an event without destroying time, or a molecule without destroying space? The answer is No. The destruction of a physical particle could not be thoroughgoing without destroying the portion of the space-time field occupied-or-affected by that particle; and by the all-or-none principle the destruction of that segment would destroy the whole.

It is in accord with this internal relationship that Relativity theory proposes that the concept of a pre-existent or independently existent empty field is untenable. And with it falls Kant's argument that we can consider all contents of space destroyed, but not space itself. The elemental real, Relativity suggests, is the event; with the event is given the *relatableness* of the event. Apart from content, no field.

Wherever there are plural Facts of the same kind, there is a Field including them and essential to their being

Corollary: *No pluralism can be a final metaphysic.*

If, for example, the universe is considered a system of monads, there is an unacknowledged Field, indicating their togetherness and their intervals—their principle of individuation: in the case of Leibniz, the Field would be the unacknowledged mind of Leibniz himself—definitely not a monad! In the case of Whitehead's universe of "actual occasions," not wholly different from that of Leibniz, as a "one-substance cosmology" (P. R., p. 29), this unity is recognized in "The Category of the Ultimate" called Creativity (P. R., p. 31) whereby the many "become the one actual occasion which is the universe conjunctively." My comment here is the same as in regard to Leibniz: we must recognize a unity not by way of a separate creativity, but in the very fact of plurality, by way of the Field in which the many coexist. The term "Creativity" designates the essential metaphysical problem: it does not of itself contribute to the solution of the problem of the ultimate arbitrariness of the Universe as Fact. It rather sharpens that problem by separating that creativity from the primordial appreciator of qualities and essences, leaving factual creativity unmotivated.

III. Necessity

Fact and Field are categories of description. Within the time-field there are relations among events, relations of coexistence and succession. It is the business of physical theory to note regularities of succession, to call these regularities "laws" (at its peril) and to regard the law as, in some way, "explaining" the instances. But since Hume we speak charingly of Necessity. Yet as metaphysicians we recognize that until we see necessity, explanations stop short of understandings. Newton explains

Kepler; but who explains Newton? When Einstein makes Newton a special case, who explains Einstein?

The conception of a necessary order, under tattered flag of Causality, yields to statistical uniformity, in spots to indeterminacy; yet reappears in unexpected places. In biology, the old issue between mechanists and vitalists takes wholly new forms. In a literal sense there are no more mechanists nor vitalists: newer developments in physics have radically restated the biological problem.

There is a new group of "Finalists," scientific biologists, who believe that no explanations of biological evolution, of growth, of repair, of reproduction, by purely physical and chemical factors can be sufficient without a guiding influence, driving toward an end even if not cognizant of that end. Their data are more careful, their reasonings more searching than those of Bergson or Hans Driesch. On the other hand, any Finalist theory, depending on guidance of organic processes by non-physical agencies, has a heavy burden of proof. How and where does the non-physical *élan* act on the physical structures? Can any laboratory procedure find it at work? Can its existence be proved? Schroedinger brings quantum theory to his aid. Evolution by gradual chance variation becomes incredible; but mutation changes the picture; and, as he proposes, "the mutations are actually due to quantum jumps in the gene molecule." With this, he finds no need of Finalist hypotheses to explain the procession of living forms seeming to reach a goal in the *genus homo*, nor yet for "equifinality" of organic cells in the maturing or self-repairing organism.

Neo-finalism actually provokes a neo-causalism, which accuses the Finalists of treason to the established methods of science (see F. Koch, *Scientific Monthly*, Nov. 1957). We arrive at an apparent *impasse:* The Finalist cannot prove empirically that a *telos* is actually at work; the orthodox scientist cannot prove that it *is not!* Each side may take comfort in the circumstances that there is now at hand a new principle of explanation which takes care of many a formerly intractable problem. It arises from the laboratory revelations of the extent to which organisms are electrodynamic fields, capable of directing processes of growth and repair, and of regulating vital rhythms. Our colleague, Filmer Northrop, working with H. S. Burr of Yale Medical School, has developed an "electrodynamic theory of life." As far as I have been able to follow their work, they leave open the issue as to the origin of these regulating fields—whether they are established by antecedent physical conditions—chemical conditions perhaps—with which nerve impulses have commonly been associated, or whether they are direct physical expressions of non-physical end-seeking impulses.

At the moment an equipoise remains, and conscientious biologists may find themselves driven to a kind of agnosticism (to use Dr. Ralph Wyckoff's word), seeing that either to assert or to deny the effectiveness of *telos* is a metaphysical judgment to which, as scientist, he feels no right.

No one has more carefully explored this—I will not say No-man's-land, but Both-men's-land—than Charles Sherrington, who concludes with satisfying clarity, "The mental is not examinable as a form of energy" (nor energy as a form of mentality). "If you say thoughts are an outcome of the brain, we as students of the energy concept know nothing of it" (*Man on His Nature*, pp. 240, 260, 289, 291). Niels Bohr calls for recognizing an anomaly, a "separate place for 'life.'" Schroedinger, having declared for the near-determinism of brain events finds himself at last in a clear antinomy, since with this determinism he must couple an opposing certitude: "I know by incontrovertible direct experience that I am directing [my body's] motions of which I foresee the effects" (op. cit., p. 87). At this point, this throws up the sponge, suggests that the connection between conscious purpose and physiology is very probably beyond human understanding, and takes refuge in pure metaphysics of a somewhat Vedantic pattern, in which mentality the universe over is not plural but one. There *is* only mind, and each ego *is* that mind.

In this act of resignation, I see a kinship between two scrupulous scientists far apart in mode of approach, Schroedinger and Henderson. L. J. Henderson, writing on the Fitness of the Environment, and (unable to surrender either the precise integrity of the physical process in the world of living systems or the unique constellation of properties favoring the possibility of organisms in this actual planet which obliged him to describe the universe as "biocentric") feels bound to regard the entire universe as a single causally-linked configuration. *Telos* appeared, in his view, solely at one point, namely in the *choice of the original configuration* from which all else must follow without deviation. The two thinkers agree (i) that every internal event is necessitated, and (ii) that there is a single-and-total touch of *telos* in the universe. As to how this total *telos* operates, both submit, with Sherrington, and in agreement with Kant and Royce, to the ultimate mystery.

It is here that I refuse to leave the cause of metaphysics. I base myself on the empirical fact of personal freedom, which, as embodied in multiple free actions, rejects being merged in a single primordial decision on the part of an absolute will. Nor can I agree that the free actions of individuals stand alone in the universe as expressions of purpose, leaving the biological development physically explained but not understood. I must also decline to dismiss the radical particularity of this actual world as in Whitehead's term an "accident," to which as an ontological ultimate, all truth must refer. The search for meaning, which metaphysics cannot abandon, must enter new paths.

Let us note that the impasse in biological theory, between neo-finalism and physicalism, is identical in principle with the impasse in the quest for concrete freedom in personal action. In each case it is the principle of necessary sequence in physical process that we encounter. At least, I encounter it; for I am committed to that principle: I make no appeal to elements of indeterminacy that in Heisenberg's analysis seem to appear in the wake of quantum phenomena. Whatever the role of the purely statistical in physical science, the sphere of the closed-system is there. It is the plague of modern discussions of this theme that respect for science has been felt to demand a "freedom" compatible with determinism, differing perhaps only as (for Royce) an "order of appreciation" differs from an "order of description." This, the philosopher's superstition, present in Kant as well as in Spinoza and firmly rooted in Leibniz (since without it his pre-established harmony could not work) has prevented the recognition of genuine freedom, and its fruit, genuine creativity, in the finite individual. Our field-concept will enable us to win release from this illusory obligation, and at the same time, as I hope, to resolve the biological dilemma, which is, in truth, a metaphysical dilemma encountered by biologists.

Necessary Sequence as Scientific Postulate

Let me first make clear why I fully accept the principle of necessary sequence as the core of scientific method for the twentieth century and beyond. In an era of exploding certitudes and of statistical rather than perfect uniformities, necessity appears almost an operational waif, repudiated by scientists and philosophers alike. Yet the idea of energy as a self-conserved quantity continues to guide exploration—though the several conservations of energy, mass, charge, etc., have had to pool interests it continues even to offer a lever for discovery. Let me illustrate by a case at the frontier:

What happens to an atomic nucleus when it is bombarded by alpha particles? It may lose some beta particles. How does this affect the total energy of the nucleus? As Werner Heisenberg puts the matter, it is precisely "the laws of the conservation of mass and energy (that) permit us to calculate what happens." He quotes the theory of Pauli that "with every beta particle (struck out) another particle leaves the nucleus carrying the difference in energy. The sum total of the energy is always constant, and this total energy is shared by the beta particle and this new particle" (*Nuclear Physics*, p. 51). This new particle, now called the *neutrino*, has thus the conservation of energy as a cognitive midwife. Indeed, the concept of an "equation," basic to all modern science, implies a conservative system of ultimate physical reals.[2] Just what these reals are has been a matter of some doubt. (Witness the long dispute between Cartesians and Leibnizians over the true formula for "*vis viva*," whether mv (as 'momentum') or $1/2\ mv^2$ (as kinetic energy); and today we know that neither of these will stand.) But the idea of an underlying quantitative identity has roots far earlier than the era of exact measurement: they are found in a very primitive conviction, *ex nihilo nihil,* and its reverse that nothing real vanishes. This notion, at odds with the notion of chance-arising and chance-annihilation, is a presumption not only of scientific prejudice, but of all responsible living. In the early experiments of Galileo on falling bodies, it took an unexpressed turn of what we might almost call a physical morality—*nature cannot be cheated*—you can't get the rolling bodies to rise higher on the reverse journey than the level from which they started.

The assumption of necessity in physical process is, in brief, a necessary assumption. We may properly consider it an *a priori* factor of life and thought, which—as is the normal history of *a priori principles*—only finds recognition through centuries of inductive approximation.

Its basis is empirical. It is true that we do not directly observe necessitation in objective change: we observe succession and only imagine compulsion. And as to what-causes-what, we remain largely docile to fact. But in our own awareness of effort in physical work, we have a private introduction into the nature of energy-in-operation. We spontaneously use this experience in interpreting physical change: we continue, in spite of self-reproach for the animist fallacy, to sympathize or empathize when we see or feel a laboring engine-pair tugging a heavy freight over some mountain pass. We know full well that imaginative sympathy is not empirical knowledge: but neither are we deluded into mental poverty by the demand to empty our engineering formulas for stresses and strains, for pushes and pulls, for the strengths of materials, and the like, of every vestige of empirical content: abstracting from our emotional involvement, we know empirically what physical necessitation means, and that it is present in our Fields.

The summarized fruit of the race's observing and thinking about the nature of Nature is the concept of the physical universe as a *conservative system—a closed group of events, unaffected by non-physical influences, and giving rise to no non-physical effects*. The more minute our observation and measurement, the more precisely this concept is confirmed. As Dr. Ralph W. G. Wyckoff, speaking of the electron-microscope, testifies, the advance in fineness of perception brings a "deeper realization that everything that happens in the world of matter seems to proceed according to a system of inexorable law."[3]

It is the logic of this conservative system that now concerns us, especially in view of the non-physical factors, whether in the organic world at large or in human decision and seeming-free action, which—in spite of the definition—appear to interact with its group-enclosed order.

The Logic of the Conservative System

It belongs to the logic of a conservative system that its member-events take place in a single space-time field. This field has the all-or-none character we have indicated: unbounded in space, it has no outside; unbounded in time, no event is before it nor after it. Since the only explanation it permits is internal—any configuration by a prior one and the laws defining the closed group—the system as a whole can have no explanation. And as a system of facts-in-a-field, constituting a single Fact, it offers no understanding, nor any ground for understanding, nor for raising the question of its "sense." If metaphysics is nonsense for it, *it* is quite literally nonsense for metaphysics. It simply *is*.

Just because of this self-enclosed perfection, two things follow: i. The conservative system is not *the whole of existence*. For the non-measurable exists: Thinking, for example, undoubtedly exists; yet thinking, even *thinking about the system*, is no part of the system. ii. The conservative system is *not the real*. For the real is the source: and the system, which simply conserves itself, is the source of nothing, and carries no hint of its own source *Only the creative can be real;* and Nature, in so far as it is conservative, is not creative. Here I regretfully part company with Whitehead, just because I agree with him that creativity is the primary mark of that real which we seek.

By "creative" we shall mean (in the toughest sense of the word) making a difference in physical nature: inserting something that would not otherwise be there. Such creation would imply a definite breath in the enclosure of the conservative system. Have we any empirical ground for thinking that such event ever occurs?

Now the bodies of organisms, including their brains and brain-events, are members of the system, and, as such, subject to physical necessity. At the same time, their cognitions and choices are *not brain-events*, nor any function of the energies there involved (here we agree with Sherrington, and part company with Schroedinger). When therefore the knower of nature proposes to act in or upon nature, by use of his body, he is proposing to pass from the non-physical to the physical, which by the logic of the conservative system is not only impossible but inconceivable. The search for creativity may well begin with the question, How is a free act possible?

If the conservative system were the reality we seek, there would be but one answer: the appearance of effective purpose in our actions, the seeming-free pursuit of future goals set by ourselves, is but the inward translation of physical necessity: we always do what we wish to do—that is our seeming freedom—but nature makes the desire—there necessity has us! From the entire impetus of the past, there is ahead of us but one possible future. This answer, which solves at once the biological impasse, making the sciences of life a part of physics, we have definitely rejected. Here we note one clear yield of Existentialist philosophies—Sartre and Camus agree that what we will to make of ourselves not only is, but is doomed to be, our own act, not Nature's, not Society's, not God's. How this is possible, these philosophies apply no answer. We have an answer.

It lies in the circumstance that Fields, infinite Fields, *may have plurals*. Kant to the contrary notwithstanding, there may be more than one total-space, more than one total-time, more than one world-order. Because of this valid pluralism, the apparent alternatives before us, as we deliberate courses of action, are genuine alternatives—not pantomime: the term "possibility" has a literal validity, not to be dissembled as necessity in disguise.

(The technical discussion in evidence of this radical thesis I shall not here detail, having recently published it.[4] Let me simply indicate the crucial step in the argument, to the effect that since fields do not exist in their own right, but are derivative from events, as Relativity theory implies, if there can be independent events, there can be independent fields. The criterion of an independent event is simply the *absence of assignable Interval* between that event and any event in the actual space-time order. For example, if one asks the distance between the top of a tree in a painting and the floor on which the viewer stands, there is no answer: the question is nonsense; the Interval does not exist. Yet each space-field is infinite, and the two infinite fields have no single point in common.)

In the case of deliberation for future action, the deliberator has fewer degrees of freedom than the artist or writer: he is bound by his sense of the vast momentum of Fact in the world he proposes to change: he can put into the future only what he conceives to be "in his power." But he is not chained by the notion that nothing is really in his power: the events he contemplates are literally "independent events," centers of reckoning for independent space-time orders, each total and infinite, none as yet existent. His capacity to control their future existence or non-existence is his concrete freedom.

In this account of our experience of simultaneous field-plurality there is another empirical element of major importance. There is no physical transition from one field to another; but *there is* transition, namely, by a movement of attention: the Self is, we may say, time vinculum between one field and the other. Or, in view of the general thesis that wherever there is a homogeneous plurality there is a Field expressive of the relationships between individual entities, the *Self here functions as a Field of Fields*. This judgment may qualify as an inductive assertion, metaphysical in character, amid justifying that other metaphysical judgment, so baffling to Schroedinger, "I know by incontrovertible evidence that I am directing [my body's] motions" and that I can "take full responsibility for them" (op. cit, pp. 87f.).

In this, our experience of freedom, the Self is to some extent a source, and to that extent shares reality. Its contemplated events, fashioned with a realist's eye to possibility—and so far, receptive—move to a result which apart front its wish and act the world would not contain. To this extent, the Self has exhibited the creativity we have been looking for.

And if we ask, what then happens to our conservative-system, and the scientific necessities that build upon its integrity, the answer is that the phenomenal world—that of the conservative order—will maintain its rules; but that the rules are at every point subject to alteration of field-reckoning through the creative decisions of Selves. This implies that while the phenomenal world is a closed system, the real universe is to some extent "open toward the future." This phrase, which has entered metaphysical thought with an indiscriminate invitation to loose-ends, must be carefully defined. It does not imply a universal ongoing run of uncontrolled "novelty": the openness of the cosmos toward the future is solely the work of purposive agents, who use the genuine physical necessities of process as instruments of the more fundamental necessities of *telos*. In their definite alteration of Fact, they insensibly alter the space-time field for the entire actual world, which now accepts as its own futurity, the futurity and therefore the space-time field of the active self. The conservative world remains conservative in regard to its energies and masses; but in the presence of organisms capable of end-seeking, its configurations remain plastic to field-replacement, as silent and imperceptible as the field-texture itself.

[...]

IV. Creativity and Destiny

In the given space-time field, we have now recognized as empirical elements—in full awareness of dissent from current analysis—two types of necessitation-in-process; the physical dynamism most easily called causality, and an occasional touch of *telos*, namely in our own purposive action.

[...]

We have so far discovered no operation of *telos* in the universe at large. As a step in this direction, let us note that we human beings never create-in-toto: we bring into existence states of fact not otherwise involved in the conservative system; we have indeed introduced novelty into the world, but novelty of familiar kinds—a novelty of rearrangement rather than of production *ex nihilo*. Our creativity is fractional. The truth is, we *have to learn to create*; and the value of the product is in proportion to the prior docility—let me say to the depth of the generating empirical plunge. Creation in art, for example, presupposes a virtuosity of realism in experience, whose finding is issued with the personal hall-mark of the artist. The creation is the unique perception and account of value-in-existence, a report as to the nature of the real. As such it has the character, in addition to its immediate interest, of truth or falsehood. Its addition to being is at the same time a celebration or song of Being; and if it lies, its uniqueness will not justify its claim of "creativity." Rilke's poetic effort, according to Babette Deutsch, was "to encompass reality by re-creating it"; to this end he tried "to identify himself with the least and greatest things he encountered." In his own words, noting his unwillingness, as of the true metaphysician, to evade time drastic passages of experience, he writes "Es wundert mich manchmal wie bereit ich alles Erwartete aufgebe für das Wirkliche, selbst wenn es arg ist." And referring to the work in portraiture of Rodin, with whom in his early years he studied, he reports its animus in these terms: "In einem gegebenen Gesicht *Ewigkeit suchen*... das Dauernde vom Vergänglichen scheiden, Gericht halten, gerecht sein,"—there speaks time profound honor of the artist's *truth*, as he holds what can be forcefully likened to a court of justice! Bernard Shaw later attests this quality of "unflinching veracity" in the work of Rodin.

Not only is our creativity dependent on a prior realism, the new idea we call our own often arrives without our intent or plan.

As point-blank effort, the will to create is seldom successful. Tschaikowski's first purposeful attempts to write music were dismally empty of result: not till he had flung away the effort to direct his thought did the spring begin to flow. It was then—as many a fertile spirit has testified—more like reception from outside than one's own product.

I am sure that individual creativeness at its best—and this applies to creative thought, to induction, as well—requires a union of action and passivity: the more complete the power of the new idea, the less can it be invited by straining along old lines. It exemplifies the ancient adage of Ptah Hotep, "The boatsman reaches the landing partly by pulling and partly by letting go!" and still more completely the maxims of Zen in the art of archery—also "partly by pulling" but, I judge, chiefly "by letting go."

Nevertheless, the fruit of this union of effort and docility *bears the individual mark*. Tschaikowski's music was not, prior to its advent, waiting outside to come in, nor laid up in any heavenly archive of eternal essences: it enriches the life of God, if there is a God, by something God would never have thought of without Tschaikowski and the passages *pathétiques* in Tschaikowski's own experience. The birth of an idea comes only to one who has bent his caring that way: solutions only to him who has labored with the dilemmas. It is the maternal brooding, in co-operation with nature, that brings the child to the crisis of birth; and *all creativity is in this sense maternal*. Though the child has been given her, it is hers. The impersonality of the co-operation background leaves human authorship valid and salient.

At the same time, the reality of that co-operating sometimes explicitly felt as in Masefield's "illuminations,"[5] suggests that the *telos* involved has wider origins. This suggestion is enforced as we consider the destination of the created fruit: privately engendered, it cannot remain private property. It is of the essence of human creation that its product, like its gestation, belongs not alone to the author's world but to our world. For as the lesser creativity of free action implies a passage of *telos* from a private world to a factual world field, so the greater creativity means a passage from the world of private conception into the world of every man. Each such decision, and each such output of idea, is attended by the simple certitude that one's private thought is in its nature universal—the natural, unquestioned *intersubjectivity of experience*. To say this is to recognize an ultimate factor of kinship, perhaps of collaboration, in the objective source of things. It is also to say that the creative self perceives his product as having a destiny beyond himself. This, its destiny, is part of its being; and also a part of his. The idea of destiny becomes part of our empirical outlook.

Destiny as an Empirical Category

The term "Destiny," suggests at once a speculative and distant future—the reverse of anything that could be immediately felt. I realize the audacity of the proposal that Destiny, like Fact and Field, has an empirical basis. Yet it will appear less out of line if we recall our original proposition that all Fields, including the time-field, are present, if at all, in their full range: what we have before us at all times is Time, all the past and all the future—the future almost wholly empty of detail, but not wholly empty of kind, and peopled with images of things anticipated.

We have too long identified the empirical with the itemized, the separate, the plural aspects of experience. The illusory attraction of sense-data as the primary building-stuff of knowledge consists largely in the circumstance that we can count them, identify them, name them. But there is no law of being that the real, in its major aspects, must come, as it were, in spots, and unscrambled. For this reason, I have dwelt on the Field-concept which underlies all discontinuities, and which, once recognized, accounts for the simply felt unity of the world. Within this felt unity, there is a richness of experience which is at a disadvantage for recognition, partly because it is too near us, beneath the level of specific language, and partly because its aspects are mutually involved. To refer to it, we must use speech; and every translation into speech does it some injustice.

Let me refer to this region as our *nuclear awareness* of the world. Within it there is, for example, a nuclear awareness of our Self, so central, and so engaged, that Hume and many after him, interested in separate impressions, not only fail to find it but deny its existence. There is a nuclear awareness of the inter-subjective Thou-art. There is also a nuclear awareness of bodily well-or-ill being, of certain instinctive powers, of a general direction of process in time, involving what is now pertinent to us, a sense of destiny.

Its most tangible elements are the elements vaguely called feeling, at once cognitive and emotional, endlessly variable and intertwined. A few things can be said of all feeling: feeling is always *a vector*, it has a direction, an active drive forward in time. And with this directionality there is a sense of power or non-power: from the first, the process which Eddington calls "the process of 'existing'"—and of which lie doubts whether any one has the faintest notion of how (it) is performed—is guided by forecast of what "I can or cannot do."

[...]

This sense of power does not exist as a separate entity: it is called out by concrete situations that stir the appropriate "I can." All have native powers; but no one can enumerate them by introspection. There is however one native power-sense, very general, usually verifiable: the total wordless power to meet the total object-over-against-me by living the life of my species. The original infantile launch of life is one of combined trust-and-assurance, translatable (with risk): "Something is there as summons; something is here as response; that call is the direction I need." To put it otherwise, the fundamental will-to-live is always more than a mere will-to-exist: it is, even in embryo, a will-to-grow into a generic type (presumably forecast in gene-structure); it continues as a will-to-live-as-human-being, including betimes a will-to-live-by-thinking, rather than by vegetating-in-sense-aesthesis. To put it compactly, living is a continuous exercise of felt-power, under the guidance of an instinctive sense, "This way lies my destiny," and with a nuclear intimation of outer expectation.

There is here something like an incipient sense of "duty" (from which will come, in due time, science); but not of duty alone: it is at the same time the way to fulfillment. Destiny, as the elemental End, is the natural synthesis of "duty" and "happiness." Into it, there comes by degrees a specification, that of having an individual "calling," in which concept one detects (i) an undefined something for me to do, an obligation, and (ii) an undefined promise, an assurance of possible success, authoritative!

It is one of the sensitive psychological coinages of classic Chinese thought that there is for each person a "Dictate of Heaven " a *Ming*, a rendezvous with Destiny. That appointment is never explicit (though in Confucius' case he believed it had become so, "Heaven has appointed me to teach this doctrine"); it could be imagined as a secret sailing-order that one must labor to decipher: yet as part of one's self-awareness of individual right-to-be, some intimation of task-and-power is inscribed in present impulse, dimly legible.

What I am now suggesting is that we corroborate in ourselves a Destiny-sense, as an empirical element of our nuclear world-awareness. We cannot be unaware of our own *telos*, as a total directive integrating all partial ends. Nor can we be unaware of our immediate and continuing dependence on a creative real, somehow akin. Our time-vista toward the future must contain the natural synthesis of this summons and this assurance. With this intimation, we pass from the categories of description and explanation to the category of understanding. It proposes a "meaning" for our personal existence and for the world; and becomes not so much a metaphysic as the clue to a metaphysic which can absorb and interpret the corpus of scientific knowledge.

[...]

If, then, there is Destiny in this sense, and a sense of Destiny, it is a Destiny for free souls, not a Fate—a Destiny without predestination. It is a call to the finite creator, not to carry out a set of statutes, preordained, nor to realize an ideal type, but to fill a need which is a world need, that meaning be realized in his unique and factual situation, a contribution to the life of God, as the hidden meaning of creation *ex nihilo*.

Conclusion

With this interpretation of our common experience, a rational metaphysic becomes possible; to confirm this possibility has been my object. For if each one can verify for himself that this total Fact we call "the world" is present not as dead-end but as summons and invitation, hence as potential meaning, we have the necessary—let me say "Prolegomena"—for enquiring what that meaning is, for any future metaphysic. Perhaps we have already a minimal metaphysic—*There is no "mere" Fact.*

On the apparently blank factuality of physical nature we have at least this light: that just as there is a necessity of the non-necessary if there is to be any existence at all, so there is a purpose which requires a realm of the purposeless. It is only as a conservative system, inanimate and uncreative, that we can grasp nature, through all time, as a single Fact. Only as devoid of inner spontaneity can humanity treat it as stable, reliable, exploitable, a neutral area for those interacting launches of creative freedom we call History. Purpose (of the arts as well as of the sciences) demands a realm of the purposeless as the purposeless cannot demand purpose: purpose is thus the more concrete symbol of reality. It is the *telos* of the Field of Fields.

In the order of living, awareness of the whole precedes recognition of the parts: the goals of later analysis are wrapped up in the embryonic layers of instinct and intuition. The real, as object of endless search, the receding goal of the Faustian (and Jamesian) "ever not quite", the real is nevertheless *always present* as that with which we immediately have to do.

It is for this reason that the Existentialist movement has come about, a wondering exploration of the inner richness of the elemental act of Be-ing. Existentialism dwells on the nuclear *telos* toward Destiny, misdescribing its feeling-component as an anxiety, or a dread, or a being-toward-Death; yet these aversive ingredients are discernible in the continuing *exigence* of an undefined rendezvous whose detail we seem to have forgotten, yet whose finding at once lures us on and spurs us on, granting us perhaps fleeting moments of "recollection."

It is for this same reason that Whitehead's majestic work culminates—not once but often—in comment that he is but interpreting the fundamental intuitions of mankind. And it is because of this same unexplicit nuclear wealth that answers to the universal metaphysical querying have from the earliest times taken the forms of prophecy and poetry. These springs are perennial. For metaphorical truth is still truth; and the number of metaphors-of-being is as great as the number of possible human adventures, each one contributing from its unique corner of factual accident what God's life could not otherwise contain.

The destiny of all such freer frames of truth is to join the sobrieties of analysis and science in a rational total, in which the major inductions from experience slowly reveal their well-hidden *a priori* incentives.

NOTES

1. C. I. Lewis, *Mind and the World Order*, p. 54.
2. As the newer developments in physics become more difficult to model or imagine, and as simple locations and time-relatakk lose definition, reliance on mathematics grows greater rather than less. "If any absolute account of the real is possible at all, it can be expressed *only* mathematically by means of tensors" (Errol E. Harris, *Nature, Mind and Modern Science*, p. 378).
3. *The World of the Electron Microscope*, p. 2.
4. *The Meaning of Immortality in Human Experience*, pp. 226 ff.
5. *So Long to Learn*, pp. 139–141, 180.

CHAPTER 4

The Self and Nature

A Servant of Two Masters

If I say all I mean by "self," I cannot leave out the body. A self without a body, so far from being the freer and perfecter thing imagined by Plato, the Vendanta, the Sankhya, would be no self at all—at best a germinal, nascent promise of a self.

Body and mind are different: we have no intention of denying this proposition. But how are they different? Not as two distinct entities which somehow interact. Nor as two parallel sets of phenomena, each complete in itself. They are different rather as a part is different from the whole. The body is an organ of the self as the brain is an organ of the body. The self needs its body in order to be an actual, active, social, historical self.

In its day, Schopenhauer's philosophy was remarkable for the careful thought he gave to the position of the body in the scheme of things. For him, as for us, the body is certainly not something extraneous to the self. The body, he said, is the will—as seen from the outside: it is the will made visible or "objectified." The several organs of the body in different species and individuals reveal the peculiar traits of their wills.[1] The tiger's teeth and claws manifest his will to live by predation. The owl's eyes express a will to live by night-flying. The human brain and upright posture exhibit a will to live by thought and circumspection. There is a Lamarkian streak in Schopenhauer's philosophy of body: function is first and structure afterward. The goat and the bull do not butt because they have horns; they have horns because they butt. Every line of the body is what it is because the will is what it is.

No one before Schopenhauer had so fully done justice to the significance of bodily detail in revealing the traits of the volitional self. At the same time, for Schopenhauer the body was not a reality nor even a part of reality: it was a mere appearance of the self. There could be, for him, no talk of the body as part or an organ of the self, sharing the reality of the self. He thought of it in one sense as more than a part, since it revealed the whole self to the outer eye. In another sense it was less than a part, since it was only a spatial symbol and not a real entity.

It is evident that Schopenhauer was not thinking of the body as we are immediately conscious of it, but rather of the body we see in others and use as a complete symbol for them. Inasmuch as whatever is visible is necessarily spatial, and empty of sensitivity as well as volition, there was some ground for making this complete

---

From SBF, 101–142.

separation between the inner view as pure will and the outer view as pure body. But if we consider the body primarily as the body we are directly aware of, engaged in all sensation and action, we cannot effect this separation. The pure will is not fully itself without *that* body. Volition for us *is* a process of "objectification," an embodiment. And the body becomes a symbol of the self, a faithful and detailed symbol, because all the impulses of the self must realize themselves by its agency. It is, or becomes, a perfectly fit organ of the self.

But have we not proved too much, or have we not taken our hypothesis too quickly? If the self cannot exist without the body, are they not tied in an ominous union which makes them partners in life and death? And have we forgotten, in claiming the body for the self that it certainly belongs to nature? Can it completely serve two masters? And is not the claim of nature the prior claim?

Much as the self needs its body, it is not at all clear that it makes it. "Objectification" is a brave word; but it is a metaphysical mystery. Our bodies appear to be given to us; we have to learn them—a great preoccupation of our early months. It does not seem to me that I *know how* to make my body. Samuel Butler, indeed, holds that we, or something in us, has that knowledge; for, he argues, what better evidence can we have that we know how to produce arms and legs, teeth and hair, than the fact that we do produce them! But is it we that do it? If we know how, that knowledge is singularly unavailable in time of need!

Again, the body is certainly not altogether such as I will. Who is there that does not quarrel with his physical equipment? In what sense is Cyrano de Bergerac's nose an expression of *his* will to live? No doubt he required something to breathe through, but if the moulding of that organ is the work of an alien power our monism is destroyed: one's body is only in part one's own. Plato's strictures upon the body as a tool of the spirit have not wholly lost their force. To every I-can there is a limit: I can so much, but I can no more, whether for physical exertion or for thought, and this limit appears to have its seat and registration in the body, as if the body were the province of an alien power. It is not mind but body which interrupts my occupation with its demand for exercise or food or sleep.

There is an opposition here which Lord Dunsany has well put from the point of view of the delinquent member, "The unhappy body." The body complains, "I am united with a fierce and violent soul that is altogether tyrannous and will not let me rest, and he drags me away from the dances of my kin to make me toil at his detestable work!"[2] Such a soul may drive matters to the point of divorce:

> "I am tired of you. I am off," said the soul. And he arose and went we know not whither.
> "Now I can rest," said the body.

If the body is simply an element in the self, how can such incompatibilities of temper exist? It is, in fact, more like a frontier between self and not-self, and a function of both. Like most between-things, it has a wavering allegiance; and while in many moods it appears to belong to me, in others it becomes the agent and spokesman of the outside powers. When appetite becomes keen, as the appetite of Esau, it seems to take possession and work its own will without much reference to the protesting self. The passion of fear may take control of the body and its deeds even against all habit. And if fear is mastered by force of thought, it is at the cost of distinguishing once more between self and body. It is told of Turenne that at the beginning of a hot engagement he found himself a prey of violent trembling, while surrounded by members of his staff. Instead of attempting to repress the humiliating ague he turned on his body with the words, "Tremble body: you would tremble yet more if *you* knew into what I am going to take you!"

The individual will to live has not all its own way in making and managing the body—certainly not so far as it is conscious.

In order to represent the body as the direct outer expression of the will, Schopenhauer was obliged to enlarge the conception of self to its subconscious depths: and the body then becomes the revelation or confession of much in the self of which it is not aware. In Schopenhauer's view, the body could never rebel in the name of an outer power, but only in the name of a hidden and contrary impulse of selfhood.

Schopenhauer is right in pointing out these deeper reaches of the self; and I believe, too, that he is right in supposing they are echoed in some of the apparent limitations of the body. But is he right, and are we right, in *beginning with the self?* Does the will produce itself? Is not every specification of the will which we see mirrored in the body the work of outside and prior forces? The traits of bird, tiger, man, have been beaten out in conflict with the world and are handed down in the species. How, then, can the bird's will to fly be called its own? It is a transmitted impulse, the impulse of the species.

It is true that the self is to some extent its own builder: it builds itself by way of habit; it becomes its own cause at the threshold of consent. But this appears a detail, an embroidery upon the mass of inherited selfhood. The will does not create and does not know its own sources. What are these sources? Whatever they are, they reside for a time, it seems, in two germ cells: they work by way of the body. The body, then, is first the agent of the other powers: it is the port of entry of new experience, and the channel of transmission of the hereditary determinants of will. The facts we must take account of are the facts of this radical exchange between the self and what lies beyond it, in birth, sensation, death.

At birth, the self is provided with an array of instincts, the elements of its heredity. In spite of all the mythology that has been produced in the name of instinct, and in spite of all the attempts to escape the mythology by abolishing the name, instinct is an inescapable fact because heredity is an inescapable fact. Mr.

John Watson regards instinct as a "religious" concept, because it has been used in an unscientific manner as a refuge for our ignorance. But there is no scientific advantage in substituting for the word "instinct" the words "unlearned response"; and in assuring us that there are almost no instincts or that we are "almost at the point of throwing away the word 'instinct,'" but that there are "thousands" of unlearned responses! "An" instinct is, indeed, a more or less arbitrary demarcation in the body of our hereditary capital; but this hereditary deposit is the fact that counts. There are dispositions in us which we can trace to a general inheritance from the race. There are others which belong to special ancestral strains. Any self may be obliged to recognize that some part of its fight in the world is a direct bequest from a dissipated forbear. And anyone may well believe that his capacity for pleasure is the use of a capital energy built by the saving and restraint of millions of ancestral organisms obedient to their vital impulse.

The body, then, is a portal, not a possession. And through this portal the self peers *out* into a dark and cavernous background in which the perspectives of its living past merge insensibly with the vast shapes of physical nature.

The Stranger in the House

We must consider the mystery of birth, the reception of a transmitted selfhood. But this is a place for resolution in holding to what we know. We have to recall that no one, from inside or outside, ever observes selfhood being transmitted through the world of physical nature. We never observe any one of our impulses arising *from* the body, as from something beyond self, though they often arise *in* the known body. For the most part, our current impulses seem to grow within the field of consciousness, or to shoulder their way from the margin to the center. And so it has always been with us from the beginning.

As some would express the matter, these impulses, particularly the profounder, instinctive impulses, appear as emerging from the "subconscious." For the most part our impulses are ways of dealing with specific types of occasion, and if the occasion is not present there is no impulse so to deal: it is only as a set of sensations which I learn to call hunger stealthily grow from nothing to something that the impulse to seek food emerges. Perhaps it is the sensation and not the impulse which comes from margin to center. But no; there are thinkers who attribute to impulse a more permanent existence, and who think of the major streams of impulse as racial, aboriginal, primitive, coming into the self from prior selfhood and living in the subconscious realm. The Freudian psychology is of this type.

The "subconscious" as an obscure region, a mid-term between mind and matter, is under scientific suspicion. Professor Knight Dunlap says that to refer a thing to the subconscious is to refer it to an unknown and uncontrollable source; hence, to do so is "religion" and not science. And since according to Mr. Watson, it is religious to refer anything to instinct, the Freudian psychology which uses both instinct and the subconscious must be doubly religious! In spite of this grave charge, it remains true that Freud and his followers have lavished much shrewd observation upon the original sources of mental states, and I think not without valuable results.

For this school of psychology, the subconscious is the home in particular of that fundamental instinctive trend which like a turbid stream of racial impulse flows through our being, always demanding outlet and always unsatisfied and restless. This craving, or "libido," or will-to-power—it is perhaps best left nameless—is described in terms which suggest a disembodied spirit or a dark, unruly stranger whom we harbor as a secret guest while we live our overt life in a critical, suspicious, and refractory world.

The analogy of the harbored stranger is not untrue to the Freudian theory; for this primitive, brooding impulse has aims as of a self distinguishable from my conscious self, whose aims are "rationalized" for the public gate. Always uncertain of perfect welcome in this outer world, the fundamental urge dwells much in inner communion and dream. And in proportion as the given front of experience threatens more profoundly to thwart its wish, it reverts to earlier openings of the sky, juvenile outlooks, infantile, prenatal perhaps; and rather than moving forward regresses toward paths even less congruent with the demands of outer reality. Thus, for example, religion arises as an imaginative cloaking of fact by fancies drawn from childish hopes of a perfect parental care, a symptom of defect of courage, or perhaps of the essential tragedy of existence which none are strong enough to face in its bald truth.

We are not concerned with the Freudian mythology; for its *dramatis personae*, with all pretense of scientific exactitude, are imaginative figures drawn by men groping as explorers must in a psychological twilight; they need not be supposed to fit the outline of reality more closely than the names of ill-discerned constellations in the skies. But we are concerned with the truth of that great trunk-stream of tendency which seeks, as an independent being, its life in the world; which has its ancient origins and its biological rhythms; and which maintains a persistent pressure against the inadequacies of our conventional social life. There is accuracy in the observation that this impulse has its epochs of impatience and danger, as at the turn of middle life, when it begins to sense the brevity of its hours of full flame and the uniqueness of this opportunity for self-expression. These years become dangerous, perhaps, just in proportion to the regularity and respectability of one's habits; because it is just these habits, confirmed by many memberships and friendships, which promise to perpetuate an anaesthetic routine centrally false to the profounder aspirations of the man. They have lost their moral value because they proceed by a momentum which belongs to the physical side of habit. I say there is truth in this picture for psychologists and sociologists; and for social respectability as well.

But I suggest that we recognize the scientific inaccuracy of referring to this vital urge as *other than the self*. To locate it in the "subconscious" and speak about it in the third person, as of a stranger in the house, is a literary device which has its scientific perils. It is *I* who am the stranger in this world; it is *I* who am dissatisfied with my own professions and my own habits; it is *I* who lack the courage or the skill to make my social self carry the full measure of my will. This reversion now and again to the outlook of childhood is nothing else than the persistence of that hope which, we have said, is the essence of the self. The self which makes religion is not a retreating self: it is the self which we met at the outset, constructing its audacious picture of the universe, aware of its destiny to deal with the ultimate powers. Its religion is the sign of its courage, not of its cowardice. My self is my hope; and my hope is forever unfulfilled, and forever reasserted. Call this hope by the more biological term, craving, or by the more romantic term, longing, *Sehnsucht*, or by the more metaphysical term, will—it is the same hope: it is *I*, and not an alien "it."

In William Watson's sonnet, *The Mock Self*, the rôles are with greater justice reversed: it is the overt self who is the alien, and the "subconscious" self, the central reality:

> Few friends are mine, tho many wights there be
> Who, meeting oft the phantasm that makes claim
> To be myself, and hath my face and name,
> And whose thin fraud I wink at privily,
> Account this light impostor very me.
> What boots it undeceive them, and proclaim
> Myself myself, and whelm this cheat with shame?
> I care not, so it leave my true self free,
> Impose not on me also; but, alas,
> I, too, at fault, bewildered, sometimes take
> Him for myself, and far from my own sight,
> Torpid, indifferent, doth mine own self pass;
> And yet anon leaps suddenly awake
> And spurns the gibbering mime into the night.

It is, of course, the prerogative of the self-conscious animal to think of himself as of another, and to ascribe quasi-selfhood to any of his impulses. This is clearly in order with respect to those fragments of heredity we call the several instincts. They are sub-selves in the same sense as our habits. They are the raw material of habit-forming; and like habits remain attached to the conscious self by the thread of their meaning. They are all members of the fundamental hope; and meaning, which is single, descends from the whole to the parts. These instincts may be "subconscious" in the same way that habit is subconscious when represented by a point of meaning in the mind. But the great trunk of impulse from which these instincts branch out cannot be subconscious in the same way. It is not a sub-self; for it is an aspect of the whole self. It cannot be in abeyance, for it is what I am: a craving that is not felt is no craving at all, and a craving that is felt by another than me is simply not my craving. It is subconscious only as the depth of consciousness is distinguished from its content; or as *that with which* I am meeting experience is distinguished from the experience being met. To every item of experience the self is saying both Yes and No: Yes, it is good; No, it is not yet that good I hope for. Which of these judgments is more constant and emphatic, God knows. But the self, the longing, is the author of both of them, hence never away from the focus of living, though seldom occupying that focus as its own sole object. The stranger in the house is no other than the host himself.

Now all this means that when we seek for the sources of the self in the "subconscious" we are seeking the sources of the self within the self! The subconscious is no mid-term between mind and matter, no obscure passageway from body to mind: the subconscious is a region within the self.[3] The self cannot discover its own temporal beginnings by this route, nor by any other mode of burrowing from within.

If we think of the origins of a new individual solely from the facts which an outside observer can discover, it may easily appear that while the new body is continuous with the parental bodies, the new mind is quite distinct and discontinuous. It seems that the body is first formed, and that the mind then gradually supervenes; in which case, the hereditary determinant of character must have had for a time some form of sub-mental or latent existence. Each new self is clearly a consequence of conscious deeds of prior selves: but it is commonly an unpremeditated and sometimes an unwelcome consequence, and if the new self cannot be said to be *meant* by its parents there can be no volitional continuity between them and it—its will is not a carrying on of their wills. For its part, it can hardly be said to have contemplated or intended those parents. If it could regard its life as a gift, and as an unintentional gift, might it not with equal detachment pass judgment upon it and, conceivably, decline it? Is the new will not a completely new and independent fact in the world?

Assuredly these suggestions are groundless fictions: in dealing with mental origins, the external view can give us strictly nothing but the biological facts. In interpreting them, we can at least avoid the Freudian fallacy of distinguishing between the new self and "its" impulse. The new self *is* its impulse: it is a new will to live; *to be, for it, is to accept being*. It can only exist as an incipient, groping will, embodied in a few elementary dispositions to action. For the use of these instincts or unlearned responses it is in the strange position of having an initial technique, as if they were *habits*—but habits it had not itself acquired; and also some sense of the meaning of these actions, as if it had a *memory* of the outcome—but a memory not based on its own experience! Let us be clear that an impulse can only exist as having a time-direction: in its very first moment, it must have a direction toward the future, and this is inseparable from a direction toward the past. The very conception of a beginning of conscious life carries with it a paradoxical reference to something prior to that beginning—as if it were a sort of Platonic reminiscence. It thus lies in the nature of the case that as we examine our own duration in time, tracing our memory backward to the utmost, we can find no wall of partition between self and prior-to-self. I never know by introspection how old I am, or, that I have a finite age. If the impulse which is I is a "racial impulse," there is no reason to ascribe age to it: it is presumably, like energy, always new as on the first day.

It is, in fact, a gratuitous assumption that where one self begins the other must stop. The truth is rather that different selves overlap: the continuity of the body is outdone in the continuities of the mind. The selves have many objects in common; presumably they have also some community of desire and tendency. If the body of one may be, for a time, a part of the body of another, may not their impulses and memories be also shared? Here we are, indeed, thrown back on speculation. But at any rate, there is no evidence that in reproduction the mental life passes through a bodily sojourn: so far as heredity is concerned, we may still hold to our view that the body is part of the self.

Nature the Consumer

Even so, we have merely postponed the difficulty. Granted that these anterior forces which bequeath to us our bodies and therewith our instinct-capital are mental forces; and granted also that every new I-will is so far coincident with these earlier I-wills that it may fairly claim its inherited body as a part of itself. Granted that the wings of every new-hatched bird express its own will to fly and not merely a parental impulse to affirm and continue their own mode of life. Still, all such selves are immersed in the greater total, nature. Parents and offspring alike, as to their bodies, are parts of physical nature; how, then, can any self lay claim to its own body unless it is prepared somehow to lay claim to all of nature with it?

The solidarity between the body and nature is of the closest. Given the bone, Cuvier could reconstruct the fish: given the body, the ideal scientist could reconstruct the physical universe—the two are of a piece. They are of a piece, also, in respect to my will: as I need the body, so I need nature. If my need of the body implies that the body is a part of the self, does not my need of nature, by the same logic, imply that nature also is part of the self? Our hypothesis seems to lead us back by an indirect route to that subjective idealism or solipsism which we rejected at the outset.[4] If that view is to be discarded, must we not give up our hypothesis and allow that physical nature is the all-consuming totality of which selves are but peculiar parts?

Now we clearly reject the subjective view of nature: the self, as we said, is but half of the world it perceives. Solipsism is but half true! It has a half-truth which we must acknowledge, namely, this: While the self is receiving, not making, the world it perceives, and is at every point in contact with a not-self, it proceeds at once to create after the pattern of what it perceives. Shut your eyes, and the visual world does *not* cease for you: if the field of your vision contained moving objects, their motion continues before you[5]—you are actively reproducing and anticipating the course of your experience. To expect is to build in advance of the fact. The self has some power to produce from its own resources a world coextensive in quality and quantity with nature: and when we dream or day-dream we project from these inner resources an environment for the body together with the body. Imagination constructs body and world in a piece.

But imagination we regard as an imitator: its products, we say, are not "realities." In the real order of things, nature lies beyond the self, not within it: and nature claims the body. Our question, then, amounts to this. If nature is not-self, is it so foreign to us that we cannot claim *joint ownership* with its alien proprietor—if it has a proprietor—much as we claim joint interest in the transmitted impulses of heredity? An inventor receives a bequest which enables him to finish his experiments, to patent and market his invention: is the invention therefore *not his own?*

What is received is the material equipment for bringing his idea to earth: the idea is still his idea and no other's. Here we readily admit that it is the idea which determines the ownership, not the raw material: it is the idea which organizes and gives meaning to that material inheritance and determines what it is. Is there some analogy between this case of received material and that immense and continuous influx of material-for-experience we call nature?

Perhaps the description of nature as material-for-experience takes too much for granted, since it labels nature by a rôle which it plays in consciousness. The difficulty of our problem lies in the apparent independence of nature: it is something for us, but it is also something on its own account. What we have to do is to consider those qualities which make nature appear so durably self-sufficient and independent, if not an alien realm.

Two of these qualities we shall pass over briefly, not because they are unimportant but because they are involved in others—the limitless immensity of nature in space and time, and the vividness or intensity of natural fact, its inescapable thereness. The mind, as we have seen, is unspatially related to the whole of space—and more!—and untemporally related to the whole of time—and more! The self is contained in both space and time, but not *simply* contained: the relation is reciprocal. As for the vividness of natural fact as compared with imagination, impressive as it is, it is evidently a matter of quantity rather than of principle. Besides these there are three marks of nature's otherness. First, the simple *given* quality of sense-data, colors, sounds, smells, tastes; we have to discover them in order to know them, we could never have invented them, we cannot deduce them as necessary features of the universe from any known rational principle. Second, the relentless order of nature, pursued with exact lawfulness without reference to my will or yours, and apparently also without any will of its own. Third, the publicity of nature: it always appears as observable by others as well as by myself.

First, as to our sense-data, the original stuff of our experience of nature; I do not say the original stuff of nature; for what the ultimate ingredients of nature are, science is not ready to say. Our experience of nature begins with these sense-qualities, sights, tastes, etc., in space and time; and we cannot sufficiently wonder that it is just these qualities which traditional physics rejects as being in us and not in the objective world. Under the name of "sensation," psychology has commonly accepted the disowned qualities and made them, if not the head of the corner, at least the foundation of the mental edifice. But let us not hasten to claim these properties for the self; for certainly in our experience of nature these sense-data appear as ingredients of nature. Let us give full credit to that appearance, and respond whole-heartedly to the summons of Professor Whitehead to avoid the "bifurcation of nature." Only, let us be clear that when we mount colors and sounds in their proper setting in space and time, and call the whole concrete picture by the name of nature, we thereby definitely reject a common illusion, namely, that sense-data are *caused* by nature. This is the most palpable of confusions. For how can that be caused by nature which is the very fabric of nature? If we regard nature as the cause of our experience, we are bound, with Descartes and Locke, to "bifurcate," and resign sense-data once for all to the self. If we decline to bifurcate, nature is not the cause of sensations.

If then we seek a source for sense-data beyond themselves, as we must, it is *beyond nature* that we are obliged to go: and nature has surrendered its apparent independence and self-sufficiency. And so far as we are dependent upon sense-data for our experience and our being, it is not nature upon which we depend: it is rather that ulterior being upon which nature also depends.

As a second mark of otherness, we note that *strict lawfulness of nature's action*, which bends to no man's will. For many thinkers (especially those of the Kantian schools) the element of law in events is the chief element in their independence of us and of our will—their standing over against the mind as something other, their "objectivity."

Now when we say that nature is a realm of law, what we mean might be put by saying that nature is occupied in *drawing consequences*. You ask, consequences of what? The naturalist replies, Consequences of previous events, which are themselves consequences of still earlier events. Then nature is drawing consequences of consequences of consequences.... ! This answer, though it has all the form of truth, and is quite verifiable, is evidently the absence of an answer or its indefinite postponement.

We should have a substantial answer only if we could find in the world something capable of *starting* a chain of consequences. Unless our analysis has deceived us, the will is precisely such a thing: for will, we thought (see [SBF,] page 81), in the moment of decision is effecting the transition from contemplation to actuality, from possibility to being. Will is a realizing or actualizing principle of the world, as we know it: and for the sake of argument, let us hypothetically accord to it the initiative it appears to have.

Now the will is perpetually engaged in deeds whose consequences it only partially discerns. You undertake a journey with a friend and every day of it brings unexpected situations and new texts of the quality of that friendship. It is largely for the sake of such discoveries that you undertake the adventure. No man knows all that he does when he does any deed. No geometer knows all that he does when he draws a circle. Least of all does anyone know what is implied in his will to live. These implications, however, are drawn for him. Who draws them? Nature. For nature is the sphere in which all the immediate implications of any fact are instantly drawn, and in which all the consequences of any fact are drawn in due time.

We do not know in advance what is implied in our own wills; but we proceed to find out. And it is *a part of our will that we shall find out*. We desire and will this inherent consistency of experience which relentlessly annexes to every deed its consequences, and thereby instructs us in the wider reaches of our own meaning. To be in this sense responsible and rational is a part of the purpose of every purpose: it is implied in the will to live.

This lawfulness of nature; then, which seemed to set nature apart from the self, begins to appear as something implied in the nature of the self: and I can very well fancy myself in the position of our inventor, to whom what comes from outside becomes with all its laws bone and blood of his own idea. This would certainly be the case if nature were engaged in drawing only the consequences of my own will-acts.

But it is a part of nature's sublime impartiality that I receive at every moment the consequences not only of what I have done but also of what countless others, my contemporaries and predecessors, known and unknown, have done together with much which apparently nobody has done, and which has no intelligible relation to my meaning. Some of these consequences are surely alien to my will. If I can adopt them as mine, it can be only by way of some extremely hospitable ingredient of my will which I do not find on the surface. It would have to be a trait of will which establishes some community of destiny between me and these other wills, whose consequences nature bears to me. I believe that there is such a trait, and that we shall discover it in the third mark of otherness.

We have said that nature is other than self because it is *public*. It is a common object for many selves: they form an immense group in space and time with respect to this common object: if it is property for any of them, it is property for all of them, and hence private property for none of them. Each must respect it as also belonging to others.

There is much in our attitude toward nature to bear out this idea of common property. Nature is "real" as over against my private fancies, dreams, imaginations. It is real because it is the world of our common life. I have an obligation to the space and time of nature, because I have an obligation to you. Buried in my books, oblivious of my appointments, living in another space-time world, I am disloyal to my comrades. The shame of living in drug-dreams or intoxication is not its pleasure, and it would still be shameful though there were no accompanying decay of mentality: its shame is its subjectivity, the abandonment of the common task in the real world of common objects, the abandonment of these my others.

The ideal accuracy of nature indicates to what degree we are concerned in the agreements of social life, the exact courses of navigation, the location of meridians and boundaries, the precise timing of clocks. Here our wills, the wills of this vast company, are in identical accord. Perhaps no two immediate interests are in more direct opposition than those of pursuer and pursued. Each would wish his own miles to be shorter and those of his opponent longer. Yet it occurs to neither to rebel against the fundamental condition of their actions, that each mile shall be precisely the same for both.

The publicity of nature—if we may take this as its primary sort of otherness—thus throws some light on its lawfulness; for a world which is to serve many wills at once must be impartial as only an ideal law is impartial. It also helps to explain the inanimate, "dead," mechanical character which we associate with this lawfulness in the inorganic world. For whatever is animate or living we feel bound to treat with regard, in proportion to its degree of life: we cannot ruthlessly break and reshape what is conscious nor grind it in our machines. If nature were sensitive in detail to its last recesses, the work of the plow, the spade, the axe, yes, even the simple movements of men would be attended with such death-dealing and pain-giving as would render effective living at last intolerable; we should sink stages deeper into the predicament of the enlightened Buddhist; we should be beset at every turn with such questions as Mr. G. K. Chesterton propounds—"Why should salt suffer?"[6] The inanimateness of nature confers freedom to exploit and reshape: the circumstance that it is a world of facts and not of meanings[7] makes it the perfect receptacle for such meanings as we will to impose upon it. It can enter unobtrusively into works of public utility or beauty because its mechanical base is neutral and unconscious in its minutely lawful procedures. A world of conscious enterprise and especially of social enterprise would be impossible without such an impassive base: a world of meanings would necessarily include, and so give meaning to, such a world of, the meaningless as abstract physical nature affords.

Thus while nature cannot be said to belong to any single self, it can be well understood as belonging to a community of selves: it is not within any one of them, but it might be an identical part of all of them. It would be over against each one of them, as an independent realm, because all the other selves are over against each one: their distinctive concerns would lend to it for each self an "objective" character. Nature would be independent and objective in a relative and derivative sense, not in an absolute sense—a conclusion which was suggested also by our study of sense-data.

Is it reasonable to consider nature as such a common domain belonging to many selves at once? This hypothesis would explain many of its striking characters, including those which set it in the sharpest contract with the world of mind. But it would hardly be a reasonable hypothesis unless the many selves that live on this infinite world of nature can be said to have some identical element in all their wills. Can any such fundamental community of will be thought to exist? I believe that it does exist; and that it is the original relation of this enormous and loose-bound community of selves to each other. How this may be, let me now briefly try to suggest.

It needs no argument to show that our human wills are always wills to live *with others*. The least social of men is inescapably sociable, not by overt choice, but by the nature of such finite minds as we are.[8] For us, to live is to grow; and craving for growth itself grows by what it feeds on and so seizes as its own that most potent and endlessly cumulative agency of growth, association with others, reaching out through time and space. We need to be with other selves, not accidentally nor by convention and special effort but by a kind of inescapable insertion and natural access capable of all degrees of intimacy. We need that kind of with-ness which is best defined as simply being in the same world, for this kind of being together involves no oppressive closeness, and yet allows infinite possibilities of approach and rapport. It is not difficult to find groups of selves which have so organized their conversation, their distances, and their meetings, that they aid one another's growth. The members of such a group have an identical ingredient of will, namely, the will to live with each other.

Any such group is obviously very limited in comparison with the innumerable company of selves which in all time have participated in this universe. In most of these one can claim no manner of personal interest; and some he may actively wish out of existence. But in spite of himself, his will extends to them by its logic. For something of all association adheres to the growing mind: to associate with any person is to associate vicariously with his associates. To put it barbarously, the relation of mental with-ness is transitive: if A is with B, in this sense, and B is with C, then A is with C; for B, having associated with C is now, whether he likes it or not, and always, *B with C*—that is what he *is*! Such a chain of intercourse clearly extends without limit to all participants in any historical nexus.

This only states in a highly mechanical and imperfect fashion what we are intimately aware of without analysis, namely, that our wills are not so many specimens of an abstract type: they are individual wills to live with specific other individuals in an order we call *historical*, in which every event and every idea is what it is because of what has gone before it and what accompanies it. To live here and now as *this* self is to live in context with *these* others, whether I know them or like them or not. In this will to live historically with these selves we have an ingredient of will which may be called identical in all members of this vast and dispersed company. And thus to will is to require that common medium through which intercourse with them is possible, namely, nature.

I certainly do not know *a priori* that existence with these other persons implies the peculiar arrangements of my body, breathing, eating, etc. I could not have deduced my own head and trunk, arms, legs, eyes, nose: still less those complex internal arrangements which remain to me, and perhaps to all men for all time, a world of abundant wonder. No "deduction of the categories" by any philosopher has penetrated far into the necessity of these details.[9] Certainly, too, we discover in and out of the body many a fact we do not, in its separate capacity, want, many a fact which is evil, and so to be changed or destroyed. But so far as facts are unchangeable, they are the actual cost of my will to live. De Bergerac's nose is not the nose of his choice. But it is the nose which, if he were to take his place in nature, and be *himself*, the offspring of these parents, with them and their "withs," he *had to have*. His nose is a consequence of an act of his own will, the acceptance of this life; it is a consequence drawn by nature, but still his; and it is in this quality that he feels a chivalrous regard for it, and proposes to defend it against all comers.

Nature is other than me and before me. But there is nothing about nature which I cannot adopt and use, as the inventor adopted his bequest, or Cyrano his nose. In all its types of otherness, factual, legal, social, it shows itself to be fitted for taking part in the life of self—not merely fitted to be known, nor fitted to be used in the arts, but fitted in its structure for interplay in the development of the will. Its very dead impersonality, the most alien of its traits, is essential to qualify it for serving as a nonintrusive common region in the will-life of many selves at once.

We may therefore accept to this extent the at-first staggering implication of our theory that the body is an organ of the self, namely, that nature is also such an organ. I cannot be myself without all of nature in space and time. The environment of any body is a part of the fact we mean by body. To the salmon after thousands of miles of sea-wandering there is just one stream in the world where it can breed and die: that stream is carried with it in the implications of its own body, and presumably also of its sense of being. It is not less true of higher creatures that their worlds of fact enter into the definitions of their selves. But nature belongs to me only in so far as I make it mine: it does not cease to be also other-than-me. It remains, I suspect, other and prior to all of us, because it is first the work and organ of a profounder self. Our lives are spent in learning what nature may mean for us: our appropriation is still superficial. Only, we know that nothing in nature is ultimately alien. We receive first, but reproduce afterward. As in heredity, the stranger became the host, so in natural causation the consumer becomes the consumed. The self is the organizing principle: it is thus the superior, the owning principle. In this circumstance lies its freedom.

NOTES

1. The several organs "correspond to the principal desires through which the will manifests itself: they must be the visible manifestation of these desires. Teeth, throat, and bowels are objectified hunger; the organs of generation are objectified sexual desire; the groping hand, the hurrying feet correspond to the more indirect desires of the will which they express."

1. *World as Will and Idea*, tr. I, p. 141.
2. *A Dreamer's Tales*.
3. A more detailed discussion of the subconscious may be found in an appendix to my book, *The Meaning of God in Human Experience*.
4. [SBF,] 104.
5. If you are following the uniform motion of a well-marked object, as of an aeroplane moving across the sky, you will find on opening your eyes after a brief interval that your gaze has moved with the object, and still catches it.
6. *Napolean of Notting Hill*.
7. [SBF,] 85.
8. For a more elaborate analysis of sociability, see *Man and the State*, Part III.
9. It is perhaps not possible to show that a world, common to many minds, *must be a world of space*; but space as we know it is such a common world. Each self has a vested interest in the whole of this space: this space is therefore present indifferently to all of these communicating minds; and the contents of space, or nature, are a region in which minds come to coalescence. As a system of behavior, each self appears among the contents of this world as an object among objects, visible as a body to each other self. And since each body is responding to the whole of physical nature, it must contain within it a part which can be put into correspondence, point for point, with all the points it can distinguish in that world: that is, space must approach the structure of an infinite manifold; and further, that of a manifold whose finite parts are infinitely divisible. The brain, as a spatial mirror of the intercourse of its self with its world, must be able to represent, as in a metaphorical analysis, each distinguishable phase of mental life. And thus the body becomes—roughly in its superficial aspect, and accurately in its less accessible aspect—a set of signs in which the observer can read the passing states of the self there acting. He cannot see those states; but he can see the translation of them into the spatial language. And of his own brain-events, he can say, This is not my self; but it is the translation of my self into the special set of hieroglyphics which we call physical.

CHAPTER 5

Passage Beyond Modernity:
The Possible Universality of Solitude

Modern Subjectivity as Resource and as Threat

That best fruit of modernity, the free individual disposed to stand alone against corporate dictation—what is he standing for? and what is he standing on?

He is standing for his right. But note: he is not standing for his private interest under the specious flag of "my right"; for what he claims as his right he claims *for all others* similarly placed. This is the precise difference between an interest and a right. Further, for the justice of his claim he is prepared to call others—disinterested—to witness. What gives him his footing is the circumstance that this for-others-also situation is at least subconsciously a known situation—known by these others, known also by the corporate being addressed; and that he, the claimant, *knows that it is known*. He seems to "stand alone"—that is his repute; but does he? Examine closely the basis of that strange inner certitude of his: *how does he know* that his situation is known? His aloneness reaches strands far beyond himself. I venture to call the ground on which he stands *a vein of nonsolitude of the "solitary" ego.*

It is the same nonsolitude as that on which Descartes wisely and inconsistently acted when, having lighted on the solitary I-exist as his ultimate certitude—meaning for him I-Descartes-exist—he published it to the world as the basis for all future philosophy! What a load for a private certitude to carry! He instinctively sensed what his method could not justify: namely, that *his private certitude was everyman's certitude in kind*. It had an irrepressible universality. At the extreme depth of his inwardness he joins an infinite outside.

He thus refuted in action the theoretical solipsism derivable from his premises, but without noticing that he had done so. This solipsism has haunted modernity; and modernity has also failed to notice its direct refutation in Descartes' act. Stirred by his enlightening certitude, modernity has followed him gladly into his subjective depths, from which it has drawn wondrous harvests. We have had the monads of Leibniz, the subjective idealisms, *all* the idealisms that draw objects from pure subjects, the inturned romanticisms, and at last the prevailing and all-absorbing psychologisms. All-absorbing, for am not I, the nature-made self, the thinker of all my thoughts? And can any thought of mine escape the coloring of my subjectiv-

---

From CWC, 21–41.

ity, my pathology, my subconscious drifts and eddies, known only to God, and the psychologist or the psychoanalyst?

Must we not have, therefore, as the perfecting enlightenment, a psychology of all the sciences—a psychology of economics (like Marshall's), of the judicial process (like Cardozo's), of religion (in many versions)—yes, of philosophy also (for has not Jaspers proposed a psychology of philosophical varieties?), even of logic (for are not our pragmatisms, our instrumentalisms and operationalisms, a sort of psychology of thinking?) and hence of physics itself (as in Bridgman's essays)? Should I hesitate to propose a psychology of psychology? Just this was offered to the public, when the Plebs textbooks, issued in London in the twenties, announced in the preface of their text on psychology that it would be a class-conscious production—not guilty of the vice of "objectivity"! Must not our very standards of truth and right—and most obviously, of beauty—be infected with the relativity and warping of the disparate egos, whose problem of togetherness Kant himself never squarely faced?

With this splendid and not infertile depth of inbound separation, the wholeness of man's conscious world is quietly resigned. Alienation from the total-and-real in its unity for all men is aided by the equally wide acceptance of Descartes' complementary doctrine, that physical nature is a process of mathematical perfection which we must conscientiously regard as empty of all purpose and quality: between man and that physical world-total no possible sympathy.

And with this abandonment of man's native rapport with the whole, the nerve of worth in his own living and acting silently ceases to function. Here, I venture to think, is the root of our malady.

For this is the first principle of human motivation: that *meaning descends from the whole to the parts.* The second principle is that meaning ascends from the parts to the whole, the inductive element of value. In every task, the detail sheds its satisfaction or dissatisfaction upward. Driving a nail well is surely an end in itself and sends its items of cheer to the task in hand. But in this continuous two-way traffic, the significance of the whole has the deciding voice. It can override many an irksome detail, whereas without it detailed triumphs lose their charm. The worth of living must indeed have its moment-by-moment verification—total and distant objectives are not enough—but if one lives determinedly in the present in order to forget that there *is no ultimate objective,* the nerve is cut.

In childhood, whole-awareness is unquestioned and latent; it exists as a pervading will-to-live-and-grow-up in a world credited with wisdom as a firm possession; under this canopy, the joy of doing is carried by plural pleasure goals kindly proposed by nature. As we mature, this latent whole-awareness presents claim as a restless query, *cui bono,* a demand for total significance, as needed to sustain the worth of nature's continuing gift. Normally, this demand is met by one's native sense of continuity with the community, assuming unreflectively—as Descartes did—the implicit universality of one's private motivation, in the naive faith that one's world is a common world, and that one's private purposes may simply interweave with the ongoing purposes of that community, and with the dim world purpose which the unrelenting forward-leaning spirit of that community foreshadows. Participating in this thought totality, the meaning of the whole descends upon the part.

But what if it occurs to me that this is, after all, only something that "I-think"? What if my naïve faith is precisely contradicted by my philosophy, which assures me that there is no such thing as a genuine community of mind? What if this faith is explicitly rejected by the moving and triumphant science-and-world-view of the age? Then it is, I say, that the sails of one's will begin to flop in a failing breeze. The springs of motivation shift their balance; nature's ostensible pluralism of private goods tends to resume sway. In particular, that individual disposed to stand alone for his right reflects that he has no ground to stand on: for no one can stand on what may be an insufferable projection of one's private pathology. The very notion of legal right threatens to yield place to an attempted calculus of interests.[1]

It is indeed the principle of our advance that has carried the germ of our malady. Deprived of its natural and responsible objectivity, our individualism begins to show its capacity to disintegrate, even in youth. And, as an incident, a generation of educators in America seeking a corrective is thrown into a mad attempt to make education equivalent to "life adjustment," meaning thereby an artificial collectivizing of the mentality of the young, under the name of "democracy."

The Dilemma of Modernity; the Struggle with Solipsism

Our situation today is a dilemma. On the one hand, we cannot repudiate the principle of advance, the subjectivity that has given us the modern individual and his right. And for this reason we cannot, with Descartes and unreflective mankind, simply assume the universality of our private experience. On the other hand, without that universality, no wholeness and no integration of will.

Because of this dilemma, we cannot end our argument by proposing simply a return to the religious element in the premodern civilization. We may indeed infer that religion is essential, and this has often been taken as the end of the matter. Religion contains the needed element of union with the whole—this is little more than a truism, for whatever unites the soul of man with the whole is religion.

And herewith we answer at once a question which was early before us: it is clearly *not the destiny of the secular state to render the functions of a religious community superfluous*. On the contrary, with the advance of a technical civilization, a church in our broad sense (assuming that it does its work and nothing but its work) instead of tending to wither away, becomes increasingly necessary to the vitality of the state, its function being to maintain that integrity of motivation which the state requires and cannot of itself elicit or command. This conclusion I regard as valid and important.

But taken as a summons to return to a *status quo ante*, it cannot be sufficient, unless we regard modernity as a false step. If we believe, as I certainly do, that the advances of modernity are genuine, and must enter into the body of whatever faith mankind can hold, we cannot disregard modernity's philosophical quandaries. Philosophy is the good faith of Faith with human thought. The issues raised by philosophy must have an answer for reason as well as for intuition. Faith itself will be affected by what we here require—a new advance of thought which, without losing the modern depth of subjectivity, can give us a rational right to our "naive assumption" of the universality of our private experience.

In the search for a releasing insight, modernity has been held fast by its own postulates—among them this, that what is subjective cannot at the same time be shared: there is no such thing as a literal awareness by one mind of another mind. The other's selfhood can certainly not be sensed, nor can another's experience be experienced as he experiences it. The first person plural, "we," is half hypothesis. When you and I look at "the same object," all I surely know is that I look at it, and suppose there is a "you" who does the same. In brief, there is no genuine consubjectivity (or as it is commonly referred to, no "intersubjectivity") for a scrupulous modern empiricism: the word "we" is a trap for the unwary!

Hence when my colleague Whitehead, in one of our joint seminars, throws out in an amiable aside, "Hang it all! *Here we are:* we don't go behind that, we begin with it," he has implicitly brushed aside one of the theoretical bases of modernity. He speaks the common sense of mankind; and in my judgment he is entirely right. But to justify the stroke, we must explicitly alter the bases of our epistemology.[2]

In practice, each individual mind, having its unique perspective of a world, includes therein its fellow minds: each *believes* in the existence of his fellows. There are no solipsists-by-belief. Yet, on Descartes' ground, which is modernity's, we must all, with Leibniz and Bertrand Russell, be *solipsists-in-theory*. As Kant has perfectly put the matter, "The I-think must be able to accompany (and swallow) all my *Vorstellungen*"—all my ideas and perceivings. On this point, Leibniz alone is fully consistent (and more resolutely consequent than Kant, who evaded the issue of the "we"): minds are monads, each with an impenetrably private world panorama unrolling, not before him, but in him.

Could there be such a thing as a veritable consubjectivity whereby one self participates, not by imaginative or sympathetic construction, but by actual experience, in the selfhood of another? Could this be the case without destroying the privacy of the ego, so that our physical world, for example, could be literally a common world, and known as such, without any intrusion of person on person? If that were the case, we should see and judge things with *a natural universality*. The solitary experimenter would know (as he spontaneously assumes) that his results must be confirmed by everyone who follows the experiment under the same conditions: a universal science would be justified. Each man would be, not merely an I-think, but *man-thinking*. This, I submit, seems to be not only the true state of affairs, but the necessary state. And if our philosophy fails to allow it, perhaps we must change our philosophy!

Such a paradoxical immediacy of otherness—at once a true realism (for our "phenomena" would thus acquire the immediate objectivity they seem to have) and a true idealism—would constitute the dilemma-solving insight. Modernity, through the firm logic of its subjective certitude and the derived empiricism of private sense data, must reject it as impossible. It becomes necessary in our philosophy to pass *beyond modernity*.

Political Theory Makes an Effort: Partial Solution

Let us note in passing that contemporary political theory shows signs of recognizing this quandary and of moving toward a solution.

It has well outgrown the stage at which the subject's obedience has to be understood as a contract or counsel of prudence. It listens with less than half an ear to the present school of "legal realists" disposed to interpret law as a "threat," as if most of us were at heart transgressors. Without too heavy an investment in the nonrational impulses proposed by the various depth psychologies, it recognizes that rationalistic egoisms are not plausible descriptions of human nature. Primitive impulses, such as the herd instinct, and the natural dispositions of the human will to serve, through family, clan, posterity in general, aims outreaching private good, insufficient as they are for a developed theory, at least point the way to a more adequate psychology of political life.

With a realer realism, political theory now perceives that the will to obey has permanent sources in what men think and believe about their total environment—in cosmic bearings and allegiances not supplied by the visible community. With great courage, Professor Robert MacIver points out that the "web of government" is sustained in part by an element of "myth." Why myth?

Myth seems on the face of it a step into the vague—something less tangible or structurally useful than those ideal standards—truth, justice, beauty, et cetera—which ancient philosophy singled out as universal guides for the human will. These guides the Stoic legalists could specify for legal use and Justinian's codifiers hand on to the lawmakers of Europe. Modernity, however, has dealt hardly with these standards; it is bound on its own principle of subjectivity to reduce all principles (including its own) to the level of psychological variables. Are they not creatures of the subjective I-think? I look on them with a sentiment of regard; but have they a footing in the nature of things beyond my psychological setup? Here myth may inject a word.

What myth adds is the suggestion—through song and story, through its appealing store of admirabilia and detestabilia—that they *may have* such a footing. The quiet molding of wills through the pictured decisions and characters of gods and heroes is empirically near-universal. Religion goes farther: it adds the responsible assertion that they do *have* such a footing—as world view, *religion is the affirmation of the anchorage in reality of ideal ends*. Myth, as the more tentative position, may well be more agreeable to the scientific temper: it is confessed hypothesis, whereas religion is dogma. But it contains the important advance, an escape from psychological debility to the outer air of speculative metaphysics—the word "speculative" here meaning "inquiring"!

This escape is essential. But it must be justified. The dilemma of modern thought has been created by philosophy, and philosophy, not imagination alone, must resolve it. How can we keep the treasure of subjective depth, and at the same time retain hold on universal validity in our experience?

Passing beyond Modernity: Intersubjectivity and Participation

It is the present century that has met the persistent philosophical issue.

The revolt against subjectivism had begun earlier. A sturdily growing social science could not operate with closed individual selfhoods. The quandary of solipsism had to be overcome or broken through. There was an inviting path much followed prior to the turn of the century—that of resolutely dissolving the supposedly impenetrable ego in the social milieu, showing how far the development of the I-think is molded by language and social interaction. There was important truth along this path (as followed by Mead, Baldwin, and others); only, Descartes' logic was not thereby met, it was submerged in the advancing wave of psychological sociability. And if this were the whole truth, the prize of modernity's deepened subjectivity is surrendered—the proud and pregnant loneliness of free individual creativity and right.

The solution was achieved by an opposite path—one which in the end made full use of the new social insights, but which began by following further the logic through which the quandary appeared, aided by a more perceptive analysis of what we call "experience."

"Experience" is modernity's magic word of charm. "Experience" is the suggested sum, or integral, of all the items, the *dx*'s, of human empiricism. The word is conveniently noncommittal as to *whose* experience is implied—whether my sole-own, or ours—yours-and-mine, or perhaps mankind's-in-general. It suggests, without asserting, an actual world-wide consubjectivity (as we have above termed the genuine "we," p. [65]) such as would exist if the ego and its fellows shared an identical object. What the newer analysis has discerned *within "experience"*—and what Plato and Descartes and Kant had failed to find there—is *an intersubjective Thou-art*, inseparable from each subjective I-am, serving to bind their several experiences together in such wise that the loose suggestion of a shared experience with an identical object is defined and confirmed. The idea of a literal consubjectivity toward a common world object is realized.

For note: As the term "experience" is noncommittal as to the identity of the subject or subjects who are experiencing, so the term "I-think" is equally noncommittal as to the experience or experiences it includes. Descartes left the matter open:

he failed to mention the *content* of the I-think as essential to its existence, and accordingly passed no judgment as to whether this content need be *inclusive* in order that the I-think hold its identity. Now the only condition under which any self can be aware of its own existence is that it is occupied with some content; and clearly the sole possibility that any self should enter the experience of another is that *some content*, some bit of experience, should be not exclusive but *had in common*, and known to be common. If experience could thus be shared, directly or through some third subject, solipsism is at an end, and yet without the fusion of self into self.

What we can now verify is that private experiencing, as receptive, is a certain *participation* of each I-think in the experience of an intersubjective Thou-art. Through this participation, my experience acquires the substantial "objectivity" of being no private dream of my own. And so far as these participations extend to all, our common objects enter the single *world unity* common intuition has always assumed them to have.

But further, the presence of this uniting selfhood provides the assurance that the common experience of mankind has an indwelling purpose, a *telos*, in which the I-am also participates. My aims cease to be mere psychological distillates of private passions; they have "an anchorage in reality." Therewith a way of hope opens for the individual, groping for significance.

General Course of the Philosophical Argument

To sketch briefly the path by which this result has been reached:

Solipsism, we have noted, has never been believed; but it has frequently been taken as an inescapable incident of our being *selves*, each with an unsharable center of feeling and perspective reference, whose intimate continuities of experience-and-memory-and-wish are only fragmentarily communicable in the coin of common speech. The logic of solipsism has been taken most seriously by the most strenuously logical thinkers, as by the early Bertrand Russell following Leibniz, and by the later Edmund Husserl. This was the necessary course of philosophical honor, if the "egocentric predicament"—to use Ralph Perry's perfect phrase—were to be logically overcome and not simply broken through in favor of the claims of common intuition.

The first step in this logical overcoming was the recognition that the solipsist position contains a self-refutation. It is not merely inconsistent with our natural behavior, as when solipsists commune with their fellows, or when Mrs. Ladd-Franklin, solipsist by logical conviction, writes to Bertrand Russell expressing "surprise that there are not more of us." It is further inconsistent with its own assumptions. For the proposition "I am incurably alone" implies that I know what being-alone is contrasted with: the proposition is significant only if I know what it would be to be not-alone. But if I were constitutionally alone I would be unaware of that fact, having no conception of the opposing condition of being. Leibniz must get mentally out of his monadic window and circulate among the monads in order to know that none of them, including his own, has windows! In brief, no one can speak or think universally of the monads unless monadism is a fallacy. To take Descartes literally is thus, in the end, to break with Descartes.

But shall the break be a simple repudiation, or shall it be by way of a more incisive logic?

For the most part, philosophy at the turn of the century acted by repudiation, and the substitution of alternative theories of knowledge. Henri Bergson reinstated "intuition" (1903) as a cognitive resource, able to "coincide" with its objects, including other selves and the semipurposive *élan vital*. This cures solipsism in a convincing way, since Bergson's intuition is every man's intuition made systematic and responsible, and the cure is valid. But since it acts by *force majeure*, i.e., by simply endowing one cognitive function with the power of self-transcendence (as the older dogmatic realisms did for all cognitive functions), the intellectual problem remains unsolved; and Bergson, by disqualifying the "intellect" in metaphysics, waived the effort to solve it.[3]

The second and affirmative step in the overcoming of solipsism remained to be taken. It depended on a consideration closely following the first step; namely, that since we do have the conception of aloneness, it must also be true that we have the conception of not-aloneness; and that conception we could not get by solitary imagination—the materials of a solitary experience do not provide the right kind of otherness to construct the idea of other-mind. The conception of companionship is possible only if there is somewhere the actual experience thereof. *Solipsism is overcome, and only overcome when I can point out the actual experience* which gives me the basis of my conception of companionship. There must be such an experience of other-mind-present, not reducible to an I-think-enjoying-a-pantomime-companionship. The problem is to identify this experience beyond possible recapture by my all-embracing subjectivity.

The quest has its difficulties. Minds are not perceivable as are the bodies to which we attribute mentality. Our voluminous and skillful intercourse with our fellows is developed on the basis of an immensely successful hypothesis that such-and-such visible and tangible objects are *signs* of mentality-and-purpose: the hypothesis of signs implies a prior idea of other-mind-expressing-itself-by-signs. What we are interested in is *the origin of that prior* idea—an idea for which there could be no corresponding sensation. It must be present very early, for infants appear to use it; and if truly intersubjective, then pervasive, and like all continuous experiences almost evanescent. We must be prepared to think that it has no determinate beginning; that each one is always consciously participating in the life of an Other, inseparable from his own sense of being, even on the preconceptual level of bodily awareness. How can such an experience be traced or identified?

We are helped by recalling, what we have already observed, that Descartes, in singling out the I-think as the fulcrum of his lever, has left us with an unfinished expression. There is no I-think (period). It is always I-think (something). An empty mind is not even idly contemplative: the vacant mind is simply nonexistent. If the premise is *cogito nihil*, the inference has to be *ergo non sum*—an inference which the ego would be in no position to draw!

I do not mean to say that Descartes' omission of the something-thought-about was an oversight. Finding that he could doubt the existence of whatever object, and as his *chef d'oeuvre* of doubt that of the world itself, he felt free to concentrate his certitude of existence on the thinking process. Not dismissing stuff-thought-about, he was simply suspending the attribution of existence to that stuff, precisely as Husserl has done in his *epoché*. But if it is granted that my empirical existence depends on a continuous I-think-something-empirical (presumably with a rill of sense data at the base of it), I can only be sure I exist if something (else) exists also. In order to be valid the Cartesian certitude requires to be enlarged: *cogito aliquid ergo sum, et aliquid est:* I think something, therefore I exist, and something (else) exists. It still remains true that my thinking involves my existence; the point is, it involves more.

Indeed, the proposition that I can doubt the existence of every object of thought is a fallacy. For to doubt existence is to know what it is that I doubt—I must know what I mean by the existence of the object. And I can know this only if there is a knowable difference between the existent and the nonexistent object, in which case it would be impossible to doubt the existence of objects presenting the known criterion. The doubt is thus either meaningless or self-defeating.

We arrive at the position—not without a suggestion of paradox—that something of the not-self is essential to the existence of the self. The matter becomes clear when we consider what we mean by sense data. Data are things given; and what is being "given" is in transit from an outer source to a receiver—only in this case what is given is not a detachable commodity, it is an essential factor in the being of the receiver. That is what "experiencing" literally is—a process in which the not-self is continuously becoming self. In the incessant rill of the empirical strand of living, always including sensation, the self is being *sustained in being*. To that extent we may say it is *being created*.[4]

We might now take it as a self-evident proposition that *whatever creates a self can only be a self.* We should then have arrived at our goal. Our empirical receptiveness to the sensed world is something more crucial and inward than an observing of variegated qualities out-there: it is also a receiving of my own life from a life-giving entity, which can by no stretch of imagination be a physical "stimulus" and nothing more. It is not a causing; it is a communicating; it is the primitive Thou-experience. The causal account of perception, valid and necessary as accounting for relationships among sense data, ceases to be remotely plausible as the essence of the transaction.[5]

Appeal to Immediate Experience

But dispensing with further argument, let me now rather seek to evoke in the reader that awareness which must be the final evidence of our result. For what we are here asserting is an element in the experience of every person: it must be verifiable there.

We do not ordinarily consider the world we perceive as an activity upon ourselves. We perceive it as a *simple thereness* of the sense-presented expanse. And there is no I-think in the picture. We can go all the way with Hume, who discovers no "self" among his impressions: by no possibility can the self be a sense object. To catch a glimpse of one's self requires a shift of vision, a turn which we call "reflexion." One can always make this turn, and always find the I-think on duty; especially when I am in doubt as to what I see, or am challenged. "I saw an airplane." You doubt it? *"I think* I saw one"; I retreat to the asylum of certitude. Or "What is this I see? I think it's a far-off plane—it may be a bird"; I ask your corroboration.

The same turn that brings the I-think into the picture brings also the sharableness: the simple thereness is already *common* experience, common receptivity toward an intersubjective action. Yet as action it is wholly different from any activity I might perceive in the field of thereness: it is silent, unrelenting, with no insistence on change, more like a firm pressure-of-being from the unnamed, unvocal, nonintrusive Other. I recognize it as the will of another self, a purposive selfhood, purposing among other things the being of this I-think. It is the Thou-art, immediately experienced as such.

Even so, the Thou-art is not salient. In its aboriginal form, it is a constant vital fact, beneath the level of concepts: it may be intrauterine as a vague awareness of dependent being, with an equally vague possibility of address-of-discomfort to the surrounding universe. But there is a point at which this locus-of-address becomes distinct and recognizable:

"Experiencing," as a rule, while we receive what is given, is also an activity on our own part—an activity of attention, more or less awake and alert. This activity is so far spontaneous that we do not associate it with a sense of effort. There arises, however, in the course of conscious development, an issue of free effort in dealing with what is given. Sense data by themselves constitute no "world." There are two ways of taking them. We may steep ourselves in their immediate quality for the purely aesthetic enjoyment of that quality—the incipient epicure or artist in all human nature. Or we may, with an effort of thought, work them into patterns of "object" and "event" which move toward responsible living, in the end to science itself. Descartes in his view of the I-think raises no issue of this effort—his broad expression includes the whole range of sensing, feeling, willing, et cetera, as well as the intentional "thinking" involved in forming a coherent world picture. What, I now ask, is your incentive for this effort to think a world?

It is—and here I venture like Descartes, but with better justification, to interpret your experience for you—it is something like *an intimation of your destined way of living*. The world I *think*, as distinct from the nonworld I *sense*, is a range of experience sharable with others. If I am to live as my *élan vital* spurs me to live, I must live in a field of experience not mine alone. But my first note-of-call is not from these many unidentified fellows: it is from the inner source of the sense-presented expanse, with which source I am aware of a certain kinship. My impulse to live by thinking, rather than by sensing alone, is a *response* to a felt purposiveness of the real with which in experience I have to do. It is akin to that sense of duty, which to Kant was our most direct approach to being-in-itself. But it is a wider thing. It is the apprehension of a way of life that Life assigns me; it is a sort of compass needle toward self-fulfillment and duty at once, in one urge of will direction. If there is in it a sense of the right of the universe against me, commonly called "duty," there is equally a sense of my right as against the universe that has thrust life upon me: if there is any obligation at all, it is reciprocal. And both senses imply the prior awareness that the source of things is a Thou—a Being fit on the one hand to receive my note of protest where protest is due, and on the other hand to pervade my living with a sense of expected performance.

For Kant, the primary and inescapable reality of duty is the source of our postulate of God. In this order of things, the actualities of experience are reversed. Unless there is first a known being to whom duty can be due, there *can be no duty*. And there is more than duty, more than reciprocal duty, in the actual situation. There is, as I shall later emphasize, an element of faith-in-opportunity; a hopeful launching out on the effort to achieve the costly happiness of becoming what I am destined to become. All this is wrapped up in the spontaneous impulsive summoning of one's will-to-think, the simplest and most general *response* to the presence in experience of the universal Other-mind.

The strength and persistence of that response is seen in the corporate and historic edifice we call "science," a building surely not made with hands. This building testifies to the assurance whereby our monadic worlds are known as one world; and whereby the lonely experimenter, wherever he is, knows his discovered truth as unquestionably a truth for every man.

With this assurance, verified in experience because arising there, we have passed beyond modernity into the post-modern era.

[...]

NOTES

1. See, for example, Roscoe Pound, *Introduction to Philosophy of Law*, 92–99. Without yielding the field to nineteenth-century social utilitarianism, Dean Pound credits it with "compelling us to give over the ambiguous term 'right.'" His own substitute is derived from the normal expectancies within a given civilization.
2. I have discussed this point at length in "Marcel and the Ground Issues of Metaphysics," *Philosophy and Phenomenological Research*, June 1954, 447 ff.

3. The resurgent realisms of this period followed in the main the path of repudiation, asserting a natural power of self-transcendence in human knowledge, and rejecting extant attempts to express the "objectivity" of the natural world as a domain of thought or (with Royce) of purpose. Royce and others in America and Simmel in Berlin felt more definitely responsible for the underlying problem, how any awareness of a mind-not-one's-own is possible. The answers tended, as in the metaphysic of Kant, to shift from the rational to the moral: the other mind is a being we *ought to acknowledge*, not aspire to experience. Whitehead was later to offer the most radical repudiation of solipsism, by quietly discarding the entire causal account of perception (of which subjectivism is an inescapable corollary), in favor of a theory of "prehensions" involving direct other-awareness.

    Meantime Husserl, in Gottingen, with the utmost logical care and scruple, had opened his campaign against one aspect of subjectivism, *Psychologismus,* making salient the "intentional" factors of thinking, and invoking *"Wesensschau,"* a perceiving of concepts, to guarantee their validity. This analysis remained interior to the Cartesian I-think; it was, as he later called it, "egological." It was not until his Parisian Lectures of 1929 that he explicitly faced the issue of solipsism, and reached a position which he described (with a precise ambiguity) as "monadological intersubjectivity" *(Husserliana,* I, 121 *et passim,* 1950). Solution incomplete.

4. "However vigorous the impetus of advance-weaving on the part of my ideas (my active expectations of experience just ahead)... my own activity always accepts the irruptive (sense-) material as its own authority and completion. Toward that outer reality I hold myself as toward that which sustains me from moment to moment in my present being. Is not that outer activity then essentially creative... creative of *me?*" *The Meaning of God in Human Experience,* 286 f.

    We may recall in this connection a speculation of Descartes to the effect that God does not create once and then leave his world to itself, but that he re-creates the world from moment to moment. In a similar sense, the constancy of the empirical contribution to the mental being of the receiver is a reiterated creation.

5. The causal theory of perception terminates strictly speaking in brain processes, not in perception. These brain events, if they could present worlds at all, would present as many private worlds as there are private brains. The terminus of the theory is thus inconsistent with its starting point in the common physical world, even if we forget the now widely recognized necessity of assuming a miracle to translate brain event into perception; and this scandal remains unremoved. The theory, useful for relationships, is bankrupt as an account of perception.

CHAPTER 6

The Human Will

I

When Hobbes traced the roots of the state in human nature to a "pursuit of power after power that ceaseth only in death," he made it clear that the desire for power is not a separate interest, one among many, but an adjunct to all the specific desires. It is the way of less circumspect animals to follow the hint of each hunger as it arises: it is the way of man to consider his desires as a whole, expect their recurrence, and seek that which will "ensure forever the way of his future desire," namely, power. Power, for Hobbes, is but an abstract name for the condition of being in command of resources, the energies of nature, the capacities of one's own mind and body, the like abilities of fellow men, so that whatever foreseen or unforeseen thing the possessor may wish to accomplish, that he can do. Power is the means to every end.

But as nature arranges our impulses, that which is a means to various ends is likely to appear as an end in itself, the object of a specific interest. Food is such a means to all organic ends; a separate hunger presides over food-getting, we seek food for its own sake. Vision serves almost every activity: but nature does not limit sight to what is thus useful—it supplies the full field and makes the satisfaction of sight an independent good. So of the interest in power: it is not left to the intelligent calculations of prudence. In the higher animals it appears, in some form, as the object of a distinct instinctive interest. To have a store of nuts, ensuring "the way of his future desire" to eat, is a condition so far satisfactory in itself to the squirrel that he hoards far beyond the possibility of consumption.

To the human being, however, having power of this and other kinds is still more significant. To be in control of forces and to know himself in control is a *right status* for him, a status in which he feels himself in the line of his destiny. To be powerless is, so far, to fail of being human. Obversely, to live as a human being is to possess and use energy, to have the science of the powers of the world and to ride them, to be able to do and to make without assignable limit. There is an instinctive trait at the root of that part of the story of the Garden in which man was given authority over the rest of creation: every animal assumes control of his own prey, but man assumes that even the hidden springs of natural and supernatural power are to be subject to him. Man alone is the masterer of fire, the magician, the explorer, the domesticator and breeder, the scientist, the delver into the secrets of the gods, the

---

From MATS, 308–324.

being that finds a premonitory delight in probing the sources of his own terrors and pains. The will to live, in man, takes the form of the will to power, i.e., the will to be in conscious knowing control of such energies as the universe has, and to work with them in reshaping that universe.

Thus understood, the quest of power is not merely in the interest of other needs, nor is it merely a search for another independent satisfaction. Power *is an element in the good which all instincts seek*. Man does not seek power merely that he may continue to eat: he eats that he may have power; and the mere pleasure of eating is far more than a gustatory satisfaction,—it is the satisfaction of passing from relative weakness to relative potency. He seeks power in the form of wealth, an abstract symbol for the mastery of nature; and this impulse which we call 'economic' is peculiarly human, because it means that all instincts have material conditions for their satisfaction, and that these material conditions have been reduced to a common denominator and made subject to a single effort so that a thousand commands are contained in one. But he does not seek economic power merely that he may have what wealth will buy; he regards—and in spite of all the criticism of the ages directed at the man who forgets the end in the means, he rightly regards—economic success as itself a victory. There is no economic instinct, but the interest in the rational control of the material conditions of life gains its profound strength from the will to power. The social instinct, in all its forms, has in it a promise of power: for it leads men, as we have noticed, to the right mounting and full use of their mental forces,—out of society man feels his best gifts wasted. I do not say that one seeks the company of his kind because he wishes to be powerful, as if being powerful were something else than being companioned: my point is that being companioned is, *ipso facto*, being in fuller power, having the peculiar leverages of a human being.

The quest of power in this wide sense we may take, then, as an instinct which is in all instincts, the fundamental instinct of the human kind. Power *per se* is not the *summum bonum:* no one could be satisfied merely by swelling in power and using this abstraction without regard to what is achieved. But power is an inseparable ingredient of the human good, and so of whatever is desirable. Pleasure itself implies the consumption of energy, hence the possession of energy. And that more powerful concern for *reality*, which leads men to hold pleasure as secondary in worth, and even to seek pain,[1] impels the human being not alone to know what powers are in his world, and to regard such knowledge as a power, but to incorporate in himself such powers as fit him to deal with those external powers. The will to be real is one with the will to be a power among powers.

It is an error to take the phrase, "the will to power," as naming something already defined and understood, and especially as having some affiliation with arrogance, competitive selfishness, or Tower-of-Babel ambition.[2] We are using it to designate a fact prior to all ethical quality, as a name for the vital impetus itself, and as a tentative and inadequate name, whose significance is the deepest problem of self-consciousness. We have the craving for potency: life is the process of learning what this craving means, in terms of the concrete program of living: only experience can instruct us in what ways this will to power can find its fitting satisfaction. The race and the individual experiment with many partially false interpretations of what they want, in the course of finding a true interpretation: we propose now to follow—in a mythically simplified fashion—the course of the typical development of the will to power in individual life, noting how the major instincts are inserted in it. And in the course of this development we shall find the psychological foundation of the state. For the state exists for the satisfaction, not of particular needs or impulses, but of the whole man. Sociability and economic pressure are disqualified for this role by the simple fact that they are partial aspects of human nature, derivatives of the will to power.

II

The instinct of infancy is dominated by impulses making for nutrition, growth, and the building of primary habits, i.e., for power in the biological arena. It adopts from the first, as its natural relation to the outer world, the assumption that this outer reality is there to serve *me*. This outer world is taken as addressable and to this extent personal; and further, as so far concerned in the well-being of the new self as to be subject to appeal, demand, expostulation. From the first cry, the growing will shows itself disposed to exercise these social powers, as ministering to the dominant craving which makes for growth in organic capacity and control.

This primitive claim-staking on the part of the budding will normally meets with a response which encourages its assumptions. The world does in fact serve it. Under this favoring sky the will strikes a sturdy affirmative root, and childhood is commonly launched upon a second stage, an *era of violence*, in which psychologists are inclined to detect the instincts of 'self-assertion' and 'pugnacity,' evident derivatives of the will to power. The body is the immediate organ of the will: if the non-ego is hesitant, recalcitrant, or hostile, one makes use of this organ to produce compliance. Crude self-assertion of this sort has its successes and its failures; and in both cases it brings something the will does not want. No social instruction can save the incipient will from these experiences, and its inferences from them, the dialectic of pugnacity.[3] It must discover through adopting a too thoroughgoing antagonism that the destruction of intercourse is beyond its intention; and that laying aside the excesses of wrath presents difficulties, the more when one has been successful than when one has failed, since the other is a will also and makes its own conditions of amiability. In those smaller groups where the social impulse is keenest, one learns to revise one's will to power in some way so that the other will is included in its scope.

From the standpoint of the purely self-interested will a condition of hostility is one of subtracted power, a condition of amity one of added power. Further, persistent hatred is a rapid consumer of energy. Self-assertion is thus defeated by its more belligerent successes, and without altering its egoistic bent gropes its way to a *non-competitive* mode of expression, so that while reaching its own ends, the ends of others can likewise be forwarded. The era of violence gives way to an *era of ambition:* one seeks a role in which one fits with others, lives on good terms with them, and still leads, commands, and plays the hero.

Thus boyhood has usually its period of *conceit,* an imaginative and *a priori* sentiment toward self as possessed of distinguished power. This is a disease of favorable omen, implying as it does a readiness to assume responsibility and toil, and a certain acceptance of the standards of those in whose eyes one proposes to shine. Conceit concedes the authority of the invisible rulers. And the belief that one can do much is, within bounds, a favorable atmosphere for achieving something: it is normal and fortunate that the endless difficulties of our undertakings disclose themselves only after we are deeply committed. Hence conceit in the growing boy, like *vanity*, a similar pride of power in the growing girl, is one of the most forgivable because auspicious of faults.

This period and the following are often times of great mental suffering because of the suspicion of inferiority or ineffectiveness. Only a being conscious of the right of power could suffer so much from such a cause. Shyness is usually an evidence of strong self-regard which feels a lack of the current means for making its worth *tell* socially. It is the reverse of an 'inferiority complex' with which it is often confused. But both types of embarrassment are signs of the same healthy will which is destined to find its outlet as it finds its appropriate language.

In ambition and in vanity, the imagination is still so far competitive as to be grandiose or romantic, positing oneself spontaneously in the leading roles. But meantime another strand of human instinct has been ripening, destined at adolescence to merge with the self-promoting form of will to power. The tendency to *nurture* or to *lend aid,* sometimes identified by psychologists as the 'parental instinct,' but present from very early years, begins to modify one's attitude not only to the 'little,' the favorite object of childish tendance, but to the living environment at large as an always helpable object. A capacity for deliberate altruism cannot exist until there is a capacity for deliberate selfishness; but the discovered satisfaction of the nurturing instinct, a form of exercising power which normally leaves the will of the aided person free, has won by the time of adolescence a sufficient place to mitigate those types of ambition which subordinate the other will. Power *for* one's neighbors competes in interest with power *over* them. The egoism of sex impulse, itself a field of mysterious powers conscious and subconscious, is steadied by protective impulses. The conceit of leadership is less insistent on one-way domination, more willing to share control and admit a mutuality of superior gifts. The growing will is prepared for independent activity as a social being.

The social world into which the maturing will now enters, on its own account, is a mode of life governed by ideas. That is, there is a characteristic way of doing everything one has to do, from planting a field to courting a wife, from entering a college to calling a physician or getting a job; these customs, laws, economic systems, institutions, have to be *thought* in order to be lived in. And because ideas enter so deeply into its constitution, none of its forms are final; it is vulnerable to new and better ideas; it is continually being disturbed by them. And these new ideas are continually being fought, trimmed, assimilated, built into institutions where they in turn contest the place with their successors. It is a world in which all forms of power play; but in which all forms of power are subject to the power of ideas.

This world is destined to initiate the newcomer into a further form of the will to power, namely *power through ideas*. For while he enters it as a learner, an apprentice, no living mind can exist long in such a structure without rethinking it; he will have ideas of his own: except for the impossible case of finding it perfect, one's new power begins with his noting of defects, and from criticism he passes to proposals for alteration. He tries to build his idea into his society; he finds it resisted, he finds that he has something to do; and he finds that in doing it his will breathes in all its cells as if it had found more completely than before what it wants and why it exists.

And he finds, further, that in so far as he wins power through his ideas, power-over men becomes completely merged with power-for them. For an idea can gain control only by being understood by others, being rethought by them, becoming their property; to win control through an idea is in the same moment to become a servant. It is this notion of a completely mutual and non-competitive power which, escaping the notice of Hobbes and of Nietzsche, left their interpretations of human nature truncated, and of political life distorted, by the unresolved notions of domination, exploitation, and invidious class-distinction. In competitive types of power, the more one has, the less others have; in the case of power through ideas, the more one has, the more everyone has.

In the form of the will to power through ideas the will reaches its maturity; but it has further experiences to meet which may modify its conception of its aim.

Every man knows intuitively that power of this personal variety is what he wants; but this knowledge gives him no certainty as to which of his ideas or qualities fully deserves to attain power. He has his convictions,—they clash with the convictions of others; he revises his own views; he learns to distrust self-consciousness as a guide to what is most valid in his thinking. It is well enough to have the will to serve; but one may not insist on serving in his own way.

One's 'idea' is, after all, not this or that fragmentary fancy; his idea is another name for himself. And this substantial and central idea is conveyed somehow in every deed, yet never wholly visible to the owner. One must either wait for the free appraisal of others, or else find some super-social sanction for his belief which gives him the certainty of a prophet, and makes its promulgation a duty.[4] The art of subordinating the personal and conscious in one's thought to the super-personal and relatively subconscious is one which must be painfully learned; and in this discipline, the will to power is purged of the last strain of self-assertive presumption.

For the will to power must suffer its disillusionment, and not seldom its tragic transformation. It must make its reckoning not alone with external evil, obduracy, chance, but with its own limitation, untimeliness, mistake. And as individuals vary, their reading of the outcome of such experiences will vary, and no type-picture can be anything but inept.

Some, oppressed by the incommensurableness between individual powers and historic tasks, suspicious of all conscious plans for changing the face of the world, retreat into a subjective existence. This may take the form of melancholy aloofness and nerveless pessimism toward action. It may lay hold of the Stoic distinction between the things in our power and the things not in our power, and retire with Boëthius into the citadel of self-command and the routine of duty. Or it may take the form of abandoning the effort toward a unitary object of will, relaxing into that immediacy of pleasure-tasting or the cult of individual 'expression' from which the will to power was destined to save us by directing our energies outward.

Some seek an other-worldly treasure, whose earthly aspect is that of power through sacrifice and loss, and the abandonment of worldly ambition. And still others reject the whole conception of power as inevitably contaminated with the quality of self-assertiveness, and seek to replace it with some form of the love for mankind.

Some of these ways of reckoning with a disillusioned will to power, notably the last, represent simply the choice of another name for the same thing. The will to power through ideas implies the love and service of mankind.

Others, however, in trying to omit something from the too great demands of ambition, surrender some element which cannot be omitted from the good which the human will necessarily seeks, and which therefore reasserts itself. Thus, the altruist who wills the social weal and not his own, still desires something more than the social weal, namely, that this weal shall be forwarded *by his efforts*, apart from which his own excuse for existence would vanish. The world-fleer does not wholly transplant his treasure; for he still hopes that his view of other-worldly good will be transmitted to other minds of this world, and become a leaven which will transform human society. Whatever one's final philosophy, it can never be held as a purely private result: as a supposed body of truth about the living world, there is inseparable from it the impulse to knead it into the self-consciousness of that world,—a refinement, but not a surrender, of the will to power. All life has the self-propagating impulse; and when life takes the form of a person, self-propagation means incorporating in history that mode of seeing things which is at first unique in the person.

Universalize thy maxim is the Kantian imperative of duty. Universalize thyself in thy effect is the inescapable imperative of happiness, or of the satisfaction of will.

And in all alike, the will still strives for *permanence of effect*. As a biological being, man takes satisfaction in the continuance of his tribe: the promise that allures him is that his seed shall possess the land forever. As an active being, he wins his happiness in deeds and structures that have the quality of durability:—who does not remember with peculiar satisfaction the first piece of work of which he could say "This will last?" As a thinking being, man wills that a thought shall be lodged by him in the working currents of futurity.

In Plato's analysis of the will, all desires are forms of love, and all love is a form of the quest for immortality through propagation of the spiritual essence. A literal immortality in human history the individual person cannot have: but an immortality of effect, of the reproduced self, can be gained, and possibly, in some degree, always is gained.

For this definition of the object of human will does not imply, as our defective discussion suggests, the conspicuous performances of exceptional men. It implies no more than is logically contained in the desire to count for something, to be worth keeping alive as a human personality. Whiting Williams, whose study of the minds of workingmen is in the best sense empirical, thus sums up his psychology: "As a practical simplification of the instinct-theory, our thesis proposes that the motivating purpose of all of us is our desire to establish and to enjoy the feeling of our worth as a person among other persons."[5] And if this worth-while-ness or counting-for-something is not illusory, it carries positive consequences which transmit their own kind, and so persist. The conspicuous elements of history are but enlarged symbols of common experience. In some degree of clarity, a concrete or historic immortality is the unabandonable goal of the will: it is what all men most deeply desire, so far as the will can be fulfilled in human existence.

But even if the disillusionments of experience could lead men in their later years to resign their claim upon the fully human good, that claim would still be renewed by each succeeding generation. And thus the race will be held to the effort to set up such conditions as will make its fulfillment possible. What are these conditions?

III

We are asking how it is possible for men to satisfy their wills. This is the same as to ask how they can attain what they most want, or how they can reach "the highest good"; only, we are not picturing this good as any final achievement or lump sum of happiness to be obtained at some particular culminating moment; but rather as a steady report of living to consciousness, to the effect that one is rightly placed, is counting as a human being, is changing things in the direction in which they need to be changed and will stay changed, so that in one's own way one is altering the universe *for good*. This awareness of power may be like that of the oarsman who in rowing with his crew is aware at each stroke of adding to the way of the boat; or it may be like that of the scientist who pushes a step farther into a standing puzzle of nature, or of some contemplative mind that deepens its hold on the meaning of things. It is the nature of power not to be captured once for all but to grow and to continue; but our question is, how any such power as we have described is possible at all.

It goes without saying that there are some things an individual must do for himself, if his will is to be satisfied. Happiness must be tried for, and tried for intelligently. The will to power can easily be defeated by unfitness or untimeliness of performance, due to lack of self-knowledge or to ignorance of the world as it is.

Accordingly one must do, and submit to, what is necessary to 'find oneself,' i.e., to learn what one's powers are: one must keep alive his contacts with his fellows, making them significant, not numerous; one must welcome criticism, lend himself to the process of trial and error, avoid pretence and fear illusion,—at all costs be real. One must try for self-mastery in respect to his scattering impulses and his technique of habit; and for a quick sensitiveness to the truth of values, about which all life aligns itself. And first of all, one must keep alive his inherent ambition, regarding that as the metaphysical requirement within him, and therewith the faith that happiness is possible for him.

These are the things each one must do for himself. They are demands, certain of which are included in the moral law, and certain others in the maxims of worldly wisdom. We may sum them up as one's *duty*, in the sense in which duty is the price of happiness paid in advance.

But there are other conditions which no individual can supply for himself.

Clearly, no individual can provide the permanence of his own effect. He can aim and cast his missile; but once it has left his hand its course is the business of the rest of the universe. If his work is to endure, one necessary condition is that it shall fall into a context which can supplement his transiency with its own durability. And what is not less important, relieve him of the dread of hopeless relativity in action, of treadmill or meaningless circular performance, by its own persistence of direction in time.

Again, no individual can provide himself with sufficient knowledge, either of himself or of his world. It is not complete knowledge that is required; for the deed that is to last need not be in any absolute sense a perfect deed—the phrase has no certain meaning: it need only be what the situation requires; and individual experience gropes its way to such fitness of action by slow degrees. But society must help in the achievement of the insight that is to improve society. Adequate self-judgment and adequate assessment of the context into which an event is to fall, require induction into an over-individual stock of wisdom.

Finally, the best judged deed, if it is to have its due effect, must be received fairly and on its merits. It may fail through lack of a hearing, or ill luck, or prejudice, or a hundred other mischances. It may fail through falling into a too well-satisfied society: in primitive and unprogressive communities men behave as though everything were already found out,—it is precisely in those places where men have most to gain through new ideas that new ideas are least welcome, and personality most nearly meaningless. Nothing short of a world of persons can completely secure the field for any new person, persons reasonably discontent, uncommitted, hopeful, and disposed to listen to *him*. But the best idea can only be sure of its due reception in proportion as the wilder hazards are eliminated and impersonal tests of performance established in society.

These, then, are the conditions beyond individual control necessary to the satisfaction of the will to power in history: a permanent order, an available storehouse of acquired wisdom, the conquest of disorder by peace, and of chance by impersonal reason and justice.

Note, too, that unless these conditions are secured, duty itself is weakened and tends to disappear. And especially that fundamental duty of keeping ambition alive. For the will to try is dependent on the worth of trying; ambition can be considered a requirement of the universe only if the universe somehow provides the conditions for fulfilling it which the individual cannot provide for himself. Without these conditions—let us call them objective conditions—duty, and therewith personality, would be stunted at its source.

And what are these but the conditions which the state exists to provide?

NOTES

1. Cf. Yrjö Hirn, *Origins of Art*, ch. v. S. Freud, *Beyond the Pleasure Principle*.
2. Though the fact that presumption, pride, *ubris*, *superba*, have been regarded as the chief of sins by the most enlightened nations strongly suggests that they represent a corruption of man's distinguishing excellence.
3. For the general theory of the dialectic of the will and a further discussion of the dialectic of pugnacity, see the author's *Human Nature and Its Remaking*, chs. xxiii, xxiv.
4. Cf. *The Meaning of God in Human Experience*, ch. xxxi, "The prophetic consciousness."
5. *Mainsprings of Men*, p. 147.

CHAPTER 7A

The Knowledge of Other Minds Than Our Own

Our enquiry into the knowledge of God has led to this as the central issue: whether in the midst of experiences of Nature and of human extremity, using these in some way as mediators, there can be a veritable experience of infinite Spirit other than myself. We do not mitigate the difficulty of this question by pointing out that the knowledge of any other minds than our own, even in plain human intercourse, has its difficulties also. But in so far as the difficulties are similar, it will be an advantage to bring them together,—the more so since, in spite of any difficulties of theory, we believe our experiences of our fellow's minds to be real,—neither illusory nor simply working-hypotheses.

All the (substantive) objects of human attention and experience may be put into three fundamental classes: the physical objects, which with their relations we sum up as Nature; the psychical objects, which with their relations we sum up as Self; and the social objects, or other minds, which with their relations we sum up as Society, or still more comprehensively, as our Spiritual World, ourselves being included. These classes of objects seem clearly distinguishable; not mixing nor blending at their borders—when I mean another mind I distinctly do not mean either my own mind or a physical thing. Each has its own science—physics, etc., psychology, sociology. And each has its own organ of perception.

But no. We have an *outer sense,* says Locke, for things of nature; we have an *inner sense* for things of our own minds, our thoughts and feelings; but Locke mentions *no sense* by which we can discern another mind. And neither, be it said, does any later philosopher. Sociologists speak of "the social sense," social instincts, "consciousness of kind," and the like; but these practical designations are not intended to name an actual organ of knowledge differentiated for perception of other minds. *We have no such organ.* Sociology is an extended psychology, made possible by the fact that Society, as we noted, includes Self,—is built up really of psychical objects, and from the center outward, by help of ideas which work well in practice: other theory than this of social experience we shall not find in the Books. This third class of objects is, by some strange device, made knowable without a special perceptive organ:—or, perhaps we are mistaken in assuming it literally knowable.

From MGHE, 241–254.

This absence of a perceptive organ makes it probable that we are mistaken: it suggests that our social knowledge is built on hypothesis, and not at all on experience. It compels us to examine our so-called social experience directly, to see whether we can find any point of actually present and certain knowledge of another mind. Such an examination yields little that is satisfying. What I do directly experience is the physical presence of the other person; and his expressive signs and language, which are also physical. From these I infer his reality, and nothing in experience tends to shake that hypothesis; everything confirms it. What I have, then, is a perfect hypothesis. For all practical purposes, I am as certain of my social environment as I am of my physical environment: indeed, the reality of this social world of mine is the last thing I should doubt. The practical certainties here are unshakable. But if you ask for more than practical certainty; if you require a genuine social experience, in the literal sense of the word experience, I am at a loss to discover it. I am inclined to think there is no such thing.

And I must acknowledge that even this sense of practical certainty does sometimes desert me. My social consciousness is subject to extraordinary fluctuations; my sense of the presence of other souls comes and goes in an unaccountable way; it flits in its substantiality from one extreme to the other, much as does my belief in God. When I seek to grasp it, it eludes me.

There are times when my consciousness is burdensomely public, and not my own; when the social world is all too real and immediate; when I can find no seclusion in my thoughts, no privacy even behind barred doors. At such times, I can get no hold on myself, because of the incessant pressure of the other men in me, voices, postures, beliefs that pursue me and harry away all risings of individuality on the part of my self. I escape into the wilderness, and Nature becomes a chorus—there is no shape which may not take on animation—even the stones may sermonize. And yet at other times, if I deliberately *seek* contact with that world of other mind, an oppressive solitude cloaks me in. I bury myself in the rush of men; but am no better able to bridge chasms, or reach vitality of give-and-take with them. I make designs against my neighbor, I hunt him to his secret castle, I hold him at the point of my sword, I seize him bodily—he vanishes, and I have nothing. I cannot make him open himself to me; I cannot so much as open myself to him: I am a prisoner, and without ability to find where I am bound. I see that the doctrine of *monads* is no futile myth.

Such is my current social experience so-called, and it seems clear to me that if there were any absolute certainty in it, these variations would not occur. That which at times may so escape me can hardly be an empirically given presence.

Then I reflect that in the nature of the case it could hardly be otherwise: the other mind must be beyond my powers of direct experience. It can be no object of sensation, because it is not a physical thing. It must be such as I am, a thinker of its objects, not an object among objects; and as such thinker, or *subject*, it can only be *thought*, not sensed. That which makes him himself, and other-than-me, is (by definition) the fact that his thoughts are not my thoughts; so long as he remains other-than-me, his thoughts can never become identically mine, though I may conjecture them and approximately think them *after him*. Of myself, I find, and desire, an infinite thought-fund inaccessible to others, and inaccessible through all finite times to myself; it cannot be otherwise with him—he has in him an infinitude of character, only gradually developed and *made general*—infinitude at which I may only guess. Souls, by their own nature, cannot touch each other; cannot experience each other: their relations do not rise to the point of *knowledge*, they remain excursions, adventures, hypotheses, wonderfully sustained by their results, but none the less, launches from solitude in the direction of an assumed reality; which reality, if it exists, is no less solitary.

I look down from a cliff upon a beach below; the black fleck wandering there excites in me the consciousness of fellow-being: I turn away with the impression that there has been in my life a social event, an experience of another mind. But I have *verified* nothing. And if I climb down and discover that object to be in fact a human shape, what have I now verified? A physical object,—nothing more. What made that glance from above more than physically significant was clearly a contribution from within. In Kantian phrase, I had imposed this *concept* upon the appearance; I had *begriffen* it that way, and my own Begriff gave me the only sociality I experienced,—all that in fact I ever can experience.

There are more intimate relations, and less intimate relations: more work, or less, for my Begriff-social to do—but what my Begriff is *given* to work upon, as actual stuff of experience, is the *body*. Body of man and Nature—nothing more. When that body disappears, even though the other spirit persists, all that *I have* of him is gone. I have no organ for the experience of other mind; by the nature of other-mind, I could have none.

I would press the logic of this situation, if I were able, until we should cry out that it is a lie, whether or not we see *how* it is false; and that any philosophy which ends in such a situation is impossible. Human communications must be at bottom as real as we think them to be—no intricate, successful, solitary *pantomime* of each with himself and Body.

And then I would urge that we are not quit of this logic by crying out against it; and resolving for our part to treat our world *as if* we were in direct conscious relations with our fellows. For that attitude of common-sense-resolve is precisely the subjective, solipsistic sort of philosophy which we have just denounced. Logic here is the sole remaining bond of genuine mutuality among men; and if we will not patiently earn our conscious right to our fellows, we must likewise forgo our conscious right to God. We cannot dispense with either.

The problem of our social consciousness is as old as Berkeley's idealism (old in fact as Leibniz or Descartes, but not felt before Berkeley as a primary demand on thinking); and since his time thinkers have not been allowed to forget it. It has become a stock spectre, especially for idealistic theories, to show that their logic must end in solipsism. Several ways to escape the logic of separate personality have been devised. We shall examine the most important of them.

One may seek to discover and formulate *infallible criteria* or signs, by which we may certainly know that we have before us another conscious being. This way out has its plausibility; for is it not the sight of other *bodies* and *expressive movements* like or analogous to our own which actually compels our judgment that another mind is here? Or, if we learn (as from Royce and Baldwin) that 'we rather interpret our own bodies by those of others, than the reverse; and if we find (by first steps in comparative psychology) that analogies soon fail as we try to test the consciousness of animals and plants; if we abandon, as we must, the whole argument from analogy as hopeless, certainly the psychology of our impulsive social *reactions* will reveal some reliable *stimuli*, whose presence infallibly indicates other mind. Are there not as Wundt suggests "manifestations of animal life which cannot be explained without the introduction of the mental factor?" Unfortunately there are none such; every physical change must and may be referred to a physical cause. There is no reason why "educability" itself may not be a property of matter.[1] Are there not in certain groupings of actions unmistakable "signs of choice"; or as James better states it, can we not recognize "the pursuit of ends with the choice of means?" Certainly all such signs as these do guide our social judgments. Even more than by strict planfulness ("pursuit of ends with choice of means") are we guided by a certain *playfulness* or superabundance in the apparent government of movements: signs of fluidity, eagerness, emotionality are more immediately compelling than signs of intelligent end-seeking. But after all, these are nothing but signs, physical signs; and explicit language which rises out of this aboriginal expressiveness is but a further set of physical signs, which nowhere rests on a veritable experience of other mind. If somewhere we could *begin* with an actual consciousness of the social object, all these criteria would help us amazingly to continue and subdivide our intercourse: it is always easier to determine what state of mind belongs with what set of actions than to determine whether there be any state of mind there or no. (Writhings of earthworm on fish-hook express discomfort, if they express *any* consciousness at all, which may be doubted.) Even if infallible criteria could be got—which is impossible—they would still do nothing to bring us nearer the other mind itself: for all such criteria are themselves physical.

A much more adequate way is that proposed by Professor Royce; his criteria are not physical, and do undoubtedly bring us near to an original experience of the other mind. "Our fellows are known to be real," says Royce, "because they are for each of us the endless treasury of more ideas.... (They) furnish us with the constantly needed supplement to our own fragmentary meanings."[2] To anything that appears in our life with the character of a *response*, we instinctively attribute outer personality. Not thunder in general, but thunder at a critical moment in our thinking, means that

Jove has spoken. If a distant signal moves in direct answer to our own signalings, we need see no human form to infer the presence of an outer consciousness. What infallibly convinces us is the experience that our own thought is carried on to further development (and without our own equivalent *effort*). The more completely and deeply the answering and supplementing idea caps and enters into our own train of development, the more inevitable the acknowledgment. And so we may build a series all the way from the opportune clap of thunder to the continuous successful intercourse with our fellow men, a series of increasing conviction of the reality of our social experience. When we have reached the stage of voluntarily *putting questions* to our environment, and expecting and receiving conceptual answers, our faith is complete. God is doubtless most real to that person who finds his prayers somehow responded to; for, to paraphrase Royce's criterion, *response* is our best ground for believing the social object real.

Upon this way of reaching the Other Mind, we must make the following comment. That we are still left with only an inference of that Other; a faith and not a knowledge in experience. Even though we say, with Royce, that reality is nothing else than response (or fulfilling of meaning), we have not so far as this criterion goes, found that reality personal save by probability of high order. We can still speak only of "the source of our *belief* in the reality of our fellow men,"[3] not of an experience of that reality itself. The relative passivity of our reception of idea from without is no invincible proof that it does come from another mind: men have been known to dream conversations which add to their knowledge; thinking itself often takes conversational shape, ourself being recipient; in all thinking the new comes to one as if from another. We shall have a difficult distinction to make between such inner development of our own meanings, and that development which we shall regard as hailing from a veritable Other Mind. But no type of inference, however direct and simple, can quite meet our requirement; for that which we must first *infer* is one step away from immediate experience.

Are we not driven, then, to a view which closely resembles that first supposition of ours that social experience is a *practical* certainty: that view namely which interprets the social experience as a moral affirmation, an *acknowledgment* which we *ought* to make, something of which no scientific or empirical knowledge is either possible or conceivable. As Professor Münsterberg puts it in his powerful chapter on "Die reine Erfahrung,"[4]—we do experience our fellow men, but even so as we immediately experience all reality, by acknowledging them real. I cannot doubt that the last mystery of mutual contact is contained in the will, rather than in the intellect; a thesis which we shall have later to consider.[5] But all will makes use of knowledge, prior or simultaneous. There is no human will that does not contain a nucleus of *knowledge* which is not our own act; and it is this that we wish to separate out.

All of these ways—by physical criterion, by response, and by acknowledgment—have a common presupposition. They all suppose the mind to be furnished in advance with an *idea* of an Other Mind. We are able to read our signs as we do, because we already expect them to mean something, we have already framed somehow the conception of another mind. Our world responds only in so far as we have our net hung out, confident that Other Mind will fill it with usable furtherings of our own thought: apart from this Other-Mind-meaning of ours, no event could take on the character of response. So also, if we are to *will*, or *postulate, or acknowledge*, the fellow-man, it is to be asked how, apart from previous idea, we know *what* to acknowledge. The conception of the fellow-man, somehow obtained, is necessary before my duty of acknowledging him can be performed, or understood. Beside which, there remains an ulterior question,—to Whom or to What do I owe this duty? I am inclined to think that *obligation* implies a known Other: and that while duty and social experience are doubtless inseparable, it is duty that depends on social experience, not social experience on duty.

It is because all of these theories really accept the doubt of an immediate experience of Other Mind, that they must thus assume the idea of Other Mind to be there,—innate or unaccounted-for. It is for this reason that we cannot adopt any of them as final; though none of them fails to throw much important light on the actual working of our social consciousness.

The ultimate difficulty in this matter is due, as I have come to think, to our over-dogmatic ideals of knowledge, and to the explanations we adopt of the knowing process. We take our knowledge of physical things as the type and ideal of all satisfactory knowledge,—and we find naturally enough that we have no such physical knowledge of fellow minds. We explain our knowing of any object by a relation between object and subject, in which the object presumably produces some effect on the subject,—and we find naturally enough that anything which is intrinsically *subject* cannot become such an object.

But if such were the true ideal and explanation of knowledge, we could not, of course, know ourselves any more than we could know others. For we can have no physical knowledge of our own mind, nor can our own mind cease to be subject in order to become an object. And conversely, by whatever understanding of the matter we can account for self-knowledge, by that same understanding we may probably account for knowledge of other subjects.[6] When Locke suggested his inner *sense*, after the analogy of outer sense, he probably used a misleading figure; intending doubtless only to outline the fact of self-knowledge as a thing distinct from knowledge of physical sense: of special organ there seems to be none for self-knowledge, any more than for knowledge of other minds. In truth, all three classes of objects of experience stand on the same precarious footing: and of these three classes, the knowledge of other mind is the latest to be declared impossible. Each of the other types of knowledge, knowledge of nature or of self, had been shown impossible, by one theory of knowledge or another, before social knowledge had been drawn into technical question. We have only to adopt the proper axiom, and any group of objects we please becomes subject to skepticism, thus:

I. Knowledge of self is impossible. Because the thing known is always other than the self that knows it. On this axiom it might be possible to know Nature, or to know Other Selves,—only not *the Self.* The epistemological subject is unknown (Rickert). Psychological introspection is understood to reveal, not the self, but quasi-physical objects; we find never the *genuine* self.

II. Knowledge of physical objects is impossible. Because consciousness can contain nothing but experience-stuff. When I say of any object "I know it"; I have already made it a part of my experience: when I think of it, I think of it always as contained in experience,—if not my own, then another's. On this axiom, it might be possible to know Self, or even Other Selves,—only not physical things as independent substances. A quasi-physical world of orderly experience we of course have; we never find the *genuine* physical world.

III. Knowledge of social objects is impossible. This is proved by sharpening either axiom above. We may say that the object of knowledge is always other than *any* subject. Or we may say that the object of knowledge is always *my* object, belonging to *my* experience, known as such, thought of as such. In either case social experience is impossible. Quasi-social experience one does not question; it is only the *genuine* Other that we fail to find.

I am inclined to think that the three cases are alike. We have a trilemma, each horn of which is as valid as the rest. We could set up another triad, if we chose, beginning thus: Self is the one object perfectly knowable; Nature is the one object perfectly knowable; the Other Mind is the one object perfectly and ideally knowable. The last of these propositions would be as tenable as the first, and as little tenable.

It is not useless, I think, thus to point out that all types of knowledge are liable to the same type of predicament; and that all such predicaments may be traced to axioms expressing some ideal of knowledge too hastily assumed as exclusive. There is a sense in which we can know *ourselves* better than we can know any other thing, whether of nature or of mind beyond ourselves. There is a sense in which *the physical world* is more thoroughly knowable and satisfactorily holdable in knowledge than any other type of object. There is also a sense in which the primary object of acquaintance for any finite knower is his environment of *Other Mind.*

The alienness and inaccessibility which we are compelled to ascertain from time to time, not more in the Other Mind than in Nature or in Self, may well be only such alienness as we must intend them to have, meaning what they do, if we were to picture to ourselves their most ideal knowableness. May it not be, for example, that if we should become clear what kind of knowledge of Other Mind we should desire, as the most perfect possible knowledge of Other Mind, this ideal knowledge would not differ in principle from the knowledge which we actually have. I propose try this as the next stage in our search for the actual social experience; enquiring particularly whether we could desire to know Other Mind apart from just such physical mesh as has in this present chapter seemed the chief barrier to that knowledge.

NOTES

1. And herewith we exclude Binet, Bunge, Moebius, etc., as well as Schneider who appeals to "irregular muscular action."
2. *The World and the Individual*, ii, 168–174.
3. P. 169 of work cited [note 2—eds.]; italics mine.
4. Grundzüge der Psychologie, pp. 44–45.
5. Under the general topic of [MGHE,] "Mysticism," Part V.
6. More technically stated: we err in assuming to explain knowing by a *dyadic* relation between subject and object (say S : o). This explanation bears its own condemnation on its face; for if knowing were of the form S : o, S (in every act of knowing) would remain unknowns and the relation S : o must be unknown likewise. If knowledge is to be *explained*, that is, put in terms of something else than knowledge, our dyad must broaden out,—as I think and shall try to show,—into a triad.

CHAPTER 7B

Such Knowledge As We Could Desire

What is the object which we desire to know? An other mind: but certainly in no case an empty mind. It is a mind which has its own objects, and is at work upon them. There is no principle of attraction between empty minds, i.e., between minds, pure and simple: there is no gravitation between minds as between bodies.

Regarded as pure spirits, minds are very much alike; individuality begins to appear, and our interest therewith, only in so far as the mind engages in struggle with its experience. In truth, minds must be occupied with matter in order to be of interest to one another; whence it may appear that matter supplies the principle of attraction between spirits, as well as between bodies—the principle at once of attraction and separation. Character comes out chiefly in dealing with Nature[1] and what engages us in any person is an individual quality which must be described in terms of his encounter with physical conditions, and the encounter of the race with those same conditions. Every character is some epitome of the economic and artisan labors of the race. Power over nature, clearly seen or dimly divined in another, is what compels us to him. This power is first seen in the body itself, wherein wayward materials and energies are subdued under an immediate capital command, prophetical of much further mastery; and beauty of body signifies to us an ease of mastery, which finishing its task returns with abundance to control itself. Apart, then, from a world of things which resists desire and so forms the text and context of a temporal career, there is nothing in mind personal and distinctive, exciting to knowledge. These elementary strains and stresses make up our simplest thought of the man. It is the other mind as knowing and mastering Nature that we first care about.

The mind to be known is, we say, a concrete being; worthless even to itself apart from the material in which it operates. It is the Mind-in-union-with-Nature that we want to know. But the mind is still *that which* deals with this material; and we concern ourselves with the material only for the sake of that which it manifests. I make boots; but still, it is no part of my self that I make just boots—I could have found my character as well in making books or laws or music. Would it not be possible, if knowing were ideal, to take the burden of nature-stuff for granted and see that character in itself, becoming conscious of its *thinking* apart from the irrelevant stimuli of its thought?

From MGHE, 255–267.

The notion of telepathic communication seems to propose some such ideal; that of reading thoughts without taking cognizance of sensations. Since we are speaking of ideals not of facts, and telepathy has usually been regarded, whether by believers or by non-believers, as an ideal improvement in mutual knowledge, we must look into the meaning of the proposal. Telepathy would save, presumably, the trouble of expression; it would save the detour of thought, by which it must journey down into language and back into thought again. It would connect the two termini directly, without the complex series of irrelevant means.

Examine this proposal of telepathy. Consider ourselves in the act of knowing the thought of another mind in the direct manner suggested. This must mean one of two things. Either we find ourselves imagining the other person, and in imagination hearing him speak, or seeing him make well-known signs, or otherwise reinvesting himself in fancy with his usual physical media of communication. Or else, we find our own thoughts moving under some "strong impression" that this development hails from a given absent person. In either case, the value of the experience would lie in the possibility of verifying it, by communicating with the person "face to face." If such possibility of verifying were cut off, we should speedily be disabused of our preference for this sort of relation with our friends; what more unsatisfactory intercourse could be imagined than a series of "strong impressions" which had no prior nor further history? Even to the telepathic fancy, the physical presence and vocal evidence of the other's thought remains *the standard experience*, to which all other points as its ideal, however useful (telephone-wise or wireless-wise) in exceptional circumstances. Telepathy, I think, has little to offer toward defining a better way of knowing Other Mind.

The plausibility of the thought-reading ideal comes in part from the very perfection of our ordinary modes of intercourse; through their silent efficiency the physical bearers of our meaning drop out of sight, and it is to us as if we were dealing with meanings purely, without any need of sights and sounds. Our social experience is the pre-eminently developable side of human experience: as we have perfected it, it is of peculiar richness, elasticity, and depth. It is with some effort of abstraction that we look away from those regions where, with amazing technique, the play of our passing thought-exchange takes place, to the simple physical groundwork of it all. We think we might dispense with that, only because it serves us so perfectly.

There is another reason for the appeal of the proposal that thoughts may be known without reference to Nature. It is the assumption that men first have thoughts and then later express them. This is less than a half-truth; for the expression of a thought is an integral part of taking possession of that thought. The one quickest way to put stupidity on a par with genius would be to make stupidity owner of all these ideas which it *has*, but is not yet able to express. In truth, it is no hardship that friends must "descend to meet"—as Emerson has it: for such descent into physical expression is a progress into valid and active existence.

An idea shares the history of the body; it needs to ripen and mature; it must find its way by gradual processes to the surface, where it will show itself in language and in action. Hastening this birth involves loss of stamina and quality in the product. The resistance of Nature to the expression of a thought is not the resistance of a wholly hostile medium; detention is a spiritual condition for health and viability, not a physical condition solely. It seems fair to say that the more significant the idea, the more it needs to be lived with before it is uttered. Idea as well as Matter must be "mixed with labor" before it can become *property*. And perhaps also there are no ideas which are mature at birth; but they, like the young of higher species, must pass a certain time in the open under friendly protection, before they can pass current among other ideas, the tools and properties of all men.

It thus requires time and Nature in order that a mind shall *exist*; must it not also require time and Nature in order that a mind shall be *known?* We do not wish to know the mind other than as it is; we cannot wish to know it, then, except in terms of its own traffic with Nature, both in acting and thinking; in possessing its own character, and in possessing its own ideas.

It is no accident, therefore, that we begin our acquaintances with fellow-men *at their periphery*—at the point of their visible encounter with Nature, with weather and the common physical conditions of existence. It is indeed an accident (relatively speaking) whether a man work out his special career in shoe-leather or in medicine or in ink: it is no accident whether he meet the four elements and make up with *them*. And however far acquaintance progresses, we cannot omit from our concept of the man those items, even trivial, of physical behavior into which we learn to condense the significance of large vistas of his spiritual quality,—the shrug, the still glance, the nervous step, the grasp of the hand. And there is some ground for thinking that we know no man completely until we have been with him in the wild, and have shared with him some first hand measurement of idea against the old elemental human obstacles.

But Nature has other properties beside obstinacy that belong inseparably to the knowledge of souls. What we wish to know of a man is doubtless his Idea (or, as Chesterton says, his philosophy), and therewith *himself*: but we can know an idea only by knowing whatever that idea contains and *aims at*. Contents, we have considered: an idea is always an idea *of* something, and the all-available first something is physical stuff, whatever else it may be. As for the aim of ideas, we thought that all ideas aim at a lodgment in Substance,[2] doubtless first seen *behind Nature;* if so, no man can be known without knowing that object. The *identity* of personality, we thought, was bound up with some changelessness in its ultimate object; and the *unity* of personality in some unity to be found there in the world beyond:[3] but I venture to say that unless changelessness and units were discoverable in some character of physical experience, any other object would work against great odds to maintain them. For reality cannot detach itself from the experience of Nature: sensation has some of the characters and dimensions of reality elsewhere found. Sensation lends to experience its *pungency*, its *vividness*, its *particularity*. The definite separation of parts in Nature, the clear difference between position and position in space no point confused with any other—make the world of sense the place where all *definiteness* is set up, where all desire for clarity and differentiation seeks its home. If it is true, then, that we cannot know a definite idea or being save as that being has a definite object; that we cannot know a vivid being, save as having a vivid object; that we cannot individualize that being, save as that being has objects with definite differences; that we cannot measure or estimate any being, save as that being has objects themselves measurable, quantitative:—if this is true, we see that in ways affecting the very foundations of personality, the knowledge of Nature, of Nature pungent and intense with sensation, is an integral part of the knowledge of another mind. These values (vividness, etc.) of physical experience are not *like* the corresponding values of social experience,—they are, so far as they go, *identical*, with social values: *they are properties of mind and matter at the same time.*

I do not say that knowing thus the objects of another mind is equivalent to knowing that mind; I say that such knowledge of the objects is a necessary, an integral part of social consciousness, even of ideal social consciousness.

It is not indeed sufficient to know the objects; we should have further to know those objects as *being known by* the Other Mind; we must find the idea at work; we must verify in experience our simplest definition of the Other Mind—an Other-knower-of-physical-Nature. We want the center as well as the periphery; and Nature certainly cannot give the center of personality, the idea itself. But Nature can give symbol of the center.

We have so far had little to say of the *body* with which we so closely identify the Other Mind; for this identification is all-too-absorbing—we forget that our knowledge of men comes as much from observing their environment as from observing their bodies. But the body is after all that with which Nature is handled; as the idea is that with which Nature is thought. The body is a symbol of the idea: it stands as subject to the environment as object. In its relation to its physical surroundings, it presents a physical picture of the knowing-process.[4] But the body is more than a symbol.

The body is an incredibly intricate and exact *metaphor* of every inner movement of that Other Mind. To every shade of thought and motive, there corresponds some change in the body, reflecting in its own different sphere each type of variation to which the inner state is subject. Man still "looketh on the outward appearance" only, even though he were able to examine the living brain; but remarkable it is that there is nothing in "the heart" not faithfully displayed in this appearance, and at the moment of its occurrence.

With all our inability to gain the exact key to the cipher;[5] and with all our inadequacy in observing these subtle physical changes; it remains true that the body, if we will take it so, is little else than the soul made visible. If we should say that the body has no independent reality, but only exists as a bulletin of an inner process; being but that process itself, *reporting itself* to us in such terms as we can physically apprehend:—if we should conceive of the body in this way, we should hardly over-state the immediacy with which it presents externally what the mind internally is, and not in its passing phases alone, but in its most rooted habits, its oldest memories, its most permanent wills and purposes. The body is a complete metaphor of the idea.[6]

But, further, the body is more than a metaphor. In some phases, it shows what that Other's experience literally is. Thus *time* is the same for both body and mind; the time of the brain process is identical with the time of the psychosis it represents. For us who look on, the *date* of those processes—if we know what they are—may be said to be a matter of direct experience,—through the body. Also, from the position which the body occupies in space, a particular and exclusive perspective view of the visible world is determined; and we who look on, can through our own physical experience know something of the *spatial experience* of that Other. Moreover, as the place of that body alters from point to point continuously, a like continuous change takes place in the physical experience of that other; the two continuities are identical, and we observe that *continuity*. And this continuous history, which cannot be duplicated by any other mind, is taken together with its view of the Changeless, to form the groundwork of its *individual identity*,—of which, thus, through our experience of that body, we get some literal glimpse.

It is for this reason that our conceptions of disembodied spirit, or of an Other whose body we cannot locate or imagine, tend to lose just these qualities of individuality and particularity (as early survival theories and spiritism sufficiently show); we find ourselves impelled to assign them deliberately a place or *seat* in Nature, or else in some other nature accessible to us in imagination, in order to save their personality from obliteration before our minds. How little, then, from our ideal of social experience can we dismiss the experience of body.

I trust I may be pardoned for dwelling thus long on considerations that are familiar. I confess that this extraordinary device by which the Other Mind presents itself in the guise of a body in the midst of Nature seems to me each time I think of it more wonderful than before. The inseparable union of two things so disparate as social experience and experience of Nature seem to be: is there not a perpetual amazement in this? It would be less amazing, perhaps, if it were all pure metaphor, or symbol, or the mere outside of what is within; but we have noted points at which the material world, as we call it, ceases to be a metaphor and shows us, as it were, a literal edge of the Other Spirit shimmering through its physical encasements. Surely there can be no accident, or superfluous illusion, or arbitrary unnecessary sundering of mind from mind in such a union. Nature and the natural body must *belong with* the experience of Other Mind, even in its ideal condition. Of myself, I seem to have only mind; of the Other, only body: and yet, as I think it through, there seems to be nothing about that body which conceals the spirit—body seems to do no more in separating than to fix and define the simple other-ness of that Other from myself; in all other respects it does but give me that Other Mind in more tangible form than by experience of its inner life on its own grounds alone, I could have it.

Let me pursue my reflection a step further. I have sometimes sat looking at a comrade, speculating on this mysterious isolation of self from self. Why are we so made that I gaze and see of thee only thy Wall, and never Thee? This Wall of thee is but a movable part of the Wall of my world; and I also am a Wall to thee: we look out at one another from behind masks. How would it seem if my mind could but once be *within* thine; and we could meet and without barrier be with each other? And then it has fallen upon me like a shock—as when one thinking himself alone has felt a presence—But I *am* in thy soul. These things around me are in thy experience. They are thy own; when I touch them and move them I change *thee*. When I look on them I see what thou seest; when I listen, I hear what thou hearest. I am in the great Room of thy soul; and I experience thy very experience. For *where art thou?* Not there, behind those eyes, within that head, in darkness, fraternizing with chemical processes. Of these, in my own case, I know nothing, and will know nothing; for my existence is spent not behind my Wall, but in front of it. I am there, where I have treasures. And there art thou, also. This world in which I live, is the world of thy soul: and being within that, I am within thee. I can imagine no contact more real and thrilling than this; that we should meet and share identity, not through ineffable inner depths (alone), but here through the foregrounds of common experience; and that thou shouldst be—not behind that mask—but *here* pressing with all thy consciousness upon me, *containing* me, and these things of mine. This is reality: and having seen it thus, I can never again be frightened into monadism by reflections which have strayed from their guiding insight.

Any connecting medium is apt to appear as an obstacle to direct relationship; on the other hand any obstacle may discover itself to be a mediator, sign of unbroken continuity. The sea separates,—or the sea connects; it cannot do one without doing the other also. So Nature *may be* interpreted in its relation to social consciousness, as the visible pledge and immediate evidence of our living contact. If there be any social consciousness, it must include within itself just such physical appearances as we have been reviewing, even in its ideal perfection.

We have pictured such ideal knowledge of the Other; we have faith in it—but we have not verified it. We have still to seek experience of the center, the knowledge of that which knows.

NOTES

1. See [MGHE], p. 190.
2. See [MGHE], p. 119.
3. See [MGHE], p. 187.
4. And this picture is so significant that in our theories of knowledge, we can hardly escape it.

It is the inveterate source of that dualistic theory of knowledge which we have condemned. We forget that We who thus see the Other's knowing, in picture, from the outside, should be included in the picture to give the whole truth, even in symbol.

5. It is not inconceivable that the key might be accurately defined, to some degree. Such a reading of the metaphor as that proposed by Münsterberg, may offer a conception of a solution. *Quality* of sensation, says Münsterberg, is represented in the brain by the *place of excitation; intensity* by *energy of excitation; vividness* by *energy of discharge; value-tone* by *place of discharge*. A somewhat different suggestion, differing especially with regard to value-tone, will be found in an apprehended essay, page 546: but it will be seen from either that the work of key-finding is the main concern of psycho-physics,—a science of definite standing, with legitimate and infinite problem.

6. The body is the manifestation in spatial metaphor of the will-to-live as inborn and as modified by experience and choice. I do not mean that this metaphor can be read by simple inspection; for in the body other records are composed with the record of the will: the will of the world beyond, as it attacks the inner will and impinges on it, leaves its trace here also. The surface of the body is the shore-line where outgoing and incoming purposes meet, conflict and cross; and one tale confuses the clarity of the other,—yet adds the data without which the other were less than true.

CHAPTER 7C

That Knowledge We Have

Any experience of an Other Mind which I could either wish or fancy must contain in it, we have thought, a World, full of sense and variety, full of obstinacy, and with substance at the back of it—like this present world. In a truly social experience, such a world would be known *as being the world of the Other Mind.* That world would be known by me; but as it were through the eyes of the Other Mind. It would be in some sense a world common to both of us; known by both at once.

And though it would be perhaps conceivable that we might carry on mutual relations, each of us having his own separate world (as, for example, I might imagine myself in dream conversing with some resident of heaven or hell, having at the same time a vision of that spirit's world and reaching some understanding of him thereby) yet all real understanding and mutual measurement, mutual judgment, appreciation of character and so even of self-knowledge, must come through having the same world with him throughout. A perfect social experience would require that this present world of Nature should be known as being the World of the Other, precisely as it is my World.

And here begins our final enquiry. For as it seems to me, this present World of Nature *is* known by me as being, in just this sense, a common World: it seems to me, indeed, that it is *not otherwise known*—that is, that a knowledge of Other Knowledge is an integral part of the simplest knowledge of Nature itself.

It is more readily granted that social consciousness involves nature-consciousness, than that nature-consciousness involves social consciousness. If for no reason, than at least for this: that our experience of Nature is constant; whereas our social experience is, at best, *intermittent*—we can and often do experience Nature by itself. It is enough if we can find a genuine social experience now and then—we have not yet done so much as this—but to make such experience an organic part of nature-experience would be to make it perpetual.

Yet I confess that I cannot find a genuine social experience at all, except as a continuous experience. It appears to me that all three types of object are intermittent in the same sense, and continuous in the same sense. Intermittent enough is self-consciousness; yet self-consciousness is always with us. Intermittent is also the consciousness of Nature, as an object of direct attention; yet the undertone of

---

From MGHE, 268–281.

Nature's presence never deserts me, even in deep sleep. In a way closely similar to that persistent awareness of my Self, which is compatible with the most fitful movements of attention to Self, is the awareness of Other Mind persistently present in experience, though doubtless less readily discoverable than any other. Inseparably bound up as I think with the continuous experience of Nature. And such continuous experience is the foundation of all the rest. I shall attempt, first of all, to make clear that *there must be such continuity, if there is to be any social experience at all*.

The chief elements of intermittency in social experience are removed when we look away from the body of the Other and regard his environing world of objects. It is in these, we have said, that we know him, quite as much as in his body. His body appears and disappears to our sight; but his environment does not disappear. It is true that these immediate objects of mine do cease, when he is gone, to occupy his consciousness, and can no longer be counted in his environment. But his experience of Nature was not limited to immediate objects, and never is so limited. Any idea of a thing, is an idea of that thing *placed* in a world of space and energy which remains a constant object. Our space does not move as we move about in it, nor does our idea of it alter; our placings are successful, coherent, unconfused, and for any moment absolute, only because our ideas reach an unvarying field for these varying locations. If, therefore, at any time I have known an Other; and in knowing him have known Nature as his Object; then this same Nature,—with its Space-field, Force-field, and the like—does not cease to be *his Object* when he disappears.

As my own physical world is not bounded, at any time, by the partition or forest or hill that happens to limit my vision, but extends with my Space in all directions indefinitely,—so does his physical world indefinitely extend, wherever he may be—reaches throughout my Space, reaches me and my place, reaches Substance—that same Substance which I also reach as my ultimate object. If I have once got into his world, I cannot get out of it while he endures,—any more than he can get out of my world, so long as I can mean him; these fundamental objects of mine, which I sum up in the word Nature, if they have ever been common objects, common to him and me, can never thereafter cease to be common objects. If my own continuous experience of Nature has ever been a *social* experience it can never thereafter lose its social reference.

But I seem to imply that there can be a *beginning* of social experience, and so a time when it was not—a time when my experience of Nature was mine alone. What I am required to show is that social experience *has no beginning*, except with physical experience itself: that my knowledge of Nature and of Other Mind are in their whole history interlocked, and inseparable. If Nature is ever common object, it *has always been* common object.

Let us consider how a social experience might be supposed to begin, as at times it does appear to begin, even abruptly. I think myself alone, for example, and with uncomfortable surprise find myself observed. It seems to me that I experience a jarring change of scene: my various objects have now to be connected up, in swift series, with the intruder's eyes. They have been exclusive objects; they have suddenly and perforce become common. They are all seared with this new relationship, as with a running breath of flame, and delivered over to joint ownership. Such readjustments often take perceptible *time* to effect. Have we not here a sufficient contrast between solitude and society, showing that social experience may *begin*—being imposed as an addition upon an experience not social?

What such a transition does unmistakably show is that exclusive property in the contents of experience is possible and may have distinct value attached to it. Such exclusive property is made possible by sensible barriers, such as opaqueness and distance. When I say, "I am entirely alone and unobserved," I am putting my trust in these barriers. But when I resort to a barrier, I confess that the objects which I thereby seek to monopolize or conceal are in some danger of being known by Others. They are already thought of by me as being sharable. And if they are sharable, it is because they are already in the World of an Other Mind; there are continuous lines through space between him and me; our world of Nature is already common. Is it not clear that when I suppose myself alone, and regard my solitude as an achievement, I am in that very thought acknowledging my world of Space and Nature to be a world common to me and Others? My negative sociability has a very positive social consciousness as its basis.

What such experiences imply and illustrate may be more compactly stated in terms of the logic of communication, as follows: *In order that any two beings should establish communication, they must already have something in common.* For when I consider the two beings, prior to their communication, as apart from one another, I must consider at the same time the beings wholly independent, having no common region to measure their distance from one another, having between them no continuity through which to travel *toward* each other, are lacking in any "toward"—are unable therefore to *approach* each other, cannot come together. All actual approach implies a deeper-going *presence* as an accomplished fact.

Given a minimal core of communication, and further communication may spin itself out upon that core, may grow intense and varied, develop its ups and downs, its relative presences and absences. But given nothing at all—nothing at all can happen. If then, experience ever becomes actually social, it has, in more rarefied condition, always been so; and hence is, in the same fundamental sense, continuously so.[1]

There is some satisfaction in reducing our question to this alternative: that social experience is either always present or never present. If now we can show that we have at any time a veritable experience of Other Mind, we show that we have such experience continually. I believe that this can be shown.

For suppose that experience is never social. In making this supposition, we mean to contrast the supposed non-social experience with a supposed social experience. In imagining my experience to be confined to myself and my objects, I admit or assume that I have an Idea of my experience not-so-confined; that I know what a social experience would be like. Now I submit that *this Idea of a social experience would not be possible, unless such an experience were actual.* Otherwise stated,—In any sense in which I can imagine, or think, or conceive an experience of Other mind, in that same sense I *have* an experience of Other Mind, apart from which I should have no such Idea.

For every supposition we may make to the effect that our idea of Other Mind is a "mere idea" to which no real experience corresponds,—that our supposed social experience is, in reality, subjective,—implies that we have in mind a type of experience in comparison with which we can condemn our supposed social experience as merely subjective. But the only type of experience in comparison with which any experience can be judged as merely subjective, is a non-subjective experience. *The only point of view from which our supposed social experience can be criticized as incomplete is the point of view of social experience itself.* The only ground upon which this idea can be judged a "mere idea" is the ground of this same idea as *not mere,* namely, as actually bringing me into presence of Mind which is not my own.

Leibniz, for example, judges that all experience is monadic, and that monads do not in actuality experience each other, though to themselves they seem to do so. In making this hypothesis, Leibniz presents to himself the world of monads, and *he* knows their relations to be other than they seem: *he* at any rate occupies a non-monadic position, is for the time being an inter-monadic Mind. And any one who judges that he—and God—know the actual reach of ideas to fall short of their apparent reach, does thereby assert that *his* idea has not thus fallen short. There is no degree of outwardness of which we can think; no degree of reality which we incline to *deny* to idea; but in that thought we have claimed it for our idea. Let me represent to myself the Other Subject, his living center, as inaccessible to my experience; then either I deny myself nothing conceivable, or else I have that which I deny.

An objection (or, let me say, *the* objection): may not this idea of a genuine social experience, which you say guarantees the experience, be an *ideal,* i.e., a conception of something we may desire and think of, which we may well use to criticize what we have, admitting that we have it *not?* Surely, not every ideal implies the experience, but rather the contrary.

Answer: An ideal is either an extension of experience as given, or an innate standard.

The idea of a genuine experience of Other Mind is not an extension of other types of experience. Imagination has its ways of building improvements on experience by combining, enlarging, extending what is given, according to known types of relation. But if the idea of Other Mind were not already given, it could not be built up in this way. Certainly not by any arrangement of physical ideas in physical relations; nor yet by any arrangement of psychical ideas in psychical relations; nor by any union of physical and psychical. To reach the idea from these, we must use the special relation of Other-self-hood, which is the idea itself. Since my idea of social experience is uniquely different from all such constructions within the physical and psychical worlds, it is not an ideal based on them. It is not an ideal by construction at all; what we seek is simply the thing, social experience, in its unique difference from all immanent variations of experience. If this unique difference is an ideal merely, it is not an ideal by imaginative construction,—it must be innate.

To say that an idea is innate, in Cartesian fashion, may mean simply that it is once for all there, and there is nothing more to be said about it. Or it may mean that the idea is due ultimately to some outer source (ancestral or divine); whereby we only reinvest in that Outer Source the difficulty of the idea in question—namely, how my ideas can reach that which is not-myself.

Or, it may mean, in Kantian fashion, that the idea is a native and necessary form by which the Self orders the material of its experience, as otherwise given. Of these, the Kantian form is doubtless the strongest: and our social experience does most closely resemble, as we have noticed, a form of interpretation, a successful hypothesis clothing our manifold experience-stuff—ultimately sensation—with social meaning.

As an hypothesis our idea of Other Mind has certain interesting peculiarities. That it is not framed imaginatively of materials taken elsewhere from experience, we have observed. But further, there is no way in which it could be proved false, or even brought to other test than its use. There are various ways in which my social judgments may err, and suffer correction in experience. Thus I may impute to a friend a false motive, accepting his statement that I am in error. This judgment clearly relies on the more authentic social experience for correction. So with other errors, as by mistaking the identity of a person, or by mistaking a post for a man; these are corrected with reference to a better social experience. There is no type of error to which social experience is subject which can refer me away from social experience for correction,—none which can send me back into myself for final court of appeal. As an hypothesis, the idea of Other Mind cannot be tested,—nor can it be withdrawn.

But now, when we suppose that this idea of ours is an hypothesis *only*, what more than hypothesis do we think it might be? We think, do we not, that it might be a genuine social experience, and no mere hypothesis? But "genuine social experience" is the hypothesis itself, if it is such. And the contrast between real and apparent in social experience is only such contrast as social experience has already furnished us with. My idea of social experience is then, of social experience *as it is:* my ideal and my idea are the same,—they refer me to what I have.

But let me make clear that in referring our idea of Other Mind to experience, I do not mean that it is derived, in Humian fashion, as a copy from a *previous impression*. It would be as little to the point to suggest that my idea of myself is derived from a previous impression of myself. My idea of myself is *at the same time* an experience of myself (unless my idea flies wild). So, unless as frequently happens I use some paper currency in referring to Other Mind, *my idea of Other Mind is at the same time an experience of Other Mind.* Let me but think what I mean by the Other Mind, and there, as I find my Self, I find the Other also. As an idea of a fundamental and constant experience, bound up with my equally permanent experiences of Self and Nature, this idea is not *prior* to experience; but is indeed prior to all *further* social experience, to all such as is intermittent and subject to error. This fundamental experience, and its idea, deserve, from their position in knowledge, to be called a *concrete a priori* knowledge.

Of the logic of this proof that we have actual experience of Other Mind I shall have more to say in a later chapter. It stands before us now somewhat barely. Unconvincingly, too, unless we can clothe with some living sense that strange assertion that Nature is always present to experience as *known* by an Other. That we cannot genuinely conceive ourselves as mentally alone in this cosmos, though we can well imagine ourselves bodily alone. That the inherent publicity of Nature, the fitness of all its objects to be communally experienced, is no empty potentiality, but a potentiality, founded (like other potentialities) on some actuality. We must now try to bring that experience more vividly before us; for we can hardly believe in an experience which we are yet unable to disentangle, or verify in ourselves. But let this conviction stand as a firm ground in our further search: that we should have no idea of an Other Mind or of a social experience unless we had the experience itself. That in whatever sense we can think, or imagine, or even *deny,* the reality of that experience,—in that same sense it must be and is real to us.

There are, I think, three natural difficulties in the way of distinguishing the undertone of social experience amid the general rumble of the ground-levels of experience. First, that we cannot identify that constant Other with any *particular* individual, yet an Other must be an individual. Second, we cannot help regarding the experience of Nature as sufficient in itself, the presence of Others in the world being additional and wholly separable fact—that the experience of Nature *may* be at the same time a social experience we can more readily believe than that it must be. Third, that we cannot verify the social experience *socially*, in the same way that we verify the facts of Nature. I shall consider these three, beginning with the last named,—reserving the others to the following chapter.

An object of knowledge or experience is, for the most part, a thing which you and I can verify together. I assert that something is true, in history, in physics, in mathematics; and when I make such statements *to you*, I mean that you also can go to the same facts and experiences and find the same thing that I have found. The truth of my assertion means that it is valid for you and other real persons in the same way that it is valid for me. This association of minds which we call " we," accustomed as it is to sit in united judgment upon facts external to itself, cannot in like fashion sit in judgment upon itself. If we doubt "we," we know not to whom to appeal. We can hardly find our fundamental sociality, because we can hardly get so far away from it as to doubt it.

Nature is pre-eminently the world of socially verifiable things, the world of scientific research—which is general human collaboration on a common object. We look at Nature through the eyes of a social world. As we look at physical things through two eyes at once, and our prospect thereby acquires something in solidity and depth; so in quite similar fashion we see objects and truths in general through two *pairs* of eyes, through indefinite multitudes of eyes, and thereby acquire that deepest solidity of judgment which we call "universality." Universality is a social habit; the necessary habit of looking at any truth as if not I alone but the whole conscious universe were looking at it with me. The simplest judgment of physical things is universal in this sense; the most particular matter of fact, as I place it in my world of Nature, is so placed by help of this deep sense of the "cloud of witnesses" to whom this fact belongs, as well as to myself. Without this habitual democracy of judgment, this habitual loss of my life in the universal judgment, I can have no life at all in Nature or in the world of truth.

And just because my social consciousness is *that with which* I am thinking my world, I am not at the same time and in the same way thinking *of* it, as one does not see his own eyes in the usual processes of seeing things. When we speak of *experience*, what is called to mind is usually experience with the experiencers left out; experience just so far as it can easily be common object and no farther. Hume in his examination of experience, found no Self: he had gone out of his house, as one noted rejoinder had it, and looking in at the window was unable to find himself at home. In truth it is not I alone, but *we* who go out, and cannot be discovered by ourselves in that house. And that same reflexive turn of consciousness which takes notice of Self, as of something always present, must, if we are right, discover the Other also, my other I, perpetual sustainer of university in my judgments of experience.

When, then, we think of "experience" as something solitary and subjective, we are cutting it off from ourselves, and calling upon the Other Mind to view it so, together with us. Holding it thus, at arm's length, we criticize it, and as we thought, by means of an idea of something better: we criticize our solitary experience by the standard of a conceived social experience which would be more comprehensive. And this idea of a better, we thought, confessed the reality of that better. In truth, we should read the situation the other way. That experience, thus held off at arm's length and criticized, is not the Real Experience, judged by standard of an Idea of a better. That criticized experience is but a conceptual part of reality, abstracted from its context, and criticized not by idea (alone) but by the reality itself. The real and the conceptual have changed places. It is through my present inseparable community with The Other that I know that abstracted "experience" to be incomplete.

NOTES

1. There is indeed no sufficient reason for supposing that the sociality of my nature-experience continues to exist after my fellow has gone in any different sense than before he appeared. The episode of this coming and going does not change the physical aspect of my world; those objects of Nature seem intrinsically *ready to be observed* by an Other Mind, to be essentially public in their constitution. If I were actually alone in this same cosmos, it is difficult to think that I should be without the idea of possible Others, conceived of as sharing it with me: it is difficult to believe that Nature could be experienced as simply *meine Vorstellung*—for the physical object itself, the common *thing*, seems to present itself as numerously knowable, having many unused knowable aspects or valencies which I with my single point of view can never exhaust. Nature seems *structurally* common, or let us say *commune*; made up with reference to many co-experiencing minds. My thought of Nature suffers no jar as men come and go, for sociability is its element. In experiencing it, I am potentially experiencing the Other, and continuously.

CHAPTER 8A

Are Group Minds Real?

The psychology we have been working with is individual psychology. It is the needs and the initiative of individuals that have made the state, and continue to make it. This implies that the individual is prior to the state; it also implies that the state is prior to the completed individual. He needs the state to become the person that he has it in him to become.

But what is the state in itself,—this entity which grows so naturally and inevitably from the overflow of men's wills to power? We have now to meet the long-deferred and crucial question whether the state, whatever its origin, is itself a mind over and above the minds of its members, a super-mind. Are social groups in general, or at least the natural groups, mental individuals of a higher order; and must we consider, beside the psychology of men in groups a "group psychology" dealing with the mentality of these composite beings?

The evidence which leads to the belief that group minds may be real is of two sorts. There is the testimony of experience:—the experience in moments of intense group feeling of being merged in something greater than oneself and greater than one's neighbors; the experience also of doing things with groups, of being carried along by a current of impulse and resolve which emanates from no particular person, but from the spirit of the group. Groups are visibly agents; and if one has felt their temper from within, he can easily credit them with having wills of their own.

The second sort of evidence is the extreme theoretical and practical embarrassment of the opposite view, when we are consistent with it. To define groups as merely composites of individual wills is indeed the natural view: our eyes make individualists of us,—we see the many, not the one. But this is most certainly a view of the first look, hardly more than a natural prejudice. Some of its difficulties we encountered at the outset[1] and hastily considered. But they have disturbed for centuries the minds of philosophers and jurists who have been obliged to reach some usable conception of the capacities of groups and their liabilities. If a nation makes war, are its citizens one by one accountable? If a trade union of a thousand members breaks an agreement, must one try to recover from its members one by one? If a partnership is dissolved, and the members continue to do business separately, is nothing destroyed? Is my obligation to the state simply equivalent to my obligation to all my fellow citizens severally, as so many wills to power? Is the mentality

---

From MATS, 339–362.

in any group merely the sum of the mentalities of its members? These difficulties are fundamental; we must give them a more careful hearing.

I. The Difficulties of Social Atomism

The essential difficulty is that groups have mental qualities which do not appear to be derived from the qualities of the unit-members.

A crowd may be indefinitely more vicious than its members severally; or, with the right union of heads, a joint wisdom may emerge greater than that of any member. The deeds of the group are not mere magnifications of individual deeds. The property of the group is not always the property of its members distributively: when the Athenians wanted to divide among themselves the income from the public silver mines, and Themistocles persuaded them to use it for building a fleet, he was enforcing upon their minds the distinction we have continually to repeat between the commonwealth and the wealth of its units. And the group as a whole has a unity and a distinctive character which may persist while individuals come and go.

Thus, the interests of the group are not found by taking the common interests of its members singly. The massing of men does not make a human group; and, conversely, no human group is a simple aggregate of human units.

Perhaps the nearest approach to such an aggregate is the combining of men for simple physical labor, as in the case of a gang of diggers without an overseer, one of whom so far directs that their efforts are actually added in the common task. What is the mental structure of such a group?

It is the essence of the bond that at the moment of receiving his directions, each man waives his physical self-government in its main object, allowing the thought and will of the leader to take control of his muscles and purposes. Within this general scheme, each makes use of his own mentality, skill, and effort. They constitute together not a sum of minds, but an extension of the directing mind and body, a multiple mentality under the control of a single plan and will. To achieve this unity it is obviously necessary that they first understand that plan, so far reproducing the leading mind in their own. It is then necessary that he should know that they have understood, reproducing their minds in his, together with their reproduction of his mind. They, in turn, will be aware that he knows they have understood, and so on, as far as one cares to pursue the series of mirrorings whose totality is a simple unity of will. Thus far removed is the mental meshwork of a simple group from the setting of minds as it were end to end.

It appears from this instance that atomism is operating with a false view of the self, as something enclosed and bounded after the fashion of the body.

Purely as a physical being, the self cannot be truly pictured as enclosed in its physical outline, crossed as that outline everywhere is by streams of matter and energy. Cut away earth and outer air, and what meaning is left within the brave figure? But we are particularly liable to be misled when we assign boundaries to the mind. We distinguish between a mind and its objects, as if the objects were something wholly distinct. But omit the objects, and have you still a mind? Certainly not. A self, we have said, is a process of intercourse with reality: cut away the objects and there is no process, the mind becomes a seeing without light. The empty mind is equivalent to no mind; hence we speak of the outworld as its 'contents,' and draw the mind's boundary not at the eyes but far and away in front of them. The self must include something of its objects.

But among its objects are its fellow selves, its society; the boundary of the self must be so drawn as to include something of them also.

It is true that the self is something without society [MATS, 235-237]; but it is also true that when society is there, the self entertains something of it within its own proper domain. To know a single other person is, for the time, to see the world as that person sees it; and that view of things remains part of oneself. To know a hundred persons is to incorporate a hundred visions with one's own. To reach maturity is to see and think—as a self—but at the same time as an epitome of a society.

Hence the self is, as it were, a multitude brought to a common focus. The voice with which it speaks is the chorus of all the voices of all the souls it has met, immortalized within its own proper voice; its vision is a confession of its social history. Tolstoi is Russia; Russia teems out of him. The social instinct implies the essential boundlessness of the self where humanity is concerned. It is the destiny of the human individual to be a mart for the mental commerce of the world, receiving first, transmitting afterward. It harbors a universal life.

In fact, if minds were the well-bounded monads of our atomistic view, such mutual understanding would be impossible; for communication would be shut off from the beginning, and therewith all building of social groups.

For however we picture our units proceeding to open their dealings with each other, we assume that they can *approach* one another. Unless two physical bodies are in the same space, there can be no physical approach; for approach means a lessening of distance, and distance is a relation of two positions in the same space. Similarly, unless two minds start with some objects in common, and *known to be in common*, they can neither find each other nor begin conversation. Given an identical physical world which establishes known relations between their bodies, given means of expression known by both to be such, given certain general interests in food, drink, shelter, weather, which are shared as objects of common human nature,—with so much in common communication can begin and grow: with nothing in common, the two minds are simply not in presence of one another and have no way of knowing or guessing each other's existence.

This implies that before two selves can communicate, some objects must belong to both of them, and not to each severally. This space is mine, but not mine alone: it is 'ours,' it is attributed by each of us to a 'we.' It is as if this 'we' stood for a real and aboriginal fact, prior to all further social grouping, coexistent with the self.

II. The Analogy of the Organism

One way of expressing the fact that selves reach out beyond their apparent limits into regions which prove to be possessed in common with others is to say that they *inhere in a common life*. Social groups, or some of them, are "organic" in structure. It is an ancient speculation that a society differs from an assemblage of individuals somewhat as each of these individuals differs from an assemblage of unit-parts. Mental organisms are capable of uniting in organisms of the second degree.

The analogy is alluring; and it has been indefatigably pursued—with some advance in seeing what is pertinent. We have reached the point, after hundreds of years, of realizing that there is no sense in asking "whether society is an organism" until we know what we mean by an organism, and whether we have in mind the organism of a man or that of an oyster, a banyan tree, or a zoöphyte. The one thing that matters is, what characters of an organism help us to understand the structure and life of social groups.

We may take it as characteristic of organisms that their parts depend on the whole for their important qualities; i.e., they cannot be extracted from it without withering in some respect. It is likewise true that the whole, though it has qualities of its own, depends on the parts.

The mark of an aggregate is that its parts may be not only set together but separated again without internally affecting them, as a set of balls at pool may be framed, scattered, and framed again, and still remain to all intents the same. Their relations are 'external.' But the parts that enter into an organism become something other than they were, taking on the quality of the whole organism. The soil and air that enter into the pumpkin become pumpkin tissue, characteristically pumpkin throughout, while the neighboring turnip makes of the same soil and air turnip tissue, without confusion or mistake. The relations of the parts are 'internal': cut the organism to pieces and the parts can neither return at once to their former character nor hold the character they have had as parts of the living total.[2]

To some extent every social body shows these organic qualities. Even relatively casual groups, our gang of diggers, camping parties, etc., begin to differentiate the functions of their members and to develop an *esprit de corps* in which each member participates. Within the group each member becomes something else than he was. And were it only for the facts of memory and habit, he can never emerge from it the same man. To this extent the analogy always holds.

It is equally evident that this organic quality invades different types of human grouping to different depths. In our gang of diggers, the men can separate, take other work under other masters, and remain more or less the same men. No doubt something of dear life goes into all work; and something of experience, of team-play, of the habit of subordination, have made the units different from what they were: it is as somewhat other men that they will take up their next job. But they have contracted for nothing but their labor; their labor is all but detachable from themselves. And similarly for all groups made by deliberate contract: the assumption that a man can extricate himself from the group the same man, as from an external relation, remains nearly true. The organic quality is here at a minimum.

It is more evident in associations whose kind has been long enough in the world to develop settled internal arrangements, such as partnerships, which are almost as old as human coöperation.

The partnership (the *societies* of Roman Law) is sufficiently an individual being so that it is thought of as one, and its component individuals as *its* members. It is considered by its public to have unique mental resources such as the participating minds strike out in each other. A firm of architects today will naturally include one partner whose skill is primarily of the engineering variety, another whose talent is mainly in the field of art. In such an association each learns to depend on the other, and to relax somewhat on the side of the other's strength: they become different persons, and cannot rightly withdraw at whim or will from the association. The "we" acquires a character, and can act more competently than either alone.[3]

In the corporation (the *universitas* of Roman Law) the unity budding in the partnership becomes so far full-fledged as to receive legal definition. Selfhood is conferred upon it from above: it becomes a juristic entity, to be treated as if it were a personal owner of property distinct from the property of its incorporators, a maker and payer of debts, a subject of other assigned rights.

But while in respect to the unity of the whole the organic quality of the corporation seems well-developed, the fact that it is a derived and artificial unity, especially devised in many modern forms to make its members extricable and intact, leaves it in a puzzling and uncertain position.

This ambiguous character of the corporation led to one of those instructive confusions in legal history which throw light on our special problem of the nature of the state. The great canonical jurists, impressed by the made-up quality of the corporation, applied to it an assertion which the Roman lawyers did not make, namely, that the *universitas* is *nothing but* a juristic entity. If so, then it is not a real being, but a *persona ficta,* as Pope Innocent IV phrased it. But that which is not real cannot have real members: the incorporators therefore are not members of the corporation. What, then, is their relation to it? Are they guardians, as of a ward *non compos mentis?* It is not clear that a nonentity can have guardians any more than it can have servants, agents, or members. Again, having no immortal soul, it is not to be judged in the next world; but if incapable of sin or crime, how can it be judged in this world? Yet it must be held responsible. And would not the same reasoning disqualify it from holding property and exercising the other rights which are its sole *raison d'être?*

These puzzles are themselves fictitious, as Oldradus and Bartolus saw: if fictions are to be admitted at all, it is arbitrary to set a limit to what shall be thus invented,—the state may be allowed to endow its creations with whatever powers it will, and with whatever liabilities should logically go with those powers. But if we assume that the personality of the corporation is a fiction, the question is made more insistent, What then is the state, which is the author of this fiction?

Is the state, in turn, a fiction or a juristic entity which we treat *as if* it were a real individual with an organic life of its own? This involves the absurdity that a fiction can be created by another fiction. The Romans were clearer than to fall into such an error: the making and unmaking of the *universitates* was the prerogative of the *princeps,* a substantial and living being. It requires a reality of some sort to set up a fiction. If corporations are made by the state, then either the state or some other real being acting through the state must be real.

In a higher degree than any lesser group, except the family, the state has the marks of organic *character.* There exists a clearer interdependence of parts, a completer division of the total labor of life among organs mutually supplementary. The assimilation of every member into the total (national) character is a conspicuous fact. In their formative years, members are inseparable from the life of the state without mutilation; and they acquire apparent detachableness only when they are so far imbued with its tradition that they carry it with them.

But we cannot say that the organic quality is fully realized in the state: the analogy fails, in respects which, in almost every biological type, would be vital.[4] We can only say, within bounds, that the state behaves like *an organism in the making.* It is rather like a disembodied organic principle invading the mass of individuals and struggling to clothe itself with an appropriate equipment of organs for life and action-as-a-whole. In the case of human beings, the growth of the body appears to precede and at times outstrip the growth of mental individuality. In the case of the state, the unity appears to exist first in the sphere of the mind and only by slow degrees in the sphere of physics.

The analogy of the organism is supposed to lend credence to the belief in the mental reality of the group. In the best instance, it lends but a shattered and distant support. The state resembles the lower organisms far more nearly than the higher; the analogy on its own strength could render probably only a confused and imbecile mentality. But if it is conceivable that the mind of such beings should be in advance of their visible appearance, and the process of history one of the materialization of an existent but imperfectly incarnate spirit, then we should understand the crudity of organic character, but we should be driven to rest our conclusions on the independent reasons for believing in such an over-mind. The organic analogy lends the theory little aid.

III. The Conception of a Super-Mind

The human self inheres in something beyond itself; and that something is mental. Is it the social milieu, either in the form of minor groups or in the form of the organized nation?

In our own country, Professors Royce and C. H. Cooley have committed themselves, perhaps, most completely in favor of such a view.[5] Royce accepts Wundt's judgment that certain objects,—language, custom, art, religion,—since they are made by man and yet by no one man, are the work of the human community: whatever produces real effects must be a real author. "The creator of the English speech is the English people. Hence the English people is itself some sort of mental unit with a mind of its own."[6]

All the difficulties of atomic individualism make for belief in such super-minds. But against it stands a great initial difficulty, that of conceiving what mode of thinking or willing such minds might enjoy. It is fully recognized by these writers that the group-mind must first be made conceivable if it is to be removed from the realm of superstition; and they have done much to remove the difficulty.

They point out that within our own minds there are situations analogous to the situation of such a unit mind to its individual members. Some of our mental states survey, and in that respect include, other states, as when we remember what we were previously thinking, or as when, hesitating between two or more motives, we conceive ourselves in each of several possible cases. Indeed, so far as we know our fellows at all, we develop, as we have been saying, an internal community-character. As our one self is to these many selves, so the hypothetical super-self is to the actual many of the group. And as our own reflective states include our sense data without displacing them, altering them, or needing in any case to duplicate them, so the super-self might be supposed to use the sense-data of individuals' experience without need of an additional sensorium of its own.

William James, who began his scientific life with a strongly marked individualism, came in time to regard that view as a product of abstract intellectualism whose units are unreal. Aided by Fechner, and by Bergson's view of the interpenetration of mental states, he saw that each single mind is internally compounded into a many-in-one, and was ready to argue that "just as we are co-conscious with our own momentary margin, may not we ourselves form the margin of some more really central self in things which is co-conscious with the whole of us?" Since "the self-compounding of mind in its smaller and more accessible portions seems a certain fact... the speculative assumption of a similar but wider compounding... must be reckoned with as a legitimate hypothesis. The absolute is not the impossible being I once thought it."[7]

I quite agree that if a super-self can be made psychologically intelligible, we need not be too much deterred by the psycho-physical difficulty of finding an appropriate organic basis for its consciousness. But if we adopt the view that this super-mind is the mind of any human group or any set of them,—that the expression "the group mind" with regard to them is more than a metaphor,—we lose the advantage of metaphor in using it, i.e., of applying the conception where it is convenient to do so, and laying it aside where it is inconvenient. We must accept it in all its consequences; and some of these, I submit, are formidable.

a. A real mind will have thoughts, purposes, actions, not identical with those of its members; hence it will have a character or moral quality distinct from theirs, its own capacity for rights and duties, its own responsibility and liability to praise and blame.

If the group-mind can be made responsible in this way, this is indeed an important datum for jurisprudence, and for the everyday action of men as well. Someone must be the owner of common property, and some real person,—for the subject of rights must be real. Someone must be responsible for common debts and for the carrying out of common contracts. Someone must be summonable into court in case of failure to fulfill common obligations; someone must be liable for damage done by common action; someone must be condemnable and punishable for injury or crime committed by the group. How to identify this legal subject: this is an ancient problem, and a modern one as well.

The simplest solution, common to rude times, is to hold each member responsible for common debt or misdeed; so that if the whole cannot be brought to terms, any member may be seized, and punished or held as security for the performance of the obligation.[8] It is not so long ago that Italy on a similar principle seized Corfu as a 'guarantee' for an assumed obligation of Greece as a whole. But these rude ideas were also capable of making a group responsible for the misdeeds of single members:[9] In the Corfu incident Italy seems to have employed this principle also, which is to the effect that as a union for mutual protection, a group would be inclined, other things equal, to abet and shield its members in any conduct not too flagrant, or perhaps even without that reservation, and thus make itself a sharer of his guilt; and that unless it took the alternative, always open to it, of ejecting and renouncing the guilty member, or delivering him over to justice, it must be understood to accept responsibility as a whole. The joint application of these two principles would evidently result in making each member of a group responsible for the misdeeds of every other member, unless one wished to find and denounce the wrongdoer. How little this disposition to 'betray' a comrade could be counted on, where clan feeling ran high, may be abundantly illustrated from Scotch and Irish history of recent times.[10]

This primitive type of justice feels no need to distinguish between the guilty group and the guilty individuals, nor between the guilty members and the innocent members. It proceeded, upon an unavowed postulate to the effect that in a guilty whole there *could be no innocent parts*. In early mediaeval Europe, villages, towns, districts might be fined, excommunicated, or even laid waste, for delicts imputed to them as wholes. The bann was commonly pronounced expressly against "town *and* burghers." Time was bound to bring efforts to limit punishment more nicely to the guilty, and especially to determine how to reach the guilty group.

Innocent IV, revolting against the notion of whole-sale excommunications, denied the premiss of the whole problem, namely, that groups are capable of crime. And certainly, if they are as he held, fictions, devoid of souls, the dictum would follow: *impossibile est quod universitas delinquat*. But the sense of retributive justice was too powerful for this logic: the followers of Innocent, to this day, have been far more ready to accept the view that the group is a fiction than to excuse it from the consequences of delict. They discussed, therefore, not so much whether groups can do wrong, as *when* the wrong is that of the group, and when that of individual members or officers; and how punishment is to be fitted to the criminal and no others.[11] The juristic mind found relief in a variety of distinctions: there are wrongs done by official action, by majorities, by representatives acting under instructions, by representatives acting without instructions, by members in their private capacity; there are wrongs which can only be carried out by a physical person, such as murder and violence, and wrongs which can be committed by the group itself, there are various degrees of consent on the part of the membership, as of children, or irresponsibles, or the absent, or those who oppose the action; and there are kinds of punishment which can affect the group as such (as fines and deprivation of privileges) and those which can only affect members (as flogging, imprisonment, decapitation). But it was found impossible to devise a way of punishing the group which did not transfer itself to the membership, and more or less indiscriminately. And the quandary remained until the shrewd Bartolus of Saxoferrato made the crowning distinction: that between delicts whose guilt is confined to the perpetrator, and those whose guilt *extends through the group*, as 'from father to son.' High treason and heresy were such crimes: for these it was right that a whole city should be condemned *aratrum pati*, to suffer the plow as had Troy and Carthage of old. Or, the *jurisdictio et civilitas* of a group might be taken away, in which case its members lost their civil rights and became *vagabundi* in the eyes of the law. The exemplary rigor with which Pope Clement and Philip the Fair of France had proceeded against the Knight Templars under allegations of sacrilege and bestiality, not alone against the rich property of the Order, but against the persons of its members, was considered an instance of the principle.[12]

To the individualistic eye this convenient distinction might seem the reverse of an advance and the instance exceptionally unfortunate;[13] but it cannot be said that we have overcome the difficulty. Burke professed himself unable to find an indictment against a whole people; yet modern war with increasing deliberateness becomes an affair of whole populations against whole populations: the group is treated as a joint and several culprit. The futility of denying the existence of an agency which was powerfully affecting the community had much to do with the ultimate recognition of the trade union in England: whatever *strikes* is real,—such seemed to be the common sense of the matter. So to-day the corporation is an agent whose responsibility we must fix: those who say that 'corporations have no souls' mean to imply that they have souls, but of an unscrupulous sort. Instead of arguing with Pope Innocent from the circumstance that such groups are not mentioned in scripture as beings to be saved to the conclusion that they have no minds and can commit no sin, we are rather prone to argue from the experiential certainty that they can commit sin to the reality, and hence the liability, of the mind behind them.

But I press the question: what precisely is this experiential certainty? Its core is that a wrong has been done, and that the wrong emerges from the group: it is not that the group *per se* is its author. If our canonists and jurists had succeeded in finding a way of punishing the group without punishing its members, this same sense of retributive justice which rejected the theory that groups can do no wrong would have assured them that the real culprits had escaped. Whatever type of reality you attribute to groups, if you ascribe to them a moral personality distinct from that of the members as these are from one another, you commit yourself to finding a type of punishment for its delicts from which *no human individual need suffer;* and this would be indistinguishable from no punishment at all.[14] The moral sense would be outraged hardly less than by the primitive indiscriminacy. On this ground it has been said that wherever you find a person attributing personality to groups, there you find one who wishes to escape responsibility. The statement is too sweeping, but that an actual evaporation of responsibility must logically ensue cannot be doubted.

b. Again, a real mind will be capable of pleasure and pain, joy and suffering; hence it will be a necessary object of humane consideration, beyond its imputed rights of property and contract. It would be at least a putative subject of the rights of life and liberty. The creation and destruction of groups would take on a gravity comparable with that of the causing of birth and of death.

As applied to the more intimate relationships, Royce did not shrink from this conclusion: disloyalty to a friendship is a dealing of death to the 'we.' And that group-life ought to be encouraged and protected is certainly a widespread feeling. The long struggle for the right of association is analogous to the struggle for individual rights of life and liberty. The traditional right of the prince to dissolve *collegia illicita* was seldom held to imply a right to dissolve any group at his whim.

Yet, if groups are minds, the ease of their multiplication and destruction is appalling! We should have to recognize the marks of group-entity in simpler and more transitory groups as well as in the more pretentious and permanent; lines would be hard to draw; wherever two or three were gathered together in the name of some common interest we should perceive or suspect the mystical presence. And since the number of groups actually formed within any modern nation far outnumbers its population,[15] we should be forced through the sheer impossibility of considering them all as subjects of possible suffering to fall back upon our present care-free practice of considering none in that light. The burden on finite intelligence and sympathy would be comparable to that of attributing high sensitivity to the entire vegetable kingdom.

c. In the most stable groups, such as nations, the deeds of the group vary in intelligence and morality with changing rulers and administrations. If these are ascribed to a distinct and identical personality, it must be one strangely hampered in expression by the individual tools it employs.

The existence in history of persistent national tempers may be granted, such as von Treitschke had in mind when he exclaimed, "Can we think of the Romans as cultivating art and humanity? Can we think of the Germans without weapons?" Without subscribing to these particular Denkunmöglichkeiten, we may acknowledge a pride of policy in any great historic people such that any lowering of the morale of public action by individual administrators provokes public revulsion. The 'deeds of the state' are products of the variable elements with some relatively constant factor, which is the national mind.

But the national mind, on this showing, *is not the sole author of any deed:* it appears to dwell in the minds of statesmen as an influence to which they are more or less open rather than as a distinct being capable of autonomous thought and decision.

For this reason, and because of the other consequences we have mentioned, I cannot accept the hypothesis that groups are minds, numerically distinct from the minds of their members. Admitting all that can be said of the incompleteness of the individual without the group, we can neither reduce the individual to a mere transmitter of the universal life, nor place the authorship of group deeds outside his consciousness and selfhood. If, finding that the individual voice comprises a chorus of other voices, we identify him with that community, we must make each of those other voices, in turn, an echo of many more; so that the individual becomes in the end a mere echo of echoes with no original sound to begin the series, hence in all consistency a pure nothing. If we say that the group deeds which he must execute are not his, but those of a super-mind, we make him a tool of a power which evades human reckoning and control. Gierke regarded it as a token of the richness of the old German conception of personality that it was thought of as divisible, so that it could part with some of itself for the building of a higher *Gesammtperson;*[16] but the true dignity as well as the wealth of personality consists in the power to *retain within the circle* of its own selfhood and responsibility those thoughts, decisions, and acts which it undertakes in the name of its group, and so distinguishes from its private acts. Group deeds are deeds of individuals, and the minds behind them are individual minds.

But the difficulties of building a unitary group life from such individuals are not banished by the impossibilities of group-realism. And the habit of personifying the group-entity seems to me neither fanciful nor groundless. Lecky's words remain valid:

All civic virtues, all the heroism and self-sacrifice of patriotism, spring ultimately from the habit men acquire of regarding their nation as a great organic whole, identifying themselves with its fortunes in the past as well as in the present, and looking forward anxiously to its future destinies.

We must do justice to this motive as well as to whatever is true in our individualistic bias. How this is to be done I shall now try to propose.

NOTES

1. [MATS] ch. iv §§ 24 and following.
2. In greater detail, an organism may be said to have the following characters:
(1) It is an identifiable group of parts, fairly marked off from its environment, while constantly exchanging matter and energy therewith; (2) it has a character as a whole which is impressed on every part, as implied in the word 'assimilation' when outer materials are taken in and by the word 'intolerance' when an attempt is made to substitute for its own tissue that of a different type; (3) it persists as a whole, and is aided to persist by what each part does, the parts in turn being sustained in their activity by all other parts; (4) this mutual service is most readily expressed by using terms of purpose rather than terms of mechanism, saying that each part serves every other and also the whole as a means to their ends, and is served in turn by them as an end to which they are the means; (5) it fails in this conserving activity, has a finite life cycle, fairly regular and characteristic for all of its kind, and dies after reproducing itself; (6) but since the life-cycle includes reproduction, the life of the kind persists, and may be regarded as the true organism.
3. Here I find myself unable to accept the terms of the contrast which Maitland makes between the Societas and the Universitas, the former marked by a contractual, the latter by a conferred unity. The element of contract must enter into all conscious associations for mutual benefit: it cannot therefore be distinctive of the Societas. On the other hand, neither the Societas nor Universitas is a merely contractual group. In each case the whole has a certain reality and effect in law: it may do business as a whole; it may be taxed as a whole; its members acquire an altered status within it. In the hands of Hobbes, as Maitland rightly observes, the contract principle was used to set up a Societas; but Hobbes was clear that the status of every member was definitively altered thereby. Thus *contract is not properly contrasted with legal status or estate;* but only with the status of birth, with which Maine was alone concerned when be drew his famous distinction.
4. To resume briefly these failings:
(1) The organs of the state-life are not locally distinguished as are those of the typical organic body, nor is there a definite totality of them. The circulatory system is well-marked, and there is a seat of government which might pass for a head. But it remains true that, as in primitive organisms, digestion is everywhere, thought and reaction everywhere. Any fractional region remains capable of developing whatever organs the whole has; may grow a head of its own: while the most definite heads of all are those of the individual "cells." (2) There is no definite

life-cycle; no inevitable old age and death; no regular law of development. Reproduction and birth have no exact parallels. A sequence of political revolutions may impose on a given nation a series of lives wholly foreign to the biological world. (3) The state is not demarked from its environment as is the organism. There is about it no empty region: its neighbors are immediately against it. The physical environment of the state is within the state itself, its soil, its air, its resources. And because of this (4) there is no such thing as a normal limit of mass for the body of the state. No doubt a state can be too large or too small for existing powers of organization. But the addition or subtraction of a piece of the geographic exterior creates no such organic embarrassment, not to say absurdity, as the like treatment of an organic body. (5) The autonomy of the units, which enter and leave the inner organs and the whole body at will, if not with impunity, is such as would disintegrate any actual biological unity.

5. C. H. Cooley, *Social Organization*. Josiah Royce, *The Problem of Christianity, War and Insurance, The Hope of the Great Community*.
6. *The Problem of Christianity*, II, 27.
7. *A Pluralistic Universe*, pp. 289–292. James is here thinking not of the political but of the religious super-self. But the conception of the state as a super-mind has been aided throughout its history by religious conceptions. Cf. Jellinek, *Allgemeine Rechtslehre*, p. 146.
8. Thus Gierke, Das deutsche Genossenschasftsrecht, II, 385: "Die mittelalterlichen Rechtsanschauung erlaubte daher sowohl bei Schulden als bei Delikten einer Gesammtheit, sobald von dieser unmittelbar Befriedigung nicht zu erlangen war, em beliebiges Mitglied derselben herauszugreifen, zu pfänden oder zu verhaften. Es mochte dann der Genossenschaft überlassen bleiben, wie sie unter ihren Genossen eine Ausgleichung herbeiführen wollte."
9. As late as 1260, according to Trouillat, II, 722, "die wegen unbefugten Fischens und Holzens auf Klostergrund verklagte *universitas villanorum* de Oheim verspricht dafür einzustehen, dass Jeder von ihr, der das noch einmal thue, Busse und Ersatz geben werde." Gierke, op. cit., p. 387, n. 7.
10. R. L. Stevenson, *Kidnapped*, gives a genial picture of the spirit of clan loyalty, as it affects clan crimes.
11. Even churches, it was agreed, might sin: for though it stood as an axiom that "ecclesia non patitur damnum propter culpam praelati," this, it was thought, must refer to the misdeeds of single prelates, not to those of prelates in groups.
12. Gierke, *Genossenshaftsrecht*, III, 409. Cf. H. Finke, *Papsttum u. Untergang des Tempelordens*.
13. The historian Döllinger said of it that "if any day of European history deserved to be called *dies nefas* it was the 10th October, 1307," the day when the Templars were thus attacked in France.
14. Cf. E. A. Ross, *Sin and Society*.
15. Consider that the number of possible groups among any number of individuals greater than three begins to exceed the number in the group by a factor which rapidly becomes vast—among six persons, forty-two different groups are possible,—and that if each person were to make but two friends in his life there would be as many groups of two as individuals.
16. *Genossenshaftsrecht*, II, 40.

CHAPTER 8B

Will Circuits

We must take our beginning once more with the fact that human individuals are not self-sufficient monads. This fact has been taken to imply that they inhere in society as in a higher organism. If this inference is, as I think, too hasty, we are bound to consider what this fragmentary character of the individual does imply; and we may begin by asking how it makes itself good in the ordinary course of living.

We have seen how, in order to be fully itself, the intellect, like the body, needs to take in much of the outer world, the world of its objects. Let us extend this observation to the self of will and habit.

Consider the round of activities that belong to the life of a single instinct and its allied habits, such as the food-getting instinct of a human or animal hunter. These activities will lie within a roughly defined region, and will follow a more or less regular routine. For the habits of the hunter must be built upon the habits of his game, those of the fisher upon the habits of fish, etc. Just how and where the particular victims will appear is unpredictable; but the kind of situation in which they may be expected is known; hence the series of objects that make up the path of the prowler is relatively constant and recurrently used. They become identified with the life of instinct, and are regarded by the food-getting creature as his *own* in a sense only more attenuated than that in which he regards tools or weapons, claws or teeth, as his own.

What is true of food-getting habits is evidently true of others: every instinct has to make use of some 'external' objects, has to make its home in the world, and what is at first but accidentally related to it becomes indispensable to its activity. So to the mechanic his particular bench and tools; to the writer his workplace, his equipment, and for the time the characters of his book; to the farmer the familiar acres, utensils, stock, and seasonal routine;—all these become part of the persistent body of an enlarged self. They involve excursions beyond the original self, yet they belong to the self: deprived of them, the instinctive functions would be interrupted much as they would be interrupted by the loss of a limb.

Now a limb belongs to the body because it is held within the vital circuits of the body, its nutrition, elimination, sensori-motor arcs, etc.; similarly, these recurrently used external objects are included in vital circuits but newly established and

---

From MATS, 363–379.

farther flung. Such extensions of the self of will and habit we may therefore refer to as *vital circuits* in a generalized sense, or specifically as *will circuits*.

A vital circuit need not be exclusively the property of one individual and his wishes. A group sharing the same hunting ground, a gang of workmen on the same job, partners in the same business, have vital circuits partly coincident; as their intellects meet in terms of certain objects, space and its contents, which are identical for all, so their wills find a region of actual coincidence in the objects of common concern and use.

It is not the existence of the same instinct in different persons that makes their vital circuits coincident. Hunters in different regions have similar impulses; but there is no fusion of their wills. This fusion requires *identity of the physical objects used*, and this is commonly brought about by limitation of the physical supply and by propinquity of the users. If in a group of nine boys there is a unanimous wish to form a baseball team; and if in the group there happens to be one bat, one ball, one mask, one mitt, etc., the prophetic eye need hardly sharpen itself to see nine vital circuits falling into a coincidence shaped by fate. Universal needs alone do not bring men together, but when universal needs conjoin with the presence, commonly accidental, of a set of objects necessary and available for the vital circuits of each, they are likely to determine a vital circuit for all.

In the case of the baseball team, it is not alone the material property that establishes the vital circuit. Each player requires not alone the ball and bat in order to satisfy his thirst for ball; he requires the other players. They become integral elements in his vital circuit.

And the relation is usually mutual. He is a part of the vital circuit of each of the other eight. And for any two members of the group, A and B, the others C, D, E, etc., fall with the physical properties into the coincident parts of the circuit.

There is always a part of such mutual circuits that is not coincident: A and B cannot use the same bat at the same time, nor can they hold the same position in the team, nor have precisely the same shade of concern in each play. But as the number of participants, the amount of physical property, and the time of joint activity grow large, the ratio of the coincident to the non-coincident parts of the circuits becomes indefinitely great, and it would be accurate for most purposes to speak of them as simply coincident. We have now to note some of the properties of these coincident vital circuits.

As the number of participants becomes great, the circuit itself seems to approach autonomy, and to impress not alone observers, but the participants also, as having a life of its own, other than their own lives. This characteristic is suggested even to the eye in such a schematic symbol of the situation as the accompanying diagram.

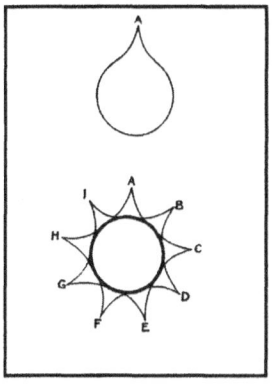

Individual will circuit and coincident will circuits, showing how this union of selves appears to give rise to a group-self.

Any work men undertake tends to set up demands of its own which hold a certain sway over their wills as from outside. What they begin, they wish to finish; and the work itself determines when and how this is to be done. A work undertaken in concert with others has this independent character in still higher degree; for one is bound by the conception which the other wills have formed of the end to be reached: a game of solitaire one may give up at will, a game of chess less freely, one's part in a crew of racing oarsman only with friction and reprobation. So it is also with occupations which consist of continually renewed enterprises, and not of one common effort, the trades and professions: each such activity is accompanied by a tradition of its own worth, invites the sinking of unlimited energy in improving its practice, clamors for sustenance as if it were a separate self. The mere fact that the life of other wills is flowing through the circuit tends to draw my will into it: I am impelled by all the silent arguments of suggestions and authority to look upon that activity as something which ought to be carried on, which *ought to live*.

And in fact the vital circuit *is a living thing*, not a mere abstraction or fiction. It is living in the same concrete sense as is the limb which it resembles: and the suffering and loss of energy which occur when a limb is severed are also experienced when the vital circuit is broken or destroyed. Life is by so much diminished. The value of selfhood becomes transferred to the vital circuit by the same logic as that which one who hurts my hand hurts 'me': because one cares for selves one must care for the integrity of whatever forms an integral part of their lives. He who injures a vital circuit injures a self.

Coincident vital circuits have thus an individuality of their own, affect the wills of their members as *an other will* to all of them, are alive with a verifiable life exhibiting itself in experience of pain when injured, and so develop a definite self-preservative tendency. These properties make it possible and convenient to regard the vital circuit for many purposes as an actual will or self, make it inevitable that language should attribute to it a kind of derived personality.

But seeing how the resemblance is produced, we see at the same time that the vital circuit *is not a self.* The only selves present are those of the participants or members.

The properties which we attribute to the whole as distinct from the individual members are in reality to be found in each of the members severally. This is possible because the members are minds, and not physical things or organic cells; for minds have certain powers which no other entities enjoy. Thus, minds can *include each other.* If box A includes box B, then box B cannot include box A: but mind A can take in mind B, while mind B is also taking in mind A, and much beside. And further, in the world of minds, *the part can include the whole,* and is continually engaged in doing so, however partial a member it may be of any whole to which it belongs. Consequently, whatever qualities the group has are qualities which each member is aware of, when acting with the group. When hydrogen and oxygen unite to form water, the atoms as such do not possess the qualities of the liquid, nor did they possess the qualities of the gases that preceded the liquid state. But when minds unite to form groups, they are themselves conscious of the difference in their own mental operations. Unless they themselves knew that groups have different tempers, powers, and behavior than those of the members apart from the groups, no outside observer would be able to convince them of the fact. The qualities of will circuits are thus inseparably affections of the minds involved in those will circuits.[1] The capacity of the individual mind for making itself a community of represented minds, without assignable limit, has been frequently taken as a justification for regarding the group, by analogy, as a self, since it also is just such a community. But it is this very capacity which makes the assumption of the group mind superfluous. And if it is superfluous, then to fill the universe with that plenum of intermediate beings between man and God becomes little other than a superstition, a source of confusion to mind and feelings alike.

It is worth observing that a mind can *mean* far more than it can *image* or *think.* It can mean, for example, to act with another mind, and so to endorse what the other mind may think and will, however little it may be able to fathom the devices of that other mind. The least in mental scope may in this way mean to think with the greatest, and, so far, the horizon of the greatest is included in his horizon.

One may *mean* an identity of will with persons whom he has not so much as thought of individually, as the children of Israel mean to be coworkers with countless unknown others in the patriarchal purpose: each one is Israel in intent, and in their collectivity they are by this common intent, still 'Israel.' Similarly every testator leaving funds in trust reaches forward in intention to minds whom he will never concretely touch, and calls confidently on them to mean what he means by his bequest, even if they change all the pictures which he regards as fitting to that meaning. His trustees must become his Israel.

This kind of identity from generation to generation is not like the identity of an individual which maintains itself as it were biologically without conscious effort, through the presentations of memory. It is an identity that must be made by each individual will in its effort to achieve continuity of meaning with its contemporaries, its predecessors, its posterity. It is thus not an over-individual self; it is reborn in the fidelity of every generation of selves. Its security of continuance does not lie in its own substance; it lies in the fact that the desire to create this continuum is for every mind of man a *necessary desire*.

What does this general theory of social groups as coincident will circuits imply as to the nature of the state?

If all the stable wishes of men tend to establish vital circuits, the total will to power will presumably require one of its own. The whole will of man is not provided for by providing for its several fragments: its circuit will not be a mere hodgepodge or imagined totality of the rest, but a distinct launch of will which helps to give them a certain unity, proportion, and place. The will to power, like the food-getting instinct, needs its physical objects, its territory as habitat and scene of action, its 'nature' as source of supply. Since each such will can be satisfied only by finding its place in a more or less developed culture, each requires *the whole domain* which such a culture must occupy: its circuit can be established only if many wills coincide. And since each will needs all the others, not alone as sources of self-knowledge through law and of permanence through force but as constituting the very receptacles for the ideas in which one's power is vested, the circuit must include this multitude of neighbors, their predecessors and successors, as well as the physical domain common to all of them.

Our hypothesis is that *the state is the circuit required by the will to power of each member, coincident for all the people of a defined territory, and including them.*

The mental structure of the state is similar to that of many another cooperating group, as to our group of ball players. But it has peculiarities which are due to the peculiar structure of the will to power and its position in human nature. The will to play ball is more or less at fancy; the will to power is inevitable and universal. The will to play is intermittent; the will to power is incessant. The will to play may or may not help others to play; the will to power can only win its ends by helping the same ends of others, i.e., it makes the type of environment in which other wills to power can find their way.

Thus, while the will to power is incessant, and undertakes an endless task, its structure promotes the fulfillment of that task. For, as Professor Whitehead has finely pointed out, when you have an entity which, like the trees in a Brazilian forest, provides by its own growth an environment favorable to the growth of others, you have an entity whose type is most likely to survive.[2]

To conceive the state in this way, as the coincident circuit of the wills to power of a people, aids, I believe, in solving a number of the standing problems of political philosophy.

It explains why the universal need calls into being not a universal state, but a number of those irregular and tenaciously individual entities called *nation-states*.

For beside the universal will to power, the same in its general conditions in all persons, the circuit involves the local individuality of the domain, the geographical character which permeates every deed of the general will. It involves also the time-individuality of its history-making action, an activity which deals uniquely at every moment with unique data. The material conditions of action must be taken as the facts provide them, always accidentally related to the will that adopts and uses them, and yet necessary to it if that will is to act in time. The will of the state is a general will, but it is not will-in-general: it is a will to secure the destiny of the will in a definite area and by definite deeds. It is the will of a nation.

It explains, further, why we cannot conceive of the state as the result of a contract entered into by men-in-general, or by such men as are able to achieve a happy agreement on terms of union, leaving the others free not to enter.

For it is these men, these who are now on the ground, that must agree if any are to find the way of their wills: all or none must come into the group. A given plot of ground cannot at the same time be used as a ball-field and for general public strolling. Still more definitively does the obligatory game of state-action preëmpt its territory, since the very notion of a public order becomes void unless it applies to all. And the domain once taken for such joint enterprise, as an unending enterprise, it can never thereafter admit any character inconsistent with it: it is thenceforth defined as the place where we, its inhabitants, seek together our wills to power.

But especially this hypothesis explains how it is that the wills of the citizens of a state constitute a genuine unity without fusing into a mystical and inoperable corporate personality. It is a genuine unity of will, and not simply the similarity of the wills of the members.[3] Our ball players are not simply alike in their tastes: they are playing identically the same game. It is not that you and I as fellow citizens have similar territories,—we have the same territory. It is not that we take part in similar histories,—we are immersed in the same stream of history. There is but one set of deeds which qualify as the deeds of our state: in that set of deeds our wills actually overlap. What we have here is not likeness in plurality; it is unity in plurality.

For the same reason the state is something more than an *idea or principle* which its members have in common. Idealists of to-day are inclined to fall back upon this solution. "Perhaps," says Ernest Barker, "perhaps the identical is neither a real person nor a nominalistic fiction";[4] what, then? Perhaps this identity resides "not in any single transcendent personality, but in a single organizing idea, permeating simultaneously a number of personalities," a view in which Professor Muirhead seems to concur.[5] But surely the will of the state is not merely the public acknowledgment that my general principles are the same as your general principles. The will of the state includes such an acknowledgment: it externalizes the "better reason" of both of us. But the will of the state is a particular will, carrying out definite undertakings. It is a woven totality of wills which are doing the same thing;—having the same idea, to be sure, but embodying it in a specific and growing purpose. The General Will is not merely the judicial arbiter; it is an active and concrete reality, its commotive processes (which are particular) carrying its universal principles with them.

On this ground we can understand how the state attains, not only an over-individual character, as an externalized reason might do, but also a growing appearance of personality, and without actually being a person. The number of will circuits which coincide in it is large; and its stable material elements tend to accumulate. The circuit will include whatever property this enduring 'we' acquires, its routes of travel, its public works, its treasures, its specific history. This present is perpetually becoming its past. And as this past can never be the past of any other group, it is only this particular 'we' that can carry on political life on that base. We cannot drop out of the projects of those past minds into whose circuit we are born: it imposes the expectation of its continuance upon us. The state thus appears to each of us as an external being, having a will of its own.

At the same time, it is still we, the individual members, who are the realities. The tie between these members and the tie of all of them with the past and the future resides in each several individual who enters the state, not in any sundered over-mind. The state exists only so far as its circuit is actually used by the will life of its extant members: it lives only so far as it is thought, meant, and reaffirmed by them.

We understand, finally, how responsibility in group action rests upon every member of the group. It is a problem of procedure, not of theory, how the various members of a large and scattered group are to be made answerable for the actions of the whole. But once the theory is clear, the procedure becomes a matter of legal ingenuity.

The state is in the same case with other groups in this respect. As a human artifact, the state will be what its members make it: in it they build their earthly Providence. They accept therewith an individual responsibility for all that the state does, for better or for worse. They cannot wholly extricate themselves from complicity even in the crimes which a government, without their vote or against their protest, commits in their name.

Our ears still ring with the stirring words in which Tolstoi essayed to repudiate his share in the Russian state because of the execution of twelve peasants without trial. Yet neither for that crime nor for all others could Tolstoi disavow his will to work out with the Russian people an historical destiny which, in spite of his theories, required some form of state; hence his repudiation remained a noble gesture, not an effective fact. When all such as Tolstoi recognize as he did that the deed alone done in their name stands as their deed; and when all such as he thereupon renounce such deeds; then will they be repudiated in deed and in truth, for they will be repudiated through the state. For those deeds, I repeat, are ours; and to attribute them to a super-mind removes them at once from the only province in which they have a promise of cure.

There is, indeed, an over-individual self, more real than men, but it is not the state.

The conception of coincident will circuits does nothing to make clear to us how a meeting of human wills is possible: it simply assumes, with all experience and common sense, that it *is* always possible for such minds as find themselves sharing the same planet, to make common cause. But this leaves untouched our argument that this everyday process of 'finding themselves sharing the planet,' together with every mutual understanding growing out of this discovery, implies that these selves have always had some region of unity, or identical experience, known to be such.[6] This aboriginal core of unity must be prior to all social relationships: it cannot be any result of historic achievements; it cannot be the state. It is an object not of social but of metaphysical reflection; our practical dealings with it are matters not of politics but of religion.

As contrasted with this metaphysical super-self, the state is a product of the human will. Man makes it, to be sure, in the image of his god, endowing it with powers to protect him, to answer many of his prayers, to lift him into a better condition of mind, body, and estate, to serve him on his way to immortality by making possible an historic counterpart of that metaphysical attainment. Yet the state remains a pseudo-deity, not necessarily mortal, as Hobbes has it, but certainly finite and artificial.

The religious unity of men thus lies far deeper than their political unity: the given deity precedes the made deity. It is as important to distinguish them as it is to see their connection, and particularly important at present. For men are always more widely conscious of the fact of underlying unity than they are of its nature: and in proportion as they lose their grasp of metaphysical reality, they incline to recover their loss by making gods of social groups, of 'society,' or 'state,' or 'humanity,' to the boundless confusion of political theory, and to vast practical losses in terms of liberty, as will appear in due time.

Are we to conclude, then, that the state, since it is no super-mind, is no end-in-itself, but a means to the welfare of its members?

The state, we answer, has no value which is able to subordinate, and so on occasion to defeat, the welfare of its members. They owe nothing to it as to a superior order of being. Having no separate selfhood, no capacity for enjoyment or suffering, it has, literally speaking, no 'welfare' proper to itself: *there is no welfare in the case except their welfare*. Statolatry we can dismiss as having no shred of sense.

But this is far from saying that for any one member the state exists only as a means to his private ends. Unless the other individual lives, whose welfare and perfection are involved in that will circuit, are nothing to him, the state must hold something of their dignity in his eyes. Even though it were only man in all the universe that could stand as an end-in-himself, it would not follow that any man could so stand alone. Our conception of the vital circuit implies that no man can have worth to himself, i.e., can gain the selfhood that has worth to him, without breaking into and including his own concern the circuits of many other wills. Allow that truth in the abstract and justice in the abstract are not eternal values shining by their own light; still *just men*, and men in whom truth and beauty have their due rule, are objects which it is worth the travail of history to produce, and no man can get 'welfare' for himself who refuses to take part in that labor. If the state is inseparable from the age-long effort to bring such men into being, that 'individual' of ours will have no course but to value the state as he values his own happiness. The state embodies no realized perfection except the will to realize perfection; yet in this respect it is nothing less than mankind in gestation with the better mankind to be. The state is not, but has that in it, which the individual is bound to serve with his life.

NOTES

1. It is true that in every such will circuit, there is immediately set up a process of mutual accommodation which makes it "an organized system of mental or purposive forces"; and this is Professor W. McDougall's definition of a mind *(The Group Mind*, pp. 13, 66). But since McDougall himself intends to reject the assumption of a collective consciousness it would seem better not to court the confusion which must come from speaking as if there were a single and distinct subject of mentality for the group as such.

    In holding to the reality of the group mind McDougall is governed in part by the conviction that mind need not be conscious. But granting that there is a subconscious limb of mind, so that mind and consciousness are not coextensive, it does not follow that a subconscious mind can exist by itself. We have no empirical grounds for assuming subconsciousness except as filling out gaps in a whole whose focus is conscious, much as we fill out unperceived portions of physical nature by the demand for continuity with perceived portions. The ground for the appellation 'mind' lies always in the conscious focus, not in the subconscious supplement. The concept of subconscious mind affords therefore no foothold for that of a group mind whose center as well as periphery should be subconscious.

    And since the qualities of the group are *known* qualities, appearing in the consciousness which each member has of the group when in the group, and constituting for him what we might call if we like *his* 'group consciousness,' the assumption of any other form of group mind would appear otiose.
2. *Science and the Modern World*, p. 289.
3. L. T. Hobhouse is inclined to accuse believers in the General Will of mistaking the likeness of different wills for their identity, or of confusing identity of character with identity of continuous existence. *Metaphysical Theory of the State*, pp. 62 ff.
4. "The discredited state," *Political Review*, May, 1915, p. 111.
5. *Mind*, October 1924.
6. See [chapter 7a, section I, "The difficulties of social atomism"—eds.]. For development of the argument that the meeting of minds implies a primitive unity or super-self, see my book, *The Meaning of God in Human Experience*, Part IV.

CHAPTER 9

Institutions and Change

Ideals and laws are fragments of institutions: institutions are permanent clusters of ideals, customs, laws. An institution, like a law, has to meet two needs and not one only: it must be serviceable to society; it must also inform a groping individual what, according to racial experience or national experience, he wants, and hold him to that meaning. The institution of property must make clear to him the completer sense of his acquisitive and grabbing instincts. The institution of the family must interpret to him his instincts of sex and parenthood. Individuals do not always take kindly to the discipline of the institution, any more than to other discipline; nevertheless, when the postulates we have set up are complied with, the hardships of this discipline have a meaning: they are part of the normal remaking of man.

But the postulates are never complied with. The specific social arrangements we have described which tend to hold our institutions to their rightful purpose are but partially successful. We cannot say that social strains as we find them are pre-eminently informing and full of meaning. If it should be whispered of our institution of property that the results of competition and its hardships are largely without human significance, I should not know how to refute such a judgment. Hegel was never truer or more illuminating than when he said that property and contract are essential ingredients in development of personality. Yet Hegel was surely a false prophet when he said that personality has no interest in the *quantity* of property a man has, its only concern being in the fact of having some property.[1] As long as opportunity lurks in spots and is given chiefly to him that hath; as long as there are dearths of common mental food if not of other food; as long as barrenness and absence of beauty and the burning out of health destroy spiritual hunger itself; as long as man power can be reckoned as horse power, intellects and loyalties flung into the hopper as trade assets, and women and children weighed in the scales of their present efficiency without regard to any future, not to say sacred or immortal possibilities,—so long personality has a stake in the *amount* of property one has and not in the fact only. And one who calls for 'discipline,' in the sense of a hearty "I accept the social universe" and its rules, may find himself deservedly crying in the wilderness, if he blinks such residual deformations of the social order. Social unrest and undiscipline are founded on something more than untidiness of mind;

From HNR, 211–225.

they are built upon a belief that what has to be done had best be done by rebellion, overt or syndicalized.

But the worst enemy of a real grievance has always been the sham grievance; and the important thing is to aim our shaft at the right target. We dare not assert that these residual deformations are wholly without meaning for the freedom of human nature. It is a curiously distorted and unreal picture of human instinct that appears when we imagine each craving satisfied as it arises. Though such Utopias have often been tried; and are the food and drink of our superficial rebelliousness, the thing is—I do not say practically, but intrinsically—impossible. I venture the statement that the chief evil of most of our social hardships is not that they exist, but that they persist beyond their time. They play their part in a process which elicits the most subtle and most characteristic aspects of human nature; we can only estimate this nature rightly if we grasp this process in its entirety.

I

A satisfied man is certainly a man whose instincts are satisfied; but yet we cannot satisfy a man by satisfying his instincts in their severalty. History is an immense laboratory for this experiment. The cushioning of human nature is always proceeding apace, according to the means and inventiveness of a social order. It is accelerated by the high premiums paid to one who finds new ways to minister to old wants, or who finds new wants to cater to. Whoever discerns a bump in the cushion, or what is as bad, a point of non-support, is made wealthy; and his device swiftly runs the gamut from luxury to necessity. Thus the self-consciousness of all tends to the level of the most epicurean (though there is always a privileged region of society which receives first aid in this elimination of discomfort). The history of all this careful study of ease is everywhere the same: the more our satisfactions, the less we are satisfied.

Accordingly there is everywhere a contemporary criticism of the results of this "progress," a criticism taking many forms,—often of ascetic practice and moralizing, or of a pessimistic denunciation of life itself as an embodied illusion, a cosmic hoax. Or another alternative dominates: the active satisfactions of instinct are set up at odds with the enjoying end;[2] a gospel of active rather than passive self-sacrifice is preached, a gospel of work or of heroic Uebermenschlichkeit, a call for the strenuous life, for 'energism' rather than hedonism, or even a clamor for war itself as an opportunity for venting the energies of men. The suggestions are many; but for us, one inference is clear.

The human being is *adapted to maladaptation*. This is perhaps his supreme point of fitness to survive on this planet. We are better fitted to walk over rough and rolling country than over the dead level of city pavements; a day's continuous marching over this artificially 'adapted' footing leaves us with a greater fatigue than a day's tramp across country. Endurance and patience are not in the first instance Christian virtues, or even virtues at all: they are biological qualities (closely related to the 'delayed response'), fitting us for dealing with the unfit. A dog can hold for a long time the memory of an injury, cherishing without loss the unappeased impulse of revenge. What is sporadic in the dog, is distinguished in man, and applies to all his major passions. Man is the animal that can wait, the animal fashioned for suspended satisfaction. This power makes it possible for him to live in an uncomfortable situation while deliberately surveying it, and selecting the thrust most fitted to remove it. The extent of this power makes him in effect a divided being, who enjoys in the present knowing his enjoyment to be partial, while harboring a larger hunger, destined to indefinite deferment, yet identified most closely with himself and hence not suffered to decline.[3] The man is to be found in his *Sehnsucht*, his longing or yearning, rather than in his accomplished ends. Were it not for this capacity to retain wholeness of prospect in the midst of very fragmentary satisfaction (aided by a large power for vicarious enjoyment), it is hardly conceivable that we could tolerate, still less take as a matter of course, the actual suppressions of talent suffered in the ordinary specialization of activity, or even in the necessity (suffered by man alone) of choosing among many possibilities of action merely because the narrow time-channel is overcrowded with our plans. No being is so domiciled in mutilations as man. Whatever shape institutions must take to give completest vent to the possibilities of his nature, it would certainly not be a shape which allowed him nothing to criticise or to reform. His fitness for the unfit must have its scope.

II

A completer view of the meaning of this paradox is gained, I believe, in what we have already learned of the structure of human happiness. The happiness of man consists in the satisfaction, not of his primary instincts in their severalty, but of his total or central will,—the will to power. And power, while it need not be competitive, can only exist where there is something to *push against*, and will be in direct proportion to such resistance.

Now the most humanly satisfying type of power, so we thought, is the power of an idea, whether in persuading other men or in shaping institutions. The exercise of any such power presupposes that in institutions there are changes to be made; the same type of maladjustment which might dispose us to pessimism may, from this standpoint, appear as a necessary condition of complete welfare. An unwitting, and hence all the more cogent, testimony to this fact may be found in the biography of pessimism, in the curious circumstance that when pessimism becomes a doctrine or propaganda, it brings with it the first stages of its own cure. And for this reason: That wherever pessimism assumes poetic or philosophic garb, it has already lifted its head above its preoccupation with instincts, and has begun a campaign in the world of ideas, if only to decorate with a cosmic frame its own sense-experiences, as did Omar Khayyam. The dissatisfied spirit has begun, in its fancy, to be a creator of other worlds, having well shattered its own to bits,—a creator of other polities, natural laws, monopolies, markets, pieties, scenes, adventures. And as within itself, the eternal Ideal plows up the field of a sodden humanity, it discovers in the career of its own condemnation of life, as a form of thought, a life that is worth clinging to. For the pessimist, it is just his pessimism and its preaching that is of value. For this is *his* edition of the will to power through ideas.

A world in which there were no institutional misfit would be a world in which such a will to power, or indeed any other, would be as nearly as possible without human occupation; it might provide a type of happiness bovine or angelic, but certainly not human.

It would be natural, but still perverse, to infer from this psychological truth the desirableness of preserving or courting or importing a degree of evil in order that human nature may gain full satisfaction. Men find, or once found, for example, a certain happiness in war: war is one way of bringing the will to power into operation against social evils, changing institutions, or at least leaving one's mark upon them; and there are occasions when because of abnormalities in political growth, social construction must take, like surgery, the paradoxical form of destruction. Yet no folly could be blinder than that of prescribing or seeking war as a remedy for the maladies of the human spirit: for no war can act as such a remedy unless it is just; and no war is just unless it is inevitable. The place of a just cause of war, or of any other evil, as a *pou sto* in the process which makes our happiness, does not logically admit it to any other place. The knight errant without a dragon or other foe may be a melancholy figure; but he must still kill the dragon when he meets him, and not coddle him along to keep an exercise for his mettle. Likewise with our social misfits: he who should counsel others, or himself, to put up with such an evil because it affords pleasing activity to contend against it, is guilty of something more than a bull. Evil has its own sources; and there is no cause for anxiety lest there should be enough of it to make permanent opportunity for the powers of all men. For a large part of evil is an incidental product of social progress itself.

III

The improvement of institutions, and social progress generally, is responsible for a certain amount of our *awareness* of misfit. For progress enhances sensitivity and desire, and both of these bring an increase of suffering.

Everyone has noticed the ineffective efforts of children to place and diagnose their own pains. They are slightly cold; they do not know that they are cold, but only that they are "uncomfortable": an older person must interpret to them their own restlessness. If we think of the child as more sensuous than the adult, we are mistaken. The adult is much more alive to sensations; he has keener discrimination and keener enjoyment. Only an adult can be an epicure, or a colorist, or a musician. The child is incapable of being "dissolute"; for nature entrusts only by degrees the more poignant experiences of sense. The fitness of the arrangement is that the appeal of sense should increase only as the policy of the self develops to judge that appeal. The adult is defined as the person who can let things *hurt*, while keeping them subordinate to his central will. On the march, knowing that water is not to be had, one is able (as the child is not) to put thirst out of mind; busy, one forgets his hunger; conversing, bodily weariness drops away. Yet the same sensations, when they get their hearing, have a definition and force proportionate to the force of the central will. Mature self-consciousness means that every impulse of a many-stringed nature has a more perfect individuality. The organism can afford to be plural because (and only so far as) it is firmly one. This is hardly a merely happy adaptation of unrelated forces: it is more likely that the added mentality and horizon are direct agents in promoting the keenness of sense-experience.[4]

A similar relation holds good between earlier and later stages of culture: the race is but gradually let down into the pit of the knowledge of evil, for it is an incident of the same process which, increasing goods and their appreciation, we call progress. Primitive culture is by definition a culture preoccupied in the external struggle, hence little free to delve into itself. The same changes of occupation that have brought economic power, have brought separateness of interest and the self-consciousness that is born of contrast: herding and agriculture make occasion for setting my labor and its products against your labor and its products, bring private property with its relative solitude and concentration upon self, generate the scheming Jacob and the thieving Hermes. Division of labor likewise means a relative privacy in the midst of the day's work, and promotes comparisons of value and pains. Money, as a medium between production and consumption, means the necessity of enquiring into my wants before I set about purchase and enjoyment. All these things together mean increased attention to pain and desire; quite apart from the similar result of gathering wealth, leisure, and the hastening of the cushioning-process above referred to, with its inequity, bitterness, and reflection. Those who fall behind in the uneven social movement are hardly worse off in the physical life than in the wealth-less stages; for the most part they are better off—there is no new suffering except in status and pride. But old physical evils have now become social wrongs, and hurt with a new pain; the social difference sharpens self-awareness, and those who lose share as equals with those who gain in the added consciousness of the risks of fortune in goods and evils. Thus maladjustments which were tolerable and relatively unnoticed, because kept in the obscure margins of the mind, become intolerable, and begin to press upon the shapes of institutions. The very process by which discomforts are relieved creates the capacity for new discomfort.[5]

IV

The circumstance of the origin of a part of social misfit, created as it is by growing social good, suggests that at least this part of evil is such as human nature is well fitted to cope with, and to take up into the activity of its own will to power. And this will be the case if institutions are plastic to the pressure upon them. The very misfits of the social order will be grist for human nature provided this postulate is complied with:

Whatever in institutions tends at any time to deform human nature shall be freely subject to the force of dissatisfaction naturally directed to change them.

Any residual dissatisfaction with social arrangements may, in point of fact, be regarded as a constant force acting upon these arrangements, and sure, in the course of time, to have its effect upon them. There is an old physical experiment in which one is to put into a glass vessel a mixture of shot, corn, sawdust, iron filings, etc., and place the vessel on a window stool subject to constant jarring by passing traffic. In course of time the mixed contents stratify themselves in order, with the densest at the bottom. It requires no great force, but only a constant force—if there is sufficient motion—to ensure that any tendency shall reach its goal. And so, wherever social shiftings take place, there is the opportunity for the edging forward of human nature. And as this changing and shifting has been going on for many ages, the probability is great that all the coarser and more serious maladjustments have been remedied, and that we have in our present institutions a *fit in sketch* of human nature in general.

If institutions have not always submitted themselves to this pressure, it might seem that in our Western world at any rate, where all complaint is legitimate, every idea has a hearing, and the art of representative, if not of popular, legislation has appeared, a miracle and a godsend, legislation participated in by the consumers thereof,—it might seem that all institutions, after ages of cakedness had now finally reached a state of sufficient flux. And in truth, the chief impediment to a free human nature is now, not social unreadiness to entertain remedies that are certain to cure, but *ignorance*,—ignorance of its own desires and how to secure them.

Legislation must, indeed, always lag behind the market-place in its part of the cushioning process; because its inventions, as distinct from the commercial kind, must be so far thought through as to take their place at once in an imposing system of ideas, The Laws, and must be suited to universal and compulsory consumption. In both cases we must get on by making multitudes of experiments and selecting from the results; but experimenting with a law must always be a graver thing than experimenting with a new breakfast food. Law-making is a most philosophic undertaking,—or should be. Otherwise it is either entangled in its own technique, and becomes a sinecure for all the self-interest and intellectual viciousness of its promoters; or else, thrown wide open to the direct popular argument from sore to salve, it loses itself in temporizing, inconsistency, and rudderless drifting. Laws can only be competently perceived through institutions, institutions through history, and history through human nature.

Nevertheless, a radical with a conscience and an intellect even moderately equal to his task has at this hour the world before him, a world desirous as never before to do justice through its institutions to all human needs. This world requires to be convinced only (1) that his remedies will remedy, and (2) that they will not at the same time destroy more than they create. And as a guarantee for this second and greater interest, it will require in him an understanding of the history of institutions which sees in them something greater than shifting arbitrariness or rough expediency or folly and oppression,—which appreciates their slow tendency to bring humanity into the full birthright of its own freedom.

V

For if society is conservative, it is so, at least in part, because it has something to conserve.

If nature could not allow the growth of sensitivity in individuals apart from their growth in will, neither can society, except at its peril, lend itself to the liberty of clamorous desire unless there is sufficient substance in men's grasp of what is necessary and common. The license that has commonly followed sudden grants of liberty[6] is no argument against grants of liberty; but it has its argument. It shows that men had conceived the restraint that was over them too inimically, not perceiving how far the social order was, in Rousseau's phrase, compelling them to be free. It shows, then, that the protest was, in part, inconsiderate and unjustified; and that the conservative party was, to just that extent and no more, right in regarding the liberals as rebels.

He who would change an institution or experiment with it must know his own will far enough to see that he wishes the innovation itself to be a conserved and protected structure. The only value any experiment can possibly have is that something may be *established*. It is not an accident that the noisiest criers for tolerance, when they have secured free way for their own idea, have commonly shown a wish to enforce that new idea with the old intolerance. They are but waking up to the logic of their own ambition; which was, not that institutions should weaken and soften or disappear, but primarily that some particular stubborn institution should yield, and the same good force be spent on maintaining something worthier. There is literally speaking no such thing as being too conservative: but it is terribly easy to be conservative of the wrong objects. Hence place must be made in all our institutions for our common ignorance, our need to learn through the free clash of convictions,—this is the valid element in Mill's plea for social liberty, the valid element in American experimentalism. The principle is, that

Conserving force shall be proportionate to certainty,—

certainty that the institution furnishes for the given society the best solution so far proposed of its own problem. This fourth postulate we must place beside the last.

NOTES

1. *Rechtsphilosophie*, § 49. The whole attempt to eliminate *quantity* from the realm of spirit, in which Bergson is at one with Hegel, seems to me unequivocally mistaken.
2. As in Holt, *The Freudian Wish*, p. 132, etc.
3. See Brown's poem, The Roman Women.
4. This is in accord with our view of the nature of pleasure and pain. See [HNR], pp. 81 f. and 123, note.
5. This is the social form of that endless chain which Schopenhauer found in the life of individual will. But it is not a treadmill. The evils are in new places. And old issues—some of them—are permanently *settled*. We have—as the flux-philosophers tell us—a perpetual movement, self-renewed: but it is not as they suggest a meaningless and directionless movement.
6. See Arthur T. Hadley, *Freedom and Responsibility*, pp. 40 ff.

CHAPTER 10

The Dialectic of Liberalism

We have mentioned three ways in which our liberal principles have been working badly. If we are to follow a pragmatic philosophy, that which does not work is not true, and should be changed off for something else. This admonition, which has already led to the vehement rejection of democracy and all its works in various quarters, does not of itself indicate where the trouble lies, nor how much should be discarded or changed. Our analysis may help us to avoid "throwing out the baby with the bath." But we may gain some insight from a principle which has kinship both with pragmatism and with the common sense of experimental science in social affairs—I mean the principle of the "dialectic" in history.

Now the dialectic is a sort of logical movement which history is supposed to manifest when we consider its major turns or changes. As Hegel used the idea, he conceived human history as a long, continuous argument. The theme of this argument is the philosophy of life: human beings, having to work out by trial and error the right ways, or the most auspicious ways, of living, make their experiments together. These experiments are at first hardly conscious and formulated—had they been, they would not have given the color and flavor to entire civilizations: they are at first subconscious, semi-instinctive ways of taking the world which find expression in customs, art, myth, religion, politics, and ultimately in philosophy. Thus China, India, Persia, Egypt, Greece, develop characteristic qualities, and transmit them as so many ideas into the stream of human thought. As qualities, they have no quarrel with one another: each civilization contributes a permanent flavor and beauty in its art to the cumulative treasures of the race. As ideas, however, they are in apparent conflict. They contribute to the wealth of human insight, but they do so at the cost of being superseded by more adequate statements: they seem to their own time to be final, but they lose that position in the organism of advancing truth. It commonly happens that when a culture has reached the point of complete self-conscious formulation of its own spirit, it dies, gives way to another.

Progress in the arts of living, according to the dialectic view, is not a steady forward motion, but an alternating movement. An idea incompletely valid will lead by reaction to an opposing mode of thought; the thesis calls forth an antithesis. Mankind tries out the extremes before it finds a middle path, which is not a compromise, nor a golden mean, but a union of valid elements in both of the contrasting

---

From LEI, 64–102.

positions. The synthesis, in Hegel's terminology, supplants the thesis and antithesis, but also conserves them. Nothing which the human mind has once seen and lived by is ever, in this way of reading history, rejected as wholly false; it is retained, sublimated, in the successive new perceptions that emerge.

One sees that the dialectical method of reading history is a variety of the experimental method. This slow tacking progress occurs because truth is not revealed at once to the human mind, whether as a set of axioms or as a finished revelation; the race has had to mingle thought with experience, its logic is spread out through long stretches of time. But it is a form of experience in which each imperfect thought *furnishes a clue* to its successor. This is its chief difference from the haphazard experimentalism of the pragmatic philosophy.

Karl Marx, as a rebellious follower of Hegel, kept his belief in this dialectical principle in history. But in his view the dominant theme of the historical argument is not, as Hegel thought, metaphysical truth and human duty; it is economic efficiency and the consequent ordering of society. The ultimate necessity, whether or not men are conscious of it, is that any social order shall use the most effective modes of production available: the true revolutions are the turning points marked by the great inventions. With the industrial revolution has come the sharpened individualistic economy characteristic of capitalism and the sharpened class struggle: these by working out their own logic will lead to their opposite, socialism, where—for some reason not fully explained—he supposed the dialectical process would settle down and rest.

If Marx were alive today, he might feel that the course of events in Europe was beginning to prove him right. While the Russian Revolution, he might argue, is the only one that sets up an economic socialism, and does so in his name; the other forms of collectivism, in Germany and Italy, inspired in large part by a fear of the Russian sort of thing, equally indicate the failure of the capitalist individualism, and are themselves only half-way stations on the way to the conclusion dialectically necessary. Many of his followers read the situation in just that way.

Others are inclined to say that the course of events tends rather to vindicate Hegel than Marx. For Hegel also regarded individualism as an "abstraction," and therefore bound to be superseded; but its element of falsity lay partly, in his view, in its giving too much importance to the economic man. The modern state, he argued, shows its immense strength by allowing its members the degree of free action that they have, ascribing rights to them, encouraging them to compete with one another and to regard the property accruing to them from this competition as somehow sacred, and even inviting them to forget the state's existence, as if that were the best state that governs least. But this, to Hegel, is merely the sort of game we always play when we concentrate attention on one factor of the situation to the exclusion of the rest: it is a concession to our mental limits, not a final truth. The complete truth recognizes that it is the state which grants these liberties, and which is justified in doing so only so long as it maintains its own inner power and unity. The individual is one pole of the social process; the community is the other pole: the state includes them both, and when the individual forgets that he is merely an abstraction, the state will resume its self-assertion. This, think the Hegelians, is what is happening today.

For our part, we are impressed by the fact that these various contemporary movements toward social unity show no resemblance to the dialectical process proposed by either Hegel or Marx. The Russian Revolution, which is the only one from which Marx ought to derive much comfort, takes place not in a great industrial country, but in a vast rural civilization. Its immediate object of attack was not a keen, driving capitalism, undermined by class struggle in which the rich had been getting richer and the poor poorer; but a rather stupid and venal union of church and state, which had begun—too late and too slow, to be sure—to make things better for the peasantry. Nor would Hegel be much better satisfied, either here or elsewhere. For a true dialectical process, in his view, must run slow and deep; its motives lie below the surface of most and perhaps of all contemporary minds; it is only the great minds which here and there catch a glimpse of the over-arching rational necessity of the change. Instead of this, what we seem to witness is a series of sudden revulsions in which shallow analyses are aided by impatience, or perhaps we should say, in which impatience is rationalized by superficial analyses. It is the tragedy of contemporary history that its rapid rate of change gives a premium to impressionistic thinking and to fashions in action: it is motivated by impulsive swings away from "our present discontents" not by deep-felt verdicts of long experience. Any judgment which takes the form, "The old regime has failed, away with it," stamps itself at once as the product of petulance, not of the dialectic of history: for the dialectic, there is no complete failure of any historic principle.

It is therefore important for us, as for all college men and women of this generation, to give renewed attention to this idea of an historical dialectic. In the form given to it by Hegel, it was regarded as a buried dogma a generation ago, imposing an artificial scheme on the fluid, unpredictable course of free historical action. Bergson rejected Hegel out of hand on that account and regarded it as a weakness of his friend Croce that he held this element of the Hegelian system one of its living parts: "There can be," he said, "no dialectic of history." Yet the presence of freedom in history does not exclude the presence also of law. And the whole conception presents itself to us today with a renewed demand for careful consideration. For dialectic, I repeat, is not forcing an *a priori* mold upon the facts, or need not be: it is an appeal to thought-filled experience rather than to blind groping; it is consecutive induction.

If there is any dialectic in the destiny of the liberal principle, we shall find it at work in the best or culminating expression of that type of thought. I shall therefore invite your attention to one aspect of the thought of John Stuart Mill, namely, his masterly and widely effective plea for freedom of thought and expression. No one formulated the philosophy of Liberalism with greater insight and sympathy; no one felt more confident that the ideals expressed in his *Political Economy*, his *Representative Government*, his great essay *On Liberty*, were moving toward realization. Yet his younger contemporary, Herbert Spencer, was already aware of the reverse currents in the undertow, and wrote one of his most vigorous pamphlets on *The Coming Slavery*, as he described the socialistic principle. Mill appears to us today as a thinker of fine mold, standing on the edge of a turn in the lane of history, and sublimely unaware not only of what was happening, but of the fact that he bore the seeds of that change in himself.

A. Mill's Argument for Liberty of Thought and Discussion.

You will pardon me if I remind you briefly of the familiar doctrine of Mill on individual liberty. His thought has by no means lost present pertinence, as the teaching profession has reason to recall. He believed that men should be free to live their lives each in his own way, with but one restriction, that neither this freedom nor its consequences should encroach upon the interests of others. Particularly important he felt it to be that a man should be free to speak his mind and to argue for his opinions. There were, as you recall, three main reasons for this plea.

First, if society allows itself to display the natural hostility we all feel toward divergent ideas by suppressing their utterance or penalizing it, we are likely to lose important new truth. Mill is willing to concede that as a matter of statistics most new ideas may be bad; but among the new ideas there are some good ones, and they will provoke the usual antagonism toward the unusual and unorthodox, somewhat in proportion to their importance. Discussion itself is the sifting process through which, normally, the wilder and more foolish variants among proposed ideas are killed off, and the more promising ones are handed on to the later stages of the tourney. Society therefore may safely intrust the elimination of "dangerous thought" to this normal struggle for survival; and unless it does so, it cuts itself off from those occasional new thoughts which are the rarest and the most important agency of progress.

In the second place, suppose that we are in the happy position in which we like to fancy ourselves, of being in possession of the truth, as far as humanity can have it. Under such circumstances, the first argument loses its point. But if this possessed and final truth is no longer challenged, doubted, denied, and then defended, it begins by degrees to lead a somnolent and semiconscious existence, until it becomes "just one prejudice the more." We lose our own perception of its reasons; it forfeits the character of an understood truth; it reverts to subconsciousness. Hence one who seriously challenges a truth, though under the premises his challenge is based on error, is doing that truth at least the service of revivifying its foundations, and so reinstating its meaning in consciousness. On this ground alone dissenters are rather to be encouraged than repressed.

Third, systematic repression of the utterance of opinion tends to ruin one of the most important assets of the community—moral courage. For though the temper of dissent may often seem rather impertinent, conceited, and destructive than courageous, there is in the willingness to oppose an established attitude of society at least a glint of the true metal without which all social life and conversation run off into a murk of tepid conformity and yes-saying.

Mill's recommendation, then, is simply, *No penalty* for opinion and opinion-spreading, no matter how outrageous the opinion may appear to us to be. By this he means to exclude all legal punishments as a matter of course; but he is thinking primarily of social punishments—exclusions, ostracisms, boycotts, loss of repute and standing. In his view there should be not only no rack, no torture, no inquisition, but also no social anger against dissent, no unfriendliness, no deprivation of patronage, no avoidance, no looks askance—complete freedom and welcome for the living thinker, no matter who he is nor what he thinks. In brief, he conceived a society in which everybody felt free to speak his mind on all points at all times, and in which nobody molested anybody for doing so, nor put him to any sort of disadvantage.

As we contemplate the ideal of such a society we are struck with a certain wonder that Mill should have regarded it as a condition under which moral courage would be developed! Since we would have here a perfect example of a costless privilege, it would seem that every occasion for moral courage had been removed, and the development of moral courage therefore rendered impossible. Where there can be no danger, there can be no courage.

But aside from this, think of the staggering price society would have to pay for such a situation. No idea, false or true, could be permitted to attain social or political power; i.e., no idea could be allowed to "prevail" as a guide to common practice. For whatever idea takes hold of human behavior *ipso facto* places all contrary ideas at a definite disadvantage. To believe an idea is to begin to form habits about it; and when habits have become established it is far more difficult to unseat the original idea than when it was in the position of pure theory, with its pro and con on equal footing. Social habits involve a greater momentum than individual habits; the outs have a correspondingly greater disadvantage of position relative to the ins. And those who hold to the outview have to suffer the natural incidents of this disadvantage, the least of which is that they have to work harder for a hearing.

Suppose, then, that to avoid this painful consequence, we prevent ideas from having any effect on behavior, gaining any social power, making any general difference: ideas become first unimportant, then meaningless, and truth being eviscerated is no longer worth getting: your realm of costless toleration is a realm of devaluated truth. So far from favoring the growth of knowledge, it promises a condition in which no one cares enough about ideas to put its new increments together into a working whole; the truth-thinking, truth-announcing business loses its romance and acclaim, and becomes like a sea of incandescent jellyfish at night—a million vague luminosities and no general light.

The normal destiny of an idea is to come to some sort of power. Our interest in discovery lies partly in the fact that truth ought to be a principle of social order; or to put it the other way around, our social order has a natural hunger for the truth which it can incorporate, and to incorporate a better truth is to dislodge a poorer. It is always possible to keep applications out of sight, indeed, for the most part they ought to be in the background of consciousness: the active meanings of ideas can add themselves to the theoretical meanings, so long as the channels remain open. But close the channels, and thought becomes a higher form of play. And since it suits the average man only too well not to think, and still more not to have to act according to any hard-won thought, Mill's ideal state would have a Chinese sort of stability, a purely literary culture, a contraceptive order avoiding all the pains of travail and milling around in the same political spot forever. Mill's saving of pain to the thinker is the Western counterpart of "saving the face": the rule, No thinker shall suffer for his thought, is equivalent to the rule, Nothing important shall ever happen.

The right of freedom of speech ought to be a right to the facilities for winning the ear of men in an uphill fight, in the face of public disapproval. The acceptance of that disapproval and its consequences is the occasion for moral courage and a token of sincerity, further a certain insurance to society that the speaker has soberly weighed his thought. Spinoza was excluded from the synagogue; and so he should have been—he did not belong there. He should have been deprived of any position which implied a belief he did not possess. So far, the social penalty for his unorthodoxy was normal.

But it did not stop there. It proceeded to those excesses which have provoked the counterexcesses of Mill's theory. It tried to cut him off from intercourse and from all livelihood within the Jewish community. The effect of this was to deprive him of his power to persuade within that community, and to throw him back upon the slower, quieter, and more impersonal influence of speculative thinking. Through this excess punishment, the Jewish community shielded itself from disturbance and the possible fascinations of falsehood, but also from stimulus and the possibilities of a leap of life. In this excess, it was wrong to Spinoza and to itself. But had Spinoza been given the choice, I do not doubt that he would have preferred to live when he did, rather than in our day when he would be tolerated everywhere and probably ignored. For in that intolerant time, truth was at least given a rating of high importance; whereas indifference to what is rare and difficult, an evaporation of the emotional significance of truth, is one of the symptomatic traits of our contemporary Liberalism.

Our principle, then, is not one of "No penalty" but one of "Relevant penalty" as against "Irrelevant penalty." The deviator ought to suffer and ought to expect to suffer; but his suffering should be such as to leave him all the means to make his case good. The right of freedom of speech does not consist in the privilege of saying anything I please without exciting any reaction. It consists in the right, and the duty, to express what I have seriously and responsibly thought, and to take the consequences of that statement. If I come to the conclusion that there is no God, I ought to be permitted to state and to argue for my atheism; but certainly not to remain within a church whose chief function is to maintain the worship of God; nor can I insist on the right to preach atheism in the primary schools. If I become convinced of the public importance of nudism or polygamy, I should have the privilege of speaking to this effect; but I have no right to demand a hearing from those who do not care to listen, nor a continued reception in the society of those who regard the prevailing manners as signs of a right mind. Ostracism is one of the things which I ought to be prepared to face without complaint.

Suppose I believe in communism, and in the value of a revolution by force for setting up the new order. I have no manner of complaint if the country protects itself against any actual revolution I may start. And if the country is so far disturbed that a talk revolution tends to become an actual revolution, it is justified in treating the talk as an incipient deed. But supposing the country to be in an ordinary state of self-possession, I should be encouraged to state my belief and my reasons for it to audiences who are disposed and able to think the thing through from first principles. I have no place in the public schools. In fact, if any man professes to believe that we should have a revolution and does anything else except prepare men's minds for that event, he convicts himself of insincerity. For if a man is dissatisfied with the political constitution under which he lives, the rectification of that basis of life takes precedence of every other concrete purpose. He cannot do that and teach school!

Suppose, again, that without accepting communism nor believing in revolution I am convinced that the evils which lead the minds of many people in those directions are real evils, and that young men and women of college age ought to begin to think about those evils and the various remedies proposed in our time, then I should be heard not only in public but especially within the colleges and universities of the country, which are committed to the wide exploration of social forms and philosophies. In no other way can new and radical proposals receive that complete aeration which they require; in no other way can they be honorably met or, indeed, be met at all since the only answer to a false theory is a true theory. The college is therefore precisely the place in which such views as communism presents ought to be known and discussed. The primary and secondary schools are the places for the conveying of prevailing tradition, together with the reasons which have supported it: the college age is the age for philosophical inquiry, and for the recognition of the problematic and unfinished aspects of our civilization. Propaganda and inflamed exhortation have no place there; but the man who can present steadily, fairly, and without fear all the facts and experiments of the contemporary world (including the facts of propaganda and inflamed speech) within the frame of a reflective and earnest judgment is a man of the greatest value for any university. The government which cannot honor the freedom of speech of such a man in such a place displays an unworthy evasion and acts to its own hurt. There is a world of difference between such teaching, and the teaching of revolution and discontent to children. Society is wholly within its right in suppressing this latter sort of abuse; it has only to beware lest the mere fact of a political inquisition bring it into worse evils.

B. The Illiberal Basis of Mill's Plea for Liberty.

So far, I have pointed out that Mill's unduly amiable attitude toward every spouter of deviation robs the truth-getting business of its proper virility, and ignores the normal destiny of truth to social power. But there is a more serious defect in his argument, from the point of view of the individual and his rights, namely, that the basis of his argument is treasonable to these interests.

The original basis of individualism, as we saw, was that the individual man as such has rights. These rights are addressed to any conscious agency that may affect them, whether the fellow man or society or the state itself. Thus, in this view, my property is mine, as against the casual thief, or a trespassing neighbor, but also against an irresponsible monarch. Magna Charta is much occupied with the ways in which the royal power may and may not dip into private pockets. There were things which society, whether for its convenience or its welfare, could not rightfully do.

Now the basis of Mill's entire plea is not the inherent right, but the social utility. This is his principle. He very seldom uses the word "right"—I believe it occurs once or twice in the text of the essay *On Liberty*, but as it were inadvertently; for the whole point of the argument is not that intolerance infringes a right but that society is likely to lose by it. On this ground, the moment it can be shown that society stands to gain by intolerance Mill can have no word to say in behalf of liberty.

Once [we] adopt this standard of measure, namely, that the individual has no rights in the literal sense of the word, but may have such privileges as are consistent with the public welfare, one is but a step away from the question, Who is to decide what is consistent with public welfare? And then we are at the door of Leviathan and Mussolini.

Thus we see in Mill the strange spectacle of a collectivist, in respect to method, arguing for individualism; the precise counterpart of Hobbes, an individualist in method arguing for collectivism. Neither could reach other than a pseudo-result. Mill, in particular, had abandoned the philosophical basis on which alone the type of Liberalism he recommended could stand. His sympathies were there—he was a great and liberal soul; but he was also one of the third or fourth generation of Liberals in whom the utilitarian method had dimmed the former sense of principle, while a certain gentility of existence had veiled from him the actual conditions of the life of the British workman, and a scholarly bent to generalities had obscured the sense of those very particulars, which as an empiricist he needed in his system.

The glaze of totality is over his eyes; he does not see the individual subject, perceiving and thinking; nor does he feel the movement of history about him as a great argument in which the thinker fights, suffers, creates. In all of these respects he stands in sharp contrast with a contemporary thinker, whose stormy life oscillated between England and the Continent, and who has done much to make the history whose tug he felt and whose dialectic he attempted to interpret.

C. The Marxian View of History.

Karl Marx, most of whose active life was spent as a refugee in France, Holland and England, knew well in his own person, as Mill never knew, the hard lot of the unpopular idea; yet he made no plea for costless toleration. He saw struggle as an aspect of life, a necessary aspect: and sharing something of Spinoza's intellectual reconciliation to what has to be, preached the class war without complaint of its incidental rigors and social ignominies.

In the year when Mill issued his *Political Economy* (1848), a bible of economic individualism, Marx and Engels brought out their Communist Manifesto. Eleven years later, when Mill published his work *On Liberty*, in which social conflict over ideas is deprecated and history seems lulled to sleep, Darwin published his *Origin of Species*, with its note of struggle for existence as a method of biological advance, and Marx his *Critique of Political Economy* with its note of economic struggle as a method of dialectical advance. Surrounded by the economic fruits of Liberalism in the shape of a growing volume and intensity of private interest, Marx foresaw its dialectical reversal to an intensity of commonwealth and a reassertion of the lost wholeness of society.

The synchronism of the work of Mill and Marx is as striking as its contrast of direction; and so far as the sense for the forces of social change is concerned, we should have to judge Marx, in view of present facts, a truer prophet than Mill and the deeper man. And upon the truth of one of his major judgments, there will be little difference of opinion. Capitalism, he thought, has solved the problem of production; it has not solved the problem of distribution. Mill would have said that if by the problem of distribution we mean *equitable* distribution, that problem will be worked out in due time but is not of first rate importance, because for society as a whole security of property is more important than any exact system of apportionment. Hegel had said something of the same sort, namely, that while it is of vast importance that everybody have property, it is of little importance *how much* property one has—philosophy has little interest in mere matters of quantity! Marx recognized the shallowness of this complacency, seeing that the quantity of property a man has is of fundamental importance, especially toward the lower end of the scale of incomes; that a difference of quantity may well make the difference between freedom and no freedom, between personal development and the stunting of all distinctively human life; and that, for these reasons, the problem of distribution could not be deferred. But in his view, it could not be met under the present system. It is here that his reading of the dialectic of history concerns us.

Modern man had been living under the system of manufacture, which displaced the system of gild handcraft and landed property, by introducing a better division of labor and releasing new productive forces. In this system, in which we were seeing the arrival of the economic individual, Marx sees rather the arrival of an economic class, *the bourgeois*. What we have thought of as its individualism, with its trust in reason, Marx thinks of rather as a class trait, allied to biological energy, a self-seeking enterprise, which is bound in the nature of the case to work out its own principle to its limit, and in so doing to prepare its own death.

This working-out, as he sees it, has led naturally to large scale industry, with an increasing mastery of mechanical power. Through its very scale, big industry begins to wipe out the early traits of individualistic (bourgeois) production, introduce a new psychology, create new problems. It brings about "on the one hand an ever increasing proletarianization of the great mass of the people, and on the other hand an ever greater mass of unsaleable products.... Overproduction and Mass Misery, each the cause of the other,—that is the absurd contradiction which is its outcome," and which of necessity calls for a new method of economy. This picture of a superabundant production, stuffed warehouses, and a hungry populace, unable to buy what had been produced by their own hands, dependent on a subsistence wage and uncertain of that—this picture familiar to us today as the outstanding puzzle of our economic order, and long ago stamped out in letters of passionate force by Thomas Carlyle, was the picture which Marx in the [18]50's was seizing upon as the fatal criticism of our order. He felt that the dialectic of history required things to get worse before they could get better by the complete overturn of the social pyramid, placing the proletariat in corporate control.

Let us compare the diagnosis which leads Marx to this result with our own diagnosis.

On the point of the unity of society, Marx feels the need of it, but does not regard it as a characteristic defect of the bourgeois system. His appeal to the proletariat is, "Workmen of the world, unite"; and to achieve this first condition of success he attempts by every method to strengthen class consciousness, which implies a curbing of individual self-assertiveness. But he assumed that Capital and the entity we have called Business are already well united and trending toward the greater unities of large-scale production as a part of the automatic drift of the dialectic—an assumption which our own observation does not support. It is true that immense aggregates of capital are the order of the day, bearing a rough proportion to the dimensions of the undertakings attempted, and the number and variety of labor organized in such undertakings. But it is also true that the relations between these aggregates, frequently competitive or partly competitive, are difficult to describe by the term "unity," or even "harmony"! They reveal, only on a larger scale, the essential individualism and divisiveness of the economic motive in its purity. Nor can we say that Marx's hope of attaining an ultimate unity of society through the medium of class war shows a deep perspicacity regarding the problem of unity.

On the point of rights and duties, the sense of dialectical necessity in things renders Marx even more silent than Mill. But the ethical basis of his movement, cloaked under the disguise of economic determinism, is his judgment that the wealth of the world is produced by the workers, is in this sense *earned*, and is their right! Duty has preceded right in this case. And since in the ideal society there are to be no idlers, there are to be no costless rights. His complaint that the problem of distribution has not been solved indicates that right-without-enough-duty is to him also a central defect of the individualist scheme.

We should have to say, however, that Marx has little interest for the general problem of rights-and-duties; his philosophy allows him to concentrate almost exclusively on the economic aspect of things. He believes too easily that all the interests of personality will take care of themselves, once the economic problem is solved. On this point he is radically mistaken: one might go so far as to say that concentration on the economic problem is likely actually to prevent the solution of that problem itself, which in our time is primarily ethical. The justification for the singlemindedness of Marx was the prevalent neglect of the economic factor, especially in the top-lofty idealism of the Hegelians; his great contribution to the philosophy of society was his thoroughgoing redressal of that neglect; it is not surprising that he fell into the opposite one-sidedness.

It would be quite possible, however, to carry Marx's critique a step beyond Marx, and on the same analogy. We might say that individualism has solved the problem of producing men, but has not learned how to distribute them into the common life. The Liberalism of "private rights" (with the muted rumor of duties far away) has produced in this country an admirable race of men; a rural population without a peasantry; an industrial population without a proletariat. I say this with deliberate defiance of those who import irrelevant European population analyses to this land; forgetting that such a term as "proletariat" is a psychological term as well as a term of relative income, and that proletarian psychology does not exist in America. Of what other nation can these things be said? This same regime has produced the men of Business, men of ability and magnitude and of not a little magnanimity, a breed to be proud of. And yet if one asks of these rugged individuals as a class whether they are wholly satisfactory as a human type; and if not, what is the matter with them; one would have to admit that they tend to come to a dead end, not knowing how to branch out into the community. There they are, handsome torsos of humanity, stuck around in well-built private estates on the edges of a thousand cities; too many of them with nothing important to do but to enjoy themselves, their wealth, their self-esteem; devoid of mission and therefore of moral dignity; helplessly dismayed at what is becoming of their children on whom they have lavished every care, sometimes including their own, and for whom they have purchased the most scientific models of education! The American individual, whether workingman or employer, capitalist or noncapitalist, is as good a product as the planet can show; he is not as a type mean nor greedy, callous nor ruthless; he takes pride in service, and if he is a business man, in the service connected with his business; he is imaginative (to start with) and sympathetic, and has a liberal sentiment toward the world at large; he has an instinctive sportsmanship; is strong in emergency; is the best giver the world has yet known. The picture of the employing class conventionalized by purveyors of the class war is a caricature which only distance and an artificially cultivated rancor make possible. But *he* is responsible for the distance, and as a rule he does not know his responsibility. He has defined his success, and his service, and having attained them he is finished: he is not distributed into the common life, either in his activity or in his thought.

On the third point of our diagnosis, that of emotional defect, we find a similar partial agreement with Marx. After the sentimental wash of unredeemed benevolence proper to the Liberal writers, the hard pugnacities of the Marxians afford a momentary relief. The missing salt is here in quantity. One is no longer dodging the actualities of conflict, want, clashing-interests under agreeing-interests; one is no longer put off by polite reticences; one is initiated into a more virile psychology, and into a sociology rich in its vein of realism. To some minds, this emotional flavor once felt renders all other outlooks insipid. Yet, as a sole diet, brine is meager, and pretends more realism than it has. The basic emotion of any stable system must be positive. In Marx, it is the felt and sought solidarity of the workers, essentially liberal in quality. His pugnacity is attained by drawing about this group—and in the Bolshevist regime about a much smaller group—the skin of a partisan exclusion, and by defining its relation to the outside portion of the community in the simple term, war. There is an emotional gain in simplification; a sensible strategic advantage. But no emotion can last which is so consciously canalized at the expense of truth. The emotional quality of the socialist movement has rightly excited the admiration of mankind; it has tended to the level of a humane religion. But alike with the Liberalism it eschews with just disrelish, it falls short of attainable realism.

D. Mill and Marx as Thesis and Antithesis.

The two thinkers whose work has now come before us instituted no comparisons between themselves, even if they knew of one another's existence. The instructive contrasts were there, but were latent, and are only now becoming significant to us some seventy-five years afterward. Let us bring them together in summary form.

The most striking contrast is that of the optimism of Mill and the pessimism of Marx with regard to the immediate social passage. It is optimism which allows a thinker to become as nearly unconscious of historical movement as Mill was. He felt that on the whole stability and security had been achieved and could be kept; he was willing to contemplate that government should now and then step out of its *laissez faire* role in order to help the weaker party to the wage bargain. With these occasional aids, the individual forces of society would normally tend to work out the welfare of the social whole. To Marx, these individual forces had already set up an unbearable strain, a situation the reverse of stable, and were steadily bringing things to a worse pass of inequality and suffering. It was not a situation which reason could remedy. The thoughts of men, not free, but molded by class interest and economic necessity, were to be a part of the equipment by which this process should be carried to the point of overturn. These thoughts must be the thoughts of fighters, who must add to the pain of the economic stress these other evils of class hatred, class warfare, class subjugation. Beyond these evils, an eventual happy state, perhaps; though even here man's so-called higher nature remains the creature of his material situation.

We have pointed out the inconsistency of Mill in supporting an individualist scheme of society for the sake of the collective good. Marx has the reverse inconsistency; arguing for a collectivist scheme of society for the sake of individual good. We have said that the central point of Marx's economic attack is the matter of distribution; but this word "distribution" betrays the motive as divergent from that of the socialist. Distribution is the process of getting the social product into the hands of you and me, the consumers; and we are individuals. It is this sense of the individual workman and his lot—a sense that Mill never enjoyed—which constitutes, as I think, the real strength of Marx's writing. When the workingman reads his Marx, he feels that he reads a man who not only knows his situation, and has his personal interest at heart, but who is actually "one of us," an illusion from the biographical point of view, but true enough in motivation. To Marx, the social collectivity is after all merely a means to the end of the individual liver. His inconsistency is thus the precise complement of Mill's inconsistency.

And now, as so often happens in contrasts of this kind, both types of policy reach the same result in one respect: both, if given free and exclusive rein, would involve the ruin of the individual personality.

How Liberalism, as a welfare philosophy, produces men who find the meaning of life where they have been taught to find it, namely, in a sum of personal satisfactions, and having gained these are at a loss for anything more to do—this we have already seen. Many of these individuals find something to lend further meaning to their existence; and this is to their credit, they were not helped to it by the ideal of "greatest happiness to greatest number !" Others rest in their rights to enjoy, lusty sunflowers, well grown, devoid of fragrance, neighbors to the weeds.

But the socialism of Marx aims consciously at the same result, only for a different group of individuals. The whole purport of the social process, as conceived by Marx, is the social dividend for the benefit of the workers. The human member of this process is taught to think of himself as a determined function of the economic mill-of-the-gods, these dialectical overruling laws being the ultimate Bourgeoisie of the Universe! The flower of Mill's philosophy is the economic gentleman, independent and freethinking; the flower of Marx's philosophy is the economic workman, dependent and unfreethinking. Both as pictures of the complete man are human failures.

In this result we come on the trail, I believe, of the true dialectic of history. This dialectic is not, as Marx thought, a paradoxically intelligent result of nonintelligent forces. Nor is it as Hegel thought a pure and superhuman logical necessity. It is the slow consensus of freely thinking and groping human minds, as they perceive the inadequacy of the thoughts which have been guiding them, and turn toward something better. Ideas contain action as the valley walls contain the stream. Great ideas are like the reservoirs created by mountain barriers, over which the waters find no outlet, though they seek through a thousand diverging ravines. There is no automatic motion onward. There is no leap ahead until at some level a breach appears in that barrier; then all the waters conspire to enlarge it and to enter the next valley. Thus a dialectical turn in history can only come on those rare occasions when men reach a common feeling of confinement within categories that have appeared final, and an equally general intuition of a way to move beyond them. It waits the arrival in human heads of a truer idea.

Whatever this new idea may be, it will not cancel the insights of Mill or of Marx over against each other; but will preserve much of each, including something of that reference to social wholeness which guided Mill, and something of that subconscious individualism of Marx. But it will have to present us an individual more complete than either had in view. This individual will have a moral quality which is not a mere derivative either of the social relations in which he stands or of his economic situation; and while having some properties of the self-sufficient being, he will have also what I venture to call a "joining function," which implies a need for something beyond himself.

This notion of a joining function may save us from the idea of a prior "social organism" in which the individual is embedded as a cell in a body, and at the same time submerged and lost. It is this "organic" conception, present in Aristotle and Hegel, which has hitherto been the chief alternative to the theory of abstract individualism. But I stand on the view that there *is no prior social organism:* there is an organism to be built, to be built by individuals endowed with the joining function. Let me conclude this chapter by a suggestion of what this strange phrase may mean.

I may illustrate this idea by an older conception of the chemical atom, once supposed to be an unchangeable ingredient of the universe. Each atom had a kind of self-sufficiency, in the sense that it could never be destroyed. But it also had its habits of combining with other atoms; and each kind of atom has its own invariant capacity for such combination. Some could take on two atoms of hydrogen as partners in a molecule, some one atom, some four, and so on. This uniting capacity was called the "valence" of the atom. When an atom had become disjoined from a given molecule, its "valence" might be regarded as a seeking activity, as if a definite number of hooks or hands were reaching out into the neighboring region for other unoccupied valences. It has a latent joining capacity.

Now the human individual, like this imaginary atom, can exist apart from other individuals: but he has a joining function, which makes him not alone capable of social life but desirous of it. In this joining function we may discern such elements as the law of "reason" which each man assumes to be the same as the reason of his neighbor. He is therefore able to coöperate with his neighbor in everything making use of logic, mathematics, science. We may also see an idea of the good, which—underneath all divergencies of taste and preference—each individual assumes to be in fundamental agreement with that of each other individual. Because of this agreement, ideas of right can be set side by side, compared and discussed; working systems of law can be set up and active enterprises involving the morals of satisfied coöperation can be carried through.

Since these common systems of thought and value are valid not only for contemporaries, but also between different periods of time, they have a character more enduring than the individuals who employ them; and they are therefore sometimes erroneously regarded as "eternal objects" existing or subsisting out of time. They are, however, but parts of the constitution of this joining power; which has in it other qualities and impulses into which we need not now enter. But because of this joining function, each individual is not merely "I-thinking" but also "We-thinking"; he uses the first person plural, the simplest name of a unitary society, as easily as he uses the word, I. Man is not by nature a solipsist, confined to his own consciousness and his own interests; he is by nature an active agent in an active world, and a personal agent in a world of persons and things. In all his economy, his hunting, his animal husbandry, his road and bridge building, his mining and manufacturing, his invention of systems of science, industry, finance, security—the entire economic structure of his mastery of nature—he is still the being whose prime interests are in that region of reason and value which make him capable of society.

The entity we call the state is the spontaneous unity of these joining functions, a unity formed, as a rule, about something-to-do in the world of concrete activity. This state does not preexist, and we are not here to serve it. But it exists because we first exist, and because its existence may enable us to be more completely ourselves. The individual apart from his joining function, purely as economic man, cannot create a social whole; the individual with his joining function may do so. Here we have the paradox of social structure; and we have now to develop in detail the solution to which this conception may lead us.

CHAPTER II

The Future of Liberalism

There are five things I would like to put forward on this subject. Let me first mention them all, and then comment on three of them.

First,—making an obvious distinction between Liberalism and the liberal spirit—the liberal spirit has not finished its work in the world, nor is it likely to do so. It belongs to human nature, not to any party, religion, or historic movement. Its business is to correct the infinite self-centeredness of that same human nature when flattered by the enjoyment of those powers which society perennially creates as it becomes complex and unequal.

Second, Liberalism as a special historic pattern of political and economic ideas has already passed: it has no future. It has been the reverse of a failure; but its unexampled success in the last two centuries has given it the value of an experiment, whose purport we now very clearly read. Its once negligible weaknesses have developed into menacing evils. Many of its ingredients will persist; but the pattern as a whole will give way to new patterns.

We are asked to prophesy regarding these new patterns; but prophecy can arise only out of diagnosis.

Third, then, my diagnosis is this: That Liberalism has shown itself incapable of achieving social unity; that it has created a pernicious separation of individual rights from individual duties; that it has lost its emotional grip because its emotional basis was in a serious degree unrealistic.

Fourth, passing from diagnosis to prophecy: Present reactions against Liberalism, crude, bedevilled and alloyed as they are, move under the necessity of an historical dialectic, so far as they tend to reassert the reality of the total interest of society. The liberal spirit itself demands the reversal toward an element of what is sometimes called an authoritarian or collectivist form, a more unified society, capable of using its voice and its muscles, with a sterner internal discipline and a new emotional basis.

Fifth: Individualism of some sort remains a necessary ingredient of any modern society. The human person can never again accept the position of a means to the state as an end; nor can his rights be reduced wholesale to the status of public utilities, as in the Fascist ideal, which the state may grant or withhold.

From *Journal of Philosophy* 32 (April 25, 1935): 230-247.

The kernel of the problem lies in the opposition of points four and five. It is comparatively easy to gain social unity at the cost of the individual; contemporary dictatorships have taken the easy path. The real problem is far more difficult, to gain unity while redefining the individual so that he too may grow strong.

It may aid our perspective to consider that while the West is reefing its Liberal sail, the new states of the Orient are moving with increasing momentum toward certain parts of the Liberal program: they are bent on national strength, and they have not misjudged that among its conditions are a degree of democracy, general education, individualism. They may avoid our diseases; but they have truly discerned some of our sources of power.

With this preamble, let me begin in the middle of things with a development of the third point, that of diagnosis. For if we who look forward differ in our forecast, it is only as we differ in our judgment as to the points in which experience has shown Liberalism defective.

I

Liberalism, we have said, has shown itself incapable of bringing about or maintaining social wholeness; and the capacity for united thought and action has become imperative. In its early days it was a habit inherited from feudal society.

It was natural to assume that a group of representatives whether of localities or of interests would sum themselves up into a fair representation of the whole state. This might have occurred if each member of Parliament, let us say, regarded his own function as that of representing Britain and not merely Bristol: but when the survival in Parliament of the member from Bristol depends on his bringing home local results, the facile assumption vanishes. It is just the total-interest that is nowhere represented in such a body. When, further, the acting sovereign is divided into three branches, specifically advised to "check and balance" one another; and when an administration is composed of fragments from a litter of competing parties, each one animated by a strong passion for party-existence, political life is reduced to a mere trickle. We have brought together a set of limbs thinking they will compose a body politic; but they disclaim one another, and the "general will" snuffs out. Political unity has to be born from unity.

In the economic realm we have the same situation. Washington foolishly professing not to represent Business, Business represents itself at Washington. And what or who is "Business"? A lot of Able Heads, each representing millions of individual transactions in going concerns, each individual transaction entered into willingly, and therefore presumably benefiting both buyer and seller—ergo, in sum total a happy country? Not at all. Each individual transaction ably manipulated so as to leave the largest net in the hand belonging to the Able Head; each Able Head, then calling on Washington for a further individual blessing, to improve not the product, not the lot of the buyer, not the Greatest Happiness, but the Net. And will not a collection of handsome Nets constitute a prosperous land? That seems to be the fallacy. They seem to constitute rather a set of prosperous spots, like pimples of prosperity on a visage predominantly pale! They do not add themselves into the General Health.

It is quite true that a land none of whose citizens have any margin is necessarily a poor land; it is also true that a land some of whose citizens have large margins has *potential* public resources, for private wealth can always be tapped by taxation. But the question is whether these private reservoirs have any regular *working relations* to the public concerns. The answer is that under Liberalism they are not so much as invited to do so. A few have deliberately laid lines from private resources to public benefits; they have acted against the inertia of the system. It is not that private owners are devoid of good-will; it is simply that there is no regular way, in the Liberal theory of things, whereby private wealth normally constitutes a working commonwealth. There is a defect in our morals, no doubt; but there is also a defect in the system of ideas. It is not merely that great private wealth is consistent with widespread private poverty, but also that by the theory of *laissez faire*, the social whole has been as a matter of principle kept on starvation rations for all the great common ends which constitute national life.

The second point in our diagnosis is that Liberalism has infected the Western mind with the disease of Rights-without-Duties. Its music has been bound up with the theme of Natural Rights; and if rights are natural, belonging to the individual by birth, they are not alone costless but also inalienable.

To think of himself as so endowed was a radical encouragement to the individual member of the Demos, an encouragement which he needed in his hour of struggle with authority; it had this pragmatic truth. But now that the conflict is over, it has become a bald flattery. There are no unconditional rights.

And the society which feeds on this diet of invincible self-esteem becomes corrupted in a vital respect; for the conditions of all rights are moral conditions. If Liberalism had recalled its modern charter in the works of John Locke it could not have forgotten that being "born free and equal" meant simply an immunity from exploitation which carried with it an imperative to refrain from exploiting others. For every right-receivable, there are innumerable duties-payable: that right of "equality" which defends me from the arrogance of a thousand pretending superiors defends a hundred thousand against my own arrogance. Hence the cry of "rights" should never have been uttered except with the undertone of a vast humility: instead of which it has been taken as a pure birth-gift of Fortune, and the question is insidiously suggested whether, after all, there is any such thing as duty. "The world owes every man a good break," owes him not the pursuit of happiness but happiness itself; and since rights are inalienable, it is irrelevant what his actions or sentiments are whether toward himself or toward others; not even crime can forfeit what nature has kneaded in with his being. This is simply to spread through the whole community the moral virus of privilege which Liberalism professed to hate.

The third point of deficiency in Liberalism is the natural root of the others. Liberalism's emotional appeal, tremendous in its fighting days, has slowly oozed away. It was founded on an unsalted amiability, arising from *a priori* principles, hopeful postulates about human nature, valid enough but untested and incomplete. There is always a rush of kindly sentiment toward the fellow man as presented in imagination; we have but to hear of a Good Samaritan, and forthwith we are he. The strength of Liberalism is in the universal appeal and universal validity of this attitude; its weakness is that it has not borne the burden of living with this abstractly defined fellow being, and thus has no proposals for dealing with his seamy side; it has not defined the place for pugnacity; it is so far unreal.

The assumption that you have only to educate men alike to make them effectively equal as citizens was allowable as a working hypothesis; taken as a dogma, it could not be observant and critical enough to make the necessary revisions. As a result Liberalism has bred a race of self-confident, vigorous men; but it has not bred a race that can be trusted with power or wealth. The atmosphere of faith which released their genius has failed to maintain their solicitude to be worthy of the new trust; there has been no tonic in the air to breed compunction in them,—they don't know the word! In the general softness all honest standards tend to disappear. The chief suffering and discontent of the passing Liberal age is not that of poverty nor injustice nor political ineptitude; it is the experience of a prevalent flabby mediocrity of mind and character which begins, especially in our more virile moments, to inspire a sort of moral loathing.

One of the tests of any system is whether it tends to beget and improve in its own kind. The art of music will not vanish so long as it continues to elicit musicians who want to absorb and add to its tradition. Liberalism has ceased to beget Liberals. As an educational temper, its products tend to be progressively weaker than the original stock. Liberalism was born as a set of principles worth fighting for; its beneficiaries of to-day number few fighting men, and fewer who have principles to fight for. Perhaps the difficulty is that with the principles of Liberalism there went a spirit of indulgence; that this spirit tended to foster self-indulgence in its protégés; and that self-indulgence can achieve no principles, Liberal or otherwise.

If a dour critic were to say that Liberalism as a dominant note in American education had produced a nation of spoiled and juvenile minds, unable to think, devoid of the power of self-criticism and incapable of mature political responsibility, we should have to accept the half-truth. Souls of this sort are necessarily illiberal at the scratch, because the consistent exercise of the liberal spirit is one of the difficult ways of living. And since a Liberal constitution can not be worked by a nation of illiberal souls, the emotional decline of Liberalism brings with it the inner decay of Liberal institutions.

Let me illustrate these comments from Mill's conception of liberty, and what is perhaps his strongest case, his argument for freedom of speech.

Mill conceived a society in which everybody felt free to speak his mind on all points at all times, and in which nobody molested anybody for doing so, nor put him at any sort of disadvantage. His ideal was one of costless liberty. Strangely enough he seemed to regard this as the best environment for the development of moral courage; whereas in fact, it would remove every occasion for moral courage in uttering one's thought.

But suppose such an ideal achieved, and then think of the staggering price we should have to pay for it, namely, that no truth should be permitted to gain any political or social power. For wherever an idea takes hold of human behavior, it *ipso facto* puts contrary ideas at a definite disadvantage. And if to avoid this, we prevent truth from having any effect on behavior, truth becomes first unimportant, then meaningless. Your realm of costless toleration is a realm of eviscerated truth. So far from favoring the growth of knowledge in the community, it promises a condition in which no one cares enough about truth to put its new increments together into a working whole; the truth-thinking, truth-announcing business becomes like a sea of incandescent jelly-fish in a night sea, a million flashes, and no general light! Since it suits the average man only too well not to think, and not to have to act according to any thought-out plan, Mill's ideal state would have a Chinese sort of stability, a purely literary culture, full of pragmatic adjustments, and politically milling around in the same spot forever.

The normal destiny of truth is to come to some sort of power; and in so doing to impose upon contrary ideas the burden of gaining the ear of men. The right of freedom of speech ought to be a right to the facilities for winning that ear in an uphill fight, in the face of public disapproval. Spinoza was excluded from the Synagogue; and so he should have been,—he did not belong there. He should have been deprived of any position which implied a belief he did not possess; but he should not have been deprived of his means of livelihood, nor of communication with his fellows. His disadvantage should have been, as it was, the occasion for his courage and the measure of his sincerity. Spinoza, I believe, would prefer to have lived when he did rather than now, when he would doubtless be tolerated everywhere and probably ignored. For indifference to what is at once rare and difficult, a loss of the emotional significance of truth, is one of the symptomatic traits of the Liberalism we have before us.

It is worth noting that while Mill was writing, an answer was already in existence. Mill's *Liberty* was preceded by the *Communist Manifesto* of 1848; and Mill's *Representative Government* by Marx's *Critique of Political Economy*, 1859.

Indeed, Mill's own writing had abandoned the philosophical basis upon which alone that type of liberalism could stand, and was so far treasonable to his own cause. For he built his demand for liberty, not on the ground of right, but on the ground of general utility. It was not that an individual has a *right* to utter the truth that is in him, but that society without toleration *may lose something* new and valuable; and that all truth when held as dogma, unopposed, sinks to the level of "just one prejudice the more." Mill is one of the third-generation Liberals, for whom the sense of principle had already begun to fade into pragmatic adjustabilities. He does not see the individual thinker: the glaze of totality is over his eyes. But neither does he see what Marx saw, the consecutive, dialectical movement of the controlling ideas of a time and people.

Marx knew well enough in his own person, as Mill never knew, the hard lot of the unpopular idea, but he made no plea for costless toleration! He saw struggle as an aspect of life. In the year when Darwin published the *Origin of Species,* with its note of biological struggle, Marx brought out his *Critique,* with its note of economic struggle and dialectical advance. Mill seems hardly to have dipped into the currents of history deeply enough to have felt their direction; Marx felt the tug of social movement as a vast argument, into which his own thought must enter and work its way through. Surrounded by the economic fruits of Liberalism in the shape of a growing intensity of private interest, he foresaw its dialectical reversal to an intensity of commonwealth, and a reassertion of the lost wholeness of society.

So far, Marx was the truer prophet and the deeper man. We are forced to agree with his judgment as then uttered; capital can produce, it may be regarded as having solved the problem of production; it has not solved the problem of distribution.

But we must generalize from this purely economic thesis. Not merely property rights, private rights of all kinds can produce—they can produce men; they have made in this country a nation of men such as nowhere else can be found; but they can not distribute those men into the common life. These rugged individuals at their maturity remain truncated torsos of humanity stuck around in handsome private estates on the edges of a thousand cities. They have nothing to do but to enjoy themselves, enjoy their wealth, enjoy their self-esteem. They have no mission, they are mere promissory futilities, empty of moral dignity; and the rights they claim become more and more a social protection to a low grade esthetic consciousness. They might as well not exist. The society that flowers into these sturdy unfragrant weeds as its best blossom is a moral and cultural failure. So much for our diagnosis.

II

Turning, then, to look forward, our thesis is that the social whole is bound to reassert itself. This can hardly qualify as prophecy in view of what is happening all around us. The element of prophecy lies solely in answering the insistent question whether this drift to centralized authority is a temporary palliative for a passing disorder or a new stage which will remain. We are prepared by our analysis to take the latter view. These movements abroad and at home toward enabling the central executive power to do something, however bedevilled and improvised in the face of acute distress, are in their general direction neither first-aid, nor mere pragmatic groping; they are a dialectical necessity: something of the sort had to come.

The new self-assertion of the social whole naturally takes on first a political character. For the whole-interest has to be *enacted*, not merely thought of. Nor can the requisite central thought and central control come by the happy congruence of numerous I-thinking individuals. Unity comes from unity. Political unity has to come by the political assertion of some We-thinking individual or group who can arouse in the Demos its latent unitary "We." This involves in most Liberal states a definite breach with tradition—it is a matter of taste, or perhaps of noise and violence, whether or not you call it revolution: but it is not necessarily hostile to democracy. It may well be that democracy will for the first time exist, because for the first time a true general will can find its way to action. A strong central government may be a tyranny: but if so that is a consequence not of its strength but of its perversity. A strong government need not be perverse: it may be a right government—whereas a weak government is necessarily a wrong government—and if it is right, it will appear as the first condition of a new liberty. For where there is no power to act, there can be no liberty.

Given this political power, the economic unity lacking to *laissez faire* can be brought about; and it is hard to see how otherwise it can be created. For it, too, requires enactment. Economic processes constitute a single and healthy organism only when the totality of persons in a community who have a right to consume *determine what is produced;* they can never constitute an organism when it is the producers who determine what is produced, and who in doing so also determine who is to consume, since no one can consume who has not taken part in production! And since there is no way at present of discovering *rightful consumers'* demand, and only the guesswork of producers for discovering the probable demand of *consumers-who-can-pay*, the original spring of the economic system is unknown and unprotected. Society has no more important business than to identify rightful demand and turn it into actual demand.

Marx supposed that the economic problem would be solved by a social control of distribution which would begin with the abolition of profit. This does not reach the core of the trouble. It is true that distribution can not be left to the contest of pressures among factors in production in which one factor, capital, has all the cards. But it is not true that you can *begin with production*, and solve your economic problem by working out a just scheme of distribution *among the factors of production*. It is the people who are *not* factors of production that make the difficulty. It is always possible in such a plan to leave out millions of rightful consumers; the unemployed can exist in a Marxian scheme as well as in any other, and they do exist in Russia to-day—if Rakovsky is right, they exist in undiminished numbers. You must begin with the rightful consumer.

The proposal that the state take over the direction of capital and industry is due to faulty analysis. Why should the state supplant producers when the problem of production has been solved? Why should it replace employers with politicians any more than it should replace employees with politicians?

What the State has to do with production is to drive into economic practice the truth that there is little or no capital whose use is not "affected by a public interest." It must represent that interest. And it must break the lockjaw into which frightened individual producers fall when each insists that the other shall first risk his economic neck by action.

The present impasse of production is not wholly but largely a moral impasse. It reveals the astonishing impotence of the most marvelous of human systems, when, thoroughly infected by greed, dishonesty, and irresponsibility in the organs of control, it is confronted by a situation which requires just one simple thing, mutual confidence! Never has there been such an occasion for the laughter of Diabolus as this universal self-created futility of the whole array of our mighty men of industry and finance.

The demand that the whole business of production be turned over to the workers, the proletariat, is mightily enforced by this spectacle, when it is interpreted by the theory that these "leaders," blinded by their fixation on profits, are hopelessly sunk in an unworkable ideology. The alternative economic proposals require consideration on their own ground; but so far as any proposal turns on a shift of *personnel*, it is of a piece with the unrealistic nonsense of the elder Liberalism. It assumes that the worker is somehow better than the employer or the capitalist—morally better and mentally at least as good. No evidence is offered for these views, nothing except the Liberal presumption that poverty purifies, and that one who has long been an underdog must be a worthy, pious, and able man. No one who knows the inner history of labor and its leadership can retain any such illusion; no sober proletarian will make any such claim. There are honest and able men on both sides; there are crooks on both sides; and except for the love of change or of punishment there is no sense in substituting one set of crooks for another. The greed of the profiteer is bigger, but not morally worse, than the greed of the man who envies him.

Between the honest men and the crooks on both sides there are many men, perhaps a majority, who are less honest than they would like to be, but who feel that they are caught in a system which puts them to a bad choice between curly dealings and business failure. It is these men whom a new order will particularly help; for the state, given sufficient authority, can *create the conditions under which honesty is not self-destructive*. No state can prevent strict honesty from being a disadvantage if one is dealing with devious men; it can and must prevent honesty from being ruinous. By establishing uniform practices and controlling the rules of competition it can meet a moral and economic reform halfway, and develop in due time the lacking morale of the business community.

But we ought not to delude ourselves with the hope that either the economic reform or the political reform will of themselves bring about a stable new order. There can be *no new polity without a new emotion.*

The central malaise of Liberalism lies in this quarter: its picture of the "general welfare" as a sum of individual enjoyments gains all its allurement from a contrast effect with spots of social misery. It offers no real and positive general good, because it builds no common purpose. Its ideal of a do-nothing State is inconsistent with the idea of a State with a mission in the world: and with a static State, there can be in the long run nothing but *static men.* Liberalism failed to see this inference; but the inference is drawn for us by the facts. There they are; we have been looking at them—men without a calling, men who can no longer take themselves seriously, and by consequence can take nothing else seriously. They have succeeded, and in doing so have reached the end of their significance: the pathetic failure of our civilization is at the top, not at the bottom. Contrast the moral condition of such a community at its best with the fierce idealism which flames up here and there among the youth of Russia or of China, to whom the nation itself, with a program which appears glorious in proportion to its difficulty, has become the absorbing business of life! The puff-cheeked bombast of Italy and Germany at the moment is far less attractive, because the national program is still loaded with the primitive goals of bigness and self-importance; there is too little of the notion of contributing ideas to a general historical movement. It is an inferior brand. But crude as it is, it is still superior to the ideal of a State whose standard it is to avoid entanglement, and to hug in isolation the fragments of a disturbed national prosperity.

III

All this sounds like collectivism, and collectivism of a sort it is.

But it is not a collectivism of either the Fascist or the Communist sort. We have not to choose between the headlessness of Liberalism and the headiness of these two devices.

Communism in Russia has the great negative virtue of a successful revolution; it has destroyed ancient abuses. It is now put to its mettle to show its positive worth. It has that worth. But that worth does not lie in its common wealth, which is rather a common poverty. The effective part of Sovietism is in those elements which it has in common with Liberalism. By removing a static tyranny and substituting a dynamic tyranny directed toward liberal ends, it has released the genius of a greatly gifted people. It has destroyed the spell of fatalism and has spurred humanity, as Liberalism has done, to think for itself and, assume responsibility for its own destiny. It has established a passionate sincerity in the center of government; for when men are sincere, then their philosophy becomes incorporated in their deeds, and it becomes a vital concern as it now is in Moscow what that philosophy is. When on the contrary, philosophy is held to be an indifferent matter for the politician, the inference is that he has no sincere intention of bringing his beliefs into his deeds. The awkward frankness of Soviet diplomacy may yet force some of the decencies of Liberalism into the venal currents of international bickering.

But Communism is not the solution we need; it has not communized the souls of Russia, and communization of property can go no farther than communization of the minds that use it, without loss of public morale. This has been amply shown by the experience of the Soviet Republic.

It is as a very intimate inside observer that Rakovsky, writing from Astrakhan about conditions in Russia in 1928, points out the decline in the "activity spirit" of the masses. He attributes this in part to the inescapable fact of differences in social function which breed differences in temper: it is impossible for the manager to retain the psychology of the worker, the more so if he is a good manager; nor can the worker maintain the spirit of mental initiative and command which the manager requires: the bureau man, in proportion to his experience, develops a public and responsible cast of mind (whose caricature is the bureaucrat). And this class-psychology of control, which deepens with his experience, can be broken up only by depriving the State of continuity in the services of its better men,—for there are such beings! But then, the nonresponsibles tend to slump; there is, Rakovsky declares, "arrivism, selfishness, cowardice" and a general moral decline, on whose details there is no point in insisting. It is clear that communism has not bred a tolerant fraternity; that the factional differences signalized by the names, Trotzsky, Stalin, Bukharin, run deeper than the party differences of the ordinary bourgeois state, which commonly stops short of banishment and death-penalties. The terms in which our communist brethren characterize each other, when they differ, and their attitude toward the mendicant and pauper (out-of-Party) classes, indicate that an enforced sharing of life at the economic level, may exacerbate rather than relieve the ordinary bitterness of inter-human criticism. Communism does not appear to have solved the problem of Public morale.

Nor can Fascism do better. The unity that is required must be a unity of thinking beings, not a unity of the drill squad. The State must be unified; and in its public purposes individual purposes must merge. But they can so merge, only when the public purposes are prolongations of individual purposes, and derive their life therefrom. The individual remains mentally prior to the State. The principle of the modern State is this: that *every man shall be a whole man*. This is the principle upon which democracy has been based, and which none of the fallacies of parliamentarism have any tendency to destroy. It is this principle on which the new nations of the Orient are building their policies; for so long as individual citizens are mentally cramped, ungrown, deprived of political, religious, or ethical autonomy and therefore unaccustomed to thought in these fields, there can be no national consciousness, and no genuine State. Men must unite; but they must first separate in order to unite; they must first be full-fledged men, before their unity can have anything but a quasi-mechanical character.

It was this principle which Marx felt, and it is this sensitivity to individual suffering which makes his work so living in its appeal to those very workmen of the world whose uniting he conceived as a voluntary and moral deed. It was precisely the deformations of human nature which most aroused his hatred of the existing system: he saw in the industrial order the beginnings of an industrial pathology. In the first volume of *Capital* (ch. 14) he quotes an English writer to this effect:

"To subdivide a man is to execute him.... The subdivision of labour is the execution of a people."

Adam Smith had already commented on the fact that "the understandings of men are formed by their ordinary employments," and that machine-tending is likely to make men stupid. Adam Smith made the observation with scientific calm; Mill, if he noticed it at all, remained politely undisturbed by it; Marx felt the crime of it in every fiber of his being. This was the measure of his greater moral depth and the secret of his enduring power.

But how could Marx fail to see that his socialized state would even more radically sin against the principle, Every man a whole man? It would remedy the unequal mutilations, under industrialism, at the cost of the equal mutilation of everybody. For the forcibly collectivized life of the communist state as of the fascist state takes the upper inch off from every head, the inch which thinks, aspires, and exercises individual judgment. And it is just this inch, most precious to the individual, which is also most precious to the modern state.

For in the last analysis, the thought and conscience of the individual man are the *only thought and conscience there are*. We talk about the state as if it were a single organism with a mind and will of its own; for the most part this figure of speech serves well enough, but it is a mere analogy, and at this point it fails. There is no public mind, in literal truth; there are only the minds of the persons composing the public. There is no public conscience; there is only their several consciences. Dry these functions up, or bind the life out of them, and all the mental and moral life of the public is stopped at its source.

Hence the new and unified state, for its own sake, must limit the scope of its effort at unification. It can not live in distraction and chronic dissent; neither can it live in a forced assent which is no assent at all. It can assume and enforce assent to its existence, and to *participation* in such measures as define the current experiment in corporate living; but it can not assume nor enforce unanimity of opinion as to the wisdom or success of these measures. It must submit its experiment from moment to moment to the judgment of free judgers, as guide to the next experimental stage. The dictatorial state attempts the self-contradictory plan of trying to live without the risks of living; but there is no life without risk whether for man or state, and conversely, *what is riskless is lifeless*. The state which refuses to risk its own continuance to the free approval of its members, and that means risking their disapproval, gets no approval at all; for what it gets is mere compulsory conformity. In making itself mechanically secure, it ensures its own mental death. Since the dictatorship there has been no cultural life in Italy, and no philosophy but Echo; and in Russia, the cultural life of the theater and of letters makes its way just in proportion as the irrepressible vitality of the Russian soul escapes the themes of political determinism.

Fortunately for man and state, the ultimate inner life is noncollectivisable. It can be killed; but it can not be bound. This part is the germinal man, the creative source of ideas and standards, of imagination and belief. We talk about the freedom of thought, as if it were a moot point; but thought can never be anything else than free,—it is only the expression of thought that offers a handle to public control. Here lies the ultimate right. The "rights of man" as assembled under Liberalism were too many and too costless. But there is one right, which is at once a right and a duty—the right and the duty of thought, of the inner germination, to get into the open, and to work its way to power! For this *is* the destiny of man, and the meaning of human life. This is the incompressible atom of individual and social life. What happens to a man's property is of minor importance—the importance of property is derived from the importance of the living man, and not *vice versa;* the two should correspond. But what happens to his voice, the voice of his feeling and belief—that is of the last importance, both for him and for his state.

To the Fascist slogan, "Outside the State there is nothing," we must rejoin that *if so, the State is nothing:* for outside the State is the source of the State itself. Man the breeder of idea and feeling is outside the State, man the deviser of new experiments, man the thinker, man who spontaneously puts himself *in loco Dei* to other men; this is the thing in the psyche of the "political animal" which perennially gives life to every political form. And if man, the responsible thinker, is in control, the liberal spirit is in control, whatever the form of the State.

Indeed, this element of liberty, the liberty to generate ideas and to get them worked into the social order, is the soul of the old Liberalism. And that soul is immortal. Among other reasons, it is immortal because this part of the Liberal program is chronically unfinished business. We have been nearer a genuine "freedom of speech and of conscience" than we are now. How much safer is it in America to speak for Communism than in Russia to speak against it? The professional defenders of our Constitution are ready to defend all of it except the liberty which gave it birth. It is foolish to suppose that Liberalism can be dismissed in wholesale while its legitimate battle is so far from won.

But here we approach our last topic. How can the strong and unified state be compatible with a strong moral individualism?

IV

How can we combine the strong individual and the strong State? By enlarging the region of conscious agreement among the members of the State, and diminishing the region of conscious disagreement.

The State is founded upon a basis of unanimity of will which for most men at most times is subconscious; only a public emergency brings to the surface the latent assent, with the feeling which we call "patriotism." The *laissez faire* State prefers that its silent mental tie should remain beneath the threshold. It renounces in this way the emotional basis of all vigorous political life; for there is no reason why the agreements of men in the life of the State should not be conscious; and they would be conscious if the State had a program of public action, both internal and external, in which citizens can actively participate.

The new emotion is the emotion given to the nation when that nation has something better to do than to exist. The older conceptions of State-action were merely modified forms of the will to exist: for the aggrandizement of empire, with its lofty prayer, "Make us mightier yet," simply magnifies existence. And when the State has nothing to do but to grow big, its citizens will naturally follow suit. The newer conceptions realize that there are qualitative changes to be made in the world; the idea of a just community is not a Platonic idea—it has its special *agenda* for every situation; there is also an international society to be built. Experiments are in order; on every experiment opinions may differ as widely as you please, except on one point—that to *this*, the going experiment, we give our best effort; here the State may be unanimous, while holding that experiment open at all points to public discussion. Nationalism as the self-glorification of States is the great political disease of the day. Nationalism as the local origination and trying-out of ideas having world-wide utility may well be the next stage of political advance.

When the State has something to do, the meaning of the whole is transmitted to the parts: the individual citizen has something to live for. He becomes willing to submit to a discipline which otherwise he would find irksome—more than this, he *wants it!* Training for public life becomes a serious matter; it is not inconceivable that even in America young men might undergo severe mental gymnastics, including the study of philosophy, such as makes membership in "The Party" the primary social distinction in Russia! The strong State, when it knows wherein its strength lies, calls out the strong individual. It is not the "executive State"—as if efficiency in management were its highest quality; it is certainly not the coercive State: it is the *co-agent State*, an obligatory cooperation in an experimental program for an improved social order.

With the enlargement of the region of conscious agreement in State action, the region of conscious disagreement is *pari passu* contracted. It can then be realized that the new State in taking action that appears to limit liberty, is in point of fact deepening its channel.

The older Liberalism lacked the sense of paradox: it could not see the half-truth that liberty has to come by way of constraint, peace by way of pugnacity, sympathy by an honest hardness, the individual by way of a pre-established harmony. Its positive judgments were just; but it was "once-born."

For example, it was right in demanding freedom of thought, and we have joined in that demand; but freedom of thought, we should add, is *for thinkers*. Disgust with Liberalism is due more to this fact than to any other, that it has assigned liberty of thought to non-thinkers; its institutions have broken down because they have assumed that folk in general think—voters, legislators, administrators, lawyers—people who ought to think, and who only pseudo-think! Men imitate, pretend, rationalize, adhere, far more than they think; and because of this their very beliefs become hollow. Millions of communicants of the old Russian Church acquiesce in the new order with little protest and less martyrdom; they thought they were believers, they were only adherents. The lash of political necessity may have been good for the sincerity of their souls; it is very probable that Russia will now do some real thinking on the subject of religion. As for our own "intelligent and educated" classes in and out of the colleges, there is some thinking done; and there is a good deal more of the wish-wash of ideas which would better be called the cerebral wave-motion of vapid up-to-datists. Idea-bearing should be as solemn a business as child-bearing; and we have turned it into a public promiscuity in which every Hornblower, Influential Editor, and National Clown mingles his say with that of Ambitious Priests and Leading Ladies to turn the General Will. What vast damage would be done to our social life if some stern political resolve were to frighten all this vain Conceit-of-Thought under cover until it were ready to make a dangerous stand for something it had really come to think?

The truth is that we live under the stress of two perils, not of one only. To the hideous perils of the Censorship, we must join the hideous perils of No-censorship; and so for all the items of the Liberal program. In every point, men must be free; and in every point they must be subject to a sobering objective judgment which checks their freedom. The new State must accordingly do two things where the Liberal State attempted but one: it must solve the apparent contradiction of these two demands.

In reaching its solution, the co-agent State will be driven to recognize what is, in fact, axiomatic—though all the tradition of nineteenth-century legality is against it—that the Absolute of individual liberty which has to be recognized at all costs and protected by the State against itself is a liberty of *the inner man* and not of his external person. The State, in spite of itself will have to deal with human motives.

It has already been compelled to do so in the case of religious liberty. No physical line can be drawn between true and false religion. But just because the State seeks liberty for true religion (if it does), it has to eliminate the swarming frauds in this field. It attempts no positive judgment, but it draws a line where public order, decency, good morals are involved. It runs the risk of destroying some of the real prophets; it can not do otherwise.

It will extend this principle to all the rights of man. They are genuine rights, not expediencies; the State is for them, and not they for the State. But the State will have to take the line that rights belong to the good will and to nothing else; and it will clamp down on the specious claims to make way for those that are genuine.

In taking these "strong lines," the co-agent State maintains one clear distinction from all dictatorship; it gives hostages for its own good faith. If it "indoctrinates" in education, it makes a place for the philosophical criticism of all doctrine. If it "rescues the children from the claws of the clergy," it will provide a rescue from the claws of its own prepossessions.

The ultimate reason for this self-limitation is its realism: it is its view of what the human individual really is. Liberalism dealt with human nature with a cheerful hopefulness, based on an incomplete psychology and a defective metaphysics. Its inability to unite a critical pugnacity with its benevolence was due, not to the greatness of its faith, but to the smallness of it. The faith that is required is faith in the invincible growing power of the normal human self, its appetite for discipline, and its resilience under social strain. Liberalism has worked its miracles: the co-agent State will do greater ones. But only on one condition—that its faith is metaphysically valid.

CHAPTER 12

Astronomy, Physics and World-Meaning

1. The Original God-Banishers Revisited

It was physical science which first, at the opening of the modern era, determined to get on without God. It was the great emancipating deed of the seventeenth century to dismiss purpose, human or divine, as irrelevant to any hypotheses which physics or astronomy had to frame. Yet it is just to this field that we must now turn for the positive correction of an overconfident humanism, which takes too lightly the problems set for it by the cosmic frame of human life.

I mean by this in the first place simply that any picture of mankind which touches religion must take into account what the physical sciences have to say about the great universe as the scene of human life. We smile today at the disturbance which the innocent calculations of Copernicus stirred in the religious mind for a full century after 1543. What difference does it make to religion whether the sun revolves around the earth, or the earth around the sun? Not much, I agree; but what we call "man's place in Nature" is always relevant to religion. And so the questions, Out of what do we human beings come? How long is human life to last in the astronomical calendar? What comes after we vanish?—these questions belong to man's judgment of himself, and their changing answers affect his view of his total destiny. The bare facts and prognostics of descriptive astronomy do not wholly settle them; it would be foolish not to consult them.

I mean, in the second place, that physical science has something new to say about the place of *purpose* in the world-process. Not that the physical science of today is any more inclined than it was in 1700 to revert to purpose as a principle for its own explanations of events,[1] but that it sees that it can no longer *deny* purpose such a place, in our total contemplation of things. The logic of its own work compels it to recognize the possibility of purpose—and be it said that physical science is much better at logic than it was in the seventeenth century. It no longer takes for granted that expelling purpose from the equations of physical theory is tantamount to expelling it from the universe. What has happened is that physics (and let "physics" stand for astronomy also) recognizes its view of the world as *partial*. It is partial, not because the two-hundred inch reflector and its line of future successors will fail to discover the periphery of the cosmos, but because everywhere it deliberately omits

---

From SIG, 85–115.

from its view aspects of the truth which are certainly there. Physics used to think of itself as the most concrete of all the sciences, dealing with the veritable stuff of things as they are. It now sees that it is an *abstract* science, and for that reason cannot tell the whole truth.

For example, it limits the range of questions it proposes to answer within its own subject matter. Nothing is more the business of physics than "energy." And physics will undertake to say a good deal about how energy behaves, but about what it *is*—not a word. Advances in the analysis which aims at finding the ultimate units of physical being, having opened up a whole galaxy of subatomic *dramatis personae*, converge upon the electronic energy-unit as the typical world-stuff. If we ask a physicist what an electron is, or what a quantum is, or simply what energy is, he is likely to answer that his business is with the phenomena that can be explained by using these concepts in a set of differential equations, not with the inner nature of energy. Sometimes he passes the question on (with a vague hint of skepticism) to "the metaphysician"; or possibly he calls the logical positivist to his side, to assure the questioner that his question is strictly meaningless. But more probably, today, he recognizes that the question is both pertinent and significant—only, not in his field.

And if some philosopher proposes that physical energy has something in common, in its nature, with what we know as life, or are aware of in ourselves as mind, as has often been done in recent years,[2] the physicist will be tolerant of the hypothesis. Now and then a physicist will refer to the notion of Herbert Spencer that "the force by which things manifest themselves as existing" is of the same kind as "the force which manifests itself within us as consciousness," akin to Schopenhauer's older notion that physical causality is identical with what we know in ourselves as "will." And if some hardy seeker for first principles leaves the field of literal thought entirely and finds himself driven to symbolic and poetic expression, he will not be read out of court. The scientist may easily be restless or skeptical, but not dogmatically negative, toward such a statement as that from the newer *Logia*,

"Cleave the wood, and thou wilt find Me there,"

so reminiscent of the words of the *Chhandogya Upanishad*:

That invisible particle (in the broken seed)
That is the universal soul;
That art thou, O Svetaketu.[3]

2. What Is It That Physical Science Omits?

I believe it worth while to enlarge on this matter of the "abstract" character of physical science. For whatever is abstracted, or extracted, from a whole leaves something behind; and as we consider what physics deliberately omits from its province, the significance of the omission grows on us.

We were just mentioning that the *qualities* of the experienced world are omitted. To the seventeenth and later centuries it became clear that physics was destined to be a mathematical discipline and had nothing to do with color and sound as conscious qualities. Precise measurableness was taken to be a universal character of nature. This was never proved, it was assumed. It is still assumed and not proved. But the conviction grows into such a degree of firmness that any small differences from our calculations which events may show are immediately attributed to our own faults in calculating or observing, and not to any irregularity of the nature-process itself. (I believe that Heisenberg's so-called principle of indeterminacy constitutes no exception to this rule.) The disposition to take advantage of the incomplete predictability of some phenomena, especially the phenomena of life, as sign of the intervention of God has all but disappeared.

Indeed, it may be said that it is just the minute differences that offer the best footholds for scientific advance. For example, the chemistry of two generations ago presented the atomic weights of the elements as multiples of the weight of the hydrogen atom. The actual weights as determined by experiment came so near to whole-number multiples—carbon was 4, nitrogen 14, oxygen 16, etc.—that minute deviations in the third and fourth decimal places seemed a pedantic pretense of greater accuracy than actual technique could support. When Professor Richards announced his four-decimal atomic weights, there were audible murmurs: "Call it even!" Just these slight departures have become the footing for new chapters in chemistry. Again, the whole development of relativity theory depends on a correction of Newton's simple formula for gravitation by a very small fraction. And the theory itself has as one of its tests a very small displacement of the apparent position of stars in the visual neighborhood of the sun, through the gravitative bending of their rays. Experimental support of the theory required a meticulous estimate of the extent of this displacement. The first test of this phase of the theory was to have taken place in 1914, on the occasion of a solar eclipse best visible in the Crimea. Professor Freundlich of Berlin was there with equipment to observe the eclipse. The outbreak in August of war between Germany and Russia placed him in internment, and the opportunity was lost. Soon after this disappointing event, Einstein found reason to make a small change in his first estimate of the small displacement. When the next eclipse was observed, the displacement was verified, and was found to be in close agreement with his *second calculation*, not with the first. The seeming misfortune of 1914 thus proved to be most fortunate for the reception of his theory; for the impression on the learned world would have been far different if Einstein's revision had taken place *after* his first estimate had been shown slightly wrong. So significant is the present meaning of almost indiscernible differences.

Thus the ideal notion once made notorious by Laplace of a world equation which should describe the motions of all particles in the universe through all time loses none of its theoretical validity, though its attainment seems yearly more remote. And if the physical network of all history is thus in principle a matter of the most precise determination, we are presented with a world-scheme from which are absent not alone all the sense qualities of sound, color, taste, smell, but as well all the feeling, passion, and meaning from which, for human experience, physical events are inseparable. For man, no event is neutral; for physics no event is anything else.

This "bifurcation of nature" into quality and quantity is no new thing; it was well known to Descartes, Locke, Galileo. It was regarded as another way of reading the difference between the subjective and the objective. The world of quality was simply a mental affair, having nothing to do with the facts. Physics could fairly consider itself to deal with the whole of the *real* world; the qualities of things, especially the "tertiary" qualities of beauty, worth, rightness, were subjective prejudices devoid of influence on the course of events. It is this easy reading of things which the twentieth century destroys.

The plausibility of identifying the physical with the real depended largely on the imaginability of the picture. Everyone can imagine, or thinks he can imagine, an atom flying through space. No one can imagine an electron, nor picture in any model the nature of a quantum of energy. Not only is physics a field of mathematics; it is a field with which we can deal *only* by mathematics. It is from physics itself that the query now arises, Can this unpicturable world be, in truth, the real world? Gustav Fechner once revolted against the "Night View" according to which, since light is only there for consciousness, the whole physical history of the cosmos unrolls itself in darkness. Though the physical energy of light pours itself from all the suns over all the worlds, it is a light which illumines nothing unless there are "minds" to see it. Today, the protest is brought in the name of the integral Nature we know, not against a methodological theft which would deprive Nature of half of her being, but against the supposition that the physical half is anything more than an algebra of event. No one ever discovers a quality apart from a quantity, nor a quantity apart from a quality. Why then adopt the weird hypothesis that the quantitative is objective, the qualitative only subjective?

With this question, we seem to return to sanity. But if the real Nature is the Nature we perceive in its integrity, qualities and quantities together, then physics must present itself in the light of an abstraction from the whole. The revolt against the bifurcation which mistakes this abstraction for the real—a revolt strongly pushed by Dewey and Whitehead—is in part a revolt of observation against "abstract thought." It is in part, however, a moral revolt; for it seems increasingly incredible to common sense that the only things that have any importance—namely, feelings and qualities—are the things to be omitted from "reality." The real is unimportant; the important is unreal. This, we say, cannot be true.

3. What, After All, Are Space and Time?

But this line of thought might well have failed to dislodge so well-established a conception of the world if it had not come to the same conclusion with another line of thought within physics. I refer to the new position assigned to space and time by relativity theory.

In the classical physics, space and time were entities in their own right, independent of the things and events located in them. That there were puzzles about their nature, everyone realized. They were evidently not "things," but rather non-things providing a room within which things could be. But they were also different from each other, two different kinds of nothing; and how nothing could have varieties it was hard to say. At any rate they were there, and in a logical sense were there *first*, before anything physical could either be or happen, since the world process had to unfold itself within the arena constituted by infinite space and endless time. For the same reason, space and time were eternal and unchanging, since everything in the nature of change presupposed their presence and stability as a background. If space itself were a moving thing, motions could obviously not be measured by reference to space; and if time "flowed" or "marched on" as it is sometimes reputed to do even today, then the flowing of events could not be measured with reference to time. In brief, it was thought, Nature *presupposes* space and time.

Now the twentieth century accustoms us to get on without these fixed regions of reference. It reminds us that we do not in fact either locate or measure events by reference to positions in space or time, for there are no markers in either. We locate events with reference to each other; we know intervals first and adopt positions afterward by purely conventional decisions; we know relations first, and terms as implied in relations. Further, as Minkowski observed, we know nothing of place except at a time, and nothing of time except at a place. Space and time are inseparable in experience, and as he proceeded to show, inseparable also in respect to measurement. What we have in hand is the concrete system of events. The abstract scheme of space-time against which we project this system is something we construct on the basis of the concrete data. Space and time thus lose their independence and their firstness for our thought; for our knowledge they are derived from events, and are not as Kant had said "ready in the mind" to receive the events.

It might still be true that what is secondary for our knowledge must be thought of as first in the order of reality. It still seems to us that, however slowly we arrive at the ideas, we recognize space and time as regions without which no events could take place, and in this sense as prior to events. But this reflection is countered by the awkward fact above mentioned—first clearly stated in Minkowski's memoir of 1908, and implied in the entire development of relativity theory—that space and time have no determinable or absolute quantities. The question, how far is point a from point b has no unambiguous answer, for we must first know whether we are to take them as at rest or in motion and in what time-interval the measuring process is carried out. Our answer will vary with the assumed position and motion of the observer.

We are driven, then, to accept space and time as abstractions from events. And the events themselves so far as physics is interested in them—i.e., in their centimeter-gram-second-measurabilities—are abstractions from the concrete experience of the observer. Physics begins with *his* observations, his sense-data, and if its calculations are right predicts future events which will be verified again in his sense-data. Physical science becomes an intricate system of theory enabling inferences to be made from one phase of experience to another. Then the real thing with which we have to do is not the intangible terms of the equations which embody this theory, but just experience in its immediate fullness of quality and meaning.

To some physicists, this means that physics is forced to return to the mentalism (commonly called idealism) of Berkeley and of Kant's Transcendental Aesthetic. Herbert Dingle carefully enquires how physical objects are "constructed" by us out of sense-stuff. Hermann Weyl asserts that the mental character of the world we find before us is the inescapable beginning of all rational thought about physics. Sir James Jeans is prone to exhibit the physical universe as a system of mathematical thought. Sir Arthur Eddington protests that there is one difference between a purely mathematical universe and an actual universe—one may be imaginary, the other real. But he proceeds to say that the only way we can necessarily distinguish the one from the other is that the actual universe has "the accent of consciousness." Hence the real remains even more emphatically the mental.

Whitehead and Dewey resist the drift toward mentalism, and insist that the return of the observer to the physicist's calculations does not require the absorption of the world into the observer's mind; it is still there in its full independence. It is premature to press this matter as if it were a foregone conclusion of contemporary physics. It is in my judgment inappropriate for metaphysics to take advantage of the embarrassments of a stage of physical enquiry which is so evidently in flux, and which involves so many makeshifts of terminology with which no one is very well satisfied. The late Professor Ehrenfest once said to me that the effort to teach mathematical physics in its present confusion had given him an insight into the Hegelian dialectic, "a succession of leaps from one lie to another by way of intermediate falsehoods." All that we need gather from the situation is the willingness of the most fundamental and characteristic branch of modern science to acknowledge the incompleteness of its own body of truth as a sufficient account of the "real world." When physics declares itself "abstract" in this sense, an epoch has taken place in human thinking.

4. The Totalities of Pattern in Events: A Human Concern Which Physics Omits to Judge

We have spoken as though all that is quantitative in the world comes within the domain of physics. This is not quite correct. Suppose, for example, a physicist were explaining to us some of the newer discoveries about the behavior of electrons, and we were to put the question, "How many electrons are there in the universe?" we might expect the answer (unless the physicist were Professor Eddington), "That does not concern me. I am simply interested in the laws they exhibit, not with their population; their number may be finite, it may be infinite." We might persist, "Of course, the total number could hardly be known unless we had determined whether the universe has a spatial limit, but the question of their density or distribution could be settled without that knowledge. Could you tell us the range of their concentration, let us say, from the densest portions of the sun to the rarest regions of interstellar space; and how they are arranged under each of those conditions?" Here our speaker might reply, "Of course, the electron within an atom would behave differently according to the degree of propinquity of other atoms. We are much concerned to examine these differences. But the actual facts of distribution of electrons or atoms belong rather to the history of the universe than to physics."

Now the questions we have asked are quantitative: How many physical units are there? How are they arranged? How much empty space is there, if any? And why is there so much mass and no more, so many suns, galaxies, dark clouds, or why so few? Physics gives attention to such questions, but it offers only fragmentary answers. Its attention has been given to laws; it has taken only a sidelong interest in *total quantities and "configurations,"* or patterns. Let the mythmakers play with the constellations; science is unconcerned whether your fancy sees a particular group of stars as a unit (knowing well it is not a unit) nor whether you call the group a Great Bear or a Great Dipper.

Nevertheless, physics has at least one strong vested interest in pattern: it has a concern for *the repeatable* just because it has a concern for law. For a law can be thrown into the form, "If A occurs, B follows; if temperature falls, water freezes." Such a formula makes no assertion that A ever happens, still less that it continues to happen; but it is evidently the business of physics to deal with what does happen, and the body of its theory is important just in proportion as it refers to conditions which occur or can be made to recur. It would not be too much to say, that physics survives as a science only because it is successful in seeing the world of events as a scene of innumerable repetitions.

We may go a step farther. Some of these processes tend to reinstate their initial member and so to provide for their own recurrence. This gives us the special pattern we call a *rhythm*. All vibrations and swinging motions are of this sort, and movements of planets in their orbits. Rhythm often has the property of being compoundable, as small waves ride the backs of great waves, and the rhythm of day and night rides the great rhythm of the solar year. This property lends a factual foundation to the leap which human thought has often made from the part to the whole. May not the story of the universe itself be conceived as a vast rhythm, such as Herbert Spencer expressed in his law which was to include all laws—the law of alternate evolution and dissolution?

Physical science has hitherto been inclined to turn this question of total pattern over to the speculative thinkers, since it cannot yet survey the total universe at any one time, not to speak of a long period of time. And the speculative thinkers have tended to decide the question, not on scientific but on moral grounds. Some like Nietzsche have been attracted by the notion of Eternal Recurrence, *das ewige Wiederkehr*; the Stoics long ago had taught the periodic absorption of the stellar field into the great celestial fire, and the re-enactment of its play. But early Christianity set its face hard against any such cosmic cycle. It was asking a good deal to think that Plato and his school reassembled at long intervals to rethink their high thoughts and to be puzzled anew by the same ancient questions, having returned to the same original state of doubt. Somehow the winnings of thought ought to be *kept* by the world. The notion of repetition reduces the great work of Socrates to the level of the child's game; for the characteristic difference between work and play is that play, accomplishing nothing, is by nature repeatable. For Augustine, however, the deciding consideration was not that the idea of cycles made Plato repeat but that it made God repeat. Hindu speculation might conceive God as playing with his world, which was after all a source of partial illusion; but for Christianity the world is the scene of the labor and suffering of God in the tragic history of redemption. And whether or not Socrates might through innumerable ages repeat his struggle of thought from doubt to partial certainty, it was inconceivable that Christ should come and die again. His work, like every divine work, was "finished" and was so pronounced; it was done once for all time. To the Christian, therefore, the notion of a cosmic cycle was a crowning impiety.

Now science can have no interest in the ethical aspect of this debate. But it has certain comments to make on the factual situation which may help us in judging it.

First, it points out that all talk of repetition or rhythm is a simplification: *no exact recurrences are known*. When science perceives and formulates a "law," it does so by singling out a facet of a process which in actuality may be endlessly complex. (This is another phase of the "abstraction" of science.) The earth returns each year to the same phase of its orbit, but not to the same point in space—if that phrase has any meaning—and never to precisely the same track with reference to the surrounding bodies. These surrounding bodies, each of which plays on the earth's motion with a different pulse, never repeat the pattern of their own positions. It might be imagined that after untold aeons some common multiple of the periods of these bodies would be realized, and a precise pattern of motion over great time announce itself. If the whole outer sidereal universe could be neglected, such a possibility is conceivable. But it is dashed by another consideration, with which contemporary astrophysics is now much occupied.

I refer to the fact that *some of the changes of the universe are unidirectional* in the sense that they cannot be reversed, and therefore prevent the recurrence of any processes into which they enter.

It has long been known that the available energy of the universe tends to run down, and that the state of universal equilibrium which this "increase of entropy" appears to forebode must be a state of universal death. Hence there has been much interest in the question whether there are compensating processes (short of the cosmic catastrophe on which Spencer relied to re-establish the original nebula) tending to restore what is lost. On this point we have no clear evidence. We can only say that the chart of the interplay of mass and energy is far more complex than when the second law of thermodynamics was first recognized.

But now a new question is raised: whether the entire sidereal system may be in process of expansion. Expansion and contraction are one-way processes, one of which points to a definite beginning, the other to a definite end. If the universe in all its parts were expanding at a known and constant arithmetical rate, it would be possible to calculate backward to a time when any finite segment of the universe must have been as small as you please. If on the other hand it were contracting, it would seem possible to predict a moment when it would vanish. The world of science adjusts itself with difficulty to either beginnings, or endings, having long been accustomed to the idea of endlessness in both directions. Professor A. A. Milne has proposed a way to reconcile the expanding universe with an infinite retrospect in time, by a regressive diminution in the unit of time-measure—an expedient which would raise a fair question whether something would not then happen to the corresponding measure of space. Fortunately, these are not questions which we need here resolve. It is sufficient to note that the scientific picture of world-change allows one-way processes a certain likelihood, and that where they are *present, cycles cannot occur*. This suggestion is confirmed by the third remark I have to offer.

This third remark comes not directly from physics, but from the mathematics of infinite collections. It plans to show that our existing system belongs to a class of patterns which *cannot recur*. Roughly stated, it consists in showing that the number of patterns which can be taken by a collection of electrons in space is in general far greater than the number of moments in an infinite time series. The possible patterns for even a small group of bodies moving independently are too many to be run through in a continuous series of moments. This can be seen if one reflects that a single body moving continuously in a line takes a different position at each moment forever, whereas a second body could be assumed to be in an infinite number of different positions for each position of the first body, and a third body in a similar infinitude of positions for each *pair-position* of the first two, the number of possible patterns being multiplied by an infinite factor with each new member of the group. Recurrences are possible therefore only if the number of patterns assumable by the system of bodies is restricted. If their mutual motions are tied together by such laws as gravitation, elasticity, etc., a given system is limited in its array of possible patterns. If we take four equal bodies and set them at the four corners of a perfect square with zero velocity, then under gravity and perfect elasticity the four are bound to move toward the center of the square, click together at the same instant and rebound precisely to the initial position, from which an exact repetition takes place, and so on forever. In general, symmetrical patterns will recur, and will be at every moment symmetrical. In general, non-symmetrical patterns will not recur and can never jump over from non-symmetry into symmetry. There is an intermediate class of patterns which are non-symmetrical but whose stations correspond to fractional numbers or to recurrent decimals. These may follow a more complex recurrent pattern. But these symmetrical and proportional patterns, as we may call them, are artificially set up from the far more numerous class of collocations of which any ensemble of elements is capable. How seldom, for example, will a throw of dice even approximate a regular hexagon? Allow, then, that the stellar universe, so far as we know it, belongs to the class of irregular patterns. Just because it moves under laws, its pattern can never jump over into regularity, and it is *incapable of recurrence*.

Most children who speculate on the cosmos, and many of the grown children of past time who have thought of the subject, have preferred the symmetrical patterns as more beautiful. They failed to consider the fate of symmetrical beauty—a finite course of variety, and thus recurrence. It is only the irregular configurations that are endlessly fertile in new forms.

For the same reason, it is only an irregular world which can support a *history*. History is more than a series of happenings, it is a series with a meaning. And a series with a meaning is one in which meaning accumulates in the parts. In such a series there is no repetition. This is true even when parts of the series have a rhythm, as in the recurring night-and-day beat of human life; for the position of each recurring phase is different in relation to the whole movement. A second day cannot repeat a first day which had none to precede it. In history there are no exact precedents.

Thus, the present outlook of astrophysics favors the application to such stages of cosmic history as we can discern of the much-abused term "unique." We live in the presence of *das Einmalige*, that which occurs once only. It seems less probable than it did that other times and other worlds may be or have been the abodes of life, since the pattern of energies which here brought about the first living molecules may easily have been a unique pattern. And whether or not Henderson's argument for the biocentric character of the universe applies in full force only to this earth, it is still more probable that uniqueness may be restored to that much humiliated product of evolution, the human animal. Via the uniqueness of pattern-phases the astrophysics of the twentieth century does something to restore a geocentric picture which in the seventeenth century it destroyed.

5. The Place for Purpose

Irregular total patterns have the advantage of being always new, but there is in the fact of irregularity no guarantee that the novelties will be propitious. Chaos is irregular, and might conceivably have begotten more chaos through all time. If an irregular configuration moves out of shapelessness into describable form, that is because it was already "loaded" with that possibility. Irregularity by itself is irrational. From the standpoint of physics any pattern of the world is irrational in the sense that it has to be taken as pure fact. No physicist dreams of deducing the existing arrangement of stars or atoms from any rational principle. His highest hope is to deduce it from the next prior arrangements, and these from their predecessors, which leaves open the whole question why *this particular succession* of patterns exists, rather than some other succession, far better for us, or far worse. The total pattern is a *datum*, which is another name for an irrational.

Since physical law faithfully transmits the inherent irregularity of the world from moment to moment, we may say that for physics the whole story of the cosmos conveys a fixed burden of irrationality. It is a unique fact, out of an infinite number of equally possible facts, whose actuality instead of theirs is wholly devoid of meaning. Had we been able to intervene ten million years ago to the extent of altering the position of one hydrogen atom, the entire subsequent course of the world would have been different; and no one at that time would have been able to say that the universe as it was had any greater reason for existing than the universe after our alteration. Physics takes the pattern it finds and asks no questions; another pattern would have been equally acceptable, even though it might have involved—no men, ergo no physicists!

Once we are clear that physics renounces all interest and claim in the explanation of total pattern, and also that total pattern holds in it the whole issue of human existence or non-existence, we are prepared to ask whether this, for us, fateful enquiry must forever be left blank: *Why does this particular configuration exist?*

The answer may be suggested by the fact that the causal sequences with which physics deals reach no *goals*. That is why, for physics, cyclical and other reversible processes are just as satisfactory as the one-way processes. Where nothing is achieved, going backward undoes nothing; and men whose minds are thoroughly physicalized can work themselves into a state in which they fancy they are as willing to read time backward as forward. But purposive processes are irreversible because it is their nature to *reach goals*, and then to hold to what they have achieved.

If then the causal processes of the universe do something which it is not in their nature to do, achieve patterns which from our view are goals (such as the existence of life and human existence), and conserve these achievements; and if, as the preceding analysis shows, such attained patterns are involved in the original configuration of things—that "burden of irrationality" carried along by the physical process—then to interpret that whole "irrational" factor of the world-process as a purposive factor is a proposal to which physics can interpose no objection. Such a proposal would fill what is otherwise a vacuum of meaning.

But we should still hesitate to enter the vacant place unless there were positive grounds for doing so. Such grounds exist.

We may here recall the circumstance we have already alluded to, that science is itself a purposive activity and that its exclusion of purpose from its own business is a purposive exclusion. Outside of that special object, the exclusion ceases to be pertinent, and the grounds which led mankind to think of the universe in purposive terms resume their full force. The scientist cannot deny the nonphysical fact of his own purposes; and since purpose can never be extracted from causes, the existence of purpose in his own being has to be referred to an outer order of its own kind.

Beyond this is the fact of the interdependence of events and the nature of that interdependence. The extension of field-theory has brought into the picture of the universal interdependence involved in gravitation a more general interdependence of each event on all other events in the same light-cone. If any one event in that system is a "goal" all the conspiring events become related to it as the cells of an organism are related to each other. It is this which gives the universe the appearance of a society and forms the mainstay of Whitehead's "philosophy of organism." The togetherness of things is a significant togetherness.

Now certainly the whole of things is not a mere aggregate or collection of independent details—the new phase of physical science leads us to doubt the applicability of the word "independent" to any feature of nature, fully as much as does the philosophy of Josiah Royce. Quite literally the universe of electrons, which is at the same time a universe of infinite electronic fields, presents a minute (though no longer instantaneous) interdependence, justifying at once Whitehead's emphasis on togetherness and Francis Thomson's lines,

> All things by immortal power
> > Near or far
> > Hiddenly
> To each other linkèd are
> That thou canst not stir a flower
> > Without troubling of a star.

Yet I cannot follow this logic with Whitehead to the point of calling the whole an organism. There is more looseness among the parks of the world, more waste, wider flung oceans of emptiness, more *relative* independence than is compatible with organic unity. The inner rhythms and changes are not the proportioned movements of organic processes. What the universe seems to present is a true system of interdependent motions *within which* organic groupings take place and run their life course—the whole presenting the character of a *single environment* for the living fragments rather than being itself a total organism with no environment. What interests us is not that everything shall be living and of mental kind, but rather that the universe should offer itself as an arena for life and purpose, an arena whose very wildness, waste, vastness, unspanned gulfs of distance, offer incentives without limit to an ever-growing mentality. Seen in this way there is a purpose in the purposeless aspects of the world; the personal finds use for the impersonal, the living for the mechanical, the intense focuses of consciousness for the infinitely expansive unconsciousness of mass and energyfields. If the world is definable as an environment for purpose, then by this definition it *has* a purpose, and is referred to a purposing being for its ultimate account.

To think of the universe as an organism is to think of it as the body of a life rather than as the object of a conscious subject. In my judgment, most of Nature is object and not organic body. It is something known, estimated, thought about, sought or shunned, named and adopted as "path" or "home" or "terra incognita" or "light-giver" or "the tumbling main" or the "region of frozen glitter and death"—all the furniture of meanings, adventures, and the social welding of common dangers and efforts. What happens to Nature when there are living beings in it is its infinitely varied coloring according to its bearing on our concerns. All those facts which were once mere way stations or intersections of causal lines become charged with goal-quality, positive or negative. The strength of Whitehead's view is to show that this goal-quality pervading everything may *coexist with the causal scheme*: wherever there is consciousness, there purpose rides along with the causal flood, and the movement of events becomes a "creative advance." The weakness of his view is in his attempt to make everything at once goal and seeker, to conceive all "actual entities" on the mental pattern, and thus to ruin his noble picture of the ingressive goal-qualities which lure and guide the striving of the relatively few foci of purpose.

His vision of the transformation of the physical by the realization of qualities waiting to be born, as if Plato's eternal ideas abandoned their impassivity and at the touch of divine persuasion entered the world of change and addressed themselves to our suffrages—this is Whitehead's poem and the valid message of his philosophy. The universe is indeed a scene in which causal momenta, repetitious and non-creative, form a mere core of the real event. We have no full reality until conscious life sees every object in terms of a glow of quality and *caring* turns process into history. And the meaning of these conscious centers and their striving is not seen until beyond their factual goal-seeking, and through it, one perceives a nonmaterial will, finding its own life in the solicitation of these myriads of beings toward the fulfillment of their possibilities.

What Whitehead has shown is that physical science cannot exclude such a vision. He does not show that physical science requires it, nor does he present his view as one which is proved by the evidence. He would persuade by presenting an "adequate" in place of an "inadequate" description of experience. He exhibits the bankruptcy of the traditional physics as a substitute for metaphysics; he presents his alternative with a challenge to all comers to do greater justice if they can to the infinitude of the world's qualitative wealth. He persuades by the amplitude of his hospitality to the abundance of universal possibility. He has made it impossible—one would like to believe for all time—to forget that goal-qualities and their responding purposes are an integral part of the concrete on-going of world-process.

6. The Supplement to Astrophysics

It is natural that a scientist should be content with an hypothesis in metaphysics. And an hypothesis such as Whitehead's which other scientists cannot reject, and which serves human life greatly by a firm comprisal of values with the facts of nature, has a strong descriptive appeal.

But it is still a description of something other than and distant from ourselves. The very sweep and majesty of its world-view lifts its object away from the simple immediacy of our living and our problems. Since it is cosmology and cosmography, it must remain conversant with the immensities and the infinitudes. This is one of its great merits. It recovers the nobility of the proper object of man's contemplation; in an age of minute specialization and of triviality masquerading as the height of man's achievement in analysis, it stands as a monumental rebuke to the seeming-wise. It "recovers altitude." In doing so, it recovers also the loneliness of altitude. It parts company with that illusory domesticity wherewith modern man deceived himself into thinking that his classifications and statistics were giving him a mastery of nature and of himself. It has shown the poverty of the cosiness of humanistic self-preoccupation. Nevertheless, without something of that domesticity, the universe remains hollow at heart; and what we only suspect as an hypothesis leaves the emptiness uncured.

I judge that this is the point on which Bruno seemed to his clerical associates to have missed the truth of things. Infinitude was Bruno's special point of piety, and also his point of heresy. To him, no one who thought God's work less than infinite thought adequately of God, to his colleagues no one who thought God's world shapeless and devoid of center as the infinite must be could think adequately of God. Bruno's world could have no domesticity, and a God dispersed everywhere as the "principle of connection among things" could not be found. It is indeed an incomplete God and an incomplete universe. What it requires, and what all cosmographical metaphysics requires, is a cure for the *illusion of vastness*.

This cure the mystics have always professed to have. To the mystic God is felt as an immediate presence. The voice of the mystic has little credence in the halls of high argument, for he declines to argue: he speaks simply of what he sees. He brings out no new categories, for he has no trust in any categories. He holds no brief for a more adequate description, for he denounces all description of the real as a misdescription. He rejects hypothesis, for he claims certitude and will be satisfied with nothing less than certitude. He makes a poor witness under cross-examination, and we do not bring him here for his testimony but we point out that we can have no confirmation of that of which we are in search—the presence of purpose in the whole of things—until the mystic's directness, immediacy, and assurance can be recovered in the common experience of men with the facts of nature. This step we are now in a position to take.

Let us recur to the position of those contemporary scientists who are willing to find themselves once more in the vein of Berkeley's "idealism," even to the point of sacrificing what they ought not to sacrifice, the objectivity of the physical entity. They are reliving the first insight of the modern revolution, that which discovers that the truly concrete thing is conscious experience, for it includes the object and in addition the enveloping awareness, "I think." Let us go with them to the simplest fragment of this conscious experience, the sense-datum, a single pulse of sound or of pain or of fragrance or of color. Surely this experience stands at the remotest pole from the astronomical reaches of the cosmos: it is local, punctual, immediate.

Now this sense-datum can be taken as a finality. It is the fact *par excellence*, the absolute kernel of what all "ideas" mean, and at the same time the absolute essence of agreeable-quality or disagreeable-quality, the pure stuff of value. Take it that way, and your humanity is firmly tethered to the earth. This is the hopeless way of beginning a philosophy, most plausible and most false. You have foredoomed your end by thus taking your beginning. The trouble is that the sense-datum is *not a finality*. No sense-datum is a simple, neutral, blank, opaque plaque of being. As a "*datum*," it is something "given" and that means given to a receiving self by an outer activity; it is a surface of contact between a living mind and a living world. And because of this, with the quality is presented also *a moral alternative*. What! The sense-datum a moral problem? Just that. For there are two things in this one thing—the stuff, and *how I take it*. And there are two ways of taking it: as a subjective self-enjoyment—sinking myself in the sense-quality and becoming identical with it—or as a *summons to think*. If the sense-datum appears to me as a *phase of an object*, let us say the fragrance as the fragrance of a fruit, I have made a decision: I have resolved to live by thinking sense-data as signs of an object-world. This is the primitive moral choice. The life of the man and the life of science itself depend on rejecting the first alternative, and going in for the second; it is the rejection of solipsism, and therewith of solipsistic enjoyment; it is the beginning of conversation.

But if science recognizes the "ought" at the base of its own existence, it has asserted by implication that this "something beyond me" which gives the datum is a source of obligation. And only a living self can be such a source. This is not argued out by the incipient consciousness of the infant; its attitude is far more substantial and direct. It does the primary ethical deed of living outward rather than inward, as no proof could either require or reach, because it already perceives that which is not itself as a Thou, an Other, and accepts its destiny as a life of conversation with that Other. This is the immediate presence of purpose in the nucleus of the world, precisely there where science begins, and also the mystic.

It belongs to one of the conceptions of space dealt with in non-Euclidean geometry that a "straight" line indefinitely prolonged will rejoin itself at an assumed origin, constituting a vast circle. Let this be a symbol of the fortunes of the determined out-bound interest of physical astronomy, so trained away from all self-consciousness that the physicist habitually omits from his world-picture his own existence as a being of emotion and purpose. Just the sharpest physical analysis of today, just the utmost reach of penetration of the physical object, has brought the scientific thinker around to *himself*, first as an experiencer of sense-data, and then as a persistent duty-bound interpreter of these data, to set up a thought-world which shall be a public, a social world, a world for Other Mind. Without this element of duty, sense-experience would never become "science." Here, then, science—consciously or not—responds to a cosmic demand. There is, as the breath of life for science itself, an *ever-acting law of normal thinking*, a non-interfering activity, in the requirement for a truth which shall be "objective" truth. And here again, the experiment of getting on without God has led to a new perception of his presence.

At the same time, whoever thus perceives the infinite universe as an edifice of truth to which our momentary feeling and thinking are instantly responding has been cured of the illusion of vastness, for he has touched, as directly as sensation itself, the garment of the living God.

NOTES

1. Biology since Darwin, it is true, is more or less tempted to fall back into the language of purpose because of the very device by which Darwin got rid of it. For when Darwin talked about "adaptation to the environment" and "fitness to survive"; and rigged up his pretty mechanism of natural selection, he created a standing invitation to the physiologist to see the *usefulness* of an organic arrangement as the sufficient reason for its existence. Hence biology has acquired a shop-habit of substituting a means-to-end way of thinking for a cause-to-effect way of thinking. But with a rigorous scientific conscience it rejects any notion of an external purpose or plan, and insists that the "fortuitous variations" from which Nature selects the fittest (by killing off the less fit) arrive in the sober order of causal necessity. These lectures are incomplete without a separate chapter on the biological sciences. For the present I shall have to content myself with certain general references to the concept of fitness.
2. As by Lossky, Montague, Whitehead. One of the schools of Marxist philosophy in Moscow, teaching the "autodynamic" character of matter, might also be mentioned.
3. *Chhandogya*, VI, xii, 3.

CHAPTER 13

Faith and World Order

[…]

The Resources for World Order Apart from Faith

By a world in order we do not mean a world in which there is no trouble, but a world in which the trouble that arises can be met and settled without throwing the whole into turmoil. In all families, I am told, there are troubles, in the sense that there are issues of policy. But a family is called "disorderly" only if such issues reach the point of physical violence or disturbance of the neighbors. The essence of social order is the existence of *a means for decisive settlement*. And for this, there are three available resources in the world community, apart from faith; namely, *force, authority*, and *law*. We shall look for a moment at each of these.

1. *Force*. The word "power" is not one from which Christians ought to shrink. Power, in physics, is capacity to do work. This capacity is morally neutral; but one might argue that if one *can* have capacity to do work, it is both idle and immoral *not* to have it. The state, as a vast concentration of the powers of individuals, has something to do in the world, and so long as it sticks to its legitimate job, it cannot have too much power. We must always thank God for power, as the opposite of impotence and frustration.

Now an order based on force may have the qualities of prompt and final decision. The potential disturbers of world peace, no matter what their motives, will be driven to peaceful methods of attaining their objects if an umpire is available with sufficient power to make the challenging of its decision imprudent.

There are obvious objections to a world order based solely on power, if there could be such a thing. First, is the matter of justice. If the settling power is genuinely disinterested, its settlements would approximate justice, solely because it is human, and justice tends toward peace. But powers great enough to keep the world quiet by main force could never be disinterested. Such power always acts so as to increase its own control, or at least not to diminish it. And the self-perpetuation of dominant power is not, as a rule, to the long-distance benefit of mankind, chiefly because of the lack of perfect wisdom on the part of any fixed grouping.

2. *Authority*. There is a disposition in men to refer their actions to a habitual

---

From *The Church and the New World Mind* (St. Louis: The Bethany Press, 1944), 14–42.

source of authority. They are open to suggestions from that source as from no other. Within the state, a government which can claim the title "legitimate," even though it is the legitimacy of a hereditary house, can command a certain obedience on the part of those who accept that line, quite apart from its power, and often apart from its actual ability or worth. The presumption of such obedience is that the legitimate government has a certain spiritual fitness, for which there is no substitute on the part of rivals, who might show greater material efficiency. In fact, authority is essentially a *moral* bond. The prestige of the Supreme Court of the United States is due not alone to high-level ability, but also to the tradition of moral responsibility which that bench has maintained through a long period of years.

But how can a world order be based on authority? There is no legitimate rule, for there is no world ruler; there is no weighty Supreme Court; there is no panel of great publicists giving authoritative interpretations of international issues. Nevertheless, I dare say that the conduct of states has always been influenced by a type of judgment we might fairly call authoritative. We remember that the authors of our own Declaration of Independence thought they ought not to proceed to the radical deed of separation without due "respect to the opinions of mankind." They assumed that there was such a thing as a public opinion of the civilized world in regard to such disturbing actions; they knew that the new state would require the intangible which business calls "good will"; they respected what has sometimes been called "the verdict of history." And vague as that phrase may be, it is quite clear that every world disturber is troubled by the reality behind it and endeavors to set up through his speeches a reasoned justification of his course.

Now this vague authority is felt in the rise or fall of the reputation which individual states enjoy for fair dealing, keeping their treaties, paying their debts. It is also a part of the prestige which is sometimes credited solely to power. For behind the power of great states, there is felt to be an element of reason, in so far as political and military power testify to cultural and scientific advance, and to whatever moral qualities are evidenced in the political solidarity of large populations. Since men are never governed by fear and force alone, but always in part by conviction and loyalty, no state, modern or ancient, can be a great power unless it is also in some degree a spiritual fabric; and if it adds to its present cohesion a century-long durability, it will enjoy a position in the international field of moral weight not at all identical with nor limited to its striking force. And this authority will be all the more impressive because there are no international organs to make that authority compulsive.

It is for this reason that the League of Nations, in its origin, decided to make its chief reliance its appeal to public opinion and not an appeal to power; advocates of a "League to Enforce Peace" put their case in vain. A series of wise decisions would have built up, by degrees, a moral authority which would have strengthened its position and rendered further decisions more effective. It could not at once bring to bear on political problems even such wisdom as it had, because the prestige which would have made its judgments effective has to be a product of time.

I judge therefore that a world order based on authority is at least possible. Whatever institution takes the place of the League will have to depend on authority, rather than on power, if, as I certainly trust may be the case, there is no world government endowed with preponderant power. The difficulty with such an institution is primarily, again, the self-interest of great states, which makes them biased judges in their own case. Their moral weight may be high when they can serve as true umpires, and very low when their own interests are involved. And an institution whose policies were governed chiefly by a group of great powers would be suspect from the start. It would have to win its authority by a strict regard for an independent source of judgment. Such a source, in domestic matters, is the law. What value can this factor have in international affairs?

3. *Law.* Where law is known and accepted, human behavior is stabilized. Quite apart from a written law, every human being lives according to an inner law of some sort, because he will always produce some kind of reason to justify his conduct. (If you doubt this, just try to go through a single day on the fixed principle of not having any reason for what you do, so that the proper reply to every question of, "Why did you do that?" should be, "For no reason, but because I chose to.") But the reasonings of different persons do not coincide, nor the judgments of the same judge on different occasions—unless there is *an announced rule* on which dependence can be placed. A community composed entirely of men disposed to be reasonable, but not under law, would differ from that same community under law, by the important circumstance that in the latter each citizen would know what to expect from the others in the ground covered by the law.

If these divergent opinions about what is reasonable could thus be reduced to one, then the law in such a community would need no other legislative or enforcing agency. For the desire to be rational is inseparable from human nature.

Why should this principle not also apply to a community of nations? This was certainly in the mind of those seventeenth century jurists who so hopefully drew up the outlines of a system of international law. If there is a right and a wrong for individual action, why is there not also a right and a wrong for state action?

The question was natural, and the dreams of men from that day to the period following Versailles have been governed by it. But one of the great obstacles to the success of that law was born about the same time, the theory of the sovereignty of the nation-state, which we have already encountered. The state must be the source of law, and in that sense the creator of legal obligation; but no law can bind such an author of law. It must be in a strict sense, "above the law." On this theory, international law can have no force beyond the free consent of the several states to abide by it; if this consent is not given, at any point, there is nothing over the sovereign state to compel its obedience, or to make it a duty.

But one reason why the principle of sovereignty has been so insisted upon is just the point at the beginning—the many ways in which a group of nations is *unlike a group of persons*, so that the whole attempt to transfer the rights of men to the rights of nations is in danger of breaking down. Let me give an example or two.

During the last war there were a number of very intelligent people in this country who retained their German citizenship and who thought that we were taking the events of that war too much from the legal and ethical point of view. One of them said to me: "You Americans are making a mistake. This war is not over a moral issue. The issue is this: Here are the Germanic peoples, multiplying in number and in strength and pressing eastward. At the same time the Slavic peoples are multiplying in number and strength and are pressing westward. At some time a clash was bound to occur. But surely you cannot say that the increase of populations is a moral issue."

This plea by no means disposes of the moral issue which presents itself in every modern war; but it does indicate one root of war for which there are no exact parallels in the relations between individuals. The natural growth of person A does not bring him into collision with the natural growth of person B, so that a contest is bound to arise in order to decide which one shall absorb, dominate, or displace the other! And if such a situation should arise, by what rule of justice could a community decide whether to have one full-grown individual or two individuals, each permanently flattened on one side?

Or, consider the issue presented by the Panama Canal project in the days of Theodore Roosevelt, where the security of the United States was on one side and the political integrity of a small nation on the other. It is hard to say that there are differences in the magnitude and importance of nations which affect one's judgments of what is right; and it is equally hard to say that there are not. But at least this is clear, that there are no quite similar problems in the cases which come before our civil courts. For it is not a simple situation in which the great and the small, the rich and the poor, stand on the same level before the law; it is a situation in which the position of one of the parties gives it a preponderant influence on the peace of the world, and thus gives it responsibilities that reach far beyond its own borders.

I have mentioned the two great obstacles to the very notion of a community of states governed by an international law. I do not think that either one of them is decisive.

As for the idea of sovereignty, that is, in substance, purely a matter of definition, a useful legal convention, which is already yielding on many sides to the many lines of interdependence which make the notion of complete autonomy, law-unto-oneselfness, out of drawing with the facts. The legal theory of sovereignty must be revised so that it shall not be destroyed by this increasing interaction. When this is done, it becomes simply another name for final responsibility; there must be some identifiable executive, legislative, judicial body in each state whose decisions can be taken as the decisions of that state. But the reason for this is obvious: it is in order that some definite agent *may be held accountable*, which is quite the reverse of any conception of sovereignty that makes it free from all accountability. And if the "reign" is simply the responsible decider, then, like other human moral agents, he becomes subject to the superior law that he must keep his promises (*pacta sunt servanda*), pay his debts, refrain from injuring his neighbors, and carry out the duties of a respectable state in regard to keeping order at home and giving his own citizens the basic rights of man. These points are the basic principles of international law.

The second obstacle is more serious. But the difficulty of the questions raised under the "nonjusticiable" title does not mean that they are to be determined by arbitrary will. The basic rights to be affected are not the rights of nations, but the rights of the individuals in nations. However boundaries may be shifted, it is *the effect on individual human lives that matters*. There must therefore be such a thing, in each case, as a "reasonable" decision, as distinct from any result reached by appeal to force. And where there is reason, there is already the possibility of law.

The idea of a world order based on law, therefore, is one which the human race cannot give up, and which ought to be a main object of the foreign policy of our own country.

But all law is weak unless there is something beyond it as a source of obligation. Specific laws are weak because they are changeable. No one of them is "the" eternal law. The more completely international law is codified, the less permanent will any one of its articles be. What men have formulated, they can reformulate. International statutes or precepts will for many years lack the prestige of rules sanctioned by long and widespread usage and confirmed by a series of decisions of an international court. And finally, every system of law is weak in the respect that it cannot *generate the emotion* which will hold nations to its observance when it contravenes their momentary interest. It is especially for this final reason that a world order based on law *must be supplemented by a world order based on faith*.

To summarize the situation, our resources for world order add up in some such way as this:

No one of these three is ever relied on alone, though there are theorists who try to rely on power alone; in fact, they all cooperate. Power requires authority to give it any sort of moral quality, without which it disintegrates. Authority requires law to give it justice in its temper and world-wide acceptance. But law, weakest of all secular resources, requires faith—weaker still, from the secular point of view—to launch it into effectiveness as the spirit of a working community. Apart from faith, the whole pyramid loses its inner harmony and sense, and therefore its vitality. It tends to become an inconsistent mixture of power politics mitigated by fragments of morality out of place.

The question is whether religious faith is in a position in the world today to make this whole setup a living unity.

What Are the Resources of Faith??

On November 11, 1931, there was dedicated a new Buddhist temple at Sarnath, in the Deer Park in which Buddha was supposed to have preached his first sermon. This event was a notable one in the return wave, on which Buddhism is coming back into India, from which it had practically vanished several centuries ago. It was made notable by two special circumstances, a gift of relics of the Buddha, presented by the British Government of India, and a speech by Narendra Nath Dasgupta, head of the Sanskrit College in Calcutta, and in that capacity a prominent member of that Hindu community which had formerly been most influential in the expulsion of Buddhism from its native land. In this speech, Pundit Dasgupta made, in effect, the following concluding statements:

> Christianity has failed in Europe to prevent Christian nations from attacking one another in deadly combat, though for centuries it has preached there a gospel of peace and good will. Buddhism has actually promoted peace on the continent of Asia. It has never spread itself by means of force nor by the use of methods of compulsion. It has brought a genuine fraternity among the lands to which it has spread. I therefore welcome this event, which symbolizes a milestone in the march of the future Hindu-Buddhist culture of Asia.

At the time of this speech, Dasgupta's statements were approximately true, though Japan had already struck in Manchuria. The ideal of a Hindu-Buddhist culture rather than a Christian culture for Asia was alluring, plausible, and, to the Christian conscience, a problem requiring thought.

It indicated, among other things, the belief of Dasgupta that the problems of world order were at bottom problems of religious faith and that there existed in Asia the promise of sufficient unity on this matter to give reasonable ground for hope.

Since that time, the Buddhist world has split asunder by the widening of the breach made in September of 1931. Japan, the most actively Buddhist of any Asiatic power (though not the most exclusively Buddhist), has made herself the political enemy of China, the potential enemy of India, and the absorber, under the pretense of friendship, of the other Buddhist lands of Southeastern Asia. What we can say on behalf of Buddhism is that the Japanese policy seems less dictated by Buddhism than by Shinto, so far as it has a religious basis at all. But in Japan, two of the leading sects of Buddhism are deliberately pugnacious in their spirit; and the Goddess of Mercy, Kwannon, has been pressed into service as the divine patroness of the Asiatic campaign. To this extent, it has taken the mold of official Shinto, the nature of whose faith contains the prophecy of the present conflict.

In a temple of the Tenrikyo sect of Shinto near Nara, Japan, there is an important brass plate in the middle of the floor. This plate marks a place memorable in

[187]

the history of the universe, for directly under it, the sun-goddess began the creation of the earth. From this center, creation expanded to form the Japanese islands; then beyond a stretch of the primeval waters, the mainland of Asia was congealed. And after Asia, the rest of the earth. During my stay in Japan I never heard any discussion of the relation between symbol and literal truth in religious tradition and I am unable to say how many of the six million Tenrikyo adherents follow this myth as history, nor to how many of the rest of Japan the other similar myths of Shinto have a basis in fact. But as a symbol, it represents a wide belief that Japan is the radiant center from which enlightened government of the world must some day spread.

In judging this application of a religious outlook in Japan, there are certain things to be remembered. Many Japanese, including not a few Japanese Christians, continue to believe in the beneficent mission of their country. They are ignorant of the conduct of their soldiers in the field. They have no practical acquaintance of any kind with a political order based on freedom. Hence the note of faith in a divine structure of history, which must eventually govern human affairs, lacks any effective release from the nationalistic plan of promotion.

At the same time, this very fact testifies to the inherent weakness of Buddhism before the heavy strains of world politics. For had Buddhism offered an alternative way of promoting Japanese culture abroad, instead of falling in with the primitive statecraft of Shinto, the liberal elements within Japan would have had a more effective religious support.

It is true that Hinduism and Buddhism have never abetted war on their own initiative. But it is now evident that, being above the battle, they have not been able, any more than Christianity, to prevent it.

In its own nature, religious faith is universal; and, binding all men to the same spiritual source and goal, it creates a supernational fraternity, out of which a genuine world order can be born, and must some day be born. But all religion has proved itself, so far, ineffective to bring that day near. And we have to look at the reasons for that ineffectiveness.

The simple fact that we have many religions in the world, instead of one world faith, is itself one answer to the question. The very intensity of religious conviction and its supreme importance to the life of the individual have made the differences matters of vital import, so that in fact religious leaders have spent much energy in denouncing the errors of other religious leaders—and the colder world of politics has inclined to accept both sides as correct on this point. We shall later have something to say on this matter, but I doubt whether today it is as great an impediment as it was a generation ago. The reasons lie rather in the attitudes of different religions to the whole political situation of man. Of these attitudes, Buddhism and Shinto are typical.

There are two types of religions in respect to their effort to become universal. There are the religions originally identified with a particular group of mankind, such as Judaism, Hinduism, Shinto, which realize their universal mission by group diffusion or mastery. And there are religions universal in their very definition, which realize their universal mission by appeal to individual assent; such are Buddhism and Christianity. The obvious peril of the group mission is its political entanglement and its provincial outlook. The peril of the individual mission is its abstraction. Preaching the principle of love and the insignificance of race, sex, nation, in the eye of God, it runs the risk of discounting the true value of the dynamic human group and thus of losing influence over it.

The result of this dilemma is that the local type of faith tends to develop a universal faith, whose conquest can take place by individual assent. Let us call these the faiths of amiability. Islam gives rise to Bahaism; Hinduism, to the Ramakrishna variety of Vedanta. Judaism develops a liberal version which is hardly distinguishable from varieties of liberal Christianity: I have heard distinguished Jews, like the late Rabbi Voorsanger of California, say that Judaism and Unitarianism were practically identical in creed.

But all these faiths, or forms of faith, by definition universal, seem to share the same feebleness of political impact. Men do not unite for heavy work on the basis of the abstract man, but on the basis of the historic man and his issues, and his future.

If Christianity has an advantage in dealing with politics, it lies here. Judaism is historical, and in its history strong. But it has become too much the religion of "return," with an attachment in the past, seeking the "restoration" of Israel, the restoration of something that once was on the hill of Zion, and must be once more. Christianity, inheriting this valid historical trait, has broken with the past anchorage and has set its anchor in the future. It lives in the eternal, but in the moving eternal which is alive in time; it believes in the God-man, the God who is at work in the historical process, and who therefore summons his followers to redeem that process, and make it in its full sweep a movement toward a Kingdom of God on earth.

Further, as I think, Christianity has an inherent pugnacity of its own, rather stimulated than dashed by repeated failure. It is for that reason that I have a special word to offer to the Christian community of this country at this time.

The Program of Faith for World Order

There are various things which hearten us as we look around the world, even the disturbed and tragic world of our time, and one of these is the fact that nations as well as men are often better than their professions. There have been nations who through their monarchs have pretended to be concerned with nothing but the interests of their own state; there has never been such a state in fact. Much of the accusation of hypocrisy leveled against Great Britain is due to the fact that it has mingled morality with self-interest frequently, indeed almost regularly, and then been naturally inclined to give the most laudable name to the mixture. This is far better than not having any mixture of morality at all. And the very fact that the ethical name has been chosen is a sign of the perennial power which the moral prejudices of the public exercise on the acts of statesmen. The more democratic a regime is, the more the conscience of men will carry over from private to public affairs and international affairs, even in defiance of the logic of the situation.

This indicates one principle of Christian statecraft; namely, the eternal *working from inside*, in the confidence that state egoism will be modified even when it cannot be finally cured. In the inner self-renewal, and the increased knowledge of international fact, lies the most immediate hope that foreign policies will be bent toward a world of just and durable peace. With this should go the following external objectives:

1. That all nations should be urged to provide in their constitutions for the effectiveness of the citizen's conscience on the acts of government as a factor in external peace. This means the adoption of at least one element of a democratic constitution whereby there is guaranteed not alone freedom of conscience, but a channel for its political influence. In the nature of the principle of freedom, this cannot be an imposed requirement on any people, but it can be recommended by the inner strength of democracies themselves as they renew their own faith and duty.
2. A demand that the economic roots of world disorder be not concealed under the calls for political and ideological reform. Not that religious faith has competence in the economic sphere; but that it has an inalienable concern (*a*) in honesty and truth, and (*b*) in the living standards of man in all lands.
3. A demand that no human being, and no group or nation, be held as the property of any other human being or nation; but that every soul of man be respected in terms of his own capacity to grow and master his destiny. The principle of empire must be revised.
4. Unremitting pressure for an adequate setup for the principles of international law, revitalized and applied, with especial attention to the refractory questions of status.
5. Reconstruction of a league of nations on the principle of authority, backed by an instructed world opinion, in which the thought of the church shall play an increasingly vital role.

The inherent power of faith is that it directly undercuts the series of world envelopes with their diminishing intensities of loyalty.

Being world-wide, it is wider than the empire, but it is also more intimate.

It is the only power which directly commands by an inner and inescapable voice. We completely misrepresent it if we think of it as one wider sphere.

It has an inherent importance because it supplies the scale of importance. Hence it is always more powerful, if one listens at all, than the voice of national advantage, which is in many ways a pseudo voice.

The national entity has no intrinsic necessity as to its boundary.

The religious being has an intrinsic necessity in his relations to mankind. He cannot keep his faith with his Maker if he destroys his duty to his fellow man.

Confucius said, "He who offends the gods has no one to whom he can pray."

Christ said, in effect, "He who offends one of the least of these my brethren, has no one to whom he can pray." And men reach the time sooner or later when they realize that prayer is their breath of life, far beyond the political sphere in its necessity and its realism.

CHAPTER 14
Vox Dei

In the transforming of man, society intends to civilize him, religion to save him. In these terms there is a suggestion that the work of society is more or less superficial, that of religion more radical and thorough. Man conforms his mind and habits to social requirements and becomes 'polite': he submits his soul to religion and becomes 'holy.'

But there is reason to question whether this traditional distinction can be maintained; or whether there is any legitimate distinction at all between the work of society and the work of religion on human nature. To make man a social being, to lead him out of his egoism and barbarity into the liberal interpretation of his interests afforded by civic life and its destinies, is not this to make him a religious being in the only sense of religion that has valid meaning?

In the early days of human organization, the distinction between the social and the religious could not have been drawn, not because all religion was social, but because all social requirement was religious. The setting-up of ideals, the defining of customs, the giving of laws were understood as the voice of God to the people. *Vox populi* had no other existence than in *vox Dei*. If the interests of society were at all divergent from those of religion, there was little opportunity to discover the fact: for when the ordering of life is singly and simply from above, there is no comparison of standards, and hence no rebellion in the name of a social value.

But the time was bound to come when the two rules, the sacred and the secular, should fall into contrast, if only because of their diverse methods of origin, the sacred relatively a priori, the secular relatively empirical and pragmatic. And when this opposition has occurred, history seems to show that the destiny of the sacred is to yield to the secular. Tabus accumulated beyond endurance; were long protected by faith and fear; but they have been swept away. Holy men fell into the way of announcing counsels of perfection such as would mutilate or destroy human nature,—the sacred books are full of such counsels: for these, practice provided an interpretation, such as all laws need; and the interpretation quietly superseded the announced ideal. The establishments and ordinances of religion became extremely costly to society, in men and time and treasure abstracted from social use, and not infrequently too, in moral integrity: neither social utility nor social ethics would sanction many ancient forms of sacrifice. But the race has believed in its social standards as against the oracles,

---

From HNR, 273–279.

and these extravagances of religious requirement have dwindled or disappeared. Today it is frequently asserted by the exponents of religion themselves that our best insight into the will of God is the verifiable welfare of society. Our religion seems to become, in effect if not in name, the religion of humanity.

Thus the question has become acute whether the reference to God is any longer significant. Is it more than an imaginative widening of the horizon under which the same acts and qualities are required, a changing of names, as from 'goodness' to 'holiness,' or from 'crime' to 'sin'? The tendency of history is unmistakable. From "The voice of God is the voice of the people" we have come to "The voice of the people is the voice of God"; and it may well be that the time has come to drop the "voice of God" as otiose, frankly acknowledging our final insight into human standards as "from below," i.e., from experience, socially transmitted. If we any longer maintain a separate place for religion in the work of transforming human instinct, the burden of proof is upon us.

I accept the burden. And I begin by pointing out an error in the logic of the argument we have just reviewed.

The course of history seemed to show that the will of God has tended to coincide with the weal of society; the inference was that the weal of society is the independent fact, and hence the only fact that need be considered. The inference is hasty. We may accept the proposition, Nothing contrary to the welfare of society can be accepted as the will of God. But the postulate that A must not clash with B does not in the least inform me what A is. I must plan my house so as not to destroy the trees on my lot: this condition does not supply me the plan of my house—would it did! Religion must not tear down social values:—this condition does not supply me with a religion. What history suggests, at most, is that the welfare of society has a negative or critical bearing on the interpretation of the religious standard. We may be *negative pragmatists* in the matter.[1] But there is not the slightest evidence, so far, that the will of God is deducible from the good of society as an independent fact.

And there is a large volume of evidence to the contrary. Let us make the questionable admission that we know and can define what social utility is; it is still true that the socially useful has never been reached by directly aiming at it, but has always come as a result of aiming at something else, as an independent object. Social cohesion, loyalty, lawfulness are dispositions upon which every social structure depends, but which society cannot directly produce. Already in the speculations of Plato and Aristotle we find a deep anxiety as to what education, what myth, what music, what lie if need be, will be likely to generate the spirit from which socially useful behavior would naturally follow. Arguing from history, it looks rather as if there could be no social good, unless there is something more than social good as a primary object of pursuit.

In point of fact, society has always had its religion in some form,—a principle of devotion which has pervaded the social tissue, acting more or less like an enzyme in furnishing energy and loyalty at points needing support. Law-abiding behavior could not be reached by the separate attention of each citizen to each law: it has to be reached for the most part through a disposition which of its own motion is "the fulfilling of the law," or the major part of the law. The man who measures each step by the law is not the good citizen: he who watches the law, the law needs to watch. There is a "spirit of the laws," something which one might call a moral substance, which shows itself in a spontaneous faith in current institutions and ideals and fellow citizens, a willingness to serve them and work with them, a spirit which society can neither give nor take away, and yet without which there is no society.[2]

I prefer to describe this spirit as a moral substance, because when we look into it more closely it is not simply a subjective temper but also a world of objects engaging each individual 'a interest and will in logical independence of his social entanglements; and in this world of objects we recognize the accumulated goods of both religion and art. These goods do not arise apart from social conditions, and are commonly reckoned as social products; but they appeal to the individual as an independently appreciating being, as an original self. Because this substance has always pervaded society, its real relation to society is obscured; and an attempt to define society apart from it would be felt as a mutilation of society. But this circumstance only makes stronger the contention that social good, defined apart from religion, is not self-sufficient. And I shall try to indicate a method of comparing the relative functions of each which will admit the comparison with justice to both sides.

It is characteristic of the development of human beings that the will to power tends to assume from time to time the character of some leading interest, which becomes the center of values for the whole life. This leading interest may rise to the level of a passion. In a boy's growth to maturity we can trace a series of these absorbing concerns, seldom coincident with the tasks set for him by his elders, but merging at last (generally speaking) in an 'ambition' which at some time or other struggles for supremacy with a personal affection. To these two major passions, ambition and love, correspond two major groups of institutions, those of the public order and those of the private order, as we shall name them. These together constitute 'society' in so far as society has a definable entity apart from religion and art.

Now what society does for human nature depends on *how completely it can satisfy* the individual will. A man can be said to be saved (to adopt the religious terminology for the sake of our comparison) not alone when he is reclaimed from rebellion or criminality; he is saved in so far as he is *not wasted*, in so far as the human material in him gets a chance at self-expression and utilization. In this sense the question for society is *how much of each member* it can save, not merely *how many* it can preserve from disaffection and rebellion.

Putting the question in this way, it is clear that society never does save the whole man. In general, society saves, or conserves, *as much of a man as can, at any time, find a valuation*. It saves as much as it knows how to use or esteem. The remainder is wasted. And it may easily be that the better the case any set of institutions can make out for itself as a whole, the worse the plight of that portion of human nature (if there is such a portion) which it cannot satisfy, because it does not understand.

We shall attempt to estimate what part of human nature can be thus 'saved' by the public and the private orders, at their best.

NOTES

1. For the meaning of the phrase 'negative pragmatism' see my book, *The Meaning of God*, preface, pp. xiii f [see chapter 2—eds.].
2. Mr. Graham Wallas has shown, in a fascinating study, how the practical art of politics is concerned with what is instinctive and emotional, not alone with what is reasonable or reasoned. He regards it as somewhat ominous that this art betakes itself so frankly to "exploiting the irrational elements of human nature which have hitherto been the trade secret of the elderly and disillusioned" (*Human Nature in Politics*, p. 177). The chief peril, as I see it, is not that political managers will address themselves to the unreasoned, but that they will make a wrong guess as to the nature of the unreasoned sentiments they have to deal with. When one leaves the rigorous path of influencing the will of one's fellows by argument alone, everything depends on what passions one attributes to them. If with Bolingbroke (to use Mr. Wallas's illustrations) one fancies himself dealing with 'that staring, timid creature, man,' the result is likely to be supercilious and deceptive political action. But if with Disraeli one realizes that 'Man is only truly great when he acts from the passions, never irresistible but when he appeals to the imagination,' there is room at least for a generous interpretation of the unreasoned motive. Benjamin Kidd seems to have been near the ground of experience in judging that the unreasoned element in politics, in its last analysis, is a loyalty of religious character. The ebullition of national feeling at the outbreak of the war showed, especially in France, how politics in times of public stress tends to avow a lurking religious ingredient, while patriotism tends to coincide for the moment with religion.

CHAPTER 15

The Unifying of History

Our historic existence with its immense contingencies we take for the most part with a certain poetic remoteness: we only half believe in it; we hope well of it—that is to say, we hope well of the luck that seems to prevail there. We live still in a semi-savage dreaminess, incredulous of the distant contingency, incredulous therefore of the present moment, veiled from the actual conditions of action, circling at planetary distances about our own practical center. The fanciful is too real to us, the real too fanciful. The evil that is in this world, and especially in this spirit of meaningless accident—the luck which we hope will be *for us* good luck—this evil does not rouse us: it benumbs us, rather, and confirms our somnambulism. This is our ingrained irresponsibility, our original sin.

It is the last fruit of religion to produce, or approximate, a prophetic consciousness, that is to say, a natural historic consciousness, wholly wakened, literal, and real, capable of seeing the divinity of its own present fact and acting upon it. It is the work of faith to face the bulk and detailed circumstance of nature, banish its luck, remove its mountains. Religion must labor long, but aims at last to bring about such a faith, literal, prophetic, responsible.

But we are right in our incredulity, so long as religion comes to us only as a psychological necessity. The conditions for prophetic control of fortune lie without as well as within, far out on the borders of the universe. Science and the State, under the encouragement of faith, may banish luck gradually to these borders: but from them, luck streams back upon human life—distributed, perhaps, in its incidence, yet none the less menacing and vast. Unless the original sources of history, the ultimate arrangements of natural facts, the configurations of physical things which set the last limits to the hopes of all living beings, are already subject to some other control than our own, there is no such thing as absolute certainty of historic action. I cannot hasten the missile that has once left my hand; every workman must leave his work at last to a world that he can no longer govern; the whole race of prophets and world-builders stands helpless in the presence of a wider agency whose name is either Fate or Providence. Without the cooperation of an environment not less than infinite, the best prophet comes at last to zero—the worse because of his concrete hopes. The mystic must give reason for his dogma that there is no "realm of chance"; that beside the work of God which we have been tracing in the individual mind, there is a supplementary work of God in the world beyond the human will,—there at the

---

From MGHE, 515–524.

origins of the plot which all events work out. Thus the theory of religion rests back upon cosmology and the philosophy of a wider history for its final justification.

I cannot here follow out into this wider world the question of the right of the religious consciousness in its immediate practical assurance. But at least one principle prevailing in that world is already in our hand, and I will touch upon it in closing. So far as our own human history is concerned—a small part, no doubt, of our total environment—we can see that the religious will tends to create the conditions for its own success. Note what these conditions are.

It is in our human environment, as we said, that our natural will-to-command finds its first successes: our power extends from this center outward. Yet taking the human world as a whole, it presents a problem to prophetic ambition not less baffling than that of the control of nature: in fact, these two problems are precise counterparts of one another. Dealing with the social environment has always the guidance and encouragement of response, pro and con, which nature lacks. On the other hand, dealing with nature has always this element of satisfaction, that nature is a single order, persistent, invariably faithful to its own principles whether against us or for us. The obstacles to prophetic confidence in dealing with the human world consist in the absence of just these qualities. He who intends to accomplish something permanent must appeal to an environment that treasures and faithfully conserves values. The fluid mass of free wills conserves nothing, holds itself bound to nothing. A world which can promise to conserve must itself be unitary and eternal: it must have a principle of persistent identity and reliability like that of nature. To introduce into this mass of free individuals an order, unity, and inflexibility of purpose like that of nature would indeed be something of a miracle. Yet without this, the prophetic attitude is not justified; this, as I see it, is precisely what the prophet must require. He must *find in the current of history a unity corresponding to the unity of the physical universe, or else he must create it.* And what I want to point out is that it is just such a conscious unification of history that the religious will spontaneously tends to bring about.

We can see that the type of power which we have called prophetic, unlike that power which Nietzsche celebrates, tends not to compete with and destroy the like power in its neighbors, but rather to develop and to propagate it. As laughter begets laughter, and courage courage, passing from mind to mind and crystallizing a social group or a social world upon its own principle, so does the world-conquering temper of religion beget its like. No human attitude is more socially contagious than that of worship, except the practical attitude toward facts which comes out of worship: namely, enthusiasm for suffering, conscious superiority to hostile facts of whatever sort or magnitude, knowledge of their absolute illusoriness, so far as they pretend finality,—in a word the practical certitude of the prophet. When religion has thus acquired a clear-sighted and thorough *contemptus mundi*, religion begins to be potent within this same world of facts: it was within the scope of the stoic to become impregnable, but the religious spirit finds itself more than impregnable,—irresistible. The prophetic attitude begins at once to change facts, to make differences, to do work; and its first work is, as I say, its social contagion: it *begins* to crystallize its environment, that is, *to organize the social world upon its own principle.*

And if this temper is actually spread through the social world (not rising and dying out like the wave of laughter, but reaching the threshold of self-perpetuation), something more has happened than the dissemination of a *type of will* by 'social imitation'—namely, that *environment* is created which this same type of will requires. The human world has taken on a certain unity of mind and purpose; for whatever may be the special field of action of any religious will, every such will must desire that unification of the conscious world as a necessary part of its own purpose. So far, all have common cause. Every prophetic will is something of an environment for every other; as the group widens, and pervades human life with its principle, it becomes, as an environment, more adequate to its task, and may reach complete adequacy.

We may conceive some such group as becoming fully conscious of the nature and extent of this task; and adopting as its own special responsibility the extension of its own unity, for the sake of making this same will accessible to all men. It would thus make it, so to speak, its own prophecy that prophetic will shall be possible; that no human being shall be obliged to let his prophetic impulses die for lack of that unity in the human world which must justify them. This, I believe, is the essential purpose of the *religious institution.* It is this purpose, as I conceive it, which brings religion to earth in the form not simply of a system of truth, not simply as a type of personal experience, but in the form which religion everywhere takes, that of the positive historic body with work to perform.

Positive religion in its primitive phases *makes history possible*, cultivating what we might call the tribal and national memory. In its more developed phases, it tries to achieve a more general, non-political, but none the less historic solidarity among men. It undertakes, we may say, to do for the sporadic prophetic impulses of men what the State does for their sporadic impulses of justice and public power. Let me develop this idea a little.

As I look over the circumstances of religious development, I observe that there are four striking changes in the religious consciousness which usually occur together: as religion becomes 'redemptive' (that is, world-over-coming in one way or another), it detaches itself from the national life, it begins a universal propaganda, and it refers itself and its adherents to some distinctive historic object or person as the beginning of its temporal undertaking (and so, as a special point of irruption of the divine into history). Thus Islam points to its shrine and its sacred book; the Buddhist convert must take refuge in the Buddha, as well as in the doctrine and the order; Christianity asks men to regard its founder as the unique way to God. How are we to understand this remarkable concurrence of characteristics at this stage of development?

It is the analogy of the State which best helps me to understand what these things mean. The political organization affords to the individuals under it what Bagehot well describes as a "calculable future." In the State I have some prospect of a tangible immortality. I acquire property that may affect in one way or another my children's children. I promote laws, perhaps, that influence more or less all lives to come within the scope of that government. I can do my small part anywhere in art or industry or science with a sense of worth; because the State is there to give permanence to the growing treasures of one generation after another. The State *lends to my deeds its own permanence,* so far as these deeds are legitimate and within its own province.

In the same way the religious institution (I am speaking now of the ideal, as reflection shows it to me, certainly not of the entire body of instituted religion as it now is)—the religious institution seems to exist to lend its own permanence and immortality to the deeper and wider prophetic purposes of men. In severing its fortunes from those of the State, it assures to the individual his right to live and take part in an infinite history, though outside all States, and in spite of the defects of all earthly States. It stands between the creative individual will and that unordered, or unstably ordered, human social mass, before whose free mobility and passion that will is indeed in a hopeless plight.

Religion defies the clash and decay of the political attempts of men, whose mission in their own sphere is similar; but it is historic religion which chiefly renders those political attempts hopeful. Religion from primitive times the protector of the stranger, the market-place, the truce, is the forerunner of international law; because it alone can create the international spirit, the international obligation; it alone can permanently sustain and ensure that spirit.[1]

It is this function, as I think, which the greater religions have more or less clearly perceived. They propose to bring into human affairs that most general unity, not interfering with nor displacing any more special undertaking, without which no such special undertaking—whether of art, or of science, or of law—is worth while, being without promise of permanence.

We customarily think of the religious institution as a way of arranging for *the social side of worship*. Worship is imperfect unless when I worship, I am joining the race in worship.[2] Instituted religion has accordingly made worship public; at its best, it does much to join the minds of all sorts and conditions of men in worship, of all present human worshippers, and with those of the past and of the future. Further, we think of the institution as *an educating body*, or as propagating the religious type of mind by that social imitation we were speaking of. But we usually fail, as I think, to see what the institution does to justify that type of mind; namely, that it brings to the individual soul not only its moral ideal, its psychological norm, but also the *kind of world* wherein such a mind can alone rightly assert itself. It is a unified and responsible world, one which cares for the individual in his concrete character, and will bear out his rightful will to endure,—a human world which religion itself has made.

It is a sign of the good faith of the institution that it brings to the individual, who seeks assurance of his own absolute worth, its assertion of its own power and permanence. It encourages him to prophesy, only in so far as it itself is based on prophecy. It asserts its own universal scope and indestructibility—the gates of hell shall not prevail against it. If this is a true assertion, the individual may always knit his prophetic action to that. The attitude which as a solitary being he could not rightfully assume is made possible to him by this external agency which is throwing over all history its most general unity, bringing men everywhere to a singleness of mind and a singleness of purpose. Through that agency, and not otherwise, he may win, in the language of religion, his (historic) salvation, the forgiveness of his ingrained sin.

In our current consciousness, we feel little need of these external assurances, nor of the institution which offers them. The sense of sin grows foreign to us: the suggestion that we any longer require what our fathers called salvation strikes with a note of unreality. We feel ourselves morally secure; and historically,—as secure as need be. But when beneath this over-socialized surface of consciousness we penetrate to the actual basis of such certainties as we have, our self-respect, our belief in human worth, our faith in the soul's stability through all catastrophes of physical nature, and in the integrity of history—this history of ours—forever, we must recognize there a mass of actual deed, once for all accomplished under the assurances of historic religion. A *system* of deed, I might rather say, organized about a prophetic purpose once planted in history and now perpetually reproducing itself all around us.

The work of positive religion is largely silent; like the work of positive law, it is as great in what it prevents as in what it noisily accomplishes—perhaps greater. But the work is there, and if we are just we shall acknowledge it. Our confidences with regard to history must be built in history as well as in universal thought,—in both of these, welded together. Unless we can discern at its silent work in human affairs this power, self-consciously eternal, actively communicating its own scope to the feeble deeds, the painful acquirements, the values, the loves and hopes of men, we have no right to such faith as we habitually assume. And without such faith there is for us no valid religion.

NOTES

1. By such super-nationalism in religion, national individuality is not obscured, but rather promoted. We require a world-religion just because we do not require, nor wish, a world state.
2. We have regarded worship in its mystical aspect, as a solitary adventure of the soul: but we have also noted from time to time that before the mystic may make his lonely flight to God, he must assert as fully as possible his unity with his human spiritual context. Unity with the Absolute becomes significant in proportion as the worshipper is first one with the spirit of God as already established in the world.

CHAPTER 16

The Last Fact

> "Whether the world we live in is or is not the world of Christianity is a question of fact." [HNR, 425—eds.]

I doubt philosophy can affirm the existence of this fact. It can show that if such a fact were extant our dilemma would be solved. It can show, further, that certain characters of the world are in harmony with such a fact. Thus, the dialectic of experience, as we look back upon it, may be understood as a part of the strategy of "The Hound of Heaven." The world is so devised that "All things betray thee, who betrayest me": the will, apparently driven by dissatisfaction in its own false definitions of good, may to a deeper knowledge be seen as driven by the wind of a god's desire. And as for all the irregularly distributed individual deprivation, it is at least conceivable that it is part of the individual appeal of that same god:

> All which I took from thee, I did but take
> Not for thy harms, but just that thou
> Mightst seek it in my. . . .
> I am he whom thou seekest.

But the power of so understanding the dialectic, or so interpreting evil, is retrospective. The force which could lift the mind into a position from which this reading seems *the truth* does not lie in the dialectic itself. It must come as a positive datum, something itself personally experienced or 'revealed.' It is here that religion takes the issue out of the hands of philosophy.

For religion in its historical forms is empirical: it appeals to the realistic temper: it deals with facts. Its function is not to prove God but to announce God. For this reason, its doctrine is stated as *dogma;* and the fundamental dogma of religion is *Ecce Deus,* Behold, *This* is God. Such a dogma certainly appeals to the reason of every man, for it can mean nothing to any one except in so far as he is capable of understanding his own needs; but beyond that, it appeals to his power to *recognize what he needs in what is real.* Recognition is an act of the mind which thought can lead up to, but never quite enforce. Hence religion calls upon every man for an individual and ultimate "I believe," which means, "I recognize this to be the tact," or, more simply, "I see."

From HNR, 426–439.

In the last resort, it is by his own vision that every man must live:—when we call a man an individual, we are thinking of the solitude of his ultimate relation to reality. He must live by what he, for himself, can recognize; and his power of recognizing is an integral part of his instinctive equipment.

For as hunger may be trusted, for the most part, to recognize what will serve as food, so all instinct may be trusted to recognize what it needs in the world, if what it needs is there. Animal instinct will recognize its needed physical facts, human instinct its needed physical and metaphysical facts,—if they exist.

Conversely, whatever beliefs, or metaphysical findings, men have lived by are to some extent corroborated (certainly not by 'general consent,' but) by the circumstance that they have formed part of the vital circuit of human instinct, have been the feeders and shapers of instinct. The more durable of these beliefs are not wholly illusory: "*l'action ne saurait se mouvoir dans l'irréel.*"

But in the composition of these working beliefs, fiction and mere hopefulness may mingle with positive metaphysical finding in unknown proportion. The mystic in man, the original seer of ultimate things, learns but slowly to discriminate between his perceptions and his dreams. The critic in man, the judgment based on experience and self-conscious reason, rises but slowly to the task of releasing what is significant and true in dogma from what is irrelevant and false,—condemning sometimes too little, quite as frequently too much.

The individual, then, who realizes that his metaphysical questions are questions of life and death for instinct and will, can give no exclusive credence either to the mystic in himself or to the critic; he will require them to act in co-operation. He will be satisfied neither with pragmatic beliefs, chosen for their promise of satisfaction (ghosts of human desires offered as substantial food to these same desires), nor with true general ideas (entities which taken alone make no difference and do no work).

He will realize that his instinctive appetite for knowledge is an honorable appetite. It is in the existing world that instinct must grow and work out its meaning; and the existing world is distinguishable both from pragmatic dreams and from true general ideas: it is a union of general ideas with matter of fact in a living fabric of historical movement and change. It is to this living mesh that mystic and critic must direct their vision. Whatever is real and significant for instinct must in some way exist in the active surface of history,—some of it no doubt *built into history* at various points of the working edge of time in such wise that we could not now unbuild it if we would.

As an inseparable part of the question, What sort of world is it that we live in? he will thus be driven to enquire, What sort of world *have we been living in?* What have been the metaphysical foundations, real or supposed real, for those qualities, those instinct-shapes, which characterize our present human type?

The qualities which have made and are making our contemporary civilization are not qualities of intellect more than qualities of character: they are such qualities as integrity, reliability, legality, practical force, love of liberty. At the root of them is a capacity for facing and absorbing the increasing pain which is incident to increasing contact with objective reality. To surrender ourselves without flinching to the findings of natural science is something we have had to learn by painfully slow degrees; to accept the unflattering position of man in the Copernican world and in the evolutionary scheme; to regard and burrow deeper into the human mind as an object in nature; to submit to the hardship involved in making a social order on the principle of a thoroughly objective impersonal justice,—all this has required the 'virtue' of Rome together with a sympathy and sensitiveness to what is not-ourselves that has not come from Rome. Our civilization is one which has once for all put away vested interest in illusions, and has dared to stand naked before the last facts so far as it could find them. In this there is much of the plain 'grit' such as Joseph Conrad loves to celebrate: but grit is not necessarily attentive to the weak, the incipient, the minute, the growing,—and it is here that our peculiar strength and promise lies. It is a union of strength and tenderness which has brought us to the best we have so far found.

The strength that we have is not the strength of physical instinct; nor has it ever been for mankind 'pure' grit. In former times, with the zest of original pugnacity and the conviction of mounting passion, men could throw themselves without reserve into the issues of battle; and battle became for them a quasi-religious orgy in which the spirit of the fathers and of the tribe drew near almost to touching and filled the frame with unwonted power. Grit and enthusiasm went together. And now without the aid of primitive feeling or hope of individual glory men of more sensitive mould go simply to a mill of war whose portent of possible suffering is incomparably more intense. What do these men stand on? Not on any consciousness of the heroic, but on the plain sense of what is necessary; and they profess thereby a faith of some kind that facing what is necessary is better than muffling the head in a lying dream. Effectively and actually men care more for reality than ever before, and behind that confidence lies some kind of creed, or let me say, some kind of contact with the spirit of the world.

Neither is the tenderness we have the tenderness of physical instinct. We tend, we teach, we legislate, we try our hand at justice and reform. We do this not from any pure outflow of kindness: we do it with a certain joy of power which is at the same time fully awake to the defect of our performance. The parent who deals with his son and the publicist whose thought becomes the rule for millions are well aware in these days of the human equation in their judgments. We are democratic: no authorities among us dare set up as absolute. They live, we all live, at the requirement of the movement of things over a gap unbridged by our own competence. Earlier men acted thus instinctively, with the confident affection and protectiveness of the animal parent or leader. But if we act thus it is because, while self-doubts emerge and continue to emerge, they have seemed to receive from the world we live in assurances that satisfy, as if at least the kindlier enterprises of living were, or might be, a partnership with power more intimately attuned than our own to the inner facts of history, capable of reaching its goal in the midst of our inadequacies.

If the spirit of the world is actually such as to justify to the growingly self-conscious being this kind of confidence and sensitiveness, we should doubtless, as with all pervasive utilities, better recognize the ingredient which does this work if it were experimentally withdrawn.

And as it happens, such aid to vision is not wholly lacking at this moment. A calamity having the force of a ghastly experiment occurs, vivisection of this vaunted Western life, with all its sources, material and otherwise, putting a harsh end to all mere momentums of belief, to all complacencies, sanctimonies, and infallible prescriptions, to all sleepy tugging at dry paps. *How much can you do without and still live?*—this searching experimental question war presses home to soul and body, abolishing stroke by stroke gross quantities of wealth, gross quantities also of life, beauty, happiness, personal and public. But with all these abolitions spreads another,—the swift and easy abolition of that supposed 'sanctity of human life' together with other sanctities formerly potent: this, too, we are called upon to do without if we can, or perhaps rather to see it for what it was,—a glamour of some sort, a conspiracy to hold high the level of self-esteem, mutual palaver of polite society, valid enough so long as no serious business is on, no occasion for telling one another cold truth.

Cold truth being now in order, we measure humanity in the mass as so much force, resistance, morale; feed it into the hopper by regiments, brigades. A comrade, a friend, changes in an instant into débris, so much wreckage to be cleared away. Once more we see man in terms of his yield: *er ist was er ist;* and that will of his, that morale and mentality, is a bit of equipment, an *appareil,* working best when nearest the ground, fit for short flights, better avoiding long ones and certainly all infinite flights. 'Infinite value'? Infinite conceit!

When this sentiment about human value is thus unsentimentally challenged, we perceive that it has had much to do with sustaining those qualities of confidence and tenderness which we thought distinctive of our civilization. It is not itself a metaphysical belief, but a by-product of such a belief, doubtless the belief of which we are in search, and whose character we may now dimly make out.

There is an instinct in us as yet unnamed by psychology, perhaps the deepest instinct of all: it is the *total infantile response to the maternal impulse.* This instinct knows what kind of metaphysic it needs, namely, a world maternal not in part only, but altogether. What has happened, then, is obvious, is it not? That benevolent god with a trillion equally dear children, that picture of world-familydom, or of world-shepherdhood, that impossible Absolute engaged in countless simultaneous 'seeking and saving' enterprises,—all of this is but the poetry of childhood, valid there in fact, and holding over into the more sheltered corners of mature hopefulness, lingering to comfort minds that insist on being comforted, minds incapable of genuine maturity,—or perhaps even to protect certain subjectivities and prides, personal, racial, genealogical, remnants of stale human provinciality liking to believe itself the chosen strain. This persistent metaphysics of the motherhood of history or grandmotherliness of history,—is it not the most palpable of pragmatic fictions, or instinct-beliefs? And if so, it can no longer serve us, *having been found out.*

But what becomes, then, of these contemporary qualities of justified strength and tenderness? They do not disappear; they are merely replaced by more elemental editions of themselves, suited rather to a world aloof, preoccupied, or indifferent than to a parental world.

If 'justified confidence' is unavailable, there is always a well of instinctive confidence to fall back upon, the simplest, least-borrowed thing in human nature, least needing to be justified,—the now admittedly *pure* grit of man at bay in a world neither his own nor anyone's; confidence original, titanic, defiant; confidence *ueberhaupt*. There is an attitude needing no metaphysics, an attitude, well so-called, which few are incapable of striking if necessary. We can always act *as if* men, or some men, were worth while, and had rights, ourselves included. For the human life authentically valued by an absolute valuer, substitute the instinctive self-valuation of the human animal, particularly the masculine animal; and for the deference due to beings objectively worthy of reverence, substitute the warmth of a maternal sympathy spreading from the center outward as the vital economy permits. Give these well-founded sentiments an artificial extension by the device called the State; so that a degree of parenthood enters into an entire community in its relations to its own members,—competing and warring from time to time with similar sentiments of parenthood on the part of other communities; and as there is no real parent, parenthood may be said to exist just so far as it can forcibly make itself valid in the world.

This is the alternative into which we may seem driven by the disillusionments, the down-crashing of all current sentiments, in this day of reckoning. And in that case history, having reached its summit, turns downward.

Let it be clearly understood that this reversal of direction is involved in the proposed change. For animal confidence can no longer sustain a fully human effort as we have come to understand it, not even a human war.

The flame of war can leap into life among common people only because of the presence there of a metaphysical outlook that seems to make a number of things, including human life, objectively valuable and 'sacred.' If the aims of war, or the activities of war, contradict this belief; or if self-consciousness in the midst of the carriage is driven to press its questions, Do I matter? Does any deed or thought of mine matter? Does any other deed or thought or interest or life matter? Does the 'cause' itself finally matter, or the nation and all its wars, holy or unholy?—the spirit inevitably seeps out of the fighting. It is possible for fighting to undermine one's sense of the only things worth fighting for.

And what is true of war is true to an even greater degree of the long upbuilding effort of the creative arts. If 'progress' must bring disillusionment and the harsh daylight of a denying realism, progress is destined to devour its own children.

Values, human values, can survive only if, reaching out toward a metaphysical condition which their dream-shapes foreshadow, they *find it*. They need reality to climb on; they need a reality they *can* climb on. They want an independent source of standards, a mooring outside of nature, such as we surmised at the beginning of our study. Their own *poussée vitale* droops, half-grown, unless it meets an equivalent *attrait vital* streaming into its environment from some pole outside itself.

And thus this experiment, this world-surgery, begins to make so much unmistakable: That what human nature has been responding to is not its own instinctive self-esteem, codified in institutions, or uncodified, but a valuation believed real and objective, supposedly hailing from beyond nature, authoritatively requiring of man that self-honor and that honor of his kind which his own impulse achieves but fitfully and from the center outward.

And this valuation, be it noted, has appeared to him not as a proclaimed theorem regarding human value in the abstract, but as actual *valuedness*, i.e., valuation acted upon in multitudes of deeds, struggles for human rights and guarantees thereof, sacrifices and martyrdoms without number; in all of which an authentic divine will and activity were supposed discernible by those having eyes to see. To many of these human doers their own deeds appeared to be utterances not alone of their private wills but also of the ultimate will of the world. In brief, we of this age have been living on an aggressive valuation, built into history, and supposed whether wisely or not to transmit an absolute judgment.

And not strangely, mankind seems to have counted most on the costliest of such deeds, the most deliberately defiant of the natural appearance. As at this moment, so it has always been: it is the negation by the brute forces of the world, the negation and contempt of what humanity has held most precious, which has split opinion into its concealed extremes.

For it is just such negation which creates the opportunity for deeds most audaciously experimental, deeds of self-immolation of which the onlooker must say that they embody either the wisdom of the gods, or else infra-human unwisdom.

It is upon the great *experimental sacrifices* of history that men have climbed to their positive metaphysical insights; or to what they have taken to be such, be it only their passionate assertions that such sacrifices, such blottings out of man's evident best, cannot have been folly, and shall not have been vain.

It is not for us, here, to assert or deny, either passionately or otherwise; but as students of human nature and its destiny to state deliberately the connections of cause and consequence, and face our alternatives. Our metaphysical finding, our last fact, may be such as to release and encourage the growth of instinctive meaning, warming out its inner logic and wider linkages; it may be (as with Schopenhauer) such as to wither and repel it; it may be no finding at all, but an enigmatic silence of a noncommittal world which denies only by refusing to affirm. In no case is it indifferent.

Absence of belief that the world as a whole has an active individual concern for the creatures it has produced need neither destroy happiness nor the morality of compassion. Life would always be worth living and worth living well, so long as free from the major torments. Instinct has its satisfactions in an uninterpreted or partly interpreted condition: it will reach some accommodation to the world that is. Nothing would necessarily be destroyed or lost from the good life which some at least of the human race now know and many hope for,—nothing except the higher reaches of curiosity and sympathy, and the wisdom of developing them. It is only the enthusiasts for a far-off good, for an endlessly progressive humanity, for a profound and logical love of life, that would be cut off; it is only the martyrs that have played the fool; only to saints and sages the world has lied.

CHAPTER 17

Confessio Fidei

[...] Working out a philosophy [...] is an inevitable activity for a rational being: if it is, in addition, a 'duty' and also a 'source of happiness,' that interesting conjunction indicates something about the nature of the universe in which this philosophizing takes place.

In a dead or meaningless universe there could be no such thing as a *duty* to reflect about the whole of things. On the contrary, it might be a human duty to forget about it and attend to the day's business. There could be no utility in contemplating what no human technique can control and no human purpose survive. There is only one absolute source of duty; that is, the way to one's destiny, which means, in practice, the way to one's next stage of growth. (Thus one says of a particularly good play or opera or book, "You ought not to miss that"). Only one thing could make philosophizing a duty; and that is that the universe has an intrinsic meaning which one ought not to miss, but perceive and enjoy. In fact, unless the universe has meaning, philosophizing becomes a meaningless occupation; for we might define philosophy as the effort to interpret experience as a whole, that is, to find the meaning of things. If things have no meaning, philosophy is ideally futile.

It follows that every philosophy of whatever type is bound to assume that the universe has a meaning (or a system of meanings); a meaning which is objective, in the sense that it is there whether or not you or I discover it, but which can be discerned by us.[1] And since meanings are something more than the bare facts of the natural order, all philosophy is, in its assumptions, contradictory to naturalism, taking naturalism strictly as the negative doctrine that Nature is all there is.

And since meanings are abstractions unless they are somehow known or felt or appreciated, the existence of objective meaning in the world implies some kind of mental life at the core of reality. To this extent, I believe that idealism is not so much a separate type of philosophy as the essence of all philosophy, an assumption whether recognized or unrecognized of the philosophic enterprise itself. I take idealism, then, so far as this argument carries us, as the centre of my metaphysics. And I take this as a point of certainty, established by the dialectical method of which we were speaking. One who should say "The world has no objective meaning" would, as I see it, contradict himself.

From TP (1929), 436–450.

This amount of idealism one may regard as a sort of philosophic minimum. The mystic, I believe, is much more adequate in his judgment that the world is an almost untouched reservoir of significance and value, whose quality we sense in passing perceptions of beauty in nature; or in love, which always comes as a surprise strangely reflecting on our previous inability to see, so that we say of ourselves,

> Atheists are as dull
> Who cannot guess God's presence out of sight;

or still more continuously in that vague but inescapable sense of impending possible good for which we continue to hope while we live. What is living? Striving? Yes: incessant striving, but not 'dumb striving.' Living is reaching out to the reality of things as a region in which the discovery of value need never end. In philosophy, this conviction counts as the mystic's; but in this respect, I believe, again, that every man is an avowed or unavowed mystic,—even the Schopenhauers.

But why not be content with the judgment that the world has a meaning (and that the old teleological argument was essentially right after all)? Why believe in such a plenum of meaning? Surely this is an *a priori* prejudice. It is not 'optimism' in the sense that good has to happen to everybody in the long run: the good has to be found, and we all run a chance of missing it. More than that, every one does, as a matter of fact, miss much of it, perhaps most of it. That is the essential and pervasive element of tragedy in the world. But I believe that the meaning is there: and how does that agree with our intellectual duty to take things as we empirically find them, the meaningful and the meaningless mixed together in experience?

There is, to be sure, something matter-of-fact in all discoveries of good. We could never deduce music, for example, from any previous knowledge about sound; and certainly not from any general theorem to the effect that objective values exist. We have to be as empirical as you please about the flavors of olives, a boat race, the Syrian desert. Values 'emerge.' Does not this pure unanticipable discovery of quality carry with it an equal requirement to be empirical toward the meaningless? There is much in the world we can only accept: it is blank datum,—there it is! The realistic temper in us demands that we rub our noses against such facts, and acknowledge them.

Willingly; but for how long? Philosophies which run into a wall of blank datum and end there are either tentative or lazy. They dare never say, These things have no meaning, but only, We have not found any, and regard it as not worth while to try. Such terminal empiricism toward the meaningless is but a personal confession: it implies nothing about the world, but only that the speaker should make way for the poet or the artist, who can see. Empiricism can set up no negatives: and we know this of the world, that values *keep emerging* as we enlarge our capacity and learn the adjustment of our instruments of vision.

I should go farther with idealism, and say that the world is a self. And I should immediately add, in explanation, that the self, so far from being a wholly evident and graspable being, as Descartes and Berkeley seemed to assume, is infinite in its depth and mystery. It is only with this understanding that it can be used as a concept for the whole of things: the infinite is measured by the infinite and the unknown by the unknown. Here again mysticism is nearer the truth than much current idealism.[2] This word self indicates chiefly that the mental life within the world has its unity, and that all the meanings of things cohere in a single will.

May not all the selfhood in the world be a manifestation of something more profound or higher? No. For there is nothing higher than selfhood, and nothing more profound. Spinoza's Substance, with an infinitude of other attributes, unless it were conscious and self-conscious, would be lower in being than the simplest of mankind. Within the Selfhood of substance there is room for all the unfathomed majesty of reality.

The human self, which we take as an imperfect image of the whole cosmos, is a thing of nature and also something more than that.

This human self must be made an object of scientific study, in its relations to its environment, as the naturalistic program requires. There are laws of learning, of habit, and the like which (since they are not used to 'manage' us), we have no reason to disown or to break across. Psychology, as a natural science, may explain a great deal about ourselves; provided we understand by 'explaining' not deriving one thing from another, but simply showing a law of variation. Thus vibration does not explain color in the sense that color is derived from vibration; but differences in vibration-rate may explain variation in color. The physical fact does not produce the mental fact; but changes in the one correspond with changes in the other.

The human self is more than a thing of nature, because it is more than a fact: facts are not conscious of facts,—the self is; facts are not values,—the self lives on values and is a value; facts are particulars, not universals,—the self is both; facts are present,—the self spans past and future. And because of these things, while facts are as they must be, the self is free: it determines, out of a matrix of plural possibilities, which one shall be the fact of the next moment.

The self is thus a union of opposites. And because precisely the same opposites are discernible in the composition of the larger cosmos and must somehow be united there, we may transfer the problem of this 'somehow' in part to the world within, as we do when we recognize that the whole is a self. The ultimate evidence for the selfhood of the whole is not primarily the evidence of argument, however, nor of analogy, but that of immediate experience, interpreted by the dialectic. We, as a group of human selves, know that we are not alone in the universe: that is our first and persistent intuition.

This proposition, that the world is a self, I regard as a point of certainty in philosophy. And therewith I confess another belief,—the belief that *philosophy aims at certainty*, and can be content with nothing less. If one wishes to be emphatic, one may say absolute certainty,—there is no logical difference between certainty and absolute certainty. Some such certainty is necessary to give structure to our system of knowledge, as well as to the experimental business of daily life. The life of knowledge as well as the life of action swings, I believe, in irregular rhythm or alternation, between this pole of certainty and the region of exploration, tentativeness, probability, hypothesis.

"Absolutism" I know, is a word of reproach for the present age of thought. Rigid codes of truth and law and morals are recognized as deadly: it has been the genius of our age to get away from their shackles. The scientific spirit is open to the perennial revision of ideas: we must be ready to accept a new hypothesis to-morrow. Yes: but by *how much* is your hypothesis new? By all that you have believed to-day? Then you are no longer the same self from day to day, and your mental world has become an insane place not worth living in.

There is a certain illusion in our estimate of the degree of change that is going on: it is the fascinating aspect of experience, also the aspect which requires our *qui vive* and so holds attention. But the history of all social revolutions reminds us that there is a law of continuity in history: there is a similar law in the revolutions of thought. There is more than continuity: there is a *principle of changelessness* in the basis of things, on which certainty can take hold and remain certain. That is the objective counterpart of the changelessness of the self which apprehends and enjoys change.

It is true that we must be ready to revise our hypotheses: that is why we call them hypotheses. We must likewise be ready to revise the laws of our life. But what if in doing so we dismantle also the spirit of lawfulness and the 'rule of law'? Then the change of laws becomes nonsense. We rely—when we talk about changing laws—on the stability of the 'that' while we experiment with the 'what.' When a contemporary prophet, urging "the transitional character of our times" (all times are transitional), admonishes us that "as nothing is permanent either in institutions or in thought, we must stand ready to revise all the old rules of religion and sex, art and letters, politics and law," we hear what is in a sense a truism rather excitedly proclaimed; but what, if presented as the whole truth, is an exemplary untruism. It can never be a question for religion, sex, art, letters whether all things change. It can only be a question what things are changeable, what are relative to time and place, and what things are stable. It is the first business of philosophy to make evident what is stable, in order that change may go on with freedom of conscience and success. Instrumentalism, in the interest of its polemic, neglects the one thing needful.

The true experimental spirit is that of the mystic, who regards every fixed habit as tentative, and every conceptual standard as provisional, not because there is nothing absolute, but *because there is*: and because—since there is this absolute standard—every conceptualized mental property must recurrently be brought to court to bear comparison with it. By renewing from time to time his perception of that absolute real and good he prepares himself for those fresh contacts with reality in social and natural experience, which are destined to revise no one knows how much of the crusty shell of our assumed axioms and prejudices.

The scientific method itself (which every contemporary philosophy hastens to claim as its own peculiar ally, realism, naturalism; pragmatism in particular) is no partisan of unlimited relativity and change. For the scientific method would be nothing without the logic and mathematics it persistently uses. Probability itself must be reckoned by a calculus which is beyond the reach of probability. The realists have done well in asserting for this aspect of truth a certain independent finality. The pragmatic declaration that the experimental method is the only method, and that therefore all truth must be held tentatively, is a prime example—in so far as it regards this thesis itself as permanently true—of a self-refuting position.

Thus realism also agrees that there is certainty in philosophy: but certainty of an abstract sort; whereas the intuitionist adds to this abstraction the effect of experience, making it a concrete certainty. This concrete certainty however must be rationally—in this case, dialectically—established. It is this which makes the distinction between philosophy and art. Rationality is the genius of philosophy: and in this sense *all philosophy is rationalism.*

As on the side of epistemology, so on the side of practical philosophy, I believe in a mystical realism, which is the only tenable sort of realism.

We must treat things in the day's work as if they were independent, naturalistic, over against us and *against* us, or at least, not for us. Struggle to build a human habitation in the midst of an alien universe; unremitting effort to expel by the aid of science whatever is evil from our point of view; expecting no good from the universe except what we human beings construct in the face of nature and except the universe itself; and admitting no wrong as inherent in the constitution of things: —this is the programme in which we join the realist.

But who has the eye for this humanistic work, and the endless patience and energy for it, in view of the fact that the task defined is nothing short of infinite? Who can wait until the end of evolution for an achievement which only remote posterity can ever see? Only one who in some way already is at the goal, as the mystic is (who for us represents the religious spirit). For him, reality in its fulness is always accessible where he is: he is always in the middle of time and space and history; he is never neurotically anxious to catch the *dernier cri*, nor hurried on to a remote goal. He alone can labor with endless resources and patience for what may yet be; for he knows that the nature of things is with him. He knows that there can be no incommensurable relation between the task and the power to deal with it. He knows that what is in him is the same substance that has set the object and established its over-againstness. He is assured, with Confucius, that the "good man is a ternion with Heaven and Earth."

It was one of the strengths of naturalism that it had an explanation for the propensity of the race to religion. The mystical-realism which we are here presenting has its corresponding explanation of the propensity of the race to naturalism, as the mode of thought fitted to the outswing of the alternation of life.

But this is naturalism on its positive side, not on the side of its negations. It is, let us say, a transfigured naturalism, which enlarges physical nature by making it a province within a greater nature.

Of this enlarged conception of nature we may say what we say about the self: it is not in reality a scheme of mathematical phenomena shifting lawfully through endless space and time. It is infinite with an inner life of its own. The reality of Nature is the sum of all the meaning that can be found in it. Taking Nature as Schelling took it, or Bruno, or Royce; not reading its inner being from the atoms upward but from consciousness in all directions:—taking nature in this way, it and its laws become the expression of an ultimate purpose and significance. And nature in turn, with its vast impersonality, removes that taint of arbitrariness which is likely to cling to our usual conceptions of 'mind' and of God.

Thus, in Dante's Inferno, the literal element of the allegory presents the punishments of the damned as having been inflicted by the will of God. In the deeper sense of the poem there is nothing arbitrary or conventional in the fortunes of these spirits; but the poet is working out, in pictorial symbols, the inherent logic of various forms of vice, wrong, or simple absence of positive good. He is considering the lots of these souls as a working of a natural law; only, a type of law which like the Hindu law of Karma, applies to ethical distinctions, and so works out perfect and invariable justice. Such a conception is akin to naturalism; but a naturalism so transformed that the inner mechanism of nature is not a lifeless, but a moral lawfulness; and the destiny of the self is not limited by the exigencies of any single; time-space order.

Some such naturalism as this, so far from being inconsistent with an idealistic metaphysics, is an essential part of the world-picture. It is only the mystic-idealist who is justified in exploring all the 'hard facts' and facing all the risks of a naturalistic system of experience, neither defying them nor running away.

Humanism some one said, is a sort of "class consciousness,"—we men banded together in solidarity against the universe outside. Yet to fix our mind upon the human interest is to lose the best things that have come to mankind. These have arrived by way of a love of art or of science, as we say, for its own sake; with humanity relatively out of the focus. How can you do good to individual men, each of whom contemplates eternity, unless you yourself contemplate eternity? Consider a man as a group of instincts hailing from animal ancestry, best understood by looking backward, and you can do him a limited amount of good, and that at the cost of his humiliation. Consider him as a group of impulses tending forward to a will to be immortal, and you find material interests taken care of as incidents. Humanism can be fulfilled only in a world that sustains the zest of doing one's human job as a religious observance. This can continue only if the world is worth that kind of devotion. Humanism depends on a transfigured naturalism which is idealism.

This view does justice also to the pragmatic outlook. For the unfinished part of the world, in which the will to believe has its rightful play, is vaster than idealism usually represents. Human life as we find it *is* not free, sacred, immortal. It must be made free; its sacredness must be conferred upon it; its immortality must be won. In these respects we are the creators of our own destinies: even beyond the humanistic limit, the world of our destiny shall be what we believe and make it.

NOTES

1. For a further development of this idea see the article "What Does Philosophy Say?", *Philosophical Review*, March 1928 (xxxvii, No. 2) [see chapter 1—eds.].
2. When I speak of what the mystic knows of the self, I am distinctly not referring to an element of semi-occultism which runs through contemporary psychology under the head of the 'subconscious.'

    The subconscious is a veritable fact, and a vastly important fact in mental life. That is no reason for making it the home of a host of mythical hobgoblins, complexes, and ghosts; or speaking of it as the 'unconscious' and imagining one understands an unconscious mental state, as something half-way between mind and body, when one uses the word 'force' or 'impulse' and thinks of swimming with ones' eyes shut!

    Under the veiled and mechanized form which the 'subconscious' has assumed in contemporary psychology, following the lead of Schopenhauer and von Hartmann, it has been the means of concealing from view all the fertile (though weirdly expressed) inquiry into the self as ethical agent, as judge and creator of art, as logician and philosopher, which the early idealists were chiefly concerned with. These activities represent far more nearly what the self is than do either laboratory reactions or mysterious subliminal cravings. The nearly complete loss of all this earlier work to psychology is the penalty which science pays when one form of obscurantism finds itself unable to speak or interpret the language of another.

Hocking as Seen Today

CHAPTER 18

Hocking's "Transfigured Naturalism"

John Howie

A great deal may be said concerning the career and interest of Ernest Hocking. His foremost human relationship was a lifelong love affair and enduring friendship with Agnes O'Reilly, his wife for more than half a century. This interest had its beginning in a Sunday morning class on friendship started by Richard Cabot. It did not end there, as Agnes continued to add new dimensions to it. It was she who required him to write the first chapter of his magnum opus *The Meaning of God in Human Experience* thirteen times. But she influenced and helped to focus his career in many other ways as well. She was involved in every academic career choice that he made including teaching at the University of California (1906–1908), Yale (1908–1914), and Harvard (1914–1943). In addition Agnes served on the Layman's Commission, which wrote *Re-thinking Missions* together with Ernest Hocking, and was responsible for one of its reports. And, as we shall have occasion to note later, she provided the example of his "direct evidence" for the basic notion that being is always *being with*. The "comrade" referred to in the quotation is Agnes. She died in 1955 after a long illness that confined her to her room in the big stone house to which they retired near Madison, New Hampshire.

Ernest Hocking has been called "the people's philosopher" and "the last of the Golden Age of American Philosophy." Both labels put him in the company of William James, John Dewey, and Alfred North Whitehead. This is a group to which his achievements certainly commend him. He published eighteen original books, 270 essays, and delivered the esteemed Hibbert and Gifford Lectures. Hocking, we may say, has earned himself a place among the best American philosophers.

His stature has been recognized by the eminent French philosopher, Gabriel Marcel. Marcel said that Hocking "was a man who, through the visible world, has never ceased to have the presentment of what is eternal" (1963, 2). Despite his massive scholarly achievements Hocking was a man of genuine humility and singular moral focus. To him scholarly endeavors were of secondary importance. "The one achievement worth noting," he said, "is the creation of a certain individual beauty in living and in the environment of living ... one's Task" (Hocking in Ethridge and Kopala 1965, 211). Hocking once remarked to his friend Lee Rouner: "I could sum up my life in [a few] words—I have enjoyed living. I have found it a wonderful and holy thing!" He had a lot of it to relish because he lived into his ninety-third year.

And during most of that time he was one of the foremost active and productive philosophers in America.

Turning to Hocking's philosophical perspective, one encounters difficulties in understanding his viewpoint. Three of these may be noted in passing. First, his writing style often provokes reflection rather than providing precise cognitive meaning. This is not by accident, we need to underscore, but rather by intent or design. Typically, his style is meditative, dialectical, often metaphorical, or aphoristic and poetical. This gives his statements a genuine warmth and appeal that is lacking in the salty, almost bitter, fare of today's analytic professionals. To give you a sample of what I mean, here are a half dozen aphorisms plucked at random from his writings.

> Living is a continuous marriage of idea with fact, and like every bridal, on one hand it fulfills one's destiny and on the other limits one's infinitude. (MIHE, 17)

> Truth is a form of love. For love involves a will to overcome the ostensible world; it harbors a will to make immortal what we see as mortal. It carries a will to project purpose, our own finite purposes, beyond the visible curtain of death, and to recognize behind the literal facts of our world a continuing care. (1959, 163)

> In bringing forth man [humankind], the universe has brought forth a mind which is free and creative. Its freedom implies its power to determine the future from conceived alternatives; also its power to err, to reject duty, and to injure. Its creativity implies its capacity to add to creation and to cooperate with the original purpose in the finishing of the world. (PTP, 504)

> It is worth observing that a mind can *mean* far more than it can image or think. It can mean, for example, to act with another mind, and so to endorse what the other mind may think or will, however little it may be able to fathom the devices of that other mind. (MATS, 370)

> Death is not *ipso facto* the extinction either of the space-and-world creating powers which that self, in its receptive apprenticeship, has developed, nor of that principle of growth which determines it to a pursuit of concrete value in common with other selves. (SBF, 177)

Second, in addition to this bent toward aphorisms, Hocking, unlike some other philosophers, does not typically seek to "prove" or demonstrate his ideas. Nor is his approach "systematic" in the usual sense of that term. Rather, his effort is intended to prompt or induce the reader or listener to search his own experience and to examine his most cherished beliefs. It is an invitation to self-reflection and to self-examination, not far afield from the time-honored procedure of Socrates. It is by taking this path that truth is often disclosed or uncovered.

Third, Hocking invites his readers to subject their experience to the method of "empirical dialectic" (see R. Hocking [son of WEH], 1978). It seeks to combine the methods of empiricism, rationalism, and pragmatism. For this, Hocking's "widened empiricism," continuities and discontinuities of experience as well as the very constituents of reality are to be taken into account. By "dialectic" Hocking means the testing of an hypothesis by thoughtful experimentation. This procedure includes within itself an appeal to "negative pragmatism" (MGHE, 23). It enables us to understand the inadequacy or falsity of certain propositions or assumptions. Yet, Hocking is confident that from every false thesis there is a "thrust" or "nisus" toward a more adequate viewpoint. What superficially yields only negative results actually provides us with a positive directive. The "empirical dialectic" is a method or process for understanding the world rather than merely describing it. To this extent it goes beyond a rigorous scientific naturalism. It would add spiritual insights to those of a strict naturalism.

Hocking uses the metaphor of "transfigured naturalism" (TP, 319) to characterize the broader perspective that is an indispensable part of what he calls "perennial philosophy." A transfigured naturalism is more inclusive. It is sensitive to the spiritual as well as to material concerns. It does not allow that the dictates of science be taken as literal metaphysical accounts. It enlarges our own view of human consciousness and enables us to envision physical nature as a mere province within a vaster, more inclusive universe. Of this transfigured nature we may say (as we may say of the human self) that it is boundless with an inner life. It is pregnant with a meaning of its own, a meaning that extends in all directions from consciousness in a manner similar to the way Schelling and Royce took nature. As a transfigured naturalism it acquires purpose and significance. Nature can no longer be fully understood from the atoms upward but only from consciousness or selfhood outwardly. Ordinary science begins and moves in piecemeal fashion. If it goes no further, it misses its transfiguration. The wide-angled picture proposed by Hocking gives religious zest to life and captures the human striving to be immortal. There is a hint that experience of this nature is somehow necessary to the development of mind.

Nature, with all of its beauty and splendor, had a special place in Hocking's life and thought. He had a special fondness for the grand "out-of-doors." In retirement Hocking lived in a stone house that he had largely constructed with his own hands. It was built in relative isolation from his nearest neighbor but in full view of the magnificent Presidential range of mountains near Madison, New Hampshire. But, it is of a "transfigured" naturalism that he speaks approvingly. It is neither a sentimental nor a romantic view of nature.

Our plan to explore Hocking's "transfigured naturalism" requires us to make an initial distinction between two kinds of naturalism. First, we need to note what is generally called a "methodological naturalism." This naturalism is the name for the scientific method that tends to construct its pattern of thought on the basis of natural causation. For this use of scientific method Hocking has high praise in many of his writings.

His criticisms are reserved for a second type of naturalism, namely, metaphysical naturalism. It is variously characterized but it includes the view that reality is nature and that the ultimate is within the framework of nature. It is in distinction from and in opposition to this view that Hocking calls his own view a "transfigured naturalism." It is our purpose to explore what Hocking means by this metaphor.

First, we explore what Hocking means by his criticisms of metaphysical naturalism. Then, after looking at what such criticisms mean, we provide a sampler of some sorts of experiences that a "transfigured" naturalism would invite us to consider, especially those that give a social dimension and require a cooperative effort from the human and divine.

Metaphysical naturalism refers to the sum of material things, in a single space and time, the system of causes and effects, their regularity and productivity. The metaphysical naturalist claims that this measurable and controllable context *is* the whole of reality. But, Hocking responds, naturalism is mistaken in its claim that nature is self-sufficient as a complete system of causes.

Such nature *appears to be* independent in three regards. That this is only appearance and not reality can readily be grasped. First, take the simple, given quality of sense data (colors, sounds, smells, and tastes). This is supposedly the original stuff of experience; it is a refractory configuration. On our part it requires reception by our knowing processes and acceptance by our feeling and willing processes. But, of course, it would be incorrect to claim that nature "caused" these sensations. For one may ask: How can that which is the very fabric of nature be caused by nature? And we are lead to the conjecture that these sense qualities are caused by something other than nature.

Second, nature *appears* to be independent because of its relentless order and apparent indifference to human strivings and efforts. Nature cannot, however, start a sequence because it is a single causal network that is only capable of conserving, repeating, and continuing. In other words, there are some situations that a merely causal series cannot explain. These include the *initiation* of a sequence and the *creation of something both new and different*. (And creation, after all, has to do with the new and different.)

Third, another mark of nature's apparent independence (or otherness) is its public character. Events may be observed by others as well as by the individual. Nature or at least parts of it are (as we say) a "common object" for many selves. This public character of nature makes possible joint endeavors with other human selves and provides a shared context for all activities.

These three alleged marks of nature's independence all in actuality attest to the dependence of nature and its function as a context for the creative activities of human selves. What Hocking wishes to avoid is a damaging solipsism. Solipsism is only half true. The self does receive, not make, the perceived world, but this is surely only half the story. Just as an inventor claims ownership of the idea that organizes and bestows meaning, even so the self is the originator of what is new and different.

A chief inadequacy of metaphysical naturalism is its attempt to reduce mind or human selfhood to brain. Brain and mind, Hocking insists, can be contrasted in five different ways.

First, the human mind can reflect upon itself, while the brain cannot. This reflection makes possible self-correction and self-development. It is indispensable for the growth of moral character and for morally principled existence. Also, it is a necessary precondition for all progress in society. Human reflective judgment enables us to be both critical and constructive—to devise new ways to assess and remedy social problems.

Second, the mind is not confined to a single space-time context, while the brain is so confined. It is this important trait that leads Hocking to the metaphor of "Field of Fields" to refer to the self. The ability of the human self or mind to make the transition from the mental field to the physical field is pivotal. The making of this transition in part constitutes its creativity.

Third, the mind can extend its temporal range to past and future, while the brain is confined simply to the present. Past, present, and to some extent the future are all within the range of mind.

Fourth, the human mind holds representational capacities, while these capacities are totally lacking, and unwittingly so, in the brain. For the mind, one thing can stand for another or represent another, and entire schemes of representation can be formulated.

Fifth, the mind gives meaning to everything, apprehending qualities and experiencing pleasures and pains. The brain, however, cannot apprehend qualities, and, for it, qualities are devoid of meaning. For the brain, qualities simply are what they are with no representational or leading capacity. The brain per se is simply incapable of suffering or enjoyment. For the human mind all experience is enriching, while none is simply neutral.

Hocking shows the inadequacy of a naturalistic view by offering a more complete perspective on the relationship of causality and purpose. Employing the method of "empirical dialectic," he shows first that causality and purpose are compatible, and then specifically in what way causality is purposive. His perspective seems to express a new teleology.

To begin with, neither causality nor purpose is observed as it occurs. What we actually do observe is a sequence of events. We see or notice the sequence: the sunflower does turn toward the sun. The sequence is observed, not the actual cause. Similarly, a train is in the station. A man runs toward it and boards it. We seem to see the man running to catch the train. But, in fact, we have only observed a sequence of events, and we infer or conjecture that the rays of the sun cause the flower to turn or that the man was running for the purpose of catching the train. Both causes or purposes, then, are imputed or conjecturally attached to an action sequence or to an event. And it is at least logically possible that an event could have both a cause and a purpose.

Consider two matters concerning the relationship of causes to purposes. First, let us acknowledge the resemblance between causal and purposive sequences. Compare a man hammering a stake in the ground with a steam pile-driver. You cannot observe the purpose or the cause passing into its effect as the weight hits the pile. We have said that this is imputed in either case. Now, it is important to underscore that we cannot prove that either cause or purpose is actually present. Both processes employ causes and effects and the sequence for both of them takes time. For the purposive process the blows of the hammer, in addition to being causes, are "means-to-an-end." And the difference appears at the end. The man knows when to stop; the pile driver does not. Purposes can and do include causes while causes do not and cannot include purposes.

Notice further that whenever causal processes seem to result in the achievement of some "goal," *all the causes* leading to that goal assume the character of means-to-the-end. They do not depart from the causal order in order to do this, nor do they deviate a single decimal point from their precisely measurable behavior. Rather, it is the whole sequence that is renamed "purposive" when it is directed to a goal. Similarly, a word processor does not cease to be a machine when it is set up to send and receive e-mail.

In this "new" teleology purpose and causality do not mutually exclude each other, and, in fact, are compatible. The sort of purpose being sought is a comprehensive one. It would need to be a purpose ascribed to the whole causal order, rather than one attributed in piecemeal fashion. Such a purpose would not interfere with the causal order.

But, why believe in such a purpose? Here Hocking locks horns with the metaphysical naturalists. He offers a threefold support for such a belief: (1) Does the causal order provide an assignable value? (2) Does the causal order preserve what is so valued? (3) Is there direct or indirect evidence of a selection of means? (TP, 62–66)

First, the result of the causal order would need to be an assignable value. Without value there can be no comprehensive purpose. But what assignable values are we entitled to attribute to the causal order?

Now, if we take evolutionary theory seriously, there seem to be three stages of assignable value: (1) the development of organic or living forms from inorganic or lifeless forms or entities, (2) the development of mental from nonmental forms, and (3) the development of rational from subrational entities.

Surely a living entity has more value or value-possibilities than some nonliving entity. What is distinctive about a living being? Disagreements will loom large in trying to answer this question, but perhaps one can say that living beings can function in ways impossible for nonliving entities. What are these? Living beings carry out processes of metabolism that are not possible for nonliving entities. Living entities can grow, nourish themselves, repair themselves, and protect themselves. Moreover, living beings behave as if they can act purposively, and for this some account needs to be provided. Again, they also make provision for the preservation of their species. A living being with conscious mental functioning has more value than one without those functions. And, surely a rational organism, capable of deliberating and thinking, has more value than one without these functions.

Each of these transitions seems to be a step forward. In each case something of value is produced and so far as we can presently say is preserved. Two reasons for this belief have been mentioned.

Can something more be said for this teleological view? I think so. Let us suppose that these transitions can be explained by chance occurrences. Are we not stretching our credulity more by making such an explanatory claim? Does it stretch our credulity less to ascribe them to purposive behavior? The fact that something of value is preserved adds weight to the purposive claim.

What of the third warrant? Is there evidence indicating a selection of means? Are nature and the features of nature the result of causality and purpose?

Think of the matter in this way. The situation we seek to explain is asymmetrical. A cause-and-effect account could explain such a situation without loose ends. But, one must reflectively push the matter further. We need to ask: Can a symmetrical situation bring into being an entirely new being? Can one account for a genuine emergent in terms of symmetry? Can the narrow naturalism or cause-and-effect account offer a convincing explanation of the newness and difference of what comes to be? On such a view the emergent in each of the three transitions—living from nonliving, conscious from nonconscious, and rational from nonrational—cannot have its arrival explained. Causality may account for the present on the basis of the past. Whatever is a result of the past, causally speaking, is capable of repetition, and repetition leaves the new out of account. Can cause-and-effect networks account for the different? Ask yourself if an effect can be wholly incommensurate with its cause. Can we, for example, account for the differences between brain and mind by a causal scheme?

We also need to ask: Will chance or random occurrences bring about the newness and differences emergent evolution insists come into being? No monkeys jumping on word processor keyboards, even though for an infinite period of time, will ever produce *As You Like It* or *Macbeth*. And the common assumption of the strict naturalist that given infinite time living organisms were bound to emerge from nonliving elements is an error wide of the mark.

"Emergent evolution" to the extent that living organisms do arise, would, then, seem to require some selection of appropriate means from a number of alternatives. The entire configuration of this particular universe would represent in some sense an original choice with these values anticipated by the purposive agent.

[223]

A most distinctive contribution of Hocking's view is his characterization of the human self as a "Field of Fields." We shall have more to say later about the origin of this insight. For the moment we are concerned with the manner in which using this metaphor contrasts his view with that of the metaphysical naturalist.

For Hocking the human self is bipolar; it has an "excursive" and a "reflective" pole. While such naturalism can in some measure account for the excursive pole, it fails to explain the reflective pole.

The metaphor of "Field of Fields" helps us understand human selfhood as a reflexive-excursive system. It was a "word form" in which insights about the self initially came to him in personal experience (see Rouner 1978).

Consider briefly what this metaphor may mean. The self (he is saying) is a "field" that includes other different fields, and whatever transpires in an event in one field is not obviously related to another field by either space or direction. He first set forth this notion in an article entitled "Theses Establishing an Idealistic Metaphysics by a New Route," which was published by *The Journal of Philosophy* at a most unfortunate historical moment, December 4, 1941. As world affairs were rushing toward the precipice of a second world war, Hocking's article went completely unnoticed.

By using the "Field of Fields" metaphor Hocking wished to combine the insight of non-Euclidean geometry (Riemann and Lobatschewski) that space can have a legitimate plural with the insight of the mathematicians (Dedekind and Cantor) that infinitude has a legitimate plural. Joining this to the relativity theory of Minkowski and Einstein, Hocking thought that space and time (or space-time) comprise infinite fields. These fields are infinite, and when one undertakes an action in any field it alters that entire field. All events within a given "Field" are related to all other events in that field, and all such events are *unrelated* to events in any other field. Now, a strict naturalistic view of the self would leave it confined to acting in only one sphere or field (namely, the field of physical space-time).

Can the naturalistic view adequately account for the power of the human self? For Hocking the answer is "no." For it is the human self that overcomes space-time plurality. In moments of decision, the self moves from one field to another by deciding what is to be done and by actually doing it. By enacting a decision it moves from the field of imagination to the field of physical reality. As a "Field of Fields" it has this unique creative power.

The power of the self puts something in the physical world. This *creativity* of the human self is "power through ideas." Through its decisions the self literally translates possibility into actuality. It changes the physical world by its action and its infinite field not alone for itself but for all other selves who participate in that field. Thus, while the physical world is a closed system of cause and effect, it remains open to whatever purposive agents (human or divine) may add. It is open to human selves who may wish to use causal processes for the fulfillment of their purposes. And it is open for cooperative actions by human selves with the divine self. A strict naturalism cannot offer an account of either of these types of creativity.

Hocking is well aware that selves, in formulating ideas, are also shaping their own character. This is the core of one's religious "Task," which he mentions as the creation of a thing of unique beauty. But, there is a "mutual creation" (MIHE, 232) between ideas and deeds. The self brings ideas into being, and this actualizing discloses their full meaning. At the same time ideas shape the consciousness that begot them. In changing nature, then, the self indirectly changes itself or alters its own character. It can also directly build its character through its own decisions.

How does a purposive action (or a decision) differ from a cause bringing about an effect? First, a decision may be postponed or delayed, in contrast to a causal process. This means that the human self can to some extent control the time factor in its execution of a decision. Second, in the case of a causal process, the alternatives are definable in advance and limited by the nature of the situation. For human decision, by contrast, alternatives are *invented*. Human selves adapt the world to suit their needs and purposes and, then, change themselves to accommodate the revised environment. We may find that we continually adapt ourselves in relation to our own mistakes perpetrated upon nature!

For Hocking the human self can create, change, or alter the world in a manner that the world cannot replicate. Decisions by human selves bring into being new and different configurations of facts. The world has (as Hocking calls it) "displaceable causality." Beethoven's music simply did not exist prior to his composing it. It is at once both new and different, even for God. "Mind can beget world as world cannot beget mind" (MIHE, 235n). This clearly points toward a metaphysical idealism.

Three personal experiences served to confirm Hocking's perspective. Upon reflection each of these experiences brought in its wake its own special insight, and these insights offer a more inclusive frame within which to understand nature. By doing so each is illustrative of what a "transfigured naturalism" would include.

First was the "insight" Hocking acquired very early in his life while working as a teenager with a railroad surveying crew. He reports the experience with the suggestion that it had a bearing on his views on personal immortality. In a broader way the experience provides an understanding of how the self is related to nature. At an even earlier time (at the age of thirteen) he had read Herbert Spencer's *First Principles*, in spite of his father's admonition against it. Spencer convinced young Hocking that the most humankind could hope for was a mechanical and soulless universe with death as the ultimate reaper. It was a picture of sweeping desolation, and Spencer's relentless logic left no ray of hope. But, listen to Hocking's own description of this surveying experience:

> The time is 1892.... The scene is the right-of-way of a single track railroad, between Aurora, Illinois, and Waukegan—the Elgin, Joliet, and Eastern Railroad, then a new belt line around Chicago. It is a summer day. A lone figure carrying a pot of white paint and a brush, stoops every hundred feet to cover a chalk mark on the inside of the rail with a vertical line of paint, and every

500 feet to paint a number. The crew of the civil engineering department are measuring the track of the railway for inventory purposes. The chalk markers, with the steel tape, have moved ahead of the painter, who doesn't mind being alone. He has become interested in the numbers.

He is, at this moment, in a cut. The banks rise on either side of him above his eye level; the breeze is shut off; the heat is oppressive. The only sounds are the humming of insects and the occasional nervous flutter of a disturbed grasshopper's wings. The painter is painting the number 1800. He is amused to note the possibility of putting this number series into one-to-one correspondence with the years of the century. He begins to supply the numbers with events, at first bits of history—Civil War and family background. This imaginary living-through-past-time be-comes as real an experience as the rail-painting, and far more exciting! 1865, 1870—suddenly 1873, my birth year: "Hello! Hocking is here!" Every mark, from now on, numbered or not, [is] entangled with personal history. But very soon, 1892, the present: I paint the Now! From this point memory is dismissed; it gives place to anticipation, dream, conjecture—there is something relentless in the onmoving of these numbers, to be filled with something—but with what? 1893—will it be the new Chicago University? 1900—where shall I be? 1950, fairly old, very likely gone. 1973, a hundred years from birth—surely gone: "Good-by, Hocking!" I see myself as dead, the nothingness of non-being sweeps over me. I have been for four years an ardent disciple of Herbert Spencer, unhappily but helplessly convinced that man is as the animals; the race moves on, the individual perishes, the living something has become nothing; ... For the first time I realize, beyond the mere clack of words, the blankness of annihilation. And no doubt, just because of this swift sense of no-sense, the shock was intense as I realize, with the same swiftness, that it was I as surviving, who looked upon myself as dead, that it had to be so, and that because of this, annihilation can be spoken of, but never truly imagined. This was not enough to free me from the spell of Spencer, but it cracked that spell: the rest of the day was spent in a new lightness of heart, as if I had come upon a truth that was not to leave me. I was glad to be alone.

Obviously, this situation was most artificially built: the mechanical action of brush and paint must inevitably run past the relived life and compel a sharp vision of the end, and then of the long time the world shall last. Yet the unfading impression left by this experience carries the question of whether this doubleness of self may not have a natural reality: may not the observing self be enduring, while the observed self drops away? (MIHE, 214–215)

What is the insight that accompanies this experience? Is there not a hint of doubleness in the self, something more and other than the "natural" observed self of which Spencer and strict naturalists speak? Does not the existence of such a self fit more comfortably with a "transfigured naturalism?" Spencer's error was not in his analysis of nature, but rather in thinking that natural fact was reality's only dimension. Thinking of the self metaphorically as a "Field of Fields" permits us to understand how the self as living might observe the natural self as dead!

Hocking's "transfigured naturalism" shows its development in his "widened empiricism." It intends to account for the factual world (cause and effect) and the insights and grasp of reality that the religious (mystics) claim. Both realms, spirit and matter, affect each other dialectically. Hocking felt that these sorts of experiences (if not actually subject to scientific analysis) were at least not contrary to it.

Generally speaking, the experience of nature is something over against us as essential to our development as human selves. The human self is at once part of nature and not merely a part. It is simultaneously within nature and transcendent over nature.

Many years later when Hocking worked on his doctoral dissertation, he returned to this philosophical puzzle. His dissertation bore the unwieldy title of "The Elementary Experience of Other Conscious Being in its Relation to the Elementary Experience of Physical and Reflexive Objects." It was (in large measure) an attack on the problem of solipsism. His solution (if we may call it that) insisted that there were three basic elements in all human experience: our selves, other selves, and physical objects. Just as natural objects by their stability, reliability, tangibility, vividness, and distinctness enable us to known our own minds, even so (insists Hocking) these same objects as the focus of our attention enable us to know other minds directly.

This insight came to Hocking many years later. He describes the moment of insight in *The Meaning of God in Human Experience* by referring to Agnes his wife as "a comrade." (Do we need to remind ourselves that he dedicated this major work to Agnes as an "unfailing source of insight"?) Let us hear Hocking's own statement of the experience:

> I have sometimes sat looking at a comrade, speculating on this mysterious isolation of self from self. Why are we so made that I gaze and see of thee only thy Wall, and never Thee? This Wall of thee is but a movable part of the Wall of my world; and I also am a Wall to thee: we look out at one another from behind masks. How would it seem if my mind could but once be within thine; and we could meet and without barrier be with each other? And then it has fallen upon me like a shock—as when one thinking himself alone has felt a presence—But I am in thy soul. These things around me are in thy experience. They are thy own; when I touch them and move them I change thee. When I look on them I see what thou seest; when I listen, I hear what thou hearest. I am in the great Room of thy soul; and I experience thy very experience. For where art thou? Not here, behind those eyes, within that head, in darkness, fraternizing with chemical processes. Of these, in my own case, I know nothing; for my existence is spent not behind my Wall, but in front of it. I am there, where I have treasures. And there art thou, also. This world in which I live, is the world of thy soul: and being

within that I am within thee. I can imagine no contact more real and thrilling than this; that we should meet and share identity, not through ineffable inner depths (alone), but here through the foregrounds of common experience; and that thou shouldest be—not behind that mask—but here, pressing with all thy consciousness upon me, containing me, and these things of mine. This is reality: and having seen it thus, I can never again be frightened into monadism by reflections which have strayed from their guiding insight.

Any connecting medium is apt to appear as an obstacle to direct relationship; on the other hand any obstacle may discover itself to be a mediator, sign of unbroken continuity. The sea separates,—or the sea connects; it cannot do one without doing the other also. So Nature may be interpreted in its relation to social consciousness, as the visible pledge and immediate evidence of our living contact. If there be any social consciousness, it must include within itself just such physical appearances as we have been reviewing, even in its ideal perfection. (MGHE, 265–266)

In the human interrelationship of love we are the most convinced of the independent reality of the other. At the same time this relatedness to other selves helped Hocking understand how mind and matter are related.

Is the world comprised of two radically different kinds of things as Descartes supposed? Descartes's formulation of the problem has troubled generations of Western philosophers. Matter, it is said, is the kind of thing that occupies space and can be located in time and place. But, mind (as we have noted) isn't this sort of thing. It is not an extended thing, and it seems to defy location. Hocking agreed with Whitehead that this "bifurcation of nature" needed to be overcome. What needed to be formulated was a broader conception of nature, a nature (as it were for Hocking) "transfigured." This would allow for nature's recalcitrance as natural fact, against which ideas would be made clear and distinct. For Hocking it is the clear, over-againstness of physical nature that brings to mind and bestows upon the work of thought its purpose and structure.

Hocking sees as a prime obligation the call to think and, in his view, nature presents mind with a vast problem to consider. For how would a purposeless factuality of nature be indispensable to mind's development? For Hocking matter and mind are dialectically related and, properly understood, function in a living harmony.

The third experience that seems to express this "transfigured naturalism" is one that evolved through his reflections on the metaphysics of selfhood. His earlier statements on how minds were related seem to be somewhat loose and largely metaphorical. What does it mean, for example, to say that one is within the mind of another? Nature seems to have a place, but mind does not. Ernest and Agnes might have presented to their respective consciousnesses the same objects and have seen them differently. Nature's objects are simultaneously "out-there" as treasures to be shared in the forefront of consciousness, and at the same time it is our minds that bring together these objects by our imaginations on the basis of our life-experiences. How does one's theory do justice to the complex facets of perception? How can one capture this complexity and variety without losing the inner integrity of selves? Hocking wanted to avoid the reductionist approach of some strict metaphysical naturalists. He wanted to avoid the sort of naturalism that takes away the original mystery of experience and leaves only that portion that can be quantified.

Here is Hocking's description of how this third resolving insight came to him:

> After a meeting of the seminar, late Wednesday afternoon, October 21, I went for a lonely walk along the Charles River bank.
>
> The sun had already set. A new crescent was standing over the far end of Andersen bridge. The mass of Business School buildings was reflected in the river as a dimly waving blackness. Under the blackness the river was silver. Against the silver, a Harvard eight at belated practice, was silhouetted, oarsmen and coxswain posturing rhythmically like gondoliers.
>
> To the West, over the line of grey-blue hills, a rim of brownish-red glow, shading upward into a sky-depth of luminous darkness. It was as though for the moment Nature were holding still—caught in a spell of quiet and tense glory, unwilling to fade.
>
> Illusion or not, the beauty and infinite quietude of a scene, whose inner texture was doubtless infinite motion, invaded the witness, as if its repose were the truth. Here was quiescence—no seminar, no discussion, no labor of categories, also no war. Time had stopped, and the world was not drenched in unmoving space. Space was endless; it was my space, running also through the earth, and out the other side. There were armies at night, minds full of battle-plans for tomorrow's action. Was it truly the same space? Could that space, crowded with fighters' strategies be the same as my space, spell-bound in peace?
>
> Yes, it must be the identical space; it is the same world for all of us. Yet it cannot be the same. For no one else saw the world I saw; if I had not happened along, that marvel of a sky-moment might have passed unknown. It was certainly not known to itself, was it? Those colors, lights, shadows, shapes, could exist only for a creature with eyes, stationed at or near where I was standing.
>
> Our various spaces, all infinite, must be and cannot be identical. The answer? Space is not single, but plural. There is a world-space, identical for all included persons. But for each one, there is also a private space, perhaps spaces, holding private responses to qualities, holding also futurities, not yet existent—plans, battle-plans perhaps, plans that can be detained, modified, cancelled, as events in the identical world-space cannot be.
>
> Space must have a plural—this we were saying in the seminar. And more than this, each person envisages plural spaces. Then, the position of the person, the self, toward this his plurality, how shall we describe it? Each space can be called a "field," a continuum in which infinite positions, potentials, etc., can be

distinguished and held-together. Could the self, as envisaging plural fields, be a field of fields?

The walk away from the seminar had brought me back to the seminar; or no: it had brought the seminar back to me, but in a vivid picture-presence. What I there thought, I was here seeing. It was all simple and self-evident; but I had a feeling of admission, as if a difficulty had dropped away. (MIHE, xiv–xvi)

Hocking's "transfigured naturalism" emphasizes these three experiences and their importance for an idealism he *hoped* to develop. For him such an idealism rests upon the broadened empiricism that is open to new and deeper insights.

Unfortunately, Hocking never develops this "new route" to an idealistic metaphysics. Instead, he offers wisdom for our times and insights garnered from a rich and full life.

Hocking's idealism would have been compatible with a "transfigured naturalism" that took as its core, belief in a living, active God that provides the ground of both scientific progress and creative action. In Hocking's own words:

The oneness of an identical Thou constitutes the VINCULUM [or FIELD] among worlds that appear as "actual" to receiving subjects.... Whatever human experience continues its experimental conversation with that Identical Thou is itself "real," whether its space-time context is of this world or of some other world. (MIHE, 240–241n)

[This conversation involves] an immediate summons to live by objective thought (including science) and by creative action: and in so far as the individual responds, partially or completely, to this imperative, God is literally, through him, at work in history. (CWC, 183)

WORKS CITED

Ethridge, James M., and Barbara Kopala, eds. 1965. *Contemporary Authors*. Vols. 13–14. Detroit: Gale Research Co.

Hocking, Richard. 1978. "Dialectic in the Unfolding of Hocking's Thought." In *The Wisdom of William Ernest Hocking*, ed. John Howie and Leroy Rouner, 1–11. Washington, D.C.: University Press of America, 1978.

Hocking, William Ernest. 1926. *Present Status of the Philosophy of Law and Rights*. New Haven, Conn.: Yale University Press.

———. 1959. "Man's Cosmic Status." In *Search for America*, ed. Huston Smith. Englewood Cliffs, N.J.: Prentice-Hall, Inc.

Howie, John, and Leroy Rouner, eds. 1978. *The Wisdom of William Ernest Hocking*. Washington, D.C.: University Press of America, 1978.

Marcel, Gabriel. 1963. *The Existential Background of Human Dignity*. Cambridge: Harvard University Press.

Rouner, Leroy. 1978. "Insight." In *The Wisdom of William Ernest Hocking*, ed. John Howie and Leroy Rouner, 23–25. Washington, D.C.: University Press of America, 1978.

CHAPTER 19

Passion for Meaning: W. E. Hocking's Religious-Philosophical Views

Bruce Wilshire

William Ernest Hocking is a major thinker unjustly forgotten. The reasons for this neglect are several and throw light on our current situation: His addresses and publications, spanning the first years of the twentieth century to the 1960s, are of great subtlety, complexity, and variety; we live in the age of the fast read. We are as much driven as our European ancestors who colonized this continent and who—compulsive, acquisitive—disgusted and terrified indigenous people.

If one were forced to play the labels game, one might call Hocking a rationalist, a mystic, and a genuine public servant. With the neglect of all these roles in our secular, hyperspecialized, often cynical age, it is not surprising that a thinker who somehow combines them should be dismissed as eclectic and consigned to the dustbin of history. Hocking seems to be one of those old-fashioned thinkers who had the temerity to feel responsible for assessing and maintaining the fabric of civilization. But what knowledgeable person in the fast lane of today's multilaned relativistic world would even use the singular "civilization" (but probably without much understanding of other civilizations)?

Finally, there is his great hospitality to the world, the many powerful philosophers East and West whom he received gratefully and whose influence is clearly evident (his ego is not fragile): for example, both William James and Josiah Royce (!), in about equal degree, and Edmund Husserl and Gabriel Marcel. All these get woven into a tapestry that is huge, original, distinctly American, and hard to take in at even several glances.

Trying to get an initial fix on the whole pattern, I employ at crucial junctures a phenomenological lens. Even without knowing that Hocking spent three months of his formative years studying with Edmund Husserl, we could see a version of phenomenology in his works themselves (see Hocking 1959).

But Husserl is a German philosopher, and the word "phenomenology" has today a distinctly continental flavor (though Charles Peirce used it or a cognate term). What does this have to do with Hocking? A lot. First, classic American philosophers are greatly influenced by continental thinkers of the nineteenth century, particularly by those who developed identity-philosophies (identity of subject and object). This is true even though they interweave these influences with distinctly American concerns and enthusiasms. Second, and even more important, phenomenology responds to a crisis of meaning and living felt throughout "advanced" North Atlantic culture. The crisis arises over the very successes of science and technology. So totally do they take over our lives that the vast prescientific matrix without which life cannot be meaningful and vital is eclipsed and begins to crumble. Indeed, without prescientific meanings and practices to supply a matrix for living, science and modern technology would themselves be impossible.

Very simply, phenomenology is the attempt to see clearly what we typically take completely for granted, what we feel we can ignore. In other words, it is the attempt to see the primal and pragmatic: the meaning of being selves that are bodies, selves ineluctably in situations or circumstances, selves ecstatic or depressed, gripped by responsibilities and enlivened thereby or wayward and listless; selves often very different from moment to moment, yet ones who remember what they've been through, and what they've promised, and know they will die. It is completely understandable that indigenous peoples, torn from their land and their lives, send up a lament that mingles achingly and strangely with the lament of thoughtful Europeans or Euro-Americans who, caught in vast tides of history, also feel dispossessed, alienated, uprooted, desiccated.

The connection between phenomenology and existentialism, on the one hand, and primal or indigenous life, on the other, is deep and direct. These ways of thinking aim to see deeper into the life we actually lead, to unmask what seems to be obvious and evident. Particularly clear in the later work of the existential phenomenologist, Martin Heidegger, is the connection to indigenous life-ways. Heidegger (1971) writes of "the play of the fourfold," of thinking as thanking, of dwelling as being open to the sky; of the pouring out from the jug of wine as a giving that echoes the giving which is Being itself; of the spring from which the water is drawn for the wine which reflects the sky; of the earth into which the wine grapes root. Earlier than Heidegger—or Marcel—Hocking's unique phenomenology opens the way for recovery of primal values: of ecstatic expansiveness, wholism, kinship, reverence, basal gratitude, ultimate responsiveness, and responsibility.

As an advanced graduate student at Harvard, Hocking was the beneficiary of a traveling fellowship to Germany. Once there, Paul Natorp suggested he study with the barely known Edmund Husserl in Göttingen. None of Hocking's advisors had suggested this, but Natorp's sketch of Husserl's attack on psychologism—his critique of the assumption that an empirical science of psychology can speak definitively on meaning and truth—resonated strongly with Hocking's "gropings," and with trepidation he went to Göttingen and was warmly received into Husserl's sparsely attended course on logical investigations. When he sent to his superiors at Harvard the mandatory report on his activities, he was told in effect not to waste the university's money on this "unknown" phenomenologist, and sadly he moved on after three months. But in this time Husserl made a profound impression, and my entry into Hocking's work will be by way of it.

How do we begin philosophizing without cheating? How do we avoid being sucked into the magnetizing and dazzling funnel of natural-scientific explanation, which must reduce or ignore our sensuous, immediate situations in which primal meaning gets made. This meaning-making contributes massively to our very being. Just because it is presupposed so unquestioningly and completely, seems so obvious and banal, we tend to think that we don't need to think about it, protect it, discover its ways of working.

Husserl was developing a way of unfolding and protecting it. He amended Hegel at a fundamental level, an amendment Hocking much appreciated. How does the world "give itself out" primordially; how does it appear initially as phenomena and phenomenon? Hegel replies that it is the poorest content or "what"; it is merely the phenomenal certainty of the "that," sheer existence, "something there."

With daring genius, Husserl makes a distinction that allows him both to appreciate Hegel's point and to supercede it: Yes, it's a that, but it's not completely empty of content, and, moreover, this content is not given isolated and alone, but rather in a fundamental network of meaning, ultimately the primordially given world itself—difficult to describe just as it appears. To expose this content, to avoid burying it under the epithets "obvious and taken for granted," we no longer simply assert or assume its existence in the everyday tunneling and practical way, but we just entertain this world-assumption as what it gives itself out to be—as phenomenon—namely, "unquestioned assumption." In Husserl's technical language, we suspend (without eliminating) the assertive or positing aspect of minding in order to allow the constituting aspect (constitutive of meaning) to freely unfold itself.

Paradoxically, perhaps, but really, release from everyday tunneling behavior that benumbedly asserts existence allows the meaning of existence to billow out. This disclosure is augmented by what Husserl calls free variations: we freely vary in imagination how any phenomenon presents itself, and when we encounter the limits of variation along its various parameters, these points mark out its essential structure, its scope, meaning, or essence. In other words, when a phenomenon presents itself as one of a certain sort, its essential features (essence) are those that can't be varied beyond certain points without destroying the identity of the phenomenon presented. For example, we cannot vary anything presenting itself as an actual thing beyond what "presents itself incompletely to any glance or series of glances," hence, that pertains to the meaning or essence of an "actual thing."

Hocking's most famous book is *The Meaning of God in Human Experience* (1912). Nearly 600 pages, it is an epochal, multifaceted achievement: in intellectual sophistication, breadth, and sensuous depth, it is without parallel in the twentieth century. I treat it here as a de facto phenomenological study. He gives a clear clue in the heading of part III, "The Need of God: A Series of Free Meditations." Free meditations for Hocking do much the same work as free variations do for Husserl: they allow primal meaning to exfoliate and exhibit itself.

Hocking does not try to assert and to establish the existence of God until page 301 and the subsequent chapter. Clearly, it's as if he had first suspended the positing or asserting of God's existence in order to display how the phenomenon of deity is constituted, what it means. When he finally offers a "proof" of God's existence ("proof" always in quotes), it is a rich, highly motivated version of the so-called ontological argument, not the threadbare, glaringly abstract schema of argument that most philosophers from Thomas Aquinas to Kant to those of our day love to explode.

If one comes to Hocking's 1912 book after having been steeped in mainstream twentieth-century analytic philosophy, it is like being let out of a barrel into the open air. Even the less rigid forms of analytic thought seem pinched, pale, and reductivist. Not only do we find in Hocking a kind of Husserlian billowing out of meaning, but, unfettered by that philosopher's mathematicism (if I can call it that), Hocking anticipates in certain ways the existential phenomenologists Marcel and Heidegger, besides developing key points in Royce and James. Heidegger, for instance, reminds us that humankind has grown up and taken shape in the presence of the gods, in the richest panoply of presences that draw us into themselves and constitute us ecstatically. Do the gods exist? But why raise the question until we know how our existence and experience feels and what its intended subject matter means?

The primal given is not some circular coin-size visual sense datum, say—such data are not building blocks of knowledge and being, but are derivative from analyses and assumptions furtive and unacknowledged. The primal given is the primal gift. Given before all reflection and analysis, is that we are environed, moodily and totally, before any analysis can begin to pick our environedness apart. For Royce, we begin as world creatures and end that way, hoping only to have thematized some of the embeddedness before we die. For James, we are engulfed in the world of practical realities which is the baseline against which all other worlds—mathematical, fictional, insane—are to be judged: an engulfedness or circumpressure that he calls belief, the feeling of reality. This he develops later as pure experience, primally given "thats" and "whats" that antecede the very distinction between self and other. For Husserl, perception is the protodoxic basis, the foundation upon which all other belief, no matter how sophisticated and complex, must find its place or be wayward and nihilistic. For Heidegger, again, we cannot be understood apart from how we find ourselves having already been found by the world, given back to ourselves moodily by the world that has already held us and assessed us in some way—*Befindlichkeit*. This includes, of course, our having already been engulfedly with others—*Mitsein*. For Marcel, recuperative reflection can only try to comprehend where we already are caught up in and by the world. It requires the most personal digging and rumination, work that we try to make understandable to ourselves and others. Rumination for Marcel is like tilling soil. No simplistic division should be made between appearance and reality. Likewise, no simplistic line should be drawn dividing the personal and the universal.[1]

Hocking knows that every mood has its idea, its notion of where we are and how we stand in the whole, and that every feeling moves to consummate itself in some ideation-realization of this place. Profound pleasure is finding ourselves confirmed as whole beings in the whole place, in the world-idea, as he calls it. He writes with amazing perception: try as we might to find ourselves isolated, "the undertone of Nature's presence never leaves us, even in deep sleep" (MGHE, 269). This Harvard professor speaks in a way an indigenous person would immediately appreciate.

Again, Hocking writes of that "one background field" that is "beyond all use" (MGHE, 119). Here he criticizes James's pragmatism and would outdo his mentor's notion of environedness and circumpressure. Yes, things must work and work out, that is necessary for meaning and truth; Hocking holds to a "negative pragmatism." But pragmatism itself cannot be sufficient, for the very reason that the one background field within which all uses and triumphs and failures must occur is itself beyond all use, beyond all manipulation and comprehension (though he will speak of world-idea). Differently put, it is presupposed by all that we typically mean by "use," so cannot itself be just another use. James is not blind to this point about the world but does not make enough of it.

Hocking's phenomenology of where we find ourselves in primal experience is patient, penetrating, and relentless. Our original sin, he writes, is failure to be engaged and aware:

> We still live in semi-savage dreaminess, incredulous of the distant contingency, incredulous therefore of the present moment, veiled from the actual conditions of action, circling at planetary distances about our own practical center.... The evil that is in this world, and especially in this spirit of meaningless accident—the luck that we hope will be for us good luck—this evil does not rouse us: it benumbs us, rather, and confirms our somnambulism. (MGHE, 515)

Awake, Hocking unpacks everyday phenomena (but I'm not sure what he means by "semi-savage dreaminess"— "savages" have to be intensely alert most of the time if they would survive). For example, "Every [generalized] optimism implies a judgment about a reality which has a character and is therefore One" (MGHE, 168). Or again, every generalized resentment implies—though we may be shocked to realize it—a personal character for the world as a whole (MGHE, 145–147). For we can feel resentment only toward persons.

Hocking penetrates to the uncanny level of immediate involvement, and banalities and stereotypes lose their grip. He develops (without naming it, I think) William James's phenomenology of pure experience, of experience so fresh and perhaps so shocking that it is only a "that" though ready to become all kinds of "whats" (James [1911] 1979, "The Thing and Its Relations," 46). Probably influenced by James, Hocking gives an example of being dazed (MGHE, 66). Husserl, probably likewise influenced, gives perhaps the best example—consider it again: Absentmindedly reading at a table, I reach for what I think is a glass of water. It is really fruit juice, say. At the moment the liquid touches my tongue, it is neither water nor juice; it is a mere "that," mere "sensuous matter." So alien to us creatures who must identify and form ideas of what things are, no wonder we may spit it out!

Or, again, James gives examples of "thats" that are simultaneously floating "whats": Watching the moon through the clouds I may not in the instant know whether it is the moon, the clouds, or I that moves (James [1911] 1979, "The Place of Affectional Facts," 35–36). But if in that instant I do not make the primal distinction between self and other, my own self loses its everyday identity. It is uncanny. Or take the pure experience of regard. It is not yet clear that I regard the other or that the other regards me. Regard floats in the situation. At the primal, immediate, or primitive level of experience, I attend to the world, and, strangely, it attends to me. Though things may appear to everyday practical awareness to exist independent of one another, they do not. Everything draws out everything else. Everything is a means for the fulfillment of everything else. To sense that is to sense what is of final importance.

Hocking takes this idea and develops it far beyond James (and way beyond Husserl's monadism). His first vantage point is on interpersonal phenomena of the human sort. I think we can call it the first free variation on the nature or meaning of God, the-person-but-more-than-person. For this idea must be built up on a founding level of human persons being-together. As the human phenomenon immediately gives itself out, it is a necessary condition for understanding the divine. And on the human level, no isolated I-self presents itself to fresh perception, no Cartesian egocentric predicament presents itself. Hocking writes:

> How would it seem if my mind could but once be within thine; and we could meet and without barrier be with each other? And then it has fallen upon me like a shock—as when one thinking himself alone has felt a presence—But I am in thy soul. These things around me are in thy experience. They are thy own; when I touch them and move them I change thee. When I look on them I see what thou seest; when I listen, I hear what thou hearest. I am in the great Room of thy soul; and I experience thy very experience.... This world in which I live, is the world of thy soul: and being within that, I am within thee. I can imagine no contact more real and thrilling than this; that we should meet and share identity, not through ineffable inner depths (alone), but here through the foregrounds of common experience; and that thou shouldst be—not behind that mask—but here, pressing with all thy consciousness upon me, containing me, and these things of mine. (MGHE, 265–266)

Directly evident to sharpened perception, we contain others' objects of experience and can modify these and others' experience of them. We participate in each other's lives. In so far forth, we contain each other.

We may think ourselves alone, but suddenly with a shock, the presence of the other is with us. In certain circumstances, we may be unable to identify just who the other is. Hocking builds on the example given by Emerson: riding horseback into the woods, we feel we have interrupted something and are now being observed. By whom exactly? We may have no idea. We feel contained in the largest Room, the Whole. The phenomenon to be seized and described is this: we may feel ourselves regarded by the Supreme Reality, the Ground of all that is.[2]

Here the meaning of God in human experience obtrudes itself, a fascinating, fearsome, perhaps protective all-surrounding presence and power, that can melt down, recast, and unify the self. Though not necessarily a focalizable object, nothing could be more objective in its sheer presence and meaning. Dewey maintained that every "this" is a system of meanings focused at a point of stress. Perhaps he would disallow the encompassing presence in question the status of a "this," on the grounds that it is not focused at a point of stress. Hocking would not be thus deterred, I think. In any case, Hocking believes that the worship or reverence induced by this overwhelming presence is the primitive propulsive source of all distinctly human accomplishments in art, religion, science, and philosophy. But regard on this all-engulfing immediate level floats dangerously. It can also result in the most destructive fanaticisms in corporate and personal bodies. One feels regarded by Divinity, but the regard is attributed to groups or corporate individuals less than the Whole that pretend to be the Whole. Groups can be caught up in genocidal madness.

He uses what he calls a "rapid survey of . . . historic phenomena" as a de facto free variation on the experience of this stunning, all-pervasive regard and mana power.

> If man's religion is first embodied in his exclamations, these . . . were at once cognitions and prayers, incipient transactions . . . but behind all these pictures [of rewards and punishments] there is, even from the beginning, a residual importance in being right with deity which we might call an ontological importance, i.e., affecting somehow the substance of one's self, the soul and its destiny, opening up some bottomless depths of being such as the eye is hardly fitted to gaze into. The amount of power that can be released when the religious nerve is pressed is quite out of proportion to the belief in the more definable pleasures and pains. . . . To keep God friendly there are few efforts that men will not make. . . . But these necessary moments of approach have their own terrors, when some one must take it upon himself to break through the habitual taboo of Holiness; a cloud of oppressive gravity deepens over the event, supportable only by fierce resolution, wrapped probably in mutilation and blood. And when the act is accomplished in safety, an exultancy equally fierce floods the brain;

exhibitions of savage gaiety, the license of supermen, can alone satisfy the spirit. We are stranger now to this vehemence, whether for better or for worse; but we can still catch from afar the pulse of this ancient ocean, its terrors and its glorious liberations. We can understand how this strange sense of ontological importance must condense in any phase of human experience in which the actual remoteness of deity seemed overcome. We shall expect to set excessive value upon those states of enthusiasm, ecstasy, intoxication, in which heaven and earth were felt to flow together. (MGHE, 346–347).[3]

At this primal level we can expect Hocking to have little respect for arguments for God's existence that assume a contingent Nature in itself and argue to a necessary Being, a Creator, as its source. For there can be no Nature in itself. Nature as it is actually given as phenomenon in experience is Nature-regarded. It is Nature interpreted by and within itself, Nature pictured, storied, sung.

So arguments that go from contingency or design—"Because Nature is, God is"— are out. Hocking writes piquantly, "Because Nature is not, God is" (MGHE, 312). That is, tuning in reverently on Nature regarding itself through its members sets us beyond the mere abstraction, "Nature," and the participatory naming of this all-pervasive regard—God—must be one with the immanent being that is named: so it must be true. Hence, Hocking's "broader empiricism": his phenomenological insertion in world-process-as-meaning-returning-into-itself, delivers its own version of the ontological argument. But, as always, the "argument" is not so much that as it is insight: the universe celebrates itself through us as God—comes home to itself—and shows itself perfectly adequate and self-sufficient in doing so. How could this feeling-awareness of conjunction possibly be false? So it must be true. Hocking makes that point clearer than ever before in history.

If one must play the traditional labels game, Hocking is first a rationalist. His idea of ideas grows up within the tradition of Hegel, Schelling, and Royce broadly conceived: ideas as concrete universals. Concrete, as they take shape within individuals residing in definite cultural situations and institutions of the period. Yet also universal as that life of consciousness that sorts the world into kinds, symbols, archetypes that not only determine the expectations of the period in which they arise but have a life of their own and cumulate through history as a kind of destiny.

Yet Hocking is also a mystic: one who doesn't believe that the logistic intellect in any form can build up an Absolute system of necessarily connected ideas that subtends—or is—the Whole. He doesn't believe we can think God's thoughts after Him, in the manner of Hegel. Also he is a mystic who attends keenly to the sensuousness and moody kinship of daily life, which leads him into a kind of existential phenomenology, or what he calls his broader empiricism.

This mix holds in solution metaphysical elements that are more traditional.

He designates these the Self, the Other, and the Thou (see Hocking 1959, 7). Let us hazard a sketch of how he tries to put all this together.

The scientistic strand of analytic philosophy in this century constricts meaning-making and hence our lives. Hocking opens us up—throws the windows wide onto a broad sky and singing air. The extent of a person is the extent of his or her ability to grasp the world. Or, much better, the extent of their ability to be grasped by the World-idea. The value of any particular thing in the world—a hat, say—is the extent to which we can find our self's nature, our "idea-stuff," instantiated, confirmed, extended in the hat (MGHE, 131).[4] We grasp the hat zestfully if it simultaneously grasps us and draws us out. A recent ad for a car touches the nerve of this point: "What am I looking for in a car? Myself." If only our advertisers could put things together and help us be wise!

The life of our ideas is voluminous, enwrapping, and propelling. He gives the concept of idea an exceedingly broad range: from sensuous images to the vastest universals or mathematical systems, each section of the range needing to be balanced and supplemented organismically by all the others if a human life is to be cohesive and effective. What is most distinctive about us, he thinks, is that we make pictures (and not merely "in our minds" as sense-data). Imagine on a wall a picture of a tree. How far up from the floor is the top of the tree (and he doesn't mean the bit of pigment that iconically signifies the top)? The question is absurd. But we have no trouble keeping the world of the tree and the world of the room in which we stand distinguished, and they nicely complement each other. We are creatures of interlacing systems or worlds of meaning.

The expansive life of new ideas has the power to break through closed systems of them, and through ossified behaviors (MGHE, 472–473, 482, 489). We can't help but think today of addictive systems, short-circuitings of what Emerson called "Circular power returning into itself," "the inexplicable continuity of this web of God" (and which Hocking echoes in his own way). The bodily self fails to trust the regenerative powers of the world; it generates sure but short-term pleasures and satisfactions—by addictively ingesting drugs, say; but this impairs the regenerative powers of that part of Nature that is our own bodies and brains. One is dependent. One's freedom to choose—or, better, freedom to be grasped by alternative possibilities or ideas—one's very self is impaired.

This is a tough test for Hocking's view of Self and the life of ideas. Can he show us how to break through the body's self-closing addictive circuits: an emptiness in the stomach and a falling away that demands instant support by any means now; an urging in the groin that might find satisfaction in an appropriate situation, but the self lacks the momentum and assurance to wait; a waning of energies that might signal an upcoming period of dormancy within the regenerative cycles of Nature, but one cannot trust these cycles and becomes a workaholic, say.[5]

Or, related in the most intimate ways to individuals' addictions are the society's, the corporate body's: groups caught up and intoxicated in their false Whole-idea, their insecure and counterfeit totality, ethnically cleanse any other groups who threaten to pollute their purity and hegemony. The experience of Divinity easily short-circuits into terror and aggression.

The sixteen years that elapse between *The Meaning of God in Human Experience* and *The Self: Its Body and Freedom* include the agony of World War I and Hocking's pursuit of the question: Can persons be basically modified? (SBF, 120–121).[6] His interest in instinct, in the primal and atavistic, always deep, is deepened, and he confronts the human body in a way he has not done before. I give only the sketchiest account of the horizons he points to.

Very significantly, Hocking writes, "Whatever my [whole] body does, I do" (SBF, ix, ff.). But he does not affirm the converse: Whatever I do, the whole body does. He does not assert a simple equivalence between self and body. Perhaps his reasons are these: For him, again, "Nature itself" and "bodies themselves" are abstractions. The reality is Nature-and-bodies-regarded-or-regardable. So when that part of Nature that is my bodily self regards itself, it transcends itself as a mere physical thing presented at any moment. I—my self—am the whole body regarded through the whole-Idea, so we cannot affirm a simple equivalence between what I do and what the body does, though there is profound overlap.

In other words, the functioning of the mind cannot be reduced to the functioning of the body, no matter how essential the body's functioning is. To take perhaps an overly simple example, if I perceive the twelfth stroke of a clock, it is not just that stroke that occupies my mind and myself at that instant, but also, at the very least, the eleven that preceded it. The twelfth stroke perceived as such is not just one sound in my ears or one demarcatable electrical event in my brain.

He extrapolates: I cannot be merely a causal mechanism because any cause perceived as such is not merely a cause. Reflected upon, it must receive my consent, tacit or explicit, in order to work. He anticipates the field of psychosomatic medicine: As certain advanced physicians have suggested, the body is the "outside of the mind" (SBF, 80).[7]

But Hocking goes on, "Now there is nothing in the field of natural causation entering into me upon which I may not thus reflect" [151]. That claim seems to me to be an inflation of the powers of mind that is metaphysical in the objectionable sense. He himself pointed out that a feeling may consummate itself in a false idea. And as John Dewey, for example, found through decades of sessions with the psychobiotherapist F. M. Alexander, it is maddeningly difficult to even begin to enlarge the veridical awareness of one's own bodily reality. Before another person manipulates one's body so that certain new sensations are generated, one could not even have imagined them. Recall the crucial passage in Dewey where he says we engage in an immense multitude of immediate organic adjustments of which we are not aware (Dewey 1925, 227).

We need a phenomenology of the body—a highly applied phenomenology, if you will—which might reveal the actual scope of our abilities to disclose its workings. Interestingly enough, Hocking himself initiates at least such an approach to body as we actually live it and regard it in the first person, before it is objectified by the sciences. It is not "the biologist's body": not *Körper*, as the Germans put it, but *Leib*, the body lived, its capacities my self's. He writes in *The Self: Its Body and Freedom*, in the chapter "Why the Mind Needs a Body":

> I open the gate with so much exertion: I walk with ease at such a rate, and not much faster. These are my coefficients. And . . . it is only by some afterthought that they are referred specifically to my body: the power of my limbs is my power—and in fact I never learn the physiology of my muscles: as I use it, I seem to live in it. (SBF, 79–80)

Marvelous, but notice he does not say I "live in" the body that I am.

Now just how—according to Hocking—does thought penetrate and grasp with its ideas this preobjectified and prereflective body? (I assume here that *Leib* is the sense of body most germane to his observations just above.) Perhaps he confronts the question, but I do not find it yet. His view of mind and body seems to me to remain parallelist, for the most part, with mind over matter, and matter conceived at times in a somewhat mechanical way as a reliable appliance for the use of mind (body conceived as *Körper*).

I do not find a univocal sense of "body" in Hocking, nor a clearly multiple sense. And I confess I keep wanting him to affirm a double-aspect rather than a parallelist-with-mind-dominant view, keep wanting him to say that what we call thought and what we call body are but two aspects of one energy. One of the advantages for him if he would say this, I think, is that he would connect what he says about body as *Leib* with his powerful thought about God. If he emphasized more body as lived, as what I-myself do (*Leib*), he could more easily connect with potent divine regard. What if my regard for myself melds in experience with the personified Whole's or God's potent regard for myself? Swelled and buoyed by this grace, what might be the disclosure of body-self's workings then? Expanded and deepened?

A religiously informed phenomenology of body-self suggests itself, a far horizon pointed to by Hocking but not much explored. Indeed, I don't think it has been really explored yet by anybody (though Marcel must not be ignored): a phenomenology, a rational reconstruction if you will, of yogic and shamanic experience of the body as phenomenon, just as it is experienced. Such a phenomenology might, for example, flesh-out, refine, reform Alcoholic Anonymous's dictum that belief in "a higher power" is necessary for recovery from addiction. For "higher than the body" might itself be addictive, may leave the person free of drink, but still burdened with addictive traits and personality.

Hocking's Gifford Lectures of 1938 have never been published as they were delivered. A piece in *The Review of Metaphysics*, "Fact, Field, and Destiny," (vol. 11, no. 4 [1958]) develops points in the second series. It's a powerful expression of what might be called religious existentialism, with even a qualified nod to Nietzsche's will to power. Most significantly, taken together with his lectures published as *The Meaning of Immortality in Human Experience*, it might be read as presenting a third view of body, neither *Leib* nor *Körper,* neither body-subject nor body-object, as inchoate (so it seems to me) as it is fascinating.

What if—I may be pressing too hard here—body-subject and body-object are but two aspects of a single energy, a more basic free energy that, gropingly, we might call body-mind? This may be what he is suggesting. Hocking writes: "If the impulse which is I is a 'racial impulse,' there is no reason to ascribe age to it: it is presumably, like energy, always new as on the first day" (SBF, 120–121). Body-self or body-mind as energy always regenerative, always new!? I believe Black Elk would understand instantly and completely. (See "William James, Black Elk, and the Healing Act," in my *The Primal Roots of American Philosophy: Pragmatism, Phenomenology, Native American Thought,* Pennsylvania State University Press, 2000.)

Hocking offers a fascinating piece of speculative metaphysics coupled with some volatile pieces from twentieth-century physics. The world of art-inspired energy and imagination may open onto another system of space-time. How about the tree's world in our picture on the wall! Yes, the possibility boggles the mind, but why not unboggle the mind, try out at least that seemingly impossible possibility? Might absolutely strange transformations occur in a universe that passes through "black holes," say, and through the unmappable domain generally of what we don't know we don't know? Perhaps, as Hocking says, the body is a hinge, a vinculum, that—as body-mind—might take another form in another space-time when its death in the space-time system of this room occurs. There might be a form of immortality.[8]

Couple all this with his general phenomenological, existential, and pragmatic approach to philosophy: what we must posit if life is to be meaningful. He writes in *The Meaning of Immortality:* "To be able to give oneself whole-heartedly to the present one must be persistently aware that it is not all. One must rather be able to treat the present moment as if it were engaged in the business allotted to it by that total life which stretches indefinitely beyond" (MIHE, 155). Might systems of space-time and energy, that most of us today cannot even imagine, have already opened themselves to such passion and commitment? Yes—but of course I don't know.

Hocking is an inspiring explorer, a marvelous antidote to the straitened and desiccated world of most professional philosophy today. Perhaps nothing better sums up the flames and generosities of his heart and mind than his remarks celebrating John Dewey's eightieth birthday:

Ten years ago, when Mr. Dewey was only seventy years old, a session of the Association meeting in this place was devoted to a phase of his philosophy. I seem to remember reading a paper at that session in which I recounted the tragedy of thirty-two years occupied in refuting Dewey while Dewey remained unconscious of what had happened!

I have now a different and happier report to make. Not, I hasten to say, that Dewey has changed, but that I have largely ceased to read him with polemical intent: I read him to enjoy him. In this I succeed far better, in fact I am almost completely successful! Only, the question continues to trouble me whether Dewey, if he knew about this, would regard it as an improvement on my part or as a retrogression. (Hocking 1940, 228)

This exhibits the faith that both philosophers showed in unfettered dialectical exchange no matter where it might lead, the faith in each other, the faith in the world and the beckoning horizons it displays to us, the faith that might yet save humanity from its fear of awareness—its original sin, as Hocking put it—a faith lacking which the prospects are bleak.

NOTES

1. For Marcel's indebtedness to Hocking, see Marcel 54–55. Marcel's image for rumination as tilling soil is found in his introduction to Henry Bugbee's *The Inward Morning*.
2. Trying to express the numinous, mythic, or archetypal meaning of key terms, I capitalize them.
3. Compare Jonathan Edwards, "I often used to sit and view all nature, to behold the sweet glory of God in these things; in the mean time, singing forth, with a low voice my contemplations of the Creator and Redeemer.... it was always in my manner ... to sing forth ... I was almost constantly in ejaculatory prayer."
4. The taproot of value seems to be delight in unfolding our being. Compare Dante: "In every action ... the main intention of the agent is to express his own image; thus it is that every agent, whenever he acts, enjoys the action. Because everything that exists desires to be, and by acting the agent unfolds his being, action is naturally enjoyable" (quoted in Csikszentmihalyi 1993, 191).
5. Hocking retrieves regenerative cycles in his "principle of alternation" (SBF, 404ff). See my *Wild Hunger: The Primal Roots of Modern Addiction* (Lanham, Md.: Rowman and Littlefield, 1998).
6. In the 1920s Hocking recommended to Marvin Farber, a graduate student of his at Harvard, that he study with Husserl and write his dissertation on Husserl's philosophy. Farber subsequently founded the journal *Philosophy and Phenomenological Research* and became known as the foremost Husserl scholar in the United States. See Peter H. Hare, "Marvin Farber," *American National Biography*, vol. 7. Oxford: Oxford University Press, 1999, 707-710.
7. Candace Pert, former chief brain biochemist at the National Institute of Health, writes, "Consciousness isn't just in the head. Nor is it a question of mind over body. If one takes into account the DNA directing the dance of the peptides, [the] body is the outward manifestation of the mind" (quoted in Northrup 1994, 25).

8. Notice below in "Shamanism, Love, Regeneration" how I discuss nonlocality phenomena as they figure in quantum physics. I am not sure that this matches exactly what Hocking means.

WORKS CITED

Csikszentmihalyi, M. 1993. *The Evolving Self.* New York: Harper-Collins.
Dewey, John. 1925. *Experience and Nature.* Indianapolis: Open Court. Reprinted in *The Later Works: 1925–1953,* vol. 1, ed. Jo Ann Boydston. Carbondale: Southern Illinois University Press, 1983.
Edwards, Jonathan. 1959. *Devotions of Jonathan Edwards.* Grand Rapids, Mich.: Baker Book House.
Heidegger, Martin. 1971. *Poetry, Language, Thought.* Trans. A. Hofstadter. New York: Harper and Row.
Hocking, William Ernest. 1940. "Dewey's Concepts of Experience and Nature." *Philosophical Review* 49 (March): 228–244.
———. 1959. "From the Early Days of the '*Logische Untersuchungen.*'" In *Edmund Husserl: 1859–1959,* ed. H. L. Van Breda and J. Taminaux. The Hague: Nijhoff.
James, William. [1911] 1979. *Essays in Radical Empiricism, The Works of William James.* Cambridge: Harvard University Press.
Marcel, Gabriel. *The Philosophy of Gabriel Marcel.* LaSalle, Ill.: Open Court, 1984.
Northrup, Christiane. 1994. *Women's Bodies—Women's Wisdom.* New York: Bantam.

CHAPTER 20

Hocking's Critique of Modernity: Countering Solipsism and Cultivating Solitude

Vincent Colapietro

"The disorder of the human world is at root a metaphysical disorder."
William Ernest Hocking (quoted in Reck 1964, 44)

Introduction

William Ernest Hocking's philosophical project can easily be related to the central concerns of some of the most prominent contemporary philosophers, analytic and otherwise. For example, anyone familiar with his writings who reads, say, Robert Nozick's *Philosophical Explanations,* Charles Taylor's *The Sources of the Self* as well as many of his essays ("Modernity and the Language of Inwardness" or "Use and Abuse of Theory"), Donald Davidson's "Three Varieties of Knowledge," or any number of Paul Ricoeur's books cannot help but see numerous and deep affinities between Hocking and these contemporaries of ours. Of course, the affinities between Hocking and those working out of the rich heritage of classical American philosophy, most notably, John E. Smith, John J. McDermott, John Lachs, Sandra Rosenthal, and Beth Singer, are even greater and deeper still. Moving closer to home (though at the regrettable risk of slighting those not mentioned), anyone conversant with Hocking who then engages the work of Stanley Rosen, Robert Neville, Daniel Dahlstrom, Victor Kestenbaum, or Lawrence Cahoone, would discover important points of contact between Hocking and these members of the department at Boston University.[1] It is easy to imagine Hocking applauding, for instance, the arguments put forth in Rosen's *The Limits of Analysis,* appreciating the analyses of eternity and of the three dimensions of temporal flux presented in Neville's *Eternity and Time's Flow,* endorsing the diagnoses offered in Cahoone's *The Dilemma of Modernity* of our deep cultural pathologies and of their buttressing philosophical fixations. In turning to Hocking, then, I do not suppose myself to be taking flight from the present, or to be cultivating an antiquarian interest, but rather suppose myself to be taking aim with his aid at the very heart of the present.[2]

Toward a Philosophical Recovery of Human Experience in Its Most Vital Forms

Let me lead into Hocking by noting yet another similarity between him and one of those already mentioned. Recently, Stanley Rosen has undertaken a series of lectures based on the premise that "everyday experience provides us with the only reliable basis from which to begin our philosophical reflections" (1995, 41). As Rosen goes on to suggest, philosophy should not only set out from but must continuously return to such experience. The value of our philosophical projects ultimately resides in their contribution to illuminating the totality of human experience (Rosen 1995, 56; cf. Whitehead [1929] 1978, 15).[3] A persistent danger is that a delimited field of human experience is taken to make up the whole of experience; another is that the appeal to personal experience is immediately—and unquestioningly—interpreted to be an appeal to an insular subjectivity. But (to name but three fields) art, science, and religion, each taken in isolation, are delimited fields within an encompassing totality; moreover, the personal transcends the subjective, for the personal is always linked to the interpersonal (or intersubjective).

Accordingly, as philosophers it is to our experience, at once personal and communicable, that we must turn and return. Certainly, not the least of our experiences is that of communication (or communion) with others, of being one with others without ceasing to be other than those others.[4] The communicability of our experience suggests that the personal cannot be equated with the private or subjective nor can the personal be severed from the interpersonal or intersubjective.

(1) The Context Making this Recovery Necessary

To trace out the implications of this insight would, according to William Ernest Hocking, point toward a passage beyond modernity.[5] In fact, nothing else would release us from the otherwise inescapable snares of a solipsistic worldview. The only way of transcending modernity is by overcoming solipsism,[6] and, in turn, the only possibility of overcoming solipsism is by recovering human experience in a more robust form than that acknowledged in the dominant traditions of Western philosophy, including professed empiricists of a traditional stripe (British empiricists such as Locke and Hume or logical empiricists such as Carnap or Ayer). Put positively, we need a *wider empiricism* than that offered by traditional empiricists.[7] Indeed, Rosen's proposal only makes sense if we mean by *experience* something quite different than what Bacon or Locke, Berkeley or Hume, meant by this word. (Of course, Rosen is cognizant of this need.) So, too, the passage beyond the modern privileging of subjectivity demands parting with the modern understanding of experience.[8] It requires a *postmodern* stance (a term Hocking himself used in the preface to the 1963 edition of *The Meaning of God in Human Experience* [xiii]).

Recollecting the ethos of Harvard at the time Whitehead joined him there,

Hocking asserted that the "cleavage [between Sir Charles Snow's 'two cultures'] characteristic of the 'modernity' stemming from Descartes, and imperfectly mended by a series of great unifiers from Spinoza and Leibniz to our own day, was rejected in practice and moving toward philosophical solution" (1959, 509). At the heart of modernity is a cleavage (cf. Cahoone 1988, 19): this unmediated division is constitutive of the very identity of the modern sensibility. One of the paradoxes of modernity, then, is that our identity resides in this division. Hocking points to this division when he proclaims that: "I call modernity the era of thought dominated by the two contrasting aspects of the philosophy of Descartes, the subjective certitude of one's own existence, and the objective certitude of a nature whose process lends itself exhaustively to mathematical expression" (TP, vi). The experiment of modernity (and this is an expression Hocking himself uses regarding this epoch) is one in which solipsism is wed to mechanism. This marriage is ultimately doomed. For a solipsistic vision of the self linked to a mechanistic vision of nature is an untenable and thus unstable position. As it stands, this position underwrites an utterly inexplicable dualism between what is in effect a supernatural self (a self completely alien to nature) and what is in intent a disenchanted nature (a nature utterly estranged from spirit).[9]

As a result of an awareness of the difficulties inherent in this position, one move has been to absorb nature into the self, another to engulf the self in nature. But the loss of the natural world as an objective, impersonal order is no more acceptable than the loss of the human self as an irreducible, efficacious being. Hence, neither dualism nor the corrective of either subjective idealism or reductive naturalism truly marks a passage beyond modernity (see especially TP); rather each one of these types of philosophy is a defining movement *in* and thus moment *of* the modern epoch.

The vision of nature as an objective, impersonal order is not a timeless intuition but an historical experiment and, beyond this, an experimental result. Other ways of envisioning nature have been tried but have not worked nearly as well for the purposes of description and explanation, of prediction and control.[10]

The historical achievement of this effective vision of the natural order is inherently linked to the systematic cultivation of what Hocking called an *empirical conscience*. At the source of the rise of experimental science is the cultivation of an empirical conscience, of respecting the heuristic imperatives to consult our actual experience at critical junctures in our ongoing investigations. But the formation of this conscience was, in deep but largely unnoticed ways, the work of antirationalists, inquirers determined to limit the scope of reason to a much narrower realm than that accorded reason within the premodern periods of Western philosophy.[11] Accordingly, the appeal to experience so decisive for generating the distinctively modern vision of the natural world marked, at once, an advance in our understanding of nature and an impoverishment in our understanding of experience. Moreover, reason's command over nature increased as its own scope decreased.

(2) The Discovery Making the Passage Beyond Modernity Possible

In the last decades of the nineteenth century and the opening ones of the twentieth, the most important figures in the pragmatic movement in the United States devoted themselves to revising the dominant understanding of human experience. But they were not alone in this effort. Indeed, what John E. Smith says in an article entitled "The Reconstruction of Experience in Peirce, James, and Dewey" regarding these three pragmatists might be said with equal justice regarding Royce, Bowne, and Hocking. These American thinkers "were developing a new and broader conception of experience based not on what experience 'must' be if it is to serve the purpose of founding knowledge, but on what actual experience shows itself to be in the course of human life" (Smith 1992, 17; cf. Dewey 1917). In fact, Smith himself makes this very point regarding Hocking in another essay devoted to "The Philosophy of Religion in America" (1970, 162–163).

Human experience in its most vital forms is truly a *vital* affair. That is, it concerns, above all, living, not knowing. In making this point I do not desire to imply a wholesale opposition between the vital and the epistemic. Life need not be a mindless groping, any more than knowledge must be a deadening possession. Indeed, living reflectively (and how can one live reflectively without living inquiringly and, to some extent, knowledgeably?) can be an intensification of life. And if the green of life does all too often fade into the gray of theory, if reflection is life-fleeing rather than life-enhancing, it is not theory or reflection in itself that is at fault. For the sources of this degradation of intelligence, we must look rather to the manner in which reflection is undertaken and to the motives animating and informing our interpretations, inquiries, and analyses.

As the German word *Erlebnis* suggests, experience is what we have *lived through*, and it is also the process of living through a series of distinct but overlapping situations. So understood, experience is primarily a vital process in which the cognitive (or epistemic) is inextricably intertwined with the affective, the volitional, the aesthetic, and so on.[12] Hence, simply to equate experience with a species of knowledge or to consider it only as a factor in the generation of knowledge is, in effect, to adopt a reductionist approach, one in which a complex reality is reduced to a relatively simple matter.[13] Hence, John Dewey stressed that human experience is not first and foremost an epistemic process but rather the continuous, ongoing, and transformative transaction between an organism and its environment. It is, in other words, the life of the organism viewed from a certain angle.

Human experience in its most immediate shape is the singular course, the unique history, of an individual life; as such it is not simply a source of knowledge. But the biological emphasis of the Deweyan approach tends to eclipse the irreducibly personal dimension of human experience (cf. Richard Hocking). In his opposition to subjectivism, Dewey also tends to undercut personalism (cf. Stuhr). Experience in a *biological* sense is a continuous series of life-sustaining interactions between organisms and their environment, whereas in a *biographical* sense (as when you speak of *your* experience or I of *mine*) it is a dramatic sequence of self-shaping encounters with (for the most part) other selves.[14] The encounters by which any self has been shaped are, overwhelmingly, encounters with other selves—so much so that, for example, all of my dealings with my self bear the marks of my encounters with others.[15] Hocking makes this very point with his characteristic simplicity and force when he notes that "social experience is an integral part of individual experience; since individual experience has neither its complete data nor its working tools apart from social interaction" (HNR, 173). The subject of experience is unquestionably an organically embodied self but, *qua* self, an irreducibly personal agency. Herein lies a deep difference between Dewey and Hocking: Dewey's conception of organism is effectively replaced by Hocking's conception of self.[16] Hocking's self *is*, nevertheless, embodied.[17]

Not only is "experience *by* a self, a 'subject,'" it is also "*of* a not-self, an 'object'" (Hocking 1951, 320).[18] In other words, "experience is of 'a world': it is a special sort of *meeting between a self and a world*" (Hocking 1951, 321). Just as experience is, in Dewey's account, *of* as well as *in* nature (Dewey 1925, 12), so for Hocking experience is *of* and *in* a world. Experience itself is a reality in its own right, but it is also a medium of disclosure in which realities other than the self or its experiences are directly encountered. What is revealed by such experience is "a common environment having a persistent character of its own" (Hocking 1951, 321). A common environment is nothing less than a shared world, a world in which I, Thou, and It are equally primordial: there is no I without you and it (cf. Davidson).

In Hocking's account, then, both what C. S. Peirce would call the secondness and thirdness of experience are given their due.[19] The category of secondness points to opposition, confrontation, to one thing being over against another, whereas the category of thirdness points to mediation, intelligibility, to one thing being brought into connection with another by means of some third thing. Experience is an encounter in which irreducibly distinct beings confront one another; herein lies its secondness. But it is not simply a dyadic affair in which brute opposition is the final or even the first word; it is, as Royce no less than Peirce would insist, always a triadic process; herein lies its thirdness. But, like Peirce and unlike either Royce or James, human experience is an irreducibly triadic process in which possibilities of mediation are grounded in the largely unacknowledged actuality of mutual penetration.

So, one reason why Hocking was so fond of quoting Whitehead's assertion ("Hang it all! *Here we are*. We don't go behind that; we begin with it" [see, e.g., Hocking 1961, 505; CWC, 27]) is that he interpreted the force of this assertion in this way: Here we are, i.e., here you *and* I are, where the "here" might designate a common task as well as a shared space. My being *with you here* is not an external juxtaposition, but an interpersonal exchange in which we are truly present to one another. Like Martin Buber and Gabriel Marcel, William Ernest Hocking was a tireless defender of personal presence.[20]

In light of these considerations, it is easy to see that traditional empiricism severely limited the scope of human experience, so much so that such empiricism deserves to be called (as Walter Kaufmann wittily suggests) empiricide. The traditional conception of human experience did so, most often, by identifying experiential data with sensory impressions of an utterly discrete character and, in turn, construing these discrete data as invincibly private contents accessible only to an essentially solitary consciousness.[21] Accordingly, the broader conception could not fail to be a heterodox one (cf. Hocking 1954, 449). But when the orthodox doctrine gives us nothing better than a Procrustean bed into which a complex phenomenon is fitted and thereby mutilated, we have no recourse but to be heterodox empiricists. Heterodoxy here means rejecting the dogma that experience is the ingestion of a totally foreign substance or the dogma that experience is the totally passive submission to an utterly tyrannical reality.

Even so, Hocking insisted that "empiricism, if it means anything, means a certain receptivity toward a content one finds but does not make. There are *data* in experience, and the word *datum* refers not only to material accepted but to a need to accept, an incapacity of our knowing processes to operate without a raw material actually presented as gift" (1956, 60; the use of "gift" in this connection deserves emphasis). Even philosophers who move significantly beyond the narrow understanding of human experience pervading modern thought (philosophers such as Royce) fail in important ways to give experience its due. For example, "Royce's empiricism was [in Hocking's assessment] limited, not only by his voluntarism, but also—and concurrently—by his conception of the individual and the whole range of experience to which this conception applies. We have, he [Royce] maintained, no direct empirical knowledge of ourselves, nor of other minds" (Hocking 1956, 61). Here is the point at which Hocking will most dramatically diverge from his teacher. While the receptivity definitive of experience is slighted by Royce, the directness of our experience of others is quite simply denied by him.

Human experience is at once a passionate affair and a disclosing medium (cf. Smith 1995, chap. 1). Ironically, the epistemologically fixated understandings of experience slight the epistemic reach of experience and, at the same time, overlook the positive role of the passions.[22] In contrast to these, Hocking contends that: "'Experience,' once considered as [nothing but] a process of sense awareness, is now recognized as a process of awareness of the real, not in spite of its inescapable feeling-component but *because* of it! Experience is passion-laden, and the passion in it is not without pertinence to the nature of the world it reports [to which it bears witness]" (CWC, 176). Put more strongly, experience is revelatory of reality *because* it is laden with passion. Passion per se is not necessarily an obstructive or distorting factor, though some particular passions (e.g., uncontrollable lust or rage) are, in their characteristic operation, blinding or benumbing. It is for this reason that Hocking speaks of "the ontological empiricism of feeling" (CWC, 179). It is not his intention to deny the importance of sensory experience but rather to stress the severely limited authority of such experience. Sensory experience cannot legitimately authorize the wholesale negations championed by traditional empiricism. It needs to be seen for what it is: "the empiricism of sense data is but the limiting edge of the widening empiricism of the ontological passions, including those of the lover, the artist, and the prophet, which open the door to reality" (cwc, 185). The ontological passions are thus truly revelatory emotions, not merely subjective responses.[23]

Experience might be taken to be simply a process that naturally occurs. On such a construal, it is as easy as falling off a log. But this approach misses something crucial, something Hocking stresses when he proclaims that "experiencing is an art, not a gift" (1930a, 294). This perhaps draws the contrast too sharply, but the point being made here nevertheless needs to be appreciated. Human experience is a precarious process evolving toward the status of conduct; it both happens to us and is orchestrated by us. Our capacity for experience is, at once, an instinctually rooted ability to learn from our worldly involvements (in this sense it *is* a gift) *and* a set of (more or less) refined skills to cope with and respond to a staggering array of complex situations (in this sense it is an art). "[E]very moment of experience, while meeting its own occasion with the existing equipment, is adding to its equipment for meeting the next occasion!" (1951, 322). In any experience, reality is really but insufficiently encountered.[24] We are ill-equipped to meet what we confront: we are experientially semiliterate, the meanings of our encounters largely escaping us.[25] The task of reflection is not so much to transcend experience as to penetrate it, not to condemn the muteness of reality but to enhance our own ability to read the meaning of our experience.

Experience is, at bottom, a dialogue between the self and the world, in which the other confronting the self always (at least according to Hocking) conveys intimations of personality, however indirectly.[26] Our experience is irreducibly triadic; that is, minimally three terms in ultimately indissoluble union define the structure of our experience. I, Thou, and It are inextricably intertwined in our experience, though the confrontational dimension of human experience prompts us ordinarily to focus on two, rather than three, of the strands woven into the fabric of our experience. Experience concerns the ways we are addressed by impersonal objects as well as personal agents and, moreover, the ways we respond.

The philosophical recovery of personal experience along the lines sketched here suggests that philosophy is always a discourse addressed ad hominem. But such discourse is not only addressed *to* persons; it also is produced *by* them. Hence, it might not be amiss to say something *about* the person being honored in this collection, of which my own chapter is but a part.

What Manner of Man Was He?

"There is," according to W. E. Hocking, "some analogy between philosophy and biography" (1928, 149). In the context of this assertion, the analogy concerns imagination: the philosopher, no less than the biographer, must rely upon imagination to enter into the topic being explored. In other contexts, however, Hocking suggests an even deeper affinity, such that personal existence and philosophical reflection are inextricably intertwined. One such context is the preface to the 1963 edition of *The Meaning of God in Human Experience:* Modernity was unable—or unwilling—to acknowledge "an experience of other selves" and, from this, followed its deeper inability to acknowledge any experience of the divine Other (MGHE, xii). After making this historical claim, Hocking immediately links the historical to the personal: "I had for some time been of the belief that these barriers [between one human self and another as well as between the human and divine self] could be surmounted and that they would fall together. In my own experience they did; this book is to that extent *autobiographical*" (MGHE, xii; emphasis added).[27] From his own philosophical perspective, then, what kind of philosopher Hocking was is connected to what manner of man he was. So it seems appropriate to say a few words about his person. But it is difficult, if not impossible to speak justly about Ernest in isolation from his wife Agnes. So a story or two about her seems pertinent here.

In a collection of pieces entitled *I Knew a Phoenix* and subtitled *Sketches for an Autobiography*, May Sarton (the daughter of George Sarton, the Harvard historian of science) opens Part I ("The Fervent World") with a sketch called "'In My Father's House'" but opens Part II ("The Education of a Poet") with one called "I Knew a Phoenix in My Youth." The fervent world was the world of her parents (see, e.g., 1954, 39), but the education was Sarton's own. The title itself is taken from a poem by W. B. Yeats: "I knew a phoenix in my youth, so let them have their day" (119), but the use to which Sarton puts this image is uniquely her own.

In her sketch of her father, she notes that, as a young man in Ghent, George "wandered, smoking and composing the early romantic books he wrote under the pseudonym of Dominique de Bray, when he thought he would be a poet, and with no idea yet that he would soon be getting a doctorate in celestial mechanics, then leave Belgium forever as a refugee in the 1914–1918 war, and eventually become the first American professor of a new discipline called the History of Science—nor, for that matter, that the poet in him would take root and reappear in his daughter, a generation later" (Sarton 1954, 24). If the roots of her poetic self can be traced to the frustrated hopes of her father's poetic sensibility, she acutely sees that her education as a poet must be traced to a maternal figure of uncharacteristic charm. After recollecting her math, science, and art teachers at the Shady Hill School (assessing them as "magnificent" [111]), Sarton emphatically asserts that none of this was "the very core of the school under Agnes Hocking. For the core of the school and its unique strength lay in the one fact that here poetry was made centrally active" (111). In retrospect, Sarton realizes that Agnes "did not tell us about poetry; she made us live its life" (112). She recalls: "I have seen Agnes Hocking . . . create such a stillness in a hundred or more boys and girls of all ages that they themselves quite clearly heard the silence above the noise of a passing trolley and the crackle of the fire"

(112). She also recollects that one day she and the other students "discovered that Sir William Watson's poem about April, for all its sentimental diction, was absolutely real" (113). While reading

> April, April,
> Laugh thy girlish laughter;
> Then, the moment after,
> Weep thy girlish tears!

a shower fell upon teacher and student, prompting laughter of a distinct cast—"the laughter of recognition." Sarton wonders: "Did Agnes Hocking summon that cloud herself" and confesses that "It would not have surprised us at all if she had" (1954, 113–114). On another occasion students *and* teacher "all became seals, a thing rather easy to do if you are already sitting in a gray woolen bag" (112). While lying on their backs in their bags, the Big Room of the Shady Hill School became an ocean as they murmured:

> Where billow meets billow, there soft be thy pillow;
> Ah, weary wee flipperling, curl at thy ease!
> The storm shall not wake thee, nor shark overtake thee,
> Asleep in the arms of the slow-swinging seas.

Not only did the floor sway like the ocean and the children roll over like seals, but "Mrs. Hocking, also in a gray bag on the floor, was the Seal of Seals!" (112).

Early in her memoir, Sarton also wonders "Why did we [students] believe in our inalienable right to feel like djinn bursting with mysterious power?" (1954, 103). She quickly answers her own question: "this creative state of mind stemmed in those early years from the genius of Agnes Hocking, the school's founder and moving spirit" (103–104). After claiming this, Sarton recollects that:

> Mrs. Hocking was the wife of the philosopher, William Ernest Hocking, and the daughter of the poet, John Boyle O'Reilly; revolutionary blood flowed in her veins. The school was born of this marriage of poetry and philosophy, and though philosophy was worshipped, poetry ruled. Mrs. Hocking never referred to her husband otherwise than as 'Ernest Hocking,' and always with the same intonation, which suggested that she considered him a deity. Once, discovering in the subway station at Harvard Square that she had forgotten her purse, she walked right past the collector, uttering the magic words 'Ernest Hocking will give you five cents tomorrow' and sailed through the wicket. (1954, 104)

Sarton recalls that as a youth at the Shady Hill School, she was acutely aware that "the emphasis on creativity and spontaneous expression was always balanced by a sense of responsibility of each child toward the community, and above all respect not only for the talent in each other, but for the ethical qualities summed up in the word 'citizenship'" (1954, 106).

She also recalls that: "Ernest Hocking, in the early days of the school, [himself] helped keep this balance."

> When some crisis arose, it was he who descended, as it were from Olympus, to tell us a short parable, as we 'gathered to ask the Lord's blessing' and sat on the low wooden benches unusually gravely, mesmerized by that serene smiling presence. Once an outbreak of anarchy rocked the school when a boy and girl from the twelfth grade got into a furious argument and tore up, to use for ammunition, a huge plasticine relief map of Europe that the smaller children had made. After the crime, the atmosphere of the school was funereal for several days, and finally Ernest Hocking, ineffably pink and serene, quietly glowing, drew us gently up from Hell by telling us a short but harrowing tale of two doves who destroyed their [own] nest. I remember the relief with which we, the whole school, watched the two culprits stand, red to the ears, and solemnly shake hands. It seemed beautiful and good beyond words that there was saving grace after all, and we never forgot the bliss of mutual forgiveness as we witnessed it that day. (1954, 106–107)

Let us now recall a recollection by Hocking of his own adolescence, a recollection of a decisive moment in his intellectual development.[28] It concerns an early, illicit affair not of the heart but of the mind. Since the medical practice of Hocking's father "took him out of the office for several hours of each day, the son from the age of around ten "was called upon to take his school books to the office, surrounded by his father's own books, instruments, and drugs (Hocking 1930a, 386). Over forty years later the younger Hocking recalled that:

> I soon began to find an interest in the books of medicine: they became my first independent field of curiosity. I dipped into the forbidden *materia medica.* One experiment in this field bade fair to be costly.... During one of my solitary sessions I undertook to inhale the gas [used at the time to treat pulmonary diseases], and finding the effects pleasant, continued to do so until I lost consciousness. (1930a, 386–387)

From his illicit dabblings and excursions, Hocking lost more than temporary consciousness. To continue with his own account:

> It was partly through this medical browsing that I was prepared to appreciate my first philosopher. In the 'eighties [the 1880s], Herbert Spencer was still the great name in English philosophy. At the moment when reflection came upon

me, I fell under his spell. In our household he was, I promptly learned, a forbidden writer; nevertheless I made my secret way through *First Principles*. As a lad of fifteen I had nothing to oppose to his plausible dialectic. Thoroughly against my will, and with a sense of unmeasured inner tragedy, Spencer convinced me. For years I plodded through his volumes. It was an unmixed discipleship, and so far an experience of great intellectual joy. Spencer had the truth—such modest truth as was to be had. He had written blank mystery over the original splendour of the uncharted world. His view demanded unqualified resignation in the outlook of animal death—to me a sweeping desolation; for I had been seized almost violently with a sense of the uniqueness of individual life and I could hardly endure the thought of annihilation. But Spencer's philosophy explained all things, the extra-beliefs [over-beliefs?] of religion among them, only too well. (1930a, 387)

The spiritual crisis was a defining moment. Hocking was a philosopher who came to philosophy through his encounter with Spencer and who moved beyond Spencer because of his discovery of James (Hocking stresses his hitting upon James's *Principles of Psychology*). It is difficult for us today to appreciate the immense stature of Herbert Spencer in the nineteenth century. His grave in Old Highgate Cemetery, largely hidden by overgrowth, stands opposite that of Karl Marx, a fitting but sad symbol of the obscurity into which he has fallen.

Hence, it is instructive to recall that William James's first publication was a spirited critique of Spencer's definition of mind. The vision of mind (or consciousness) to which James was led by this critique was one for which *he* is duly celebrated and still remembered. In his first publication, "Remarks on Spencer's Definition of Mind as Correspondence," James concluded by stressing that "the knower is not simply a mirror floating with no foot-hold anywhere, and passively reflecting an order that he comes upon and finds simply existing. The knower is an actor" ([1878] 1978, 21). Indeed, "there belongs to mind, from its birth upwards, a spontaneity, a vote. It is in the game, and not a mere looker-on; and its judgment of the *should-be*, its ideals, cannot be peeled off from the body of the *cogitandum* as if they were excrescences, or meant, at most, survival" (24). This vision is reasserted in *The Principles of Psychology*, the work that enabled Hocking to liberate himself from Spencer: "The conception of consciousness as a purely cognitive form of being ... is anti-psychological.... Every actually existing consciousness seems to itself at any rate to be a fighter for ends, of which many, but for its presence, would not be ends at all. Its powers of cognition are mainly subservient to these ends, discerning which facts further them and which do not" ([1890] 1983, 144).

Not only James but also Peirce self-consciously articulated at critical junctures his own philosophical outlook in explicit opposition to Herbert Spencer. In a frequently quoted text from "The Architecture of Theories," Peirce insists that "philosophy requires thorough-going evolutionism or none" (Peirce 1935, 6:14). The halting or incomplete evolutionism against which he is pitting himself is Spencer's doctrine that mechanical laws rigidly determine the evolutionary process. Just as the Spencerian conception of mind forecloses the possibility of mind as truly creative, as an agency by which the novel is brought into being, so the Spencerian vision of evolution limits the possibilities of growth, the trajectories of evolution, to those that are mechanistically foreordained. For Spencer, growth is in the grip of law; for Peirce, the laws of nature are themselves the emergent results of cosmic evolution. Thus, the cosmos is, for Peirce, a scene of irreducible novelty no less than the mind is a source of unpredictable innovation. An evolutionary cosmology uncompromisingly committed to cosmic evolution would insist upon such irreducible novelty, just as an account of mind truly faithful to our experience of our own mindfulness (cf. Desmond) would insist upon such unpredictable innovation.

My own sense is that, though Hocking's vision of the universe was not influenced by Peirce's evolutionism, his vision of mind was a development of James's insistence that consciousness is above all a fighter for ends which, but for the presence of consciousness, would not be ends at all. This is perhaps no more evident than in an essay entitled "Mind and Near-Mind." Though it is was originally presented in 1927 at the Sixth International Congress of Philosophy, this paper has direct relevance to contemporary discussions and unsurpassed insights into the nature of mind. What Hocking observed then might with no modification be said of, say, the most recent developments in cognitive science: "the extant science or sciences of mind have presented us not the mind itself, but substitutes for mind,—systems of objects which are equivalent to mind for certain restricted purposes,—Near-minds, we may call them" (297). To move beyond near-mind and toward what is properly understood as mind, we must not simply conceive of mind as a synoptic or synthesizing capacity but resolutely focus on "particular and salient syntheses" (302). We must note that: "The mind holds together, for example, past, present, and future; it holds together fact and value; it holds together the actual and the possible." The "characteristic activity of the mind" is, according to Hocking, "conceiving a possibility and bringing it to birth." He goes so far as to suggest that "Mind is directed primarily toward the non-existent essence—the thing hoped-for but not seen" (302). Is it possible for anyone familiar with James's writings to avoid hearing echoes of them in these passages from Hocking?

Experiencing our own mindfulnesss and, in turn, minding our experiences define complementary aspects of Hocking's philosophical undertaking. The experience of our own minds, at once direct and irreducible, reveals them to be no passive mirrors; the minding of our own experience in turn reveals it to be no subjective screen interposed between our minds and the world.

But, regarding these crucial matters, the modern sensibility is mindless, not mindful! "Modernity completely failed to resolve the dilemma of 'solipsism'; and with its inability to find an experience of other selves would follow its deeper inability to find an experience of God" (MGHE, xii).[29] The resolution of this dilemma would entail nothing less than (to use Hocking's own expression) the "passage beyond modernity." This "book is to that extent autobiographical" (MGHE, xii; cf. Miller 1978). In recollecting his friendship with Edmund Husserl, dating from 1902, Hocking suggests that "the route one follows, be it direct or tortuous, must always be one's own: in the original passages of thought there is a (frequently unconscious) element of autobiography" (1959, 5). But he is quick to point out that "The central mystery of thought is that the most intensely personal, autobiographical, private—as in Descartes' course of doubt—is potentially the most universal" (6).

Two actual experiences in particular seem to be crucial for Hocking's own efforts in surmounting the alleged barriers between one's one self and other selves (be these other selves either human others or the Divine Other). The first experience is reported in one of the most famous passages in any of Hocking's writings. Before quoting it, however, let me set the stage a bit. Recall that Hocking went to Harvard to study with James.[30] In addition, recall that in the most famous chapter of *The Principles of Psychology*, the one devoted to "The Stream of Thought," James boldly asserted:

> Each mind keeps its own thoughts to itself. There is no giving or bartering between them. No thought even comes into direct *sight* of a thought in another personal consciousness than its own. Absolute insulation, irreducible pluralism, is the law. It seems as if the elementary psychic fact were not *thought* or *this thought* or *that thought*, but *my thought*, every thought being owned. Neither contemporaneity, nor proximity in space, nor similarity of quality and content are able to fuse thoughts together which are sundered by this barrier of belonging to different personal minds. The breaches between such thoughts are the most absolute breaches in nature. Everyone will recognize this to be true, so long as the existence of *something* corresponding to the term 'personal mind' is all that is insisted on, without any particular view of its nature being implied. ([1890]1983, 221; Colapietro 1989)[31]

In the report of his own experience, Hocking begins by echoing the Jamesian thesis but then interjects, quite jarringly, a radical doubt regarding our psychic insularity, our absolute insulation. In a manner recalling James, Hocking confesses that he has "sometimes sat looking at a comrade, speculating on the mysterious isolation of self from self" (MGHE, 265). Such speculation prompted him to ask:

> Why are we so made that I gaze and see of thee only the Wall, and never Thee? This Wall of thee is but a movable part of the Wall of my world; and I also am a Wall to thee: we look out at one another from behind masks. How would it seem if my mind could but once be within thine; and we could meet and without barrier be with each other? (MGHE, 265)

In response to his own question, however, he offered this startling answer:

> And then it has fallen upon me like a shock—as when one thinking himself alone has felt a presence—But I *am* in thy soul. These things around me are in thy experience. They are thy own; when I touch them and move them I change *thee*. When I look on them I see what thou seest; when I listen, I hear what you hearest. I am in the great Room of thy soul; and I experience thy very experience. For *where art thou?* Not there, behind those eyes, within that head, in darkness, fraternizing with chemical processes. Of these, [even] in my own case, I know nothing, and will know nothing; for my existence is spent not behind my Wall, but in front of it. I am there, where I have treasures. And there art thou, also. . . . I can imagine no contact more real and thrilling than this; that we should meet and share identity, not through ineffable inner depths (alone), but here through the foregrounds of common experience; and that thou shouldst be—not behind that mask—but *here*, pressing with all thy consciousness upon me, *containing* me, and these things of mine. This is reality: and having seen it thus, I can never again be frightened into monadism by reflections which have strayed from their guiding insight. (MGHE, 265–266)[32]

The second experience is reported in his preface to Gabriel Marcel's book on Royce's metaphysics. It is the experience of having one's own experience accredited by another whom one deeply respects. Hocking recalls that, in an essay submitted to Royce during his last year of graduate study at Harvard, 1903–1904,

> I ventured to differ from one of his central doctrines, namely, that we have no direct knowledge either of our own minds or of other minds. For, as he held, selves are individuals; and individuals are beings such that, for each one, there can be in the whole universe no other precisely like it: this is what we mean by our individual attachments. Such uniqueness can be no matter of empirical knowledge: it is rather a matter of will: 'it is thus that the mother says, There shall be no other child like my child' (*World and Individual*, 458–460), ergo no possible substitution, no recompense for loss. In this particular essay, I reported an experience in which, as I read it, I was directly aware of another mind and my own as co-knowers of a bit of the physical world, a 'Thou' and 'I' as co-knowers of an 'It.' (1956, vii-viii)

After submitting this essay, Hocking was expecting "a radical criticism from my revered professor" (1956, viii). What he received instead was Royce's comment, as he pointed to the dissenting passage upon handing back the essay, "'This is your insight: you must adhere to that!' Without assenting to my view, he had given me his blessing for its development" (viii).

The courage to attend to our own experience, to accredit its authority sufficiently and thus to probe its depths unstintingly—such courage—is not a solitary achievement. We are encouraged by others or, tragically, discouraged to have such courage. We can distrust our experience to the point where its disclosures are overlooked. We can even perpetuate a social hallucination by disregarding the direct disclosures of our personal experience. Is this not the moral of the folk tale regarding the emperor's new clothes? Hocking as a student made polemical use of his direct experience of the personal presence of another self: he appealed to this experience in order to refute his teacher Josiah Royce, according to whom selves are neither perceived data nor conceived universals but rather interpreted. He did so in a term paper during his last year as a graduate student (cf. Robinson 1966). I hope that it is not too obvious to point out that May Sarton's experience at the Shady Hill School was analogous to William Ernest Hocking's experience in one of his graduate seminars (recall Sarton 1954, 103–104). In an article entitled "On Royce's Empiricism," Hocking recollects that "It was Max Otto of [the University of] Wisconsin, himself an uncompromising truth-seeker, who remembered that Royce had once told him [Otto] that he wanted to give his students 'a small plot of ground on which they could set their feet'" (1956, 57). As a graduate student Hocking staked a large piece of ground, and Royce replied by saying that he must adhere to his insight, though it contradicted a central tenet of Royce's own philosophical idealism. Lest anyone suppose that I am advocating a one-sidedly affirmative approach to pedagogy, let me quote approvingly Hocking's own insistence in *Man and the State* that "the new idea is seldom fitted at birth for a public career; its needs to win its substance and its spurs, through being tossed about in the tempered ruthlessness of friendly give-and-take" (MATS, 260).

The nub of Hocking's criticism of Royce's position is that, if Royce is correct, then "we are still left with only an inference of the Other; a faith and not *a knowledge in experience*" (MGHE, 249; emphasis added). But such an inference and faith are insufficient to account for our experience of encountering others, of being with them in an intimate and interpenetrating manner. Our knowledge of other selves is, at least on Hocking's account, rooted in a *direct* experience of their personal presence. Such experience provides a unique species of human knowledge. We are *with* others in such an intimate and inextricable way that "if a pure solitude is possible, it is perpetual. Experience is always and necessarily social, or never—these are our alternatives" (MGHE, 282). "In order that any two beings should establish communication, they must already have something in common" (MGHE, 272; emphasis omitted). Any communicative exchange is always the realization of an antecedent community, however implicit and inchoate this community might be.[33]

The language of interiority or inwardness cannot be simply dismissed or discarded, but it needs to be used only with the utmost care (MGHE, 379). Our direct experience of personal presence is an encounter of something *not* fully present, *not* finally disclosed, but always suggestive of (to use the Jamesian expression) an "ever not yet." The self as creative entails that our experience of any self (including our own selves!) is always partial and (in important respects) superficial. Hocking's attunement to the mystery of the person was, more than anything else, his motivation for identifying himself as a mystic. The mystic realizes that, in actual fact, solipsism does not need to be surmounted but rather solitude needs to be cultivated: the mystic, like the child looking upon the nearly naked emperor, sees plainly the self apart from objects and other selves.

What Manner of Reflection Was His?

Hocking's passage beyond modernity is both a movement beyond the dualisms definitive of this epoch (above all, the dualism of subjectivity and objectivity) and a transformation of reflection, including the manner of reflection characteristic of the philosopher. Thus, his distinctive manner of philosophical reflection along with his defining philosophical commitments deserves careful attention here.

Hocking's philosophical outlook has been identified in various ways. In an early treatment, W. H. Werkmeister identified it as "individualistic idealism" (1949), while more recently and accurately Andrew J. Reck has called it "empirical idealism" (1964, 42). Early on Hocking himself confessed that: "I know not what name to give to this point of convergence [in my own thinking], nor does name much matter: it is realism, it is mysticism, it is idealism also, [but] its identity, I believe, [is] not broken" (MGHE, xix–xxx). The sense in which Hocking was an idealist is that he took the universe to be a universe rather than a multiverse, a totality rather than a miscellany. It is not utterly inappropriate, and, in some ways, it is a philosophical imperative to conceive of this totality as a self. Though the human self is "an imperfect image of the whole cosmos" (TP, 316), the failure to leave uninterpreted the totality of things amounts to nothing than the suicide of reason (TP, 313, 315). Thus, for Hocking "the world is a self." He explains that: "The ultimate evidence for the selfhood of the whole is not primarily the evidence of argument . . . nor of analogy, but that of immediate experience, interpreted by the dialectic. We, as a group of human selves, know that we are not alone in the universe: that is our first and persistent intuition" (TP, 316). Herein lies the principal basis for his identification with the idealistic tradition.

But Hocking also identifies himself as a realist. For he is committed to the view that "We must treat things in the day's work as if they were independent [of us and our activities], naturalistic, over against us and a*gainst* us, or at least, not for us" (TP, 318). But he qualifies this realism as mystical. His reason appears to be that mystics are persons who experience the unity of their lives with what is most important and real. They do not live in exile from the cosmos. For mystics, then, reality in its fullness is always accessible where they are; they are *in medias res*, but in such a way as to be in intimate, sustaining union with the ground and goal of their own existence. Mystics can labor with endless resources and patience for what may yet be, though only far off in the future; for they know that the nature of things are with them.[34] So in the concluding chapter of *Types*, entitled "Confessio Fidei," Hocking affirms that "I believe in a mystical realism, which is the only tenable sort of realism" (TP, 318).

In addition to his identification with idealism, realism, and mysticism in the respects indicated, the defining commitments of Hocking's philosophical outlook include not only a widened empiricism (a topic discussed at length above) but also negative pragmatism, inductive metaphysics, a carefully stated set of *"second* principles." Each of these, including Hocking's modifications of empiricism, deserve comment here.

Negative Pragmatism

In 1912, Hocking observed that: "The pragmatic test has meant much in our time as a principle of criticism, in awakening the philosophic conscience to the simple need of fruitfulness and moral effect as voucher of truth" (MGHE, xxiii). For Hocking, however, the only viable form of this critical principle is a negative one: Negative pragmatism, as he called it, is the principle that "'That which does not work is not true.' The corresponding positive principle, 'Whatever works is true,' [he regarded] ... as neither valid nor useful" (MGHE, xxiii). In Hocking's estimation, positive pragmatism does not work, therefore it is not true!

Inductive Metaphysics

Metaphysics cannot undertake to present a comprehensive system composed of necessary inferences from self-evident principles. It is a much more groping, tentative, experimental undertaking than the deductivist systems of so many traditional metaphysicians would ever suggest. Metaphysics is inductive in that it sets out from experience, but its commitment to experience does not entail a rejection of the a priori. For Hocking, then, "the best verification is to arrive at an insight. Hence 'ways of seeing' may naturally adopt 'ways of groping' as subsidiary tools whose destiny is to give way to perceptions" ("Outline-Sketch," 254). Hocking thinks that it is reasonable to hope that the empirical might lead to the a priori: "For the seeing we speak of is not mere perceiving that something is [or just happens to be the case], but also discerning that it must be" (254).

Hocking's metaphysical categories are thus "all empirical inductions from human experience" (Reck 1964, 66). His three principal categories are fact, field, and destiny. There are obdurate data which cannot be gainsaid; hence, Hocking subsumes them under the category of *fact*. These facts are not only obdurate but also connected in countless ways to one another. No single fact is encountered or, beyond this, known in complete isolation from other facts. The relatedness of facts to one another constitutes *fields*, exemplified by space and time. Whereas we describe both facts and their relationships to one another, the description of facts can in some measure be a movement toward explanation; for we partially explain something by relating it to something else, that is, by tracing out the patterns of particular connection with a field of encompassing relationships. At the very least, such descriptions invite explanation.

For Hocking there is a field of fields inclusive of all that is. This is the Absolute, since it is not related to anything outside of itself and, thereby, not conditioned by anything other than itself. The Absolute as the totality of all things cannot be viewed as either miscellaneous or impersonal. The intimations of ever wider and deeper unity suggested to Hocking that the totality of things is something more than a miscellany. In addition, the felt presence of not only a sustaining but a creative Thou within the innermost recesses of his own personal consciousness convinced him that the human condition is not one of cosmic solitude (TP, 316). The field of fields can be discerned as nothing less than an absolute Self who is the creative source of all other selves and, indeed, of all finite things. For reasons not at all clear and thus not convincing to me, Hocking maintained that "whatever creates a self can only be a self" (1956, 37). This precludes the possibility of emergence.

The world as a whole has a meaning (Reck 1964, 42). Moreover, the world both as a totality in all of its unity and as an unimaginably complex array of irreducibly unique particulars has a creative, not merely sustaining, source. The ultimate intelligibility of the world required, for Hocking, a divine creator of that world. For the presence of finite selves can only be traced to a principle of divine selfhood; and the failure to explain this presence would be a fatal flaw in any philosophical system, especially one put forth by a finite self!

Just as the relationships of facts to one another yields the inductive category of field, and the inclusion of narrower fields within wider ones ultimately leads to the metaphysical conception of a field of fields, so the understanding of this all-inclusive, self-conditioned field in terms of selfhood yields the (allegedly) inductive category of *destiny*. Though Hocking originally went to Harvard to study with James, the influence of Royce's absolute idealism was more profound than that of James's radical pluralism. As James and Royce sitting on a stone wall in New Hampshire were waiting to have their photograph taken, the puckish James tried to make Royce laugh by his famous outburst "Damn the Absolute!" (for reproductions of this photograph, see Meyers 2001, page following 306; Rouner 1969, 29). Hocking, however, was disposed to defend rather than to damn the central idea of the dialectical tradition with which he most deeply identified. This is evident in numerous places and ways but perhaps nowhere more vividly than in the manner in which Hocking's *Coming World Civilization* (1956) echoes Royce's *The Philosophy of Loyalty*. Royce proclaimed in explicit opposition to Jamesian pragmatism that while truth does indeed mean "the fulfillment of a need," "we all need the superhuman, the city out of sight, the union with all life,—the essentially eternal" (Royce 1916, 346). He goes on to say that: "This need is not invention of the philosophers."[35] Hocking staunchly maintains: "Human purpose ... acquires the sense of bringing something to pass which apart from this, our finite act, would simply not exist" (1956, 184). Such purpose "takes the shape of a creative task within a process having an affirmative and universal goal in history, even though the city to be built, already present in its conspectus—*universus hic mundus jam una civitas*—is still in its architecture out of sight." This goal was Hocking's category of destiny, expressed here more robustly and confidently than in the cautious formulations in "Fact, Field, and Destiny."

Widened Empiricism

Hocking was a robust empiricist, so much so that (as we have just noted) Andrew Reck (1964) characterizes his philosophical outlook as "empirical idealism," and Hocking himself asserts that "God is to be known in experience if at all" (MGHE, 229). In fact, "Everything that is worth knowing about the world, including metaphysical knowledge, is to be known in experience; for experience is metaphysical—it is dealing with reality. This does not exclude a priori knowledge, for experience contains a priori elements which subsequent reflection brings to light. Thus a priori knowledge is the last in the order of time to be recognized and isolated" (1930a, 394).

"We have too long," Hocking contends, "identified the empirical with the itemized, the separate, the plural aspects of experience," an allegedly subjective experience at that (1958, 545). Experience is "an interplay between an active Self and an active External Reality" (MGHE, 285). My self "carries on a spontaneous self-projection, a running-ahead in anticipation of experience; and no experience can come to me which is not an answer to certain organic questionings set out to receive events" (MGHE, 285).

"But empiricism, if it means anything, means," Hocking insists, "a certain receptivity toward a content one finds but does not make." He adds: "There are *data* in experience and the word *datum* refers not only to material accepted but to a need to accept, an incapacity of our knowing processes to operate without a raw material actually presented as gift. There must be a prior docility before there can be construction" ("On Royce's Empiricism" in Hocking 1956, 60). It is inadequate to characterize Hocking's reconstruction of experience simply as a widened empiricism, for it is also a deepened perspective; moreover, it is not only enlarged in terms of depth as well as scope but also is reconceived in its innermost character. At the heart of experience is not a causal nexus but a communicative exchange, a point to which we have already called attention and one to which we will return.

Second Principles

In "Some Second Principles," Hocking's contribution to *Contemporary American Philosophy: Personal Statements*, he suggests that "Second principles remain for our philosophy more wieldable than the first principle [or any allegedly exhaustive list of first principles], and on the whole more useful, provided always that they are *well known to be second*" (1930a, 399). (Is it possible to dissociate this modest emphasis on some second principles from Hocking's disaffection with the partly concealed arrogance of Spencer's *First Principles?*) After offering an instructive sketch of his intellectual development, Hocking confesses that "There is something about thinking which dissolves away its historical roots, even to the personal knowledge of the thinker" (1930a, 393). So he breaks off his narrative of his development and offers, albeit reluctantly, a small set of second principles. His reluctance is rooted in a warning from his daimon that "the thing is bound to be a set of rough logs rather than a building"; even so, he sets "down some of the views to which he has come, simply as materials for a philosophy. For the most part, they are not provable; nor are they in any general sense axiomatic" (1930a, 393). But they are for Hocking *personally* axiomatic.

These second principles are ambiguous simplicity, initial empiricism, inclusive rationalism, tentative mysticism (explorative pluralism), union of fact and value (the *fact* of value as well as value of fact). *The principle of ambiguous simplicity* is, in effect, a denial of metaphysical atomism. The "task of analysis is never done; and were we to depend on it for our bearings we should necessarily despair of any result" (1930a, 393). Complex phenomena manifest a simplicity, just as the most rudimentary elements of any successful analysis are themselves in some respects complex. That is, any complex reality is in certain respects simple, whereas even the simplest units are in some ways complex. Herein lies the ambiguity of simplicity. "Atomism is a necessary expedient in physics; in philosophy it is a will-o'-the-wisp. There are no indivisible units of the world"; there are no absolute simples. What is true of things in general is, of course, true of selves in particular. So, this second principle has special relevance to the question of solipsism.

Second, *the principle of initial empiricism* is that everything worth knowing is to be known through experience. What makes this empiricism initial rather than ultimate? In explaining this principle, Hocking quietly marks his opposition to both James and Royce. In unannounced opposition to James, he asserts that "from the first experience presents wholes as well as parts. Empiricism cannot consist, then, in going from the parts to the whole. Empirical knowledge grows from a sketch" (Hocking 1930a, 394). Of course, it was James who contrasted empiricism and rationalism by insisting that the lover of facts goes from the parts to the whole while the champion of reason proceeds from the whole to the part. Again, in implicit opposition to Royce (opposition elsewhere stated quite directly and forcefully), Hocking observes that "There are many thinkers who feel obliged to be Kantian with regard to our social experience who are not Kantian anywhere else." They feel this obligation because they assume that any "other mind than our own is not given, and in the nature of the case cannot be given. We can only *interpret* our world as social, imposing upon its plain, natural stuff, object *for me* [emphasis added], the new category of other-observers, so that nature becomes *object for us*" [emphasis in original]

(1930a, 396). There is, from Hocking's perspective, a complex interplay between the experiential and the a priori. He even insists that the a priori is ordinarily not prior in the order of explicit knowledge, for the a priori is likely the last thing to be arrived at (Hocking 1961, 513). Inductive steps and dialectical maneuvers support each other in helping us move toward a vision of the whole (TP, 316). Again, this second principle has special relevance to our principal concern, for it demands that we give our initial experience of other selves in its full weight.

Third, the *principle of inclusive rationality* means that while experience has the first and instigating word, "reason has the last and inclusive word" (Hocking 1930a, 396). "It is necessary to leave the realm of 'facts' in order to derive facts" (Hocking 1951, 335). In other words, the brute facticity of experiential data is not the final word. Facts are, to be sure, accorded categorial status in Hocking's metaphysical "system."[36] The obduracy of fact needs to be acknowledged philosophically, but so does the intelligibility of facts, especially when they are located in fields and, moreover, when the trajectories inherent in some of these fields evolve to the point of having the status of a destiny. The obduracy of facts cannot be gainsaid (Reck 1964, 45). For Hocking, nothing short of the Absolute as an all-inclusive and self-sufficient domain can render facts fully intelligible. The Absolute is the field of fields within which facts are encountered and destinies unfolded. It is best rendered intelligible when interpreted as a self. The matrix of finite, conditioned selves is, accordingly, an infinite, unconditioned Self.

"It is, indeed, impossible, as Spencer alleges, to avoid assuming self-existence somewhere. But it is an error to suppose, as this proposition suggests, that it is a matter of complete logical indifference where you assume self-existence" (Hocking 1930a, 397).[37] To assume that experiential fidelity requires us to accept submissively experiential data or that natural piety demands us to accept blindly natural facts is to deny human reason its defining hope: "The understandableness of things is a necessary assumption" (1930a, 396) not a pathetic pretension.

Since Hocking's commitment to this particular principle of inclusive reason is both so central to his philosophical project and so at odds with many contemporary tendencies, it bears fuller comment than his other second principles. Reason cannot rest content with description nor even explanation; it must drive toward understanding. Note that there is a triadic hierarchy here: description, explanation, and understanding. In practice, there are no hard and fast boundaries between any of these pairs. As Hocking notes, "Exact description always does more than describe; it yields a measure of 'explanation'" ("Outline-Sketch of a System of Metaphysics," 251). "Understanding is the perception of meaning" (252). "Metaphysics must postulate that the world is not meaningless: it is fact, but not 'mere fact'" (252). Not *mere* nor *brute* nor *dumb* properly modify fact, philosophically conceived. "Fact . . . receives in common speech the resentful title of 'brute fact.' As it first presents itself, it is certainly not brute: it is the measure of our vitality" (Hocking 1950, 6). For a living being, especially one of highly varied susceptibilities, the factual order is a finely differentiated field in which ever more nuanced discriminations and inclusive configurations than the initial distinctions drawn and patterns traced by this being are intimated by its own vital involvements. Fact "becomes brute only if it remains to the end *dumb*. To end, as we must begin, with a simple acceptance of fact is, for philosophy, prudent, plausible, comradely, and fatal. It is to accept, not merely the universe, but the opacity of the universe" (1950, 6). Philosophy is an experiment in articulation. The alleged bruteness of facts is, in the end, more of a reflection of our dumbness (in a twofold sense: lack of penetrating intelligence and also of our discursive failures) than of anything else.

The drive toward radical understanding pushes toward a recognition of irreducible creativity. In order to explain reality, principles of conservation and of alteration are insufficient; nothing less than a principle of creativity is needed. An account of the universe that limits itself to explaining the conservation of what exists is inadequate, for what we encounter changes not merely in the sense of mutations compatible with conservation but also in the sense of the real emergence of radical novelty. Only one that seeks a principle of generation or creativity will approximate adequacy. Reality comes to be identified with creativity: the real is not so much what is other than us but what is dramatically in process of becoming other than itself. For the "criterion of reality is creativity, both for the world and for the individual" (MIHE, 243). "[T]hat which only conserves cannot so much as explain its own presence in the universe" (MIHE, 245). "[T]hat which is in nature self-conserving ... must be ontologically secondary to that which in its nature creates.... Only what creates can be real" (Hocking 1959, 280). But, here as in all other inquiries, we must turn to experience in order to understand the meaning of our terms and the force of our assertions. "We need an example of creativity in action. Does experience supply any such example?" (1959, 280) Hocking contends that it does, in particular, in the action of selves. To become *other than* a socially conditioned self is to win the solitude requisite for the higher forms of human sociality; in turn, to become other than a narcissistically preoccupied self is to win the connectedness with others so important for the deeper forms of human solitude. Given these two points, the relevance of this principle to our topic should be obvious.

Fourth, the *principle of tentative mysticism* is that our conception of any object but especially of the totality is never adequate to that object or the whole (Hocking 1930a, 397). The "obverse of this tentative mysticism" is a commitment to *"explorative pluralism"* (397; emphasis in original): "just in so far as the One eludes definitive characterization, the sphere of the clearly definable remains plural and open towards future experience" (397–398). "No one can pass judgment on the value of existence without considering the report of the genuine mystic" (400). The other whom we encounter is never able to be grasped or known, once and for all. The other ever eludes our characterization just as we always experience this other as other but also as a being in whom we dwell.

Fifth and finally, there is the principle proclaiming the *union of fact and value*.

On the one hand, our values and valuations are themselves facts with complex linkages to our actual circumstances. On the other hand, facts are highly valued. The discovery of good has mainly two conditions: "First, a rather ruthless and uncompromising objectivity of mind"; "Second, a conscious recovery of the practical presuppositions which live in the 'subconsciousness'" (Hocking 1930a, 399). Since this principle is of less immediate relevance to our main topic, it suffices simply to note it.

The extent to which Hocking is an inheritor of the rich resources of modern philosophy should be evident from this survey of his manner of reflection. But his crucial departures from some of the first principles of modern philosophy, especially as encountered in the inaugural texts of René Descartes, should be equally manifest. To these departures we now turn.

"The Passage Beyond Modernity"

Hocking himself conceived his project to be one of transcending the problematic of modernity. In "ordinary human communication" we witness nothing less than "an experience of receiving-and-invading in which the solitary I-think of Descartes becomes the We-think—so simply [and effortlessly] that we fail to note the momentous transition" (TP, 309; cf. MGHE, xii). The way that the I emerges out of the You-and-I (i.e., the We) is, if anything, even more primordial than the way the I carrying on the task of its own meditations takes the form of the We. Phenomenological attention to these momentous transitions points toward another transition: in Hocking's own phrase, they indicate the direction in which the "passage beyond modernity" becomes possible.

In the chapter of *Types* entitled "The Rebirth of Philosophy," Hocking alleges that: "If our interpretation of the present era is correct, we *have experienced* . . . the dissolution of the characteristic outlook of what we call 'modernity,' the period governed by the antithetical insights of Descartes" (TP, 311; emphasis added). Part of Hocking's task is to make manifest the import of this experience, to win in reflective consciousness what we have actually lived through in our cultural lives. Descartes's antithetical insights are, first, his radical affirmation of the finite self and, second, his mechanistic vision of the natural world.[38] The only way *beyond* the epoch defined by these antitheses is, however, by going *through* them; and in turn the only way through them is to push them to their own *inherent* extremes: in the disarray of modernity is to be found not only its dissolution but also its solution. "That solution could come only through pursuing each antithetical insight to its limit, until subjectivity, finding inter-subjectivity at its center, could rejoin objectivity" (TP, 312). It is only through descending to the depths that the solution takes shape and thus becomes recognizable. But this descent took time. It also defined our time and, to a significant degree, still defines it, for the passage beyond modernity is not yet complete.

In *What Man Can Make of Man*, Hocking observes that: "Like every other historic epoch this modern period has had to work out its principles with great leisureliness, seeing what they mean in terms of what they lead to. Scholars think things out in hours [or days or weeks or years or at most decades]; man's experience thinks them out in centuries" (WMCMM, 9). Modernity is at bottom an experiment. Unlike the explicit, intentional strivings so characteristic of modern science and, more generally, modern life, modernity itself is, in its encompassing significance, an unintentional experiment (CWC, 4; cf. 41). Experience is given an insurmountably subjectivist interpretation, whereas reality is given a reductively naturalistic interpretation (because reality is equated with nature, and, in turn, nature is given a thoroughly mechanistic meaning). The self apart from others and even its own body is presumed to be an omnicompetent knower; humanity apart from God, humanity as nothing but a part of nature, is likewise presumed to be either fully intelligible or ultimately unintelligible due to the absurdity of the universe itself. There are presumed to be absolute or impenetrable barriers between one self and another. In addition, there are limits to the sense we can make of things; provisional, piecemeal meaning is always possible, whereas unconditional, inclusive sense is ever out of our reach. So modernity is, as we have already stated in other ways, the shotgun marriage of solipsism and naturalism (cf. Reck 1964, 44).

To recall another one of Hocking's characterizations of modernity, it is "the era of thought dominated by the two contrasting aspects of the philosophy of Descartes, the subjective certitude of one's own existence, and the objective certitude of a nature whose process lends itself exhaustively to mathematical expression" (TP, vi). In the opening chapter of *What Man Can Make of Man*, W. E. Hocking asserts that: "Man's self-consciousness is an active destiny, partly a magnet luring him toward what he thinks he is, partly a lash driving him to self-change" because of a critical sense of what he is *not* (WMCMM, 3). Modernity is an epoch of reflexivity, an era in which the exigencies and authority of self-consciousness become part of a *self-conscious* destiny. Hocking concludes the opening chapter of *What Man Can Make of Man* by contending that "everyone knows, not by rumor but by introspection, that modern man is tired of himself" (WMCMM, 7). The sense of modernity's dissolution is not hearsay but experience: it is a felt condition of the modern psyche. Chapter 2 of that work is entitled "Modernity Ushers Itself Out." How this occurs is via the experience of modernity itself, an experience that brings into the focus of our attention our experience of others.

"The conception of companionship is possible only if there is somewhere the actual experience thereof. *Solipsism is overcome, and only overcome when I can point out the actual experience* which gives me the basis of my conception of companionship" (CWC, 35). "But no type of inference, however direct and simple, can meet our requirement; for that which we must infer is one step from immediate experience" (MGHE, 250). Hence, Royce is wrong about how we know others: it is not through interpretation that we obtain access to others, for what interpretation actually achieves is never more than gaining fuller access to the significance of our own experience of, or encounter with, others. Interpersonal involvement is a primordial datum, an irreducible phenomenon. ("Hang it all! *Here we are*. We don't go behind that; we begin with it.")

For Hocking, then, solipsism can only be surmounted phenomenologically. But the surmounting of solipsism does not carry a devaluation of solitude. Quite the contrary. Solitude must be painstakingly cultivated. Hocking insists that "This present existence ... is an apprenticeship in creativity. At the same time (and as part of the same fact) we acquire the power of solitude, jutting out into the alone—alone perhaps even with reference to God" (MGHE, 299). But it is important to feel the full force of Hocking's own emphatic distinction: *"we do not begin as solitary beings and then acquire community: we begin as social products, and acquire the arts of solitude"* (MGHE, 299). Hocking connects these arts with worship and further connects the experience that they yield with the mystic. "Worship must be always in some measure, as Plotinus puts it, a flight of the Alone to the Alone" (MGHE, 329). "A philosophy of mysticism would be a philosophy of worship" (MGHE, 349). There is of course no reason to connect these arts of worship with one religion or a tightly knit family of historical faiths. Indeed, it is important to resist such a reduction.

Mystics are, as we have already noted, ones who experience themselves to be in medias res but nonetheless in the most intimate contact with the ground and goal of their existence. But this experience is not so much given as it is won by disciplined practices of meditative attention. "Solitude ... is," for Hocking, "the essence of mysticism: and ... the basis of its supreme social importance" (MGHE, 403). "Mysticism in its true character is precisely *the redemption of solitude:* it is the process which enters one step farther than we have yet explored into the heart of our own infinite subjectivity" (MGHE, 404).

These points return us to one of Hocking's most important self-descriptions. "I believe in a mystical realism, which is the only tenable sort of realism" (TP, 318; cf. Hocking 1961, 516). As a realist, Hocking insists that: "We must treat things in the day's work as if they were independent, naturalistic, over against us and *against us*, or at least, not for us" (1961, 318). But, in identifying himself as a *mystical realism*, Hocking was obviously not aligning himself with reductive naturalism or mechanistic materialism. He was calling for a transfiguration of nature herself. Hence, he speaks of transfigured naturalism (1961, 319), a vision of Nature inclusive of Spirit as source and soul of the totality. The totality might compress itself into a moment, and this compression might be experienced by the individual in her solitude. Such is, in Hocking's account, the essence of mysticism. Given this understanding, it is not hard to see why he maintains that solitude is the essence of mysticism. Such solitude, however, has sociality as a condition of its own emergence; moreover, it has a community of autonomous selves as one of its possible trajectories.

On the one side, we find Feuerbach, Marx, and Nietzsche; on the other, Augustine, Royce, and Hocking. Feuerbach, Marx, and Nietzsche are atheists who contend that, within the deepest depths of divinity, we find nothing but reflections

[269]

of our own human selves. Their opponents assert that, within the most interior recesses of our own psyches, we find an Other at once threatening and sustaining, a source of law and also of life. From the first viewpoint, the divine other is no other at all, but an unacknowledged projection of finite human traits and roles stripped of their finitude and imperfections. From the other perspective, human solitude is always transitory and indeed ever an achievement, whereas an original solipsism to be transcended is always only an illusion of apartness. Solipsism is surmounted by acknowledging the Thou ever within us, whereas solitude is achieved only by cultivating, alternately, defining attachments and centering moments of perfect detachment. The self-enclosed consciousness of fanatics makes us aware of the extent to which solitude is "the home of stagnant growths and morbid consciousness" (MGHE, 403). But the solitude sought by the mystic is a transformative encounter with an irreducible Other: "his intention is that his absolute Object [which is not an Object at all but a Thou] shall gain strength pari passu with his entrance into himself" (MGHE, 403–404). Our spiritual health depends significantly upon a resolute will to cultivate a silence and apartness with which few individuals today are at all comfortable. The wisdom of Hocking's own words on this matter invites quotation: "We cannot live well, I judge, unless there is something in our lives which offers us from time to time the possibility of absolute detachment and solitude.... The mystic is simply the person who does consciously and with the whole man that which we all are doing spontaneously and in fragmentary fashion in every moment of our effective living" (MGHE, 404).

Conclusion

Near the conclusion of *What Man Can Make of Man* Hocking asks, When humans fall back on devising myths, do they not thereby show themselves to be despairing of reason? Of course, Plato's recourse to myths is central to his own discourse. One might even claim that in the *Discourse on Method*, Descartes slyly opens with a personal narrative as a crucial part of a case for the authority of mathematical reason against the pretensions of narrative discourse. Both examples suggest that the relationship between *mythos* and *logos* is not one of simple opposition, a point keenly appreciated by Hocking. He answers his own question by asserting that recourse to myth is unavoidable: "Myths there must be, since visions of the future [connected with prophecy] must be clothed in imagery" (WMCMM, 58). The crucial question is not whether or not we ultimately fall back upon narratives to render our lives comprehensible, but what is the character of the narratives to which we appeal. For "there are myths which displace truth, and there are myths which give wings to truth" (WMCMM, 58). This difference is of the utmost personal and cultural significance. In contrast to the transitory myths of demagogic manipulators, "there are deeper myths, born of the permanent and universal aspirations of men [and women], such as the dream of a future human fraternity" (WMCMM, 58).

At the very conclusion of his presidential address to the American Philosophical Association, this master of dialectic himself turned to the weaving of a tale. After proclaiming to his professional colleagues that "the only answer to an imperfect myth is a truer one" (Hocking 1928, 154), he tries his own hand at weaving a truer one:

> According to an old Welsh legend, Merlin, the magician and prophet, after spending some years as counsellor at the court of King Arthur, suddenly and mysteriously disappeared. It was supposed that he fell prey to the sorceress Nimu, who having coaxed his secret from him, used it to throw him into a trance and imprison him alive in a great rock.
> Many years later, a wanderer lost in the mountains fell exhausted to the ground, and was startled to hear a voice coming as it seemed from the depths of the earth, and speaking in an ancient and uncouth form. He understood that the voice purported to be the voice of Merlin. . . .
> But he could distinguish only a few syllables. And though they stamped themselves upon his memory; and he set them into a ballad, which he sang up and down the mountain roads . . . there was no deliverance. Now every seventh year a traveler is lured to that spot and another fragment of the spell is recovered and another song is made. But Merlin cannot be released until the travelers meet and join their fragments into the complete saying.
> We philosophers, the travelers of the myth, are taking part in the age-long labor of release. The meanings we find are actual possibilities buried in the heart of the world. Our different reports are, in part, our own creations, wrought by imagination. . . . But they are, first of all, our debt to the infinite imprisoned meaning of the world. (1928, 154–155)

As long as the presence of such philosophers as William Ernest Hocking is felt, the magic of Merlin will not be utterly absent from the discourse of philosophers. This might recall for some of you, however, James's disparaging remark about traditional metaphysics and thus serve not as a compliment to Hocking but as a basis for suspicion. Recall that, for James, "Metaphysics has usually followed a very primitive kind of quest. You know how men have always hankered after unlawful magic, and you know what a great part, in magic, *words* have always played. If you have the name . . . you can control the spirit. . . . 'God,' 'Matter,' 'Reason,' 'The Absolute,' 'Energy,' are so many solving names. You can rest when you have them. You are at the end of your metaphysical quest" (James 1907, 31–32).

But what if the name of God and other names associated with the divine (e.g., self, absolute, one) are invoked not to close but to open human experience to its own transcendent ground and destiny? What if they are used to probe the meanings inherent in experience itself, by enabling us to turn experience back upon itself and even perhaps inside out? What if the solution is itself a program for determinate work in the ever hazardous realm of obdurate fact? What if our most cherished metaphysical words are not magical incantations but passionate responses betraying more than the puny, pathetic character of the human figure from whom they issue? What if they are as revelatory as they are passionate? Animated by a hope that these questions might be answered in the affirmative, Hocking produced a body of work worthy of careful study and critical assessment. He knew before many of us were born that we moderns are tired of ourselves (Hocking 1942, 7), that modernity is in the process of ushering itself out (chap. 2 of *What Man Can Make of Man* is, after all, entitled "Modernity Ushers Itself Out"), that in understanding the triumphant (triumphalist?) march of the modern spirit in European culture we are passing beyond it and truly entering what he himself dubs "a postmodern era" (MGHE, xii–xiii). Moreover, he realizes that at the center of this passage is a confrontation with others and indeed with otherness. That in crucial respects he conceives this encounter *other than*, say, Lyotard or Derrida or Foucault or their legion of imitators makes his critique of modernity all the more, not less, relevant to our own urgent task of envisioning our historical present. With the aid of William Ernest Hocking, then, we might take sharper aim at the heart of our own elusive moment. "Hang it all! *Here* we are." In Hocking's appropriation of Whitehead's utterance, there is no counsel of despair. It is an invitation to insert oneself in the present, to reflect upon *our being with* one another, here and now. His is an invitation it would be wise to accept, at least in broad outline if not always in specific detail.

NOTES

1. This paper was first presented on December 4, 1996, as a lecture at Boston University. The reference here is to several members of the Department of Philosophy at that university. Lawrence Cahoone is no longer there.
2. I am borrowing this expression from Jürgen Habermas, who used in it reference to Michel Foucault. This expression, however, applies to Hocking, as does Habermas's question: "How does such a singularly affirmative understanding of modern philosophizing, always directed to our own actuality and imprinted in the here-and-now, fit with Foucault's [or Hocking's] unyielding criticism of modernity?" (Habermas, 1986, 106). My essay is intended to provide suggestions for how this question in reference to Hocking might be answered.
3. In *Experience and Nature*, Dewey goes so far as to suggest that we have "a first-rate test of the value of any philosophy which is offered us: Does it end in conclusions which, when they are referred back to ordinary life-experiences and their predicaments, render them more significant, more luminous to us, and make our dealings with them more fruitful? Or does it terminate in rendering the things of ordinary experience more opaque than they were before, and in depriving them of having in 'reality' even the significance they had previously seemed to have?" (Dewey 1925, 18). A complex philosophical relationship existed between Dewey and Hocking, one involving deep affinities and fundamental disagreements.
4. "Of all affairs communication is the most wonderful. That things should be able to pass from the plane of external pushing and pulling to that of revealing themselves to man, and thereby to themselves; and that the fruit of communication should be participation, sharing, is a wonder by the side of which transubstantiation pales" (Dewey 1925, 132). It is certainly significant

that when Hocking turned to revising his dissertation, a work entitled "The Elementary Experience of Other Conscious Being in Relation to the Elementary Experiences of Physical and Reflexive Objects" (Harvard University, 1904), he originally envisioned a work entitled "The Philosophy of Communication." As we will see, his philosophy of communication was deeply rooted in an actual experience of immense personal and philosophical significance for Hocking. Whereas James's experience of the catatonic boy in the asylum was deeply terrifying ("He sat there like a sort of sculptured Egyptian cat or Peruvian mummy, moving nothing but his black eyes and looking absolutely non-human. This image and my fear entered into a species of combination with each other. *That shape am I*, I felt, potentially."), Hocking's experience of the personal presence of his own wife Agnes was truly saving. A world without walls and persons without masks were, in that moment of revelation, directly experienced by Hocking.

5. There is a phenomenological recovery of what Hocking calls "nuclear experience." At the heart of this recovery is the insistence that "In this nuclear experience there are always three factors, an I, a Thou, and a common subject matter, let us say an It. Taken in its totality, this It is simply the world in which the I must work out its life. But the Thou, discerned as always present, lends to the world, the It, a character which completely effaces the privacy-limit of Descartes' 'I think, therefore I am: the It is no longer merely My world, the It is Our world.... The triumphant march of modernity [whose ultimate failure is rooted in its decisive successes] is now understood. And understanding it, we pass beyond it: we enter a postmodern age" (MGHE, xii–xiii).

6. As we shall see, the experiment of modernity concerns the attempt to grant absolute autonomy to humanity as well as to attribute insurmountable privacy to the self. Hence, it is in effect and especially in its later developments often in intent a secular movement, a movement toward secularization (cf. Smith 1995, 180-205).

7. Two important works for understanding what Hocking means by this expression are "Marcel and the Ground Issues of Metaphysics" (1954) and *Coming World Civilization* (1958). Also, Rouner 1969 is extremely—and characteristically—helpful in illuminating this central feature of Hocking's philosophical project.

8. Two points need to made in reference to the eclipse of subjectivity by intersubjectivity. First, the attempt to grant primacy to intersubjectivity (or what Hocking calls in *Coming World Civilization* consubjectivity) should not be construed as entailing the elimination of subjectivity. Especially in his political theory (but not merely here), the distinctively modern subject is in some respects retained. In light of the horrific experiments in collectivist politics, it is of course no surprise that one of Hocking's ambitions in politics, practical as well as theoretical, was to defend (as the title of an important book signals) *The Lasting Elements of Individualism* (1937). *Coming World Civilization* is divided not into chapters but into studies; study 2, "Passage Beyond Modernity: The Possible Universality of Solitude," opens with a section entitled "Modern Subjectivity as Resource and as Threat." And a later section of this study concludes by claiming that "The dilemma of modern thought has been created by philosophy, and philosophy, not imagination alone, must resolve it. How can we keep the treasure of subjective depth [itself something carved out by the passionate efforts to affirm radical autonomy in one form or another—think here of Luther's resounding words "Here I stand. I cannot do otherwise" or of Descartes' efforts to take radical possession of his own thought via a deliberate method of radical doubt], and at the same time retain hold on universal validity in our experience?" (Hocking 1954, 30; cf. Polanyi 1958). Hocking was convinced that the resource of modern subjectivity might be mined but its threat averted. His position seems to be identical with that of Maurice Merleau-Ponty, who asserted in "Everywhere and Nowhere" that "There are some ideas which make it impossible for us to return to a time prior to their existence, even and especially if we have moved beyond them [or at this moment in

the process of such movement], and subjectivity is one of them" ([1960] 1964, 154).

Second, here is an important point of contact between Hocking and Dewey. Dewey speaks of "the absurdity of an experiencing which experiences only itself, states and processes of consciousness, instead of the things of nature. Since the seventeenth century this conception of experience as the equivalent of subjective private consciousness set over against nature … has wrought havoc in philosophy" (Dewey 1925, 21). As he also suggests, "experience is something quite other than 'consciousness,' that is, that which appears qualitatively and focally at a particular moment" (Dewey 1925, 369).

9. The spirit of modernity is in numerous and important respects the spirit of *analysis*, the process of arriving at ultimate irreducible elements and of supposing that these elements are more real than the composites resulting from the intermingling of these elements. Analysis is of course an indispensable intellectual procedure. But when undertaken in a certain manner it cannot help but generate dualisms. As C. S. Peirce suggests, "dualism in its broadest legitimate meaning [is] … philosophy which performs its analyses with an axe, leaving as the ultimate elements, unrelated chunks of being" (Peirce 1935, 7:570).

10. Here we see an important example of what Hocking called negative pragmatism (a doctrine to be explained in the section of this chapter entitled "What Manner of Reflection Was His?"). Whereas the fact that this vision of nature has worked thus far does not guarantee its truth, that the alternatives have *not* worked as well does count against their claim to truth or at least adequacy.

11. In chapter 1 of *Science and the Modern World*, "The Origins of Modern Science," A. N. Whitehead makes just this point.

12. "The fundamental fact about experience is," according to James, "that it is a process of change" (1909a, 220). This might be true, but human experience is an ongoing process having more or less enduring consequences. Hence, James's claim and indeed my own need to be qualified, for experience is *both* a process and a product. John E. Smith makes note of this fact in an especially illuminating way when he asserts that "In the most basic sense, experience is the many-sided product of complex encounters between what there is and a being capable of undergoing, enduring, taking note of, responding to, and expressing it. As a product, experience is the result of an ongoing process that takes time and has a temporal structure" (1968, 23).

13. Of course, it is virtually impossible with a reality as complex as experience to avoid oversimplifying in one's theorizing about experience. As Dewey astutely notes, "Not safely can an 'ism' be made out of experience. For any interpretation of experience must perforce simplify; simplifications tend in a particular direction; and the direction may be set by custom which one assumes to be natural simply because it is traditionally congenial" (Dewey 1925, 366).

14. I am using "biographical" here in a broad sense, one inclusive of the "autobiographical." To be able to describe and narrate one's own life or experience is intimately connected to the way one's life is described and narrated by others.

15. The genius of Freud is to map some of the important ways in which the dramas of intrapsychic life are modeled on those of interpersonal existence. Hocking was himself concerned with what he called "subconsciousness."

16. Dewey contends that "one can hardly use the term 'experience' in philosophic discourse, but a critic rises to inquire, 'Whose experience?' The question is asked in adverse criticism. Its implication is that experience by its very nature is owned by some one; and that the ownership is such in kind that everything about experience is affected by a private and exclusive quality" (Dewey 1925, 178–179; cf. Smith 1992, 31). Against this view, Dewey argues that experience "has its own objective and definitive traits; these can be described without reference to a self, precisely as a house is of brick, has eight rooms, etc., irrespective of whom it belongs to" Dewey 1925, 179).

17. One might object that Dewey's organism *is* personal—for it is in certain circumstances, due to processes of enculturation, a self. Personalists (including Hocking) tend to deny or downplay this point.
18. The metaphor Peirce uses in reference to consciousness might with even greater justice be used for experience: "everything which is present to us is a phenomenal manifestation of ourselves. This does not prevent its being a phenomenon of something without us, just as the rainbow is at once a manifestation both of the sun and of the rain" (Peirce 1935, 5:283).
19. Given his sympathy for mysticism, it seems that the firstness of experience is also accorded a place in Hocking's account.
20. The sort of presence intended here is untouched by the critiques of the metaphysics of presence associated with Derrida and other postmodern authors.
21. In articulating a wider empiricism, Hocking took himself to be joining a distinctive development in contemporary philosophy, not inaugurating a wholly new doctrine. (Indeed, herein lies an important difference between his own project and that of Descartes, the widely acknowledged father of modernity.) For example, he notes in the 1963 preface to *The Meaning of God in Human Experience* that there is "a notable *general* turning from the sense-data-mental-data pattern of admitted experience" (MGHE, xii; emphasis added). Every appeal to experience carries, however implicitly, a theory of what counts as experience (Smith). The only experience admitted into the court of inquiry and, indeed, put in the position of judge has been experience that follows the pattern indicated by Hocking here. I might add that the mental is effectively identified with the private, thereby generating the problem of solipsism. "The great vitality of the twentieth century is due," according to Hocking, "to its rejection of that pattern, its appeal to experience neither physical nor ego-centered" (xii).
22. Before noting a parallel between Hocking and Dewey on experience as shot through with emotion and passion, let me quickly suggest that Buber, Marcel, and Hocking might be taken to represent the way the principles of dialogue and intersubjectivity can be defended in three different religious traditions (respectively, the Jewish, the Catholic, and the liberal Protestant).

    Dewey bemoaned "how far away from the everyday sense of experience a certain kind of philosophic discourse, although nominally experiential, has wandered.... I would rather take the behavior of the dog of Odysseus upon his master's return as an example of the sort of thing experience is for the philosopher than trust to such statements [as 'What I actually experience when I am looking at a chair are only a very few of the elements that go to make up the chair']. A physiologist may for his special purpose reduce Othello's perception of a handkerchief to simple elements of color under certain conditions of light and shapes seen under certain angular conditions of vision. But the actual experience was charged with history and prophecy; full of love, jealousy and villainy, fulfilling past human relationships and moving fatally to tragic destiny" (Dewey 1925, 368).
23. William James makes a related point when he suggests that "Things reveal themselves soonest to those who passionately want them, for our need sharpens our wit. To a mind content with little, the much in the universe may always remain hid" (1909b, 205). This claim, of course, needs somewhat to be qualified, for it all depends upon what specifically are the passions animating and guiding us in our quests and inquiries.
24. One of the motives for Hocking's insistence upon mysticism is that the mystic appreciate the extent and perhaps even the ways in which reality outstrips our ability to articulate its depths and contours.
25. In this connection, it seems appropriate to recall the lines from T. S. Eliot's "Dry Salvages": "We had the experience but missed the meaning; / And approach to the meaning restores the experience/in a different form."
26. One problem with this interpretation is how to square it with some of Hocking's most

27. The title of Gabriel Marcel's essay and also Leroy Rouner's recent Hocking Lecture.
28. In a recollection other than the one being quoted in the text at this point, Hocking stresses that "My life is not a time-string with events strung on it like beads. There are plenty of events, but to tell them would not be 'my life.' For I have lived several lives abreast, or rather braided; and the events often belong at once to two or three strands. For instance, my wife and I went to the Near East in 1928; that was 'an event.' My job was a study of mandates—philosophy, political theory—Egypt, Palestine, Syria, Turkey, ending in Geneva. At the same time, it belongs on the education strand.... It was also on the art strand: I made various drawings for the hypothetical illustration of a book that appeared in 1932, without illustrations. And it was also on the strand of one's loves—the most important of all—for I fell in love with the Arabs and out of love with the Zionists" (451).
29. In one place, Hocking actually identifies "a trilemma, each horn of which is as valid as the rest." He explains that "Self is the one object perfectly knowable; Nature is the one object perfectly knowable; the Other Mind is the one object perfectly and ideally knowable. The last of these propositions would be as tenable as the first, and as little"(MGHE, 253).
30. "I came to Harvard to find James. James was not there; for two years he was absent in Europe [giving the Gifford Lectures]" (Hocking 1930, 389). When James returned in 1901, "I went to him with the enthusiasm of deferred hope. He read his marvellous manuscript on religious experience. The stuff of that work was grist to my mill: James was indeed a liberator, and in his presence life was in the saddle. Yet James's method, or lack of method, and his results left me confused and unsatisfied. My days of discipleship had passed with the passing of Spencer's domination, and with the most ardent desire to do so, I could not again become the disciple of any" (389).
31. In *A Pluralistic Universe*, however, James—in some places, though not in others—radically modifies this position. For example, in one text, he asserts that "The particular intellectualist difficulty that held my own thought so long in a vise was ... the impossibility of understanding how 'your' experience and 'mine,' which 'as such' are defined as not conscious of [or accessible to] each other, can nevertheless at the same time be members of a world experience defined expressly as having all its parts coconscious, or known together" (1909b, 226). Cf. Ford 1982.
32. Any student of Peirce will be reminded of a famous passage in which Peirce asks: "Are we shut up in a box of flesh and blood? When I communicate my thought and my sentiments to a friend with whom I am in full sympathy, so that my feelings pass into him and I am conscious of what he feels, do I not live in his brain as well as in my own—most literally?" (Peirce 1935, 7:591).
33. See Hocking's brilliant essay entitled "Marcel and the Ground Issues of Metaphysics."
34. These sentences are such close paraphrases of a paragraph in *Types* as to be virtually quotations. I have done so to make the language more inclusive (using the plural rather than "he").
35. It is significant that, in *The Meaning of God in Human Experience*, Hocking himself tries to establish just this point. The titles of two chapters in particular signal his loyalty to Royce and his qualified but deep differences with James: "The Need of Unity" and "The Need of an Absolute."
36. To what extent does Hocking truly have a metaphysical system? In a recent conversation I had with Leroy Rouner, he remarked that he was struck upon rereading Hocking how much looseness there was in his philosophy.
37. In "Humanism and Truth," James asks: "Must not something end by supporting itself?" He answers his own question in this way: "Humanism is willing to let finite experience be

self-supporting. Somewhere being must immediately breast nonentity. Why may not the advancing front of experience, carrying its immanent satisfactions and dissatisfactions, cut against the black inane as the luminous orb of the moon cuts the caerulean abyss? Why should anywhere the world be absolutely fixed and finished?" (1909a, 222). See also chap. 2 of James 1911.

38. Given the importance of this point, it is perhaps also important to recall Hocking's own exact formulation of these antithetical insights: "The present century [in particular] has seen the extreme assertions, both of the subjectivity of the I-think, and of the objectivity of the purposeless physical world" (TP, 311–312).

WORKS CITED

Blau, Joseph L. 1952. "Varieties of Idealism." Chap. 6 in *Men and Movements in American Philosophy*. New York: Prentice-Hall.

Cahoone, Lawrence E. 1988. *The Dilemma of Modernity: Philosophy, Culture, and Anti-Culture*. Albany, N.Y.: SUNY Press.

Colapietro, Vincent M. 1989. *Peirce's Approach to the Self: A Semiotic Perspective on Human Subjectivity*. Albany, N.Y.: SUNY Press.

Dewey, John. 1925. *Experience and Nature*. Indianapolis: Open Court. Reprinted in *The Later Works: 1925–1953*, vol. 1, ed. Jo Ann Boydston. Carbondale, Ill.: Southern Illinois University Press, 1981.

———. 1927. "Politics and Human Beings." [Review of Hocking's MATS.] *New Republic* 50: 114–115. Reprinted in *The Later Works: 1925–1953*, vol. 3, ed. Jo Ann Boydston. Carbondale, Ill.: Southern Illinois University Press, 1981.

———. 1930. "In Reply to Some Critics." *Journal of Philosophy* 27 (May 8): 271–277. Reprinted in *The Later Works: 1925–1953*, vol. 5, ed. Jo Ann Boydston. Carbondale, Ill.: Southern Illinois University Press, 1981.

———. 1940. "Nature in Experience." *Philosophical Review* 49 (March): 244–258. Reprinted in *The Later Works: 1925–1953*, vol. 14, ed. Jo Ann Boydston. Carbondale, Ill.: Southern Illinois University Press, 1981.

Ford, Marcus Peter. 1982. *William James's Philosophy*. Amherst: University of Massachusetts Press.

Habermas, Jürgen. 1986. "Taking Aim at the Heart of the Present." In *Foucault: A Critical Reader*, ed. David Couzens Hoy. Cambridge, Mass.: Basil Blackwell, 103-108.

Hocking, Richard. 1970. "Event, Act, and Presence." *Review of Metaphysics* 24:37–56.

Hocking, W. E. 1910. "How Ideas Reach Reality." *Philosophical Review* 19:302–318.

———. 1927. "Mind and Near Mind." *Proceedings of the Sixth International Congress of Philosophy*, ed. E. S Brightman, 203–215. New York: Longmans, Green & Co.

———. 1928. "What Does Philosophy Say?" *Philosophical Review* 37:133–153. Reprinted as chap. 1 in this volume.

———. 1930a. "Some Second Principles." In *Contemporary American Philosophy: Personal Statements*, vol. 1., ed. George P. Adams and William Pepperell Montague. New York: Macmillan.

———. 1930b. "Action and Certainty." *Journal of Philosophy* 27 (April 24): 225–238. Reprinted as an appendix in John Dewey, *The Later Works: 1925–1953*, vol. 5, ed. Jo Ann Boydston, 461–476. Carbondale, Ill.: Southern Illinois University Press, 1981.

———. 1940. "Dewey's Concepts of Experience and Nature." *Philosophical Review* 49 (March): 228–244.

———. 1941. "Theses Establishing an Idealistic Metaphysics by a New Route." *Journal of Philosophy* 38 (January–December): 688–690.
———. 1946. "Metaphysics: Its Function, Consequences, and Criteria." *Journal of Philosophy* 43:365–378.
———. 1950. "Fact and Destiny." *Review of Metaphysics* 4:1–12.
———. 1951. "Fact and Destiny (II)." *Review of Metaphysics* 4:319–342.
———. 1954. "Marcel and the Ground Issues of Metaphysics." *Philosophy and Phenomenological Research* 14 (June): 439–469.
———. 1956. "On Royce's Empiricism." *Journal of Philosophy* 53 (January–December): 57–63.
———. 1958. "Fact, Field, and Destiny: Inductive Elements of Metaphysics." *Review of Metaphysics* 11:525–549. Reprinted as chap. 3 in this volume.
———. 1959. "From the Early Days of the 'Logische Unterschungen.'" In *Edmund Husserl: 1859-1959*, ed. H. L. Van Breda and J. Taminaux. The Hague: Martinus Nijhoff, 1-11.
———. 1961. "Whitehead As I Knew Him." *Journal of Philosophy* 58:505–516.
———. 1966. "History and the Absolute." In *Philosophy, Religion, and Coming World Civilization: Essays in Honor of William Ernest Hocking*, ed. Leroy S. Rouner. The Hague: Martinus Nijhoff, 1966.
James, William. 1878. "Remarks on Spencer's Definition of Mind as Correspondence." *Journal of Speculative Philosophy* (January): 1–18. Reprinted in F. H. Burkhardt, ed., *Essays in Philosophy*, 7–22. Cambridge: Harvard University Press, 1978.
———. [1890] 1983. *The Principles of Psychology*. Cambridge: Harvard University Press.
———. 1902. *The Varieties of Religious Experience: A Study of Human Nature*. New York: Longmans, Green, & Co.
———. 1907. *Pragmatism*. New York: Longmans, Green, & Co.
———. 1909a. *The Meaning of Truth: A Sequel to* Pragmatism. New York: Longmans, Green, & Co.
———. 1909b. *A Pluralistic Universe*. New York: Longmans, Green, & Co.
———. 1911. *Some Problems of Philosophy*. New York: Longmans, Green, & Co.
Krikorian, Y. H. 1958. "Hocking and the Dilemmas of Modernity." *The Journal of Philosophy* 55 (March 27): 265–275.
———. 1966. "Hocking and the Dilemmas of Modernity." In *Philosophy, Religion, and Coming World Civilization: Essays in Honor of William Ernest Hocking*, ed. Leroy S. Rouner. The Hague: Martinus Nijhoff, 1966.
Kuklick, Bruce. 1977. *The Rise of American Philosophy*. New Haven: Yale University Press.
Marcel, Gabriel. 1966. "Solipsism Surmounted." In *Philosophy, Religion, and Coming World Civilization: Essays in Honor of William Ernest Hocking*, ed. Leroy S. Rouner. The Hague: Martinus Nijhoff, 1966.
Merleau-Ponty, Maurice. 1964. *Signs*. Trans. Richard C. McCleary. Evanston, Ill.: Northwestern University Press.
Myers, Gerald. 2001. *William James: His Life and Thought*. New Haven: Yale University Press.
Miller, John William. 1978. *The Paradox of Cause and Other Essays*. New York: W. W. Norton & Co.
Neville, Robert Cummings. 1993. *Eternity and Time's Flow*. Albany, N.Y.: SUNY Press.
Passmore, John. 1957. *A Hundred Years of Philosophy*. Harmondsworth, England: Penguin.
Paz, Octavio. 1990. *In Search of the Present*. San Diego: Harvest/HBJ Original.
Peirce, C. S. 1935. *The Collected Papers of Charles Sanders Peirce*. Ed. Charles Hartshorne and Paul Weiss. Cambridge: Belknap Press of Harvard University Press.
Polanyi, Michael. 1958. *Personal Knowledge: Towards a Post-Critical Philosophy*. Chicago: University of Chicago Press.

Reck, Andrew J. 1964. *Recent American Philosophers: Studies of Ten Representative Thinkers*. New York: Pantheon Books.

———. 1966. "Hocking's Place in American Metaphysics." In *Philosophy, Religion, and Coming World Civilization: Essays in Honor of William Ernest Hocking*, ed. Leroy S. Rouner. The Hague: Martinus Nijhoff, 1966.

Robinson, D. S. 1966. "Hocking's Contribution to Metaphysical Idealism." In *Philosophy, Religion, and Coming World Civilization: Essays in Honor of William Ernest Hocking*, ed. Leroy S. Rouner. The Hague: Martinus Nijhoff, 1966.

Rosen, Stanley. 1980. *The Limits of Analysis*. New Haven: Yale University Press.

———. 1989. *The Ancients and the Moderns: Rethinking Modernity*. New Haven: Yale University Press.

———. 1995. "The Metaphysics of Ordinary Experience." *The Harvard Review of Philosophy* 5 (spring): 41–57.

Rouner, Leroy S. 1969. *Within Human Experience: The Philosophy of William Ernest Hocking*. Cambridge: Harvard University Press.

———. 1996. "Solipsism Surmounted: Ernest Hocking's Philosophy of Community." Reprinted as chap. 21 in this volume.

———, ed. 1966. *Philosophy, Religion, and Coming World Civilization: Essays in Honor of William Ernest Hocking*. The Hague: Martinus Nijhoff.

Royce, Josiah. 1899. *The World and the Individual*. New York: Macmillan.

———. 1908. *The Philosophy of Loyalty*. New York: Macmillan Co.

———. 1912. *The Sources of Religious Insight*. New York: Charles Scribner's Sons.

———. 1913. *The Problem of Christianity*. New York: Macmillan Co.

Sarton, May. 1954. *I Knew a Phoenix: Sketches for an Autobiography*. New York: W. W. Norton & Co.

Smith, John E. 1962. Foreword to *The Meaning of God in Human Experience*. New Haven: Yale University Press.

———. 1970. *Themes in American Philosophy: Purpose, Experience, and Community*. New York: Harper & Row.

———. 1992. *America's Philosophical Vision*. Chicago: University of Chicago Press.

———. 1995. *Experience and God*. New York: Fordham University Press.

———. 1996. "Hocking's Insights About the State and the Individual." Reprinted as chap. 25 in this volume.

Spencer, Herbert. 1878. *First Principles of a New System of Philosophy*. Vol. 1 of *A System of Synthetic Philosophy*. New York: D. Appleton & Co.

Werkmeister, W. H. 1949. *A History of Philosophical Ideas in America*. New York: Ronald Press Co.

Whitehead, A. N. 1925. *Science and the Modern World*. New York: Macmillan.

———. 1929. *Process and Reality*. NY: Macmillan. Reprint, corrected edition, ed. David Ray Griffin and Donald W. Sherburne, New York: Free Press, 1978.

Wilshire, Bruce. 1996. "Passion for Meaning: William Ernest Hocking's Religious-Philosophical Views." Reprinted as chap. 19 in this volume.

Woodbridge, Frederick J. E. 1930. "Experience and Dialectic." *Journal of Philosophy* 27 (May 8): 264–271. Reprinted in John Dewey, *The Later Works: 1925–1953*, vol. 5, ed. Jo Ann Boydston, 487-495. Carbondale, Ill.: Southern Illinois University Press, 1981.

CHAPTER 21

Solipsism Surmounted:
W. E. Hocking's Philosophy of Community

Leroy S. Rouner

Ernest Hocking wrote some twenty books on a wide variety of topics—law, human rights, religion, ethics, world politics, and more—but each of them was grounded in a central metaphysical position. That position was first explored in his doctoral dissertation at Harvard in 1904 and later expanded in his first and most important book, *The Meaning of God in Human Experience* in 1912. The dissertation had an unfortunate title: "The Elementary Experience of Other Conscious Being in Its Relations to the Elementary Experience of Physical and Reflexive Objects." He had been studying in Germany, and it shows. He might better have called it "Our Experience of Other People in Relation to Our Experience of Ourselves and Nature." Nevertheless, his purpose was plain. He had set out, he tells us, "to restore the stinging reality of contact with the human comrade." In other words, he set out to solve what technical philosophers call "the other minds problem." The business at hand is to show why that problem lies at the heart of modern philosophy and why we require what he called "a passage beyond modernity."

Briefly put, the modern problem of knowledge is that major philosophers like Descartes have argued that the knowing process takes place entirely within the mind of the individual knower. This leads to solipsism, the view that the only thing we can really know are the inner states of our own minds. Now, it may be possible for us to live with this limitation in relation to nature, but when it comes to people, it is a different story. We need to know that we really *do* know the other person. If you are ever called on as a character witness in court, you have to be able to say, "I *know* this and I *know* he could not have committed this crime," for example. So the issue of solipsism weighed heavily on Ernest Hocking—a Midwesterner who came from a strong family and took community for granted—and his whole philosophical enterprise is one of showing how we really are in community with one another in a wide range of human experiences.

His metaphysical reflections on all this will strike you as thin and abstract, however, since in our day, community has become a visceral issue. To be in community with ourselves, others, and the natural world around us is to be at home in those worlds. And the most primal and instinctive sense of being at home comes to most of us not through metaphysical reflection but through the natural bonds of blood, region, language, caste or class, and religion, which are the bonds of traditional and tribal cultures. They are not as strong with us mobile, modern people who live most

[280]

of our lives in urban industrial centers as they are with Indian villagers, Asian peasants, and African tribespeople, but we feel their power nevertheless. Deep in us all, beyond the rational specifics of economy and political ideology, there is a visceral instinct that makes us gravitate toward our own kind and fear the stranger. We still feel the old bonds, and they give us what we now call our roots. To be part of this family, however contentious; to be familiar with this place of childhood memory; to know this language's local accent and intimate meanings; to have a place, however low, in this community; and to share with others the celebration of this religious belief and commitment, in which the deepest in us meets the deepest in our community—this is what it means to be at home.

Those whom we perceive to be different from us are outsiders, aliens, strangers. We may be fascinated by them and occasionally even join forces with them, but when it is them against us—Protestants against Catholics in Ireland, Tamils against Sinhalese in Sri Lanka, Arabs against Israelis in the Middle East—what is at stake for us is deeper than economic self-interest or even ideological commitment. What is threatened is our sense of being at home in our world. And our need to be at home is deep and powerful.

The problem that this raises for us is the pluralism of what Ernest Hocking called "the coming world civilization." These *others* are now not only our neighbors in the global village but also our partners in the task of human survival. I confess that my enthusiasm for this situation is qualified. I like novelty, occasional change, and people who are different from me, but our current cultural pluralism is a thunderstorm, a flood. There is no way that any one person could encompass it all or make sense of it all, or even survive it all if we were honestly open to its total impact. Pluralism makes us all bobbing corks on its cultural ocean, in the midst of a hurricane. But here we are, and the only serious question is how we are to ride out the storm.

Philosophy seems like a weak vehicle for that ride, especially when compared to the thick, strong bonds of our natural identities. But it provides a universality that natural bonds do not, and even a weak conception of universality may help. If philosophy can provide some thin, overarching, vague rationale for who we are, and how we can find common ground with these strangers who are now our neighbors and partners, that is no small service. That was the service Ernest Hocking's metaphysics intended to provide. His metaphysics then became the superstructure upon which his philosophies of history, religion, and world culture were built.

He begins with the three fundamental elements in human experience: ourselves, other selves, and physical nature. Everything in experience is an I, a Thou, or an It. As he read the story of modern philosophy since Descartes, he saw that the philosophical connections among these three had been severed. The most serious aspect of that fragmentation of experience was the isolation of one self from another. Modern philosophy had robbed us of our ability to explain how we know the other person to be a mind like our own. Social knowledge had been reduced to behaviorism. We know other persons only through what their bodies do. We have no direct access to the mind, spirit, or soul of the other. Hence, the characteristic spiritual affliction of modernity is loneliness, and solipsism (the view that we can know only the internal states of our own minds), the metaphysics of loneliness, became for Hocking the contemporary philosophical problem most in need of solution.

The Idea of a Purposeless Nature

The medieval interpreters of Aristotle integrated the human philosophical desire for understanding the "reasons why" (*to dioti*) things are as they are with the divine love that is God's will that things should be the way they are. Medieval science was therefore human wisdom conjoined with divine truth. In the Elizabethan period, however, there was a major shift in the understanding of science, popularized by Francis Bacon and his insistence that the aim of science is *useful* knowledge. Knowledge now became power over the forces of physical nature. As Bacon put it so eloquently,

> I will give thee the greatest jewel I have. For I will impart to thee, for the love of God and men, a relation of the true state of Salomon's House.... The end of our foundation is the knowledge of causes and secret motions of things, and the enlarging of the bounds of human empire, to effecting of all things possible. (1620, 1.14)

For the Greeks, science was elegant explanation, a fit pursuit of lofty minds for whom affluence had granted the leisure to reflect on principles of understanding. For medieval Christianity, science was a faithful uncovering of the ways in which God affected God's will in world. But for Bacon and his successors science explored the laws of matter in motion in order to command nature. The purpose of scientific study was "to turn heaven and earth to the use and welfare of mankind" (Bacon 1.14). This was in sharp contrast to the medieval view of science, inherited from Aristotle. For Aristotle, a theory of knowledge was precisely a theory of the world's intelligibility, in which the power of the knower to know a thing joined with the power of the thing to be known.

Notable here is Aristotle's understanding of nature. Everything has a material cause, the stuff of which it is made; an efficient cause, the process whereby it comes to be; a formal cause, the particular kind that makes it this sort of thing rather than that sort; and a final cause, which is Aristotle's name for the purpose of a thing. The purpose of a maple tree, for example, is to be a real, or perfected, maple. In its career from seed to sapling, the maple tree is aiming at something. Just as a growing boy is aiming at manhood, so a growing sapling is aiming at becoming a properly full-grown tree.

This notion that the natural world has purpose of some sort is part of Aristotle's view of the world as intelligible, and intelligibility is not radically different for natural things and for persons. Natural objects are not "objects" or "things" in the modern sense because they have an active role to play in the knowing process. For Aristotle a yellow wall has the power *to be seen* as yellow. We do not have the power to know it apart from its power to be known. So knowing something is not solely the function of an individual mind. It is a natural function that takes place in an intelligible world, and it requires both the power of the individual knower to know a thing and the power of the thing itself to be known.

In contrast, modern theories of knowledge, from Bacon and Descartes to Kant, think of knowledge as an event taking place within an individual mind, made possible by the power of the individual mind to know. This view understands nature primarily in terms of Aristotle's material and efficient causes. The formal cause—the natural kind of thing that this particular thing is—is no longer inherent in the thing itself, or derived from participation in some Platonic idea. Formal cause is now only the way we understand it and talk about it, and the name we arbitrarily decide to give it. Formal cause becomes a function of signs and symbols of understanding in the mind, rather than the inherent intelligibility of the thing in and of itself. And final cause is removed from metaphysical analysis altogether. We no longer speak of a tree as having any natural purpose.

The Divorce Between Nature and Mind

Building on the view that all knowledge is grounded in the absolutely certain and immediate knowledge that one has of one's own mind, Descartes admits that our knowledge of physical nature, and our knowledge of other minds than our own, becomes problematic. Aristotle's natural realism celebrated a sunny and untroubled confidence that the world is a coherent whole in which my mind, other minds, and physical nature are integrated by a *Nous* (world mind) which, while primarily evident in the workings of your mind and mine, is also evident in the structure and purposive operations of physical nature. Hence, the entire experienced world is illumined with the light of intelligibility. In such a world human minds are not radically separated from nature, nor is my mind fundamentally at a loss to explain its instinctive assurance that you, who are distinct from me, also have a mind of your own.

With the Cartesian shift, however, illumination no longer floods the world. The light of reason illuminates the inwardness of the individual mind. "Cogito ergo sum" (I think; therefore I am). The mind of my neighbor, however, although not quite covered with darkness, is, to me, a twilight of confusion. We all know perfectly well that the neighbor has a mind precisely like our own, but our other-minds problem expresses our inability to explain to ourselves how we know this. The natural world, on the other hand, is not in twilight; it is cast an epistemological outer darkness. To define a physical object simply as something that takes up space, a *res extensa*, is to announce a mystery. We know that there is something out there, and we know how it appears to us, but we cannot know what it is in itself.

Aristotle and the medievals knew the "treeness" of the tree from the inside, so to speak, because they knew its purpose in being that kind of tree. The implications of the Cartesian view were later made specific by Kant, when he pointed out that all knowledge begins with the reality of the individual knower. He observes, irrefutably, that I can only know what I know. All that I know is logically preceded by the realization that I am knowing it. This "I think" must be presupposed in any knowledge claim by any mind. Any particular act of knowing is thus radically relativized. What the object may be in and for itself must always be unknown to me. For the modern mind, therefore, knowledge of nature became knowledge from the "outside."

The individualization of the knowing process aggrandized the power of the individual mind as the sole active agent in the knowing process. Our perceptions grasp and shape bits and pieces of experience from which our concepts construct a world. We are thus the creators of our world. Perception is now a raid on the unknowable, a bequeathing of status and reality on that which, apart from the mind's gracious attention, must remain dark and dumb. Aristotle's nature, enlivened by the purposive presence of the world Mind or *Nous*, here becomes shrouded and alien.

Aristotle's world, and the medieval world that built on it, was a metaphysical community. Its lines of connection made intelligible relations among individuals, their fellows, and the natural world that was their setting. In breaking down our understanding of these relations, modernity has sacrificed that visceral sense of community that lets us feel at home in our experienced world of ourselves, others, and nature. It was this metaphysical community Hocking sought to restore.

He was not willing to go back to Aristotle or the medievals, however, because he believed that something significant had been achieved in the Cartesian shift that he wanted to preserve. That achievement was precisely the distinction between the world of mind, *res cogitans*, and the world of matter, *res extensa*. This distinction is true to our experience—people are different from trees or rocks. It opens up the creative possibilities of modern science.

It is currently popular to criticize dualisms of all sorts in the name of integrated holisms, but Hocking was persuaded that dualism was a problem that each culture needed to work through. When the Chinese neo-Confucian scholar Hu Shi announced proudly that China had had no Descartes, Hocking responded that that was part of their problem and that it had prevented them from creative engagement with the possibilities of modernity. Modern life requires a purposeless nature, he believed. He insisted that that purposelessness had been given to us for a purpose: the creative purposes of modern science and technology. Even the kind of ecology we could all be happy with would require that we dam *some* rivers and fell *some* trees, and we are not morally free to do that if nature has purposes with which we are interfering. Perhaps even more to the point are those quantum leaps in modern medicine that have made a better and longer life possible for increasing numbers of people because we have learned how to subdue natural viruses and control them.

His primary commitment was to fashion a metaphysics that would be true to our experience. The problem is that our experience is not unified in a simple way. His colleague Whitehead had a nice way of putting it. He remarked that "sometimes I think that I am in the world; and sometimes I think that the world is in me." In other words, we have two radically different kinds of experience of ourselves in our world.

One Hocking called natural realism. The world was here before we entered it and will be here after we leave it, and we know ourselves now to be in that world. The other he called subjective idealism. The world I know is always, inescapably, the world as known to me. Natural objects, for example, are known to me only through sense perception, and my knowledge of these objects is a conception that lives in my head. That world is *in* me.

Hocking wanted to do justice to both these experiences, and his metaphysics is therefore dialectical, in a manner that distinguishes his view from that of his teachers, Josiah Royce and William James. James's pragmatic and pluralistic philosophy of radical empiricism understood reality as a forward flow of "pure experience," a view that has since endeared him to Buddhists, Whiteheadians, and other "go-with-the-flow" philosophers. Royce's metaphysics of the Absolute, on the other hand, had trouble moving at all. His metaphysics never entirely escaped Ralph Barton Perry's criticism that he was proposing a static "block universe" because the really Real in Royce's world is an unchanging transcendental idea.

Hocking thought reality moves, but not in a forward flow. It zigs and zags. Reality, he thought, is like the learning process, and in Hocking's system even God learns because God does not know the future, and the unfolding future of free human activity is endlessly instructive to the mind of God. Learning is the process whereby we get an idea about something, only to have it countered by a different idea, which we then incorporate into our original understanding, for a better idea of the thing. As in Hegel, the meeting of thesis and antithesis produces a synthesis. The question is then: What kind of synthesis can resolve the crisis in our experience between the natural realism of our conviction that we are in the world, and the subjective idealism of our reflection that our experienced world is really in us?

In search of a solution, Hocking went back to Descartes, whose famous "Cogito ergo sum" (I think; therefore I am) seemed to him only half right. He agreed with Descartes that immediate knowledge of our own minds is the certitude that makes philosophy possible in the first place. The reality of a thought necessarily requires the reality of a thinker. But, as it stands, the statement doesn't really make any sense because it is impossible simply to think. You have to think *something*. So the objects of physical nature, the things I think *about*, are *necessary* for thought.

That's the key point. I couldn't think unless I had something to think about. It is nature that lends clarity, pungency, definition, specificity, to thought. In that sense, natural objects, as the content of mind, are mind-stuff. And since it is nature that thus makes mind possible and gives us the objects that become the content of mind, Hocking goes on to note that nature is therefore "creative of mind in me."

That may sound animistic, but at least it was not simply speculative. Hocking used to say that metaphysics is an "out-of-doors" business. Virtually all the major turning points in his philosophical development involved specific experiences that took place out-of-doors. The crucial one here is described in a key passage of *The Meaning of God in Human Experience* (265–266). He says, in effect: Why is it that when I look at you I see only your exterior, your body, the forehead that encases your mind; and never the real you? This exterior wall of presence is only a movable part of my world, and I am also only a wall, a facade, to you. Your mind is lurking there, behind your forehead, "fraternizing with chemical processes," as he can't resist saying. But then he asks himself, Is that really where *my* mind is? Well, no. When, with Descartes, he said that the mind, which is the self, is necessarily presupposed by any thought that that mind may have, he wasn't talking about chemical processes gurgling away back there in the brain. He notes that he doesn't have any experience of chemical brain processes. His experience of his mind is purely an experience of its content. Here Hocking agreed with James. Consciousness, as some sort of separate substance, doesn't exist; or at least, we don't have any distinguishable experience of it as existing apart from the content of consciousness. *My* mind *is* its content. It is what I am thinking *about*. And if your mind is also its content, then we both share the same content insofar as we share the same experienced world.

We sit here, out of doors, looking at the same mountain, and that mountain is the common content of our common mind. Yes, you see it from a slightly different angle, and you don't feel about it quite the same way I feel about it. Your mountain is not quite the same as my mountain because you are you and I am me—and *vive la différence!* Otherwise Sameness would be King, and we would all die of boredom. But the major characteristic of this particular mountain is the common reality that you and I absorb in our own slightly different ways, and that objective point of departure is the same for all observers. If we didn't have these objects in common, we would all be crazy and life would be impossible.

So nature is known as the content of other minds. But what if there is no one else sitting there with us looking at the mountain? Do we still experience the mountain as "creative of mind in me?" Yes, we are still persuaded of its objectivity. Scientific objectivity, he notes, is established by the confirmation of another observer. We know that we are seeing something real when another observer knows that he or she also sees the same thing. And that is the way we experience the mountain, even when there is no other mind immediately present to view it with us. We know it as objective, that is, as known by another mind.

But what sort of Other Mind could confirm that objective reality? *Our* minds are passive. We must take the world as it is given to us. Hocking finds nature as "creative of mind" in him. That is to say, nature is the stuff of an *active* mind, not one that knows passively and empirically, one that comes and goes from any particular scene as our minds must do. Nature is the stuff of an active mind that does *not* come and go, but is present always and everywhere in the mind-creating work that is nature presenting itself to our thought.

Once again, this notion of all-encompassing thought is not speculative. We have an experience of this thought in the form of an idea of the Whole. It is difficult to establish the significance of this Whole idea because it is not the specific content of our ideas but the unspecific background which makes those ideas possible. The Whole idea is not what we are thinking *about;* it is the basic idea we are thinking *with*. In order to make his point Hocking casts about for the simplest and most unlikely example. Well, what about hats? With what idea do I think *hat?* What intellectual framework gives meaning to my notion of a hat?

> With the hat-idea, to be sure. Yes, but is the clothing-idea unconcerned?—or the city-street-idea? or the civilized-society-extraordinary-requirements idea? or the man-and-woman idea? or the whole mass of aesthetic notions, and political, historical, even religious opinions? With all these, and with all other ideas summing themselves up currently in my whole idea, hat is thought. (MGHE, 131)

The dialectic of our experience of nature thus begins with the thesis of natural realism and is countered by the antithesis of subjective idealism. The synthesis of these two notions is that nature is the realm of other mind. The new exploration begins with this thesis of nature as the realm of other mind and is countered with the notion of our own empirical minds, which must know nature passively and only occasionally. The synthesis in this second movement of the dialectic is of a mind that knows actively, creating mind in us—an absolute mind that does not come and go. This mind is experienced by us as that Whole idea which we know prior to any specific content of natural objects, and which is the possibility of our having a coherent context for any specific knowledge. This idea of the Whole or Absolute is part of what we mean by God, and it is this idea that reestablishes our community with nature and with our neighbors.

> As simply as Nature presents itself as objective, just so simply and directly is the Other Mind present to me in that objectivity, as its actual meaning. I do not first know my physical world as a world of *objects* and then as a world of *shared* objects: it is through a prior recognition of the presence of Other Mind that my physical experience acquires objectivity at all. The objectivity of Nature is its community, not two facts but one; but the whole truth of this one fact (the whole I do not see unless I note what I am thinking with)—the whole of this fact is community. (MGHE, 288–289)

Conclusion

In *The Rise of American Philosophy* Bruce Kuklick concludes his chapter on Hocking with the comment that since Hocking disputed Royce over the issue of solipsism, he did not accept Royce's view that other selves were social constructs. Clearly, Hocking "desired to distinguish idealism by making selfhood social. Here, however, he disappointed. He wrote that God's creations were not apart from God, that God 'included' other selves and their objects. What was the relation, then, between God, the world, and other selves? Hocking wanted to avoid absolute solipsism, but he never clarified his position" (1977, 489 [Kuklick's reference is to MGHE, 298]).

I agree with Kuklick that Hocking needed to write a systematic metaphysics in order to clarify his position. The Gifford Lectures on "Fact and Destiny" were to have been his "duty book" (as Whitehead called *Process and Reality, his* own systematic metaphysics), but he never published them. He did some new work on the philosophy of selfhood on the basis of field theory, and the idea of the self as "a field of fields" became important enough that a revised sketch of his unfinished metaphysics was entitled "Fact, Field, and Destiny." On the other hand, Kuklick's criticism doesn't focus on the crucial unfinished issue. That issue is whether or not Hocking can make his qualified metaphysical dualism coherent. The problem is not that God "includes" the creation. Of course God does, in some sense, "include" the created order of self, nature, and society. That idea is virtually inescapable in any Christian philosophy where God is creator, sustainer, and redeemer of the world. Nor is the problem that creation is not "apart from" God, another way of putting the same idea. The issue is not that Hocking put his position this way; it is that he did not fully spell out what "include" and "not apart from" were to mean in his dialectical system.

Some things can be said about his intention in this regard. Charles Hartshorne once admitted that he could not see the difference between Hocking and Berkeley, but it is clear at least that Hocking did not intend Berkeley's subjective idealism and its view that the natural object is an idea in the mind of God. Nor would Hocking have been happy with my colleague John Findlay's notion that the natural particular is an "instantiation" of a transcendental idea. Hocking was a neo-Hegelian, not a Neoplatonist—a distinction that Findlay would not have admitted but that seems significant to me.

For Plato, dialectic is a method of knowing our world of phenomena. As in Socrates' illustration of "the divided line" in the *Republic*, dialectic functions only on the phenomenal side of the line, not in the realm of the transcendent ideas. Dialectic leads you to a "synoptic intuition" (Windelband) of the ultimate nature of things, the idea of the Good. That ultimacy is not, itself, dialectical. But for Hocking, dialectic characterizes the entire nature of things, the world of the transcendent as well as the world of natural phenomena. Even God is a learner. As in Hartshorne's dipolar theism, Hocking's God is, in one sense, unfinished, because God cannot know the future, the future not yet being available as an object of thought. Hocking loved to say, "God does not know what I am going to do tomorrow."

Hocking intended to do justice to the contradictory nature of experience with a view of reality in which God both includes and is in some sense distinct from the world, and in which we are both free from and inextricably bound to God. He intended to defend the realism of objective physical nature and its purposelessness, and to say that its purposelessness had been given to us for a purpose. Dialectic does not dissolve objectivity into subjectivity. It announces instead that physical nature is both fact and idea, that selves are both individuals and inextricably bound in community, that even God is both Whole and unfinished.

Had Charles Peirce lived to befriend Hocking the way he befriended Royce, he might well have given him the same advice: that his system needed logical tightening. Some revision or elaboration of the principle of noncontradiction is required in order to make dialectic more coherent. But I suspect that Hocking never wrote his "duty book" because he never believed it possible to provide a logical argument that would be philosophically compelling. What he sought was a system that would be experientially appealing. What he wanted to say was, "This is my experience. Is it yours also? Does it have something of our common humanity in it?"

I find his philosophy fairly successful in those terms. My experience is complex, not simple; ambivalent, not smoothly forward-moving. My life does not "go with the flow"; it bobs and weaves. I yearn for a sense of community with my neighbors and with nature, and I accept the fact that the visceral, natural bonds of blood, region, language, caste or class, and religion have become destructive in the larger community of the coming world civilization. I do think he overstated our need for a purposeless nature. As he himself argued, there is probably no such thing as an absolute right to anything, and I don't see why the right of a tree to fulfill its purposes may not be morally subservient to my right to shelter. But that change would require only an adjustment in his system.

Can the thin gruel of philosophy substitute for the thick bonds of natural identity? No. We are always going to love and die for our parents and our children before we take on the universal community of the coming world civilization. But Hocking's metaphysics of community goes on to a philosophy of history in which metaphysics makes contact with the religious foundations of culture. In so doing he resolves the cultural problem of incommensurability which plagues philosophers of communitarianism today, and gives historical pith and cultural substance to his reflections on community.

If there is to be a human future, we need to be guided by some general, inclusive notion of who we are and what we are supposed to be about as a human community. And for that task, I know no better guide than Ernest Hocking.

WORKS CITED
Bacon, Francis. 1620. *Novum Organum*.
Kuklick, Bruce. 1977. *The Rise of American Philosophy*. New Haven: Yale University Press.

CHAPTER 22

Institutions and the Making of Persons: W. E. Hocking's Social Personalism

Tom Buford

Consider the nature and role of institutions in the philosophy of William Ernest Hocking. I do so for two reasons. First, we are in a crisis of institutions in our country. Institutions are under intense scrutiny and heavy criticism for failing to accomplish the ends for which they were formed. For example, consider higher education; it was formed in an attempt to mold human life, to remake human nature, in Hocking's language. With Allan Bloom's *The Closing of the American Mind*, what found expression was what many felt—viz., that institutions of higher education have failed us. Though Lawrence Levine's recent *The Opening of the American Mind* presents a counter, it is accompanied by Bill Readings's *University in Ruins*. Beyond higher education, Judge Robert Bork in his *Slouching Toward Gomorrah* gazes into the heart of most institutions in America and does not like what he sees. And, the suspicious eye finds fissures in secure icons in the pantheon of American leaders such as Thomas Jefferson, almost an institution himself. For many, clearly articulated skepticism has escalated to loss of trust. The second reason for my invitation is that in the philosophy of Hocking we find one of the few theories of institutions developed by a philosopher. Seeking help with the institutional issues of today, we shall ask what, if anything, Hocking teaches us about institutions that helps us ferret out worthwhile from gratuitous criticism? Further, what, if anything, ought we expect of institutions? What is unfair to expect of them? Such questions also place us in a position to critique Hocking's views.

How shall we approach this aspect of Hocking's thought? Hocking tells us that he seeks "the valid basis of an individualistic theory of society" (HNR, xi). A well-known charge against such philosophies is their failure to provide an adequate basis for community. The charge is rooted partly in individualism's dual emphasis on the moral, personal growth of the individual person as well as on the moral critique of social practices and institutions that hinder that growth. The crux of this charge is that such individualists find themselves in the throes of a dilemma (one aspect of the dilemma of modernity): the institutions that form or civilize human nature must be reformed because they hinder that very civilization! Hence, the central question before us is whether Hocking's thoughts on institutions can resolve that dilemma. We focus on one aspect of that dilemma, the remaking function of institutions, and return to the question of trust.

Consider three questions. First, what is Hocking's account of the social life of persons? Second, what is the place and function of institutions in Hocking's social thought (a topic usually omitted in the literature on Hocking's social philosophy)? Third, does the remaking function of institutions pose a problem for Hocking's theory of institutions? Let's turn to the first question.

I. What is Hocking's Account of the Social Life of Persons?

To begin, let me state succinctly Hocking's view of institutions. Hocking believes that though we are individuals we are inherently social creatures. Forming groups, human beings solidify them with institutions. All institutions are fabricated, quasi-personal, and maladaptive. Their character is influenced by the nature of the humans who made them, and their purpose is the development of individual persons. Though maladaptive, we should not abolish institutions; we should challenge and attempt to change them. For a standard against which to evaluate institutions, humans appeal to the absolute. To uncover the roots of institutions, consider the following aspects of the psychology of human nature: instinct, will to power, will circuits, and conscience.

Instinct

Society is formed by persons, though persons find themselves in society. What can that paradox mean? Begin with natural man, our biological life and associated instincts. Appealing to what we know from biology and psychology, Hocking finds specific instincts that form a hierarchy and central instincts that form a linear progressive structure. Each specific instinct is rooted in the microstructure of the biological organism; these specific instincts are primary, and each belongs to "a set of motor organs which may be assembled, in structure, as a single organ group, or may be dispersed.... There is thus a very rough correspondence between bodily shape and instinctive equipment: the instincts are inherited with the body, as its behavior-charter, so to speak" (HNR, 39–40). Though instincts function successfully with a minimum of training "it is the untaught and unteachable skill that marks the instinct." We see "numerous clear-cut instincts of simple patterns which we may call 'units of behavior,' because they are used in various combinations." Examples are reaching, grasping, pulling, shaking. In man they are left in fragments, and in animals they are unified (HNR, 51).

Built on the primary instincts are the second-order instincts. They fall into pairs: "general physical activity and ... repose (including the various modes of rest and sleep as unity of behavior); curiosity and aversion to novelty; sociability and antisociability" (HNR, 5). Think of second-order instincts as ordering the course of the primary instincts. For example, "pugnacity is ... *an instinctive control of instinct, an instinct of the second order.*" There are four second-order instincts: pugnacity, play, curiosity, and fear (HNR, 54). From this short discussion of instincts we see Hocking working with the natural materials of human life. These materials are not ordered along the lines of phenomenal causality. Rather, the more basic instincts find direction through the higher ones. For example, grasping and other rudimentary instincts may find themselves fulfilled in play.

Now, turn to the central instincts, the linear, action order of instincts. Central to these is the will. As Rouner points out, "The question which interests [Hocking] most, and which he regards as most important, is the question of the integrity of these several instincts, the manner in which they cohere in a self; or, more simply, their relation to the one fundamental instinct of an individual—the will" (1966, 155–156).

Will to power

What is the will, or will to power, to use Hocking characteristic phrase? Here instinct is self-conscious, unifying, evaluative, creative, and purposive. Consider each of these in turn. First, in the will to power, instinct becomes self-conscious, unifying, and evaluative. Though equipped with instincts, humans have successive experiences or successive interests; those experiences are united. But how? Consider what sign would indicate that one experience belongs to the *same mind* as the other and not to someone else's mind (HNR, 69). The two experiences would have a common value meaning. But a common value meaning can arise only for a self. Hocking explains, "Only when successive experiences, whatever their differences of content, have this in common, that they affect for better or for worse an identical concern in fortune, is there any self at all. And conversely, wherever there is a self, there all experiences are referred to a common interest: they are being perpetually sorted as satisfactory or unsatisfactory by a test in which no one can instruct any mind but itself" (HNR, 70). A self is "a permanent principle of selection" (HNR, 70). Experience presents possibilities from which the self chooses and evaluates as agreeable. The self "learns empirically what *things* are good. But what good is, it cannot learn empirically; since the use of this knowledge is implied in the first judgment.... The dawning of such self-possession means the achievement of a more or less stable *policy* toward incoming suggestions and impulses. And to have a stable policy is to have, in the specific sense of the word, a *will*" (HNR, 71).

What is it to have a stable policy? Hocking explains, "The policy of a self is its acquired interpretation of its own central and necessary interest. And thus, if men are alike in nature, we should be able to perceive at the center of all 'central instincts' and 'necessary interests,' and indeed within all instincts whatever, a nucleus of common meaning which we would be justified in calling the fundamental instinct of man, the substance of the human will. No one description of this central instinct is likely to be sufficient; but the phrase 'the will to power' is capable of conveying a large part of the truth" (HNR, 71).

Further, the will to power is the fundamental *creative* instinct of man. Hocking points out that "the will to power is perhaps the nearest name that has yet been found for the most central instincts." More than the will to live, the will to power involves "dealing with a world of objects and resistances, and holding intact one's validity in the midst of that intercourse. More than that, it implies the process of the artist, that of imposing upon the external mass an element of form and order that is first one's own. This active and creative quality is better suggested by the phrase, the will to power" (HNR, 73–74).

Next, the will to power is purposive. It is the single most significant aspect of the will to power. Though each instinct has its own particular goal and a way to achieve it, none is independent of the purposive direction of the will to power (HNR, 115).

In sum, Hocking claims that "it is the business of psychology to find first what the common clay is, and only then to enquire how it assumes its individual shapes. But if there is a common clay, a craving which in some way underlies and explains the rest, we are bound to take at least a glance at the question *what this clay itself is made of*, or whether it must be taken as an ultimate fact" (HNR 78). The root metaphor arising from our exploration of human nature is the artist. Hocking observes, "If we can anywhere catch a glimpse of the ultimate character of the will, it should be in our answer to the work of an artist. For it is his work to bring the deepest things in us into active response to the deep things of the world outside" (HNR, 80).

So far, we have outlined the psychology of the individual person. How can relations with others persons develop from such an individualistic understanding of human nature? We turn to Hocking's notion of will circuits.

Will circuits

A will circuit is the extension of the self of will and habit. Extension requires both an external environment and internal impulses.

One root of will circuits is the commotive impulse in the human organism. It consists in focusing the scattered intentions of several minds on a common purpose and moving them into the current of its achievement (MATS, 14–15). To be common it must be instituted. Once the common interest is instituted the group is "held together by its pursuit" (MATS, 16). The other root of the formation of a will circuit requires coincident external elements, wherein humans coincidentally share a common external environment. What fuses the wills of social groups is not only that the individuals have similar impulses but also that they share common objects. "This fusion requires identity of the physical objects used, and this is commonly brought about by the limitation of the physical supply and by propinquity of the users" (MATS, 365).

Consider now some properties of these coincident vital circuits, fused by the pursuit of a common and instituted purpose. First, they develop and possess autonomy. Hocking observes, "As the number of participants becomes great, the circuit itself seems to approach autonomy, and to impress not alone observers, but the participants also, as having a life of its own, other than their own lives" (MATS, 366). We find autonomy as workers gather to build a house; building the house takes on a life of its own.

Second, will circuits possess both solidarity and authority. "The mere fact that the life of other wills flowing through the circuit tends to draw my will into it: I am impelled by all the silent arguments of suggestion and authority to look upon that activity as something which ought to be carried on, which *ought to live* (MATS, 367).

Third, will circuits tend to become quasi selves. Calling on the metaphor of personality, Hocking says that "in fact the vital circuit *is a living thing*, not a mere abstraction or fiction. It is living in the same concrete sense as is the limb which it resembles: and the suffering and loss of energy which occur when a limb is severed are also experienced when the vital circuit is broken or destroyed" (MATS, 367). The social group takes on a life of its own. Once a group institutes common goals, it takes on the characteristics of personality: purposiveness, autonomy, authority, and will to power (MATS, 375). However, Hocking resists moving beyond personality as a metaphor. The group mind has no reality, no facticity beyond that of the individual persons in whom it is rooted (MATS, 368).[1]

Finally, the individuals who formed the social group find their identity and value through it. But how does the individual identify itself and find its value in terms of the now formed society? "The value of selfhood becomes transferred to the vital circuit by the same logic as that which shows itself in the turn of speech according to which one who hurts my hand hurts 'me': because one cares for selves one must care for the integrity of whatever forms an integral part of their lives. He who injures a vital circuit injures a self" (MATS, 367–368).

Conscience

We have given Hocking's account of the formation of society. But what is lacking is the moral element in that society. We return to human nature to determine whether its roots must be there. We are interested, also, in how a human becomes a moral agent; it is central to the remaking of human nature (HNR, 90). In persons, is the moral sense original equipment or is it developed socially?

Hocking's answer is clear and definite. "It is impossible that the 'ought' as we mean it in its current use should be a social product, as will appear if we consider how the meaning of this word is ordinarily conveyed" (HNR, 93). Why is this the case? Hocking explains,

> The history of the mastering of ... [ought] ... is not outwardly different from the history of the mastering of other difficult words: it is late in finding a firm

place in the mind. But when it arrives, there is a clear distinction in meaning between 'I ought to do thus and so' and 'It would be prudent for me because others prefer it.' This distinction has been called out by something in the attitude of the person who uses 'You ought' not noted in the foregoing derivation. The 'You ought' is neither a command, nor an item of information concerning the general will. The reaction to one who is supposed to have violated the 'You ought' is not one of simple anger; it has an ingredient of regret. It addresses itself not alone to his future discretion, but also to his past decision: it deplores the process by which he reached his choice. It assumes, rightly or not, that he was capable of a better process, and that he knows it. In brief, the 'You ought' addresses itself to an answering 'I ought' within; and unless the 'I ought' responds, it has missed its target. This 'I ought,' since it is presupposed in the meaning of 'You ought,' cannot be conveyed from without by means of the 'You ought.' It can only find its way into our sign-language by being taken as understood.... We know that every new person must find this angle for himself. The social use of the word [you ought] is thus never purely instructive: it is also, and primarily, awakening. It appeals to a strand of self-judgment which is original with every individual, and in this sense belongs to original human nature." (HNR, 93–94)

If it is not a social product, is conscience an instinct, one that can be accounted for in terms of biological evolution? Conscience resembles general instinct in behavior; it craves for an object of loyalty, which it seeks in its social context (HNR, 97). But standing outside the instinctive life, it can self-consciously perceive the direction of that life and guide it toward integration. It appears that all branches of the human family have a conscience. Though human societies vary, we should be able to find what is constant among and through the variations.

What is it about conscience that sets it apart from "all other innate tendencies" (HNR, 98)? "[C]onscience is the principal inner agency for the making of human nature; hence it must stand as a critic over against everything that is to be remade, and so over against all instincts ... it is cognizant of every act of will, and of the total policy of the self.... On this showing, original human nature would contain, beside all its instincts, something different from instinct, a self-consciousness applying certain standards of value to the control of behavior" (HNR, 98).

What are these standards? What is their source? It is tempting to think that Hocking must be referring to Platonic moral universals. But he is not. To answer these questions, turn to Hocking's discussion of sin. In the sinful act "the moral nature comes to its most vigorous and definite expression" (HNR, 100). What is sin? And, where in human nature is sin found? Sin is found in the life of the instincts. Yet no instinct is sinful by itself; to be sinful it must have an environment (HNR, 114). Sin is found "in the relation of an impulse to its mental environment" (HNR, 114). Recall our analysis of the instincts and their hierarchical and linear structure. We pointed out that the central instincts collectively were a single tendency, the will to power.

However, the specific instincts appeared to have their own goals, though none were independent of the will to power. Belonging to the mind, the specific instinct must appear consistent with the will to power and satisfy that will in its own domain. But the relation of the specific and central instincts may be strained, and they may become uncooperative. The specific instincts "may reject the responsibility to carry any further meaning than that of its own direct goal" (HNR, 115).

Here the specific moral issue arises. It arises "from this conflict: not the conflict between one person and another, nor the conflict between one impulse and another in a given mind; but the conflict between a given impulse and the central will, or between the separate and restricted meaning of an impulse, and the wider meaning which because of its human belonging it 'ought' to carry." Negatively, "Sin ... is the refusal to interpret crude impulse in terms of the individual's most intelligent will to power" (HNR, 116). Positively, "Sin ... *is the deliberate failure to interpret an impulse so that it will confirm or increase the integration of selfhood.*" For example, "If ... I allow ... [an impulse] to assume its primitive and separate meaning of destruction, I give it an interpretation inconsistent, in general, with as much of my will to power as I am capable of grasping. I sin. And I am aware of the fact, however vaguely:—this is my conscience" (HNR, 117). It is obvious then that all have sinned and continue to do so. This implies that all that humans make as artists, all the will circuits that they have formed and in which they live, are fallen, less than what they ideally could be.

Why do men sin? The explanation is their freedom to act on an impulse without due regard to its wider meaning. It is not a breakdown of rule following. There is no law of learning for morality. Right is not a matter of technique, following an objectively definable standard—such as Franklin did (HNR, 127). Sin or morality "is in all cases a matter of history, or better, of biography.... It might be possible to show the entire history of sin as a history of moral growth" (HNR, 172).

The biography, or better autobiography, is not a matter of the individual alone, for every autobiography is written in an environment. It is deeply social and institutional. "No man can live a moral life in aloofness from society and its various alliances; yet all alliance is alliance with the imperfect.... It is at the cost of losing all effect that one refrains from attachment to whatever is historical and organized in the world. Institutions exist to lend to each individual member their over-individual dimensions and scope. It is not alone a practical but a moral peril if I reject their aid.... It is equally evident that there are no perfect institutions" (HNR, 127).

Now we can return to the standards of value to which conscience must appeal in controlling behavior. Sin leaves in bold relief the standard, the *fully integrated self.* All of man's life is infected by his failure to achieve such full integration. Such failure is his expression of natural finitude. But this is not simply a matter of individual deeds; it is also deeply his status in the world. Listen carefully to Hocking:

> To lose life, to lose the quality of life, to lose the possibility of responding to what we believe to be the best, and hence the possibility of being with the best,

> ... to be unable to love, and *to know this inability and this loss*: this is a torment to man as it is not to the other creatures. If man must recognize in himself a status of natural finitude, we must also admit, as an element in his original equipment, an impulse which repudiates that status and demands a being at the level of his appreciation. This is not something different from the will to power; but it is the deepest expression of it. It is the *will to overcome death*.
>
> Religion has had this service to render: it has co-operated with this human unwillingness to accept mortality. It has constantly reminded man how easily he may remain mortal, and how hardly he may earn immortality. It has made him pray with a touch of fear, "Take not thy holy spirit from me." (HNR, 143)

What is this? Anxiety neurosis? Maybe. Some have called it the divine spark.

We have now quickly worked our way through Hocking's psychology, his understanding of the formative bases of social relations, of the roots and character of human morality, of human sin, and of the ideal to which conscience appeals in evaluating the will to power. And we noted in passing that institutions are infected by this natural finitude. Less than what they ideally could have been, they are maladaptive. We turn now to institutions, those agencies that attempt to remake human nature.

II. What Is the Place and Function of Institutions in Hocking's Social Thought?

We shall begin with a definition of institutions. Bellah defines an institution as "a pattern of expected action of individuals or groups enforced by social sanctions, both positive and negative.... Institutions are normative patterns embedded in and enforced by laws and mores (informal custom and practices)" (Bellah et al. 1991, 10–11).

In light of our analysis of human nature, what are the roots of institutions? As patterns of behavior they are rooted in the commotive impulse, conscience, and will circuits. Once a common purpose is instituted, the social group achieves autonomy, solidarity, authority, and quasi personality. One can say metaphorically that the instituted purpose can be seen as a norm governing the quasi personality; it is its thoughts. Viewed jurisprudentially, the thoughts of the social personality are laws. Viewed socially, they are the norms of institutions. And viewed metaphysically, laws rest in what is beyond particular institutions, the aboriginal unity, a super-self.

To grasp the importance of the super-self, consider Hocking's explanation:

> The conception of coincident will circuits does nothing to make clear to us how a meeting of human will is possible: it simply assumes, with all experience and common sense, that it *is* always possible for such minds as find themselves

> sharing the same planet, to make common cause. But this leaves untouched our argument that this everyday process of 'finding themselves sharing the planet,' together with every mutual understanding growing out of this discovery, implies that these selves have always had some region of unity, or identical experience, known to be such. This aboriginal core of unity must be prior to all social relationships: it cannot be any result of historic achievements; it cannot be the state. It is an object not of social but of metaphysical reflection; our practical dealings with it are matters not of politics but of religion.
>
> As contrasted with this metaphysical super-self, the state is a product of the human will. Man makes it, to be sure, in the image of his god....
>
> The religious unity of men thus lies deeper than their political unity: the given deity precedes the made deity. (MATS, 376–377)

Succinctly, social groups arise as the wills to power of individuals combine with those of other individuals in a will circuit. And the reason for their coming together lies not in the individual wills alone but in the aboriginal unity of the absolute.[2]

With this background, we come to the function of institutions, specifically the remaking of human nature. To grasp the function of institutions, consider society without them. We can do so by examining Hocking's view of experience. By experience, Hocking means "simply that inner digestion of data of all sorts whereby the outcome of every essay in behavior becomes a basis for modifying the next similar essay, and excluding the influence of all deliberate suggestion and training" (HNR, 150). As the life of instinct thrusts individuals into their environments, a particular emergency arises, a gap between the impulse and the means of satisfying it. "It is in this gap between the broad thrust of instinct and the particular emergency that 'intelligence' finds its first employment" (HNR, 150).

What is intelligence for Hocking? It is "the idea of a total end regulating the ways and means to its fulfillment—spans this gap, I do not mean that it acts unaided" (HNR, 152). This activity occurs in an environment of instincts and suggestions from Nature. As the intelligence guides the human toward ends, it will occasionally modify its plans. In such modification "consists the education or self-education of the animal: they are the work of 'intelligence,' so far as they are guided by the persisting idea of the general end, that is to say, by a mind or self" (HNR, 153).

How does intelligent experience work in transforming instinct? It does so by "wielding the tools of pleasure and pain.... Whatever experiment of mine results in pleasure will be confirmed, and its occasion will be sought again. Whatever experiment results in pain will tend to be checked or much modified at its next suggestion" (HNR, 156).

On what do these results depend? They depend on (1) definite sense experiences, (2) general depression or elation, and (3) mental after-images, that which remains with one after the event. The after-image is crucial in modifying human nature; "it is the reaction of the *whole will* upon the partial impulse, when the full meaning of that impulse is perceived in the light of its results" (HNR, 162). Hocking explains, "If the after-image is negative, the natural result will be a new hypothesis for dealing with a similar situation. And the transformation of instinct, under experience, consists essentially in the series of hypotheses which a given mind adopts,—hypotheses about the ways in which impulses are to be followed in order to satisfy the complete will.... And inasmuch as each successive hypothesis is built on the error of the preceding one, the process might well be called, in analogy with Plato's method of finding true ideas, a dialectical process. The work of experience is the dialectic of the will" (HNR, 163).

To confirm the dialectical work of experience, Hocking asks if institutions tend to "carry (human nature) in directions which of its own momentum it would not follow" (HNR, 167). His answer is that the "dominant trend of the human will is, at least roughly, parallel with the demands made upon it by society" (HNR, 167).

"As we consider the guidance society gives immediately we recognize that it works through social modeling" (HNR, 171). This is the process by which "custom continues the direction of development struck out by individual experience, and facilitates it.... More in detail: it abbreviates the tedious process of learning from experience; it saves from experiments too costly for the individual,—such, for example, as might cost him his life, or his health; it speeds the whole process of interpretation, through its own acquired skill of imparting its maxims.... Society is to each of its members a storehouse of technique: and as little as the learner could spare the mechanical technique of the socially transmitted arts and sciences, could he dispense with the accumulated capital of wisdom in the ways of behavior, the folkways of his own tribe and time" (HNR, 177). That is, as custom (the instituted common purposes that are normative for the will circuit) assumes the work of the after-image, humans appeal to the accumulated experience of the group instead of their individual experience alone.

Hocking raises an important question, "If human instincts, left to the teachings of experience, would grow very much as society tries to model them, why not leave them more completely to their own growth?... And further, so far as society loses the invaluable guidance of that still, small voice, the mental after-image, which governs growth, how can we be assured that its transformations shall, in the main, be other than deformations?" (HNR, 171).

Unfortunately, we cannot; though society is not primarily repressive, in actuality it has been, especially in three ways: (1) its standards are shaped to its interests rather than mine, (2) "the material equipment and scope which it offers me is curtailed by the competing needs of others,—and there are too many of us for the supply;" and (3) "the permitted modes of behavior fall into fixed institutional forms, and hamper the movements of any life that grows beyond them. Social modeling can be good, from the standpoint of the individual, *only if all these tendencies are corrected*" (HNR, 181). And, how can they be? "We have set up the individual life, with its natural dialectic, as the standard to which social pressures must conform; and by the aid of this standard we propose now to outline a set of tests whereby we can distinguish a good social order from a bad social order" (HNR, 182).

To do that Hocking locates the basis of obligation in the relations of the society and the individual. He says, "This is the primary and original 'right' in the relations of whole and member: a man's right is to his own development; the right of society exists only where its own interest and that interest coincide.... The test of a good social order, then, will be this: that I am not obliged to adopt any rule of conduct because of what others prefer I should do or be, unless I also have or can have that same preference" (HNR, 184).

To meet that test, under appropriate circumstances, four restrictions should be placed on institutions. And a discussion of each will aid our grasp of the repressive tendencies and the remaking possibilities of institutions. **Postulate 1:** "*What others wish me to be must be identical with what I myself wish to be*" (HNR, 185). This is the *postulate of identical ideals*. "In point of fact there are arrangements apparently as natural and as old as society itself which help to secure precisely the agreement required by the postulate" (HNR 185). These include the family, recommendership, the interested ideal, and the anatomy of admiration.

Postulate 2 is this: "*Every competitive interest must be so transformed or interpreted as to be non-competitive, or an ingredient in a non-competitive interest*" (HNR, 200). How do we bring about such noncompetitive relations among humans? It is done through agencies or institutions. The culture of a social group is its ideas, and its ideas are its laws and ideals. As we have seen, "Ideals and laws are fragments of institutions; institutions are permanent lusters of ideals, customs, and laws. An institution, like a law, has to meet two needs and not one only: it must be serviceable to society; it must also inform a groping individual what, according to racial experience or national experience, he wants, and hold him to that meaning" (HNR, 211). For example, "property must make clear to him the complete sense of his acquisitive and grabbing instincts" (HNR, 211). And family "must interpret to him his instincts of sex and parenthood" (HNR, 211). When humans comply with the institutional demands placed on them, "the hardships of this discipline have a meaning: they are part of the normal remaking of man" (HNR, 211). Since humans seek to be better and since institutions, being created by humans, bear the imprint of the sinful nature of their creators, "the human being is *adapted to maladaptation*. This is perhaps his supreme point of fitness to survive on this planet" (HNR, 214).

Now we can understand the place of institutions in the developing life of humans, in remaking persons. Hocking says,

> Man is the animal that can wait, the animal fashioned for suspended satisfaction.... The extent of this power makes him in effect a divided being, who enjoys in the present knowing his enjoyment to be partial, while harboring a larger hunger, destined to indefinite deferment, yet identified most closely with himself and hence not suffered to decline. The man is to be found in his

... longing or yearning, rather than in his accomplished ends. Were it not for this capacity to retain wholeness of prospect in the midst of very fragmentary satisfaction (aided by a large power for vicarious enjoyment), it is hardly conceivable that we could tolerate, still less take as a matter of course, the actual suppressions of talent suffered in the ordinary specialization of activity, or even in the necessity (suffered by man alone) of choosing among many possibilities of action merely because the narrow time-channel is overcrowded with our plans. No being is so domiciled in mutilations as man. Whatever shape institutions must take to give completest vent to the possibilities of his nature, it would certainly not be a shape which allowed him nothing to criticize or to reform. His fitness for the unfit must have its scope.... The happiness of man consists in the satisfaction, not of his primary instincts in their severalty, but of his total or central will,—the will to power. And power, while it need not be competitive, can only exist where there is something to push against, and will be in direct proportion to such resistance.... Now the most humanly satisfying type of power, so we thought, is the power of an idea, whether in persuading other men or in shaping institutions. The exercise of any such power presupposes that in institutions there are changes to be made; the same type of maladjustment which might dispose us to pessimism may, from this standpoint, appear as a necessary condition of complete welfare. (HNR, 215–216)

We turn now to **Postulate 3**: "*Whatever in institutions tends at any time to deform human nature shall be freely subject to the force of dissatisfaction naturally directed to change them*" (HNR, 221). The point here is "the very misfits of the social order will be grist for human nature provided this postulate is complied with" (HNR, 221). Hocking does not condone attacking institutions and laws simply for the sake of doing so. Rather, "There is literally speaking no such thing as being too conservative: but it is terribly easy to be conservative of the wrong objects. Hence place must be made in all our institutions for our common ignorance, our need to learn through the free clash of convictions,—this is the valid element in Mill's plea for social liberty, the valid element in American experimentalism" (HNR, 224–225). Experimentalism must be carried out with care; "Law-making is a most philosophic undertaking,—or should be.... Laws can only be competently perceived through institutions, institutions through history, and history through human nature" (HNR, 223).

Finally, we have **Postulate 4**: "*Conserving force shall be proportionate to certainty*,—certainty that the institution furnishes for the given society the best solution so far proposed of its own problem" (HNR, 225). But "is there any part of our institutional life which can claim such wholly certain and irreplaceable value? Nothing, unless what is necessary to meet a necessary interest. Such a necessity we have recognized in the simple existence of a social order, and of a political form thereof. But we cannot argue from this necessity that any given society or state is necessary; it is only that some particular state is necessary" (HNR, 225–226).

We have before us the main outlines of human nature, of the moral life developing within human nature, of the origin of society and the state, and the nature and function of institutions within that society. One important question remains: Could not the social order so necessary for the development of human nature to its full potential become a deity? It could, but only if the moral roots of society and its laws are ignored. Hocking contends that, as with individuals, "institutions and all institutions must *save their lives by losing them*" (HNR, 330). This means that "as for society and the State, it is the death of every institution when it begins to regard itself as self-sufficient or worthy of devotion in its own right" (HNR, 331). What, then, takes precedence over society and the state? It is the person. Here we find the role of religion in institutions. "Religion has no choice but to place the child in man, the total unexpressed self, above the institution; and to provide for that self a kingdom not of this world" (HNR, 332). This implies that "religion as the office of referring men to the absolute; not the absolute which removes them from the relative, but the absolute which by establishing a point of rest within the flux of change, gives all change, with its effort, and its hostilities, its total meaning" (HNR, 354).

III. Does the Remaking Function of Institutions Pose a Problem for His Theory of Institutions? Or, Hocking's Solution of the Dilemma.

Revisit now the issue that prompted us to begin this investigation. Can Hocking with his individualistic theory of society resolve this dilemma: the institutions that civilize human nature must be reformed because they hinder that very civilization! Considered another way, persons are deformed through institutions, yet recognizing they need reforming, persons depend on institutions for that reforming. How can institutions that deform, reform? Can Hocking resolve this dilemma? In one way he can, but in another he cannot.

Hocking can resolve the problem in a theoretical sense. We have seen that institutions are central to making persons on the level of instinct. Though they bear the imprint of man's sin, central to institutions is a common purpose formed and evaluated by conscience. The standard to which conscience appeals is the super-self, the absolute. The laws of institutions are informed by that standard, the fully integrated self. Thus, at the core of institutions is an absolute standard. As a self seeks self-reformation, or remaking, though it appeals to institutions for assistance, it can appeal to the standard governing the institution itself for help in its own remaking. Without the unity of the super-self, institutions could only repeat their deforming work. But by appealing to the standard, both the individual person and the institution can be reformed. In this way the individual can achieve the freedom of a more fully integrated personality, and institutions can be modified to better achieve their purposes.

But in a pragmatic sense Hocking cannot solve the problem. Within the framework of a society, consider the relation of persons to institutions whose morale has been destroyed by those institutions and who psychologically and socially can find no hope in them. Hocking has nothing to say to them. He is theoretically correct; the institutions of society that formed persons can be appealed to reform them. But if individuals have no trust in the institutions, they will not appeal to them for help. And Hocking offers no help with restoring trust. Paradoxically, Hocking's negative pragmatism, "That which does not work is not true" (MGHE, xiii), returns to haunt him. He has advanced a view of persons and institutions that fail the test. And it is not hard to understand why. His negative pragmatism is heavily dependent on the environment as the testing ground for the truth of the claim. If the environment changes, so does the truth of the claim. And that is what has occurred here. Hocking's view of institutions is appealing, if one assumes the essential trustworthiness of institutions themselves. But, if that trustworthiness has eroded, the ground is cut from under his criterion. Offering no way to restore trust in the root of institutions, the instituted common purposes of group life, its laws, this view of institutions will not work for those who do not trust them. Now, if I am correct that a loss of trust in institutions permeates our society, Hocking offers us no help with that loss.

NOTES

1. It is interesting to note that Hocking does not believe the community formed is consciously intentional. As he points out:

   > It is worth observing that a mind can mean far more than it can *image* or *think*. It can mean, for example, to act with another mind, and so to endorse what the other mind may think and will, however little it may be able to fathom the devices of that other mind.... One may *mean* an identity of will with persons whom he has not so much as thought of individually, as the children of Israel mean to coworkers with countless unknown others in the patriarchal purpose: each one is Israel in intent, and in their collectivity they are by this common intent, still Israel.... This kind of identity from generation to generation is not like the identity of an individual which maintains itself as it were biologically without conscious effort, through the presentations of memory. It is an identity that must be made by each individual will in its effort to achieve continuity of meaning with its contemporaries, its predecessors, its posterity. It is thus not an over-individual self; it is reborn in the fidelity of every generation of selves. Its security of continuance does not lie in its own substance; it lies in the fact that the desire to create this continuum is for every mind of man a *necessary desire*. (MATS, 370–371)

2. Hocking believes that the meeting of minds implies a primitive unity or a super-self. See MGHE, Part IV. A confusion is likely to arise at this point between norms that apply to a specific institution at a specific time and place and those norms that are universal in character. To avoid that possibility, we distinguish between natural and artificial institutions. Consider the family. In one sense the family is natural, in the sense that the voluntary acts of choice

and consent that enter into it are mounted on an involuntary base. Marriage is a matter of will: the disposition to marry is not. But in some groups the intelligence and will that form them act in the services of *permanent mental needs* which if not satisfied in one way and time will seek satisfaction in some other way and time. From this we infer that natural norms are the instituted common purposes formed on the commotive impulse and rooted deeply in the instinctive life of persons. They are universal in character. Specific norms are those formulated and instituted for artificial institutions.

WORKS CITED

Bellah, Robert N. et al. 1991. *The Good Society*. New York: Alfred A. Knopf.

Rouner, Leroy S., ed. 1966. *Philosophy, Religion, and Coming World Civilization: Essays in Honor of William Ernest Hocking*. The Hague: Martinus Nijhoff.

CHAPTER 23

W. E. Hocking and the Liberal Spirit
Douglas R. Anderson

I am confronted with the unusual task of providing a glimpse of the philosophical concerns of a talented, but now little recognized, philosopher in the American tradition. Perhaps it is too much to say that I can provide even a glimpse; William Ernest Hocking, who lived from 1873 to 1966, has a bibliography that runs to nearly 300 entries including at least a dozen significant books. Moreover, his life interests, which he took to be intimately related to his philosophical interests, were extensive. He earned money to pay his way to Harvard to work with William James by teaching mathematics and by working at surveying. While at Harvard he earned one hundred dollars a year as an organist for the Harvard Divinity School. He drew with pen and ink throughout his life, and at age 60 took up oil painting. Having earned a Harvard Walker fellowship for foreign study in 1902, Hocking spent the year in Germany. There he heard of the young Edmund Husserl and went to visit him at Göttingen; when Harvard chairperson Hugo Münsterberg learned of the visit, he wrote a brief note to Hocking stating that the philosophy department "did not grant Fellowships in order that students might seclude themselves in provincial universities" (Rouner 1969, 11). Together with his wife, Agnes, he founded the experimental Shady Hill School in Cambridge, Massachusetts in 1915. Hocking carried on correspondences not only with Husserl but also with Gabriel Marcel, Robert Frost, John Dewey and others. Interesting as these features of Hocking's life may be, however, if there is to be a retrieval of his philosophical work, it must be generated by something admirable or useful in that work itself.

Just getting started with Hocking's work, however, is not easy. One of the lessons learned in the recovery of Charles Peirce's work over the last sixty years was that there needed to be some association or correspondence established between Peirce's thought and philosophies that were already on the table. This occurred in two ways with Peirce. On the one hand, scholars found that he had actually influenced thinkers such as Josiah Royce, James, and Charles Morris. On the other hand, they learned that he could be situated in the trajectory of nineteenth-century American thought that ran from transcendentalism through to the influence of evolutionary thought and the origins of pragmatism. For my own retrieval of Hocking, I think some similar relational work is necessary. In different ways, Hocking's influence appears in the thought of Marcel, Charles Hartshorne, John William Miller, and John E.

Smith. Moreover, there was significant exchange between Hocking and his Harvard colleague Alfred North Whitehead.

Hocking himself was a student of both James and Royce, and this fact gives a unique flavor to the career of his philosophical writing. That he was aware of the dialectical tension in his own being is revealed in an interesting discussion of "pragmatic idealism" in his first book, *The Meaning of God in Human Experience*. The Roycean-idealist dimension of Hocking's work is not so easily foregrounded in the present intellectual climate as is his Jamesian-experiential dimension. So, it is through the latter that I try to offer a glimpse of his philosophical task.

This Jamesian dimension placed Hocking squarely in the American philosophical tradition of the twentieth century. "Philosophy," he maintained, "is the common man's business and until it reaches the common man and answers his questions it is not doing its duty" (Howie 1972, 249). His is the same down-to-earth frankness that earned pragmatism the genuine disrespect of more traditional philosophers who made such sober claims as that of Albert Schinz related by Paul Carus: "Pragmatism is nothing but this adulterated philosophy; philosophy sold to democracy" (1909, 474). Indeed, Hocking was a longtime friend and sometime philosophical adversary of the key common person's philosopher, John Dewey. As with Dewey, Hocking's commitment to philosophy's relation to ordinary human experience led him to write not only about metaphysics but also about art, education, religion, and politics. It is from this last quarter of Hocking's thought, the political, that I launch my present discussion. Specifically, I aim to say a few things about what he called the "liberal spirit" and its social and political import. To try to keep the discussion within the scope of present interests, I keep in mind Hocking's relation to Dewey and pragmatism and occasionally try to place Hocking's thought through its opposition to some features of the neopragmatic "liberalism" of Richard Rorty. My hope is not to persuade anyone to take up a discipleship of William Ernest Hocking. I work with the more limited aim of piquing an interest to inquire into the ideas of a first-rate mind whose work was marginalized by the midcentury political shufflings of philosophy in the United States.

Looking into Hocking's conception of the liberal spirit offers an occasion to recall a central, though sometimes forgotten, thread of the pragmatic tradition with which Hocking's thought was entangled: the close quarters maintained between our philosophical thinking and the habits by and through which we conduct our lives. More directly put, the living relation between philosophy and our attitudes. In the first of his Lowell lectures on pragmatism in 1906, James remarked that the "history of philosophy is to a great extent that of a certain clash of human temperaments" (1907, 6). Later, in the same lectures, and following a trail Peirce had marked out, James shifted his conception of pragmatism from that of a formal method to that of a habit of mind: "No particular results then, so far, but only an attitude of orientation, is what the pragmatic method means" (54). There *is* no static recipe for inquiry, but there is a pragmatic character to be looked for. Dewey, who shared James's sense "that philosophy expresses a certain attitude, purpose and temper of conjoined intellect and will" (James 1919, 6), took the same focus into the realm of political philosophy, maintaining that democracy was not centrally a matter of the structure of the polis. In his essay "Creative Democracy—The Task before Us," he made the point as follows: "In any case we can escape from this external way of thinking only as we realize in thought and act that democracy is a *personal* way of individual life; that it signifies the possession and continual use of certain attitudes, forming personal character and determining desire and purpose in all of the relations of life" (Dewey 1940, 222). This focus on attitude seems to me directly linked to the Bainian conception of belief that the pragmatists adopted, as well as to the earlier transcendentalist fascination with the work of moods and temper. It was a focus Hocking shared: one that kept him inextricably linked with the American philosophical tradition despite his worries over the pragmatic emphasis on instrumentalism.

Hocking brought his interest in the relation between philosophy and attitude to bear in his query concerning the future of the liberalism spawned by Locke and pursued by Mill. He drew from our culture's experience in the first third of this century the conclusion that "Liberalism as a special historic pattern of political and economic ideas has already passed: it has no future" (FL, 230). His diagnosis admitted the obvious successes of liberalist culture, two of which he took to be an increased tolerance and a somewhat more generalized higher standard of living. For several reasons, inherent in its own history, liberalism, as Hocking saw it, began to fail itself. Specifically, he maintained, "Liberalism has ceased to beget Liberals" (FL, 234). He noted a loss of "the universal appeal and universal validity" of a liberal "attitude" of "unsalted amiability" and "kindly sentiment toward others" (FL, 234). In a remark that, despite its incipient cynicism, retains some relevance today, Hocking stated his concern more strongly: "If a dour critic were to say that Liberalism as a dominant note in American education had produced a nation of spoiled and juvenile minds, unable to think, devoid of the power of self-criticism and incapable of mature political responsibility, we should have to accept the half-truth. Souls of this sort are illiberal at the scratch, because the consistent exercise of the liberal spirit is one of the difficult ways of living" (FL, 234).

For Hocking, it was, in part, an active liberal spirit that had accounted for liberalism's initial successes. And, it was, in part, the further generation of the liberal spirit by liberal cultures that enabled their ongoing success. Thus, as he worked through the failures of liberalism's version of individualism, Hocking maintained that one condition of the possibility of our moving beyond liberalism without rejecting its successes was a recovery of the liberal spirit—a functioning individualism, he believed, required this recovery. The attitude found in the liberal spirit is one that, for Hocking, underwrites any political and social revision and growth. There is in this claim a *prima facie* likeness both to Dewey's organic model of social development and to Rorty's description of social change through the ironist revision of final vocabularies. The first likeness, I think, is rooted in some actual affinities; the second, as I will try to indicate, although real, is less deep and overlays important differences.

Just as James and Dewey offered no recipes for achieving the pragmatic and democratic attitudes for which they fought, Hocking presented no formula for creating the liberal spirit. Nevertheless, we can distill from his writings a sense of some of the generic traits he took to be constitutive of the spirit. These might be enough to establish a heading for assessing the liberal attitude and its relevance for our own efforts in the conduct of life. Whether or not we make any headway in assessing Hocking's philosophical project, in establishing some of what seems to be at stake for him may awaken a dialogue concerning our own attempts to be twenty-first-century liberals.

Insofar as Hocking sees liberalism effecting its own negation in its own dialectical career, it makes sense to begin by a negative route in our approach to the liberal spirit. The failures Hocking believes we have experienced tell us something about what he thinks the liberal spirit is not. And the failure most relevant for this purpose is to be found in the attitude and orientation of the type of person liberalism in the United States has steadily generated. These are, as Hocking saw it, rugged individualists with a talent and energy for business. What this type of liberal individualist experienced and understood was the impact of negative freedom—the clearing of constraints by a liberal state so that individuals could exercise their abilities. In its productivity, this type embodied the success and revealed the experiential "truth" of liberalism. As Hocking saw it, however—and as Dewey saw it—this truth is a half-truth. The "successes" of liberalism were at the same time, in other ways, serious failures, especially inasmuch as they were accompanied by the loss of important features of the liberal spirit.

Hocking often referred to these business individualists as "Able Heads," and he sought to assess the social import of their conduct of life:

> And what or who is "Business"? A lot of Able Heads, each representing millions of individual transactions in going concerns, each individual transaction entered into willingly, and therefore presumably benefiting both buyer and seller—ergo, in sum total a happy country? Not at all. Each individual transaction ably manipulated so as to leave the largest net in the hand belonging to the Able Head; each Able Head, then calling on Washington for a further individual blessing, to improve not the product, not the lot of the buyer, not the Greatest Happiness, but the Net. And will not a collection of handsome Nets constitute a prosperous land? That seems to be the fallacy. They seem to constitute rather a set of prosperous spots, like pimples of prosperity on a visage predominantly pale! They do not add themselves into the General Health. (FL, 232)

In short, liberalism has had the consequence of affecting an illiberality among its beneficiaries—a character of closure, insulation, self-indulgence, and self-engrossment. The philosophical source of this result, Hocking suspected, was an over-emphasis on negative freedom. Liberalism has so emphasized rights that it has lost sight of the necessary dialectical relationship between rights and duties. Hocking identified this loss as a cultural disease—one perhaps still at work for us—whose upshot is a thorough demoralization. "Hence the cry of 'rights,'" he argued, "should never have been uttered except with the undertone of a vast humility; instead of which it has been taken as a pure birth-gift of Fortune, and the question is insidiously suggested whether, after all, there is any such thing as duty" (FL, 233).

The further effects of this absence of humility among the Able Heads include their self-identification as "receivers" not "givers" and their ongoing blindness to the public welfare and to the actual conditions of the "many" in liberal societies. They have learned, Hocking said, to put "the 'I' foremost," and they "may well have brought us to a pass where no genuine political 'We' can get a voice" (LEI, 46–47). "The question," Hocking said, "is whether these private reservoirs have any regular *working relations* to the public concerns. The answer is that under Liberalism they are not so much as invited to do so" (FL, 232).

Finally, working from this negative direction, the lack of a sense of the "we" was accompanied by another element of failure: the loss of a purpose more significant than the accumulation of private satisfactions. This absence in the lives of the Able Heads meant for Hocking that they brought little back to the culture that produced them. In contrast, he saw in the liberal spirit an infinite purpose in its task of creating the self and an environment for the realizing of all selves. The self, for Hocking, "so far from being a wholly evident and graspable being, as Descartes and Berkeley seemed to assume, is infinite in its depth and mystery" (TP, 440). The individual self, as for Dewey, is made not found. This larger purpose seemed to get lost in the self-engrossment generated by liberalism; for liberalism tends to produce persons "who find the meaning of life where they have been taught to find it, namely, in a sum of personal satisfactions, and having gained these are at a loss for anything more to do" (LEI, 96). I am reminded of Rorty's repeated advice for intellectuals to lighten up and not take themselves so seriously, especially since no one else seems to; if we look close to home we may find that presently we are the persons "without a calling," about whom Hocking was concerned.

In concert with Dewey, Hocking established a resistance to these effects of the liberal experiment, a resistance that stands pretty squarely in opposition to the "liberal ironism" of Rorty, whose conception of "human solidarity" is "a matter ... of sharing a common selfish hope, the hope that one's world—the little things around which one has woven into one's final vocabulary—will not be destroyed" (1989, 92). Or, as Richard Shusterman puts it in articulating a similar distinction between Rorty and Dewey, for Rorty "the prime value of liberalism is its privileging of negative liberty over any positive conception of self-realization or empowerment, its 'ability to leave people alone, to let them try out their private visions of perfection in peace' (Rorty 1991, 194)" (Shusterman 1994, 395). Hocking embraces the possibility of empowerment and banks our ability to move beyond liberalism's present condition on the recovery of the liberal spirit, which we now see begins with a resistance to the blindness and closure instantiated in liberalism's product, the business individualist. "Making an obvious distinction between Liberalism and the liberal spirit—," he asserts, "the liberal spirit has not yet finished its work in the world, nor is it likely to do so. It belongs to human nature, not to any party, religion, or historic movement. Its business is to correct the infinite self-centeredness of that same human nature when flattered by the enjoyment of those powers which society perennially creates as it becomes complex and unequal" (FL, 230). As I turn to Hocking's positive indications of the generic traits of the liberal spirit, I want to keep in mind that his purpose is in awakening us to a lived attitude and not in presenting us with a programmatic recipe for social cure.

From this initial negative route we might say that Hocking's "liberal spirit," in its widest sense, seems to involve a creative and experimental attitude in the remaking of human nature—an overcoming of "self-centeredness" and a return to a larger purpose. He takes the remaking of our nature to be an "art peculiar to man" (HNR, 10) and in general takes life to be "an apprenticeship to creativity" (MGHE, 153). Creativity, for Hocking is, however, not an act of sheer domination; creative activity begins with an openness or receptiveness to the possibilities actually available. The liberal spirit thus exhibits a liberality towards ideas themselves, treating them with what Hocking occasionally called "creative love;" an "idea, once conceived, must be free to live its prenatal life" (MIHE, 232–233). This attitude of reception, working with initial philosophical reflection, eventuates in experimental activity, such that the liberal spirit moves adventurously out from the creative self. Indeed, Hocking found in Dewey's *The Quest for Certainty* "one value which no future experience can dislodge," the value "of discovering the possibilities of the actual and striving to realize them" (1930, 236). It is in this striving to realize that one brings the liberal spirit into the public sphere.

In conjunction with this openness and receptivity, Hocking finds in the liberal spirit a willingness to think, to work with the possibilities at hand. For him, a willingness for philosophical work is a feature of the liberal attitude; the liberal attitude *is* a philosophical attitude. Hocking agreed with Whitehead that all human belief and conduct are metaphysical at root: "Long before the term was heard of, human beings were asking questions we now classify as metaphysical. These questions continue to be asked by persons who would be horrified to learn that they were talking metaphysics" (1946, 366). He understood metaphysical inquiry to derive "from a primitive and inescapable human concern, man's ambition to know where he is, what he is, why he is, and what the whole thing means" (1946, 367). Philosophical—and metaphysical—thinking, consciously undertaken, is thus crucial to the liberal spirit, in part, precisely because it provides a "world" in which the liberal spirit's concern for the whole can gain a purchase. This I should acknowledge, however, is a two way street—a matter of reciprocal or dialectical dependence. In the direction I am presently taking, the liberal spirit reveals a need for metaphysical thinking to avoid being homeless. But it is also the case that, for Hocking, the spirit or attitude orients thinking such that metaphysics itself stands to gain in both flexibility and richness under its influence. Indeed, Peirce often exercised a distinction between science as a way of thinking and science as a body of propositions, opting for the former. The distinction influenced both James and Royce, and something of this influence, as I will try to sketch below, remains in Hocking's thinking about philosophy and metaphysics.

Metaphysics, then, establishes a working sense of limits and constraints, of what is actually possible. This is especially important for the experimental dimension of the liberal spirit, since it provides the background or the environment without which measurement and judgment in experiment would be impossible, or, at least, arbitrary.

A willingness to philosophize is likewise crucial in providing a working foreground for experiment. Philosophical speculation, in dialectical relation with the receptive attitude, works out possibilities: ideals, aims, and ends-in-view toward which we drive our experimental activities. Experiment requires an orientation, just insofar as it means to establish something, and, Hocking maintains, "the only value any experiment can possibly have is that something may be *established*" (HNR, 251). Consequently, there can be no experimentation without philosophical thought. And particularly where the stakes are high, experimentation needs philosophy: "experimenting with a law," says Hocking, "must always be a graver thing than experimenting with a new breakfast food. Law-making is a most philosophical undertaking,—or should be" (HNR, 249). The creative generation of aims and ideals is central to Hocking's interest in the remaking of human nature, and the reflective work it entails brings a responsibility to experimentation. As Hocking suggests, "if our attitude toward the matter were purely empirical, we could have no manner of objection to having anyone experiment with anything, for instance, with killing off the surplus population, as one humanitarian old Pharoah is said to have done by throwing 80,000 beggars into a quarry, both for their sake and for that of the survivors" (1940, 243).

Interestingly, Hocking shares with Rorty a sense of urgency in the use of creativity and experiment in the revising of human living. The difference is that where Hocking sees a need for philosophical/metaphysical thinking in enabling the liberal spirit to carry out its reconstructive work, Rorty sees a need for jettisoning metaphysics altogether. Rorty's reasons are several, and I will try to deal with each in its place. The reason relevant at this juncture is his belief that metaphysics cannot fulfill its promise to "ground" or "found" our ordinary beliefs concerning the world and the conduct of life, and that therefore we can, and should, get on with life without looking for any metaphysical "backup" for our beliefs. Pragmatically speaking, metaphysical beliefs are superfluous.

Hocking was well attuned to the sort of criticism Rorty presently brings to bear on metaphysics. Referring to an earlier antimetaphysical turn, he remarked that "This engaging prospect of relief from metaphysical travail is new in its sweep but not in its principle" (1946, 365). His philosophical response was that the "backup" conception of metaphysics, if taken in a hard-nosed way, is misguided in supposing that metaphysics is of use only if it can establish a deductive certainty from which other claims can be derived and through which they can be sustained. Hocking, like Peirce and Dewey, had another assessment of metaphysics' function. He maintained what he called his "rooted heresy": "that *metaphysics is first of all an inductive science*: it is only through the temporal, factual, refractory, irrational aspects of experience that first principles come to a light that holds steady. They have to be found *in rebus*" (1958, 275). The backgrounding of principles, limitations, and possibilities that metaphysics effects is, for Hocking, a reflective response to the undergoing, suffering side of experience. Its function is to establish and maintain working certainties (see 1930). Indeed, one of his own reflective responses was to reject the possibility of Rorty's suggested overcoming of our metaphysical urges: "We cannot solve our metaphysical problems by preventing them from arising" (1940, 238). For Hocking, every particular metaphysical stance remains, in principle, open to revision and development. However, what the liberal spirit, in its project of remaking human nature, cannot countenance—or survive—is the absence of philosophical thinking. From Hocking's angle of vision, the "need for metaphysics is . . . not remote and eventual but concrete and actual" (1946, 378).

The concreteness and actuality Hocking had in mind have to do with the close relationship between thought and action that he, like the pragmatists, believed to be at work. In an essay assessing the importance of Dewey's work, Hocking noted with applause that "Dewey's philosophy is not a set of propositions" but "a national movement" (1930, 225). Philosophy construed as a set of propositions or propositional beliefs loses its vitality—its concreteness and its actuality. Philosophy only gains vitality insofar as it is "believed" in a pragmatic way, insofar as it informs human habits and action: "The blank face of a proposition is deceptive: its very self is in the working out" (1930, 225). In the case at hand, for example, it is just insofar as liberalism as idea has been fought for and put into practice, as we say, that Hocking feels confident in assessing its value: its failures and successes.

This "working out" of our philosophies—our ideas—discloses, in addition to receptiveness and a will to philosophize, an emotive dimension in Hocking's conception of "liberal spirit." The first trait of this dimension is the courage to bring ideas into the public realm: a willingness to risk one's thought in a public experiment. It is precisely this sort of risk that Hocking took to be diminished both by excessively liberal and by fascist cultures. On the one hand, liberalism tends more and more to establish a market in which all ideas are accepted. In this "safe world," Hocking argued, "ideas become first unimportant, then meaningless, and truth being eviscerated is no longer worth getting: your realm of costless toleration is a realm of devaluated truth" (LEI, 135; see also FL, 235). Fascism, on the other hand, tries to effect a risklessness by eliminating any need for ideas: "The dictatorial state attempts to live without the risks of living; but there is no life without risk, whether a man or a state, and conversely, what is riskless is lifeless" (LEI, 135). The liberal spirit requires an environment that can sustain its requisite courage; without it, its project comes to a close, and the culture is left with stagnation at whatever present status it has, a culture, suggested Hocking, "full of pragmatic adjustments, and politically milling around in the same spot forever" (FL, 235). Despite his differences with Dewey's pragmatism, Hocking claimed to have learned from it what he called the "fighting-value" of ideas and to have seen the "fighting-value" of pragmatism itself at work in American culture as a sustainer of the liberal spirit: "The great public work of the instrumental philosophy has been to limber up the ways of knowing of this people, to reduce fixed dogmas to working hypotheses fit for experiment; to give the intellectually traditional, authority-seeking, hero-worshipping American the courage of his own experience" (1930, 227). A recognition of and willingness to pursue the fighting-values of our ideas and purposes is a clear mark of the liberal attitude.

The liberal spirit's courage is attended by a second emotive trait: steadiness of commitment. The purposes, ideals, and aims generated by our thinking require a conviction on our side to see them through. Not only must we bring them to the public, we must see to it that they are given room to manifest success and/or failure. Taken together the emotive traits enable private notions to be worked out in the public sphere. However, they also have the capacity—especially in the twenty-first century—to provoke a fear of totality (see Rouner 1969, 184). This, I think, is another reason for Rorty's suspicion and rejection of metaphysics. That is, as he sees it, the courage and commitment that go into the publicizing and actualizing of our philosophies can easily develop into a kind of fanatical and dogmatic adherence to these ideas and the habits of conduct that surround them. Most notably, we blame the existence of national socialism on this sort of courage and commitment gone astray. If, as Rorty supposes, metaphysics has no use as a foundation for cultural habits *and* it bears with it the opportunity for such extensive degeneracy, it makes even more sense to try to get over our habit of philosophizing. The "air of light-minded aestheticism" he adopts toward "traditional philosophical questions," says Rorty, is important because it "helps make the world's inhabitants more pragmatic, more tolerant, more liberal, more receptive to the appeal of instrumental rationality" (1991, 193).

Hocking was fully cognizant of this danger of courage and commitment. Nevertheless, he would see Rorty's response—especially in light of his resistance to Mill's similar line of argument—as too extreme for the reasons adduced at the outset. If over-commitment leads to totality, under-commitment results in something like

"The Wasteland" or "The Hollow Men"—no consummatory bang, but a whimper. When metaphysics fails in practice, in being worked out, the answer should not be to end metaphysics and our sense of commitment but to get a better metaphysics. In a letter to a former student, Hocking acknowledged "that Germany's aberration was metaphysical" and "that the deep suffering of our age, its loss of bearings, is metaphysical," but he also maintained "that the cure for all of this must be metaphysical" (Robinson 1968, 116). In order to sustain this commitment to metaphysics in the face of the actual aberrations in history, Hocking saw the need for two further traits in the liberal spirit. Put in a less transcendental fashion, he understood through experience the importance of being self-aversive and of attending to what lies beyond one's immediate interests and concerns.

To be self-aversive is to attend to one's own fallibility even in the midst of one's commitment; it is to understand that our thought and action is, in part, experimental. Hocking's insistence on the inductive nature of philosophy builds in a kind of methodical aversiveness; that is, it keeps the critical dimension of philosophical thought up front. Nevertheless, Hocking, I believe, had in mind for the liberal spirit a more direct awareness or sense of our openness to loss and failure: a lived orientation, not merely a method. Only under the sway of this aversiveness can we move beyond *ourselves* (see MGHE, 472–481). The "true dialectic of history" for Hocking is "the slow consensus of freely thinking and groping human minds, as they perceive the inadequacy of the thoughts which have been guiding them, and turn toward something better" (LEI, 97–98). The import of James's meliorism was not lost on Hocking; he simply adapted it to his own version of historical idealism.

The second attentiveness returns us to the earlier separation of liberalism and the liberal spirit. Liberalism, Hocking perceived, led eventually to self-engrossment; the liberal spirit, to effect its purpose, required an outward-moving interest as well. In bringing our ideas to bear on our cultures, we must attend both to the needs of other individuals and to the public health. Such attention serves to temper the "erotic" or self-directed element in our thought and action. It is precisely for this reason that Hocking identified the good Samaritan as a bearer of liberal spirit (LEI, 61). A liberal attitude must reflect Hocking's claim that "Man is not by nature a solipsist, confined to his own consciousness and his own interests; he is by nature an active agent in an active world, and a personal agent in a world of persons and things" (LEI, 101). The upshot of this attentiveness was for Hocking a genuine openness to cultural differences, so long as these could be construed as genuine experiments aimed at cultivating self-realization; it is this strand of Hocking's thought that Daniel Robinson identified as his "cultural pluralism" (Robinson 1968, 108).

Finally, Hocking required of a liberal spirit an attention to the actual conditions of others; it was this attentiveness in Marx's thought that Hocking found most compelling. Without such attention, the liberal spirit might spend its efforts in misguided ways and in dead-ending directions. If, as Hocking suggests, "the heart of the liberal consciousness" lies in the "spirit of compassionate and creative aid for the exploited" (LEI, 61), one must become acquainted with the conditions of the exploited. The irony is that this last trait of the liberal spirit is made more difficult to achieve in the midst of liberalism's actual successes: "It is only the direct experience of humanity-under-duress that can supply the clues for understanding the behavior and motives of other humanity-under-duress. There is such a thing as being too fortunate for judging the less fortunate. The U. S. A. . . . suffers under this handicap at just this juncture" (SMN, 6). We indeed have little feel for life in Sarajevo; most of us have only peripheral acquaintance with the conditions that cultivate the life (and now death) of a "Notorious BIG" or the likes of Nine Inch Nails; few men have any direct grasp of the experience of women who live under the threat of violence. The liberal spirit should neither pretend to know what it does not nor romanticize what it does know; it should seek an acquaintance with the actual conditions of other human lives.

These last two traits of attentiveness are closely linked to Hocking's articulation of a revision of liberal democracy. The two central features of his revision—what he called the commotive function in building community and the co-agent state—directly reflect the need for and difficulty of the creation of a political space in which free individuals might not only remake themselves but might at the same time choose some common purposes for which to strive. These are matters for another time, but they serve to indicate Hocking's own struggle to think his way toward an environment in which the liberal spirit might more effectively undertake its task.

Conclusion

Having marked out this skeletal structure of traits of Hocking's conception of the liberal spirit, I am left wanting in time to try to cash out its significance. One might make a quick attempt to bring this spirit to life by listing an array of exemplary historical figures. However, perhaps it is enough that each of us can think of more ordinary persons who in their own ways have brought something of a liberal spirit to bear on our own lives; if any of us has literally sensed the significance of such a spirit, it will stand as a bit of evidence in the direction of Hocking's conception. Let me close, then, with a brief abstract of the philosophical import of Hocking's interest in enabling this liberal attitude and with a question concerning its relevance for the unhandsome elements of our own present condition.

The lived upshot of the liberal spirit, it seems to me, is an achieved freedom and responsibility. Hocking, like Dewey, sees in such an attitude the possibility of self-realization. For Hocking, a freedom that is empowering, that is more than a liberty from external constraint, is achievable only through an awareness of constraints and only with discipline. And it is this freedom that makes us responsible. We are not, as he puts it, born responsible; the maintenance of a liberal spirit yields a kind of Thoreauvian ownership of our thoughts and actions; responsibility comes with this ownership of our creativity and experimentation. Again, responsibility is not a matter of having a particular philosophical doctrine, but of being philosophical in concert with the rest of the liberal spirit.

In Hocking's view it is just this positive freedom and responsibility that enable the liberal spirit to engage in the ameliorative project of remaking human nature.

I have, pretty much, worked the drier, descriptive side of Hocking's work. It would be unfitting to conclude without some attempt to return his thought to our own concrete condition. So, I end by asking what is left of the liberal spirit at our American universities and colleges? My own sense, and I make the point earnestly, not as a dose of cynicism, is that many of our universities are now run by the Able Heads of business. I suspect also that those of us who work the scholarly trade have entered into an entrepreneurial game: a game perhaps driven by the measuring practices of deans, but one in which we have nevertheless become complicit. Among students, negative freedom seems to have been pushed to its limits: the "right" not to have exams before vacations, the "right" to avoid classes and study through purchased notes. Student life seems a feast of rights without duties. If I am at all right in these guesses, I find it hard to see how the liberal spirit Hocking conceived can put in much of an appearance in our schools. And if such an attitude does not reside in a culture's universities, where else is it likely to find a home?

My question, however, may do no more than raise the question whether Hocking's liberal spirit is wanted. Perhaps Mill and Rorty are right in suggesting that being left alone is enough; and perhaps we have already achieved that aim and, as Rorty thinks, merely need to preserve it. To begin to think through these issues both individually and in community is beginning enough for Hocking: "political life" for him "is a philosophical enterprise . . . and a democracy is peculiarly committed to the effort to think it through" (MATS, x). To fail to think it through in our contemporary culture of abundance might, however, put us in the company of those products of liberalism who drew Hocking's fire in the mid-1930s: "These rugged individuals at their maturity remain truncated torsos of humanity stuck around in handsome private estates on the edges of a thousand cities. . . . They have no mission, they are mere promissory futilities, empty of moral dignity; and the rights they claim become more and more a social protection to a low grade aesthetic consciousness. They might as well not exist. The society that flowers into these sturdy unfragrant weeds as its best blossom is a moral and cultural failure" (FL, 236). I hope at least, even if we disagree with Hocking's philosophical diagnosis, that we of the thinking trade, offspring of a liberal culture, can avoid cultivating ourselves into the suburban weeds he documented. In a more positive vein, I am willing to risk that a living version of his liberal spirit might help us take a run at what he called the "one achievement worth noting": the "*creation* of a certain individual beauty in living and in the environment of living—one's Task" (Howie 1973, 250).

WORKS CITED

Carus, Paul. 1909. "Anti-Pragmatisme." *The Monist* 19 (July): 474–75.
Dewey, John. 1940. "Creative Democracy—The Task Before Us." In *The Philosopher of the Common Man*, ed. Sidney Ratner. New York: G. Putnam's Sons, 220–228.
Hocking, William Ernest. 1930. "Action and Certainty." *Journal of Philosophy* 27 (April): 225–237.
———. 1935. "The Future of Liberalism." *Journal of Philosophy* 32 (April): 230–247. Cited as FL. Reprinted as chap. 11 of this volume.
———. 1940. "Dewey's Concepts of Experience and Nature." *Philosophical Review*, no. 2 (March): 228–244.
———. 1946. "Metaphysics: Its Function, Consequences, and Criteria." *Journal of Philosophy* 43 (July): 365–378.
———. 1958. "Response to Professor Krikorian's Discussion." *Journal of Philosophy* 55 (March): 275–280.
Howie, John. 1972. "Metaphysical Elements of Creativity in the Philosophy of W. E. Hocking, Part I." *Idealistic Studies* 2 (September): 249–264.
———. 1973. "Metaphysical Elements of Creativity in the Philosophy of W. E. Hocking, Part II." *Idealistic Studies* 3 (January): 52–71.
James, William. 1907. *Pragmatism*. New York: Longmans, Green, & Co.
———. 1919. *Some Problems of Philosophy*. New York: Longmans, Green, & Co.
Robinson, Daniel. 1968. *Royce and Hocking: American Idealists*. Boston: Christopher Publishing House.
Rorty, Richard. 1989. *Contingency, Irony, and Solidarity*. Cambridge: Cambridge University Press.
———. 1991. *Objectivism, Relativism, and Truth*. Cambridge: Cambridge University Press.
Rouner, Leroy. 1969. *Within Human Experience: The Philosophy of William Ernest Hocking*. Cambridge: Harvard University Press.
Shusterman, Richard. 1994. "Pragmatism and Liberalism between Dewey and Rorty." *Political Theory* 22 (August): 391–413.

CHAPTER 24

The Defects of Liberalism: Lasting Elements of W. E. Hocking's Philosophy

John J. Stuhr

> ... there is no way of plotting a living thing upon a flat sheet.
>
> William Ernest Hocking (MATS, xv)

I. A Blind Date with a Negative Pragmatist

Believing that life is short, too short for long prefaces and windy introductions, I begin directly with a statement of fact and a postulate. Moving from this fact and this postulate, I seek to establish a general conclusion.

As I begin, I want to tell you that, the so-called problem of other minds notwithstanding, I know just what you're thinking. You're thinking: Is a book focused on an obscure, dead American philosopher really worth my time and effort? You're thinking: Don't I have better things to do than read an essay drawn from a lecture about an obscure dead American philosopher that is part of a series of lectures sponsored by an organization funded in part by the obscure dead American philosopher's family? You're thinking: This is going to be really bad.

Now, I admit that this sounds like a recipe for a tedious and unrewarding intellectual blind date. However, I think this obscure dead American philosopher, William Ernest Hocking, may surprise and engage you. (This essay is drawn from chapter 2 of Stuhr 2003). Of course, I won't promise love at first sight; few blind dates are that easy or effortless.

Instead, let me promise only critical honesty. Let me begin with this statement of fact: William Ernest Hocking is today an obscure philosopher. Of course, to note that Hocking is an obscure philosopher is to engage in redundancy. In American culture today, philosophers typically are unfamiliar, inconspicuous, and remote, and so to be a philosopher in America today typically is to be obscure. Even so, Hocking now is especially obscure, or doubly obscure, because his work now is unfamiliar even to most philosophers. It is simply a matter of fact that even professional philosophers rarely read, write about, or discuss Hocking's thought. Almost all of his many books are out of print. There are hardly any references to his work in scholarly citation indices. Professional conferences do not include papers about him, and graduate students do not write dissertations about his thought. His views are very seldom taught, even in courses on American philosophy and even in courses on twentieth-century American philosophy. The recently published *New Oxford Dictionary of Philosophy* includes no entry on Hocking, while the 1967 *Encyclopedia of Philosophy* devotes to Hocking's life and work a single column squeezed between longer entries on Leonard Trelawney Hobhouse and Shadworth Hodgson. At Penn State University, most of Hocking's books aren't even housed in the massive main library; instead, they gather dust in a warehouse annex filled with books that aren't used enough to merit shelf space in the stacks. In short, it is a matter of fact that today Hocking's philosophy is very rarely read, analyzed, or utilized.

This neglect of Hocking's philosophy is remarkable because it stands in sharp contrast to the serious and sustained attention devoted to, and the importance ascribed to, his philosophy during his long career, from his first published philosophical essay in 1898 at age twenty-five through some 300 publications right up to his death in 1966. During much of this time, Hocking was generally regarded as a major thinker of lasting importance and real originality, a philosopher mentioned in the same breath as James, Royce, and Dewey, a thinker one could not avoid.

As such, Hocking is a striking case study in the processes of canon formation within professional philosophy and the humanities more generally. How, why, and in whose interests has Hocking been so thoroughly marginalized, excluded, and erased? Just when did he move from professional philosophy's Top 40 playlist to its discount dustbins of genuinely alternative music? What are the consequences of this dramatic reversal of fortune? What follows from it? Who is implicated in it? How has it shaped our own thought?

I think these are very important questions. They are questions to which philosophers, despite their proclaimed interest in self-knowledge, devote surprisingly little attention. Still, any adequate genealogy of the virtual disappearance of Hocking's philosophy from our intellectual horizons must include at least the following three concerns. First, Hocking has vanished in part because the sweeping scope of his thought stands in opposition to the present narrow specialization of most professional philosophy. Drawing on realism and mysticism, empiricism and Christianity, naturalism and intuitionism, Asian thought and Marxism, and modern philosophy and currents of reflection that eighty-five years ago he recognized and labeled as postmodern, Hocking ranged over problems in religion and politics, education and ethics, biology and psychology, and epistemology and aesthetics. In doing so, he displayed a stunning intellectual breadth and wide and generous sympathies that readily seem outdated in an era in which philosophical portfolios are considered diversified if they include, for example, both Quine and Davidson, or both Heidegger and Derrida, or both wild deconstruction of Searle and superficial analysis of Foucault. Moreover, Hocking's philosophy outstrips and undermines the intellectual partitions that professional philosophy now has established for itself. He attended seriously and carefully to the writings of American pragmatists, British analysts, Continental metaphysicians and antimetaphysicians, and Indian mystics. As such,

Hocking embodied in abundance the pluralism and respect that is in such short supply in professional philosophy today.

Second, just as the scope of Hocking's philosophy stands in opposition to the intellectual specializations and subspecializations within professional philosophy, so too the orientation of his philosophy stands in opposition to contemporary professional philosophy. Like John Dewey, Hocking believed that philosophers should address the real, living problems of men and women rather than the artificial issues, formal methods, and retold histories and marginal comments of so many professional philosophers. Accordingly, Hocking wrote without the jargon, conversational name-dropping, nearly endless footnotes, and other trappings of the academy. He aimed at an educated public. Today, sadly, that public may not exist in sufficient numbers to provide him with readers. His books certainly have no place in the chain bookstores that fill their philosophy sections with bestsellers on new age metaphysics, pyramid power and the healing properties of pyramids and crystals, the Zen of business downsizing, and the application of total quality management principles to intimate personal relationships. In addition, this orientation now is largely ignored by scholarly audiences that judge such work insufficiently technical and demand that their philosophy be less public and more professional. Hocking, however, took seriously the view that philosophy is concerned with wisdom—and not just with knowledge. He took seriously the view that wisdom is a shared good, such that successful philosophy must be public philosophy. As a result, his writings are a virtual chronicle of public problems and transformations in twentieth-century America—from his books on nationalism and world civilization, experiential faith and living religions, and science and values, to his essays and articles on war and military psychology, diplomacy and the League of Nations, foreign relations with the East and Mideast, law and human rights, the atomic bomb and international responsibilities, the treatment of ex-enemy nations following World War II, the role of unions and labor strikes, the mission of public education, the Cold War, the meaning of the death of President Kennedy, and the public role of the free press—an analysis recommended to its readers by *Time* magazine. By contrast, professional philosophy today finds little time (or space) for this commitment to illuminate practice by theory and to test theory by practice.

Third, Hocking's philosophy is ignored today not just because of its broad scope and public orientation but also because of its content. Hocking was an idealist, and idealism has long been out of fashion in philosophy. In the twentieth century, European phenomenologists, existentialists, hermeneuticists, critical theorists, and poststructuralists and postmodernists have attacked idealism. British and Anglo-American ordinary language philosophers, positivists, analysts, realists, and materialists have rejected idealism. And, American pragmatists, naturalists, and empiricists have criticized idealism to the point that they rarely bother any more even to engage it. By itself, of course, none of this hostility toward idealism establishes that idealism is fatally flawed, or even flawed at all. To demonstrate that idealism is incorrect requires a detailed analysis of the validity and soundness of the arguments set forth by idealists and their enemies. It does, however, establish that idealism now seems to most philosophers to be something musty, something stored in library warehouses and metaphysical museums, something more important to the history of philosophy than to the present life of philosophy. For most philosophers today, idealism is no longer, in the words of William James, a "live hypothesis"—a hypothesis that stands in relation to an individual as a real possibility, a hypothesis that scintillates with credibility for that individual, a hypothesis on which that individual is willing to act and to live (and not just to sit passively while reading an essay like this) (James [1896] 1979, 14). Hocking's own description of the movement of thought and changes in philosophical climate seems to apply to idealism today: "The formulae that were once potent here too begin to fail: ideas and phrases, gritty a generation ago, a decade ago, are already worn smooth and lend no more friction to any human work" (MGHE, ix).

Hocking surely tried to render idealism a live hypothesis, a potent, gritty philosophy. He recognized that this is not an easy task. Writing to a friend in 1954, he observed:

> I have for a long time been concerned over what we might call the "bad press" which idealism has been suffering under. In spite of the irrelevance of the notion of "fashion" to the world of ideas, there is no doubt that in this country, and to some extent in Europe, there has ruled an anti-idealistic fashion. And strangely enough in a field where care in the use of terms should rule, this current has been opposed less to idealism than to subjectivism with which it is too easy to identify idealism.... It is a matter of great importance to get idealism as a metaphysic presented as it is, and not as those who seek the air of novelty by an illicit contrast would like to present it.... I am giving myself to the same effort so far as circumstances permit—to write that paragraph in which the meaning of idealism is so transparent and radiant that it will compel its own attention and conviction, and spread through the whole network of human mentality. That may take a hundred years, but what does that matter? (to Daniel Sommer Robinson, May 11, 1954; in Robinson 1968, 159–160)

Hocking attempted to spread idealism by engaging tirelessly its critics—particularly pragmatists such as James and John Dewey. Indeed, in many respects, Hocking's metaphysics and philosophy of religion constitute a sustained attempt to set forth an idealism that can not only withstand but also incorporate the insights of pragmatism. Hocking viewed pragmatism not simply as a challenge to idealism but above all as an opportunity for idealism to release its forces, to render itself more complete, self-consistent, and ultimately reasonable. Thus, Hocking wrote that pragmatism had laid bare the weakness of classical idealism by demonstrating that idealism "does not do the work of religious truth" and, so, "is not the truth of religion": "The salvation [idealism] offers men seems still to be, in effect, a salvation from the particular in the general, the ideal; even though it names the concrete as its goal, it has not yet been able in this matter of religion to accomplish union with the concrete ... so that when the pragmatic test comes, a religion which is but a religion-in-general, a religion universal but not particular, a religion of idea, not organically rooted in passion, fact, and institutional life, must fail" (MGHE, x, xii).

Because Hocking accepted this pragmatic argument against traditional idealism, he endorsed what he calls "negative pragmatism"—the view that "that which does not work is not true." Hocking explained:

> if a theory has no consequences, or bad ones; if it makes no difference to men, or else undesirable differences; if it lowers the capacity of men to meet the stress of existence, or diminishes the worth to them of what existence they have; such a theory is somehow false, and we have no peace until it is remedied. I will go even farther, and say that a theory is false if it is not interesting: a proposition that falls on the mind so dully as to excite no enthusiasm has not attained the level of truth; though the words be accurate the import has leaked away from them, and meaning is not conveyed. (MGHE, xiii)

Hocking did believe, then, that "negative pragmatism" serves a valuable critical function, a kind of self-help function for flabby idealists who need to get out of the universal and into the particular and "just do it." However, he thought that "positive pragmatism"—a view that he bizarrely believed as committed to the view that there is "No reality yet unmade" and simplistically summarized as the theory that "Whatever works is true"—served no constructive function. Throughout his life, Hocking continued to caricature pragmatism and to argue that pragmatism, (mis)conceived in this manner, is self-refuting. Although Hocking made this argument over and over, it is a terrible argument. Hocking's argument does not establish that pragmatism is self-refuting. Rather, it establishes that pragmatism is incompatible with certain idealist assumptions about human nature. This, of course, is hardly startling. Pragmatists themselves recognize that their epistemology is incompatible with idealist metaphysics and must be coupled instead with radical empiricism, an account of experience as transactional. Given his idealist assumptions, Hocking concludes that pragmatism is false and idealism is true. However, this simply begs the question by using idealist assumptions to establish idealism.

For example, in his 1912 *The Meaning of God in Human Experience*, Hocking asserted that "the only kind of truth which in the end can comply with the pragmatic requirement ... is a non-pragmatic truth, a truth which has an absolute aspect" (MGHE, xvii). Why? Hocking answered that only belief in the absolute and ideal works in practice: "No religion, then, is a true religion which is not able to make men tingle, yes, even to their physical nerve tips, with the sense of an infinite hazard, a wrath to come, a heavenly city to be gained or lost in the process of time and by the use of our freedom" (MGHE, xiv). Only idealism, Hocking asserted, can make us tingle with the sense of infinite hazard; only idealism can give us "the unlimited right of Idea in a world where nothing that is is ultimately irrational" (MGHE, xii); only idealism can provide us "the mystical and authoritative elements of faith" (MGHE, xix). Beginning with a deep longing for the Absolute and the belief that "life is but a certain consciousness of the Absolute" (MGHE, 203), Hocking concludes that any philosophy that fails to satisfy this longing is not satisfactory: "We could not live without the Absolute, nor without our idea of the Absolute.... Thus, accepting fully the pragmatic guide to truth, we conclude that the only satisfying truth must be absolute,—that is, non-pragmatic" (MGHE, 206). This argument may be revealing from a psychological perspective—it may tell us something about Hocking and his hopes, desires, and needs—but it is not successful from a logical point of view. To presuppose that we require a mystical and authoritative faith, a world in which nothing is irrational or irreducibly plural, a sense of infinite hazard that makes us tingle, the companionship of God that renders us open to experience (MGHE, 225) is to presuppose—rather than argue for—idealism.

Hocking frequently repeated this question-begging argument, as though it might be made true if set forth sufficiently frequently. In his 1929 *Types of Philosophy*, for example, Hocking asserted that "pragmatism requires a non-pragmatic truth" and "fails by its own test" (TP, 164–165; see also 445). Why? Hocking asserts that pragmatism views truth as man-made, as intrinsically tied to human purposes and choices, as dependent on us and accessible to us. This, he continues correctly, makes impossible absolutely objective truth and reality absolutely independent of human experience. But, he asserts, it is only this objective truth and independent reality "that can set us free" (TP, 170). Thus he concludes that humanism depends on idealism (TP, 450): "God is nothing if not that on which we depend.... We cannot swing up a rope which is attached only to our own belt" (TP, 170). Pragmatists, of course, deny that there are any other belts to which we might attach our ropes, deny that humanism depends on idealism, and deny that there is, or needs to be any nonpragmatic justification or nonpragmatic foundation for pragmatism. Thus James notes that "tho one part of our experience may lean upon another part to make it what it is in any one of its several aspects in which it may be considered, experience as a whole is self-containing and leans on nothing" (James [1905] 1976, 99). Hocking's desire—a desire shared by many persons—to be able to "swing up" is no doubt real, but the mere existence of this desire does not establish the truth of his belief that there is an Absolute that satisfies this desire.

Hocking repeated this argument in his 1938–1939 Gifford Lectures, "Fact and Destiny," summarized, revised, and published in 1966 as "History and the Absolute" (Hocking 1966). Here his target was not simply pragmatism but the whole "malaise of Modernity," a deep relativity and fragmentation in our science, philosophy, and lives. The self, Hocking claimed, desires and requires "some assurance of integrity in itself, of wholeness and truth in its vision of the world," but modernity cannot meet this demand because it "suffers from an inability to find an objective and durable goodness in its many goods, a necessary unity in its aims, a radical bond between its best-justified wishes and the Facts" (Hocking 1966, 460). Modernity delivers only suffering, irrationality, the absurd, evil, and death—"the apparent finality of Tragedy"—and the relativity of our meanings and values. Once again, Hocking claims this view is self-refuting: "Relativity, on being discovered, is already in principle overcome" because "the Relative can be known to be such only in contrast to an Absolute" (461). And once again, this is an expression of hope and longing, rather than a conclusion of fact and logic. Hocking believes that given modernity, our histories and finite lives lose significance by acquiring finality. We suffer and die. In contrast, Hocking asserts that given an Absolute, living "acquires significance by losing finality." Thus he concludes: "[The Absolute] include the assurance of a continuing future, in which meanings as yet unimagined are to be proposed; and in whose fulfillment our Will-to-create and, with it our Will-to-suffer in creation, shall find its full scope. As realizing the presence of his Absolute, the word of the fully-living human being is "Lo, Thou art With me"; and because of that fellowship, problems alleged intractable—the rooted hatreds, calls for revenge, despairs—lose their finality, without losing their summons to develop within history the pertinent empirical situations" (462).

Here again the contrast with pragmatism, and the desires that underlie it, could not be sharper. In his *Pragmatism*, James writes: "I am willing to think that the prodigal-son attitude, open to us as it is in many vicissitudes, is not the right and final attitude towards the whole of life. I am willing that there should be real losses and real losers, and no total preservation of all that is. I can believe in the ideal as an ultimate, not as an origin, and as an extract, not the whole. When the cup is poured off, the dregs are left behind forever, but the possibility of what is poured off is sweet enough to accept" (James [1907] 1975, 142).

Although James claimed that pragmatism is a new name for an old way of thinking, it is Hocking's message that is an old way of thinking in philosophy and a long-standing message in religion. Hocking delivers this message in language that now seems dated and musty. More importantly, it is a message propped up by a question-begging argument and rooted in an unwillingness to accept the finitude of life, the untranscended reality of suffering, and the finality of death. It is a message that in substance does not deserve to be a live hypothesis.

II. Falling in Love with Liberalism's Critic

I began with a statement of fact: Today Hocking is an obscure philosopher. I located the tripartite basis of this obscurity in the broad scope, public orientation, and idealistic content of his philosophy. In this light, I now introduce a postulate: Some obscure philosophers deserve to be obscure. I know that this postulate may trouble Ph.D. students combing the history of philosophy for writers and issues about which almost nothing has been written; I realize that it may upset untenured philosophy professors determined to identify a novel research agenda so as to publish rather than perish professionally; and I understand that this may offend senior faculty who have built careers by developing ever greater expertise on an ever shrinking subject matter. Still, for present purposes I assert confidently that some obscure philosophers fully merit their obscurity.

Given the fact that Hocking is an obscure philosopher, and given the postulate that some obscure philosophers deserve to be obscure, the question is obvious: Is Hocking an obscure philosopher who deserves to be obscure? More generally: What criteria must any obscure philosopher meet to deserve obscurity? For example, is it enough to write dense, unclear prose? To employ convoluted, invalid arguments? To address artificial or trivial problems? To make false or merely uninteresting assertions? To write too much or too little? To fail to exhibit originality or creativity?

It may be tempting to think that Hocking's caricature of pragmatism and his repeated question-begging argument for idealism are sufficient to merit obscurity. I admit almost complete hostility toward his idealism and the longing that gives rise to it. In doing so, however, I note Hocking's own advice on the treatment of one's philosophical enemies: Love your enemy as you love your friend. This advice, preached often but practiced seldom, is more familiar than clear. It is often understood as a call to treat friends and enemies just alike, to treat them indifferently. Hocking argued that this interpretation misses the point. To take up the task of love, Hocking explained, is to seek to transform an enemy, to enlist that enemy in a "cohostility" to its own evil, thereby to render it no longer an enemy at all. He urged: "The task of love is not mere amiability toward the right-minded; it is also creativity toward the wrong-minded: it is to effect this radical change of will. We thus reach an ethical Absolute which is the reverse of indifference,—it is the making of difference." (Hocking 1966, 436)

It is in this spirit of love—"creativity toward the wrong-minded," the wrong-minded idealist—that I approach Hocking, though I approach him without any ethical Absolute. Admittedly, this tough-love approach entails major surgery: Specifically, I propose to detach as fully as possible Hocking's pragmatic social and political thought—his analysis of the state, liberalism, and individualism—from his idealist metaphysics. I propose to hold on to his requirement to effect a radical change of will and make a practical difference, but at the same time to throw out his Absolute, both metaphysical and ethical. The importance of this task is itself pragmatic: The point of this operation is not simply to save Hocking from undeserved obscurity, but rather to make available to us, and for us, Hocking's insights.

Hocking's social and political philosophy is most insightfully and fully developed in his 1926 *Man and the State* and especially in his 1937 *The Lasting Elements of Individualism*. (Hocking dedicated *The Lasting Elements of Individualism* to John Dewey, "comrade and opponent in debate through many years of deepening affection," and it is instructive to consider Hocking's now little-known books in light of

Dewey's familiar, canonical 1927 *The Public and Its Problems*, 1929 *Individualism: Old and New*, 1935 *Liberalism and Social Action*, and 1939 *Freedom and Culture*.) Hocking described *The Lasting Elements of Individualism* as a study in the philosophy of history that attempts to look forward—but not in the way that pragmatism looks forward. He explained: "It is hostile not to pragmatism, but to mere pragmatism: it believes that our experimentalism is destined to transform itself into a version of the 'dialectic method' whereby mere groping takes on rational direction and destination. Out of the flux, certainty" (LEI, xii–xiii).

Hocking did not achieve his goal. He did not transform experimentalism, pragmatism, into a philosophy of certainty, idealism. In fact, what he did for us—as distinct from what he said he wanted to do—is just the opposite: His penetrating criticism of liberalism allows us to transform it from a philosophy of history as necessary direction or predetermined destination into a philosophy of history as a contingent experiment or ongoing journey, constantly in need of piecemeal reconstruction. In short, in spite of Hocking's own intent, the lasting element of his *The Lasting Elements of Individualism* is its demonstration that out of certainty comes flux—and the need to confront this flux with intelligence.

Hocking defined individualism as "simply belief in the human individual as the ultimate unit of social structures," belief that the individual is more real than social groups and institutions generated by, and composed of, individuals (LEI, 3–4). Hocking claimed that the "plain facts of experience" do not support individualism. Rather, they support the view that "individuals are products of social groups quite as much as social groups are products of individuals." Like Dewey discussing the interrelations of individuality and community, or Mead setting forth his view of the social self, Hocking observed that "dependency seems to run both ways," and so "if we are simply reporting the overt facts of society, we should say that Aristotle and Locke are both right—the state is prior to the individual, and the individual is prior to the state: there is an alternating current or cycle in which neither can claim absolute priority" (LEI, 4–5).

Given these "plain facts of experience"—the reciprocity and interdependence of individuals and social groups such as families, neighborhoods, universities, and states—why would anyone endorse individualism—belief in the priority of individuals to social groups? Almost everyone in the modern Western world, Hocking thought, does endorse individualism. Modernism is this passage of the locus of reality to the individual, "the turning point from the dominance of the formula, to every group, numerous men and sets of men, toward the dominance of the formula, To every man, numerous groups, and possible groups" (LEI, 30). This belief in individualism, Hocking explained, rests not on the surface facts of experience but rather on a liberal faith, a "faith or intuition which is liberal toward the individual." Hocking described this liberal faith as "an attitude or confidence toward the undemonstrated powers of the units of society; it means a faith that the welfare of any society may be trusted to the individuals who compose it." He continued: "Liberalism maintains that the greatest natural resource of any community is the latent intelligence and good will of its members; and it seeks those forms of society which run a certain risk of preliminary disorder in order to elicit that resource. Since individuals can be developed only by being trusted with somewhat more than they can, at the moment, do well, liberalism is a sort of honor system" (LEI, 5). Political liberalism, Hocking argued, is simply the result of this liberal faith in individuals.

The consequences of this faith, Hocking thought, constitute the three core tenets of liberalism: equality, liberty, and rights. A liberal faith in individuals, Hocking explained, leads to: (1) "an essential equality of men, since the respects which set a man apart from the group are the same for all men" and the necessity for each man to rely on his own reason "implies a native fund of reason qualitatively the same in all"; (2) "an essential liberty, since each individual, as chooser of his group, must mentally contain all these social possibilities in himself" because "what society is to be depends on him, rather than what he is to be upon society"; and (3) "a set of rights which spring from his needs as a man," needs that "become the basis of his choice of his many possible groups" of equals, and, thus, the basis of political fraternity (LEI, 35).

Long before Ronald Reagan, George Bush, Pat Buchanan, and Newt Gingrich, Hocking, like Dewey, worried that liberalism is not working, or not working well enough, and needs to be revised, reconstructed, reborn. Proceeding just like a pragmatist, Hocking asked: What are the actual practical results of trusting the welfare of society to the individuals who compose it? He asked: What have we gained by implementing the honor system that is liberalism? The results, he asserted soberly, are mixed. Individuals have developed new energies under freer political conditions, and in this respect liberalism has been a great success. Hocking continued:

> But these energies have not infallibly been devoted to the welfare of the society; the individual has frequently seized the opportunity to make something for himself and let society take the consequences. He may be surprised and annoyed to be told that anything else is expected. For liberalism trains people to receive, and only hopes that they will give. If the group is to be liberal toward individuals, they must be recipients of its liberalty; and few habits are easier to develop than the habit of being recipients, especially if this receiving is connected with the idea of "rights." (LEI, 6)

As an honor system, as a political system rooted in a faith in individuals, Hocking concluded, liberalism needs "some kind of supplement" if it is to receive from individuals what it requires in order to succeed.

The pragmatic question, then, is this: What is the supplement that liberalism needs, and how, if at all, can this supplement be provided? Before we can offer a prescription for the ills of liberalism, Hocking thought we must have a more detailed diagnosis. What exactly is wrong with liberalism? In an analysis that is remarkably similar in many respects to Dewey's attack on outdated and ahistorical earlier varieties of liberalism in his *Liberalism and Social Action*, Hocking claims that liberalism suffers from three major defects that it alone cannot remedy. His analysis is instructive and very relevant today. First, Hocking asserts, liberalism is incapable of achieving and maintaining social unity. Although some sort of social unity is desirable, this unity is neither guaranteed nor automatic. It has to be achieved. It has to be achieved because "society is not an organism; it only faintly resembles one and that least of all when it is analyzed into individuals, each of which can set up independent life, as the cells of a body never pretend to do" (LEI, 42). Moreover, the larger the social group, the more difficult it is to achieve this unity because "the less it is possible to conceive of it as a result of the conscious consent of its individual members." This lack of unity is evident everywhere in liberal political and economic social relations. In politics, do our elected representatives represent the unified interests of our state? Can they represent the state, taken as a unified entity, when their political survival depends on satisfying a local electorate by producing local results. "In such a body," Hocking observed, "it is just the total-interest which is nowhere represented" (LEI, 45–46). Liberalism may offer us fine theories of the unified, general will, but in experience this general will is extinguished: "Our theory tells us that each individual is capable of thinking 'We' as well as 'I'; and that since human beings are born in groups, they will naturally put 'We' first and 'I' afterward. But if our individualism has trained them in the rightness and necessity of putting the 'I' foremost, it may well have brought us to a pass where no genuine political 'We' can get a voice" (LEI, 46–47). In our time of special-interest and single-issue politics, Hocking's diagnosis rings true. In economics and business, Hocking argued, we find the same lack of social unity. Have the economic transactions that liberalism has made possible resulted in a prosperous land? No, Hocking answered, we have only some prosperous individuals in certain spots, "pimples of prosperity on a visage predominantly pale." Changing metaphors, Hocking observed that these "private reservoirs of wealth" have no regular working relationship to unified public concerns: "Liberal theory of property terminates in the processes by which they receive possession; individualism has no theory of the relation of private wealth to the working commonwealth, except through the taxing power, which appears as an unwelcome intrusion from a political arm not wholly above suspicion of self-interest, and not as the normal development of the owner's will" (LEI, 50). Accordingly, social unity is not built: "Action as a whole, and for the whole, is beyond the reach of a purely individualistic enterprise" (LEI, 51). In our time of a growing gap between rich and poor, almost all of whom demand tax reform, Hocking's point, if not his language, has never been more relevant.

Liberalism's second major defect, Hocking claimed, is its attachment to rights without duties, rights that are supposedly natural and inalienable, rights that thus become privileges. Hocking called this an infection of the Western mind, a moral toxin, once a "useful encouragement" but now a "pernicious flattery" (LEI, 53). "There are no unconditional rights," Hocking wrote; "For the conditions of all rights are moral conditions; without good will, all rights drop off (LEI, 53, 54). John Locke recognized that an individual's right to immunity from exploitation carried with it a duty to refrain from exploitation of others, but Locke's liberalism now lies in wreckage in the disposition to take without giving, to receive without acknowledgment or sense of debt. This disposition is omnipresent and is at work in our economic stereotypes: from the idle rich to welfare cheats and able-bodied food-stamp recipients, from sweat shop owners to their lazy employees, from neighbors who borrow without returning to parents who demand that society provide for their children, and from faculty desperately trying to reduce their teaching loads and minimize their office hours to "frequenters of colleges"—Hocking says that he will not call them students—who expect to graduate to positions of leadership without engaging in the hard work that leadership requires. Hocking concluded: "Liberalism has not merely shown a flaw, it has undermined itself and prepared the way for a general regime of dependence" (LEI, 57).

Hocking called the third defect of liberalism "the emotional defect" and identified it as the root of the other two defects. Liberalism's original emotional appeal lay in its cheerful, amiable view of human nature as, by nature, good. But, Hocking countered, this liberal faith in the nature of individuals has produced individuals unworthy of that faith, self-indulgent individuals now incapable of putting this faith into practice in their own lives, fair-weather liberals who no longer really fight for liberal principles even though "there is plenty to be done before the world is even decently liberal":

> The chief source of suffering and discontent regarding the passing Liberal age is not that it has evolved its own special brands of poverty, injustice, political ineptitude; it is the experience of a prevalent flabby mediocrity of mind and character which begins, in our virile moments, to inspire a sort of moral loathing. To say that each man is as good as the next means only that the next is as poor a sort as the first.... Until Liberalism learns how to include in its hopeful program the provision for correction and the honorable severities of living, it will be no guide for the steps to be taken." (LEI, 60, 59, 58)

Our liberal faith, then, has produced individuals who do not justify that faith and who are incapable of taking up that faith. Liberalism, Hocking concluded, has produced individuals, liberal hypocrites, politically correct but illiberal at the scratch, for whom liberalism itself no longer has emotional appeal. Liberalism's success, Hocking concluded, now has produced conditions that guarantee its failure. Hocking's analysis of the defects of liberalism is informed and penetrating, and it remains timely and genuinely important. On this basis alone, it is a mistake to neglect Hocking; we permit his obscurity at our considerable peril.

III. Breaking up with an Incorrigible Absolutist

Can liberalism overcome these defects? Is there a solution? If so, what is it? How must liberalism be supplemented? Hocking believed that liberalism can overcome these defects—perhaps even that there is a dialectical necessity that liberalism will overcome these defects. The defects of liberalism did not lead him to champion communism, fascism, anarchy, revolution, or isolationism. A supplemented liberal state, Hocking argued, now must meet two necessary conditions. First, the liberal state can achieve social unity only in action, not in thinking alone, only in practice, not in theory alone. The liberal state must actively create, rather than passively reflect, political unity. The state must engage in uniting deeds, acts that "can embody the latent 'We' of the society or nation." Hocking explained: "This involves in most liberal states a breach with the tradition of the hampered government; but ... it may well be that democracy will for the first time exist, because for the first time a true general will exists and finds its way into action, or rather gains real existence by finding its way into action" (LEI, 106; see also MATS, 14, 44, 157). The liberal state, then, must become an active state, a state uniting in action, a state that performs what Hocking calls the "commotive function"—the unending activity of a group's constituting itself as a group, making up its unified mind, and moving together, wills and emotions and ethical passions united in a shared mission. This need, Hocking observed (with some implicit references to the New Deal), has never been greater: We simply cannot "endure the same amount of division, dissent, obstruction, delay as was tolerable a century ago" (LEI, 142). In being commotive, the state supplies the social unity that Hocking claimed liberalism lacks.

The liberal state, if it is to repair itself, must meet a second necessary condition. The individual in this state, Hocking claimed, must be "incompressible." What does this mean? Hocking explained that the liberal state can merge or unify individual purposes—that is, be "commotive"—only when its public purposes are prolongations of, and derive life from, individual purposes. He summarized: "The individual thus remains mentally prior to the state; and the principle of every future state must be this: that every man shall be a whole man," (LEI, 133) that every state must establish the objective conditions for the exercise of the will of this whole man (MATS, 325). (I will interpret this charitably, presuming that Hocking wanted women to be whole women as well!) Hocking meant that the new, active, unified and unifying liberal state must not be a totalitarian or dictatorial state; it must submit itself to the free judgment of its members; it must risk its continuation to the free approval of its members; it must assure individuals the means to differ with it. In uniting incompressible, whole individuals, the state supplies the duties reciprocal with rights and the emotional foundation that Hocking claimed the liberal state lacks.

Is it possible to unite these two necessities, the commotive state and its incompressible members? Hocking asked: "How can the strong and unified state be compatible with this incompressible individual life and liberty"; how can we have a strong state and strong individuals (LEI, 138, 143)? The answer is supplied by what Hocking called a "co-agent state"; a state "based on the unanimous action of free individuals," a state "whose primary function is the commotive function issuing in action, which is at once particular, history-making action, and unanimous action, an extension of every citizen's will" (LEI, 150, 151). A co-agent state, Hocking explained in conclusion, would differ from our liberal state in its foreign relations and diplomacy, its economic policy and educational arrangements, and its freedoms. Just one example: The co-agent state would insist that "freedom to express thought is for thinkers." It would recognize that many people who ought to think actually "imitate, absorb, pretend, rationalize, adhere, far more than they think" (LEI, 173–174). Here is Hocking at his rhetorical best: "Idea bearing should be as solemn a business as child bearing; and we have turned it into a public promiscuity in which every Hornblower, Influential Editor, National Clown mingles his say with that of Ambitious Priests and Leading Ladies to turn the General Will. . . . To the hideous perils and absurdities of the Censorship, we must join the equally hideous perils, hypocrisies and humbugs of No-censorship. . . The new state must do two things where the Liberal state attempted but one. It must restrict liberty for the sake of liberty" (LEI, 174, 175).

Unfortunately, rhetoric aside, this is not Hocking at his philosophical or political best. Let me step away from this line of thought in order to conclude with a brief critical assessment of Hocking's supplement to liberalism, the co-agent state. Hocking's introduction of the co-agent state is something like pulling a rabbit out of a hat. It is a very good trick, but it is a trick nonetheless, and a trick that can be done only if the rabbit is secretly put in the hat before it is pulled out. Of course, the difficult part of this trick is putting and keeping the rabbit in the hat; once this is accomplished, pulling the rabbit out is very easy. I have no doubt that Hocking's co-agent state, once pulled from the philosopher's hat, would repair the defects of liberalism. After all, it is a state that by definition is based on the unanimous action of free individuals, a state that is by definition a unity of responsible individuals with strong emotional attachment to their state, a state that by definition is engaged in unanimous action that is an extension of every citizen's will. It just doesn't get any better than this.

Or, at least if you are an idealist, it doesn't get any better than this—because this co-agent state is simply the ongoing realization of the Absolute in history. In this co-agent state, Hocking wrote, "it is not necessary to choose between the universal and the particular, the ideal and the real: every actual deed is a union of both" (LEI, 151). A defective liberalism, it seems, needs the Absolute or God on its side. The co-agent state, Hocking wrote, is a mortal and finite edition of God (MATS, 405). Hocking's supplement for the defects of liberalism is the God of his idealism, Christianity, and mysticism. For Hocking, individualism has a lasting element to the extent that it provides conditions necessary for the realization of the meaning of God in human experience. His co-agent state is the political embodiment of the meaning of God in human experience.

Just as he does in his metaphysics, Hocking begs the question in his politics. Here, however, the consequences are far more dangerous and less abstract. As a result, his private, self-effacing admission that "I am stupid about organizations ... and trust in God for the outcome" (Robinson 1968, 160) appears at least as ominous as it may be honest. Hocking does not ask, much less answer, any of the most obvious and pressing practical, as opposed to theoretical, problems. For example:

- In the co-agent state, only those who express themselves responsibly have a right to expression. Who, then, determines what is censored in the co-agent state? A philosopher king? A government agency? Local boards of citizens? Publishers of major newspapers and magazines and producers of television and radio programs? The companies that sponsor these publications and programs? Moreover, how is this censorship enforced?
- In the co-agent state, only those "who have a right to consume" determine what is produced (LEI, 166). Who, then, determines what persons have a right to consume what products? How will society identify "rightful demand?" Hocking wrote that there is nothing worse than a complex bureaucracy, and claimed that the economy needs only "the touch" of the co-agent state, but who directs this touch and what, if anything, prevents the light touch of a co-agent state from becoming the heavy-handed grip of massive bureaucracy?
- In the co-agent state, who secures the unanimous action of free individuals—free even if censored, free even if touched by the state? Just how is this done? By a philosophy class in critical thinking? By a national marketing campaign? By the military—be all that we can be? By propaganda? Hocking said that the co-agent state requires the commotive equivalent of war. Besides war itself, what is the commotive equivalent of war? And, if the co-agent state gives a war, how does it ensure that everyone will come?
- In the co-agent state, if the state becomes an experimenter rather than a dictator, as Hocking said, does it really become justified in dictating its experiments (MATS, 409)? What experiments? Who experiments and who is experimented on? Who dictates when these experiments are failures, when they are solutions, and, perhaps, when they are final solutions?
- In the co-agent state, rights are "conditional on good will" and "the criterion of good will is in general the disposition of the individual to submit to what is called discipline" (LEI, 172) Whose discipline? That of the co-agent state itself? Hocking did not say. He sidestepped the issue by claiming that "conscience tends to a certain universality" such that "there is a tendency to ethical agreement among men" (LEI, 171), asserting that the co-agent state

provides for the possibility of an honest and competent opposition (LEI, 177), even though the actual exercise of this opposition is incompatible with the unanimous action that defines the very existence of the co-agent state.

To leave these questions unanswered is to supply only a theoretical remedy for the real and pressing defects of liberalism. It is to abandon pragmatism in politics as well as metaphysics. Like Hocking, Dewey sharply criticized liberalism. Unlike Hocking, Dewey believed that the problems of liberalism and democracy can be addressed only by more liberalism and more democracy. Dewey's philosophy has not been implemented to any significant degree, and so it is difficult to know if this course of action would repair the defects of liberalism, particularly the emotional defect, so astutely analyzed by Hocking. Is pragmatism too amiable, cheery, pluralistic, and flabby? Or is Hocking's prescribed treatment worse than this illness itself? Listen to Hocking, carried away from his usually saner judgment by his idealism and its Absolute:

> The failure of the Liberal civilization is at the top, not at the bottom. Contrast the moral condition of such a community with the fierce idealism which flames up here and there among the youth of Russia or of China, to whom the nation itself, with a task which appears glorious in proportion to its difficulty, has become the absorbing business of life. The puff-cheeked bombast of Mussolini, the narrow fanaticism of Hitler, are less attractive, because their national conceptions are still loaded with the primitive goals of bigness and self-importance: "Make Us Mightier Yet"! It is an inferior brand of national purpose. But crude as it is, it is still something—and in this something, superior to the ideal of a state whose ambition is to avoid entanglement and to hug in isolation the fragments of a disturbed national prosperity. (LEI, 113–114)

If these are our only options—Hitler and Mussolini or Hoover and Roosevelt—then we would do better to pursue "disturbed national prosperity" without national purpose rather than puff-cheeked fanaticism and fascism, no matter how absorbing, idealistic, or co-agent.

This sort of idealism that pictures history on the side of its Absolute and, in turn, believes this Absolute "permeates the texture of history" (Hocking 1966, 463) simply does not work. As Hocking said, "if we are to follow a pragmatic philosophy, that which does not work is not true, and should be changed off for something else" (LEI, 64). Still if liberalism is to renew itself, it must confront the defects diagnosed by Hocking. This requires a liberal faith, a strenuous faith (see Stuhr 1997, final chapter). Perhaps it requires a faith that is emotionally defective because it is so strenuous and demanding, because it is a faith without guarantee or certainty, because it, unlike idealism, is a faith that discovers in human affairs no "power, self-consciously eternal, actively communicating its own scope to the feeble deeds, the painful acquirements, the values, the loves and hopes of men" and women.

Without this self-consciously eternal power, Hocking argued that "we have no right to such faith as we habitually assume." I think this is correct. Without this faith, he continued, "there is for us [idealists] no valid religion" (MGHE, 524). Again, I think he is correct. By contrast, for those of us without "valid religion," for those of us with only a pragmatic spirit and a liberal, democratic faith, Hocking's philosophy constitutes a revealing, instructive illustration of another faith. As such, as Hocking himself knew well (see LRWF, 274), it constitutes an important opportunity for us to revitalize and reconstruct our own most important and sometimes obscure loyalties. Even if this now involves a trip to a library annex or used bookstore to supplement the contents of this volume, this is an opportunity that we should seize today.

WORKS CITED

Hocking, William Ernest. 1966. "History and the Absolute." In *Philosophy, Religion, and the Coming World Civilization:Essays in Honor of William Ernest Hocking,* ed. Leroy S. Rouner. The Hague: Martinus Nijhoff, 1966.

James, William. [1896] 1979. "The Will to Believe." In *The Will to Believe and Other Essays in Popular Philosophy, The Works of William James.* Cambridge: Harvard University Press.

———. [1905] 1976. "The Essence of Humanism." In *Essays in Radical Empiricism, The Works of William James.* Cambridge: Harvard University Press.

———. [1907] 1975. *Pragmatism: A New Name for an Old Way of Thinking, The Works of William James.* Cambridge: Harvard University Press.

Robinson, Daniel Sommer. 1968. *Royce and Hocking, American Idealists: An Introduction to Their Philosophy, With Selected Letters.* Boston: Christopher Publishing House.

Stuhr, John J. 1997. *Genealogical Pragmatism: Philosophy, Experience, and Community.* Albany, N.Y.: SUNY Press.

———. 2003. *Pragmatism, Postmodernism, and the Future of Philosophy.* New York: Routledge.

CHAPTER 25

W. E. Hocking's Insights About the Individual and the State

John E. Smith

William Ernest Hocking's thought was both wide and deep. He reflected in a systematic way on the many dimensions of human experience—religion, science, morality, politics, history and education—and in so doing successfully brought the light of his own experience and insight to bear on the extensive knowledge he possessed in all these areas. Because of my belief that his insights into human nature and politics have not received the attention they deserve, I want to concentrate on some aspects of both subjects with the aim of convincing you that Hocking's thought merits what we may call a second round of appreciation.

I must begin by reminding you, as I had to remind myself when I returned to rereading Hocking's writings after some years, that he was comprehensive in his thinking so that his books are weighty in more than one sense. The two works forming the main basis of my commentary are *Man and the State* published in 1926 and *The Lasting Elements of Individualism* published in 1937. The slightly more than a decade separating these books spanned the aftermath of the first World War and growing signs of the onset of the second. I do not attempt to connect Hocking's thought in any direct way to that historical situation; it should be clear, however, that with the communist experiment, as it came to be called, already on the world stage and the fascist dictators seeking to consolidate their power, the themes of Hocking's two books—the nature and worth of the individual and the question of the scope and authority of the state—were, and indeed still are, matters of the highest moment. In surveying Hocking's views, I believe that there are three of his basic ideas that will repay our attention. The first concerns his way of presenting the ancient thesis that *will* and not *force* forms the basis of the state. The second has to do with the question whether and in what sense the state is an entity over and above its individual citizens. The third idea focuses on the role of religion in forming the conception of the individual in the West and the importance there of the concept of *contract* as opposed to the idea of *status* prevalent in the cultures of Asia.

Hocking had what I would call a realistic approach to thinking about the realm of politics in that he stressed at the outset its paradoxical or even contradictory character. "To all efforts of men to cooperate," he wrote, "fate has attached a penalty. Whenever a common interest exists, an antagonism of interest springs out of it"

(MATS, 3). In his own simple but pointed example, consider that if two individuals till a field together, each is concerned that the other not shirk his responsibility nor lay claim to an unfair share of the yield. In more general terms, the harmony and cooperation that make production possible may well disappear at the point of distribution, a casualty of conflicting interests. Anyone, he claimed, who fails to take seriously both this agreement and this divergence can be no guide in politics.

The importance Hocking attached to this paradox can be seen in his *defining* the politician as the one who confronts it in its special relation to civilized life as a whole. "The politician," he wrote, "is the man who deliberately faces both the certainty that men must live together, and the endless uncertainty on what terms they can live together" (MATS, 13). Accordingly, both the state as a reality and the political philosophy expressed in it must be seen not as something fixed but as proposed *solutions* to the most basic problem confronting the human race. What sort of institution or arrangement of human affairs will make it possible for people of divergent interests to live together in peace and stability? How are we to structure the state and its offices so that their functions can be performed in a just and orderly manner?

The first of our three ideas—that will and not force is the basis of the state—sets out by taking note of the ultimate purpose of the state, which is, as Hocking puts it, to provide a stability in human affairs that is the counterpart to the regularity we find in the natural world. It is unfortunate, he believed, that the root word for "state," which is "stat," should have come to connote what is "static" when it meant instead something that is willfully set up and is expected to remain standing in virtue of the *will* that made it in the first place. In this respect, Hocking, like Hobbes and many other political theorists, stresses the "artifactual" character of the state as the product of conscious human art. Reflection about the state begins with the simple distinction between those who govern and the multitudes of the governed. The former, he claims, must be understood as representative persons, which means that they do not speak as private individuals but in the name of the state—"Not I, but the state, commands you." As for the governed, Hocking says that although we invariably see the multitudes as a collection, to think of the people truly is to recall one by one the unique beings we know and their diverse interests, interests pursued by each individual with a concern no one else can fully share. In opposition to Hobbes, Hocking does not think of individuals simply as *egoists* but rather as distinct "wills to live," each of whom is attempting to work out the plot of their own lives. In other places he identifies this will to live as a "will to power" understood as the reasonable aim of self-realization or the power of persons to affirm themselves in the development of both body and will.

Hocking describes his conception of the state as a version of the ancient idea that the state is "externalized reason" and credits Kant and Hegel with reviving this position in the modern world. "The state," he maintained, "consists in the reality of the wills of its members, i.e., their best or most reasonable wills, so far as they have common standards" (MATS, 44). Or again, "The state might be defined ... as *the common reason and conscience of its members."* Accordingly, Hocking rejects a contract theory of the state because it envisions the relation between the ruler and the people as essentially external, since the two parties start out as independent of each other. On his view, however, the individual is related to the state by "belonging" in the sense that his or her will finds expression in the state's decisions and actions. In place of a contract, Hocking proposes the idea of a *tacit conspiracy* of each individual with his neighbor to adopt a particular source for the issuing of demands to be pressed on each by all the rest; in short, a form of authority all acknowledge and accept. The important point is the recognition by the individual of the presence of his or her will in the law of the state, an awareness that is the exact opposite of the adversarial attitude adopted by those who think of all government as "they," an alien power in which they do not participate, a force to be resisted. To underline the involvement of the individual's will in the state, Hocking proposes an arresting version of Kant's notion of autonomy; "the state," he writes, "is an arrangement whereby everyman's better judgment becomes his external ruler" (MATS, 46). Here the ruler is external but not alien; as Kant put it, when I understand that my own will is externalized in the law of the state, I also see that in obeying the state I am obeying myself as legislator.

That Hocking was under no illusions about the realities of politics can be seen in his pointing out the limitations of the view that the state is "externalized reason." The state, he says, does not embody the whole of the reason or conscience of its members, it is not the only group in the state embodying reason, and it includes much that is neither reason nor conscience as evidenced by political manipulation, diplomatic chicanery, and many forms of corruption. Accordingly, Hocking acknowledges that the state must also exist as force and with a coercive power, expressed in the form of a positive law that is no mere derivative of reason. An empirical inquiry must, in his view, take seriously the fact of force but at the same time insist on finding some rationale for it. "We absolutely reject," he writes, "that part of political realism which proposes that any force or fact in human society is its own excuse for being." And on this account, he continues, "we decline to make 'force-using' the essential and defining mark of the state" (MATS, 76). In words that hark back to the discussions of the Greek philosophers about the doctrine that "might is right," Hocking insists that the force of the state must always be based on its rightful ascendancy, not its ascendancy on its force. This relationship was, of course, to be tragically reversed by the world's dictators in the decades yet to come.

The recovery of the idea and, even more important, of the sense that government is an organization of individual wills, a "we" in which is expressed every "I," would be a major step forward in overcoming the current mind set that brands all government as an adversary, a power exercised by "them," a totally alien force. It is one thing for an individual or a group in a nation to have the sense of being disinherited, or the evidence that their interest is being ignored, in short, that they are unrepresented or inadequately represented and can find no will of their own in the interests, concerns, and governing power of their country as it presently exists. It is quite another for an individual or a group to think of government itself solely in terms of alienation and to identify law and political authority as forms of oppression to be resisted and nullified.

This attitude is manifested at present in the thought and practice of some sectarian groups and armed "militias" in America where the belief that governmental authority is inherently evil sparks efforts to secede from society and live in isolated compounds under laws of their own. These efforts often include finding ways to use the Constitution as a bulwark against the same government that provides a guaranty for their rights. This adversarial outlook is the opposite of Hocking's view of the state as the organization of individual wills. Instead of the "we" of government in which all individuals see their own "I" included, there is only the "they" of government as the oppressive enemy. The great strength of the participatory democracies, Hocking claims, resides, first, in their ability to sustain the faith of their citizens in government as representative of the people and the general welfare, and, second, in the continual struggle to overcome the power of special interests for whom the general welfare does not count.

Our second idea concerns a question that has been put in many forms—in what sense, if any, is the state an entity above and beyond the citizens who make it up? Hocking's approach is to ask "Are group minds real?" and he combines his discussion with a consideration of the idea, more familiar in the earlier decades of the twentieth century, known as the organic theory of the state, or the doctrine that the state can best be understood through an analogy with the living organism. As Hocking was well aware, whatever may be the final answer about the reality of so-called group minds, it is necessary to account for certain facts about groups, communities, and nations which cannot be understood in terms of social atomism or the widespread but scarcely coherent idea that a group is a "sum" of individual members. It makes no sense to think of the bonds of family, language, loyalty, and religion which unify the members of any community as resulting from some process of adding or compounding, and hence to speak about a "sum" offers no insight whatever into what a community is. Here let me anticipate Hocking's position on the matter; his considered view is that the individual is prior to the state in the sense that it is from individual need and initiative that the state first comes into being, but that the state is prior to the *completed* individual since all its members must have the environment and stability provided by the political order to develop their talents and capabilities. In the end Hocking found the analogy between an organism and the state unsatisfactory; he believed, moreover, that it gave little support to the case for the reality of a group mind.

We are not, however, to suppose that Hocking was a nominalist or that he subscribed to the idea that only individuals are real and that groups and corporations are mere fictions or pure creatures of the law. On the contrary, he was too good a student of the Greek philosophers and of Hegel and Royce to ignore that groups have qualities, some mental in character, which are not obviously derived from the qualities of the members as individuals. A crowd may be more vicious than any of its members; a group may arrive at a decision that is wiser than the opinion of any one member, and the property of a group is not always the property of the members taken one at a time. As Hocking points out, questions about the relation between groups and their members become especially urgent when duty, loyalty, and responsibility are involved. If a nation wages war and, as is vivid in our recent memory, seeks to exterminate an entire people, are the citizens of that nation one by one accountable? Or again, is my obligation to my nation and the loyalty I owe to it equivalent to my obligation and loyalty to all other citizens severally or even to any group of them? These and other questions have no easy answers—chiefly because they all involve either actions on the part of groups or attitudes of individuals to groups, neither of which is to be understood in terms of the relations of single individuals to each other. In these and countless other cases some clear understanding of the nature of a group, a community, a nation, is needed.

Hocking provided this understanding through his attempts to grasp the nature of the *unity* that marks every community, from the most loosely organized to the most closely knit. The first hurdle in his view is to surmount ordinary experience and common sense in one important respect; for both, what we *see* are the individuals, but the *unity* seems invisible and eludes those who go by sight alone. Hocking shows us why even the simplest group appearing to be a mere aggregate is very far from being "the setting of minds ... end to end" in some sort of compounding process (MATS, 342). Consider, he says, the mental structure of a gang of diggers having no overseer but who nevertheless need a leader from among them to direct their efforts. Each individual agrees to waive his physical control over himself and to allow the thought and will of the leader to take charge. "They represent," Hocking writes, "not indeed a sum of minds, but a multiple mentality under the control of a single plan and will." For the arrangement to work, however, requires considerable understanding among the members. They must understand the plan as it exists in the leader's mind, he must know that they understand the plan, and they must know that the leader is aware that they understand the situation. Although much of this network of understanding will remain unspoken, since past experience and habit take its place, all the members are engaged in what Royce and Peirce would have called interpretation or the comprehension by several distinct minds of the same meanings, purposes, deeds, and so on, which define and unify their project. Hocking rightly insists that communication of this sort is impossible on the atomistic view. Two selves can communicate, he claims, only if they have objects in common; *my* space is not only mine but *ours* since it is also *yours*.

Hocking is at pains to acknowledge the strong points of the view that groups, corporations, and the state have a reality that is not accurately represented by pointing to a totality of their members. There is, he notes, the familiar experience of being merged in something greater than oneself and of working with a resolve that emanates from no single individual but seems to belong to the *esprit* of the group. He also takes seriously the idea set forth by the social psychologist, Wilhelm Wundt, that certain realities such as language, custom, religion, and art, though made by human beings have not been made by any one human being, and hence must be products of community life. And Hocking is aware that what produces real effects cannot be a mere nonentity but must have some sort of reality of its own. He is, nevertheless, skeptical about accepting the group mind theory, not least because he cannot make sense of the idea that such a mind could have a moral personality or that it could be the sole author of any deed. "I cannot," he concludes, "accept the hypothesis that groups are minds numerically distinct from the minds of their members" (MATS, 360). Expanding on this conclusion, Hocking returns to his previous admission that, while the individual is incomplete without the group, we nevertheless cannot reduce the individual to a mere transmitter of some universal life, nor place the authorship of group deeds beyond individual consciousness and selfhood. In a perceptive passage worth quoting in full, Hocking writes, "the true dignity as well as the worth of personality consists in the power to *retain within the circle* of its own selfhood and responsibility those thoughts, decisions and acts which it undertakes in the name of the group, and so distinguishes from its private acts. Group deeds are deeds of individuals, and the minds behind them are individual minds" (MATS, 361).

Instead of invoking, as he calls it, an "inoperable corporate personality" (MATS, 373) as the unity that is at the heart of the state, Hocking proposes his idea of "will circuits" as the model. His claim is that every instinct, from the securing of food and shelter to the moral aesthetic and religious concerns that are the substance of culture, must make use of some external objects in order to make a home in the world. Thus, the mechanic has tools and a bench, the writer has a writing table and characters yet to be born in his novel, the farmer has utensils, his farmland, and livestock. Hocking calls these extensions of the self by the name of "will circuits"—they will later serve as a model for the state. In addition to the particular instincts or interests found in human beings, there is the matter of providing for the person as a whole, which means giving unity, proportion, and place to these instincts and, in turn, to the individual will circuits that exist. This can be done by finding a habitat and scene of action for the will to power, which is the basic political reality. The state is then seen as that circuit whereby the will to power of each member comes together in one unity that is coincident with all of them. "Other activities," he writes, "are intermittent, but the will to power is insistent."

The idea of a "will-circuit" is of great importance for Hocking's political theory because a circuit of this sort is said to be the embodiment of a unity of wills that he finds characteristic of the state. Since human individuals are not self-sufficient monads, they must take in or appropriate the outer world, the world of objects, and thus undergo a development that at the same time enlarges the scope of their own selves and the boundaries of what they can call their own. This extension of the self is often considered chiefly as a matter of intellect or the acquisition of knowledge, but, for Hocking, it is equally essential to take account of the extension of the self that expresses itself through will and habit. All instincts, says Hocking, from food getting to the works of the creative writer, find a home in the world only through the *objects* appropriate for that activity. As we noted previously, the farmer will have his stock, his fields, and his barn, the mechanic will have his work-bench and his tools; in each case the *objects* are what is necessary for the fulfillment of these instincts. Hocking calls these activities vital circuits in the case of individuals and will circuits in the case of social groups based on the coincidence of these vital circuits. He goes on to point out that vital circuits need not be the exclusive property of one individual but may involve a group sharing the same hunting ground, a crew of workmen sharing the same job, or partners in the same business. For Hocking, these individuals find that while their vital circuits are only "partly coincident," their wills find a region of "actual coincidence" in "the objects of common concern and use" (MATS, 364). Here we see Hocking's original idea, an idea that does important duty in other parts of his thought. It is not, he claims, the existence of the *same instinct* in different people that makes their vital circuits coincident—"there is no fusion of their wills"—but *the identity of the physical objects used* (MATS, 365; italics in original). This emphasis on the *world* and its objects as a major factor mediating between and uniting individuals is an important corrective to the tendency to find the unity of a community only in shared meanings, plans, and purposes. Hocking's illustration of the baseball team, elementary though it is, nicely expresses the central thought he has in mind: "If in a group of nine boys there is a unanimous wish to form a baseball team; and if in the group there happens to be one bat, one ball, one mask, one mitt, etc., the prophetic eye need hardly sharpen itself to see nine vital circuits falling into a coincidence shaped by fate. Universal needs alone do not bring men together, but when universal needs conjoin with the presence, commonly accidental, of a set of objects necessary and available for the vital circuits of each, they are likely to determine a vital circuit for all" (MATS, 365).

After his criticism of the "group mind" theory, it will be recalled, Hocking still found himself searching for that underlying unity between human beings which is essential for the existence of the state, a unity that the group mind theory cannot provide. We may anticipate his thought at this point and suggest that for him it is the idea of a will circuit that provides the needed unity and thus the proper model for the state. What, then, are the distinctive features of such a circuit? Hocking admits at the outset that a vital circuit is a living thing in the same concrete sense in which a human limb is, and he further admits that the *value* of selfhood attaches to a circuit, since whatever happens to the circuit can be said to happen to all its members as when we say, what hurts my leg hurts "me." He denies, however, that a circuit *is* a self and insists instead that the only selves involved are the individual participants. Hocking's reason for this denial is based on facts about the mind which he had pointed out in other writings. Minds, he claims, have the unique capacity to include each other, and each individual in the group can include the whole, or the others and all their relations; the group or will circuit as such has neither capacity and hence is not a self. The identity and continuity of a group, moreover, does not have the same basis as that of an individual. For the individual, biological continuity apart from human effort, and memory are the essential factors, but for the group the identity must be willed or intended by each individual in his or her effort to achieve continuity of meaning with contemporary members of the group, with those who have gone before and with those who are still to come. This form of continuity for Hocking is possible because a person can *mean* or intend an identity of will with persons whom s/he has not *thought* of individually and has never met. In Hocking's illustration, every testator who leaves funds in trust *reaches forward in intention* to minds he will never touch but upon whom he calls and depends to "mean what he means by his bequest" regardless of whatever other changes may have occurred in the meantime. Two points are implicit in Hocking's argument; the first is that there is no over-individual self involved because the identity and continuation of the group "does not lie in its own substance" but is "reborn in the fidelity of every generation of selves" who also find themselves possessed of a "necessary" desire to create and sustain the group (MATS, 370). The second is that the identity and continuity of intention that is the lifeblood of the group is a matter of *willing* on the part of each individual. For Hocking, willing is not confined to choice and decision; it embraces as well desire, intention, and meaning in the sense of "determination," as when someone says, "I *mean* to see that that inequity is abolished." Will, in short, means *power*.

The upshot of the foregoing discussion is the question, What does the theory of groups as coincident will circuits imply as to the nature of the state? The beginning of the answer takes us back to Hocking's idea of a will to power in each individual and to his insistence that, unlike intermittent instincts, the will to power is incessant. Like all instincts, however, the will to power "needs the physical objects, its territory as habitat and scene of action, its 'nature' as source of supply" (MATS, 371). Hocking is talking not about a will circuit that is merely an idea or an ideal, but about a *real coincidence* of wills embodied in physical objects with its own habitat, organization, and instruments of action. True to his experiential approach, Hocking expresses his proposal in the form of an hypothesis: "The state is the circuit required by the will to power of each member, coincident for all the people of a defined territory, and including them" (MATS, 371). Implicitly criticizing the abstract universalism of the Enlightenment, Hocking underlines that, although the will to power is universal in its reach, it calls into being not a *universal state* but individual entities called "nation states."

The reasons behind this view are made eminently clear; no will circuit ever comes to be in a vacuum, but in only some particular domain with a specific geographical character and an individual "history-making" power. Hocking underlines his point by insisting that the "material conditions" of action, both geographical and historical, are *facts* to be taken seriously by the *general* will of the state, and he continues with a most acute summary sentence: "the will of a state is a general will, but it is not will-in-general.... It is the will of a nation" (MATS, 373). In a final pronouncement he makes it clear that the state exists only so far as the will circuit it expresses is "actually used" by its members, a condition that spells out a further indictment of the idea that the state has any sort of being as a separate self.

The emphasis Hocking placed on the material conditions for action, the function of common objects and products in the various forms of human endeavor, the facts of geography and of history in the world's politics, testifies to the realistic and empirical character of his idealist philosophy. I understood upon first reading him that, although he obviously had great respect for the idealist philosophical tradition and saw himself as belonging to it, he was, nevertheless, wary of an idealism that displayed little interest in the world of nature and did not take seriously the fact that human life takes place within a natural environment and a culture that depends on physical resources no less than those of a spiritual or intellectual character. Modern idealism has often been guilty of finding intelligibility only in the realm of mind and selfhood, while regarding the world of nature as "opaque" and an ultimate stumbling block to the attainment of a fully rational comprehension of things. Without joining the issue, suffice it to say that Hocking was fully aware of the problem and was determined to avoid perpetuating the error.

The same idea of nature's role is central to Hocking's philosophy of religion, where, for him, the natural world stands as a common focus for both man and God. He does not find the significance of the world in the role it plays in cosmological arguments for God's existence, and he even regarded such proofs as running counter to the spirit of religion. As Hocking rightly sees, a God who is *only as real* as the world is not enough, especially since the quest for God has often been inspired by the sense that the world as it stands is unsatisfactory. Hence, the significance of the natural world for the religious consciousness must lie elsewhere. He describes as an original source of the knowledge of God "an experience of *not being alone in knowing the world*, and especially the world of Nature" (MGHE, 236). Seen in this light, Nature ceases to be the "unknown" reality and is endowed with the order and rationality which it is the endless task of science to comprehend (MGHE, 237).

In seeking, moreover, to understand the basis in experience for the knowledge we have of each other, Hocking makes an excellent case for the view that the world we inhabit provides the common reality that brings us together. "This world in which I live," he writes, "is the world of thy soul: and being within that I am within thee" (MGHE, 266). Nor, Hocking insists, should we look upon this connecting medium as a barrier, for, like all relations, they hold us apart while connecting us at the same time. They cannot, moreover, do one without the other. The space that so clearly separates us from one another also connects us as beings who are together in the *same* space. Hocking's idealism takes nature no less seriously than mind.

Returning to the theory of the state, understanding the state as the circuit of circuits, howsoever illuminating, still leaves open the question of how the meeting of human wills is possible. His answer appeals to a region of unity and identical experience among human beings that is deeper than the political realm. "This everyday process," he claims, "of 'finding themselves sharing the planet' together with every mutual understanding growing out of this discovery, implies that these selves have always had some region of unity or identical experience" (MATS, 377). This primal unity is said to be prior to all social arrangements and thus cannot be the result of historical achievement nor can it be supplied by the state. Instead, this unity, in Hocking's view, stems from religion—"the religious unity of men thus lies far deeper than their political unity" (MATS, 377). Harking back to an earlier discussion of desires that we cannot fail to have, he cites the will to power as the human propensity possessed by all and, more important, claims that its existence calls for an arrangement of wills which is the state. The will that the state exist, then, is unanimous; it is that primal unanimity which, in the view of most political theorists, must precede the right of any government to impose its will on citizens as if it were "their own." For Hocking, this primal unity of wills is no diplomatic achievement, but "a deliverance of human nature" (MATS, 383), and it represents his way of combining consent with necessitation, a combination possible only if everyone acknowledges the existence of a mutual will to power.

Ever realistic in his recognition of the negative side of things, the human capacity for evil, Hocking takes seriously the complaint of the anarchist—the individualist who sees nothing but the magnification of human deficiency in any government—and passes a judgment that is especially relevant for our contemporary situation. The anarchist, he contends, believes that the vices of human beings are inherent in state action as such, a belief that leads growing numbers of people to want to be done with politics altogether. Hocking regards this attitude as irresponsible since the will to power cannot be stifled, nor can the need for the organization that is the state be denied. The problem is, as before, to find the proper form of organization, but, as he insists, we receive no help in the solution of this problem from those who despair of any form of organization and retreat to the inviolability of the individual, atomic will. The position is basically a parasitic one; those who propose to secede from the state live under the illusion of their own self-sufficiency and utterly fail to see that it is the state that provides them with the only place of standing and stable order possible in an actual world of many wills to power. The state sustains them in their very opposition to it. Implicit in the anarchistic outlook is a denial that there is any *public* domain or dimension that needs to be nurtured and protected; social and political reality are dissolved into a disparate multitude of private beings and individual spaces. One of the more unfortunate consequences of this view—we experience its effects in America today—is a refusal to distinguish between law enforcement officials in their capacity as agents of the state and in their status as private citizens. This is consistent even if potentially disastrous; if there is no legitimate political authority, no acknowledged domain of public power, there can be nothing for government officials to represent and the only alternative for this sort of individualist is to see them as no more than private individuals whose efforts to enforce the law only make them guilty of coercion and of violating the rights of others.

Let me conclude this topic with a brief summary of Hocking's theory of the state. He begins with a belief in the existence of a will to power in each individual from which follows the need for the state. The existence of mankind—the deep-seated unity among human beings—underlies the unanimous will that wills the existence of the state. But it is the reality of special interests and individual willfulness which makes the state a necessity as the only way to provide a stable order in which the public interest and the welfare of all citizens may be harmonized. Hocking's view here is not unlike that expressed by Reinhold Niebuhr when he said, speaking not about the state as such but about democratic government, that man's capacity for justice makes democracy possible, but his capacity for injustice makes democracy necessary. Niebuhr called this position "realism" in contrast to the extremes of cynicism and sentimentality. Hocking was giving expression in his political philosophy to much the same position.

The last of the three ideas selected for consideration is Hocking's account of the basic conception of the individual in Western civilization. For his views on the subject I turn to his book, *The Lasting Elements of Individualism*. A caveat is needed at the outset regarding the term "individualism." This term has often been used, and not without justification, in a pejorative sense to indicate an exaggerated emphasis on the individual as a wholly self-sufficient unit and a corresponding devaluation of society and its institutions. This is *not* what Hocking means by the term. Individualism for him means primarily "belief in the human individual as the ultimate unit of social structures" and the claim "that there is something more real than the state—the individual" (LEI, 4). He connects this outlook on the political side with the tradition of modern liberalism and its belief in the powers of the individual to advance the welfare of society. There is a gamble, he admits, in trusting individuals to play so large a role in developing the resources of a nation. Those who have been trusted in our democracies to develop new energies under favorable political conditions have done so, and he sees this as a positive achievement. But, he notes, there is also the fact that the resulting goods have not been devoted sufficiently to the welfare of society, because these same individuals have used the opportunity to make something for themselves while leaving society to suffer the consequences.

In order to underline the idea of the autonomous individual as it emerged in the West, Hocking draws a contrast with corresponding ideas in some Asian countries. He speaks of the collectivism that prevails, a collectivism of the great family or clan group, which "holds the property of the group, receives into a common fund much of the individual income of its members, maintains its own discipline, decides for its members whom they marry, what and how much they study, and where they are to be employed" (LEI, 7–8). Hocking illustrates his point by citing the case of an

Asian graduate student in the philosophy department at Harvard. The student had been assigned a graduate fellowship on the basis of his academic work, but in the middle of the year he reported that his funds were depleted, and, when asked for an explanation, he responded candidly, "Brother got married." Hocking's comment sums up the point: "He had not arrived at the notion of a type of income which was a strictly personal rather than a family fund; and his first lesson in financial individualism was painful on both sides."

To express the difference between East and West in this respect, Hocking appeals to the well-known phrase of the distinguished jurist Sir Henry Maine, "the passage from status to contract" by which he meant to express the course of social evolution in the West. "The rule of status," Hocking writes in his expansion of Maine's point, "is the rule of the collective mind of a society when it has achieved a more or less stable equilibrium, so that not even the contemporary collectivity venture to alter it" (LEI, 10). Status has found its most extreme expression in the caste system of India, but the idea has been uppermost in the civilizations of China and Japan as well. Contract, by contrast, signals individual choice coupled with the self-consciousness that a person's self-expression flows not from tradition, but from his or her own accomplishments and decisions. This concept defines the position of the individual in the West, and Hocking wants to understand its origins since he believes that we have accepted too uncritically the economic interpretation according to which the modern individual is simply the "bourgeois" product of the destruction of the feudal system and its replacement by the factory system; in short, a product of the industrial revolution and nothing more.

Hocking, like the Hegel of the *Phenomenology*, was acutely aware of the important role played by self-consciousness in all historical development. Accordingly, in laying down a challenge to "the economic interpretation of history," which dominated social and political thinking in the earlier decades of this century, Hocking posed the following question: "Is there not an inherent absurdity in supposing that men could begin to act as self-sufficient individuals without preparation in thinking of themselves as such?" (LEI, 26). His answer is that the "economic factors" of modern life could not operate on people's minds unless certain other factors had prepared them to look upon themselves as individuals with some place of standing apart from a group, an occupation or a native country. Hocking proposed to point out those other factors by a brief historical excursion into the origins of individualism in Western civilization.

No one, of course, knows when the idea of individualism was born because instead of a single birth it had numerous outcroppings through the centuries. It appeared in eighteenth-century thinking about the "rights of man" and in the democratic revolutions associated with those ideas. But, he claims, we must go back still further to the dissolution of the feudal system and especially the breaking up of the guilds with the coming of new crafts and manufactures, when there arose a new personal freedom for the worker who, no longer the property of a landlord, might now choose to sell his labor to the highest bidder. This meant, in Hocking's words, that "status gave way to contract in the economic sphere" (LEI, 18).

Following many historians, Hocking next takes note of the political shift that took place as the result of the rise of private wealth stemming from the breakup of the feudal economy. "If private wealth exists," he writes, "kings will desire to tap it," but in so doing they discover, like the master in Hegel's *Phenomenology*, that royalty becomes dependent on its subjects so that "the individual will begins consciously to affect the state" (LEI, 18). "To many historians," Hocking writes, "we have here the true headwaters of the democratic-individualistic stream." While not unmindful of the importance of this political shift, he cannot accept it as a satisfactory explanation. The reason is not hard to find; for Hocking the roots of individuality must be found at a level deeper than either the political or the economic spheres, and hence he goes back further to the Reformation. The Reformation, he claims, was not interested primarily in either the economic or the political man, but "had something to say to the individual conscience" (LEI, 19). That "something," as he puts it, is not the "natural right" of the conscience to think for itself but the absolute *obligation* to do so, as stands out so clearly in Luther's appeal to the individual Christian. Royce had argued that when a person acknowledges a deed as his or her *own*, there comes a sense of unique individuality. I believe Royce was right, but Hocking seems to be going a step further in finding this sense, first, in our capacity to pass judgment on our selves and our conduct, and, second, in our acknowledging an obligation to do so. If the sense that no one else can do my deed is strong, the sense that no one else can have a conscience for me is as strong if not stronger. Another person may make much the same judgment about my conduct as I do, but if that judgment is adverse, I am the one who will have the "bad" conscience, and my neighbor will not feel my discomfort. It is no accident that Hocking places such great emphasis on conscience as the root of individuality; his chief reason, it will be recalled, for rejecting the idea that the state can be understood in terms of a "group mind" is that such a mind, even if real, could have no conscience. Conscience is a reality only for the individual.

We cannot follow Hocking further in his return journey, which finally ends with the Christian and Platonic traditions, each of which has so decisively shaped Western civilization. I should like to close with a short coda that takes into consideration a singular historical fact that Hocking does not mention but that I believe is essential if we are to understand the contribution of religion to the rise and persistence of individuality in the Western world. Despite the fact that much of the literature of the classical world has been lost, it is still true that prior to the *Confessions* of St. Augustine, there is little in the surviving literature that might qualify as instances of autobiography, of an individual recounting the story of a unique life. The great exception is, of course, the *Meditations* of Marcus Aurelius, a work that, because of its high moral resolution and personal tone, has had a great appeal in the ensuing centuries. By comparison, however, Augustine's account of his personal odyssey is deeper because it goes far beyond moral ideals and prescriptions to grapple with the religious concerns of the From Whence? and the To Whence? of human existence.

Augustine's *Confessions* is far more than an autobiography; it is a searching and candid appraisal of his entire life in the light of his belief that God is truth and that, in his well-known words, "Our hearts are restless, until they find their rest in Thee." No thought, no deed, no word stemming from the depths of his inner life is too intimate to be revealed to the God from whom no secrets are hid. Individuality and privacy come to full flower when one is confronting the truth before a God who understands. I would be less than loyal to the thinker whose ideas I have been expounding if I did not acknowledge that, while he does not use the examples of my coda, he grasped the same point. "A man's ultimate relations," he writes, "are solely to God; and perhaps the deepest thing in Christianity is the adequacy with which it presents this ultimate solitude of the soul, not alone in birth, and in death, but in the history of its own ethical problem.... This is the essential freedom of the self, that it stands for a fateful moment outside of all belongings, and determines for itself alone whether its primary attachments will be with actual earthly interests or with those of an ideal and potential 'Kingdom of God'" (LEI, 22–23).

If I were asked to single out one characteristic feature of Hocking's approach to philosophy, I would cite his spirit of *adventure*, his willingness to try out and accept the consequences of new ideas. We have seen this in his perceptive formula that the individual as such is prior to the state, but that the state is prior to the completed individual. It appears again in his philosophy of religion, where he argued that it is the cosmos, the world of things we share, that forms a medium of communication between God and human beings. And, in his later years when he had been invited to give the Gifford Lectures but was no longer up to the task, he set forth, nevertheless, a concrete program for the lectures calling for an "inductive metaphysics" rooted in experience. Consider how often the term "inductive," with its implication of attention to fact and experience, has been taken as the exclusive property of the sciences, while to metaphysics has been assigned an abstract method of deduction. These are thoughts of one who welcomes adventure; in the figure of William James, one who marks a trail on the trees of the forest before anyone has passed that way.

CHAPTER 26

W. E. Hocking on Marx, Russian Marxism, and the Soviet Union

George L. Kline

I first met William Ernest Hocking in March 1958 at the annual conference of the Metaphysical Society of America at Brown University, where he delivered the presidential address. In May of that year Ivor Leclerc and I visited him at his home in Madison, New Hampshire. We were especially interested in seeing his notes on Whitehead's first course of lectures at Harvard. (Those notes have since been published [Whitehead 1984].) I commissioned Hocking's splendid essay, "Whitehead as I Knew Him" for the Whitehead centennial issue of the *Journal of Philosophy* (1961). That essay was included in the book that I edited in 1963, *Alfred North Whitehead: Essays on His Philosophy* (rpt. 1989). I saw Hocking for the last time on March 29, 1966, less than three months before his death on June 12. I felt—and feel—great esteem for Hocking as a thinker and scholar and great affection for him as a person. I particularly appreciated his wisdom, generosity, decency, and what Charles Hartshorne has called his "large humanity" (Hartshorne 1946, 457).[1] I also prized his lively and eloquent philosophical style.

Like John Dewey, Hocking wrote not just technical treatises in the traditional areas of philosophy but also copious and persuasive essays on public affairs. In a period—from the early 1920s to the late 1950s—when passions ran high both for and against Marx, Russian Marxism, and the Soviet state, he managed to maintain a sensible restraint and a nuanced moderation in his judgments, avoiding the opposed extremes of uncritical embrace and impatient repudiation of those theorists and the movements and political systems that they inspired.

I. Marx

Hocking offers a clear and convincing statement of Marx's economic interpretation of history, justly noting the centrality for Marx of the doctrine of "class war" (*Klassenkampf*). The "feeling of class hostility must be kept alive" (MATS, 450). Marx assigns to economic factors the key "role in history which Hegel attributed to Spirit" (MATS, 284 n. 1). For Marx, economic struggle is a "method of dialectical advance" (LEI, 85),

[349]

and "class-consciousness with class-war is the destined way into the [historical] future" (MATS, 449). The dialectic of history requires things to get worse before they can get better (as a result of the proletarian revolution) (LEI, 88). The "mythology of revolution" mandates a dim view of the existing order. According to Marx, the "badness of present states [of society] is more desirable than their goodness." Moreover, reformist accommodations and liberal concessions must be flatly rejected, "every gift spit upon, in order [to preserve] the warlike temper" (MATS, 450).

Hocking puts his own criticism delicately: "Marx's hope of attaining an ultimate unity of society through the medium of class war" does not reveal a "deep perspicacity regarding the problem of [social] unity," especially since Marx is silent about rights and duties (LEI, 89).

Hocking's general critique of both the theory of economic determinism and the doctrine of class struggle strikes me as persuasive. He brands as an "illusion" the belief that the "economic drive is the dominant history-making force," noting that "[a]s long as [the] economy works through human heads, and so long as those heads have their beliefs, prides, resentments, loves, hates, just so long will our [economic problems] depend for their solution on problems of social ethics [hence on noneconomic values]" (SWP, 520).

Hocking admits that there was a certain justification for Marx's "single-minded" focus on economic factors, since those factors tended to be neglected by other theorists, especially by the Hegelians, with their "top-lofty idealism." So, to redress the balance, Marx "fell into the opposite one-sidedness" (LEI, 90). Now, I do not myself consider Hegel's philosophy to be a "top-lofty idealism." Furthermore, Hegel did not wholly neglect economic factors (see, e.g., Maker 1987). It was Hegel, after all, who—as John Herman Randall used to say—"breakfasted on brass tacks."[2] But Hocking is right to claim that, as compared to Marx, Hegel assigned economic factors a secondary and subordinate place among the agents of historical change.

Hocking notes a tension in Marx's position. Although Marx saw the whole meaning of history in economic terms, "his own fervor, and the exalted spirit of self-sacrifice often shown by his followers in their effort [to bring about] the ideal [future] society, welled up from unacknowledged springs of human feeling and from a passion for justice as they conceived justice [that is, from other than economic sources]" (LEI, 114).

After referring perceptively to Marx's "hard pugnacities," Hocking adds the wry comment that "as a sole diet, brine is meager" (LEI, 93). This, I take it, is an echo of Whitehead's critique of the Voltairian mentality: "Men cannot live on ... disinfectants [alone]" (Whitehead 1926, 87).

Hocking goes so far as to speak of the "pathetic absurdity" of Marx's belief in a historical determinism that "requires so much *resolute support* to make it work" (MATS, 451; italics added). He sees Marx's advocacy of "class hatred, class warfare, class subjugation" (LEI, 95) as "essentially perverse," because "in order to 'march toward [future] deliverance from evils' [Marxist revolutionaries] leap blindly into certain evils which reason could foresee and into still others that we know not of" (MATS, 451).

Hocking offers an intriguing comparison of Marx's position with that of his older contemporary, John Stuart Mill (1806–1873). He stresses that Mill failed to recognize what for Marx was the "crime" of machine-tending, something that rendered workers overly specialized and "stupid"—or, "if he noticed the fact at all, [Mill] remained politely undisturbed by it" (LEI, 134). This "crime" was something that Marx felt "in every fiber of his being. This is the measure of his greater moral depth, and the secret of his enduring power" (LEI, 134). However, Hocking adds, Marx failed to realize that his "socialized state" would sin "even more radically" against human wholeness. It would replace the "unequal mutilation" of the capitalist system with an "equal mutilation" of everyone without exception (LEI, 134).

Those words were written in 1937. Nineteen years later Hocking added this general comment: " [W]e are today less than ever persuaded by the Marx-Engels [claim] that the logic of his economic needs can explain man's social history or his cultural prowess, still less [determine] his destiny" (CWC, 43).

Hocking goes on to offer four specific criticisms of Marx's position:

(1) "[U]nless Marx can appeal to something other than the economic motive itself, the logic of his criticism of the capitalistic economy will turn against the socialistic economy and reduce it also to units each of whom works only *for himself*. But he does, in fact, appeal to other motives [in particular,] moral resentment of wrong and moral enthusiasm for a better order" (MATS, 294).

This means that, in effect, Marx and the Marxists have "*announced* an economic interpretation only to *abandon* it" (MATS, 294; italics added).

(2) Hocking disputes the "liberal presumption" shared by Marx that "poverty purifies, that the underdog must be a particularly good dog" (LEI, 123–124). The fact is, Hocking insists, that there are "honest and able men among laborers and among employers; [and] there are crooks on both sides." He sees no "virtue in substituting one set of crooks for another." It is appalling, he observes, how quickly those who have been oppressed learn the "arts of oppression" (LEI, 124).

(3) Marx's claim that the "ideology of law, morals, politics, religion, is not what it pretends to be, but [is rather] a function of economic interest tends to undermine its own validity." If this claim is true, then Marxism itself is only one more ideology, "economically determined, and without presumption of truth" (MATS, 295).

(4) Writing in 1959, Hocking sees Marx's neglect of national, ethnic, and religious self-identity and self-assertion as a theoretical weakness. All such forms of identity and assertion, for Marx, belong in the famous "dustbin of history." Marx had "no feeling" for what Hocking calls "a *revived na-*

tional sense, as concrete and racy [*sic*] of the soil as custom and dialect and folklore." Hocking complains that the "entire literature of the Communist Movement" is quite "empty of national feeling" (SMN, 120).

From the perspective of the late 1990s, with the recent bitter experience of the ugly and destructive expressions of national, ethnic, and religious self-identity, self-assertion, and conflict—in India, Pakistan, the Middle East, Bosnia, Kosovo, and Northern Ireland—we may perhaps wish that Marx had been right on this point. On the other hand, as Hocking was well aware, Marx's favored doctrines of class warfare and proletarian revolution also had their ugly and destructive aspects.

I note briefly two omissions in Hocking's discussions of Marx, omissions as welcome as they were rare in the literature on Marx published in the 1950s and early 1960s: (1) One finds in Hocking none of the mostly empty chatter about the "humanism of the young Marx" that characterized much of that literature. As I have argued elsewhere, Marx rejected every ethical humanism or "humanism of *principles*," a position which is present-oriented and shows basic respect for human rights. What he accepted was the much weaker, future-oriented "humanism of *ideals*," a position that is fully compatible with transitional totalitarianism of the Leninist and Stalinist type (see Kline 1969).

(2) Hocking, with one exception, avoids making the empty claim, endlessly repeated by both defenders and critics of Marx, that he was a philosophical materialist, that he developed or at least defended a materialist ontology. Engels, Plekhanov, and Lenin did that, but Marx did not (see Kline 1988). The one exception that I have discovered in Hocking's writings is the misleading contrast between "Hegel the idealist" and "Marx the materialist" (SMN, 217), where presumably the reference is *not* to Marx's economic interpretation of history but rather to a materialist ontology.

Finally, I note two minor problems of terminology, both of which make a difference to points of substance, and both of which are pervasive in the writings of Marx's critics as well as his defenders. Unfortunately, both of them sometimes appear in Hocking's writings on this subject.

(1) Although Hocking was well aware that Marx's "materialist interpretation of history" was an "economist" doctrine, having nothing to do with a materialist ontology, he sometimes permitted himself such expressions as "material necessity" (in the sense of "economic necessity") (MATS, 284 n.1) and made such claims as that for Marx "ideas and beliefs ... are the creatures of *material or economic* forces" (FP, 22; italics added). I'm afraid that it doesn't really help to identify "matter" in some not further defined sense as the "economic basis of life" (TP, 3d. ed., 224).

(2) Both defenders and critics of Marx have been massively misled by Lenin's forceful but false claim that "Marx and Engels scores of times termed their philosophical views dialectical materialism" (Lenin [1909] 1927, 9).[3] In fact neither Marx nor Engels *ever* used the expression "dialectical materialism"

(*der dialektische Materialismus*). But Marxist-Leninists as well as opponents of Marxism-Leninism have been repeating this falsehood for decades. And in at least one place—though only in a textbook—Hocking joined this chorus, asserting that Marx called his position "dialectical materialism" (TP, 3d. ed., 224). For the historical record, it appears to have been Dietzgen, in a work written in Chicago in 1886 and first published in Zurich in 1887 (four years after Marx's death), who first used the expression "dialectical materialism" (Dietzgen, 61, 75, 79). Plekhanov repeated this expression and made it current, beginning in 1891.[4]

II. Russian Marxism

Although Hocking makes scattered references to Lenin, Trotsky, Bukharin, and Stalin, he does not treat any of them as Marxist *theorists*. He refers several times to Khrushchev, but in only one connection as a theorist or ideologist, namely, with respect to the doctrine of "peaceful coexistence" of states with opposed social systems. I shall say something about this in section III. For the moment, I mention only one of Hocking's comments about Khrushchev, in a personal letter written at the time of the Cuban missile crisis (October 1962). The comment was to the effect that Khrushchev's face expressed "pure evil." This judgment went strongly against the "winds of doctrine" of the time, and since, but in my considered opinion was largely true.

The reputation that Khrushchev enjoyed, and to a considerable extent still enjoys, as a reformer and "liberalizer" is quite undeserved. To be sure, in 1956 he "de-Stalinized" the surface of Soviet society but only in order to "re-Leninize" it in its depths. In foreign affairs he brutally crushed the Hungarian uprising of 1956, caused the infamous Berlin Wall to be erected in 1961, and brought the world to the brink of nuclear war in the Cuban missile crisis of 1962. He was no less brutal in domestic affairs. His introduction in 1961 of the death penalty for crimes against (state and public) property, before this penalty was suspended in late 1988, had cost several hundred Soviet citizens their *lives*, citizens whose only crime was to have taken or abused the *property* of the state.

Other aspects of what I have called Khrushchev's "social Stalinism" (see Kline 1964) include his denunciation of modernist tendencies in Soviet art (in his famous "donkey-tail" speech of 1962) and the condemnation in 1964 of the young Leningrad poet Joseph Brodsky (who was to win the Nobel Prize for Literature in 1987) for "social parasitism," that is, for having failed to perform "socially useful labor." Brodsky would in all probability have served out his entire five-year term at hard labor in the Far North if Khrushchev had not been toppled from power in October 1964. In fact, Brodsky was released after only twenty months (in November 1965).

In a word, Hocking's characterization of Khrushchev as representing "pure evil" strikes me as essentially justified.

III. The Soviet Union

Hocking frequently said "Russia" when he meant "the Soviet Union" (e.g., FP, 38). This was a common, though unfortunate, error in his time. The Soviet Union comprised fifteen republics, only one of which (to be sure, the largest) was Russian, two others—Ukraine and Belorussia—being Slavic, and the remaining dozen non-Slavic, ranging from Armenia and Estonia to Georgia and Uzbekistan. But Hocking was right to speak, as he often did, of the creativity of the *Russian* (rather than Soviet) people or the "irrepressible vitality of the Russian [not "Soviet"] soul" (LEI, 136). After all, he knew nothing, and even today specialists in Russian thought and culture know very little, about Armenian, Estonian, Georgian, or Uzbek thought and culture.

I shall consider Hocking's views of the Soviet Union under half a dozen headings:

(1) *The Bolshevik Revolution and its consequences, including the Stalinist terror.* In some places Hocking seems to me to overstate the positive contributions of the October Revolution, although in other places he introduces severe qualifications, as when he speaks of the "crimes of revolution" (SMN, 72, 207) and of the revolutionary destruction of law and rights. He refers to the "openly professed amoralism of the founding saints of the revolution," specifically identifying both Lenin and Trotsky in this connection (SMN, 183). And he makes it clear that for Lenin the "Great End [of Communism] justifies the means, inhuman or otherwise, necessary to promote it: the [only] crime is to fail" (SMN, 183).

In my judgment, Hocking sometimes comes too close to the official Stalinist view in condemning the "old regime," both state and church. He ignores what was only incompletely appreciated during his lifetime and has been fully documented only in the past couple of decades, namely, the important movements of reform in both the tsarist government and the Russian Orthodox Church, especially during the dozen years before 1917.[5]

Here are two examples of Hocking's treatment of the Bolshevik Revolution and what he calls "communism in Russia": "Communism in Russia has the great negative virtue of a successful revolution: it has destroyed ancient abuses. It may be that some of the iniquities and corruptions of the old church-state regimes were so deep-rooted that a complete cleansing of the stables was the least painful way to get rid of them" (LEI, 115). Another statement in the same work strikes me as overly generous to Stalin's regime at a time (1937) when it was engaged in a fierce campaign of terror, especially against intellectuals: "[The positive worth of Communism in Russia] does not lie in its common wealth, which tends rather to be a common poverty. It certainly does not lie in an increase of liberty. It lies rather in the fact that for the old static tyranny has been substituted a tyranny which is dynamic, and directed toward certain liberal [*sic*] ends" (LEI, 115–116).

Hocking sensibly rejected two common slogans of the time: "Communism vs. Capitalism" and "The Communist World vs. the Free World." As early as 1945—as he himself recalled in 1959—he had undertaken "to show that there are in the world of advanced societies no purely capitalist and no purely communist economies—all are 'mixed.'⁶ The wide differences in the proportions of the mixture are due to the more essential issue of the *pattern of freedom*" (SMN, 10; cf. 34).

What is mostly wrong with the slogan "Communism vs. Capitalism" is that it presents "as economic an issue involving our deepest convictions regarding the normal bond of social and political organization," and this in turn is also a matter of *freedom* (SMN, 43). Hocking further notes that the Bolshevik Revolution took place "not in a great industrial country, but in a vast rural civilization. Its immediate object of attack was not a keen, driving capitalism, undermined by class struggle ... but a rather stupid and venal union of church and state, which had begun—too late and too [slowly], to be sure—to make things better for the peasantry" (LEI, 69).

One statement of 1932 shows, at the same time, both a penetrating insight into the workings of Stalinist totalitarianism and a certain naïveté. "Russia," Hocking declares, "exiles its scholars, or fines them, or does away with them; these deeds become known" (SWP, 498). The implication seems to be that when the brutalities of Stalin's treatment of "scholars" become known, those brutalities are somehow reduced or neutralized. But in fact much of the brutality, especially that directed at intellectuals, was carried out in secret and remained unrevealed until decades later. Examples are the ghastly deaths in the gulag in 1937 of philosopher Gustav Shpet and mathematician-theologian Fr. Pavel Florensky, which were not revealed (as to actual time and cause of death) until the late *1980s*.

Hocking sometimes showed a clearer grasp of what the Soviet regime was actually doing to cultural and intellectual life: "The forcibly collectivized life of the communist state [he wrote in 1937] takes the upper inch off ... every head, the inch which thinks, aspires, exercises individual judgment, doubts, [and] demurs" (LEI, 134).

He also makes the perceptive remark that "[i]t is a radical weakness of revolution on Marxian lines that the 'exploiting classes' in regimes dominantly agricultural rather than industrial—that means China as well as Russia—are likely, as landed aristocracy, to be the bearers of the *historic culture* of the nation; and with their liquidation—not the national spirit itself, but the voice of that spirit, is muted" (SMN, 121).[7]

Hocking adds that the Marxist-Leninist expression "dictatorship of the proletariat" is "accidentally precise: it is [a dictatorship] not *by* the proletariat but *of* [i.e., over] the proletariat *by* heads of [the] party" (SMN, 118). This is an intriguing and, I assume, unknowing echo of Trotsky's early charge against Lenin, that he was preaching and practicing an unacceptable "replacementism" in which the Party takes the place of the proletariat as a class; the Central Committee takes the place of the Party; and, finally, the General Secretary takes the place of the Central Committee.[8] There is the further irony (not mentioned by Hocking) that precisely this charge could have been quite justly leveled against Trotsky himself in the 1920s—particularly, the charge that for him, as for Lenin, the *Party* had "taken the place" of the *proletariat*.

Despite the pointed critical remarks noted above, Hocking failed—as most critics of Soviet Communism have failed—to note one of the principal philosophical and ideological underpinnings of the brutalities and inhumanities of Soviet society, namely, the powerful, almost obsessive orientation of Soviet ideologists and policy makers toward the world-historical *future*. This future-orientation had two related but distinguishable aspects: (a) a blind confidence that the historical future could be accurately predicted and that it held the certain, if long-term, promise of attaining the "radiant future of communism" *(svetloe budushchee kommunizma)* for all mankind; and (b) the more ominous assumption that, for the sake of attaining that radiant future, present communities, cultures, practices, and—especially—persons could justifiably be reduced to the status of *means* serving that world-historical *end* (see Kline 1993).[9] Marx, Lenin, and Stalin—as well as Trotsky—were enthusiastic instrumentalizers, quite prepared to sacrifice both the past and the present for the sake of their projected world-historical communist future.

(2) I note two *welcome omissions* in Hocking's treatment of the Soviet Union: (a) there is none of the talk, common at the time among Western commentators, about the "grandeur" or "nobility" of the "Soviet Experiment." So far as I can see, Hocking uses the expression "The Communist Experiment" only once, and there it appears as a rather neutral section heading and does not occur at all in his text (cf. LEI 115). (b) Hocking never draws the kind of distinction that was most forcefully—and fancifully—drawn by Roy Medvedev between the noble and constructive Lenin and the ignoble and destructive Stalin (Medvedev 1972). As recent revelations from previously secret party archives have made clear, Lenin was no less brutal and repressive than Stalin (see Volkogonov 1994). The main difference was one of scale: Lenin was in power for less than seven years, and his victims were numbered in the tens of thousands; Stalin was in power for almost thirty years and his victims were numbered in the tens of millions.

(3) Hocking's account of *Soviet anti-religious propaganda and the repression of*

believers is lively but incomplete. Thus he writes in 1944: "[N]ow in Russia we have had for twenty-five years the atheism of a great nation—not unanimous, but dominant," and adds: "We shall ... know better after a hundred years, if Russia will remain atheist so long, how this regime works out" (SIG, 66). Earlier he had asserted: "Millions of communicants of the old Russian Church acquiesce in the new anti-God regime with little protest and less martyrdom: they fancied they were *believers*; [but] they were only *adherents*" (LEI, 174; italics added).

In fact, there was considerable protest, and there were not a few martyrs, especially during the 1920s. However, both the protest and martyrdom were effectively concealed by Soviet officialdom until quite recently.[10]

Hocking is aware that the Soviet regime paid only lip service to human rights generally and to freedom of conscience in particular. But he does not appear to realize that even in the Soviet Constitution of 1937 (the so-called "Stalin" Constitution), there was no equality of rights between believers and nonbelievers, even "on paper." Believers were allowed the right to worship but were denied the right to attempt to persuade others to share their beliefs. The teaching of religion to more than three people at a time was a criminal offense, for which many Soviet believers spent long years in Stalin's gulag. In contrast, nonbelievers had not only the right to disbelieve but also the right, opportunity, and systematic encouragement and support of the Communist Party and the Soviet State (including every level of the educational system) to attempt to persuade others to share their atheism.

Moreover, charitable and other nonliturgical activities of all religious groups were banned. And no Soviet citizen who was known to have any kind of religious affiliation was permitted to receive higher education or to hold a responsible position in the society, the economy, or the culture. The social and intellectual "marginalization" of religious believers in the Soviet period was much more complete and much more destructive than Hocking realized.[11] And it did not come to an end until the eve of the collapse of the Soviet Union, when, in 1990, laws were passed that genuinely guaranteed freedom of conscience for all Soviet citizens.

Hocking's strongest condemnation of the Soviet position on religion appears in one of his latest works. He refers to our *"righteous hatred"* of evil, including the evil of the "original and continuing crimes of revolution" and to our "relentless hatred of the atheist-materialist degradation not of the earth and its fruits [alone], but of the spirit of man in its cosmic insertion. How can we make peace with a system that destroys the [spiritual] light that lifts the whole mixed tangle of history into partnership with infinitude?" (SMN, 206).

And he adds: "What ... can we feel but horror toward a regime that would stamp out this aspiring flame [of religion], which is the soul of humanity?" (SMN, 207).

(4) Hocking seems to me to overestimate the *social cohesiveness and collective resolve* of Soviet society. Thus he speaks in 1944 of a "great social enthusiasm" that provides a "good substitute for traditional religion" (SIG, 66). Now Stalinist propaganda included a drumbeat of claims about the unshakable "moral-political unity" of the Soviet people. But in fact the Soviet population in the late 1930s, the late 1940s, and the late 1950s was more ideologically "demagnetized," more diverse, more divided, more distracted, and more corrupt than Hocking allows. One of the few bits of evidence of a Soviet loss of ideological fervor that he offers (in 1937) dates from 1928. It is a statement by Khristian Rakovsky, a member of the socialist opposition purged by Stalin in 1938, frankly admitting that there had been a "frightful decline in the spirit of activity of the working masses," and noting the "ever growing indifference" of those masses toward the "destiny of the dictatorship of the proletariat." Among the Bolshevik leaders, Rakovsky detects "arrivisme, selfishness, [and] cowardice" (LEI, 119, 121).[12]

Although Hocking occasionally refers to the pre-1917 corruption of the tsarist "Church-State" alliance (LEI, 115), he takes no account of the pervasive corruption of *Soviet* society. Bribery, kickbacks, and embezzling were widespread. They were often winked at, sometimes encouraged by the system itself, with its centralized command economy. For instance, factory managers often found that they had to bribe high officials of various ministries to obtain the raw materials, machinery, and spare parts they needed to meet production quotas set by those same ministries.

(5) In the late 1950s and early 1960s many Western commentators dismissed *Khrushchev's announced policy of "peaceful coexistence"* as a propaganda ploy or, at most, a temporary tactical move. Hocking takes it with full seriousness and, in my judgment, is right to do so. He usually calls it either just "coexistence" or "competitive coexistence" or else "peaceful competition." Thus he characterizes Khrushchev's "will to coexistence in peaceful competition" as something both "realistic and genuine" (SMN, 150). Hocking is convinced that the "people of the USSR ... do not want war"[13] and that this "constitutes a tangible reassurance that Khrushchev's program of competitive coexistence" is a genuine aim of the Soviet state (SMN, 139, 140; cf. 157).

One may add that the doctrine of peaceful coexistence (of nation-states with opposed social systems, i.e., one socialist, the other nonsocialist) is not a *Marxian* doctrine. There is no such idea in Marx himself. But it is quite solidly rooted in *Leninist* thought, even though Lenin's position was ambiguous in certain respects. In any case, Khrushchev's doctrine has a serious conceptual foundation in the Marxist-Leninist philosophy of history. On this view, not all capitalist states will advance to socialism at the same time. During the interval—which may last many centuries—between the appearance of the *first* socialist state and the disappearance of the *last* capitalist state, the relations among the two kinds of states will be governed by the principle of peaceful coexistence or nonmilitary competition. Peaceful coexistence is a transitional condition, intermediate between the historically *past* condition of interrupted war among nonsocialist states and the anticipated *future* condition of uninterrupted peace among socialist states.[14]

Hocking rightly stresses the competitive nature of peaceful coexistence, but he fails to appreciate the force of the Soviet repudiation of "*ideological* coexistence" as something that amounts to a "betrayal of the cause of communism."[15] That Soviet leaders should have done everything in their considerable power to prevent their own people from *accepting* what they branded as "alien ideologies"—Christian, existentialist, pacifist, personalist, etc.—is understandable. But they also made systematic attempts to prevent their own people from even being *exposed* to such ideologies—through censorship, closed borders, the jamming of foreign radio broadcasts, etc. Hocking seems to have been unaware of this rather more sinister corollary of the doctrine of peaceful coexistence; in any case, he makes no critical comments about it.

(6) On the question of *the place and function of Marxist-Leninist philosophy in the Soviet Union*, Hocking took two rather different positions, one early, the other late. In 1937 he asserted—without justification, it seems to me—that "Communism in Russia" had established "at the center of government an intense concern for a *true philosophy*," adding that this was a "mark of *political sincerity*" (LEI, 116; italics added). It is highly doubtful that the "true philosophy," which in 1937—and indeed until 1956—was identified in all Soviet pronouncements as "Marxism-Leninism-*Stalinism*," was accepted as a matter of sincere conviction by Soviet leaders, Soviet intellectuals, or ordinary Soviet citizens. Much closer to the mark is Hocking's acknowledgment (in 1959) that there is a "cloak of [Marxist-Leninist] *philosophical indoctrination*" that has been "thrown over the whole nation [which is treated] as a *captive audience*" (SMN, 22; italics added). I think that Hocking inclined, on balance and quite sensibly, to this second view.

IV. The Soviet View of Hocking as a Thinker

Since we have been examining Hocking's views of Soviet ideology, philosophy, and policy, it seems appropriate to note briefly what the Soviets were saying about Hocking in the period 1951–1978. Generally speaking, the Soviet critique of Hocking was relatively unabusive as compared to the brutal invective that was heaped on James and Dewey. Unlike them, he was not usually attacked directly, but rather by implication as a representative of American personalism, a movement that was characterized as "one of the most reactionary tendencies in contemporary bourgeois philosophy," and as being filled with "hatred of the working people."[16] It happens that the first Soviet references to Hocking that I have discovered occur in a book marked by grotesque abusiveness, even though its treatment of Hocking himself is relatively restrained.[17]

Marx and Lenin, of course, were fierce, sometimes abusive polemicists. Soviet commentators of the Stalinist period were no less fierce and abusive, but somewhat less imaginative and a good deal more repetitious than their ideological heroes in their vituperations against "bourgeois philosophy."[18] Three of Lenin's favored expressions turn up repeatedly: his use of *ideika*, the disparaging diminutive of *ideia*, for any "idea" of an ideological adversary,[19] the use of "diploma'd lackey of" regularly followed by "bourgeois ideology" or (among Soviet commentators) "Wall Street,"[20] and the disparaging diminutive *bozhenko* (always written with lower-case "b"; see n. 36 below) rather than *Bog* for "God."

There is also much talk of ideological and philosophical "decay," "rot," "obscurantism," and "religious or priestly superstition."[21] Thus, American philosophy is branded a "philosophy of gangsterism," representing everything that is "most reactionary, rotten, [and] backward" in the entire history of philosophy.[22]

In the case of Dewey there was the extraphilosophical fact that he had chaired the Trotsky Commission, which met in Mexico City in 1937 to sift the evidence being presented at Trotsky's show trial in Moscow and to cross-examine Trotsky himself. The commission concluded that Trotsky was *not* guilty as charged, that is, not guilty of treason, espionage, etc. Dewey himself was careful to point out that the commission's conclusion did not entail any endorsement of Trotsky's principles or policies. But Stalinist critics ignored this disclaimer, labeling Dewey not only a "diploma'd lackey of imperialist reaction," and so on, but also a defender of and apologist for the despised anti-Stalinist Trotsky.[23]

The Stalinist polemic reached its abusive climax in the early 1950s. By 1959 Marxist-Leninist criticism of Western thinkers had become somewhat more restrained. In contrast to the earlier blanket invective directed at Western philosophers, which was supported by little or no direct quotation from their works, the critiques of the 1960s and 1970s included many direct quotations, mostly in adequate Russian translations, which gave Soviet readers some idea of the actual positions of such thinkers as Dewey and Hocking.[24]

Unfortunately, the use of direct quotations from an author's work, even when the Russian translations are adequate, does not guarantee fair or accurate representation of that author's views. I have noted two cases of striking and deliberate misrepresentation—one of Dewey's position, the other of Hocking's. It is, after all, one thing to be abused for a position that one holds, but quite another thing to be abused for a position that one—explicitly or implicitly—rejects.

In 1938 in a pamphlet entitled "Democracy and Education in the World Today," Dewey deplored the fact that "[i]n the present state of the world apparently a great and increasing number of people feel that the only way we can make ourselves secure is by increasing our army and navy and making our factories ready to manufacture munitions." And he added: *"somehow we too have a belief that force, physical and brute force, after all is the best final reliance"* (italics added). He goes on to say that we should try to strengthen our democratic institutions rather than "surrender to the belief in force, violence and war" ([1938] 1946, 44).

The Czech Marxist-Leninist Josef Linhart quotes only the words I have italicized above, giving as a reference only Dewey's "post-war book" *Problems of Men*.[25] He thus attributes to Dewey precisely the view Dewey was rejecting. And Iurii Mel'vil', in his introduction to the Russian edition of Linhart's book, states flatly and falsely that "Dewey declared that brute force is the 'best final reliance' for preserving the bourgeois system," and that pragmatism sanctions the use of "any and every violent and perfidious method."[26] Linhart's text adds the claim that pragmatists defend "aggression, violence, and deception."[27]

In 1947 Hocking remarked that the Italian press under Mussolini had tried "to regain an overall unity of national purpose by exciting in the masses a total vision of national destiny in whose behalf a will to sacrifice could be reborn," adding: "The Italian dream of renewed empire was corrupt and corrupted its servants" (FP 24–25). Mel'vil' quotes this passage (in an adequate Russian translation), but then makes the perverse comment that the "Italian dream of empire was corrupt because it was the dream of an *Italian* empire. However, the dream of *America's* divinely ordained world mission, undergirded by arguments about defense of the ideals of 'Western democracy,' can, according to Hocking, serve to waken in the American people a will to self-sacrifice, moving them to kill and be killed."[28] Hocking himself, I'm certain, would have been stunned by Mel'vil's conclusion.

More substantial exposition and criticism of Hocking's position is offered in an article devoted entirely to his work[29] and in several books and articles on American philosophy generally and American personalism in particular.[30] Soviet commentators appear unsure just where to place Hocking in the spectrum of American thought. They are well aware that he was not a pragmatist and sometimes cite him as one of the "bourgeois critics" of American pragmatism.[31] They usually treat him as a personalist, sometimes—along with Brightman and Flewelling—as a follower of Royce and Bowne,[32] sometimes as a "second-generation personalist."[33] But, confusingly, one authoritative Soviet source *contrasts* his position with that of the personalists: "Traditional Protestant religious philosophy exists both as 'monism' (Hocking) and as personalism (Brightman, Flewelling)."[34]

All of the Soviet commentators on Hocking make three critical points about his philosophical position. On each of these points they see a parallel with one or another "classical" American philosopher.

(1) Hocking—like Peirce[35]—is both wrong and wrong-headed in claiming that the age-old conflict between science and religion has been resolved and that, rightly understood, science and religion supplement and support each other. For all of the Soviet Marxist-Leninist commentators, religion is "unscientific" and superstitious and the further advance of science will lead to its final disappearance.

(2) Hocking—like James—is both wrong and wrong-headed to take mystical experience seriously. In epistemology his emphasis on intuitive knowledge often merges with an unacceptable emphasis on *mystical* intuition.

(3) Hocking—like Dewey—is both wrong and wrong-headed when he claims that the rivalries between socioeconomic classes can and should be resolved through dialogue and peaceful compromise. On the contrary, for the Marxist-Leninist critics, these rivalries involve deep-seated and irreconcilable "contradictions," which will eventually lead to the social upheaval of proletarian revolution and the "worldwide victory of Communism."

Although, as noted earlier, the Soviet treatment of Hocking is less abusive than that of Dewey, it is uniformly critical. In only one Soviet commentary have I found any positive comment about Hocking's position, and that concerns the quite specific question of his acceptance of Khrushchev's doctrine of peaceful coexistence. The entry on Hocking in the authoritative *Encyclopedia of Philosophy* concludes with the statement that "Hocking is an advocate of the peaceful coexistence of [opposed] social systems."[36] In this, presumably, he is being tacitly contrasted to such "warmongers" as Dewey.

One Soviet commentator offers translated excerpts from Western sources that briefly state Hocking's importance as a thinker, as well as a mildly positive assessment of Hocking's career as a philosopher from another Soviet source, but is careful to avoid praising Hocking *in propria persona*.[37]

Generally speaking, Hocking treated the Soviets a good deal more fairly and objectively than they have treated him. But there is reason to hope that in post-Communist Russia those competent and conscientious specialists in American philosophy who are now focusing their attention on Emerson, Thoreau, Peirce, or Mead may one day turn to a close and sympathetic study of the thought of William Ernest Hocking. I have no doubt that they will then treat him as fairly, objectively, and thoughtfully as he has treated Marx, Russian Marxism, and the Soviet Union.

NOTES

1. In a review of Hocking's *The Coming World Civilization*, Hartshorne added a convincing comparative judgment: "This book has a greatness possessed by very little philosophical writing today" (Hartshorne 1957, 562).
2. Randall's fuller statement is that Hegel "loved facts, hard facts and cold facts, . . . His familiar portrait suggests . . . that he has just made a breakfast of brass tacks" (1965, 277).

3. Lenin's Russian text is in *Sochineniia*, 4th ed. (Moscow: Gos. izd. polit. literatury, 1947), 14: 7. The translator has magnified Lenin's falsehood, putting "scores" for his *desiatki* (literally, "tens"). [All citations to foreign language works can be found in the endnotes and not in the "Works Cited."—eds.]
4. For further details, see Kline 1988, 175, and 182 n. 44. The Plekhanov (translated) text is Plekhanov 1961, esp. vol. 1, 478. The original is "Zu Hegels sechzigstem Todestag," in *Die neue Zeit*, no. 7–9 (1891).
5. Major contributors to this new understanding include Alexander Solzhenitsyn, Paul Valliere, an American specialist on nineteenth- and twentieth-century Russian religious thought, and Adele Lindenmeyr, an American specialist on the social history of nineteenth- and twentieth-century Russia.
6. Hocking included the Soviet Union among the "advanced societies." But we now know that, except for its huge and generally quite efficient military-industrial complex, the Soviet Union during the 1950s was essentially a third-world country.
7. I take it that Hocking is here using the ugly Stalinist term "liquidation" *(likvidatsiia)* in the ominous Stalinist sense of "total destruction" or "complete killing off."
8. The Russian term *zamestitel'stvo*, which Trotsky used, is sometimes rendered as "substitutism"; see, e.g., Deutscher 1954, 90. I prefer the slightly less awkward "replacementism." Trotsky's early text is *Nashi politicheskie zadachi* (Our Political Tasks) (Geneva, 1904), esp. 50, 54.
9. See also the revised and expanded Spanish version of this paper: "La Posible contribución de la filosofía clásica rusa a la construcción de una sociedad humanista," *Diálogo filosófico* [Madrid], no. 31 (1995): 77–90 (trans. by Maria del Carmen Dolby Mugica and Luz-Marina Perez Horna with the assistance of Leopoldo Montoya).
10. Detailed and compelling evidence is presented, for example, by Fr. Damaskin (Orlovsky) in *Ucheniki, ispovedniki i podvizhniki blagochestiia Rossiiskoi Pravoslavnoi Tserkvi XX stoletiia. Kn. 1* (Disciples, Confessors, and Heroes of Piety of the Twentieth-Century Russian Orthodox Church. Bk. 1), Tver': Izd. Bulat, 1992.
11. For details and background, see Kline 1968, chap. 6, 146–171.
12. Hocking is here quoting from Rakovsky's article in *The New International* for November 1934.
13. A year earlier Hocking had referred to a "mystical sense of social unity deep in the Russian folk" that holds the "possibility of sweeping over all bounds, as in the spontaneous welcome of our Texan pianist [Van Cliburn]" (from a private letter, June 2, 1958).
14. See Kline 1978.
15. Nikita Khrushchev, as quoted in *Pravda*, June 29, 1963.
16. L. A. Shershenko, "Amerikanskii personalizm" (American Personalism), in *Sovremennyi ob"ektivnyi idealizm. Kriticheskie ocherki* (Contemporary Objective Idealism. Critical Essays), ed. G. A. Kursanov (Moscow: Izd. sots.-ekon. lit., 1963), 376–377.
17. T. I. Oizerman and P. S. Trofimov, eds., *Protiv filosofstvuiushchikh oruzhenostsev ameriko-angliiskogo imperializma* (Against the Philosophizing Weapons-Bearers of American-English Imperialism) (Moscow: Izd. Akademii nauk SSSR, 1951). The two references to Hocking are on 46 and 186. The normal Russian term is *anglo-amerikanskii* (Anglo-American). But, presumably, in the period of the Korean War, Soviet ideologists wanted to stress that it was no longer Great Britain but the United States that stood first among the "imperialist powers."
18. Although contemporary Russian commentators on American philosophy, whose work is marked by civility and conscientiousness, find the memory an embarrassment, it *was* the case that half a century ago Soviet commentators regularly characterized Dewey, for example, as a "reactionary American bourgeois philosopher ... an ideological weapons-bearer of the American imperialists ... an active participant in filthy, slanderous campaigns against the Soviet Union" (M. Rozental' and I. Iudin, eds., *Kratkii filosofskii slovar'* [Brief Philosophical

Dictionary], 3d ed. [Moscow: Gos. izd. polit. lit., 1951], 128).
19. Iurii Mel'vil', for example, accuses American personalists of seizing upon "any reactionary, anti-scientific *ideika*" to justify the rule of the imperialist bourgeoisie" (*Amerikanskii personalizm—filosofiia imperialisticheskoi reaktsii* [American Personalism—A Philosophy of Imperialist Reaction] [Moscow: Znanie, 1954], 32).
20. Stalinist variants included "philosophizing lackeys of Wall Street" (cf. Iurii Mel'vil', "Pragmatizm—filosofiia amerikanskogo imperializma" [Pragmatism—the Philosophy of American Imperialism], intro. to Josef Linhart, *Amerikanskii pragmatizm* [American Pragmatism] [trans. from the Czech by A. Starostin] [Moscow: Izd. inostr. lit., 1954], xv). This is the kind of talk that Hocking in 1959 referred to as "ghost-chatter" (SMN, 139).
21. The Russian terms *mrakobesie* (obscurantism) and *popovshchina* (religious or priestly superstition), with their Slavic roots and their colloquial flavor, are stronger and more effectively abusive than their English counterparts.
22. Oizerman and Trofimov, 54, 55.
23. The "Trotsky connection" often remained in the background of Soviet criticism of Dewey but was sometimes made explicit; as in Linhart, 16.
24. For Hocking, see, for example, Jan Bodnar, *o sovremennoi filosofii SShA* (On Contemporary Philosophy in the United States) (trans. from the Slovak by D. K. Zvonkov) (Moscow: Izd. sots.-ekon. lit., 1959), esp. 181–187, and N. E. Shlaifer, "Teoretiko-poznavatel'naia kontseptsiia E. Khokkinga" (E. Hocking's Epistemological Conception), in *Iz istorii zarubezhnoi filosofii XIX-XX vekov* (From the History of Foreign Philosophy in the Nineteenth and Twentieth Centuries), ed. A. S. Bogomolov (Moscow: Izd. moskovskogo universiteta, 1967), esp. 151–153, 156–158, and 160–162.
25. Linhart, 15.
26. Mel'vil', ix.
27. Linhart, 250. In 1957, Mel'vil', quoting the same Dewey text as Linhart, adds: "It is difficult to appraise these words as anything but a summons to directly terroristic, fascistic methods of suppressing the workers" (Linhart, 113). But at least he gives the correct page reference in *Problems of Men*. B. A. Shabad, in 1966, goes even further in the falsification of Dewey's position, introducing the passage from *Problems of Men* with the words "Somewhat later Dewey, summing up his views in political philosophy, wrote..." (*Politicheskaia filosofiia sovremennogo imperializma* [The Political Philosophy of Contemporary Imperialism], 2d ed. [Moscow: Izd. Mezhdunarod. otnosheniia, 1966], 33). He also gives a false and misleading page reference—25 instead of 44—for the Dewey passage. [My thanks to Larry Hickman for providing materials from the Dewey database that made it possible for me to identify the source of the passage in question before I had come upon Mel'vil's correct page reference of 1957.]
28. Iurii Mel'vil', "Filosofiia mistiki i reaktsii" [A Philosophy of Mysticism and Reaction], *Voprosy filosofii*, no. 4 (1953): 169, italics added. This article is an early version of the pamphlet cited in note 19. It differs from the pamphlet in providing references for the direct quotations from foreign authors, including Hocking. The pamphlet limits its references for direct quotations to passages from Lenin (13) and Engels (24)! The pamphlet version omits the quotation from *Freedom of the Press*, replacing it with the bald assertion that "Hocking proposes that the American bourgeoisie appraise the 'healthy' political penetration of Italian fascism, which was able, by means of false ideas, to deceive the people and motivate them for war" (31). Mel'vil' then repeats the passage from the journal version beginning: "The Italian dream of empire" and ending: "to kill and be killed," and adds a generalizing conclusion that was not in the earlier text: "These misanthropic arguments reveal with utmost clarity the true face of the personalists [as] philosophizing lackeys of imperialism" (32).
29. N. E. Shlaifer, "Teoretiko-poznavatel'naia kontseptsiia E. Khokkinga," in *Iz istorii zarubezhnoi filosofii XIX-XX vekov*, 148–163.

30. E.g., chap. 6—"Filosofiia amerikanskogo personalizma" (The Philosophy of American Personalism)—in A. S. Bogomolov, *Anglo-amerikanskaia burzhuaznaia filosofiia epokhi imperializma* (Anglo-American Bourgeois Philosophy of the Age of Imperialism) (Moscow: Mysl', 1964), 202–235. The discussion of Hocking is mainly on 217–221, 223–229, and 234.
31. See A. I. Titarenko, *Pragmatistskii lzhemarksizm—filosofiia antikommunizma* (Pragmatist Pseudo-Marxism—a Philosophy of Anti-Communism) (Moscow: Izd. moskovskogo universiteta, 1964), 74. The other "bourgeois critics of pragmatism" whom Titarenko identifies are Russell, Reichenbach, Alexander Meiklejohn, and Arthur Murphy. Titarenko differs from other Soviet commentators in calling Hocking "one of the *founders* of American personalism" (132; italics added).
32. I. Balakina and K. Dolgov, "Personalizm," in *Filosofskaia entsiklopediia* (Encyclopedia of Philosophy), 5 vols. (Moscow: Izd. Sovetskaia entsiklopediia, 1967–1970), 4:242.
33. Shershenko, 351 (see note 16 for full reference).
34. B. Bykhovsky, "Amerikanskaia filosofiia" (American Philosophy), in *Filosofskaia entsiklopediia*, vol. 1 (1960): 51.
35. See, for example, Iu. K. Mel'vil', *Charls Pirs i pragmatizm (U istokov amerikanskoi burzhuaznoi filosofii XX veka)* (Charles Peirce and Pragmatism: At the Sources of Twentieth-Century American Bourgeois Philosophy) (Moscow: Izd. moskovskogo universiteta, 1968), esp. sec. 3, which is on the "fundamental contradiction of Peirce's philosophy" (27–51) and includes such headings as "The Fundamental Question of Philosophy and the Conflict of Science and Religion at the End of the Nineteenth Century" and "Scientific and Anti-Scientific Tendencies in Peirce's Philosophy." Mel'vil' concludes his book by contrasting Peirce the honest seeker of truth with Peirce the philosophical idealist who "deviated from scientific truth in the name of religious prejudices and anti-materialistic preconceptions" (489).
36. D. Lukanov, "Khoking, Uil'iam Ernest" in Balakina and Dolgov 1970, 5:439–440. The quoted sentence shows that Lukanov was familiar with Hocking's *Strength of Men and Nations*, although that title is not included in his bibliography. What I once called "orthographic atheism" (see Kline 1968, 112 n. 14) was mandatory throughout the Soviet period but is here carried to an untypical extreme. Not only is the Russian word *Bog* (God) regularly written as *bog* (god), but Hocking's titles *The Meaning of God in Human Experience* and *Science and the Idea of God* appear in Lukanov's entry as "Meaning of god in human experience" and "Science and the idea of god," respectively. In more typical cases, including all of the Soviet discussions of Hocking previously mentioned, Russian translations of such titles exhibit orthographic atheism but the original English titles do not. Of course, orthographic atheism is in full force throughout the text, including direct quotations, of any given Soviet commentator.
37. Shlaifer quotes the positive assessments of Hocking's place in American thought and culture offered by Andrew Reck (1964) and D. S. Robinson (1962). He also quotes D. V. Ermolenko to the effect that "over his long life Hocking gained fame as one of the most prominent religious philosophers in the United States and took his place as one of the chief leaders of personalism" (*Sovremennaia burzhuaznaia filosofiia SShA* [Contemporary Bourgeois Philosophy in the United States] [Moscow, 1965], 70). See Shlaifer, 149–150.

WORKS CITED

Deutscher, Isaac. 1954. *The Prophet Armed: Trotsky: 1879–1921*. Oxford: Oxford University Press.
Dewey, John. [1938] 1946. "Democracy and Education in the World Today." Address before the Society for Ethical Culture delivered on October 24, 1938. Reprinted in *Problems of Men*. New York: Philosophical Library.

Dietzgen, Josef. 1965. "Streifzüge eines Sozialisten in das Gebiet der Erkenntnistheorie" in *Schriften in Drei Bänden*. Vol. 3. East Berlin: Akademie Verlag.

Hartshorne, Charles. 1946. "Review of *Science and the Idea of God*." *Philosophy and Phenomenological Research* 6:453-457.

———. 1957. "Review of *The Coming World Civilization*." *Philosophy and Phenomenological Research* 17:562-563.

Kline, George L. 1964. "Philosophy, Ideology, and Policy in the Soviet Union." *Review of Politics* 26:174-190.

———. 1968. *Religious and Anti-Religious Thought in Russia*. Chicago: University of Chicago Press.

———. 1969. "Was Marx an Ethical Humanist?" *Studies in Soviet Thought* 9:91-103.

———. 1978. "Three Dimensions of 'Peaceful Coexistence.'" In *Varieties of Christian-Marxist Dialogue*, ed. Paul Mojzes. Philadelphia: Ecumenical Press, 201–206.

———. 1988. "The Myth of Marx's Materialism." In *Philosophical Sovietology: The Pursuit of a Science*, ed. Helmut Dahm, Thomas J. Blakeley, and George L. Kline. Dordrecht: Reidel, 158–203.

———. 1993. "The Potential Contribution of Classical Russian Philosophy to the Building of a Humane Society in Russia." In *XIX World Congress of Philosophy: Lectures*. Moscow.

Lenin, V. I. [1909] 1927. *Materialism and Empiro-Criticism* [1909]. Trans. A. Fineberg. New York: International. Reprinted in *Collected Works*, vol. 14., Moscow: Progress, 1968.

Maker, William, ed. 1987. *Hegel on Economics and Freedom*. Macon, Ga.: Mercer University Press.

Medvedev, Roy A. 1972. *Let History Judge: The Origins and Consequences of Stalinism*. Ed. David Joravsky and Georges Haupt. Trans. Coleen Taylor. New York: Knopf.

Plekhanov, G. V. 1961. "For the Sixtieth Anniversary of Hegel's Death." In *Selected Philosophical Works in Five Volumes*, trans. R. Dixon. Moscow.

Randall, John Herman. 1965. *The Career of Philosophy*. Vol. 2. *From the Enlightenment to the Age of Darwin*. New York: Columbia University Press.

Reck, Andrew J. 1964. *Recent American Philosophers: Studies of Ten Representative Thinkers*. N.Y.: Pantheon Books.

Volkogonov, Dmitri. 1994. *Lenin: A New Biography*. Ed. and trans. Harold Shukman. New York: Free Press.

Whitehead, Alfred North. 1926. *Science and the Modern World*. 2d ed. New York: Macmillan.

———. 1984. "The Harvard Lectures for 1924–1925," ed. Jennifer Hamlin von der Luft. In Lewis S. Ford, *The Emergence of Whitehead's Metaphysics 1925–1929*. Albany, N.Y.: SUNY Press, 262–302. (Hocking's notes on Whitehead's lectures)

CHAPTER 27

Metaphysics and World Philosophy: W. E. Hocking on Chinese Philosophy

Robert Cummings Neville

William Ernest Hocking (1873–1966) is to be remembered for many things, as this series of essays so persuasively demonstrates. Most of these were recognized during his long, productive, and distinguished career. But no one could have foretold during his lifetime that he would be remembered as the first Boston Confucian.

Who are the Boston Confucians, you might ask? Hocking would have known Boston Brahmins but not Boston Confucians.[1] In fact, it was not until the 1990s that the title was ever used, to my knowledge.[2] The following three points characterize the school of Boston Confucianism.

First, it claims that Confucianism is a philosophy accessible to people who are not East Asians, do not read Chinese, and are not Sinologists. This is significant because many people have believed that Confucianism is a kind of ethnic philosophy, so deeply rooted in Chinese (and other East Asian) cultural identities and family structures as not to be sympathetically comprehensible, let alone adoptable, by non–East Asians. Accessibility to Western non-Chinese readers also depends on translations of the texts into European languages and on academic travel and exchanges that bring non–East Asians into contact with living representatives of Confucianism in China, Korea, and Japan. The situation now in these respects is far more fulsome than in Hocking's day, although I shall show that he had sufficient resources firmly to grasp Confucianism.

The second characteristic of Boston Confucianism is its practice of reading the Confucian tradition intermixed with Western philosophy with all positions construed as contributions to an emerging world philosophic tradition. The other traditions of Chinese philosophy, as well as those of India and elsewhere, are to be construed the same way. On the surface this looks like comparative philosophy. But would you say that a study of Hume and Kant is comparative Scottish and German philosophy? Some Western philosophers say that the Western is "our" tradition and that treating Chinese philosophers in connection with Western ones is bringing the alien to the familiar. But the Western tradition is "ours" only if we make it so. Few Western philosophers who cite Plato and Aristotle read them in the original Greek; most American philosophers who discuss Kantian ethics, except specialist scholars, read English translations. If "we Westerners" make the tradition of Confucius and Mencius "ours" along with that of Plato and Aristotle, it is in fact ours. Boston Confucians are self-conscious heirs of both ancient sources and integrate them into a common tradition.

The third point is that Boston Confucianism is a form of contemporary philosophic practice, not exclusively or even essentially scholarship about the Confucian tradition. Contemporary philosophical problems lie in such fields as ethics, political theory, aesthetics, philosophy of religion, science, education, metaphysics, and spiritual matters, and in each field Confucianism has made important contributions. Historical resources need to be understood in order to be used, and that is a complex hermeneutical process. But from a philosopher's standpoint, historical resources also need to be used in order to be understood: their meanings do not show themselves fully until they are properly pressed into service. Boston Confucianism is a contemporary philosophy identified by the importance it gives a certain tradition's resources; the same was true three centuries ago of Cambridge Platonism, which was not so much about Plato as about England and/or heaven.

William Ernest Hocking was a Bostonian who, in the 1930s, wrote philosophy that exhibits all three traits of Boston Confucianism.[3] I doubt he would have claimed to be more a Confucian than a Platonist, but then some present day Boston Confucians are other things as well. Hocking had an understanding of Confucianism, particularly that of Zhuxi, that was extraordinary for his time and entirely respectable now. He read Zhuxi as a philosopher alongside Kant, Fichte, and Bergson, improving upon them in crucial respects. And he took Zhuxi to have an important contribution to make to the problem of democracy and science, a problem as central for our time as for Hocking's, in Boston and elsewhere.

Hocking is known for his cosmopolitan sympathies and his philosophy of a world civilization, discussed elsewhere in this book, and epitomized in his *The Coming World Civilization* (1956). I want to focus on a crucial example of world philosophy in his thought, a particular paper called "Chu Hsi's Theory of Knowledge," published in 1936. First, however, I want to comment on his background in Chinese philosophy.

Hocking, of course, is known as one of the last great systematic philosophers in the Western philosophical tradition and is also known for thematizing his systematic conceptions in practical areas. He wrote not only for academic philosophers but also for people interested in larger issues.[4] His two main systematic topics were religion and the social character of human life, and in both contexts he had occasion to study and comment on Chinese civilization, ancient and contemporary.[5] He was, moreover, of that generation of philosophers, or "public intellectuals" as we now say, who began the great conversation of East and West, including Hu Shih who visited his Harvard class in the 1920s. He participated with Charles Moore in the early East/West conferences in Hawaii, and took responsible understanding of the cultures of his friends and fellow philosophers to be a part of the philosophic life.[6]

In his discussions of world religions he spent more time on those of India, including both Hinduism and Buddhism, than on those of China. He wrote only one paper explicitly about a Chinese philosopher, the one I am about to analyze, plus a review article coauthored with his son Richard of a book on contemporary culture (1953) in China by Wing-tsit Chan (Hocking 1954). Thus his mastery of the Chinese tradition, especially the work of the difficult philosopher Zhuxi, his ability to treat Zhuxi in intimate comparison with Western philosophers, and his adroit use of Zhuxi for his own philosophic purpose are all the more remarkable.

I

His own philosophic purpose in the essay on Zhuxi was to examine how science should be conceived in a democratic society. This was one facet of his interest in the development of a world civilization. Science is important for democracy, according to Hocking, not only because its technological consequences make communication possible in ways required for democracy, but also because scientific understanding is democratically available to anyone.[7] In a world of scientific advancement, he thought, nearly everyone has a chance. Modern science might have originated in the West, he allowed, but even in the 1930s it had been appropriated by cultures all over the globe, which were developing it in ways indigenous to themselves. China in particular by then had moved out of the antiscientific, xenophobic, attitudes associated with much late Ching conservative Confucian culture into active entry into the modern scientific world. What might have entered China through Western imperialism had been Sinicized, and the Chinese could enter democratically, as it were, into the modern world.

But science requires a particular kind of knowing. In fact, Hocking opened the essay with the observation that "ways of knowing must vary with the nature of the objects to be known" (1944, 109). Science knows objects under the assumption that there is no mind in them, no teleology. Hocking the idealist, of course, was also, if not more, interested in the kinds of knowing that pick up on mental and teleological matters. But as for science, it is perfectly fit for knowing nature under certain assumptions, and its technological benefits are enormous. Only if science is taken to be the exclusive form of knowing does it become scientism.[8]

As to science itself in the modern Western sense, Hocking characterized it in the Zhuxi article as both empirical and rationalistic. The empiricism of science is a devotion to the knowledge of things, not to the knower but to the things to be known. Empiricism is a kind of denial of the self and its interests in favor of a piety before nature. Hocking sharply attacked what he calls "hearty nineteenth century pragmatism" for fudging on this matter entirely. The rationalism of science consists in its desire to integrate knowledge into a whole, to know the whole truth. This leads science to ever more general and overarching principles. Modern science has the unifying language of mathematics.

But modern science in fact is not capable of knowing the moral, teleological, mental aspects of the world, which Hocking held to be so important. He followed Bergson's critique of science as failing to include what wholly empirical and wholly rationalistic intuition can tell us. The world-picture of science is of a mechanism, whereas reality is more like an organism, according to Hocking. He declined to go as far as Whitehead in declaring the world to be an organism, or at least to be understood in the metaphors of what Whitehead called the "philosophy of organism." Hocking's counterdescription of the universe is worth quoting, not only for understanding his relation to Whitehead but also because it is so like the Chinese conception of process:

> There is more looseness among the parts of the world, more waste, wider flung oceans of emptiness, more *relative* independence than is compatible with organic unity. The inner rhythms and changes are not the proportioned movements of organic processes. What the universe seems to present is a true system of interdependent motions *within which* organic groupings take place and run their life course—the whole presenting the character of a *single environment* for the living fragments rather than being itself a total organism with no environment. What interests us is not that everything shall be living and of a mental kind, but rather that the universe should offer itself as an arena for life and purpose, an arena whose very wildness, waste, vastness, unspanned gulfs of distance, offer incentives without limit to an ever-growing mentality. Seen in this way there is a purpose in the purposeless aspects of the world; the personal finds use for the impersonal, the living for the mechanical, the intense focuses of consciousness for the infinitely expansive unconsciousness of mass and energy-fields. (SIG, 108)

Can we attain to an alternative conception of science that is just as empirical as the modern and just as rationalistic, but also sensitive to the mental? For this, Hocking appealed to Zhuxi.

II

Zhuxi (1130–1200) was the greatest of the Song Dynasty Neo-Confucians. He synthesized the reforming thought of his predecessors, all of whom responded to Buddhism and Daoism's challenges to Confucianism. Zhuxi's system provided an interpretation of the classic texts of Confucianism that was to remain the basis of the Chinese civil service examinations until the twentieth century.[9] The positive affirmations of his system were both metaphysical and moral. Hocking gave a neat and very accurate summary of Zhuxi's so-called dualism, noting the inappropriateness of the characterization of dualism. Zhuxi developed two cosmological categories, *qi* and *li*.

Qi is often translated as *ether* or *material force*. Hocking's summary characterization is accurate: "a subtle all-pervasive quasi-material entity, capable of local variation, of degrees of density and of resistance to the pure control of the spiritual principle, Li" (1944, 113). *Qi* is what is, or should be, organized or given structure by *li*, principle. But *li* is the hard category to understand. Zhuxi's translator, J. P. Bruce, translates *li* as "law," which would be neat if it is to describe a scientific universe of matter operating under the dictates of law. But, as Hocking says,

> Li has a pedigree which may disqualify it. It must be understood as one of four manifestations of the Ultimate Being, these four to be taken in a descending order. They are: *T'ien*, Heaven; *Ming*, Heaven's Decree, which is at the same time the Vocation, Bestimmung, of the creature; *Hsing*, the nature of the thing; *Li*, the individualized embodiment of the Nature, i.e., the Life-charter of the individual being. *T'ien* and *Ming* can be regarded as the active, transmitting function; *Hsing* and *Li* as the receiving function. These functions are two aspects of the same continuous activity: for Heaven is always engaged in its decreeing of destiny; and things are always showing signs of an impressed Law, the *Hsing* or Nature of the species, contained in the *Li* or Life-rule of the individual. This activity and this receptiveness, taken together, constitute what we may call the life of *T'ien*, or the manifestation of *Tao*, the Ultimate Order of the World, which for Chu Hsi is a moral order. (113)

Hocking's account is extraordinarily lucid, but it does not quite appreciate the metaphysical power of Zhuxi's conception of *li*. The Dao, for Zhuxi, is not merely the ultimate *order* of the world, as if it were on the *li* side opposed to *qi*. Rather, the Dao is the ultimate reality of the world, its process taken as a whole. And *li* is Zhuxi's word for the most ultimate on the order side, which is sometimes called "heavenly principle." The Neo-Confucian distinction between *li* and *qi* is its development in metaphysical terms of the ancient Confucian (and Daoist) division of reality into Heaven, Earth, and their conjunction, a set of distinctions found in the *Yejing*. It is the same metaphysical principle, *li*, that is to be found in every finite thing, giving it order. Most particular, *li* is the principle of harmony according to which every specific thing can harmonize itself in its environment of ongoing processes to fulfill its own unique mandate. So Hocking is right in emphasizing the overall ordering principle of heaven and also in saying that this single principle is manifested in unique ways for each individual. His phrase, "life-charter," is apt for describing the function of *li* in each finite thing. Hocking wrote with clear awareness that the Chinese did not believe that finite things are internally constructed substances but instead are specifications of larger processes that interact with one another and attain their unity or harmony in that interaction; his own description of the world quoted above, declining to be a philosopher of organism, is a neat statement of the Chinese view.

Zhuxi had much of the modern scientific temper, Hocking claimed, in being both an empiricist and a rationalist. Because *li* is always individuated in *qi*, it is necessary to look at things in their material uniqueness. Zhuxi had no sense for the modern scientific method, with controlled experiments and the like, but he did direct science outward to observation. At the same time, he also emphasized that what we find in things is their principle, or *li*, and this connects them. In principle, *li* allows things to be connected with one another and with the whole.

Now, it is the nature of *li* as principle that interested Hocking, for *li* is "mental" in Hocking's sense. *Li* is whatever would harmonize the components of a given thing or situation, and thus it is teleological. The Chinese did not believe in an Aristotelian teleology, according to which a substance contains an end or fulfillment or completion toward which it drives. But they did believe that processes need harmonization, and any thing or situation can be understood in terms of what will, would, or should harmonize the otherwise chaotic or independently progressing processes. For human life, understanding one's *li* always takes the form of identifying what processes are going on and discovering how to bring them into harmony. Because we live in a wider world, our own processes of harmonization need to be harmonized with the harmonizing needs of nature and society; Zhuxi and the Neo-Confucians interpreted this as the Mandate of Heaven, finding one's place, or process, within the process of the universe.

Now, what is true of persons is true of other animals and nature, more generally. *Li* provides a continuity from the quotidian moral concerns of human beings to the strivings of animals and the larger harmonizing processes of nature. The mind of a human being is one with the mind of the universe, Zhuxi and other Neo-Confucians said. And the "extension of knowledge," Zhuxi's phrase for science, has to do with bringing this unity of mind to mind, laying out the connecting principles, and creating a kind of moral continuity of individuals with the Dao. Hocking quotes Zhuxi's fetching remark in this regard:

> In our sense of heat and cold, of hunger and repletion, in the love of life and shrinking from death, and in the instinctive seeking for what will benefit and shunning of what will be prejudicial,—all this is common to man with other creatures. (But) the diversity of Law [*li*] is seen in the existence among ants and bees of the relation between sovereign and minister, in which there is manifested no more than a gleam of Righteousness; in the existence among wolves and tigers of the relation between parent and child, in which there is manifested no more than a gleam of love.... It is not the case that man, as the being possessed of the highest intellect, stands alone in the universe. His mind is also the mind of birds and beasts, of grass and trees. "Man," however, "is born endowed with the *Mean*, the attribute of Heaven and Earth." (1944, 111–112)

Hocking pointed out that this identifies not only a biological continuity but also the "differentia of man," which is "the *balance* which exists among his instinctive propensities, a balance which fits him for hesitation and reflection, and thus for the influence of ideas upon his behavior" (112).

III

What is most interesting about Hocking's exposition of Zhuxi is that it proceeds in a comparative contrast with Buddhism. He began the paper with a brief discussion of Dharmapala's interpretation of change. Dharmapala (439–507) was an Indian Buddhist who wrote a major commentary on Vasubandhu's founding text of the "Consciousness-Only" school of Buddhism, which was popularized in China by Hsuan-tsang, who used Dharmapala's writings. All Buddhists are concerned with the nature and soteriologically bad effects of change, and with whatever unity underlies change. Buddhism, of course, denies the reality of any entitative underlying unity but does indeed have to know how time flows. Hocking describes Dharmapala's interpretation of an ideal being, "the Tathagata Buddha, to whom this unity is evident. The Tathagata is not disturbed by transition; he understands its laws. He perceives the numerous things in the world, and recognizes their attractive qualities, but knowing also their mortality, he is not tempted to seize on any of them as his good: he is like the lotus, not disattached, not swept away by the current, and yet on the other hand not fascinated, not under illusion, unspotted by the world: he overcomes the world by comprehending it" (1944, 110). In a brilliant paragraph, Hocking interpreted this Buddhist position in modern terms:

> Things and events are not merely additive items whose sum makes up the world; science reveals them as parts of a single system, Nature. Now 'Nature' is a term of hope, rather than of scientific achievement; the final synthesis of the laws of change is never reached. Before we reach this elusive physical unity, the question recurs which in western thought we supposed we had banished—perhaps the ultimate order of things is less an order of fact than an order of meaning or value! We appear driven to assume a teleological structure in things, as a condition of completing our scientific labor. The Buddhist, never wholly succumbing to anthropomorphism, provides this teleological element by invoking a quasi-personal being as a symbol of the nature of the final coherence of things, and then develops a special branch of his theory of knowledge for the perception of this being. (1944, 110)

So far, Buddhism agrees with Zhuxi about at least the ideal of a comprehensive understanding of the world; Zhuxi's categories might be preferable, but he obviously learned from Buddhism. Yet he was also extremely critical of Buddhism, and Hocking elicited the most critical part. For Buddhism, as Zhuxi interpreted it, the purpose of knowing is to find the center of the self and retreat from the world. Quite the opposite of the purported Buddhist claim to believe in No-self, Zhuxi thought that Buddhism was a selfish religion, turning people inward, away from the world and from their responsibilities to one another, family, and society. Some Buddhists, those who have taken the Bodhisattva's vow to continue working life after life to enlighten all sentient beings, might counter the charge of selfishness. But there is a big difference between the project of enlightening all sentient beings and taking care of one's family, repairing the dikes, and nurturing people in your village—the Confucian ideal. In comparative perspective, it is not hard to see why Zhuxi would think Buddhism selfish when it encourages people to sit in meditation seeking enlightenment for themselves so that they can escape to Nirvana (1944, 117).

Selfishness is not merely a moral epithet for Zhuxi. On the contrary, it is his explanation for why true knowledge is so difficult to attain. The extension of knowledge does not progress by simply looking at more and more things with the principles. It requires what Hocking called "the ethical conditions of insight." Zhuxi knew that things are to be known *in rebus*, as Hocking said, by paying attention to them on their own, analyzing them on their own terms, discerning what principle is doing with them in their processes of harmonization. But if we are selfish, all that outward analysis is distorted. We think we are looking at the other, but we are projecting our own wish-filled images. To put it in modern terms, we are pursuing our pet theories and seeing what those theories let us see. So Zhuxi insisted upon a peculiar kind of personal character to aid the extension of knowledge, a character made sincere and chastened of selfishness. There is an extremely elaborate program of Confucian self-development to sagehood that has as its object, not the perfection of the self or its blissing out, but its harmonizing cognitive and moral continuity with the rest of the universe.[10]

This is all a bit unfair to Ch'an Buddhism, about which Zhuxi was complaining.[11] That school too would say that a lack of selfishness must be obtained in order to rid oneself of grief-filled attachments. Once a person has attained enlightenment, it is possible to see things as they are and without subjective bias, according to the Buddhist theory. Zhuxi's point was a practical one: the Buddhist meditation and monastic procedures were more likely to cultivate selfishness by always focusing on the self's enlightenment than to achieve enlightenment with its subsequent moral commitments to behave helpfully in harmony with the rest of the world. Hocking recognized, in fairness to Buddhism, that Zhuxi's strictures about attaining an unselfish approach to the extension of knowledge is more like the preparatory stages of enlightenment in the Eightfold Noble Path of an earlier kind of Buddhism than to the meditation practices of the Buddhism of his contemporaries.

IV

The lesson Hocking drew from Zhuxi is complex. Being careful not to ascribe a modern sensibility to him, Hocking nevertheless found in Zhuxi's approach a moral sensitivity that surpassed Bergson's. Hocking wrote,

If there be in the world, as Bergson supposes, a realm of mechanism, the ashes of dead life, there intuitive sympathy would have no application: pragmatic knowledge would be appropriate. But Chu Hsi, though he has a reputation of being a dualist, has no such realm of inanimate matter: he carries his attribution of life and even of degrees of consciousness throughout the universe much in the spirit of Fechner, Paulsen, Whitehead. Hence he allows no exceptions in behalf of pragmatically interested modes of knowing. All penetration into the realities of things requires a moral objectivity whose essence is unselfishness.... As compared with Bergson, then, Chu Hsi has far more for his ethically sensitized intuition to perceive. And because of this he would further disagree with Bergson in his view of the nature of scientific knowledge—he would not hand science over to the "pragmatic" way of knowing. (1944, 125)

Moreover, although Zhuxi can be called a rationalist in the senses mentioned, Hocking severely qualified the full use of that term, which had been applied to Zhuxi and his age by Hu Shih. Rationalism is usually reductive to principles. Zhuxi is more the empiricist.

Hocking went on to say that "scientific method is based on the deliberate and persistent effort to escape the circle of humanistic interests, not to say class interests, in its discovery of objective truth.... Empiricism is itself a form of self-denial, a moral will to let the object speak for itself. But empiricism holds that if we allow it to do so, the object will speak— i.e., truth is accessible" (1944, 127).

The final lesson Hocking wanted to mine from Zhuxi was political, namely, that true science aids the democratic process. Much of my discussion here has been to lift up Hocking's Boston Confucian argument that science needs to be conceived in such a way that the moral or teleological dimensions of its subject matter can be construed as part of scientific knowing, not the projection of personal views on top of a mechanistic conception. In this, Hocking supports Zhuxi over Bergson. But a serious problem remains. Hocking opened the paper with the observation that "If not an axiom, it is at least a reasonable presumption in the theory of knowledge that ways of knowing must vary with the nature of the objects to be known." He then pointed out the esoteric rigors of attaining to Buddhist enlightenment about change, and said this kind of knowing can get to the moral as well as the most real center of the universe in ways preferable to modern Western science. This point was expanded with Zhuxi's account of moral knowing, and the Buddhist tendency to turn inward was corrected by the Neo-Confucian concern to address the world in a harmonizing cognitive way, letting the world speak for itself. But does this mean that the Neo-Confucian path is as esoteric as the Buddhist? If so, then science with a moral heart cannot be a fulcrum for democracy, for it would require an aristocracy of adepts.

Hocking never suggested that Zhuxi was a democrat, any more than he was a modern scientist. But he did attempt to say that Zhuxi's approach to knowledge is exoteric whereas Buddhism's is esoteric. One branch of Hocking's argument is that Confucians of all sorts are antiaristocratic, claiming that anyone from any part of society can study, and those good at studying can go all the way in Confucian learning. Although Confucianism developed a family culture that nourishes learning, and therefore children of Confucians are more likely to be ready and willing to study than people from social strata of little learning, Confucianism indeed has been a force to break through social class barriers. Another branch of Hocking's argument is that Zhuxi's emphasis on empirical analysis, and improving the self so as to be unselfish when examining things, is genuinely exoteric and learnable. Buddhism, with its use of imaginative representations of semipersonalized Tathagata Buddhas, is far too esoteric. There is much to be said for Zhuxi's down-to-earth emphasis on study, and anyone can do it.

I doubt these arguments carry the day, however, in the claim that Zhuxi's moral science can be a democratic leveling activity. However straightforward in comparison with Buddhism, or Christianity, Hinduism, or Judaism for that matter, the Confucian project of becoming a sage is the creation of a new aristocracy. Most people around the world are in fact selfish. Most therefore could not do science in the sense Hocking advocated and would thus revert to mechanistic science. Like Dewey, Hocking would have to say that ordinary people need to become aristocratic in their capacities for democracy. Achieved aristocracy is difficult when you are born something else.

V

Now, there is a not-so-hidden villain in Hocking's argument here, namely "hearty nineteenth century pragmatism," by which he meant the theory that "knowledge is (partly or wholly) *constituted* by action." Therefore, we choose our ideas and beliefs as we choose our actions. "Our judgments about the world are instruments for guiding conduct, and are therefore to be *chosen*, rather than thought out—to be chosen for the sake of their value as instruments of living" (1944, 125). This may not be a fair understanding even of William James's sloppy pragmatism. It is exactly the opposite of Peirce's pragmatism, for which learning what is worth choosing is the most important lesson to investigate, and whose methods of correcting belief are in extremely close accord with the Neo-Confucian emphasis on learning the principles in things.[12] But Hocking does recognize a kind of vulgar pragmatism that has become all the more popular in the postmodern insistence that all knowing is a display of interest and power and therefore you ought to fight for your own. That vulgar pragmatism, or late Marxist postmodernism, does indeed insist that science be mechanistic because it wants to deny the residence of differential worths in the world.

Over against that vulgar pragmatism, which reinforces a putatively value-free conception of natural science, Hocking could only urge another vision of the world.

This was, of course, his life's work. This, more than any insistence that the world is made of ideas rather than matter, constituted his *idealism* (see Rouner 1975). He found in Zhuxi, more than in the Buddhist and Hindu philosophers he studied, an ally in presenting that alternative vision.

Here is now a more substantive reason to call William Ernest Hocking the first Boston Confucian than a mere citation of his knowledge and use of Confucian philosophy. The particular use to which he attempted to put Zhuxi, and the Confucian tradition to which Hocking gained access through Zhuxi's writings, was the creation of an alternative world philosophy for a world civilization that was being brought into existence by modern science. This is the particular aim of the so-called New Confucian movement, of which the Boston Confucians are a part, stimulated by a generation of Chinese philosophers Hocking's age or younger. One of the most influential of these, Mou Tsung-san, coined the phrase, "moral metaphysics," for his peculiar philosophy combining Western philosophical idealism with classical Confucian themes—more of the school of Wang Yang-ming than Zhuxi, but not different on the points discussed here (see Tu 1979, chap. 8, and 1989, chap. 8). Mou's student, Tu Wei-ming, is at the center of Confucianism in Boston.

It should be noted that Hocking, more than most of his Chinese counterparts, understood what is at stake in developing a world philosophy for a world civilization. The world civilization itself is only slowly coming into being, and so far it is not clear whether it is more civilized than barbaric. Philosophy can be one of the civilizing forces. Hocking recognized that a world philosophy cannot be the imperial triumph of one philosophy over the others, as some earlier idealists might have thought having read Hegel. Rather, the strong thinkers in all the world's traditions need to be heard in dialogue over the issues. Hence, we should know Dharmapala and Zhuxi as well as Plato and Kant. The syntheses that hopefully will provide the languages in which we can discuss world philosophical issues cannot be schematic charts of different positions, as our colleagues Watson (1985) and Dilworth (1989) might hope.[13] Rather, the syntheses will come from philosophers working piecemeal with as many sources as possible to construct a world vision. Plato and Aristotle did that for their time, and because of their philosophies, the West has had a language to debate not only the issues that separated them but also a great many others. Not until Plato and Aristotle was there a genuine Western philosophical tradition. Confucius, Mencius, Xunzi, Laozi, and Zhuangzi similarly created the Chinese tradition. Indian and Islamic traditions began the same way. One or more synoptic visions is necessary before we can begin to assess whether we have a philosophy whose terms pick up the real issues for a world tradition.

I have finally reached the topic announced in my title, metaphysics and world philosophy. Metaphysics in the grand tradition of the West, of which William Ernest Hocking was such a distinguished representative, is synoptic vision, a theorizing that allows us to see what things are similar and different, how they affect one another and are to be conceived together.[14] Modern Western science arose from that speculative project. But it has lost sight, in fact precluded sight, of those questions of value with moral impact that only a fool or an a priori philosopher could miss. And so, the long Western historical project of vision, or knowing things for their own selves and in their connections, as Hocking would have Zhuxi say, has come upon a series of roadblocks. Enlightenment skepticism evokes romantic reactions; the global political hegemony of the West in the last century fostered vain attempts to impose Western philosophies across the world. Postmodernism says that everything is of interest and thereby undermines the sense of the world's otherness and reality as capable of correcting our signs.[15]

Hocking urged us to come to world philosophy through two preparatory projects. One is political philosophy that is comparative and that does acknowledge the differences in political realities. The other is comparative philosophy of religion, or of culture as he generally handled it; religious studies, sensitive to the perspectives of religions other than those that framed the discipline of religious studies in the first place, is a crucial device for bringing into the conversation those voices who need to be heard for a world philosophy to be possible. His own contributions to political theory and religion are enormous.

Perhaps even more telling is Hocking's capacity actually to bring a major figure such as Zhuxi into the conversation and assess his contributions with judicious nuance. In particular, the contribution he brought from the Neo-Confucians was the missing ingredient in the Western speculative project, namely, a way to conceive of knowing that is genuinely axiological, interpreting things in terms of what they have achieved, what they might become, and what difference that makes. Only when the questions of value are related to the boundaries of imagination by which we speculatively envision the world, and then brought to the specifics of actual things whose values we can appreciate and weigh, will it be possible to work through to the lineaments of a world philosophy.[16] William Ernest Hocking saw this clearly, and he set us to work.

NOTES

1. For a discussion of the Boston Brahmins and of Hocking as one of the most distinguished of them, see C. T. K. Chari's "Human Personality in East-West Perspectives," in Rouner 1966, 381ff.
2. At a conference on Confucian-Christian Dialogue in Berkeley, California, in 1991. It was used to describe four participants from Boston who subscribed to the traits described here. I subsequently presented a paper to the American Academy of Arts and Sciences entitled, "The Short Happy Life of Boston Confucianism." Begun as a joking title, the phrase has caught on in America and China, as well as in Russia, where it was published in a translation with a commentary by Alexander Lomonov under the title, "'Bostonskoye konfutsianstvo' —korni vostochnoi kulturyi no zapadnoi pochve," in *Problemyi Dalnego Vostoke* (*Far Eastern Affairs*), 1 (Moscow 1995): 136–149. [All citations to foreign language works can be found in the endnotes and not in the "Works Cited."—eds.] See Neville 1994, which was the presidential address to the International Society of Chinese Philosophy at its Eighth International Conference in

Beijing in 1993. Now, in addition to Confucians who accept the description above, there is a working group of Confucian scholars in Boston presided over by Professor Tu Wei-ming that accepts the title of Boston Confucians. The "Boston" part is still a joke—the school includes anyone who treats Confucianism as an important resource for philosophical problems of cultures outside the East Asian sphere, particularly modern Western urban cultures (such as Boston's); the joke is that Bostonians regard themselves as living at the center of the world (*Chung Guo*), the creed of the Boston Brahmins.

3. Although most of Hocking's academic career was spent at Harvard, beginning in 1914, soon to be Royce's successor in the Alford Chair of Natural Religion, and surely part of the Harvard Boston Brahmin society, he was in fact bred and raised in the Midwest. Born in Cleveland, he was educated through high school in Joliet, Illinois, began college in Iowa, and finished at Harvard. His first academic teaching job (he had previously been a grade school principal) was in comparative religion at Andover Newton Theological School (1904–1906), then in philosophy at Berkeley (1906–1908), and at Yale (1908–1914), where he published his first major book, *The Meaning of God in Human Experience* (1912). On these biographical matters see Rouner 1969, especially the introduction, and also Rouner 1966, "Curriculum vitae," and the essays in that volume by Leroy S. Rouner, Andrew Reck, and Y. H. Krikorian. The latter volume has a comprehensive bibliography of Hocking's work prepared by Richard Gilman. Rouner 1969 is the best general exposition and critical commentary on Hocking's work.

4. Gilman's bibliography cited above lists numerous letters to the editor and what we would now call Op-Ed pieces. Hocking's work in RTM was the report he edited, and mostly wrote, of a commission to study the effects of Christian missions in China, Japan, and India-Burma. It was intended not for ecclesiastical authorities but for laypeople in churches who had been supporting missions about which Hocking was dubious.

5. His most important book on religion, already mentioned, was MGHE. His most systematic treatise in political philosophy was MATS. See also SWP. In many respects, his HNR combines both the religious and political interests, but does so by placing both in an evolutionary context with nature.

6. See Hocking 1944; this was the conference volume from the 1939 Hawaii conference that Hocking himself was not able to attend, though his article introduced the conference. See the Gilman bibliography for Hocking's numerous contributions to Festschrifts for South and East Asian scholars.

7. For a broader discussion of science, see Hocking's SIG.

8. In SIG, chapter 4, Hocking discussed science, especially physics and astronomy, as abstractions that leave out purpose and value.

9. Hocking used a 1922 translation (by J. P. Bruce) of Zhuxi's works. Hocking also knew Bruce's commentary (1923). A more up-to-date translation is available by Wing-tsit Chan, a friend of Hocking's (Zhuxi 1967); in the foreword to this volume, Wm. Theodore de Bary writes, "*Reflections on Things at Hand (Chin-ssu lu)* is unquestionably the most important single work of philosophy produced in the Far East during the second millennium A.D." (xii). A fine collection of interpretive papers is Chan 1986. For Chan's own extended analysis, see Chan 1989. Zhuxi 1990 is another selection of Chu Hsi's works, translated with a commentary by Daniel K. Gardner. For the historical context, see Tillman 1992. The transliteration of Chinese words and names depends on the system used. "Chu Hsi" and "Tao" are in the Wade-Giles system which was popular until recently; "Zhuxi" and "Dao" are in Pinyin, the official transliteration system of contemporary China, which I use. On the comic silliness to which this leads, see Neville 1995, xiii–xiv.

10. The most outstanding contemporary proponent and expositor of the Confucian project of becoming a sage is Tu Wei-ming (see Wei-ming 1979 and 1985). Most remarkable in this regard is Hocking's own *Human Nature and Its Remaking*, a Confucian project of personal and

species transformation if there ever was one, but employing only Christian metaphors, not Confucian ones. Hocking's discussions of Christian virtues are extraordinarily Confucian!
11. There were in fact many Buddhist schools that Zhuxi would have known, including Hua-yen, T'ien-t'ai, and the Yogacara (Consciousness-Only) schools. For a general introduction to each of these, Chan 1963, chaps. 22–26, which also has an extensive translation of Chu Hsi that emphasizes his criticism of Buddhism (chap. 34).
12. On Peirce, see Neville 1992, chap. 1.
13. A new synthesis will have to come from living philosophy, and the archaic analysis of Watson and Dilworth treats all philosophies as only possibilities based on principles, not living systems of thought.
14. For a logical analysis of synoptic vision, see Neville 1995.
15. See Weissman 1993 for a fierce counterargument.
16. I have followed up modestly on Hocking's axiological program with my three-volume *Axiology of Thinking*, comprised of Neville 1981, 1987, and 1995.

WORKS CITED

Bruce, J. Percy. 1923. *Chu Hsi and His Masters: An Introduction to Chu Hsi and the Sung School of Chinese Philosophy*. London: Probsthain.
Chan, Wing-tsit. 1989. *Chu Hsi: New Studies*. Honolulu: University of Hawaii Press.
———, ed. 1963. *Source Book of Chinese Philosophy*. Princeton: Princeton University Press.
———, ed. 1986. *Chu Hsi and Neo-Confucianism*. Honolulu: University of Hawaii Press.
Dilworth, David A. 1989. *Philosophy in World Perspective: A Comparative Hermeneutic of the Major Theories*. New Haven: Yale University Press.
Hocking, W. E. 1936. "Chu Hsi's Theory of Knowledge." *Journal of Asiatic Studies* 1:109–127.
———. 1944. "Value of the Comparative Study of Philosophy." In *Philosophy—East and West*, ed. Charles A. Moore, 1–11. Princeton: Princeton University Press.
———. 1954. Review of *Religious Trends in Modern China* by Wing-tsit Chan. *Philosophy East and West* 4:175–181.
Neville, Robert. 1981. *Reconstruction of Thinking*. Albany: State University of New York Press.
———. 1987. *Recovery of the Measure*. Albany: State University of New York Press.
———. 1992. *The Highroad around Modernism*. Albany: State University of New York Press.
———. 1994. "Confucianism as a World Philosophy." *Journal of Chinese Philosophy* 21:5–25
———. 1995. *Normative Cultures*. Albany: State University of New York Press.
Rouner, Leroy S. 1969. *Within Human Experience: The Philosophy of William Ernest Hocking*. Cambridge: Harvard University Press.
———. 1975. "The Surveyor as Hero: Reflections on Ernest Hocking's Philosophy of Nature." In *Contemporary Studies in Philosophical Idealism*, ed. John Howie and Thomas O. Buford, 53–68. Cape Cod, Mass.: Claude Stark & Co.
———, ed. 1966. *Philosophy, Religion, and Coming World Civilization: Essays in Honor of William Ernest Hocking*.
Tillman, Hoyt Cleveland. 1992. *Confucian Discourse and Chu Hsi's Ascendancy*. Honolulu: University of Hawaii Press.
Tu Wei-ming. 1979. *Humanity and Self-Cultivation*. Berkeley: Asian Humanities Press.
———. 1985. *Confucian Thought: Selfhood as Creative Transformation*. Albany: State University of New York Press.
———. 1989. *Way, Learning, and Politics: Essays on the Confucian Intellectual*. Singapore: Institute of East Asian Philosophies.

Weissman, David. 1993. *Truth's Debt to Value*. New Haven: Yale University Press, 1993.
Watson, Walter. 1985. *The Architectonics of Meaning: Foundations of the New Pluralism*. Albany: State University of New York Press.
Zhuxi: 1922. *The Philosophy of Human Nature by Chu His*. Ed. and trans. J. Percy Bruce. London: Probsthain.
———. 1967. *Reflections on Things at Hand: The Neo-Confucian Anthology compiled by Chu Hsi and Lu Tsu-Ch'ien*. Ed. and trans. Wing-tsit Chan. New York: Columbia University Press.
———. 1990. *Chu Hsi: Learning to be a Sage*. Trans. with commentary by Daniel K. Gardner. Berkeley: University of California Press.

Selected Bibliography of William Ernest Hocking

BOOKS

The Coming World Civilization. New York: Harper and Bros., 1956.
Experiment in Education: What We Can Learn from Teaching Germany. Chicago: Henry Regnery Co., 1954.
Freedom of the Press: A Framework of Principle. Chicago: University of Chicago Press, 1947.
Human Nature and Its Remaking. New Haven: Yale University Press, 1918.
The Lasting Elements of Individualism. New Haven: Yale University Press, 1937.
Living Religions and a World Faith. New York: Macmillan, 1940.
Man and the State. New Haven: Yale University Press, 1926.
The Meaning of God in Human Experience: A Philosophical Study of Religion. New Haven: Yale University Press, 1912.
The Meaning of Immortality in Human Experience. New York: Harper and Bros., 1957.
Morale and Its Enemies. New Haven: Yale University Press, 1918.
Preface to Philosophy: Textbook. New York: Macmillan, 1946.
   This book is coauthored with Brand Blanshard, Charles W. Hendel, and John H. Randall, Jr. Hocking's contributions are: part 1, "What is Man," 3–99, and part 5, "A World-View," 413–504.
The Present Status of the Philosophy of Law and of Rights. New Haven: Yale University Press, 1926.
Re-Thinking Missions: A Layman's Inquiry after one Hundred Years. New York: Harper and Bros., 1932.
   This book is coauthored. Hocking's contributions are chaps. 1–4.
Science and the Idea of God. Chapel Hill: University of North Carolina Press, 1944.
The Self: Its Body and Freedom. New Haven: Yale University Press, 1928.
The Spirit of World Politics: With Special Studies of the Near East. New York: Macmillan, 1932.
Strength of Men and Nations: A Message to the USA vis-à-vis the USSR. New York: Harper and Bros., 1959.
Thoughts on Death and Life. New York: Harper and Bros., 1937.
Types of Philosophy. 3d ed. New York: Charles Scribner's Sons, 1959.
   This edition was revised in collaboration with his son, Richard Boyle O'Reilly Hocking. (Chap. 1 in this book is taken from the 1st edition, 1929.)
What Man Can Make of Man. New York: Harper and Bros., 1942.

Adapted (with modifications) from a selected bibliography by Robert Byron Thigpen in *Liberty and Community: The Political Philosophy of William Ernest Hocking* (The Hague: Martinus Nijhoff, 1972), 112–116. A comprehensive bibliography by Richard Gilman of Hocking's writings is available in Leroy S. Rouner, ed., *Philosophy, Religion and the Coming World Civilization: Essays in Honor of William Ernest Hocking* (The Hague: Martinus Nijhoff, 1966).

ARTICLES

Action and Certainty. *Journal of Philosophy* 27 (April 24, 1930): 225–238.
America Does Have Something of Offer the New Era. *Alumnus of Iowa State College* 39 (April 1944): 176-179.
Analogy and Scientific Method in Philosophy. *Journal of Philosophy, Psychology, and Scientific Methods* 7 (March 16, 1910): 161.
The Atom as Moral Dictator. *Saturday Review of Literature* (February 2, 1946): 7–9.
The Binding Ingredients of Civilization. In *Goethe and the Modern Age*. Ed. Arnold Bergstraesser. Chicago: Henry Regnery Co., 1950.
Can Values be Taught? In *The Obligation of Universities to the Social Order*. Ed. Henry P. Fairchild. New York: New York University Press, 1933.
Christianity and Intercultural Contacts. *Journal of Religion* 13 (April 1934): 127–138.
Conformity and Revolt. *The Smith Alumnae Quarterly* (August 1936): 338–341.
Creating a School. *Atlantic Monthly* (December 1955): 63-66.
  Co-authored with his wife, Agnes Hocking.
The Creed of Philosophical Anarchism. In *Leviathan in Crisis*. Ed. Waldo R. Browne. New York: Viking, 1946.
Cross Currents in Asian Aims. *Asia* 36 (April 1936): 235–238.
The Cultural and Religious Organization of the Future. In *Toward International Organization*. New York: Harper and Bros., 1942.
Culture and Peace. In *The Church and the New World Mind*. St. Louis: Bethany Press, 1944.
Democracy and the Scientific Spirit. *American Journal of Ortho-Psychiatry* 10 (July 1940): 431–436.
Dewey's Concepts of Experience and Nature. *Philosophical Review* 49 (March 1940): 228–244.
The Dilemma in the Conception of Instinct, as Applied to Human Psychology. *Journal of Abnormal and Social Psychology* 16 (June–September 1921): 73–96.
A Discussion of the Theory of International Relations. *Journal of Philosophy* 42 (August 30, 1945): 484–486.
Does Civilization Still Need Religion? *Christendom* 1 (October 1935): 31–43.
The Ethical Basis Underlying the Legal Right of Religious Liberty as Applied to Foreign Missions. *International Review of Missions* 20 (October 1931): 493–511.
Ethics and International Relations. *Journal of Philosophy, Psychology, and Scientific Methods* 14 (December 6, 1917): 698–700.
Fact and Destiny. *Review of Metaphysics* 4 (September 1950): 1–12.
Fact and Destiny (II). *Review of Metaphysics* 4 (March 1951): 319–342.
Fact, Field and Destiny: The Inductive Element in Metaphysics. *Review Of Metaphysics* 11 (June 1958): 525–549.
Faith and World Order. *The Church and the New World Mind*. St. Louis: Bethany Press, 1944.
Famine Over Bengal. *Asia* 44 (August 1944): 345–349.
The Finer Arts of Pugnacity. In *The Spirit of Scholarship*. Greencastle, Ind.: DePauw University, 1940.
The Freedom to Hope. *Saturday Review* (June 22,1963): 12, 13–15, 50.
The Function of Science in Shaping Philosophic Method. *Journal of Philosophy, Psychology and Scientific Methods* 2 (August 30, 1905): 477–486.
The Future of Liberalism. *Journal of Philosophy* 32 (April 25, 1935): 230–247.
The Group Concept in the Service of Philosophy. *Journal of Philosophy, Psychology, and Scientific Methods* 3 (January 4,1906): 5–12.

History and the Absolute. In *Philosophy, Religion, and the Coming World Civilization*. Ed. Leroy S. Rouner. The Hague: Martinus Nijhoff, 1966.
How Can Our Schools Enrich the Spiritual Experience of Their Students? *Beacon* (October 1943): 195–206.
How Ideas Reach Reality. *Philosophical Review* 19 (May 1910): 302–318.
Illicit Naturalizing of Religion. *Journal of Religion* 3 (November 1923): 561–599.
The Influence of the Future on the Present. *Harvard Alumni Bulletin* 27 (April 9, 1925): 817–23.
Instinct in Social Psychology. *Journal of Abnormal and Social Psychology* 18 (July–September 1923): 153–166.
Issues in Contemporary Philosophy of Law. *Harvard Law School Record* (March 5, 1947): 1, 4.
Justice, Law, and the Cases. In *Interpretations of Modern Legal Philosophies*. Ed. Paul Sayre. New York: Oxford University Press, 1947.
Marcel and the Ground Issues of Metaphysics. *Philosophy and Phenomenological Research* 14 (June 1954): 439–469.
The Meaning of Liberalism: An Essay in Definition. In *Liberal Theology: An Appraisal*. Ed. David E. Roberts and Henry P. van Dusen. New York: Charles Scribner's Sons, 1942.
Meanings of Life! *Journal of Religion* 16 (July 1936): 253–283.
Metaphysics: Its Function, Consequences, and Criteria. *Journal of Philosophy* 43 (July 4, 1946): 365–378.
Morale. *Atlantic Monthly* (December 1918): 721–728.
The Nature of Morale. *American Journal of Sociology* 47 (November 1941): 302–320.
A New East in a New World. *Fortune* (August 1942): 107–110, 119–120, 122, 124, 126, 131.
The New Way Of Thinking. *Colby Alumnus* 29 (July 15, 1950): 3–7.
On Philosophical Synthesis. *Philosophy East and West* 2 (1952): 1117–1129.
On Royce's Empiricism. *Journal of Philosophy* 53 (February 2, 1956): 57–63.
On the Law of History. *University of California Publications in Philosophy* 2 (September 17, 1909): 45–65.
On the Present Position of the Theory of Natural Right. In *Library of the Tenth International Congress of* Philosophy. Vol. 1. Ed. F. W. Beth and H. J. Pos. Amsterdam: North Holland Publishing, 1949.
Our Western Measuring Stick Carried East. *Asia* 31 (September 1931): 554–559, 600–604.
Philosophy—the Business of Everyman. *Journal of the American Association of University Women* 30 (June 1938): 221–227.
A Positive Role for the United States. *Harvard Guardian* 6 (December 1941): 15-18.
Private Property and Property Systems. In *Post War World*. New York: Commission on a Just and Durable Peace of the Federal Council of the Churches of Christ in America, 1945, 3.
Problems of World Order in the Light of Recent Philosophical Discussion. *American Political Science Review* 46 (December 1952): 1117–1129.
Reality in Christian History. *The Crozer Quarterly* 14 (October 1937): 274–283.
Reconception Reconsidered. *Christian Century* (March 2, 1955): 268–269.
Religion and the Alleged Passing of Liberalism. *Advance* 126 (May 3, 1934): 86–88.
Religion of the Future. In *Religion and Modern Life*. New York: Charles Scribner's Sons, 1927.
Science in Its Relation to Value and Religion. *Rice Institute Pamphlet* 29 (April 1942): 143–221.
Some Second Principles. In *Contemporary American Philosophy: Personal Statements*. Vol. 1. Ed. George P. Adams and William P. Montague. New York: Macmillan, 1930.
Sovereignty and Moral Obligation. *International Journal of Ethics* 28 (April 1918): 314–326.
The Spiritual Effect of Warlessness. In *A Warless World*. Ed. Arthur Larson. New York: McGraw-Hill, 1963.

Statesmanship and Christianity. In *The Church and the New World Mind*. St. Louis: Bethany Press, 1944.
Theory of Value and Conscience in Their Biological Context. *Psychology Bulletin* 5 (May 15, 1908): 129–143.
Theses Establishing an Idealistic Metaphysics by a New Route. *Journal of Philosophy* 38 (December 4, 1941): 688–690.
This is My Faith. In *This is My Faith*. Ed. Stewart G. Cole. New York: Harper and Bros., 1956.
Ways of Thinking About Rights: A New Theory of the Relation Between Law and Morals. In *Law: A Century of Progress, 1835-1935*. Vol 2. New York: New York University Press, 1937.
What Does Philosophy Say? *Philosophical Review* 37 (March 1928): 133–153.

Index of Selected Names

Aristotle 6–7, 16, 149, 193, 282–284, 326, 367–368, 377
Augustine 13, 173, 269, 347–348

Bacon, Francis 7, 246, 282–283, 289
Baldwin, James 67, 86
Bergson, Henri 23, 36, 69, 112, 135, 138n1, 368, 370, 375
Berkeley, George xii, 7, 21, 85, 171, 180, 210, 246, 288, 309, 378–379
Bradley, F. H. 20, 33
Buddha 6, 187, 198, 373, 376

Confucius 45, 191, 213, 377

Darwin, Charles 144, 156, 181n1, 366
Derrida, Jacques 272, 275n20, 319
Descartes, Rene 34, 56, 62–65, 67, 69–71, 73n3, 85, 169, 210, 228, 247, 257, 267–268, 270, 273n5, 273n8, 275n21, 280–281, 283–286, 309
Dewey, John xi-xiii, 12, 169, 171, 217, 237, 240, 242–243, 248–249, 272n3, 274n8, 274n13, 274n16, 275n17, 275n22, 305–310, 312–313, 315, 319–321, 325–328, 333, 349, 360–362, 364n27

Einstein, Albert 34, 36, 168, 224

Fichte, J. G. 6–7, 15, 368
Foucault, Michel 272, 272n2, 319
Freud, Sigmund 51, 82, 274n15

Goethe, Johann W. von 11, 384

Hartshorne, Charles 288, 305, 349, 362n1
Hegel, G. W. F. xiii, 7–8, 11, 15, 23, 31, 128, 135n1, 136–138, 144, 149, 233, 238, 285, 336, 339, 346–347, 349–350, 352, 362n2, 366, 377
Heidegger, Martin 232, 234, 319
Heisenberg, Werner 37, 38, 168
Hocking, Agnes (O'Reilly) 217, 227–228, 252–253, 273n4, 305
Hu Shih 19n1, 368, 375
Hume, David 10, 20, 31, 44, 71, 104, 246, 367
Husserl, Edmund xii, 31, 68, 70, 73n3, 231–234, 236, 243–244, 257, 278, 305

James, William xii-xiii, 5, 86, 112, 118n7, 171, 217, 230–231, 234–236, 242, 244, 248–249, 255–257, 262, 264, 271, 273n4, 274n12, 275n23, 276n30-n31, 276n35, 276n37, 285, 305–308, 311, 314, 319, 321, 323–324, 348, 376

Kant, Immanuel 15, 17, 20, 31, 35, 37–38, 40, 63, 65, 67, 72, 73n3, 170, 171, 234, 283–284, 336–337, 367–368, 377

Leibniz, G. W. 35, 38, 62, 65, 68, 85, 101, 247
Lenin, Vladimir Il'ich 352–353, 354, 356, 358, 360, 363n3
Lewis, C. I. xii, 31
Locke, John 7, 56, 83, 88, 99, 153, 169, 246, 307, 329

Marcel, Gabriel 33, 217, 231–232, 234, 241, 243n1, 249, 258, 275n22, 276n27, 305
Mead, G. H. 67, 326, 362
Mill, J. S. 139–141, 143–144, 146–149, 155, 156, 161, 301, 307, 313, 316, 351

Newton, Isaac 15, 35–36, 168, 379

Peirce, C. S. 8, 19n3, 33, 231, 248–249, 255–256, 274n9, 275n18, 276n32, 289, 305–306, 311–312, 339, 362, 365, 376, 380n12
Perry, R. B. xii, 13, 68, 285
Plato 6–7, 12, 47–48, 67, 80, 173, 178, 193, 270, 288, 299, 367–368, 377

Quine, W. V. O. xiii, 319

Robinson, Daniel S. 314, 321
Rorty, Richard 306, 308–309, 311–313, 316
Rouner, Leroy S. 217, 276n27, 276n36, 292
Royce, Josiah xi-xiii, 5, 23, 37–38, 73n3, 86–87, 112, 115, 177, 213, 219, 231, 234, 238, 248–250, 258–259, 262–264, 269, 276n35, 285, 287, 289, 305–306, 311, 317, 319, 334, 339, 347, 361, 379n3
Russell, Bertrand xii, 13, 33, 65, 68, 365

Santayana, George xii-xiii, 5, 13–14, 18
Schelling, Friedrich von 15, 213, 219, 238
Schopenhauer, Arthur 33, 47, 49, 135n5, 167, 207, 209, 214
Smith, John E. 245, 248, 274n12, 305–306
Spencer, Herbert xi-xii, 5, 139, 167, 173–174, 225–226, 254–256, 264–265, 276
Spinoza, Baruch 38, 141, 144, 155, 210, 247

Tolstoi, Leo 11, 108, 125
Trotsky, Leon 353–354, 356, 360, 363n8

Watson, William 52, 253
Whitehead, A. N. xii-xiii, 30, 33–35, 37, 40, 46, 56, 65, 73n3, 123, 169, 171, 177–179, 181n2, 217, 228, 246, 249, 272, 274n11, 284, 306, 310, 349, 350, 370, 375

Zhuxi (aka, Chu Hsi) 368–378, 379n9, 380n11

Index of Selected Subjects

Able Heads 162, 308–309, 316
Absolute 10, 21, 26–27, 58, 81,
    112, 164, 200n2, 204–205,
    238, 262, 265, 271, 276n35,
    285, 287, 291, 298, 302,
    323–325, 331, 333
  –ethics 325
accident (as opposed to substance) 32–33, 37
action(s) 14, 16, 25, 37, 39–43, 48,
    53, 56, 62, 71, 79, 81, 90n1,
    93, 111, 113–114, 116, 123–125,
    130, 138, 149, 152, 157–158,
    163–164, 184, 195n2, 196,
    198, 200, 211, 222, 224–226,
    229–230, 235, 243n4, 266,
    292, 297, 301, 312, 314, 328,
    330–333, 340, 342–344, 376
agency 48, 59, 115, 139, 143, 184,
    196, 200, 249, 256, 295
Alford Professorship xi–xii,
    379n3
analytic philosophy xiii, 234,
    239
artist 39, 41–42, 71, 209, 251,
    293, 296
autonomy 118n4, 120, 160, 185,
    273n8, 294, 297
  –Kant's notion 337

behaviorism 281
Being 42, 46, 232
  –highest, necessary, ultimate
    13, 72, 238, 387
belief(s) 3, 84, 162, 164, 202,
    204–205, 207, 234, 255,
    310–312, 352, 376
  –Bainian conception of 307
  –in the Absolute 322–323

  –in the individual 326, 345
  –metaphysical 204, 312
  –philosophy as examination
    of 8–9
  –pragmatic 202
  –propositional 312
  –religious 24, 230, 281
biography (auto-) 14, 32, 251,
    257, 296, 347–348
  –of genius 17
  –of pessimism 130
body (bodies) 15, 37, 40, 47–50,
    53–55, 59–60, 61n9, 72, 76,
    85, 91–92, 94–95, 97n6, 99,
    107, 111, 117–118n4, 119, 126,
    149, 174, 178, 204, 214n2,
    239–240–242, 243n7, 268,
    286, 291, 328, 336
  –judicial 185
  –of the state (political)
    118n4, 152
  –social (corporate) 109, 240
boundary (boundaries) 33–34
  –mind's 108
  –national 191
  –of a concept 11–13
  –of the self 108
Buddhism 6, 187–189, 369–370,
    373–374, 376, 380n11

causality 36, 42, 167, 221–223,
    225, 292
cause 7, 10, 49, 56, 77, 86, 145,
    181n1, 207, 221–225, 227, 240
  –efficient 282
  –final 282–283
  –formal 282–283
  –material 282
China xi, 6, 136 159, 187, 284, 333,

    346, 355, 367, 369, 373, 378n2,
    379n4, 379n9
choice 26, 40, 59–60, 79, 97n6,
    141–142, 217, 295, 302, 303n2,
    323, 327, 342, 346
  –arbitrary 33
  –moral 180
  –signs of 86
  –telos as (purposive) 37, 223
civilization(s) 72n1, 136, 142, 159,
    203–204, 231, 290, 302
  –conflict of 32
  –contemporary 203
  –fabric of 231
  –Liberal 333
  –of China 346, 368
  –of Japan 346
  –premodern 64
  –rural 138, 355
  –stifling 32
  –technical 64
  –Western 345–347
  –world xii, 281, 289, 320,
    368–369, 377
communication 85, 92, 100, 108,
    155, 246, 267, 272–273n4, 339,
    348, 369
  –telepathic 92
communism 142, 160, 162, 330,
    355–356, 359, 362
  –anti- 369n31
  –in Russia 159, 354, 356, 359
community (communities)
    63–64, 66, 104, 112, 115–116,
    122, 138, 140, 146–147,
    154–155, 157, 182, 184, 186,
    205, 254, 259, 269, 280–281,
    287, 289–290, 313n1, 315–316,
    326–327, 333, 338–341, 356

[389]

community, *continued*
- —business 159
- —Christian 189
- —Hindu 187
- —Jewish 141
- —just 163
- —metaphysical 284
- —of desire 54
- —of destiny 57
- —of nations/states 184–185
- —of minds 64, 122
- —of selves 58–59, 269
- —of will 59
- —primitive 82
- —religious 64
- —universal 289

communitarianism 289

Confucian(ism) 367–368, 370, 376
- —Boston 367–368, 377–378–379n2
- —neo- 370, 372, 378

conscience 5, 22, 30, 133, 161, 190, 247, 291, 295–297, 302, 332, 337, 347
- —bad 347
- —Christian 187
- —empirical 247
- —freedom of 162, 190, 211, 357
- —good 9
- —logical 9
- —maturity of 22
- —philosophic 24, 261
- —public 161
- —scientific 181n1

consciousness 22, 53, 55, 76, 81, 82n4, 83–87, 89, 96, 98–99, 104–113, 116, 117n1, 132, 140–141, 167, 169, 171, 178, 180, 200, 203, 213, 219, 225, 228, 236, 238, 243n7, 262, 267, 270, 274n8, 275n18, 286, 314, 323, 340, 370, 375 (see also "subconsciousness")
- - -Only 373, 380n11
- —aesthetic 156, 316
- —class 145, 213, 349
- —collective 117n1
- —historic 196
- —liberal 314
- —national 160
- —religious 197–198, 343

- —self- 78–79, 98, 129, 132, 181, 206, 268, 295, 346
- —social 84–85, 88, 94, 96, 98, 100, 104, 228
- —spiritual 22

contingency 196, 235

contingent (the) 31

continuity xiv, 7, 34, 53, 68, 95–96, 99, 127n1, 160, 228, 239, 372 (see also "discontinuity")
- —biological 342, 372
- —in thought 211
- —law of . . . in history 211
- —moral 372, 374
- —of a group 342
- —of experience 219
- —of meaning 123, 342
- —of the body 54
- —of the mind 54
- —with community 63

conviction(s) xiv-xv, 6–7, 16, 24, 78, 87, 103, 134, 168, 183, 203, 209, 285, 301, 313, 321, 355, 359
- —logical 68
- —primitive 38
- —religious xi, 188

corporation(s) 110–111, 115, 338–339

cosmology 179, 197, 256
- —Whitehead's 30, 35

Dao (a.k.a., Tao) 371–372, 379n9

death 32, 48–49, 58, 74, 115, 118n4, 145, 178, 202, 218, 218, 225, 242, 255, 297, 315, 324, 348, 355, 372
- —Hocking's xi-xii, 319, 349
- —mental 162
- —of institutions 302
- —of John F. Kennedy 320
- —of Marx 353
- —universal 174

democracy 64, 136, 152, 157, 160, 306–307, 315–316, 330, 333, 345, 361, 368–369, 375–376
- —of judgment 104

destiny 31, 43–46, 52, 57, 74, 125, 138, 141, 180, 190, 208, 213, 218, 237–238, 261–263, 265, 268, 271, 275n22, 358, 371

- —empirical 25
- —human ("man's") 30, 108, 162, 166, 207, 214, 351
- —of meaning 16
- —of the sacred 192
- —of the state (nation) 64, 124, 361
- —of truth 143, 155

dialectic 136, 138, 144–145, 149, 201, 210, 219, 255, 260, 271, 288–289
- —empirical 219, 221
- —Hegelian 171
- —natural 299
- —of experience 201, 287
- —of (in) history 136, 138, 145, 149, 151, 314, 349
- —of pugnacity 76, 82n3
- —of the will 82n3, 299

discontinuity 44 (see also "continuity")
- —in nature 34
- —of experience 219

divinity 196, 237, 269
- —experience of 240

dogma(tist) 8, 138, 154, 156, 250, 313
- —religious 24, 67, 196, 201–202

domination 77–78, 310

duty (duties) 6, 44, 71–72, 79–82, 88, 137, 142, 146, 153, 162, 181, 184, 190–191, 208–209, 218, 306, 309, 329, 339, 341 (see also "right[s]")

ego 37, 62, 65, 67, 70, 231, 275n21

egoism (egoist) 192, 336
- —of sex impulse 77
- —rationalistic 66
- —state 190

empiricism (empiricist) xiii, 26, 29, 31, 65–67, 143, 209, 219, 246, 250–251, 261, 264, 319–320, 369, 372, 375
- —principle of initial 264
- —radical 285, 322
- —widened (broader) 219, 227, 230, 238, 246, 251, 261, 263, 275n21

environment 32, 55, 60, 66, 77, 84, 87, 89, 94, 99, 117n2,

Subject Index

118n4, 123, 155, 177–178, 181n1, 196–198, 206, 210, 217, 225, 248–249, 293, 295–296, 298, 303, 309, 311, 313, 315–316, 338, 343, 370–371
–social 84, 197
essence 31, 35, 70, 107, 180, 233, 256, 375
–eternal 43
–of human creation 43
–of mysticism 269
–of philosophy 208
–of social order 182
–of the self 52
–spiritual 80
evil(s) 10–11, 60, 79, 129, 131–132, 135n5, 142–143, 148, 151, 196, 201, 212, 235, 324–325, 338, 344, 350, 353, 357
existence 7, 10, 12–13, 24, 31, 35, 39, 42, 45, 51, 59, 70, 79–80, 92–93, 127n3, 143–144, 163, 176, 196, 221, 233, 266, 322, 348
–of God 234, 238, 343
existentialism 33, 46, 232
–religious 242
experience xiii, 9–12, 14, 17, 21, 23, 27, 29–31, 37, 42–46, 49, 51, 53, 55, 57, 67–69, 71–72, 73n3-n4, 80, 83–85, 87, 89, 92–93, 95, 99–103, 106, 112, 126, 137–138, 152, 169–171, 178, 180, 193, 195n2, 202, 208–209, 211, 213, 219–221, 224–225, 227, 229–230, 234–238, 241, 246–251, 259, 261, 263–264, 266, 268, 272n3, 273n4, 274n8, 274n12–n14, 274n16, 275n18, 275n21-n22, 276–277n37, 280–281, 284–288, 292, 297–299, 306–307, 312, 314–315, 322–323, 326, 328, 332, 335, 339
–immediate 27, 34, 71, 87, 210, 260, 268, 271
–mystical 362
–national 128, 300
–nuclear 273n5
–of freedom 41
–of God xii, 83, 240, 252, 256, 343, 348

–of meaning 10
–of nature 55–56, 83, 98–99, 103, 212, 227
–of others (social) xii, 65, 68, 80, 83–88, 92, 94–95, 98–103, 212, 249, 252, 256, 259, 264–265, 268–269
–private 64–65
–pure 234–236, 285
–racial 128, 300
–religious 276n30
–shared (common) 67–68, 71, 96, 228, 258

fact(s) 18, 24, 26–27, 29–33, 35, 39, 41, 43, 45, 57, 60, 176, 180, 207, 210, 218, 256, 261, 264–266, 272, 287, 289, 293, 322, 324, 348
–irrational 10
–matter(s) of 9–10, 14, 104, 202, 209
–mental 210, 214n2, 257
–natural 55, 227–228
–objective 26
–of force 337
–of life 32
–of personal freedom 37
–of plurality 35
–of purpose 177
–of self-knowledge 88
–physical 210
–religion as 22, 51, 196, 201
–society as independent 193
–Universe as 35
–"we" as aboriginal 109
–world as 29
–world of pure 16, 176
faith 20, 22, 25, 27, 63–65, 87, 154, 165, 182, 186, 190, 194, 196, 200, 203, 243, 320, 323
–in government 338
–in the Other 87, 96, 259
–liberal 326–327, 329, 333–334
–religious xv, 20, 186–192, 269
fallacy 153, 308
–animist 39
–doubting thought as 70
–Freudian 53
–monism as 69
fate 45, 120, 196, 335, 177

field 15, 33–36, 38–41, 43–44, 46, 82, 99, 221, 224, 227, 229–230, 235, 261–262, 265–266, 288
–electrodynamic 36
–electro-magnetic 34
–energy 178, 370
–gravitational 34
–mental 221
–of action 198
–of consciousness 50
–of experience 72, 246
–of natural causation 240
–of religious knowledge 24
–of thereness 71
–of vision 54, 74
–physical 221
–space-time 35, 39, 41–42
freedom 13–15, 17, 23–27, 32, 37–38, 40–41, 46, 58, 60, 129, 134, 138–144, 164, 188, 190, 218, 239, 296, 302, 315, 323, 331, 346, 348, 355, 357 (see also "liberty")
–negative 308–309, 316
–of conscience 190, 211
–of speech 155, 162
–of thought 162, 164
–positive 316

Germany xii, 22, 137, 159, 168, 232, 280, 305, 314
Gifford Lectureship on Natural Religion xii, 217, 242, 276n30, 288, 323, 348
God xv, 21, 25–27, 33, 43, 45, 53, 63, 73n4, 84–85, 87, 101, 122, 142, 166, 168, 173, 179, 181–182, 193, 198, 200n2, 201, 209, 213, 225, 230, 234, 237–238, 241, 243n3, 263, 268–269, 271, 282, 285, 287–289, 323, 331–332, 343, 348, 360, 365n36
–experience of xii, 256
–eye of 189
–finite 11
–incomplete 179
–Kingdom of 189, 348
–knowledge of 83, 343
–meaning of 236–237, 332
–postulate of 72

[391]

God, *continued*
—voice of 192–193
—web of 239
—will of 193, 213, 282
—work of 196
good(s) 10–11, 26, 53, 75, 79–81,
  119, 132, 150, 159, 194, 201,
  207, 209, 212–214, 254, 267,
  288, 292, 320, 324, 329, 345,
  373
—absolute 212
—collective 148
—highest 80
—independent 74
—individual 148
—moderately 17
—of society 193
—personal 27
—possible 209
—private 64, 66
—social 132, 193–194
—total 33

habit(s) 49, 51–53, 81, 95, 104,
  109, 117, 119–120, 140, 192,
  210–211, 293, 306, 312–313,
  327, 339, 341
—of mind 306
—of philosophizing 313
—of subordination 110
—primary 76
—social 104, 140, 313
happiness 44, 72, 80–81, 127,
  130–131, 153, 204, 207–208,
  301
—greatest 148, 153, 308
—imperative of 80
Harvard xi-xii, 5, 217, 229, 232,
  235, 243n6, 246, 252–253,
  257–258, 262, 276n30, 280,
  305–306, 346, 349, 368,
  379n3
heaven 45, 114, 201, 213, 238, 282,
  368, 371–372
hell 25, 114, 216, 254
Hibbert Lectures 21
Hindu(ism) 6, 173, 187–189, 213,
  369, 376–377
history 10, 12, 23, 32, 46, 80, 82,
  92, 103, 108, 111, 116, 124, 127,
  129, 133, 136–139, 144–145,
  149, 156, 169, 175, 178, 183,

188, 192–193, 196–200,
202, 204–207, 211–212, 226,
230–232, 238, 263, 275n22,
281, 289, 294, 296, 301, 314,
326, 331, 333, 335, 343, 346,
349–352, 357, 359
—European 118n13
—Irish 113
—legal 110
—of a priori principles 39
—of an individual 248
—of institutions 134
—of Judaism 189
—of labor 158
—of liberalism 307
—of Other Mind 99
—of philosophy 5, 306, 321,
  324, 360
—of Russia 363n5
—of science 252
—of the body 92, 95
—of the cosmos/universe 169,
  172, 175, 188
—of redemption 173
—of revolutions 211
—of the state 118n7
—of thought xi, xv
—of will circuit 125
humanism 213–214, 276n37, 323
—ethical 352
—of ideals 352
—of Marx 352
—overconfident 166

idealism xiv, 21–28, 31, 33, 62,
  64, 146, 208–210, 214, 230,
  259–261, 288, 314, 320–323,
  325–326, 331, 333–334, 343,
  350, 377
—absolute, 20, 26, 262
—Berkeley's 85, 171, 180
—dialectical xiii
—empirical 260, 263
—fierce 159, 333
—individualistic 260
—metaphysical 225
—pragmatic 306
—subjective 14, 54, 62, 247,
  285, 287–288
imagination 13–14, 17–18, 26, 31,
  55, 57, 67, 69–70, 77, 92, 95,

101, 154, 162, 195n2, 224, 229,
233, 242, 252, 271, 273n8, 378
—mathematical 16
—philosophical 16
—poetical 16
immortality 80, 126, 199, 214,
  225, 242, 297
individualism 64, 137, 143,
  146, 149, 151–152, 290, 307,
  325–326, 328, 331, 345–346
—atomic 112
—bourgeois 145
—capitalist 137
—economic 144
—moral 162
induction 30, 42, 82, 138, 261
instinct(s) 4, 6, 13, 17, 20, 44,
  46, 49–54, 75–77, 119–120,
  129–130, 193, 202–203, 207,
  213, 240, 291–293, 295–296,
  298–299, 301–302, 340–342
—animal 202
—economic 75
—food-getting 119, 123
—grabbing 128, 300
—heard 66
—of infancy 76
—parental 77, 300
—physical 203
—second-order 291
—social 75, 83, 108
—visceral 281
institution(s) 78, 128, 130–134,
  164, 184, 194–195, 206, 211,
  238, 290–291, 296–303, 303–
  304n2, 322, 326, 336, 345
—academic xiii, 290
—crisis of 290
—democratic 361
—history of 134
—improvement of 131
—Liberal 155
—of family 128
—of property 128
—religious 195, 199–200
instrumentalism 63, 211, 307
intersubjectivity 65, 67, 73n3,
  273n8, 275n22
—of experience 43
intuition(s) 11, 20, 46, 65, 68–69,
  149, 210, 247, 260, 326, 375
—mystical 362

–rationalistic 370
–synoptic 288
I-think 64–71, 73n3, 267, 277n38

judgment(s) 5, 12–14, 16, 20, 23, 31, 41, 53, 65, 68, 86, 98, 104, 128, 138, 143–144, 152, 161, 164–166, 183–185, 202–203, 209, 235, 255, 266, 292, 311, 330, 337, 344, 347, 353, 355, 376
–absolute 206
–contradictory 7
–corporate (united) 1, 103, 362n1
–metaphysical 36, 41
–objective 164
–perfect 213
–pragmatic principle of 23
–reflective 221
–social 86, 102
justice xiii, 44, 52, 62, 66, 82, 113, 127, 154, 178, 182, 186, 194, 203, 275n18, 329, 345, 350
–court of 42
–equal 248
–objective 203
–retributive 114–115
–rule of 185
–sporadic 198

knower 40, 255, 280, 282–284, 369
–absolute 21–22
–co- 258
–finite 89
–omnicompetent 268
knowledge xiii, 8, 13, 18, 24–26, 44, 73n3, 81, 85, 87–90, 90n6, 91–93, 96, 98, 103, 140, 155, 170, 201–202, 211, 234, 248, 258–259, 263–265, 282–285, 287, 320, 341, 372, 374–376
–empirical (physical) 39, 87, 89, 250, 258, 264, 369
–intuitive 362
–metaphysical 263
–modern problem of 280
–of evil 132
–of God 83, 343
–of Nature 94, 98–99, 284

–of power 75, 78
–of (the) other (minds) 83–84, 88–89, 94, 96, 98–99, 259, 343
–of self (see also "self-knowledge") 89
–organ of 83
–pragmatic 375
–religious 24
–scientific 45, 87, 375
–social 84, 88–89, 281
–theory (theories) of 69, 88, 96–97n4, 282–283, 373, 375

law(s) xi, 32, 35, 39, 56–57, 66, 78, 91, 114, 117n3, 123, 128, 133, 138, 149–150, 172–173, 182, 184–186, 192, 194, 199–200, 211, 213, 270, 280, 297, 300–303, 311, 320, 337–338, 345, 351, 354, 357, 371–373
–eternal 186
–ideal 58
–international 184–186, 190, 199
–mechanical 256
–moral 81
–of being 44
–of conservation of energy 38
–of continuity 211
–of Karma 213
–of learning 210, 296
–of nature (natural or physical) 30, 131, 175–176, 213, 256, 282
–of property 32
–of reason 150
–of thermodynamics 174
–Roman 110
li 370–372
Liberalism xv, 139, 141, 143–144, 146–148, 151–160, 162, 164–165, 306–310, 312, 314–316, 325–331, 333, 345
liberty 32, 115, 126, 134, 143, 155–157, 162, 164, 203, 315, 327, 331, 355 (see also "freedom")
–individual 139, 164, 330
–negative 309
–of thought 27, 164

–religious 164–165
–social 134, 301
logic 3, 11, 13, 54, 59, 63, 66–67, 69, 85–86, 103, 114, 121, 134, 137, 150, 166, 177, 190, 193, 207, 212–213, 294, 324, 351
–Descartes' 67
–of communication 100
–of the conservative system 39–40
–of solipsism 68
–Spencer's 225
loyalty (loyalties) 128, 183, 190, 193–194, 195n2, 295, 338–339
–clan 118n10
–obscure 334
–to meanings 11
–to Royce 276n35

Marxism 319, 349, 351, 353, 359, 362
materialism
–dialectical 352–353
–mechanical 269
matter 10, 31, 39, 50, 53, 86, 91, 93–94, 107, 117n2, 227–228, 236, 241, 271, 282, 284, 371, 375, 377
meaning 9–14, 16–19, 19n2, 26, 30, 37, 45, 52, 55, 57–58, 63–64, 86–87, 92, 108, 128–129, 148, 162–163, 169, 171, 176–178, 207–209, 221, 232–235, 237–239, 251, 262, 265, 268, 271, 287, 309, 322, 324, 339, 341–342, 373
–common value 292
–destiny of 16
–in (of) history 175, 350
–in nature xv, 208, 213, 219
–objective 16–17, 208
–of creation 45
–of God 236–237, 332
–of ideas 141, 221, 225
–of things 9–10, 13–14, 16–17, 81, 208, 210, 233
–social 102
metaphysics xiv, 20, 29–30, 33, 37, 39, 69, 171, 178–179, 205, 208, 261, 271, 281, 284–285, 288–289, 306, 310–314, 321, 332–333, 348, 368, 377

[393]

metaphysics, *continued*
—cosmographical 179
—idealistic 213, 230, 322, 325
—inductive 261, 348
—moral 377
—new age 320
—of Liberalism, defective 165
—of loneliness 282
—of mysticism 27
—of presence 275n20
—of selfhood 228
—rejection of 313
—Royce's 258, 285
—speculative 67, 242
—Vedantic 37
mind(s) 9–10, 16–17, 37, 47–48, 50, 53–56, 65, 69, 74, 78, 83, 87–89, 91, 93–95, 101, 104, 105n1, 106–108, 110–113, 115, 122, 126, 127n1, 127n6, 137, 160–161, 167, 169, 180, 192, 196–197, 199, 201, 203, 213, 214n2, 218, 221, 223, 225, 227–228, 240–241, 243n7, 254–258, 280–287, 292, 296, 298, 303n1, 314, 339–343, 369, 372
—association of 103
—Cartesian view xii
—communicating 61n9
—development of 219
—empty (vacant) 70, 91, 108
—finite 59
—genuine community of 64
—group 106, 112–113, 115–116, 122, 127n1, 149, 294, 338, 340–341, 347
—juristic 114
—national 116
—objectivity of 267
—of God 285, 288
—other 69, 72, 73n3, 79, 83–92, 94–96, 98–104, 105n1, 122, 181, 218, 227, 250, 258, 264, 279n29, 283, 286–287, 303n1, 318
—past 125
—public 161
—right 142
—Spencer's definition 255–256

—super- 106, 112–113, 116, 118n7, 126
—unity of 198
—world of 58
modernity xii, 62, 64–67, 246–247, 252, 256, 267–268, 272, 272n2, 273n5-n6, 274n9, 275n21, 282, 284, 323–324
—passage beyond xiii, 66, 72, 246–247, 257, 260, 267, 280
—problem of xii, 267, 290
monad(ism) 35, 62, 65, 69, 84, 101, 108, 112, 119, 228, 236, 258, 340
monism 48, 361
mystic/mysticism 17, 20, 22, 26–27, 179–180, 196, 200n2, 202, 209–212, 214n2, 231, 238, 260–261, 264, 269–270, 275n19-n24, 319, 323, 331
—Indian 319
—logical 11
—metaphysical 17
—religious 227
—speculative 27
—tentative 266

naturalism 208, 212–213, 219–220, 223–224, 229, 268, 319
—metaphysical 220–221
—methodological 219
—reductive 247, 269
—rejection of 276n26
—scientific 219
—transfigured 213–214, 219–220, 225–228, 230, 269
Nature xv, 18, 21, 40, 57–58, 60, 83–85, 89, 91–96, 98–100, 103–104, 105n1, 166, 169–170, 178, 181n1, 208, 213, 219–220, 228–229, 235, 238–240, 269, 276n29, 286–287, 298, 343, 371, 373
—consciousness of 98
—experience of 83, 93, 95, 98, 99, 103
—knowledge of 89, 94, 99
—nature of 39
—world of 98, 100, 104, 343
neutralism 11–12
not-self 12, 49, 54–55, 70, 249

objective (an/the) xv, 14, 17, 31, 63, 169, 190
objectivity 14, 23, 56, 63–64, 66, 68, 73n3, 180, 260, 267, 277n38, 286–287, 289, 375
ontology 13
—materialist 368
order 29–30, 82, 145, 158–159, 164, 177, 182, 186, 197, 255, 293, 350–351
—astro-physical 30
—causal 222
—economic 145
—factual 265
—group-enclosed 39
—historical 59
—industrial 161
—logical 10
—moral 371
—natural 208, 247
—necessary 36
—of appreciation 38
—of being 126
—of description 38
—of instincts 292
—of knowledge 265
—of living 46
—of nature 55, 197, 220, 343
—of reality 170
—of things 55, 72, 373
—political 188, 338
—private 194–195
—public 124, 165, 194
—real time 11
—social 14, 128–129, 133–134, 137, 141, 162–163, 182, 203, 300–302
—space-time 40–41, 213
—stable 344–345
—world xiii, 40, 182–184, 186–188, 247, 276n26, 371
organism(s) 13, 15, 36–37, 40–41, 50, 109, 111, 117n2, 117–118n4, 132, 136, 157, 161, 177–178, 223, 248–249, 275n17, 291, 328, 338, 370–371
—healthy 157
—higher 119
—human 32, 293
—mental 109
—rational 223

–self-repairing 36
–social 149
otherness 55–58, 60, 66, 69, 220, 272
–nature's 55
–world's 378

passion(s) 24, 169, 194, 199, 203, 242, 250, 275n22, 322
–for justice 350
–for party-existence 152
–of fear 49
perception(s) 31, 39, 42, 73n5, 83, 137, 139, 181, 202, 229, 234–237, 261, 275n22, 284, 373
–causal theory (account) of 70, 73n3, 73n5
–of beauty 209
–of good 212
–of meaning 265
–organ of 83
–sense 285
personalism (personalist) xiii, 248, 275n17, 359–361, 364n19, 364n28, 365n31, 365n37
phenomenology 231–232, 235, 241
–existential 238
–Husserl's xii
–James's 235
–of the body 241
philosophy xi–xv, 3–10, 14, 17–18, 20, 22–23, 26–27, 62–67, 69, 79, 85, 136, 144, 160, 162–163, 180, 197, 201, 208–209, 211–212, 237, 242–243, 246–247, 251, 253, 255, 263–264, 266, 272n3, 273–274n8, 274n9, 275n21, 276n28, 276n36, 281, 285, 289–290, 306–307, 311–312, 314, 319–321, 323–324, 332, 334, 343, 348–349, 359–360, 364n27, 367–368, 377–378, 379n9, 380n13
–American xiv, 217, 245, 319, 360–362, 363n18
–analytic xiii, 234, 239
–ancient 66
–bourgeois 360
–Chesterton's 93
–Chinese 367–368,

378n2 (see also "Confucian[ism]")
–Christian 288, 361
–comparative 367, 378
–Confucian 377
–Descartes's 247, 268
–Dewey's 312, 333
–English 254
–ethnic 367
–evolutionary xi
–German 367
–Hegel's (Hegelian) 7, 350
–Husserl's 243n6
–idealist 343 (see also "idealism")
–instrumental 313
–Marx's (Marxist-Leninist) 146, 149, 181n2, 358–359
–Mill's 149
–modern 7, 13, 267, 280–281, 319
–of communication 273n4
–of history 289, 326
–of Liberalism 139, 148
–of mysticism 269
–of organism 368
–of religion 20, 321, 368
–of selfhood 288
–perennial 219
–political xv, 123, 307, 324, 336, 345, 378, 379n5
–practical 212
–pragmatic 136–137, 285, 333 (see also "pragmatism")
–Royce's 177
–Schopenhauer's 47
–Scottish 367
–social 291
–Spencer's 255
–universal 7
–Western 246–247, 367
–Whitehead's 177–178
–world 368, 377–378
physicalism 37
piety 25, 179, 369
–natural 9–10, 265
pluralism 35, 281, 320
–cultural 281, 314
–explorative 264, 266
–irreducible 257
–nature's 64

–radical 262
–valid 40
poetry 13, 16, 46, 252–253
–of childhood 205
–metaphysical 16
–racial 19
postmodern age (era) 246, 272, 273n5, 319, 376
postmodernism (postmodernist) 320, 378
–Marxist 376
poststructuralist(s) 320
pragmatism (pragmatist) xi, 11, 22–27, 63, 136–137, 212, 219, 235, 248, 305, 306–307, 312–313, 319–327, 333, 361, 369, 376
–Dewey's 313
–James's (Jamesian) 235, 262, 285
–negative 24–25, 193, 195n1, 219, 235, 261, 274n10, 303, 322
–Peirce's 376
–positive 26, 261, 322
–vulgar 376
principle(s) 55–56, 66, 89, 111, 113–114, 124, 134, 142–143, 145, 153–154, 156, 165–167, 169, 184, 197–198, 261, 267–268, 282, 312, 320, 330, 352, 369, 371–372, 374–376, 380n13
–all-or-none 35
–contract 117n3
–liberal 136, 138, 329
–of action 16, 25
–of advance 64
–of alteration 243n5, 266
–of ambiguous simplicity 264
–of attraction 91
–of authority 190
–of changelessness 211
–of Christian statecraft 190
–of connection 179
–of conservation 266
–of contradiction 11
–of creativity 33, 266
–of criticism 24, 261
–of devotion 193

[395]

principle(s), *continued*
—of dialogue 275n22
—of divine selfhood 262
—of empire 190
—of freedom 190
—of growth 218
—of harmony 371
—of human motivation 63
—of impersonal justice 203
—of inclusive rationality 265
—of indeterminacy 168
—of individuation 35
—of initial empiricism 264
—of international law 186, 190
—of judgment (pragmatic) 23
—of Liberalism 154
—of love 189
—of necessary sequence 37–38
—of negative pragmatism 24
—of noncontradiction 289
—of peaceful coexistence 359
—of persistent identity 197
—of positive pragmatism 24
—of selection 292
—of self-help 6
—of social order 141
—of social utility 143
—of sovereignty 184
—of subjectivity 66
—of tentative mysticism 266
—of the dialectic in history 136–138
—of the modern State 160–161
—of the union of fact and value 266
—ontological 33
—pragmatic 25
—rational 55, 176
—Relevant penalty 141
—second 263–265
—self as organizing 56
—socialistic 139
—spiritual 371
—universal 125
Principles of Psychology xii, 5, 255, 257
proletariat 145–146, 158, 356, 358
prudence 17, 66, 74

psychologism 62, 73n3, 232
psychology 4, 56, 63, 66, 83, 86, 106, 145, 147, 160, 165, 204, 210, 214n2, 232, 291, 293, 297, 319
—comparative 86
—Freudian 50–51
—group 106
—Hindu 6
—military 320
—proletarian 146
—William's 80
purpose(s) 37, 40, 45–46, 57, 63–64, 68, 73n3, 80, 95, 97n6, 107, 113, 117n2, 142, 159, 166, 177–181, 181n1, 197–198, 200, 208, 213, 218–219, 221–226, 228, 256, 262–263, 282–284, 289, 293, 307, 309–310, 313, 323, 339, 341, 370, 379n8
—common 297, 299, 302–303, 304n2, 315
—individual 160, 330
—national 333, 336, 361
—patriarchal 122, 303n1
—prophetic 199–200
—public 160, 330

qi 370–372

rationalism (rationalist) 63, 212, 219, 238, 264, 372, 375
—of science 369
real (the) 7, 23, 27, 40, 42, 44, 46, 46n2, 72, 169, 171, 179, 196, 250, 266, 285, 331
realism (realist) 11, 17, 22–23, 27, 42, 66, 73n3, 147, 191, 206, 212, 260–261, 269, 289, 319–320, 345
—a priori 42
—Aristotle's 283
—critical 17
—dogmatic 69
—legal 66
—mystical 212–213, 261, 269
—natural 285, 287
—political 337
reality 7, 20, 22–23, 26, 40–42, 46–47, 51, 68, 75, 84–85, 87, 93, 96, 101, 104, 108, 117n3, 169, 202–203, 206, 208,

210, 212, 219–220, 227–228, 234–235, 237, 249, 251, 258, 260, 263, 266, 268, 275n24, 285, 288, 322–323, 326, 343, 370, 378
—bodily 240
—call of 18
—central 52
—common 286, 343
—complex 248, 264
—concrete 125
—criterion of 266
—division of 371
—external 263
—full 178
—independent 94, 228, 323
—metaphysical 126
—objective 26, 203, 286
—outer 51, 73n4, 76
—physical 224
—tyrannical 250
—ultimate 11, 371
reason 5, 7, 19n2, 20, 27, 31, 145, 148, 150, 167, 183, 186, 201, 247, 264–265, 271, 327, 337, 350
—beyond 24, 27
—common 337
—externalized 336–337
—impersonal 82
—law of 150
—light of 283
—mystic 20
—objective 14, 17
—religion of 20
—suicide of 260
relativity 212, 323
—of meanings 324
—theory of 35, 40, 168, 170, 224, 324
religion 4, 20–28, 50–52, 64, 66–67, 112, 126, 136, 151, 164, 166, 188, 192–194, 195n2, 196, 198–199, 200n1, 201, 211, 213, 237, 246, 269, 280–281, 289, 297–298, 302, 306, 310, 319, 322, 324, 335, 338, 340, 344, 347, 351, 357–358, 362, 368, 374, 378, 379n5
—comparative 379n3
—extra-beliefs of 255
—false 164

–foundations of 24
–historic 27, 199–200
–humane 147
–instituted 199
–language of 200
–of humanity 193
–of "return" 189
–philosophy of xv, 20, 321, 343, 348, 368, 378
–positive 198, 200
–psychology of 63
–science of 20
–subtle 21
–theory of 197
–true 25–26, 164–165, 322
–valid 200, 334
responsibility 24, 41, 77, 113, 115–116, 147, 158–159, 196, 232, 254, 296, 311, 315–316, 336, 340
–final 185
–individual 125
–ingrained 196
–moral 183
–political 154, 307
right(s) 24, 32, 36, 40, 62–64, 67, 72, 72n1, 85, 110–111, 113, 115, 137, 142–143, 146, 148, 150–151, 153, 156, 162, 165, 185–186, 200, 205–206, 253, 280, 289, 300, 309, 316, 320, 327–330, 332, 334, 338, 344–346, 350, 352, 354, 357 (see also "duty [duties]")
–civil 114
–individual 151
–inherent 143
–legal 64
–natural 129, 153, 347
–of association 115
–of freedom of speech 141–142, 155
–of Idea 24, 323
–of life 32, 115, 199
–of power 77
–of property 115, 156
–of religious consciousness 197
–of thought 162
–private 146, 156
–rational 65
–to consume 157, 332

–to expression 332
–to preach 142
–to real estate 32
–to worship 357
–ultimate 162
Russia xi, 108, 125, 158–160, 162–164, 168, 333, 354–355, 357, 359, 362, 363n5, 378n2

science 29–30, 37–38, 40, 46, 50, 71–72, 83, 97n5, 150, 167, 171–174, 177, 180–181, 196, 199, 212–213, 214n2, 230, 232, 237, 241, 246, 252, 268, 282, 284, 299, 311, 320, 323, 335, 343, 348, 362, 368–370, 372–373, 375–377, 379n7-n8
–abstract 167
–aim of 282
–Bergson's critique of 370
–biological 181n1
–business of 29
–cognitive 256
–dictates of 219
–empirical 232, 247
–experimental 136, 247
–history of 252
–inductive 312
–life of 180
–medieval 282
–methods of 36
–natural 203, 210, 376
–object of 30
–of religion 20
–of the powers of the world 74
–ordinary 219
–philosophy of xv
–physical 37, 166–167, 171, 173, 177–178
–presuppositions of 8
–psychology of 63
–scope of 30
–social 67
–successes of 232
–universal 65
–Zhuxi's moral 376
self 12, 15, 23, 41, 44, 47–60, 61n9, 65, 68, 70–71, 77, 83–84, 88–89, 91, 96, 99, 102–104, 107–109, 112, 119–122, 132, 165, 180, 210–211, 213, 214n2,

218–219, 221, 224–227, 229–230, 234, 236–237, 239–241, 247, 249, 251–252, 257, 259–260, 262–263, 265, 267–268, 271, 273n6, 274n16, 275n17, 276n29, 281, 286, 288, 292–295, 298, 302, 309, 312, 323, 340–343, 348, 369, 373–374, 376
–active 41, 263
–bodily 239–240
–conscious 52
–creative 43, 310
–divine 224, 252
–doubleness of 226
–embodied 249
–enlarged 119
–essence of 52
–genuine 89
–infinite 276n26
–integrated 296, 302
–nature-made 62
–new 53, 76
–original 119, 194
–over-individual 123, 126, 303n1, 342
–poetic 252
–profounder 60
–protesting 49
–receiving 180
–reproduced 80
–retreating 52
–social 52, 326
–socially conditioned 266
–subconscious 52
–supernatural 247
–volitional 47
self-consciousness 78–79, 98, 129, 132, 206, 268, 295, 346
–mature 132
self-esteem 146, 156, 204
–instinctive 206
–invincible 153
self-knowledge 81, 88, 98, 319
–sources of 123
sense-data 31, 34, 43, 55–56, 58, 112, 171, 180–181, 239
sin 111, 115, 118n11, 161, 193, 200, 295–297, 302
–ingrained 200
–original 196, 235, 243
–world 351

[397]

socialism 137, 359
—economic 137
—national 313
—of Marx 148
society 75, 78–79, 81–83, 100, 108–109, 119, 126, 128–129, 134, 137, 139–144, 150–151, 153, 156–157, 192–194, 221, 288, 291, 294, 296, 298–303, 310, 316, 326–330, 332, 337–338, 345–346, 350, 357, 372, 374, 376
—appearance of 177
—attitude of 140
—democratic 369
—feudal 152
—good of 193
—ideal 146, 350
—individual forces of 14
—individualistic theory of 290, 302
—international 163
—Marx's scheme 148
—Mill's scheme 148, 155–156
—origin of 302
—philosophy of 146
—polite 204
—Soviet 353, 356, 358
—unitary 150
—unity of 145–146, 151, 350
—welfare of 193, 327, 345
—work of 192
solipsism xii, 54, 62, 68–69, 73n3, 86, 220, 247, 260, 264, 268, 270
—logic of 68
—quandary/problem of 67, 227, 256, 275n21
—surmounting/overcoming xv, 69, 73n3, 180, 246, 268–270, 280, 282, 287–288
—theoretical 62
soul 14, 25, 64, 85, 93–94, 96, 114–115, 164, 190, 192, 200, 200n2, 204, 213, 227, 236–237, 258, 269, 282, 343, 348
—immortal 110, 162
—of humanity 358
—universal 167
—violent 48

space 10, 15–16, 24, 30, 34–35, 39, 55–56, 59–60, 61n9, 94–95, 99–100, 108–109, 120, 170–174, 180, 212–213, 220, 224, 228–229, 249, 257, 261, 283, 320, 339, 343–344
—infinite 170
—interstellar 172
—Newtonian 34
—plural 229
—political 315
spirit 24, 48, 85, 95, 194, 238, 247, 269, 271, 282, 297, 349
—disembodied 51, 95
—dissatisfied 130
—human 131
—incarnate 111
—infinite 83
—international 199
—liberal 151, 154, 162, 306–316
—living 32
—national 355
—of God 200n2
—of the laws 194
—of the world 203–204
—other 95
—pure 91
—realm of 135n1, 227
—religious 198, 212, 343
state 11, 64, 74, 76, 82, 106, 110–111, 116, 118n4, 118n7, 123–127, 137–138, 143, 150–152, 158–165, 182–186, 189, 196, 198–199, 205, 298, 301–302, 313, 325–326, 328, 330–331, 333, 335–348, 353–355, 359
—bourgeois 160
—co-agent 163–165, 315, 331–333
—communist 161, 355
—dictatorial 161, 313, 330
—do-nothing 159
—laissez faire 163
—liberal xv, 157, 164, 308, 330–331
—Mill's ideal 141, 155
—modern 137, 160–161
—Russian 125
—secular 64
—Soviet 349, 357–358
—strong 163, 330–331
—static 159

subconsciousness (see also "consciousness") 127n1, 139, 267, 274n15
subjective (the) xv, 169
subjectivity 260, 289
super-self 112–113, 118n7, 126, 127n6, 297–298, 302, 303n2
symbol 16, 97n4, 181, 188, 238, 373
—body as 47–48, 94
—elements of history as 80
—Marx as 255
—Nature as 94–95
—of understanding 283
—pictorial 213
—schematic 120
—spatial 47
—wealth as 75

telos 36–37, 42–43, 45–46, 68
—fundamental necessities of 41
—nuclear 26
theory (theories) 22, 24, 60, 66, 83, 112, 115, 125, 14, 140, 158, 168, 171–172, 229, 248, 320, 322, 328, 330
—biological 37
—Buddhist 374
—causal, of perception 73n5
—contract, of the state 337
—electrodynamic 36
—evolutionary 222
—false 142
—field- 177, 288
—Finalist 36
—Freudian 51
—group mind 340–342
—individualistic, of society 290, 302
—Liberal 153, 328
—Mill's theory 141
—of abstract individualism 149
—of dialectic 82n3
—of economic determinism 350
—of experience 275n21
—of institutions 291
—of knowledge 88, 97n4, 282, 373, 375–376
—of laissez faire 153

[398]

–of mysticism 27
–of positive pragmatism 322
–of prehensions 73n3
–of religion 197
–of social groups 123
–of the sovereignty of the nation-state 184–185
–of the state 344–345
–organic, of the state 338
–Pault's 38
–physical 35, 166
–political 66, 126, 273n8, 276n28, 340, 368, 378
–quantum 34, 36
–self-refuting 26
–true 142
time 7, 15, 25, 34–35, 39, 41–44, 54–57, 59–60, 81, 93, 95, 114, 150, 156, 170–171, 173–176, 183, 189, 192, 202, 211–213, 220, 223–224, 228–229, 261, 263, 303n2, 322
time-field 35
tragedy 16, 209, 255
–finality of 324
–of contemporary history 138
–of existence 51
–of refuting Dewey 243
transcendental idea 285, 288
truth 5–6, 14, 22, 24–26, 37, 42, 46, 51, 63, 66–67, 72, 79, 97n4, 104, 127, 136–137, 139–141, 147, 155–156, 161, 167, 179, 181, 190, 201, 210–212, 218–219, 232, 235, 255, 261–262, 270, 274n10, 287, 292, 303, 313, 322–323, 348, 351, 365n35, 369, 375
–about (of) religion 21, 23–24, 27, 321
–artist's 42
–criterion of 24
–divine 282
–emotional significance of 141, 155
–final 137, 139
–form of 56
–inaccessible 26
–loss of 25
–metaphorical 46
–metaphysical 137

–necessary 3
–non-pragmatic 26, 322–323
–normal destiny of 143, 155
–objective 3, 181, 323, 375
–of liberalism 308
–of values 81
–pragmatic 153, 323
–psychological 131
–system of 198
–test of 14
–unfinished 26

universal (the) 7, 31, 33, 235, 322, 331
universality 32, 104, 281, 332
–irrepressible 62
–natural 65
–of private experience 63–65
universe 8, 24, 29–33, 35, 37, 41–42, 52, 55, 59, 71–72, 75, 81–82, 122, 127, 149, 166, 168, 171–179, 188, 196, 208, 210, 213, 218, 223, 238, 242, 256, 258, 260, 266, 268, 275n23, 370, 372, 374–375
–alien 212
–block 285
–conscious 104
–inclusive 219
–incomplete 179
–infinite 181
–mathematical 171
–meaningless 208
–of "actual occasion" 35
–of compromised worth 17
–physical 39, 54, 171, 197
–scientific 371
–social 128
–soulless 225
–stellar 175

value(s) 13, 17, 19n2, 24, 27, 32–33, 126, 132, 150, 179, 180, 197, 200, 204, 206, 209–210, 222–223, 238–239, 256, 264, 266–267, 294–295, 310–311, 320, 324, 334, 373, 378, 379n8
–concrete 222
–human 25
–inductive element of 63
–infinite 204
–of existence 266

–of liberalism 309
–of revolution 142
–of selfhood 121, 294, 341
–moral 51
–objective 17–18, 209
–primal 232
–social 192–193
–standards of 296
–taproot of 243n4
value-judgment(s) 14, 20, 32–33 (see also "judgment[s]" and "value[s]")
violence 114, 157, 361
–era of 76–77
–physical 182
–threat of 315
volition 47–48
voluntarism 27, 250

whole (the) 10–12, 46, 52, 63–64, 169, 173, 177, 180, 182, 208, 210, 235, 237–238, 241, 260, 264–266, 283, 287, 289, 324, 370, 372
–meaning of the 10, 262
–social 148, 150, 153, 156–157
will 15, 20, 47, 49, 52–57, 59–60, 60n1, 64, 66, 71, 75–81, 87–88, 97n6, 107, 119–126, 130, 132, 134, 135n5, 163, 167, 178, 194, 195n2, 196, 198–199, 201–202, 204, 210, 218, 255, 258, 292–299, 301, 303n1, 304n2, 307, 325, 328, 330–331, 335–339, 341–342, 344, 347, 361
–absolute 37
–arbitrary 186
–community of 59
–dialectic of 82n3, 299
–divine 206
–general 124–125, 127n3, 152, 157, 164, 295, 328, 330–331, 343
–good 9, 79, 153, 165, 183, 187, 327, 329, 332
–growing 76, 78
–identity of 122, 342
–incipient 76
–maturing 78
–moral 17, 375
–object of 79–80

[399]

will, *continued*
  – of God 25, 193, 213, 282
  – of the state 124–125, 343
  – prophetic 198
  – public 4
  – pure 48
  – religious 197–198
  – resolute 270
  – satisfaction of 80
  – self-interested 77
  – to be immortal 214
  – to believe 214
  – to create 42
  – to differ 4
  – to fly 49
  – to live 44, 47–49, 53, 57, 59–60, 75, 97n6, 293, 336
  – to obey 66
  – to philosophize 312
  – to play 123
  – to power 51, 75–79, 81–82, 123–124, 130–132, 194, 242, 291–293, 295–297, 301, 336, 340, 342, 344–345
  – to serve 66, 78
  – ultimate 206
  – unanimity of 163, 345
  – unity of 107, 124
will circuit(s) 120–123, 125–126, 127n1, 293–294, 296–299, 340–343
  – coincident 123, 126, 297, 342
world xiii, 7, 9–19, 21–33, 37, 41–45, 49–60, 61n9, 62–63, 65, 70–72, 73n3–n5, 74–76, 78–79, 81, 85, 88, 93–96, 98–99, 103–104, 105n1, 108, 110–111, 119, 131, 134, 136, 146–147, 150, 153, 159, 161, 163, 166, 169–173, 176–180, 182, 185–186, 188–189, 196–199, 200n2, 201–211, 214, 218–219, 221, 225–230, 233–236, 238–239, 242–243, 245, 249–251, 256–257, 260, 262–266, 271, 273n4–n5, 280–286, 288, 296, 302, 309–311, 323, 329, 336, 340–341, 343–344, 353, 361, 369–378, 379n2
  – Aristotle's 284
  – active 150, 314
  – biological 118n4
  – Bruno's 179
  – Buddhist 187
  – civilized 183
  – classical 347
  – concrete 23
  – conscious 63, 198
  – conservative 41
  – contemporary 142
  – Copernican 203
  – desiccated 242
  – experienced 168
  – factual 31, 227
  – fervent 252
  – God's 179
  – inorganic 58
  – intelligible 282–283
  – irregular 175–176
  – living 79, 180
  – material 95
  – medieval 284
  – mental 211
  – monadic 72, 101
  – neutral 17
  – objective 14, 17, 56, 247
  – of abundant wonder 60
  – of Christianity 201
  – of facts 58, 60, 197
  – of ideas 130, 321
  – of living systems 37
  – of matter 39, 284
  – of meaning 16, 58, 238
  – of mind 58, 122, 284
  – of nature 59, 73n3, 98, 100, 104, 247, 267, 276n26, 280, 282–284, 336, 343
  – of other mind 84, 98, 100, 181
  – of peace 190
  – of persons 82, 150, 314
  – of phenomena 289
  – of politics 188
  – of pure fact 16
  – of quality 169
  – of science (research) 104, 174, 369
  – of space 99–100
  – of the soul 96
  – of the transcendent 288
  – of things 91, 348
  – of truth 104
  – of values 13
  – orderly xv
  – organic 39
  – outer 76, 119, 340
  – parental 205
  – phenomenal 41
  – physical 50, 65, 89, 99, 102, 108, 224, 258, 277n37–n38, 287
  – pluralistic 7
  – private 43, 65
  – psychical 102
  – relativistic 231
  – Royce's 285
  – safe 313
  – social 78, 84, 104, 181, 197–198
  – Spiritual 83
  – structure of 14
  – unchosen 32
  – visible 217
  – Western 22, 133, 326, 347
world-idea 235, 239
world-space 229
worship 23, 26–27, 197, 199, 200n2, 237, 269
  – attitude of 23
  – of God 142
  – right to 357

[400]

www.ingramcontent.com/pod-product-compliance
Lightning Source LLC
Chambersburg PA
CBHW021814300426
44114CB00009BA/179